Newspaper organization and management FIFTH EDITION

HERBERT LEE WILLIAMS

Newspaper organization and management

FIFTH EDITION

IOWA STATE UNIVERSITY PRESS/Ames, Iowa

DEDICATED TO A QUARTER-CENTURY OF
Journalism students and practitioners

Herbert Lee Williams, B.A., M.A., Ph.D., is Chairman, Department of Journalism, Memphis State University, and has been copy editor for the Memphis *Commercial Appeal* and general manager of the Fulton, Ky., *Daily Leader.*

Composed and printed by
The Iowa State University Press
Ames, Iowa 50010

First edition, by Frank W. Rucker and Herbert Lee Williams, copyrighted 1955 and carried through four printings

Second edition, 1965, through two printings
Third edition, 1969, through two printings
Fourth edition, 1974

Fifth edition, 1978

Library of Congress Cataloging in Publication Data

Williams, Herbert Lee.
  Newspaper organization and management.

  First-4th ed. by F. W. Rucker and H. L. Williams.
  Bibliography: p.
  Includes index.
  1. Newspaper publishing.   I.   Rucker, Frank Warren.
Newspaper organization and management.   II. Title.
PN4734.R78   1978   658′.91′07   78-15799
ISBN 0–8138–1150–3

Contents

Preface

THIS BOOK HAS BEEN WRITTEN:

First, to outline and describe the best methods and practices now used in producing and promoting newspapers.

Second, to describe the most modern and practical equipment that may be used in publishing a newspaper.

Third, to show the ideal location and arrangement of equipment in a newspaper plant that will provide maximum efficiency, a proper flow of work, and speed and economy in production.

Fourth, to provide for journalism students and all others who plan to enter the field a textbook that reveals the challenging issues and problems publishers must face and explains the qualifications needed for success in directing and managing newspapers.

To keep the contents of this volume up-to-date and timely, four previous editions have been issued within a period of seventeen years. For the fifth edition an exhaustive revision of the entire text has been undertaken. This has been necessitated by the dramatic changes in newspapering during the 1970s — technological, sociological, and economic.

Particular attention is given to the improvements now taking place in newspaper publishing:

1. The almost complete changeover from letterpress to offset in the printing of newspapers of all circulation sizes (Chapter 5).
2. The great number of new newspaper plants being built or used buildings being remodeled to provide accommodation for mechanical equipment (Chapter 8).
3. The interesting changes in architectural design of newspaper plants being built; buildings of one story or one and a half stories are preferred, and more ground space is required for the plant and nearby convenient parking (Chapter 8).
4. The instituting of computer service in more newspaper plants to save time in accounting, to keep close check on growth in all departments, and to keep news facts more complete and accurate (Chapter 6).
5. The increase in the use of other electronic equipment to provide greater speed, attractiveness, and economy in newspaper production (Chapter 6).
6. Greater use of newspaper photography and improvement in the kind of equipment required and the type of pictures preferred (Chapter 7).

7. The growing trend toward color printing by newspapers to compete with color television and to add interest and attractiveness to advertising and news features (Chapter 7).

For valuable assistance in accumulating material, we are indebted to more than 300 publishers, managers, or department heads. For this generous and important cooperation we are truly grateful.

Authors of works on journalism; editors of professional journals; educators; officers of newspaper associations; lawyers who deal with newspaper taxation, labor, and law; newspaper accountants and finance officers; newspaper brokers; manufacturers of newspaper equipment; printing plant engineers; and newspaper architects have given liberal assistance.

The great assistance given by *Editor & Publisher, Journalism Quarterly, Printing Equipment Engineer, Quill,* and other publications related to the newspaper business has meant much. The American Publishers Association, Inland Daily Press Association, Southern Newspaper Publishers Association, International Circulation Managers Association, Midwest Circulation Managers Association, Classified Advertising Managers Association, National Newspaper Promotion Association, Texas Circulation Managers Association, Texas Press Association, Michigan Press Association, New England Weekly Press Association, Missouri Press Association, and Institute of Newspaper Controllers and Finance Officers also provided important facts and illustrations.

Foreword

Here is a timely book in the field of journalism. This fifth edition represents an exhaustive revision and rewriting of the text first produced in 1955 by Professor Williams and the late Professor Frank W. Rucker and widely accepted through four editions.

As manager of a daily newspaper and of a regional press association, the author is ideally suited to provide a synthesis of the complex elements with which newspaper management works today. Connections and contacts with members of the press in many parts of the nation have enabled him to assemble the experiences of other practical newspaper people to support the definite costsaving, timesaving, work-flow, and better production suggestions presented in this book.

Professor Williams has had the added advantage of teaching the subject in the classroom—at Boston University, at Michigan State University, and at Memphis State University where he heads the Department of Journalism.

This book will be read and studied with great appreciation by men and women in all areas of newspaper work. It will fill a significant need as a textbook in the field, to be sure, but it will serve another valuable end also—encouraging capable young people to enter the important, challenging arena of newspaper work.

Earl English
Dean Emeritus, School of Journalism
University of Missouri, Columbia

1

Organization and equipment

PUBLICK
OCCURRENCES

Both *FORREIGN* and *DOMESTICK*.

Boston, Thursday Sept. 25th. 1690.

IT is designed, that the Countrey shall be furnished once a moneth (or if any Glut of Occurrences happen, oftener,) with an Account of such considerable things as have arrived unto our Notice.

In order hereunto, the Publisher will take what pains he can to obtain a Faithful Relation of all such things ; and will particularly make himself beholden to such Persons in Boston whom he knows to have been for their own use the diligent Observers of such matters.

That which is herein proposed, is, First, That Memorable Occurrents of Divine Providence may not be neglected or forgotten, as they too often are. Secondly, That people every where may better understand the Circumstances of Publique Affairs, both abroad and at home ; which may not only direct their Thoughts at all times, but at some times also to assist their Businesses and Negotiations.

Thirdly, That some thing may be done towards the Curing, or at least the Charming of that Spirit of Lying, which prevails amongst us, wherefore nothing shall be entered, but what we have reason to believe is true, repairing to the best fountains for our Information. And when there appears any material mistake in any thing that is collected, it shall be corrected in the next.

Moreover, the Publisher of these Occurrences is willing to engage, that whereas, there are many False Reports, maliciously made, and spread among us, if any well-minded person will be at the pains to trace any such false Report so far as to find out and Convict the First Raiser of it, he will in this Paper (unless just Advice be given to the contrary) expose the Name of such person, as A malicious Raiser of a false Report. It is suppos'd that none will dislike this Proposal, but such as intend to be guilty of so villanous a Crime.

THE Christianized *Indians* in some parts of *Plimouth*, have newly appointed a day of Thanksgiving to God for his Mercy in supplying their extream and pinching Necessities under their late want of Corn, & for His giving them now a prospect of a very *Comfortable Harvest*. Their Example may be worth Mentioning.

'Tis observed by the Husbandmen, that altho' the With-draw of so great a strength from them, as what is in the Forces lately gone for *Canada*; made them think it almost impossible for them to get well through the Affairs of their Husbandry at this time of the year, yet the season has been so unusually favourable that they scarce find any want of the many hundreds of hands, that are gone from them ; which is looked upon as a Merciful Providence

While the barbarous *Indians* were lurking about *Chelmsford*, there were missing about the beginning of this month a couple of Children belonging to a man of that Town, one of them aged about eleven, the other aged about nine years, both of them supposed to be fallen into the hands of the *Indians*.

A very *Tragical Accident* happened at *Water-Town*, the beginning of this Month, an *Old man*, that was of somewhat a Silent and Morose Temper, but one that had long Enjoyed the reputation of a *Sober* and a *pious Man*, having newly buried his Wife, The Devil took advantage of the Melancholly which he thereupon fell into, his Wives discretion and industry had long been the support of his Family, and he seemed hurried with an impertinent fear that he should now come to want before he dyed, though he had very careful friends to look after him who kept a strict eye upon him, least he should do himself any harm. But one evening escaping from them into the Cow-house, they there quickly followed him found him hanging by a *Rope*, which they had used to tye their Calves withal, he was dead with his feet near touching the Ground.

Epidemical *Fevers* and *Agues* grow very common, in some parts of the Country, whereof, tho' many dye not, yet they are sorely unfitted for their imployments; but in some parts a more *malignant Fever* seems to prevail in such sort that it usually goes thro' a Family where it comes, and proves *Mortal* unto many.

The *Small-pox* which has been raging in *Boston*, after a manner very Extraordinary, is now very much abated. It is thought that far more have been sick of it then were visited with it, when it raged so much twelve years ago, nevertheless it has not been so Mortal, The number of them that have

Fig. 1.1. The first newspaper published in America (confiscated by the British after one issue) recognized its obligation to inform the people of events that affected their welfare.

1

The obligation to inform

> One of these days we newspaper people are going to get smart enough and care enough to edit, print, sell and deliver that perfect—or near perfect—newspaper.
>
> *Allen H. Neuhart*

Throughout their 300-year history newspapers have been transformed, particularly in recent decades, by the sociological, economic, and technological changes that have touched all other human enterprises. But the one quality of the true newspaper that remains forever constant is its purpose: *the dissemination of information.*

While there may be no other similarities between the multiedition metropolitan newspaper giants of today and the first tiny news sheet published in America, which carried the title *Publick Occurrences both Forreign and Domestick* (Fig. 1.1), their purpose links them in the single role of informing the public. The colonial editor's aim was to publish the news "once a moneth (or if any Glut of Occurrences happens, oftener)." From that time on every responsible newspaper executive has recognized that objective as the primary goal of the operation.

This sense of purpose is basic to an understanding of newspaper organization and management and is the overarching reason for the existence of the "newspaper business." As expressed at a recent gathering of international leaders, "the role of the press in informing the world public is one of transcendent importance; every newspaper is an encyclopedia of local history and world movements."

Realizing that the public wants its news as it happens—fully covered, well printed, attractively and accurately presented in a form whereby it may be preserved to become a public record—publishers generally have invested heavily in modern equipment, expanded quarters, and capable employes. Only those directly connected with newspapermaking can comprehend the various essential ways the modern press serves the public.

RESPONSIBILITY AND SERVICE

A bulletin board

A newspaper announces the time, the place, and the topic of meetings and chronicles births, deaths, and marriages. It gives vital facts about current issues. It warns when taxes must be paid, when voters must register. It proclaims elections, designates voting places, and informs parents and children when schools open and when and where the classes must register. It stimulates public interest in holidays and special days and their programs. It tells when service clubs, women's organizations, and church groups meet. It heralds coming sports events. This constantly changing community bulletin board is delivered to the reader to be perused at leisure. But speed and, above all, accuracy are essential in assembling and presenting such information, which is always important to someone.

An educator and promoter

The newspaper instructs in international relations, history, geography, economics, psychology, politics, medicine, agriculture, home economics, meteorology, and more. Through the newspaper's columns the doctor talks professionally about rare and common diseases and points out ways to avoid or treat them. The weatherman conveys to those going on an outing the cheerful news of a bright day or warns the farmer with hay on the ground of possible danger of crop spoilage from rains to come the following day. Recipes and beauty hints enlighten and please women readers. Columns are devoted to human behavior and political issues, and generally there is a sprinkling of practical advice on a myriad hobbies and activities. Such important services of the newspaper require research, selection, and direction. Plain facts are dramatized with colorful and helpful information. Photographs of individuals and groups, views, maps, and charts make news more understandable and meaningful.

Names in the news are transformed into live human beings. Persons prominent in national and world affairs are brought close to all through biographical facts and human interest material in the newspaper. During wars the press associations and special correspondents describe for newspaper readers the countries where fighting men are stationed and the habits and customs of the people.

Rendering so diverse a service requires an enormous amount of work. Such vital information does not just walk into the news columns. It must be collected, written, and published at the right moment to make it appreciated and helpful.

Most newspapers invite people to express themselves on matters of general community interest. Through the editorial columns the editor interprets the thoughts of the community. The editor speaks, and the readers talk back. Thus the public receives the opinions of both. This is a truly democratic service that requires understanding, courage, fairness, and diplomacy.

The newspaper is a prime factor in formulating a community program and in organizing the community to carry it out, in promoting the growth and development of the community, in advertising its assets to the outside world, and in pointing out its faults and weaknesses to the home people. It organizes, informs, promotes, and finances. In most communities the newspaper willingly provides space for and actively supports campaigns to raise funds for worthy causes.

The newspaper produces news and advertising. People always have had an appetite for news, and hunger for it has increased through the years. Advertising is a force that has revolutionized industry and trade by stimulating competition, which promotes greater efficiency, more and better products, and lower prices.

The newspaper builds regional business. By making shopping easy and profitable for its readers through advertising, the newspaper provides a pleasant and convenient contact between merchants and customers. The reader shops the newspaper's columns, much as a store's customer shops the counters. The difference is that shopping from the newspaper's columns may be done without tramping from floor to floor, ringing for elevators, or standing on escalators. The reader simply goes to the telephone and orders what he wants.

Business and service institutions spend billions of dollars each year for newspaper advertising — evidence that this service is valuable to those with products or services to promote.

A protector of freedom

The newspaper, a semipublic institution, is not a public utility subject to government franchise and other regulation, but in certain respects it functions as a utility. In communities where the newspaper has a large circulation and exerts a strong influence for community betterment, it is as important as a telephone exchange, a light and power company, a water company, or a gas service. It is just as necessary for families to receive light on the happenings and issues of the day as to receive light from the community power plant.

There is this difference, however, between a newspaper enterprise and a public utility: the newspaper's franchise is granted by the First Amendment to the Constitution of the United States; the public utility's franchise is determined by a government agency and is subject to change, control, or revocation.

The newspaper guards the people's interests. Officers of the law realize that without favorable public opinion they are greatly handicapped in carrying out their responsibilities. They realize also that there is nothing more effective to prevent or abate crime than publicity. Officers know newspapers can and do help them in many ways: by giving them favorable publicity when their work deserves it, by holding the threat of widespread publicity over would-be offenders if they do go wrong, by warning the public of criminal activity, by helping police apprehend criminals, and by protecting the innocent from unjust prosecution. Officials know, too, that good newspapers are as quick to expose incompetence in office as they are to commend efficiency.

The fact that the press exists through constitutionally created privilege sets it apart from other business enterprises. To fulfill their role in our democratic system, the newspapers of America are constantly called upon to protect the public and to thwart any effort to limit in the slightest degree the privileges of free expression as defined in the Constitution.

A communications leader

With so many challenging opportunities to serve, careful organization and sound management are imperative. True, the newspaper is the public's traditional source of news and the principal medium of advertising for business, but it enjoys no monopoly. The development of other means of imparting news and advertising means the newspaper must battle for the supremacy it holds.

Without question the newspaper best fitted to wage that battle successfully will be both responsible and service minded. The tremendous speed with which news must be obtained from great distances, the accuracy and fairness with which it must be handled, and the promptness with which newspapers must be circulated impose great obligation. Still other responsibilities result from the public's reliance upon newspapers for counsel and guidance in community improvement; in the shaping of better, more efficient government; and in the general promotion of better living.

In the field of advertising, great service is demanded of the newspaper by retailers, wholesalers, and manufacturers who recognize the newspaper as an effective sales-producing agency. The task of coordinating newspaper departments and stimulating them to efficiency in providing the public with the services so strongly demanded and warmly appreciated is a vital one that should not be overlooked.

In the competition that has developed—radio, facsimile, and television—and in the problems of labor, newsprint supply, and rising costs of operation and materials, there is much to challenge the ingenuity, skill, and honor of those responsible for newspaper management.

At no stage of newspaper development have publishers been more conscious of their responsibilities and opportunities or more eager to succeed in their calling. By personal study and research, by cooperation and exchange of ideas, and by sponsoring and encouraging a higher standard and wider scope of journalistic training and practice, they are seeking and promoting better ways of answering the universal call for news through the printed page.

Robert S. McCord, executive editor of the Little Rock, Ark., *Arkansas Democrat,* and president of The Society of Professional Journalists, Sigma Delta Chi, gave this compact evaluation of the newspaper's role today: "American journalism is the best in the world. I think we can defend ourselves against any attacks. But to do so, we must be standing on solid ground—ground not tainted by corruption, irresponsibility, or stupidity. And we must not be standing in concrete; we should be bright enough and bold enough to admit that we do make mistakes and to work toward the day when we can deliver information to the American people in a more accurate and more understandable way."[1]

Management is obviously the answer to the challenge confronting the modern newspaper, for without economic independence, there can be no editorial independence. And without a free press, there is no free society.

---

1. Remarks in *The Masthead,* vol. 28, no. 2, p. 15 (quarterly publication of the National Conference of Editorial Writers). Used by permission.

2
Organization functions

> Weeklies and dailies have never had a brighter, more exciting role. They have never had more challenges. Who are these weeklies and these dailies? They are people in production, in circulation, in business, in advertising. Wars aren't won without the infantry.
>
> *Rollan Melton*

A promising approach to the organizational problems confronting all management is one known familiarly as the "systems-analysis-and-systems-flow" concept. According to Professor John De Mott of Temple University, such an approach makes it possible to relate newspaper publishing to other forms of enterprise and to make comparisons that best illustrate the basic principles and functions of management.

Functions common to all kinds of enterprise management include:

1. Decision making — the process by which a course of action is consciously chosen from available alternatives for the purpose of achieving a desired result.
2. Organizing — the actions by which the structure or allocation of jobs is determined.
3. Staffing — the method by which managers select, train, promote, and retire subordinates.
4. Planning — the deliberate anticipation of the future and consideration of alternative courses of action open to management.
5. Controlling — the measurement of current performance, coupled with guidance toward predetermined goals.
6. Communicating — the process by which ideas are transmitted for the purpose of evoking a calculated response.
7. Directing — the procedure by which actual performance of subordinates is achieved to bring about the attainment of preestablished goals.

In an elaboration of the systems-analysis-and-systems-flow approach,

Joseph Massie explains: "All these functions are closely interrelated. However, it is useful to treat each as a separate process for the purpose of spelling out the detailed concepts important to the whole job of the manager. At times it may be desirable to consider several functions jointly in order to show their close interrelationships. For example, communicating and controlling must be considered together in systems planning; organizing, communicating, and staffing may be viewed together in studying organization behavior."[1]

This general concept is helpful as a beginning, but a more specific definition of newspaper organization is needed.

TYPES OF ORGANIZATION

Three types of organization, which are commonly known as pyramidic, functional, and staff and line, are employed in business and industry, but only one of these is suitable for a smooth-running and effective newspaper.

The *pyramidic type* is similar to that of a military organization. Authority is assigned by ranks and titles in an unquestioned delegation of superior and inferior positions. It is quite apparent such organization could not be applied successfully in a newspaper.

A good illustration of the *functional type* is the labor union. Here authority is assigned by levels of work or particular duties, with each function having its own final authority. A purely functional organization would not be practical for a newspaper because departments would be pulling away from and against each other instead of pulling together.

The *staff and line type* has the good qualities found in the other two. Control is graduated down in levels, with each stratum having its final authority. The departments are headed by executives who are directly responsible to a superior, but each executive is given full responsiblity and authority within the group supervised. This type of organization is best suited to newspaper operation because it provides controls over all departments yet permits freedom of operation within each.

Here are illustrations of how the staff and line organization works in the operation of a newspaper. The mechanical superintendent, for instance, may have higher staff rank than the composing room supervisor, but the latter is the final authority on composing room matters. Employes take their problems directly to the supervisor rather than to the superintendent, the business manager, or the publisher. The advertising manager who wants a front-page story to accompany an advertisement about a store

---

1. Joseph Massie, *Essentials of Management*, 2nd ed. (Englewood Cliffs, N.J.: Prentice-Hall, Inc., ©1971), pp. 6–7, as reported in a paper presented by John De Mott at the Association for Education in Journalism Convention, University of Maryland. Reprinted by permission of Prentice-Hall, Inc., Englewood Cliffs, N.J.

opening will not assign a reporter to the story, but will approach the city editor, who has full authority over local news reporting.

The managing editor who is told that carriers are folding the papers so that the front page tears before delivery to the reader will ask the circulation manager to give remedial instructions to the carriers or may ask the business manager to pass the order down to the circulation manager. Thus each department functions independently while at the same time interdepartmental coordination and cooperation are possible.

DEPARTMENTS OF A NEWSPAPER

In weekly and small daily newspaper plants the two general divisions are usually referred to as *the office* and *the shop*. The news and the ads are received in the office, where the copy is written and all general business connected with the newspaper is transacted. All the mechanical work pertaining to the newspaper is carried on in the shop. The paper is composed and printed and, in most weekly newspaper shops, considerable job printing is done as well.

In plants of medium size and for large city dailies, six general departments are set up, each requiring persons specially trained by education or experience. They are: editorial-news, business, promotion, mechanical, data processing, and administrative. Except for data processing, which has evolved during the 1960s and 1970s, these departments have been traditional with newspapers over a very long period of development.

Editorial-news department

All reading material (that is, everything except advertising) is assembled in the editorial department. This may call for several divisions, the number depending on the size of the newspaper. A large newspaper's editorial-news department will have five general divisions.

Newsroom. All general news is either prepared or processed in the newsroom. The world, national, and state news is brought in by wire for editing either by hand or through electronic editing terminals. The city editor assigns reporters to cover local news stories. News is received by telephone, by telegraph, and through personal interview. This room is a busy place from early in the day until press time, the intensity increasing as the deadline for copy approaches.

The large city newspaper also may have several specialized news departments — music, art, finance, agriculture, movies, radio, television. Nearly all newspapers have columns devoted exclusively to society and sports, the latter a major division on large newspapers.

Copydesk. Located in the newsroom but almost a separate division is the copydesk, where the stories turned in by reporters and checked by the city editor are examined by experienced copyreaders. They eliminate unnecessary and inappropriate words and phrases, correct spelling and punctuation, check facts, indicate paragraphs, and write headlines. When all the copy has been processed for the composing room, page layouts are made showing where stories are to be placed.

Editorial room. In another section of the news department or in a room to themselves are the editor of the editorial pages and the editorial writers. They handle the material that goes on the editorial page, including feature stories, book reviews, and letters from readers; they write the editorial comment reflecting the newspaper's opinion on important issues.

Picture division. Metropolitan newspapers each have a large staff of photographers who receive assignments from the picture editor, city editor, or managing editor. Space must be provided for photographic supplies and darkroom work. This division works closely with the newsroom.

Library. Connected with the news department, particularly in larger newspaper plants, is a library, popularly called *the morgue.* The library contains material that is considered "dead copy" but may be used again to "background" or fill out current stories. Filed here are clippings from past issues of the paper—stories of local history and of persons prominent in the community; facts and figures regarding local utilities, important civic improvements, rosters of community organizations and lists of their officers from year to year; facts about the city and county government and the city, county, and state budgets; and the financial statements of banks and savings and loan associations. These facts are clipped as they appear and catalogued alphabetically so they may be found easily.

During a war period many pictures of martial activities, of soldiers in camp or in action, and of important officers are filed. Mats and cuts of persons prominent in national affairs and in the local community also are filed in the morgue. Pictures of churches, school buildings, public buildings of every sort, bridges, important highways, parks, and the like are all subject to repeated use and must be preserved.

In the library are reference books—an encyclopedia, a complete history of the United States, histories of the state and local community if available, maps of the world, ocean charts, a globe, a world almanac, a book of quotations, an up-to-date dictionary, books pertaining to military operations, reference magazines, and trade journals. The larger the newspaper, the greater the demand for precise, diversified information, making the need for an adequate library imperative.

In the library also are bound files of the newspaper, files of competing papers, or microfilms of each. These will be consulted constantly not only by the editorial staff but by people of the community and visiting newspaper and magazine writers.

Business department

The business department is responsible for the efficient operation of all the newspaper's revenue-producing activites. It directs sales and collections. It receives, expends, and invests money. It supervises everything pertaining to the business side of the newspaper, including advertising, circulation, and job printing.

Advertising division. This is the most important section of the business department and is divided according to the types of advertising produced.

First, there is the group that prepares copy and sells space to local advertisers. This must be a smoothly organized sales staff because it has all local merchants, manufacturers, and service institutions as prospective customers.

Second, there is the department of general advertising, sometimes called foreign or national advertising. This department looks after advertising from outside sources, usually the advertising of distant manufacturers and jobbers who have a product sold by local dealers or for which the company wishes to find a dealer.

A third essential department deals with the smallest ads — the classifieds — and requires capable direction. The classified ad department brings in valuable revenue and at the same time builds much goodwill for the newspaper.

Some newspapers have still another division to handle legal advertising — publication of official notices that must be run in connection with settlements brings in valuable revenue and at the same time builds records of all kinds from city, county, and state.

Circulation division. Circulation is the lifeblood of the newspaper. Without it the newspaper would carry no advertising, and without advertising the newspaper could not survive.

To perform its important selling, delivering, and collecting duties effectively, the circulation division is split into several units. The largest is the group that handles the city circulation. Making the paper a welcome daily visitor to every home is a task that requires careful supervision, a large staff, and hard work. On the large city newspapers hundreds of carriers and other employes are used in distribution, while many serve as salespeople and collectors.

Because the publisher normally likes to extend the influence of the newspaper as far into the surrounding territory as possible, the circulation division is organized to obtain subscribers in other towns of the county. Papers are sold through carriers, usually boys or girls residing in the towns.

Farmers on the rural routes in the county and adjoining counties and former residents now living in distant parts of the country also want the news or their "home community." Their newspapers come by mail.

One of the continuing problems of the circulation division is to find suitable transportation for long distances. Newspapers must be on their way while the news is still fresh. Consequently, large city newspapers have a transportation or traffic department that provides trucks, cars, and motorcycles for delivery to distant points and also keeps close check on airline, train, and bus service.

Job printing division. Smaller newspapers often do job printing in a separate department in their plants. Business houses want stationery, forms, statements, catalogs, circulars, and broadsides printed. The public wants wedding announcements and invitations, birth announcements, personal stationery, club programs, and other items. In farming communities, printing auction sale bills is important business. Schools and churches frequently need printing service. All these and more are handled in the job printing division.

Promotion department

Newspapers sometimes are accused of not taking their own medicine. It is said they urge others to advertise but seldom make use of advertising themselves. This may have been true in earlier days, but it is not so in the majority of newspaper plants today.

Most newspaper managers realize the value of promoting their own wares, telling readers how well the classified ads pull, showing merchants how to increase sales and turnover, calling readers' attention to outstanding features in the news columns, and urging subscribers to send the paper to relatives and friends. Promotion has become a specialized business. The person who can produce attractive promotion material and organize campaigns is valuable on the newspaper staff.

Mechanical department

Marvelous machinery today does much of the work that was done by hand years ago. New devices are continuously being developed to save time and labor and to improve the quality of the mechanical department's work. Plants using the newer cold-type or phototype processes, instead of the traditional hot-metal method of setting type, embody the following functions: composing, makeup, photographic platemaking, and presswork. In the few plants that still depend on the hot-metal processes, this department has four main divisions: composing room, stereotyping room, engraving room, and pressroom.

In the so-called cold-type plants, news copy and straight matter are composed by electric typewriters and electronic scanners or on terminals feeding directly into a computer. Heads and display type are variously set or assembled on paper or film. Ads are composed and assembled by similar means and duplicated in photoproofs or the equivalent for the advertiser to approve. Pages made up by "pasteup" methods then go to the process camera. Completed pages on film are printed on a thin press plate; the number of pages per plate is determined by the size of the press. These steps are identical whether for web-press or sheet-fed offset.

In traditional hot-metal plants, the copy sent down by the news and advertising departments goes first to the composing room. News copy or *straight matter* is "set" by operators at typesetting machines. Pictures and other illustrations are sent to the engraving room where *cuts* are made.

Advertising copy is set by machine and by hand, and everything is then assembled in steel *chases,* page size.

These chases are sent to the stereotyping room, where plates are cast from molten metal for the press. If the press is a flatbed press instead of a rotary, the forms are sent to the press without being stereotyped.

The processes followed in each of these divisions of the mechanical department are described fully in later chapters.

Data processing department

The addition of the computer to newspaper operations has necessitated the development of an entirely new section of highly trained personnel and sophisticated equipment. From the smallest publications to the largest some degree of reliance on data processing methods is becoming generally standardized. All departments are affected by the application of the "new technology" and are thus closely interrelated with the data processing department. The nature of this interaction is made clear in ensuing portions of the text.

Administrative department

In a properly functioning newspaper, the many independent operations must be coordinated by a strong administrative unit. This unit is made up of the owners and executives whose duty is to establish and direct consistent, uniform policies.

The administrative department exercises authority over all other departments of the newspaper. Directly responsible to it are the editor-in-chief and the business manager, who in turn exercise full control over the "news side" and the "business side." The mechanical superintendent, while in complete charge of the production department, is in most cases responsible to the business manager, not directly to the administrative department.

One of the important responsiblities of the administration is to see that efficiency is maintained and that each department understands the close relationship it has with all the others.

FACTORS THAT AFFECT ORGANIZATION

Clearly, then, the stereotyped lines of organization so familiar in most industries are not followed in the newspaper field. Each newspaper evolves a type of organization best adapted to its own particular business and editorial problems — a system consistent with its form of ownership and the capabilities of the major executives or owners.

The form of organization found in one well-managed and profitable newspaper would not necessarily improve matters in another slightly less well-managed institution. Before a newspaper setup is changed, therefore, a survey should be made to determine whether the contemplated change

would be beneficial. The general structure and the divisions of responsibility within a newspaper organization depend upon several factors, as
discussed below.

The publisher

Much of the philosophy of organization depends upon whether the
administrative head is distinctly interested in the business aspect, is
primarily an editor, or is a person interested in the mechanical end of the
operation. If administrators have had a business career or by nature are
particularly interested in profits, they probably will give special attention
to dividends and other matters connected with the business office. If they
are reporters or editorial writers, they may give greatest consideration to
covering the news field and to commenting editorially on community affairs. If they have spent most of their careers in the shop, they are likely to
be particularly interested in the typographical appearance of the
newspaper and in the equipment of the mechanical department. The
wisest publishers, however, will give attention to all these phases of
newspaper work and see that they operate in balance. In other words, they
will strive for excellence in all departments.

The community

Although the internal organization of any newspaper will be in-
fluenced to some extent by the community's population, it must be
remembered that newspapers of very limited circulations often operate in
densely populated cities. Such newspapers—a suburban weekly, for
example—will have a much less elaborate organization than newspapers in
the same community that may serve fifty times more readers. Population
has a direct effect upon newspaper organization in the smaller communities outside metropolitan areas.

Daily newspapers seldom operate in communities of less than 5,000,
since such communities usually cannot comfortably support more than one
or two weeklies or semiweeklies. The organization of a weekly newspaper is
somewhat less elaborate than that of the average daily. Since many basic
functions are needed to operate some weeklies but the ramifications of
these functions are limited, the staff is much smaller and the deadlines are
somewhat more leisurely. In general, the larger the community, the larger
the newspaper that serves it and the more complex and extended the
organization of that newspaper.

If the city's corporate limits spread over a wide territory or the
newspaper is located in a city that is next to a still larger city, circulation
and news-gathering problems are greatly increased. For example, should
the newspaper concentrate its circulation and news-gathering efforts in its
own city or in both cities?

If the city's business section is scattered or encompasses a wide area,
the cost of soliciting and servicing local advertisers will be higher than in

communities where business activities are concentrated in a relatively small area. Publishers who are alert to these local problems will organize their plants and employes to meet them efficiently.

Business conditions

Cities of the same population vary greatly in the number and size of business institutions and in the extent to which their merchants and manufacturers will patronize a newspaper. Where retail stores doing a large volume of business are eager to draw from a larger trade territory, newspapers have a better opportunity to sell advertising space and there is a strong inducement to increase circulation. In such a situation, the publisher would give special consideration to the advertising and circulation departments to take full advantage of the opportunity to gain business from those sources. The emphasis within a newspaper organization is likely to be upon opportunities for increasing revenue and building the financial strength of the newspaper.

MEETING MAJOR NEEDS

Particular needs common to all newspapers must be met. These are consistent policy, quality of product, and an accurate check on the business. Proper organization provides the answer.

Statement of policy

The newspaper cannot escape periodic statements of policy regarding its news, editorials, advertising, deadlines, and business practices. Neither can it, as a highly departmentalized organization, avoid frequent internal policy conflicts.

For example, the advertising manager may want a picture feature killed to make room for additional late advertising, but the circulation manager may want it to run because it is part of a plan to increase reader interest and build circulation. The city editor frequently wants inside pages held open so that local news can appear throughout the newspaper, but the mechanical superintendent usually is eager to close these pages early to avoid extended deadlines and overtime pay. The editorial-news department may be planning a campaign for a muncipally owned and operated light plant, while the advertising department is preparing to renew the advertising contract of the privately owned utility presently serving the community. Such departmental conflicts are inevitable, but they must be resolved within the organization if the newspaper is to maintain a firmly established policy in the eyes of the public.

Maintenance of product quality

As a manufacturing industry, the newspaper has products to sell — advertising to businesses, and news and information to the public. The better the product, the better it will sell. A good newspaper is not achieved by accident but is the result of careful planning and organization, each department working in close harmony with the others to produce a constantly improving newspaper.

The newspaper must maintain consistent advertising to bring in a major share of the revenue needed to meet operating expenses. The advertising department must guarantee a strong circulation in order to sell advertising. The circulation department must have a live newspaper filled with news, pictures, and other features to draw readers if it is to build a good circulation.

Each department must be active and efficient. If one is not strong, the others are weakened, and the product — the newspaper — begins to deteriorate.

Records of income and expenses

The many functions involved in newspaper production create almost unlimited possibilities for leakage of funds and waste of valuable time and materials. When labor and material costs are high and going higher, it is especially important to watch expenses closely. Specifically, management can do these things:

1. Take advantage of quantity discounts where the operation permits quantity buying. Frequently this gives the added saving of prepaid transportation.
2. Take time discounts. They are the easiest and yet one of the most frequently overlooked ways to save money. Check laborsaving devices and streamline production schedules.
3. Check inventories often enough so orders can be placed systematically rather than suffering the penalty of extra charges from placing orders that call for rush handling and delivery.
4. Encourage workers using supplies — whether they be in the office or the plant — to give tips about better and cheaper ways of carrying out an operation. They should not be committed to a hard and fast system that is never reviewed and is purely on the "reorder of present supply" basis.
5. Make an accurate check of profits and losses daily. Only through systematic accounting practices and prudent organization will the newspaper manager be able to keep the business sound financially.

3

Types of ownership and operation

The community press truly offers opportunity for everyone, from the beginner who wants a solid journalism background to the career newsman who won't be happy until he has his own paper

Garrett W. Ray

At one time all newspapers were local, and most were individual enterprises. The earliest colonial newspaper was owned and operated by a printer as a supplement to his job printing business, and his individual ownership plan is still popular in small communities. But many communities grew rapidly and, as newpaper operations became more complex and opportunities to serve increased, other types of newspaper ownership, management, and operation were developed. Those found most commonly today are individual ownership, partnership, corporation, group or chain ownership, employe ownership, vertical ownership, and joint operation.

INDIVIDUAL OWNERSHIP

Although some daily newspapers operate under individual proprietorship, this type of ownership is more common among weekly newspapers. The owner usually is the editor and manager and when necessary serves in almost any position in the plant.

Advantages
1. The editor-proprietor is given absolute control of the newspaper.
2. The owner can make all decisions on business and editorial policies.
3. The owner receives all profits from the business.
4. The owner is intimately connected with the newspaper; in the minds of the public, owner and newspaper are one and the same.

Disadvantages
1. Individual ownership is not ~~adaptable~~ *conducive* to an expanding business.
2. Unlimited liability is placed on the individual owner.

18

3. Success of the newspaper depends heavily on the ability and credit status of the owner-publisher.
4. Long-time loans may be difficult to obtain, since creditors must consider the life expectancy of the proprietor.
5. In case of the owner's death, the paper must be probated in the estate. This may mean a temporary publisher and a decline in business.
6. The proprietor is always liable for debts of the paper, even to the extent of personal possessions.

A typical example of successful individual proprietorship is the Ellsworth, Maine, *American,* a weekly newspaper with almost 8,000 readers. James Russell Wiggins is publisher and editor as well as sole owner.

PARTNERSHIP

A partnership is formed when two or more persons make an ownership agreement, either orally or in writing, for the purpose of establishing, purchasing, or operating a newspaper.

Advantages
1. Persons of different capabilities and financial standings are permitted to pool their talents and money.
2. Needed capital may be provided by permitting persons not familiar with the publishing business to invest in the enterprise.
3. Responsibilities of newspaper publishing are divided, thereby lessening the load for each owner.
4. Judgment of more than one mind is brought into the business operation.

Disadvantages
1. Each partner is liable for the newspaper's entire debt.
2. Each person is privileged to obligate the newspaper.
3. Each partner runs the risk of becoming liable for an unusually large debt incurred by any one of the other partners.
4. Partnership may be discontinued at any time by death or withdrawal of a partner or by the sale of that interest.
5. Long-term credit is sometimes hard to obtain.
6. A partner who is irresponsible in personal or business relations may jeopardize the interest of the other partner or partners.

A partnership may take one of two forms: general or limited.

A *general partnership* is based on an agreement between two or more persons to establish or purchase a newspaper and engage in publishing it. It is the more common form of partnership, but each partner is liable to an unlimited degree. Each partner is a general agent for the newspaper, and in any business matter one partner may act for both.

A *limited partnership* enables a publisher who is a general partner to raise ownership capital with limited liability for those who provide the additional capital. A limited partner is responsible for the debts of the newspaper only to the amount agreed upon as an investment and has no right to contract for the newspaper and no control of its assets.

Another form of business association, called the *joint-stock company,* is more common in England than in the United States. While really not a partnership, it is somewhat similar. A joint-stock company is created by a contractual agreement, which usually provides for a board of directors and officers to manage the newspaper's business affairs and for the issuance of capital-unit stock certificates, which may be transferred freely or sold. Each capital contributor is under limited liability as a partner.

The Dardanelle, Ark., *Post-Dispatch* provides a clear illustration of the partnership operation. Joe Stock serves as news director and Fritz Freeman directs the advertising, both under the label of Freestock Enterprises. Thus the traditional dichotomy that characterizes every newspaper — the "news side" and the "business side" — is resolved by the expertise of two parties working independently but in cooperation.

CORPORATION

For daily newspapers the corporation is the most common form of ownership because it is more adaptable to problems of expansion, centralization, or transfer of fractional ownership.

Advantages
1. The personal liability of investors, in case of lawsuit, is limited to their share of interest in the corporation.
2. The business of the newspaper is not readily affected by changes in stock ownership.
3. Transfer of control is flexible.
4. Operations can be expanded easily by increasing capital.
5. A publisher, who owns 51 percent of the stock in the newspaper and whose powers are defined in the articles of incorporation, may control the policies and obtain, from outside sources, 49 percent of the capital needed for operation.

Disadvantages
1. Rigorous federal and state regulations require detailed reports at frequent intervals.
2. Transfer-of-stock tax and other corporation taxes are imposed.
3. Profits distributed to stockholders are first taxed as income to the corporation and again as dividends to the stockholders.

Representative of the many thousands of newspaper corporations is the Colorado Springs, Colo., *Gazette-Telegraph*. C. H. Hoiles is chairman of the board and publisher of this thriving daily in the 55,000–60,000 circulation class.

GROUP OR CHAIN OWNERSHIP

As in other branches of industry and business, chains of newspapers can consolidate financial interests, editorial direction, and administrative command.

Daily newspaper groups, now at an all-time high in total number of newspapers and total circulation, have attained an average size of 5.7 dailies per group, according to the *Editor & Publisher International Year Book*.

Advantages
1. Supplies may be purchased through a central office with discounts for quantity.
2. Advertising space may be sold nationally, with a single organization representing all newspapers in the group.
3. Accounting methods can be standardized, permitting easy comparison of properties and quick correction of administrative errors.
4. Encouragement and stamina are given to publishers within the group through exchange of ideas and experiences.
5. First rights to valuable features are obtained more easily.
6. Ownership of newspaper stock is made possible to promising journalists who otherwise might not be able to obtain it.
7. Certain details of bookkeeping and other office procedure may be centered in a common office for all newspapers.

Disadvantages
1. Managers or publishers might not feel compelled to promote the local community to the same degree that they would if the newspaper were owned by them or by a local corporation or partnership.
2. Subscribers sometimes feel that the newspaper is managed by "remote control," that they are not as close to the editor as they would like to be.
3. Permanence of management is more in question than when the newspaper is entirely locally owned.

Newspaper chains take various forms, depending on the point of operation at which cooperation is dominant. In some cases a holding company controls at least 51 percent of the stock in each newspaper. The holding company may have supervision over editorial policies of individual newspapers, or the company may allow each to formulate its own. Major materials, such as newsprint, machinery and other equipment, and supplies usually are bought through general headquarters. Daily, weekly, and monthly reports of business from each newspaper are required by the holding company.

Newspaper groups have been formed without a common holding company but with a chain of command from an elected set of officers and directors. Publishers in the organization have the controlling interest in the newspapers they publish and also may have an interest in the other newspapers. They manage their own newspapers and formulate their own policies with the advice and counsel of the officers and directors of the general organization. The cohesive force of the group comes from the men and women who compose it, who have holdings in each other's properties, and who mutually share traditions and principles upon which the group was established.

In some group organizations there is strong direction from the holding company in the naming of editors and managers for each newspaper. The editors and managers, however, may still be very influential in formulating newspaper policies in their individual communities. While a majority of the stock in each newspaper may be owned by the holding company, editors and employes of each newspaper are generally encouraged to buy shares also.

Of the approximately 160 chains in the United States, the Gannett publications represent the largest individual group, with 57 newspapers under one ownership or control. The Newhouse list of 22 metropolitan newspapers claims the largest aggregate circulation. Other giants in the field include Scripps-Howard, Knight-Ridder, Booth, Cox, and Copley.

EMPLOYE OWNERSHIP

A plan of ownership instituted by some publishers allows employes to buy stock in the newspaper corporation. In some cases the employes own a majority of the stock and control the policies of the newspaper.

Advantages
1. Employes are given an incentive to protect the best interests of the newspaper.
2. Sense of ownership on the part of employes helps to create high morale.
3. Interdepartmental barriers are more easily broken down.
4. Fewer changes are made in personnel.
5. Questions pertaining to wages, hours, and other production matters are understood better and are more easily handled.

Disadvantages
1. Length of employe service is likely to be given greater consideration than production abilities.
2. Sentiment may prevail over good judgment in matters of management and policy.

3. Opportunities for bringing new blood into the organization are fewer.
4. Sale of property is difficult, even if it should appear beneficial to the newspaper.

Employe ownership usually develops where a publisher has held the controlling interest and upon retirement or death wants the paper continued under its established policies in the hands of associates. Furthermore, the publisher appreciates the interest and the ability of employes and desires to recognize their loyalty in this way.

In some cases, the stock is willed to employes, but more often they are simply given the opportunity to acquire it. The instrument usually created to carry out the employe ownership plan is a stock trust agreement. It enables eligible employes to enjoy a beneficial interest in company shares, to vote them, and to receive dividends, but it prevents those shares from being sold to anyone outside the employe group. If a stockholder wants to dispose of the total or any portion of interest held, it may be sold to another employe or turned back to the trustees for resale.

The Fairbanks, Alaska, *Daily News-Miner* is a recent newspaper to become employe-owned. Its publisher, C. W. Snedden, devised the transfer of ownership to his employes as a practical way of keeping local control for the Fairbanks newspaper after the business had, in his judgment, grown too large for family ownership. *Daily News-Miner* employes are eligible to participate in the plan with one year of seniority and can acquire more stock as their time of service lengthens.

VERTICAL OWNERSHIP
A newspaper also may operate under a vertical ownership plan, meaning that the newspaper and the enterprises serving it are under common ownership. A corporation owning and operating a large city daily, for example, also may own and operate a radio or television station, a paper mill, a transportation system, and news and advertising syndicates. These allied institutions contribute to the success of the newspaper.

Advantages
1. Assures the newspaper of certain services and materials needed for its successful operation.
2. Ties the newspaper in with other communications media in giving service to a definite area.
3. Helps to reduce general expenses of newspaper operation.
4. Provides practical investment of newspaper profits.

Disadvantages
1. Widens publisher interests and responsibilities to the extent of a possible lessening of attention to the newspaper.
2. Capital that could be used for improvement of the newspaper might be drawn into financing of other jointly owned enterprises.

Perhaps the most outstanding example of vertical ownership has been provided by the Chicago, Ill., *Tribune*. The *Tribune* has owned and operated as many as 25 affiliates from coast to coast, including such subsidiaries as the Lower St. Lawrence Transportation Company, Marhill Mines, Tonawanda Paper Company, Manicougan Power Company, the Chicago Philharmonic Orchestra, the Ontario Paper Company, a construction firm, and radio and television stations.

JOINT OPERATION

A system of cooperative operation between two or more newspapers of different ownership within the same community is sometimes used to reduce maintenance and operation costs. The newspapers are produced in the same plant, but each has separate news and business offices and its own reporters and editors, advertising salespeople, and circulation employes; and each formulates its own editorial policy. With the introduction of web-offset, regional plants are being equipped to handle up to 20 or 30 weeklies in one plant.

For a joint publishing operation, an agreement is drawn up setting forth the financial obligations of each newspaper, or a corporation is formed representing capital from both ownerships.

Advantages
1. Maintenance and operation costs are reduced.
2. Productive hours in the plant are increased.
3. Pleasanter relations are developed among newspapers in a competitive field.
4. Attention of publishers and owners is focused more on the community than on competition.
5. Publishers may give more unified and complete newspaper service to their communities.
6. Advertisers usually are permitted to buy space either in all newspapers at a combination rate or in separate ones at the individual newspaper's standard rate.
7. Joint handling of some advertising and perhaps some news copy permits reduction of personnel in the news and advertising sections as well as in the mechanical department.

Disadvantages
1. With competition partly eliminated, efforts toward specific improvements might be lessened.
2. With reduced competition, publishers might strive for greater profits than their newspaper service deserves.
3. Use of common production facilities may lead to standardization, resulting in loss of newspaper individuality.

The Oklahoma Publishing Company combines joint operation in one plant of the Oklahoma City *Times,* an evening newspaper, and the *Daily Oklahoman,* a morning publication with Sunday editions. While the top management is the same for both newspapers, each has its own key executives such as city editor, news editor, sports editor, and columnists.

CHANGING OWNERSHIPS

It should be understood that a newspaper with a long publishing history might function under more than one of the above-described forms of ownership at various stages in its development.

A unique example is provided by the Cincinnati, Ohio, *Enquirer.* In 1848 the newspaper was under the individual proprietorship of Hiram Robinson. During the 1970s it operated as a partnership run by Washington McLean and his son. Later, the *Enquirer* was incorporated under American Security and Trust Company management. In 1952 the newspaper was converted to employe ownership. For some time it was a member of the chain operation headed by E. W. Scripps, until it was separated from that group by a divestiture order enforced by the U.S. Department of Justice in 1964. The *Enquirer* was also operated as a vertical ownership when it obtained the Washington, D.C., *Post* and held that property for a few years. And it originated as a joint publishing venture when it was formed from the combination of two early newspapers, the *Journal* and the *Advertiser.*

It is apparent, then, that the form of ownership of any given newspaper may change from time to time as personal, economic, or legal influences dictate.

4

Personnel requirements

> You must keep abreast of changing life-
> styles, and with your employes, who
> don't want to work 50 to 55 hours a week,
> who want more than two weeks' vacation.
> If management remains static, the em-
> ployes will too.
>
> *Charles Baum*

How well a newspaper succeeds in meeting its responsibilities depends on the caliber of its personnel as well as on the form and extent of its organization. It must have a sufficient number of trained and experienced persons to perform the duties required in publishing a newspaper.

FACTORS THAT DETERMINE PERSONNEL

Three factors determine the size and character of a newspaper's personnel: the size of the paper, the form of ownership or operation, and the extent and condition of equipment.

Size of paper

On a small weekly newspaper, where demands of the individual positions are not too great, it is possible for one person to handle several jobs. there are newspapers being operated successfully by a man and his wife. One may serve as editor, business manager, ad solicitor, composing machine operator, and press operator. The other may fill the positions of bookkeeper, bill collector, society editor, reporter, or machine operator. Their children, too, each may have a part to perform.

When Mr. and Mrs. Robert A. Bowling took over the Montgomery City, Mo., *Standard,* most of the work for the first few years was done by the Bowlings and their three children. Others on the work force were three full-time and two part-time employes, but the members of the Bowling family were the newspaper's mainstay.

On a large city daily, where work falls heavily on every department, there are the positions common to the average newspaper as well as many additional ones made necessary by the specialized work required in publishing a metropolitan newspaper.

When the Washington, D.C., *Post* issued a special section describing its building, it announced that the efforts of 939 persons went into publishing the *Post*. Of these, approximately one in seven was directly engaged in digging up, collecting, checking, writing, and preparing the news and feature content of each day's newspaper. Others—also one in seven—solicited and prepared advertising. Two out of seven handled printing and composition. Another two out of seven were needed to circulate the paper into distribution channels. The remainder were employed in general administration. All these 939 persons, scattered through many departments and filling a variety of positions, have a common goal: to make the Washington *Post* a good newspaper.

On newspapers falling between the "man-and-wife weekly" and the metropolitan daily, personnel requirements will vary with the service given to the communities. The Hannibal, Mo., *Courier-Post,* a daily newspaper, has a force of 49, exclusive of carriers. All newspaper promotion is done by the advertising department. In the mechanical department, the platemaking division and the pressroom operate as a unit with a single superintendent. The three press operators also run the cameras and the platemaking equipment. (See Table 4.1.)

Type of ownership

The number of persons required to publish a newspaper depends to some extent upon whether it is individually owned, operated under a part-

Table 4.1.   Departments and chief personnel of the Hannibal, Mo., *Courier-Post*

Administrative Department	*News Department*	
General manager	News editor	Reporters—3
Accountant	City editor	Photographer
Bookkeeper, assistant	Sports editor	Education-religion writer
General office—2	Society editor	Farm area editor

Advertising Department	*Circulation Department*
Manager, retail advertising	Manager, circulation
Manager, classified advertising	Supervisors, carrier—2
Clerk, classified advertising	Carriers, city—81
Salespeople, advertising—4	Carriers, outside city—135
	Motor route drivers, independent contractors—6

Mechanical Department	
Superintendent, mechanical	Press operators, camera, platemakers—3
Superintendent, composing room	Printers, journeymen—6
Superintendent, mail	Perforator operators—3
Head press operator	Assistants, part-time—4

Total personnel, including carriers: 261

nership or a corporation, a member of a group organization, under
employe ownership, or published with another newspaper from a common
plant.

Usually, in a partnership those who have invested their money in the
business are active in its operation. As under individual ownership, the
abilities and services of the owners would materially reduce the amount of
labor otherwise needed to produce the newspaper.

Borrowing funds necessary for conducting a newspaper is usually
easier for a corporation than an individual or a partnership, and the corporate owners also are more willing to assume heavy obligations when it
seems opportune to add personnel and expand the services of the newspaper.

Under employe ownership, those responsible for getting out the
newspaper have a personal interest that should react toward efficiency and
high morale; although employes may possibly retain their positions beyond
the age when they may give maximum efficiency. In either case, the size of
the newspaper's personnel is affected.

In a vertical form of operation, in which the owners of the newspaper
perhaps operate a radio station, a paper mill, an advertising service, a
feature syndicate, and a magazine publishing business, fewer persons may
be needed for the actual production of the newspaper than if it were the
sole project. Those who gather news or sell advertising for the radio station
may also provide the same service for the newspaper, and vice versa. Work
done for one of the several enterprises lessens work in the others, and some
of the labor costs customarily allotted to newspaper publishing may be
charged to another related enterprise.

A group newspaper may operate with fewer personnel than one of
similar size individually owned when some of the administrative work,
general bookkeeping, and record keeping is done at group headquarters.
A single promotion department may serve all the newspapers. Space in all
newspapers of the group may be sold to national advertisers, thereby assuring advertising linage for weaker members that they otherwise might not
obtain. A common purchasing agent might serve in buying major supplies
at more satisfactory prices than if each newspaper handled its own purchasing. Personnel to take care of these responsibilities at each of the
newspaper plants therefore might be eliminated or at least reduced.

Personnel can be reduced when two newspapers in the same community arrange to have all their mechanical work, and probably advertising and circulation as well, done in one plant by a single staff. A joint
publishing plan is carried out by the Lincoln, Nebr., *Journal* and *Star.*
Each newspaper has an independent editorial staff and separate offices for
handling news and editorial features; but the mechanical production, sale,
and distribution of the two papers are handled in one modern plant. The
two newspapers combine their news and editorial staffs for the Sunday
Journal-Star. Copy is written by the news and editorial staffs of both the
Journal and the *Star* and is edited and made up by the Sunday staff of the

Journal. The arrangement of departments and personnel for the Lincoln plan is shown in Table 4.2.

Laborsaving machinery and printing equipment in good repair reduce the time needed for many operations and make it possible for a newspaper to produce more with less personnel. Modernizing a building and rearranging the equipment also can help hold down the payroll.

By remodeling its building, rearranging departments, and adding equipment, the Columbus, Ga., *Ledger* and *Enquirer* expanded its circulation and number of pages by approximately 50 percent in a seven-year period. The number of employes increased only from 250 to 260, or 4 percent.

PERSONNEL BY DEPARTMENTS

Given the size of a newspaper and its type of operation, a careful look at the departments and the work done there provides a fair indication of the number and nature of personnel required.

Administrative department

On some newspapers, particularly those that are individually owned, one person is *general manager* and supervisor of work in all departments. He or she dictates the editorial policies, directs the business department, and watches over the mechanical department. This administrator either is the sole owner or is a responsible and experienced journalist employed by the owners. (See Table 4.3.)

On other newspapers, two persons divide the administrative responsibilities. A *business manager* directs the advertising staff, the circulation department, and the accounting department; and an *editor* writes the editorials, oversees the gathering and handling of news, and selects the features. Usually they are the sole owners or the principal stockholders in the newspaper corporation.

A three-way authority exists in some newspaper organizations. There is a head for each of the three main departments—business, editorial-news, and mechanical—and they confer and cooperate for the general operation of the newspaper plant.

Newspaper corporations have the usual officers: *president, vice-president, secretary,* and *treasurer.* Although the corporation's officers sometimes are not active in the publishing of the newspaper, usually they are important members of the administrative department. On some papers the president of the corporation is the publisher; on others he or she will serve as managing editor, editor, or business manager. On a number of papers the vice-president holds a responsible operative position such as managing editor, general manager, editor, business manager, or advertising manager.

When the president is not the directing head of the newspaper, the chief executive usually is the publisher or general manager. It is customary

Table 4.2. Departments and personnel for joint publishing of the Lincoln, Nebr., *Journal* and *Star*

EDITORIAL DEPARTMENT
(*Journal*—State Journal Co.; *Star*—Star Publ. Co.)

Journal	*Star*	Sunday *Journal-Star*
Executive Editor	Editor	Combined Staffs
2 Associate Editors		Sunday Editor

Department	*Department*	*Special Pages Feature*	
Editorial page	Editorial page	Magazine content	Church
Metropolitan news	Metropolitan news	Music	Plus same depart-
Regional news	Regional news	Art	ments as daily
Wire news	Wire news	Drama	
Farm news	Farm news	Movies	
Sports news	Sports news	Books	
Peoples' news	Peoples' news	Radio-television	
Syndicate features	Syndicate features	Business	
50 employes	33 employes		

Total editorial department personnel: 83

ADMINISTRATIVE DEPARTMENT
(Journal-Star Printing Co.)

Plant	Publication Policy	Accounting
Acquisition, engineering, repair and maintenance of building, machinery, equipment, fixtures, utilities, telephone service, and custodial service	Printing company sells advertising subject to advertising policy of each newspaper. It mechanically prints, sells, and distributes each paper.	Handles all bills and collections
13 employes	5 employes	12 employes

Total administrative department personnel: 30

MECHANICAL PRODUCTION, SALES, AND DISTRIBUTION
(Journal-Star Printing Co.)

Circulation	Data Processing	Mechanical	Advertising	Editorial Service
City—20	Computer supervision—1	Photoengraving—10	Classified—10	Photography—7
Out-of-state—10	Key punch—2	Composing—85	Local display—12	Library—4
Listroom—4	Programming—2	Pressroom—16	General display—2	Art—2
Mailroom—20	Control—1	Engineer and bldg.—10	Paper layout—2	
			Dispatch—10	
54 employes	6 employes	121 employes	36 employes	13 employes

Total production and distribution personnel: 230

Table 4.3.   Administrative department personnel

Weekly	Small Daily	Medium Daily	Metropolitan Paper
Publisher	Publisher	Publisher	Board of directors
Editor	Editor	Manager	Publisher
		Editor	Editor
			General manager
			Managing editor
			Business manager

Note: In addition to holding administrative positions, the editor and managing editor are the most important members of the editorial-news department.

in most such instances for the executive to be responsible to a *board of directors.*

On larger newspapers a business manager works under a general manager and duties will vary with the paper. The business manager may be in charge of all activities except those of the editorial and news department. Or the sole responsibility may be to direct the organization's finances. On still other newspapers duties may be confined to office routine, collections, and similar matters.

The type of administration for group newspapers depends upon the policies and preferences of the owners. In many group organizations some administrative responsibilities are centered at general headquarters, thereby reducing those of the individual newspaper.

Editorial-news department

Heading the editorial-news department is the *editor,* who on a smaller newspaper may write the editorials. If the editor is not adept at writing, he or she may merely determine the subjects to be discussed and leave the writing to an *editorial writer* (or allow the latter to do both). On most newspapers, though, the editor supervises the editorial page, confers with editorial writers, and oversees all matters pertaining to the newspaper's policies. (See Table 4.4.)

Working with the editor are the *managing editor* and the *news editor.* While they both work together in handling news material, ensuring that the editorial-news department has sufficient personnel and proper facilities for gathering the news and handling features is the chief responsibility of the managing editor; and seeing that all available news is sought and properly handled rests with the news editor.

Next in importance is the *city editor,* who sees that the community news is covered. This key person carefully lists all coming events and at the proper time directs *reporters* to cover them. The city desk is constantly open for "news tips," to which reporters may be assigned to run down the facts. Some reporters cover regular "beats" for news. *Rewriters,* who handle copy that has been previously used or fresh copy that needs revising, and *suburban correspondents,* who send in news from outlying neighborhoods, also are under the city editor's supervision. On large city newspa-

Table 4.4. Editorial-news department personnel

Weekly	Small Daily	Medium Daily	Metropolitan Paper
Publisher	Editor	Editor	Editor
Editor	City editor	City editor	Managing editor
Reporter	Sports editor	Telegraph editor	News editor
	Society editor	Makeup editor	Telegraph editor
	Reporter	Sports editor	Day city editor
		Society editor	Night city editor
		Special editors	State editor
		Copy editors	Makeup editor
		Photographers	Sports editor
		Reporters	Society editor
		Proofreaders	Woman's page editor
			Feature editor
			Sunday editor
			Special editors
			Editorial writers
			Rewriters
			Washington correspondents
			Special correspondents
			Reporters
			Photographers
			Copy editors
			Proofreaders
			Librarian

pers, the city desk is covered 24 hours a day, which requires a *night city editor* as well as a *day city editor.*

The *state editor* handles news from out in the state and usually is assisted by *special correspondents* or *special reporters* at the state capital and other important points. The Kansas City, Mo., *Star,* for example, which circulates mainly in Missouri and Kansas, has a state editor and special reporters in each of the two capitals.

Close-in news is always of greatest interest to a high percentage of a newspaper's readers. Consequently, city and state editors must take care to avoid duplication of effort. By reason of its location on the border of three states—Tennessee, Arkansas, and Mississippi—the Memphis, Tenn., *Commercial Appeal* has a tristate desk, where the news from the three states is handled. The *tristate editor* and the *metropolitan editor,* who has absorbed the functions formerly carried out by a city editor, work together closely in handling news, pictures, and features from their respective areas. All copy from the tristate desk passes through the metropolitan desk on its way to the copydesk, and the metropolitan editor meets daily with the tristate staff to plan methods and extent of coverage. This arrangement helps to avoid duplication in covering and handling the news.

The *telegraph editor* processes news that comes by wire. Since the Teletype machine grinds out far more news than can possibly be published, the telegraph editor must decide which items are to be used. Frequently, individual stories can be improved by adding facts having a local angle.

Washington correspondents keep in close touch with news and opinions at the nation's capital, sending accounts to their papers of all happenings that have a bearing on local conditions and interests.

The *society editor,* ever mindful of women's interests in community, social, and cultural life, covers meetings of women's clubs, weddings, receptions, style shows, and all other events in which women participate. The large city papers also have a *family page editor* who deals more elaborately with general news, pictures, and features of interest to men and women.

Because of the public's interest in sports, the *sports editor* holds a major position on larger dailies, organizing thorough coverage of all sports activities within the newspaper's immediate territory and compiling the scores and running accounts of national and world sports events. During the seasons for individual sports the staff of *sports reporters* and *photographers* cover all activities carefully. Editorial comment regarding teams, players, and events is provided in personal columns.

On metropolitan papers several sports reporters are employed, each covering a specific field. The transmitting facilities of the newspaper are drawn upon heavily to carry reports quickly to readers who are eager for sports news.

Since features comprise a large portion of the modern newspaper's offerings, some papers have a *feature editor* who selects from available material the stories and illustrations to be used and directs the handling of them. Some of these features may be provided by members of the news staff, and others by free-lance writers, but most come from feature syndicates, which furnish wide assortments in daily packages.

The *picture editor* has become an important member of the news staff by reason of the widening interest in photojournalism. From this desk assignments are issued to *staff photographers* whose pictures of persons, things, and events add interest to the day's news. Working under the managing editor and the city editor, the picture editor selects the photographs to be used for each issue.

Metropolitan newspapers have a number of *special editors* to cover news connected with industries that contribute to community progress and touch the lives of newspaper readers closely.

Newspapers published in the great agricultural states have farm departments headed by *farm editors. Special reporters* and *contact people* throughout the agricultural area provide articles about farm methods, crop production, agricultural experiments, soil conservation, livestock breeding, farm organization activities, and other matters of interest to rural residents.

In states where oil or some other mineral is the basis of a vast industry, an editor is maintained to cover the news of that field. Each of the large city newspapers in Texas has an *oil editor* who each week provides many columns of news material of special significance to oil producers and workers and to persons who have investments in oil.

So many transactions and movements take place in the field of finance that many city newspapers have found it advisable to have a *financial news editor* who keeps in contact with banks, investment agencies, loan companies, realtors, and contractors.

Other special editors on city papers are *music editor, dramatic editor, radio editor, church editor, fashion editor, movie editor, book editor,* and *school editor.*

With so many persons and sections furnishing news items, there must be some well-defined coordinating plan. This is supplied by the *makeup editor.* With the aid of schedules prepared by the editors and the advertising department, the makeup editor prepares a dummy or layout, which shows where each news item, headline, picture, feature, and advertisement is to be located. Most newspapers have a certain ratio of reading material and advertising which they like to observe as a standard, usually 40 percent news and 60 percent advertising. They also set limits on space for certain types of news and features, such as three pages for sports, one for financial matters, and two for comics. Other makeup practices may limit the volume of pictures. News items and features do not go into the newspaper in a haphazard manner. Although the makeup editor usually is permitted considerable discretion, there will be conferences on many matters with the *editors, composing room supervisor,* and *advertising manager.*

Special editing and paring of copy is done at the copydesk by *copyreaders* or *copy editors,* who also write headlines for the individual stories. The copydesk is traditionally a large horseshoe-shaped table with a slot in it, enabling the *head copy editor* to sit at the center and deal copy to and consult with other copy editors. Figure 4.1 shows copy editors and reporters at work in the news department of the Lincoln, Nebr., *Journal.*

The familiar U-shaped copydesk is disappearing from the scene as individual electronic editing terminals for copy editors are taking its place. The copydesk area, nevertheless, remains as an integral operating unit in the news operation.

The Sunday edition of a metropolitan newspaper has become so popular that editing, printing, and distribution are almost a separate enterprise from that of producing the other issues of the week. A *Sunday editor* and a special staff, assisted by members of the regular staff, select and produce the vast and varied material that goes into this edition.

Proofreaders carefully and quickly peruse proofs of galleys for errors that need to be corrected before the material goes into the forms to be made ready for the press. Usually those who read the news galleys have their desks in the news department and those who read advertising proofs have theirs in the advertising department, but in some plants all proofreaders are positioned in the mechanical department.

Closely connected with the editorial-news department of a

Fig. 4.1. A section of the newsroom of the Lincoln, Nebr., *Journal* showing the "slot," a term that refers to the inside curve of a specially made desk for copy editors. The person inside the slot directs the work of copy editors who gather around the outside curve. Reporters face the newsdesk and the slot.

metropolitan paper is the library of reference books, magazines, pamphlets, maps, clippings, cuts, mats, and photographs, which often provide valuable supplemental material for news and feature stories. The *librarian* and the staff keep this material in order for ready reference by editors, editorial writers, and reporters and constantly add new material. On smaller newspapers, the reference collection consists of only a few books, with cuts, photographs, and clippings; the responsibility of filing usually is with one of the reporters, the proofreader, or a person otherwise employed in the office. The collection usually is referred to as "the morgue."

An organizational diagram (Fig. 4.2) shows personnel and desk arrangement in the editorial-news department of the Lincoln, Nebr., *Journal*.

Business and accounting department

The business department is responsible for everything that brings in revenue and for transactions that require funds to be paid out. *Business managers* need to be economy minded but not so much so that they hamper the organization's operations or lessen the newspaper's quality. As good executives, they thoroughly understand the newspaper's ideals and goals as well as its resources. They must keep in step with modern methods and adapt them to the best use of the newspaper's departments. The func-

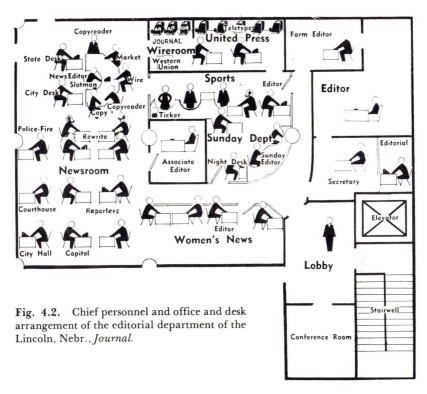

Fig. 4.2. Chief personnel and office and desk arrangement of the editorial department of the Lincoln, Nebr., *Journal.*

tion of this department is to ensure enough money to pay the running expenses. (See Table 4.5.)

A division of the business department is the bookkeeping and accounting office. There the financial records and accounts are kept; correspondence is carried on; necessary purchases of supplies, materials, and services are made; the payroll is handled, and the budget is watched. For a weekly or a small daily newspaper, usually one (or two) person takes care of all the details connected with this office. On larger papers the *treasurer* of the corporation or the *cashier* usually heads this division. This person is assisted by the *controller* and *auditor* and the necessary number of *bookkeepers, record clerks, correspondents,* and *tabulators.*

Advertising department

The chief source of a newspaper's revenue is advertising. The *advertising manager* sees that all available accounts are well serviced and keeps the advertising volume at a high level. He or she is constantly on the alert for new accounts. In the advertising department there are at least three units—local display advertising, general or national advertising, and classified advertising. On the larger papers each division has a special manager. (See Table 4.6.)

Table 4.5.   Accounting personnel

Weekly	Small Daily	Medium Daily	Metropolitan Paper
Bookkeeper	Cashier	Treasurer	Treasurer
	Bookkeeper	Cashier	Controller
		Stenographer	Auditor
		Bookkeepers	Cashier
			Stenographers
			Bookkeepers
			Tabulators
			Record clerks
			Correspondents

The *local display* or *retail advertising manager* and a force of *advertising salespeople* take care of advertising for local business firms and search continually for new accounts. They study other newspapers, trade journals, and syndicated services and keep a close check on the business districts of the newspaper's territory. Sales personnel are assigned definite territories or a certain number of accounts to serve. Their worth is determined by the number of advertising column inches credited to them each month and by their ability to satisfy the merchants served. Assisting in providing suitable copy for advertisers are *artists* and *copywriters.*

The *general* or *national advertising manager* handles the advertising that comes from sources outside the newspaper's immediate area. Manufacturers of items in general use and those with special trade names always desire to build up the demand for their products in every community. Automobile manufacturers, oil companies, food manufacturers, appliance representatives, and others recognize newspapers as effective means of increasing sales. The national advertising manager usually works with *special advertising representatives* in the large factory centers to keep the newspaper sold to these advertisers and occasionally makes trips to the large centers for personal interviews with manufacturers or with the advertising agencies handling their accounts.

Table 4.6.   Advertising personnel

Weekly	Small Daily	Medium Daily	Metropolitan Paper
Adv. salesperson	Adv. manager	Adv. manager	Adv. manager
	Adv. salesperson	Display adv.	Display adv. mgr.
	Classified	mgr.	Classif. adv. mgr.
	salesperson	Classif. adv.	Nat'l. adv. mgr.
		mgr.	Copywriters
		Nat'l. adv.	Artists
		mgr.	Adv. salespeople
		Copywriters	Tel. solicitors
		Artists	Spec. representatives
		Adv. salespeople	Research director
		Tel. solicitors	Interviewers
			Clerks

Research to ascertain the possibilities of developing advertising accounts and the results from certain campaigns is carried on extensively by larger newspapers. In addition to taking care of such details, the *research director*, assisted by *interviewers* and *clerks*, conducts surveys, wins the cooperation of local dealers in merchandising the products that are advertised, and formulates plans for strengthening and improving advertising efforts.

The classified advertising department is significant to every newspaper not only for the revenue it produces but also for the reader interest it creates. The *classified advertising manager*, who has an abundance of customers to serve, uses *street, correspondence,* and *telephone salespeople.* A great force of telephone solicitors is employed on large city newspapers.

Circulation department

Some newspapers and other publications manage to exist on little advertising and a few in modern times have survived without any, but none can hope to last unless it has the vital element of circulation. (See Table 4.7.)

The *circulation manager* has attained high respect for important contributions to the success of a newspaper. Here is a specialist just as the advertising manager, the promotion manager, the chief editorial writer, and the mechanical superintendent. With a force of *solicitors, carriers, supervisors, collectors,* and other assistants, the circulation manager sells and delivers the paper and collects for it.

The circulation areas of some newspapers are so large and the distribution of the newspaper is so widespread that the territory is divided, with a manager or supervisor over each portion. The circulation personnel of a metropolitan paper includes a *city circulation manager*, a *country circulation manager*, a *mail circulation manager*, and sometimes a *Sunday*

Table 4.7.   Circulation personnel

Weekly	Small Daily	Medium Daily	Metropolitan Paper
Duties divided among newspaper's personnel	Circ. mgr. Supervisor Carriers	Circ. director State circ. mgr. City circ. mgr. Supervisors Dist. mgrs. Carriers Distributors Agents St. salespeople Mailers	Circ. director State circ. mgr. City circ. mgr. Mail circ. mgr. Sunday circ. mgr. Traffic mgr. Dist. supervisors Branch supervisors Route supervisors Distributors Salespeople Truck drivers Carriers Agents Mailers

circulation manager. The responsibilities of each are apparent in the titles they hold. The delivery of the newspaper requires *street salespeople,* city and suburban *carriers, motor route carriers, outside country dealers, agents, mailers,* and others.

Promotion department

The promotion department prepares newspaper advertising, direct-mail material, film advertising, radio scripts, and probably television programming. The personnel of this department consists of the *promotion manager,* probably an *assistant promotion manager,* and other help that may be required, including *copywriters, artists, photographers, typists,* and *correspondents.* (See Table 4.8.)

Mechanical department

The mechanical department employes provide composition and print the material produced by the editorial-news and advertising departments. It usually is referred to as one department, although in some plants it is divided into the composing room and the mechanical department. (See Table 4.9.)

If the composing room and the mechanical department are considered a unit, the person who heads it is known as the *mechanical superintendent.* If there are two departments, they are headed by the *composing room supervisor* and the *mechanical superintendent.* The composing room works with the editorial-news department, and the mechanical department works with the business department. In other words, the final authority on any question arising in the composing room rests with the composing room supervisor and the editor, and for any question arising in the mechanical department the authority rests with the mechanical superintendent and the business manager.

The head of either of these divisions fully understands the mechanical process of putting out a newspaper and usually has had experience as a *typesetting machine operator* or *compositor.* When anything goes wrong with the machinery, the supervisor knows what needs to be done to have it running smoothly again and as head also knows whether the employes are doing efficient work.

Table 4.8. Promotion personnel

Weekly	*Small Daily*	*Medium Daily*	*Metropolitan Paper*
None	Work done by advertising manager	Promotion manager Copywriters Artists Typists	Promotion manager Assistant manager Copywriters Artists Photographers Typists Correspondents

Table 4.9. Mechanical personnel

IN PLANTS MAKING FULL OR PARTIAL USE OF COLD TYPE OR PHOTOTYPE

Weekly	Small Daily	Medium Daily	Metropolitan Paper
Typist(s)	Mech. supt.	Mech. supt.	Mech supt.
Makeup (and photographer)	Typists	Comp. supervisor	Comp. supervisor
Pasteup	Pasteup	Press supervisor	Press supervisor
Platemaker and press operator	Operator for photolettering machine	Pasteup	Markup
	Makeup	Markup	Pasteup
	Process photographer	Typists	Typists
	Platemaker	Teletypesetter operators	Teletypesetter operators
	Offset press operator	Phototypesetters	Hot-metal machine operators
	Helpers	Makeup	Floorpeople on type conversion to cold type
	News photographer (also operates electronic engraver)	Process photographer	Makeup
		Platemakers	Process photographer
		Offset press operators	Platemakers
		Helpers	Offset press operators
		Electronic engravers	Helpers
			Electronic engravers

IN PLANTS USING TRADITIONAL HOT-METAL EQUIPMENT

Weekly	Small Daily	Medium Daily	Metropolitan Paper
Typesetting machine operator	Mech. supt.	Mech. supt.	Mech. supt.
Compositor	Typesetting machine operators	Composing room supervisor	Composing room supervisor
Press operator	Compositors	Typesetting machine operators	Makeup supt.
	Makeup person	Compositors	Typesetting machine operators
	Press operator	Makeup person	Compositors
	Helper	Stereo. supt.	Stereo. supt.
		Stereotypers	Stereotypers
		Pressroom supervisor	Pressroom supervisor
		Press operators	Press operators
		Helpers	Helpers
		Engravers	Eng. dept. supervisor
			Engravers

There is always great pressure in the composing room of a daily newspaper. The material must be rushed into type and be ready for the forms at a definite moment. The composing room supervisor sees that copy is brought down from the news and advertising departments and is divided between the operators and printers so that composition may be completed in the shortest time.

At a mechanical conference in South Bend, Ind., the assistant general manager of the Dayton, Ohio, *Daily News* emphasized the important position that the head of the mechanical department fills in a newspaper plant.

"Foremen are selected," he said, "for their basic native intelligence, humane sentiments, know-how, and record—specifically, for their understanding of organization, experience with contract matters and negotiations, inherent spirit of fairness, and knowledge of their craft. In many cases the last point is given first consideration, because rarely does a man fulfill these requirements without being a good craftsman by nature."

Working under the composing room supervisor are the *operators* of *phototypesetting machines,* the *camera crew,* the *pasteup* and *makeup* personnel, and the *proofreaders,* the number of each depending on the size of the newspaper. On a daily paper of moderate size there are several machine operators. In a large city newspaper plant there will be a room filled with machines and operators. Some machines stand idle for relief or emergency duty in case something goes wrong with those in use.

When hot type is used, the makeup person in the composing room places the type in the forms according to a layout plan provided by the editor, makeup editor, or someone assigned by the editor to cooperate in setting up the pages. The pages are then moved to the stereotyping room if the press does not print directly from type.

In older plants, *stereotypers* place the page forms under the mat press and draw mats from each page to be placed in the casting mold. Each page comes from the casting mold as a curved plate, which moves on to the pressroom where it is locked in its proper place on the cylinder of the press. The *press operators* and the stereotypers often must rush to meet the deadline. In plants where offset printing is used, *platemakers* take the place of stereotypers and *electronic engravers* become compositors.

In many newpaper plants the mailing room is near the mechanical department or is connected with it. Here the papers are wrapped and labeled for their destinations and are tied in bundles according to towns. Other bundles of papers are readied for trucks standing by to deliver them to carriers or distributors in outlying areas.

In the mechanical department also, or near it, is the photoengraving department, where pictures and other illustrations are converted into cuts for use in the paper. The size of the engraving plant and the number of persons employed depend upon the number of pictures and pictorial devices used to illustrate news events and advertising messages.

Data processing department

Generally, a *data processing department manager* oversees all the applications of computerized billing, account handling, and related record keeping. Uses of the computer in typesetting, classified ad listing, or copy handling are usually under the supervision of a *production manager*. (See Table 4.10.)

The *data processing manager* must direct the overall operation of the data processing department, including full responsibility for the installation of equipment, to achieve specific objectives of the department in as efficient and accurate a manner as possible. Proficiency in accomplishing this will determine the efficacy of the organization. The selection and training of personnel is an important phase of the manager's activities. Responsibilities also include procurement of equipment and supplies, clerical procedures (procedure writing, scheduling, programming, coding), and physical-site preparation.

The *assistant data processing manager* closely coordinates the activities and schedules of the data processing department with those of outside departments and assists in the conversion to any new or changed applications. This person advises the data processing manager of major schedule fluctuations or procedural adjustments within the department and supervises the maintenance of the department's physical appearance.

The *programming supervisor* is in charge of the programming section and bears administrative and managerial responsibilities. The duties here are to receive the broad systems-design diagrams for each application from the assistant data processing manager and to prepare the broad flow diagrams for each run on which the computer programs will be based. As these are subdivided and distributed to system analysts or individual programmers for detail programming, their efforts must be coordinated and

Table 4.10. Data processing personnel

Weekly	*Small Daily*	*Medium Daily*	*Metropolitan Paper*
Computer operator	Computer operator	Data processing manager	Data processing manager
	Key punch operator	Computer operator	Asst. data processing manager
		Key punch operator	Computer operations supervisor
		Programmer	Computer operator
			Control clerk
			Key punch supervisor
			Key punch operator
			Programming supervisor
			System analyst
			Programmer

must not be permitted to overlap, so that they may take advantage of already developed routines.

The major duty of the *system analyst* is to study the operation of a portion of the business (usually assigned by the programming supervisor) to the point where he or she fully understands its objectives and procedures. The system analyst should be concerned not only with the "mainline" flow of information but also with many details and should understand the logic of these. This person should be able to obtain an understanding based upon interviews with operational and supervisory personnel. Assured that the system is right, the analyst then fills in necessary details before turning it over to programmers — details such as definitions of all input and output for each run and fields of information in each record — and also supplies necessary quantitative data to the programmers. In addition to laying out the logic of the regular processing runs, the analyst is also responsible for performing the same duties on other runs, such as file creation and cleanup during conversion. In summary, the system analyst must design the system required to process an application through the data processing department. This design includes the source data, the programs through the computer, and the reports desired.

The *programmer* must provide programs to be used in the data processing department for processing applications through the system. A programmer receives the flow charts and/or instructions (supplied by the system analyst or programming supervisor) covering the broad logic of a part of a computer run or a routine. In this work, one must deduce all logical alternatives that can occur and provide for handling them. Detailed programs must be developed strictly in accordance with standard procedures so they will not be misunderstood. The programmer also participates in the "debugging" and conversion of the program on the computer.

The *computer operations supervisor* must supervise overall operation of data processing and computer operations to achieve specific objectives of the department in as efficient and accurate a manner as possible. This involves responsibility for maintenance of the computer room, seeing that all work is put away at the end of each day's processing, and supervising and directing computer operators in preparing jobs to be run on the computer. An accurate disk-library control system must be maintained, and the supervisor is responsible for ensuring the use of proper disk files when a job is processed.

The *computer operator* processes data through the computer section of the data processing department, utilizing the computer systems available as well as related machines to produce required reports. The operator receives input data, which is programmed in machine language. Data is processed through the machine according to policies and procedures, and output information and reports are delivered to the control clerks. The computer operator sees that disk drives are mounted, dismounted, filed, and labeled properly.

The *control clerks* maintain control of all source input and report output of the data processing department. They must maintain control logs of all data processing applications and are responsible for seeing that logs of all source material being sent to the department are set up and posted to record indicative totals by batch. They maintain schedule sheets of all applications reflecting "source in," dates, and "reports out" and advise the computer operations supervisor of any source discrepancies.

The *key punch supervisor,* who is usually a female employe, is responsible for the control and supervision of the key punch section. She maintains a schedule of all applications being processed and assigns personnel within the section for proper utilization of machines and employes. She advises the assistant data processing manager in writing of any need for overtime or additional personnel within the department. She interviews and hires new key punch operators, with the approval of the assistant data processing manager, and trains new employes both in the operation of machines and in the punching of the applications.

The *key punch operator* enters data from source material into punched cards, which will be used as input data to the data processing system. Data is recorded on tabulating cards by punching a series of holes in a specified sequence. This is accomplished by using an IBM key punch machine and following written information on source documents. Cards may be duplicated by using the duplicating device on the machine as required. The operator maintains a file of program cards as required and verifies work of others as requested.

5
Modern equipment and change

> The present decade will see the newspapers of this country move from costly slow production systems to highly efficient low-cost production.
>
> *William D. Rinehart*

The acceleration of technological changes over the past decade has been somewhat mind-boggling for veteran newspaper professionals who have seen long-established methods of production abandoned for a whole new array of publishing facilities and concepts. For example:

1. Laser typesetting and platemaking processes are in use on a number of newspapers. As Laser Graphic Systems Corporation puts it, "We're totally, inexorably committed to the future advancement of laser technology as the key to electronic publishing."
2. Large city newspapers today have more than 35 varieties of "systems" to select from as they develop swifter ways of transmitting copy through video display terminals and optical scanners to the printing phase.
3. The New York, N.Y., *Wall Street Journal* is already publishing editions at its plant in Orlando, Fla., by means of signals bounced off a satellite that hovers 22,300 miles over the equator; the signals are sent from the *Journal*'s production plant in Chicopee, Mass., via WESTAR I, which was launched into orbit around the earth during 1976.
4. The Salt Lake City, Utah, *Tribune* is considering the feasibility of microfilming editions that can be projected on a screen in the subscriber's home, thus eliminating all paper costs.

An awareness of the latest improvements in newspaper machinery and equipment, coupled with an appreciation of what those improvements can accomplish, provides an unending source of interest and challenge to management today. With a knowledge of the basic principles that apply to all newspaper production situations, the current "technological explosion" becomes more understandable and therefore more manageable.

Technical terminology for describing widely different methods for the composition of type matter is well standardized. *Hot metal* covers the printing elements cast (in type and in stereotyping) by traditional use of molten lead alloys. *Cold type* includes the product of various typewriter mechanisms with manually assembled type characters on paper or plastic. *Phototype* is the product of typesetting machines on film or paper, using the camera principle, usually keyboard operated (some with tape alternatives).

Use of cold type and phototype has increased rapidly, while some plants use two or three of these basic methods. The weekly publishers were first to employ typewriter composition and offset printing. But developments in photolettering and phototypesetting machines and the application of web-fed construction to offset presses made that process practicable for dailies. Today most nondaily newspapers have "converted" from letterpress to offset, and over 62 percent of dailies are using this method. Computer uses for statistical needs have been followed rapidly by a variety of applications to typesetting and to automatic controls of other machinery.

Because the manager is more interested in the functions of the plant's physical equipment than in its technical operations, answers to the following questions are needed:

1. What operations are required in the mechanical department to produce a newspaper that will serve the community adequately?
2. How well is the mechanical department equipped to meet production requirements?
3. Should we go to a totally new system? Then how would the change affect equipment, and how can we adapt our personnel to new processes?
4. What additional equipment should be provided to increase business potential?
5. Would new and improved equipment cut production costs, step up overall plant efficiency, and produce a better newspaper?
6. Does the business and circulation volume of the newspaper justify a higher speed press?
7. Would readers and advertisers appreciate color printing enough to justify adding color printing equipment for general use?
8. Is equipment receiving proper care for maximum efficiency and extended service?

PRINTING THE NEWSPAPER

Printing is the last of several steps in the mechanical production of a newspaper, but it seems logical to discuss it first because to a great extent it governs other processes in the plant. Furthermore, no machine holds the pride and esteem of the publisher and the interest of plant visitors as firmly as the printing press.

Methods of printing

Newspaper printing employs the three most widely used techniques among the established graphic arts processes. Other methods not presently adaptable include the electronic formation of a printed image (as with Xerox) and rubber-plate printing with fluid dyes (flexography). The processes diagrammed in Figure 5.1 are letterpress (oldest), offset (most recently introduced in the field), and gravure (introduced as intaglio or roto-gravure more than a half-century ago).

Letterpress, or relief printing, transfers the impression to the paper from a raised, inked surface. One principal advantage of letterpress printing for newspaper production is its flexibility, especially for quick changes. There are four letterpress operating principles: platen — for small commer-

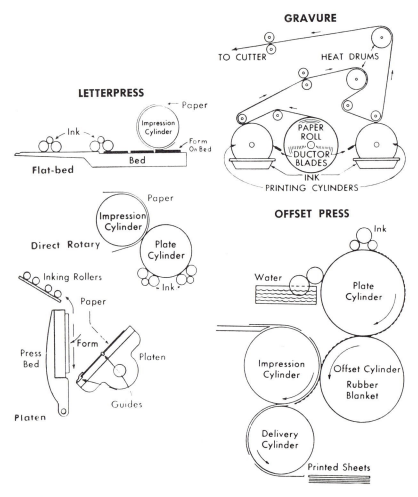

Fig. 5.1. Press operation principles. (From Hartley E. Jackson, *Newspaper Typography,* Stanford University Press. Reprinted by permission of the publishers.)

cial printing; sheet-fed cylinder—for commercial printing and small newspaper production; flatbed web—for newspapers; and rotary—for newspapers. There are two types of rotary presses, tubular and semicylindrical.

Offset printing transfers (or "offsets") the printing-ink image from a rubber press blanket on which the image has been deposited by the printing plate. The plate has been produced by photochemical procedures derived from the earlier art of lithography. As first practiced on smooth, fine-grained stone, the lithographic artist drew pictures or lettering on the stone with greasy crayon or ink. Type was transferred from a proof printed in greasy ink. When the stone was moistened, the greasy image would accept printers' ink, while the moist background surface repelled the ink and remained white on the printed impression. Stone (except for use by a few graphic artists) has now been replaced by thin plates that can be wrapped around a printing cylinder. Variously prepared of metal, plastic, or special paper, offset plates result from a series of chemical and photographic treatments.

The resiliency of the rubber surface on which they are printed makes it possible to print finer details on rougher textures of paper than is possible with letterpress. Newsprint paper is well adapted to offset, and finer details in printing permit the use of finer halftone screens, thus broadening the newspaper's use of photographs. The application of photography to platemaking permits the use of any kind of writing, typing, lettering, or composition that can be copied with the camera.

After several decades of growing importance of offset in commercial and book printing, the designing of web-fed offset presses suitable for newspaper printing has caused publishers in an ever increasing number to adopt this process.

Gravure printing carries an ink image in heavy pictorial values and sometimes seems to be the most nearly photographic among all the printing processes. The gravure image is formed in tiny dots below the surface of a printing cylinder. As compared with letterpress or offset pictures (in which varying dot sizes determine gradations from black to white) the gravure dots remain constant in size but vary in depth. Etched into the surface of a copper cylinder, they become "wells" (usually 22,500 in one square inch) that are deepest for black areas, shallower for gray tones.

On the gravure press the dots are filled with fluid ink. Then a "doctor blade" wipes the surface of the rotating cylinder clean, leaving in the depressed wells amounts of ink that print as black or gray tones according to the depth of the dots. Under heavy pressure on a rotary gravure press, the inked cylinder then deposits its pages of type and pictures on paper. Usually the dot or screen effect is barely perceptible in the pictures, but it often produces a fuzzy effect on type characters.

Mostly used for Sunday magazine sections, rotogravure is practical for extended pressruns only. Because of the comparatively long time needed to prepare the printing cylinders (for which any kind of type may be used) this process is limited to special sections that can be run in advance.

Fitting processes to needs

The publisher or general manager should study printing processes and press types to determine which is best adapted to printing and publishing needs. Each method and each press has advantages for some situations and disadvantages for others. For example, the metropolitan newspaper with its large circulation requires a high-speed, more versatile press than a medium-sized daily; and the press needs of the weekly and the small daily are more modest than those of the medium-sized daily.

WHAT PRESS TO BUY—AND WHEN

The newspaper in a growing community sooner or later will be forced to replace its press with a larger and more modern one. The change is an important event because it usually takes place amidst qualms and doubts and with what the publisher feels is considerable courage.

"When are conditions right for a press change?" "What kind of a press should I buy?" These are important questions for management to answer.

To the first, a press manufacturer replies: "If the total run takes longer than two hours, the newspaper needs a faster press." But the publisher should assemble more evidence than that. A more valid decision may be reached by obtaining definite answers to such questions as these:

1. What has been circulation growth the past four or five years and what are prospects for the years ahead?
2. What is being done by competing newspapers? Are they becoming more aggressive? Are they installing new equipment?
3. Is the community growing in population, business, and wealth? Are there prospects for new industries? Will highway construction bring more trade to the city?
4. Do advertisers reach out for more business? Will they be willing to pay a higher rate for advertising if we increase circulation and provide color in advertising?
5. Are subscribers satisfied with the kind of newspaper we are giving them and with the delivery service? Do they complain about poor print and clamor for more features? Have deliveries been late?
6. What are pressroom conditions? Have there been pressrun delays? Do we have to make double runs? Is the pressroom overtime running higher? Are repair bills going up?

If the answers to most of these questions are in the affirmative, it is time for a press change.

One publisher comments: "You can't use old equipment and pay modern-day wages." This may be a slight exaggeration but the principle is sound: *Obsolete and inadequate equipment increases operating costs.* When a publisher begins to realize that, it is time to install a better press.

Equipment buying considerations

New equipment is always preferable when a publisher can afford it and when the business will support it. Some advantages are:

1. Offers longer trouble-free life.
2. Is newer in design.
3. Is made of better material.
4. Has the most modern facilities.
5. Is easier to operate.
6. Provides a depreciation advantage under the tax law.

But when cost of new equipment is out of reach, a publisher is forced to shop the used market. And it is just as important to be a shrewd buyer here as it is in, for example, the used automobile market.

In many cases the publisher will find that the cost of replacing worn parts and putting the machinery in top operating condition will raise the price to the point where buying new will be just as economical. In short, while surveying the used equipment market, if the buyer does not understand machinery and equipment someone who does should go along or expert advice from other sources should be sought. It does not matter what is being purchased — press, photocomposition equipment, folder, stone, proof press, or what — it must be in good condition if it is to be worth the money. The publisher who begins a career with an old press always looks forward to the day when finances will allow its replacement.

Whether the press is to be new or used, installation cost is not included in the purchase price. For new equipment there are shipping and erection expenses. For used equipment, there are these same costs plus the expense of knocking down the old press, moving it, and reerecting it. This latter is important because wages of riggers and machinists are much higher in certain areas than others, and consequently the dismantling charges can affect total cost. Most manufacturers of large presses will furnish experienced factory-trained erectors.

Ample space is of first importance when planning for a new or different press. Ceiling height must be adequate for convenient press operation and for possible installation of additional units later. Space also must be provided around the press for paper-roll trucks, for carrying plates to press units, and for conveyor systems that carry newspapers from the press to the mailroom. Installation costs must be given consideration.

TRANSITION TO OFFSET

The overwhelming majority of newspapers in America are now printed by the offset method, which allows greater flexibility in adapting to innovations in the preparation of copy and printing plates. At first, the changeover was limited primarily to smaller weeklies and nondailies, but now most metropolitan dailies have made the transition from the 500-year-old letterpress process of printing to entirely new offset plants.

By equipping their older-type presses with "saddles," many newspapers have managed to find a satisfactory and efficient interim process and to maintain quality production while avoiding all-out conversion to offset. Such newspapers as the San Francisco, Calif., *Examiner;* the South Bend, Ind., *Tribune;* the Spokane, Wash., *Daily Chronicle;* and the Buffalo, N.Y., *Press* have gone to this method of printing with offset plates on saddle-equipped machinery.

In Kansas City, Mo., both the *Star* and the *Times* have converted to DeLitho, a process that uses a stainless steel cylindrical screen and an air manifold to blow the ink solution onto the printing surface of offset plates. This allowed the management to retain full usage of 45 press units already in service. A number of other major newspapers, including the Birmingham, Ala., *News,* depend on the DiLitho method. Still another approach with exciting possibilities is that of the Los Angeles, Calif., *Times,* which converted its presses to accommodate recyclable plastic plates manufactured from liquid polypropylene instead of the traditional molten metal.

The purpose of each of these innovative techniques is to take full advantage of the electronic improvements available in setting type and making plates. In making a change from letterpress to offset several problems must be understood by publisher and staff, and they will need the full cooperation of the press manufacturer in meeting these problems. Otherwise, everybody will be on tenterhooks when conversion time comes along.

Richard H. Bell, salesman for the Cottrell Company, mentions three elements to be carefully considered in the frustrating experience of making a press change: the proper hardware to be used, the proper procedures for operating the equipment, and the proper training to qualify persons to implement these procedures.

Says Mr. Bell,

My experience has shown that the greatest sins are most often committed in the training area. Many publishers feel that they'll be out the door with their first well-printed paper 10 days after the press arrives.

Unfortunately, it's not true in the majority of cases. Not only do the press operators need training, but the people in the other production departments need training as well. More realistically, the conversion process should be stretched out over a period of 6 to 10 weeks to insure proper training of all personnel in the new procedures. And, if contract work is planned six weeks to two months ahead, running time should be allowed on the paper before taking the plunge.

Dale Stafford, as editor-publisher of the Greenville, Mich., *Daily News* (now *News Banner*), was an offset newspaper pioneer. His decision to move to offset was not occasioned by the need to replace worn-out equipment. At the time he purchased the *Daily News,* the paper was printed on a new Goss flatbed press with which the newspaper had won numerous

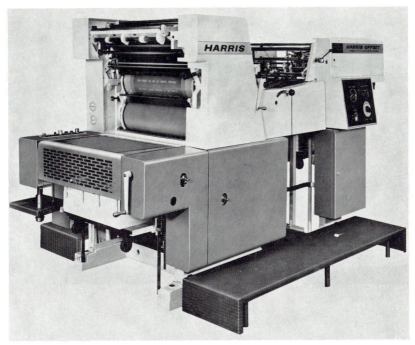

Fig. 5.2.   Sheet-fed offset presses like this Harris 23 x 29 single-color are finding increasing application for short-run newspapers. Flexibility and fast makeready make it highly adaptable for newspaper production and quality commercial work. (Courtesy of the Harris-Seybold Company.)

awards for typographical excellence. But instead of relaxing with a prosperous property clear of debt, Stafford chose to invest another $100,000 in capital equipment to switch to offset.

The first few weeks following the installation of a new offset press brought many of the problems familiar to most publishers who also have made this basic change. But the duration of this problem period was relatively short, largely because of the extensive preparations made by Stafford and his associates.

Three weeks before the change in the *Daily News* plant, the firm rented a nearby building in downtown Greenville where it set up a bank of Justowriters (electric typewriters by which operators can produce even margins on the right-hand side), pasteup tables, and other necessary equipment. Here a group of women were trained in offset composition and pasteup.

"This is the real key to offset economy. We no longer face an emergency when we lose a member of our production force. We always have a reserve of several women in the community who are trained in all

Fig. 5.3. A modern offset newspaper press, the Cottrell Vanguard Model 22, prints from continuous rolls of newsprint at high speeds with high fidelity in black and white or color. More than 850 newspapers in the United States and Canada are produced on this type of press. (Courtesy of the Cottrell Company.)

phases of offset composition and who are working for us on a part-time basis," Stafford pointed out.

Reader acceptance

Well in advance of actual conversion, the *Daily News* carried strong promotion of offset in editorial and advertising columns. This proved effective in obtaining the public's approval even though the appearance of the 9-point Justowriter type was at sharp variance with that to which the readers had been accustomed. Stafford believed it would be a bad mistake to reduce the size of the type at the time of the move to offset, as this would be objectionable to many readers. Unthinkingly, they probably would base their objections on offset rather than the smaller type. Stafford strongly recommended advance preparation of the readers through promotion by any publisher contemplating this change.

Offset equipment costs—except for the press—are low. At the *Daily News,* for example, this investment was approximately $20,000 but today would be nearer $30,000. For a weekly newspaper the estimated cost could be held as low as $12,500.

Stafford concluded, "Perhaps the single most important end result of offset newspapering will prove to be the improvement of contents . . . a

Fig. 5.4. Making up the offset newspaper. Composing room supervisor Raymond Eastman puts the finishing touches on the page-one pasteup of an edition of the Greenville, Mich., *News Banner,* with assistance from managing editor Walter Jaehnig. (Courtesy of the Greenville *News Banner.*)

better overall editorial job. This becomes possible as publishers have more time to devote to publishing rather than printing."

Arrangement of equipment is of major importance in achieving the most efficient use of employes and machines. Figure 5.5 shows a floor plan designed to facilitate a smooth flow of work.

E. J. Erlandson, executive editor of the Missoula, Mont., *Missoulian,* tells of witnessing the transformation of a small western daily from a rather drab but dutiful sheet into an aggressive, attractive newspaper with progress and community service its top goals. The transformation began with the purchase of the *Missoulian* by the Lee Newspapers in the 1920s, and not long ago it came to a new height of glory and success with the purchase and installation of an offset press of the latest model and other modern equipment. The press has a capacity of 40 pages as opposed to the 24 of the press it replaced.

The change at first shocked old-time *Missoulian* readers, but the paper assumed a bright new face. Its photos were sharper and its type easier to read than under the hot-metal process. Employes, some with years of experience in the hot-metal process, found it difficult at first to shake off the feeling of being confined to the one-column width and the old column

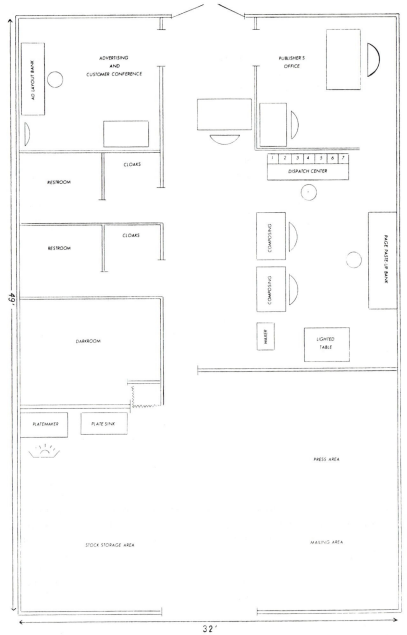

Fig. 5.5. This model layout for a newspaper printed by the offset method provides direct-line production for present efficiency, a movable partition for rearrangement, and open-end design so that future growth will not disturb the basic pattern. (Courtesy of *The American Press.*)

rules. But soon all were using white space and varying column measures to open up the pages.

The new press brought with it many corollary changes throughout the newspaper plant. The newsroom was remodeled, and space previously occupied by the stereotype department was converted into darkrooms for the photographer and lab technicians. A studio was provided with three different screen backdrops and adequate lighting. The room at the front of the editorial office, formerly used for photoengraving and as a darkroom, was converted to an editorial conference room and library.

As part of an expansion plan, the Coldwater, Mich., *Daily Reporter* went from letterpress to offset by installing a Cottrell V-15A press. Thereby the *Reporter* increased its use of process color, first in editorial then by advertising. Its new press has five units.

The Greenville, N.C., *Reflector* is printed on a Goss Urbanite offset press. The changeover marked an end to letterpress printing methods utilizing metal type by which the newspaper had been produced since its beginning nearly 100 years ago. Most of the type now is set on Compugraphic equipment, which projects the image of each letter on photographic paper to form the lines of type. The 32-page press delivers up to 40,000 papers per hour. It has full-color capability and the building has been designed to be expanded to the maximum capacity of 64 pages.

When the *Post-Star and Times* of Glens Falls, N.Y., moved into a new building, it abandoned an antiquated letterpress plant and converted to offset, photocomposition printing methods. The morning daily is printed on a six-unit Goss Urbanite press. And for the first time in its history the newspaper is able to print color. Since 1906 the newspaper or its predecessors had occupied a three-story complex in downtown Glens Falls. The *Post-Star and Times* moved to the new one-story structure a half-mile away over a weekend.

A retraining program for *Post-Star and Times* employes had been in progress for months while the new building was being constructed. Printers learned to operate Compugraphic machines and to do paste-makeup. Reporters and editors were taught to dummy pages more exactly than before. Advertising personnel mastered layout techniques they had not previously used. Press operators and stereotypers were schooled in page-camera and platemaking techniques as well as operation of the offset press.

The Eugene, Oreg., *Register-Guard* has installed a new Harris N-1680 double-width offset press at a cost of $2.4 million, which produces at a capacity of 80,000 newspapers per hour. Among other benefits the new press has reduced the total time needed for printing all issues of the *Register-Guard* from three and one-half hours to slightly more than two hours. This impressive installation was the final phase in conversion to cold-type production.

These are random examples of the universal trend from letterpress to offset printing of newspapers of all sizes. Since 1965, for instance, more than 185 Goss Metro offset presses, representing more than 11,000 in-

Fig. 5.6. News editor Grady Crenshaw checks over the first issue to come off the Goss Metro Offset press used by the Memphis, Tenn., *Commercial Appeal.* (Courtesy of the Memphis *Commercial Appeal.*)

dividual web-offset units, have been assembled and installed in newspaper plants. A recent "convert" was the Memphis, Tenn., *Commercial Appeal,* whose daily circulation is produced on 32 Metro offset units (Fig. 5.6).

LETTERPRESS NOT FORGOTTEN

It should be emphasized that many newspapers in the United States, and particularly in other countries, still depend entirely on the traditional relief-printing or letterpress method, accompanied by the hot-metal processes that have been used since early times. Because of the great historical significance of letterpress and because it is proving to be the most practical operation for a number of newspapers, attention will now be given to this kind of equipment.

Flatbed cylinder press

For some weekly and semiweekly newspapers of small circulation the flatbed cylinder press is depended upon. Single sheets are fed by hand from a board atop the press. The type pages are placed directly on the bed; and the cylinder, which makes either one or two revolutions per impression, brings the newsprint sheets into contact one at a time with the inked type, thus printing one side. The sheets are then returned by hand to the feedboard for printing the reverse side.

Most cylinder presses accommodate four newspaper page forms at a time, a few of them only two. The folding mechanism may operate separately or may be connected to the press at the proper production stage. Many older presses of this obsolete type, still in use, produce about 2,000 impressions per hour; but more recent machines are rated at 3,600 to 4,250 impressions per hour.

Flatbed web-perfecting press

A few nondailies in the larger circulation bracket and dailies with less than 5,000 subscribers may still use a flatbed web-perfecting press, which is faster and has greater capacity than a flatbed cylinder press (Fig. 5.7). While the type bed in the cylinder press moves back and forth between the ink rollers and the impression cylinder, the web-perfecting press employs the same principle somewhat in reverse. The stationary-type beds are one above the other, and each has an impression cylinder that moves back and forth over the face of the type pages.

Newsprint flows into the press automatically in an unbroken web from a large roll. The web snakes over and under steel rollers that allow it to glide over the inked type pages at just the right tension, pausing only for an impression with each revolution of the impression cylinders. The printed ribbon goes into the folding mechanism where it is folded, cut, trimmed,

Fig. 5.7. Goss Cox-O-Type press. A popular early model for small daily, weekly, and semiweekly newspapers, this unit prints and delivers 8 full-sized pages of six, seven, or eight columns or 16 tabloid-size pages. Delivery speed is 3,500 per hour. (Courtesy of the Goss Printing Press Company.)

and delivered as finished newspaper copies. Thus in one continuous operation an eight-page newspaper is printed on both sides and is presented ready for distribution at a steady rate of 3,000 to 3,500 copies an hour.

The web-perfecting press currently manufactured is single acting. Still in use, however, are double-acting flatbed presses, no longer manufactured, that will be serviceable for many more years. The double-acting press prints on *both* strokes of the impression cylinders at a top production rate of about 5,500 copies an hour. Even though output is somewhat lower on single-acting presses, they produce better quality printing and are equipped with superior folders.

The next step up is to a rotary press, and both the tubular and semicylindrical types are adapted to the needs of newspapers from large weeklies to large dailies. Rotary printing is done from stereotype plates. Instead of passing between an impression cylinder and a type bed, the newsprint passes between two cylinders, one fitted with stereotype plates and the other with an impression cylinder. Inking rollers are arranged to transfer ink to the plates for proper printing at high speeds.

Tubular press

The tubular press uses stovepipe-shaped plates, which go almost entirely around the cylinder. Chief advantages of this type of press are:

1. Only one stereotype plate is needed per page instead of two, thus saving stereotyping time.
2. Size of editions may be increased in multiples of two pages.
3. Presses may be enlarged in multiples of four-page decks or units.
4. Operation is more economical than for semicylindrical presses.

However, there are definite limits to tubular capacity. As press runs become more complicated, the ratio of complexity rises in a sharper curve with tubular presses than with the semicylindrical type. For instance, a tubular press having one folder produces a single-section newspaper only. If there is a folder with an upper former or two regular formers, two sections may be produced. One folder with an upper former and one regular folder, cross-associated, could produce four sections. This last is practically a hypothetical case because the complications involved in controlling the web make such an arrangement impractical. Generally speaking, 32 pages is the optimum page capacity of the tubular press.

For many years the most popular tubular press was the Duplex Tubular, a deck type. Many are still in use and performing well, but the press has not been manufactured since 1947. Another popular tubular model is the Duplex Unitubular (arch-type unit design), which has not been built since 1951. Later models are the Goss Unitube (arch-type design) and the Dek-A-Tube (deck-type), which have better inking systems than the older model presses, more working space, more roller and ball bearings, sturdier folders, improved design, and improved tension controls — many of the features of a large metropolitan press.

Semicylindrical press

In a semicylindrical press, two curved plates are fitted around a cylinder (Fig. 5.8). Three types of these presses have been manufactured: single plate wide, made years ago with few still running; two plates wide, referred to as single width; and four plates wide, referred to as double width.

A semicylindrical press may be run either straight or collect. In a straight run, duplicate stereotype plates are put on the cylinders and produce two copies of a newspaper with each cylinder revolution. In a collect run, only one plate is used for each page—thus doubling press page capacity—but only one newspaper copy is printed with each cylinder revolution.

A single-width semicylindrical press of eight units will turn out 64 pages (collect). On collect runs and for the same number of units it has twice the page capacity of a tubular press. Well designed for the medium-sized field is the Universal, a single-width press with a speed of 36,000 copies an hour and a folder capacity of 64 pages (Fig. 5.9).

The double-width press is required when a large portion of the newspaper's circulation must be distributed rapidly. More compact than twinned single-width presses, it has double folders permitting double delivery, is built more sturdily (and consequently increased quality can be incorporated in it), and offers much greater operating flexibility. The double-width press is equipped with angle bars for assembling the webs in a variety of section combinations.

The differences between double-width and single-width presses may be compared to the differences between large and small automobiles. More refinements can be built into the larger machines because purchasers are in a position to pay the additional cost for such tangible benefits.

Fig. 5.8. Goss Unitube press with four units, showing the operating side. Units one and four have extra color cylinders. (Courtesy of the Goss Printing Press Company.)

Fig. 5.9. The Goss Universal press is engineered especially for fast-growing medium-size city newspapers and designed for one-level operation. This is a semicylindrical rotary press that will produce 36,000 to 40,000 newspapers per hour. (Courtesy of the Goss Printing Press Company.)

Among double-width presses are those manufactured by Walter Scott and Company, Wood Newspaper Machinery Corporation, R. Hoe and Company, and the Goss Printing Press Company. These modern presses have normal running speeds up to 50,000 copies an hour, have top speeds of 60,000 an hour, and are equipped with folders having a 96-page capacity. Many of these larger presses have been modified to utilize DiLitho or other direct methods of printing discussed earlier in this chapter.

Fig. 5.10. The Jumbo Courier is a web-fed rotary press for large-city newspapers. Modern design allows more efficient use of space, less paper waste, and increased capacity. (Courtesy of Koenig & Bauer-USA.)

Convincing evidence of the viability of letterpress equipment is the introduction of the new Jumbo Courier press, which permits the "clustering" of more printing plates per unit to provide real savings on cost per page. The New York, N.Y., *Daily News,* which boasts the largest newspaper circulation in America (over 2 million), is able to print from six plates across its press cylinders in place of the customary four. The Jumbo is also capable of handling four plates around each cylinder, where other presses can accommodate only two (Fig. 5.10).

EQUIPMENT PRECEDING PRESSWORK

Because the press is the largest, the most expensive, and the most crucial mechanical installation in the newspaper in that all preceding operations — copy preparation, type composition, platemaking — are determined by the kind of press available, this chapter has emphasized the final printing phase of production. In the following chapter the "front-end" operations will be explained, especially as affected by the latest innovations in electronic equipment.

The recency of accelerating changes in technology should be kept clearly in mind as a dominant factor in the selection and utilization of equipment. William D. Rinehart, vice-president of the American Newspaper Publishers Association's Research Institute, told a convention of publishers that "more new equipment has been installed and new newspaper plants have been built in a decade than in perhaps any 30- or 40-year period before." He observed that more than 1,100 newspapers went from letterpress to offset printing in the 1970s; this transition to "cold type" has made dramatic changes in every other phase of the newspaper's method of production.

6

Stampede to electronics

The newspaper reporter of pencil and notebook memory is fast becoming an electronic journalist.

Editor & Publisher

Smartly designed precision machinery that is lighter, cleaner, swifter, and more versatile than printing technology of the previous 500 years has blossomed in newspaper plants on an almost universal scale. It is estimated that more than 95 percent of American newspapers depend on photocomposition of type in place of the hand-setting and machine-setting methods used by all publishers just a half-century ago. The demand for efficiency, cost control, and flexibility is being satisfied with computer-related equipment in an ever-widening area of support services for newspaper production and management. The development has been so rapid that some third-generation devices are finding acceptance that were unheard of a few years ago. Total expenditures for new systems designed and installed in newspapers passed $100 million in 1978.

In the newest systems everything involved in getting out the newspaper happens "on-line." From original keystroke to final composition of news, classified and display advertising copy, and virtually all other reading matter, a network of terminals, controllers, data bases, and typesetters go into action. In the complicated process, costs are reduced because of the elimination of tedious corrections, repeated handling of copy, filing problems, and other time-wasting efforts. For most large metropolitan dailies the new systems represent the first opportunity to streamline totally the pre-press functions. For other newspapers the latest equipment provides a dramatic step beyond the pioneering editorial input devices formerly depended upon.

IN THE NEWSROOM

Even the trusty typewriter of the reporter has become obsolete as a newspaper tool. In its place is the CRT (cathode-ray tube) or VDT (video display terminal). A more commonly used name is simply *editing terminal* (Figs. 6.1, 6.2).

An editing terminal links the creativity of a reporter with the speed and accuracy of a computer. Words typed at a terminal appear instantly

64

Fig. 6.1. The Hendrix 5200 stand-alone editing terminal allows the operator to compose copy directly on a television tube by manipulating a typewriterlike keyboard. This model was a pioneer in the field. (Courtesy of Hendrix Electronics.)

on the screen above the keyboard. If a writer makes a mistake or changes his mind about the wording of a sentence, he can correct it with the touch of a button. When the reporter is finished with the story, he can send it instantly to the terminal of any editor in the building.

The Detroit, Mich., *News* electronic system consists of 72 terminals and nine computers. The terminals and the programming were built to *News* specifications by Hendrix Electronics of Londonderry, N.H. The computers were manufactured by Digital Equipment Corporation, Maynard, Mass.

Editors can view a listing of all the stories waiting for their attention by pressing a button on the terminal keyboard. If they wish, they can ask the computer to display a three-line summary of each story in the file so they can decide which to edit first and which can wait until later (Fig. 6.2). An editor can display the entire story on the screen and then correct the text to whatever extent is necessary. Lines open up to make room for insertions and close up when words or letters are deleted.

Reporters working from the eight bureau offices of the *News* — in Washington, Lansing, the city-county building, and five suburban

Fig. 6.2. Editors and reporters employing editing terminals to write and edit stories. (Courtesy of the Detroit, Mich., *News.*)

locations—use specially modified IBM Selectric typewriters to write their stories. These stories are "read" by Datatype Corporation scanners, which translate the words into digital signals that are sent over telephone lines into the *News* editorial computer system. Once these bureau stories are entered into the system, they are called up on a terminal screen and edited just as if they were local stories written within the *News* downtown office.

Stories from the national wire services (Associated Press and United Press International) as well as supplementary services (including the Los Angeles, Calif., *Times;* Washington, D.C., *Post;* and Washington, D.C., *Star*) are fed directly into the computer system.

Regardless of how they get into the system, all stories wind up on an editor's screen. When the editing is complete, the editor merely presses another button on the terminal, and the story is transmitted to the paper's composing room where it will be set in type. Split screens incorporated in the new Harris 1700—made by the Harris Corporation Composition Systems Division in Melbourne, Fla.—can display 54 lines of copy for faster editing or can present two stories simultaneously to expedite the merging of wire stories or other copy (Fig. 6.3).

CLASSIFIED ADVERTISING

Copy-processing technology can make the classified advertising function an even more vital part of the total newspaper operation. As order takers record copy on the screens of their terminals, sales-prompting messages appear to encourage additional ad linage and to assure complete record gathering. The ad taker can concurrently run a credit check against such items as telephone and account numbers (Fig. 6.4).

Fig. 6.3. Video display terminals are used in all departments of the newspaper where copy has to be set. Here a Chicago, Ill., *Tribune* composing room operator uses the Harris 2200 for preparing a wide variety of typefaces and styles — text, headlines, advertising copy — to be relayed to the computer for instant typesetting. (Courtesy of the Chicago *Tribune.*)

During the phone call the system will automatically calculate the price of the ad, based upon number of days of press run, size, and rate. This data is supplied to the advertiser and to a special data base for billing. The probable classified page count can be forecast up to a week in advance by means of this stored information. On-line files permit instantaneous pickup of expired ads.

DISPLAY ADVERTISING

In systems widely used today, terminals are used to enter display advertising copy that is transmitted to on-line video layout systems. Ads are positioned, sized, and precisely fitted. The newest equipment displays ads up to 100 picas wide and can specify up to 250 type fonts (faces) (Fig. 6.5). Entire pages can be viewed on terminals and proofread for corrections before the page is phototypeset. Full-page viewers are referred to as pagination systems, of which Mergenthaler Linotype Company's Page View Terminal (PVT) is an outstanding example.

Fig. 6.4. Classified advertising is set directly on an Atex video display terminal. The operator is able to provide the price of the ad as soon as the terminal has all the information and flashes back the exact cost of the desired number of insertions in the newspaper. (Courtesy of the Louisville, Ky., *Courier-Journal* and *Times.*)

COMPOSING ROOM

In composing rooms, terminals are used to update existing text such as TV sections, legal notices, and classified ads. They are also used for proofing text on perforated paper tape, marking up ads with typesetting codes, and generating ad and news text right on the terminal.

When terminals are used for proofreading, text can be proofed on the screen right after it is perforated instead of one or two steps later after phototypesetting. Proofreading text before it is typeset has only been possible since the introduction of very reliable phototypesetting machines, where a chance of generating wrong characters is very remote.

Where the terminals are not available for electronic preparation of copy, the copy must be typed on electric typewriters before it goes to the scanner. These changes have sometimes been rather traumatic for reporters and editors who for years have pounded out their stories and editorials on manual typewriters, with great freedom to pencil in correc-

Fig. 6.5. The person in advertising makeup no longer bends over a table, working with metal slugs and cuts. The entire ad is composed on a specially designed video display terminal that, at the press of a command key, transmits the image to the control computer for phototypesetting in a matter of seconds. (Courtesy of the Louisville, Ky., *Courier-Journal* and *Times.*)

tions and scratch out errors. The whole idea is to produce copy that is ready to be scanned optically for rapid photocomposition.

At the Bloomington, Ind., *Daily Herald-Telephone*, a CompuScan OCR (optical character recognition) unit is used for converting typewritten material into punched tape in seconds (Fig. 6.6). Because CompuScan copy must be clean and nearly perfect for the machinery to handle it, retraining of reporters and copydesk personnel on the use of carefully produced electric typewriter copy is going on at the *Daily Herald-Telephone* and other newspapers converting to the system. Simple typographical mistakes can be corrected mechanically, but major revisions and deleted paragraphs are no longer allowable on newspaper copy on its way to the OCR.

The 1200 Autoreader, manufactured by ECRM of Bedford, Mass., is a typical OCR system for composing rooms. It processes copy at the rate of 1,200 words per minute and is calibrated to make no more than three er-

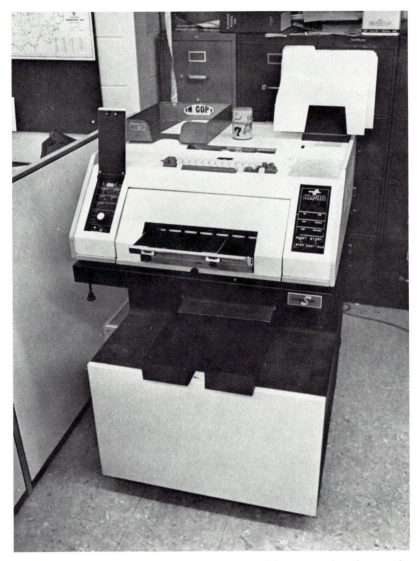

Fig. 6.6. Where electric typewriters are used for preparation of copy to be set in type, an optical character recognition scanner, like this CompuScan Alpha model, must "read" the copy and punch tape to be fed into the electronic typesetting equipment. (Courtesy of the Bloomington, Ind., *Daily Herald-Telephone.*)

rors in 10,000 characters as it converts typewritten and edited copy into machine-readable form. Editing, incidentally, is done by hand with nonscannable nylon-tipped pens, which the optical device cannot "see."

THE COMPLETE SYSTEM

The heart of the newspaper electronic system is the computer. An elaborate system will include a number of computers or controllers to which up to 380 terminals may be attached. Dozens of peripheral devices can be associated with the central controlling computer in a great variety of configurations to perform an almost incomprehensible number of services. Since all forms of information can be translated into weightless impulses, these can be assembled, processed, stored, or shipped anywhere in the world in less than one-seventh of a second, at a speed a million times faster than the speed of sound. Thus as one observer has expressed it, "When you talk about the achievements of the computer, you are talking about the intellectual capacity of the educated, creative human mind that taught the electronic circuitry what to do." The computer and its components are of use to the newspaper in direct proportion to the imaginative capacity of management.

For a simplified chart of an up-to-date computerized newspaper operation utilizing editing terminals, computers, optical scanners, pagination systems, and electronic typesetting see Figure 6.7. The chart in Figure 6.8 shows how operations in 14 cities are linked together by telecommunications serving the Westchester Rockland Newspapers in New York State; each utilizes electronic production. Whether within the plant or between plants in a group operation, the system possibilities are unlimited.

Management is confronted by many questions in the selection of an appropriate system. The right answers will be determined in large part by the individual newspaper's needs as balanced against its budgetary limitations. Once a decision is made, however, there are still many options for the manager to consider:

1. Will the supplier of equipment provide training for the staff?
2. What action would be necessary in case of power failures or malfunctions in the new system?
3. How does the system handle the present wire service facilities?
4. If electric typewriters are to be used with an optical scanner to supplement copy handling, can the OCR provide input into the system?
5. Will the system accept perforated tape inputs also?
6. What are the actual editing advantages of this system over its competitors?
7. Does the computer have adequate storage — that is, is its memory capacity sufficient?

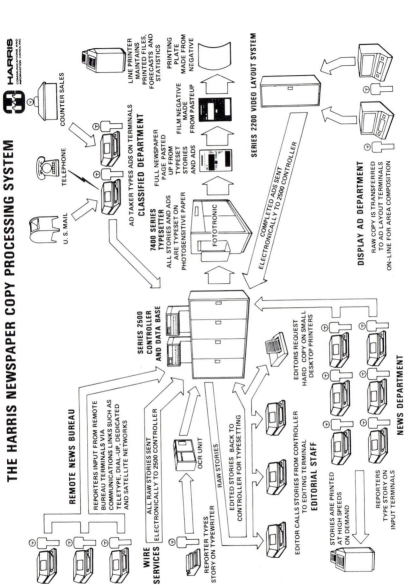

Fig. 6.7. This simplified chart indicates where all the elements of an integrated copy-processing system fit into the overall design. (Courtesy of the Harris Corporation Composition Systems Division.)

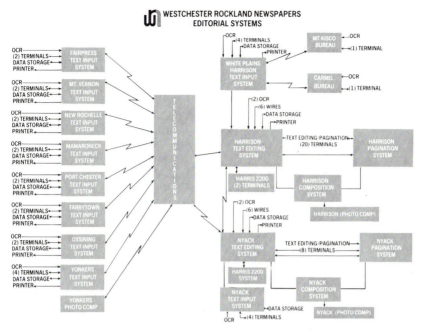

Fig. 6.8. An electronic system for the processing of newspaper copy can link together not only the production operations of a single newspaper but the editorial processes of a whole group. (Courtesy of the Westchester, N.Y., Rockland Newspapers.)

8. How reliable is the retrieval aspect of the system? If two newspapers will be using the same plant equipment, does each have absolute security of all copy stored in the memory file?

9. What are the terms of the contract for the sale or lease or servicing of the system?

10. Will the system allow for reasonable queueing—that is, an orderly waiting line for stories and advertising copy to be handled according to set priorities?

11. Does the system operate at maximum speed (about 250,000 characters per second) or at a lesser rate that is adequate for production capacity?

12. Are the screens and characters large enough for comfortable and efficient operation by personnel?

13. Are full-page display screens needed for makeup now, or can the pagination system be added later?

14. Will future objectives and changes be accommodated on this system without major reinvestments?

15. Does the system provide greater utilization of photocomposition and plate-making equipment?

16. Is final control over the total appearance of the finished page enhanced, or are editors called upon to make important sacrifices for the sake of speed?
17. Are other newspapers with similar systems satisfied with results in terms of error reduction, cost cutting, and overall efficiency?

SETTING COPY INTO TYPE

Once the impulses from the various terminals reach the computer—relaying news, advertising, and other inputs into the control center (Fig. 6.9)—the process is ready for the next step, which is photocomposition.

The transition from hot-metal typesetting was naturally one of making adaptations to existing equipment. For almost a century, the ungainly looking linesetting machine was the workhorse of the composing room. Therefore, the first phase in the move toward electronic typesetting was to convert the mechanical process by adding a conversion unit. Figure 6.10 shows one of the transitional machines that is equipped with photographic typesetting capabilities and eliminates the hand-keyboard operation.

Today's systems link terminals, via computers, directly to the type-setter, which produces and develops the image on photographic paper ready for pasteup. These typesetting units are interfaced to the computer system to minimize handling by composing room personnel, and all copy from the press associations comes directly into the computer system, thus avoiding re-input by means of punched tape (Fig. 6.11). The Compugraphic videosetter is a standard photocomposing unit for smaller newspapers, while larger publications depend on more elaborate models like the Photon Pacesetter or the giant Mergenthaler Linotron. Fonts of type contained on grids within the phototypesetter are reproduced with lightning speed.

As the developed proofs of news stories, headlines, advertisements, and other reading matter pour from the phototypesetter, they drop into a bin where they are ready to be cut apart, fed through a device that coats the back of each with hot wax for mounting on page-size layout sheets, and thus prepared for platemaking.

MAKING THE OFFSET PLATE

The offset process involves working with pasteups of page proofs rather than metal frames or "chases" filled with actual type. The pasteup area therefore is of great importance to the efficient flow of work. It consists of tilt-top tables on which the waxed proofs are laid flat onto numbered sheets of the exact dimension of the newspaper page to be printed (Fig. 6.12). The pasteup section of the composing room must be spacious, well lighted, and free of any extraneous material. For a close-up of a completed page-one pasteup see Figure 6.13.

Fig. 6.9. A workman adjusts a component of the computer control that directs the typesetting for the La Crosse, Wis., *Tribune.* Disk drives on the left hold the programmed editorial and classified advertising copy for upcoming editions. (Courtesy of the La Crosse *Tribune.*)

Fig. 6.10. Fotomatic (camera unit attached to the left side of the machine) was a transition from mechanical to electronic typesetting. It produced 8.2 lines of newspaper text per minute. (Courtesy of the Intertype Company.)

The next step is the production of a negative made of film specially designed for the offset method of printing. In Figure 6.14 the pasteup page is shown positioned in the camera frame ready for shooting; the finished negative (Fig. 6.15) is ready to be slipped into a pneumatic tube and sent directly to the platemaking department.

Fig. 6.11. The Photon Mark II Pacesetter is wired directly to a Harris 2500/20 system for on-line typesetting at 70 lines per minute, with or without punched tape. (Courtesy of the La Crosse, Wis., *Tribune.*)

Fig. 6.12. This neat, orderly pasteup area of the Rochester, Minn., *Post-Bulletin*'s composing room is a marked contrast to the work spaces of hot-metal plants. Makeup personnel paste proofs onto page-size layouts in preparation for the next edition. (Courtesy of the Rochester *Post-Bulletin.*)

Fig. 6.13. This page-one pasteup is given a final check by an editor and a production supervisor of the Des Moines, Iowa, *Register* and *Tribune*. (Courtesy of the Des Moines *Register* and *Tribune*.)

Fig. 6.14. An engraver for the Louisville, Ky., *Courier-Journal* and *Times* loads a Chemco Pager camera. This unit produces a full-page negative of the pasteup. (Courtesy of the Louisville *Courier-Journal* and *Times*.)

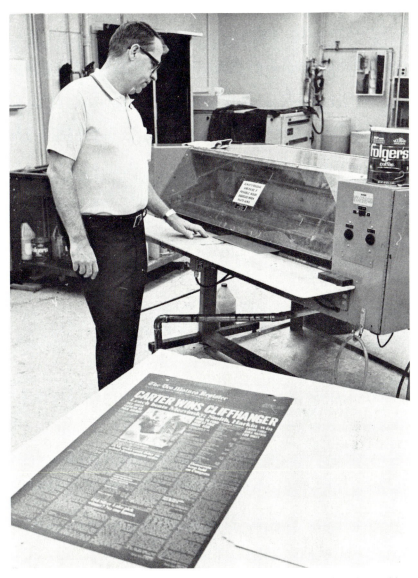

Fig. 6.15. The completed page negative is ready for the platemaking department. (Courtesy of the Des Moines, Iowa, *Register* and *Tribune*.)

Fig. 6.16. A modern platemaking department. Notice the aluminum plate, ready for printing, being delivered in the foreground. (Courtesy of the Rochester, Minn., *Post-Bulletin.*)

Many types of platemakers are available, from table-top models like the Ascor Vacuum Printer to large floor models like that used by the Des Moines, Iowa, *Register* and *Tribune* (Fig. 6.16). The most advanced systems such as the Laseriter 100 and the Chemco News-Plater (Fig. 6.17) do not require a negative but print directly from the pasteup onto the aluminum press plate. In addition to great savings in production time (a modern platemaker can turn out two press-ready plates per minute), these machines provide plates that weigh less than a half a pound each in place of the 40-pound stereotype plates required for letterpress printing.

MORE CHANGES AHEAD

The improvements in technology discussed here may seem revolutionary to newspaper personnel who can remember shops where type was set by hand, but the trend will undoubtedly continue. For example, an editing terminal already on the drawing boards will be linked directly to a platemaker via computer to create a 100-pica-wide aluminum plate without going through the steps outlined in this chapter. The plate will be pregummed and ready to attach to the printing cylinders of the press, thus

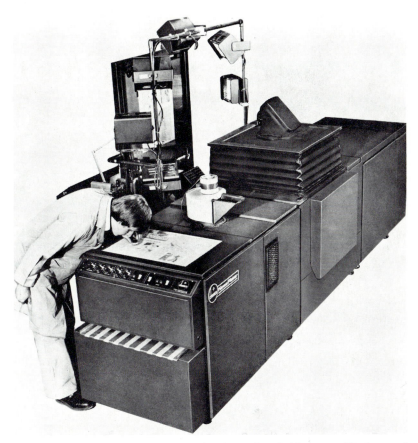

Fig. 6.17. This fully automatic platemaker holds up to 75 sheets of aluminum and turns out two press-ready plates per minute. The page pasteup is positioned on the upright copy board of the Chemco News-Plater, which requires no negative and produces the plate by electrophotographic means. (Courtesy of the Chemco Photoproducts Company.)

reducing the time lag from writer to printed page to a matter of seconds rather than minutes or hours. Such changes clearly indicate that management will be in need of vision, know-how, and a spirit of progressive advancement — perhaps more than at any time in the history of newspapering.

7

Photography and color printing

> Better photography must be instigated and motivated by photography departments and photographers. Editors can't do it. They work with formulas to get those pages out. They need formulas to make all those decisions. Photographers should understand these working methods, and editors should understand something about a photographer's thinking.
>
> *Tom Hubbard*

Editors have discovered that pictures of every kind, when reproduced on the printed page in either black and white or color, will add brightness to the newspaper and help to meet competition and build circulation. The rapid move toward the use of photography and color printing by newspapers is almost as exciting as the technological advances treated in the preceding chapters.

Practically every newspaper organization, from the small weekly to the metropolitan daily, has one photographer or more on its staff to provide illustrations for many of its reported stories. A survey of Connecticut newspapers by the Connecticut News Photographers Association reveals that the average press photographer of that state takes care of 5.1 picture-taking assignments daily. The most common assignments are in these categories: police-fire, group shots, sports, civic clubs, government, and women's activities.

"Good pictures, given good play, are important to news pages," declared Gregory Favre, when he was editor of the West Palm Beach, Fla., *Palm Beach Post,* in addressing editors at a newsphoto conference. "We have been trying to learn for years how to reach out of the printed page and grab the reader by the lapel of his coat and say, 'Pay attention.' "

The Florida editor emphasized pictures even though he is basically a

---

The photographs reproduced in this chapter previously appeared in *News Photographer* and are reprinted by special permission.

Fig. 7.1. Jay Dickman of the Dallas, Tex., *Times-Herald* got this picture of a policeman sobbing in grief at the funeral of a murdered colleague.

word man — a "three-times-a-week column writer." Announcing his love for pictures — big pictures, impact pictures, news pictures, feature pictures, pretty pictures, all kinds of pictures from A to Z — Favre observed, "I think our readers love pictures too." Favre explained that the *Post* favors one strong picture as a matter of preference over a multipicture layout. "We go for the best picture every day for A-1. It might be a sports picture and that's all right with us . . . we'll settle for anything if we think it's the top picture of the day."

To make sure the *Post* can provide adequate space for its pictures, Favre said, "Two years ago we talked the editor out of three open pages for local news and local pictures five days a week. We consider this a cornerstone of our appearance. The only way you'll ever be able to play pictures as they should be played is by having a pre-set number of pages with a certain amount of space on them. It isn't difficult to have a good looking newspaper with good pictures. Make good assignments. Brief your photographers. It is my experience that photographers, taken as a whole, don't read beyond the pictures and they often don't know what is news. So brief them well."

PICTURE PAGES

An interesting photographic feature used by newspapers, which can compete with television, is the picture page that makes photos more vivid. Professor Clifton Edom, for many years head of the photography sequence at the School of Journalism of the University of Missouri, thinks that a page of pictures built to a common theme has greater appeal than the so-called "hodge-podge" page of pictures. The best picture pages now appearing in newspapers are well designed in typography and in picture layout.

A study of six midwestern newspapers by a photo-editing class taught by Lillian M. Junas at Ball State University in Muncie, Ind., indicates that picture pages still play a prominent part in the daily newspaper, with an average of 4.8 run per day. Newspapers selected for the study included the Milwaukee, Wis., *Journal* and the St. Louis, Mo., *Post-Dispatch,* both of which have carried picture pages for many years; the Louisville, Ky., *Courier-Journal;* the Chicago, Ill., *Tribune;* the Indianapolis, Ind., *News;* and the Dubuque, Iowa, *Telegraph-Herald.* These were selected because they have used picture pages in the past and/or because of their recognition in press circles as top photo papers.

Any picture spread of more than one-half page was considered in the study, which covered two one-month periods (October and January) or a total of 54 days. The classes studied picture pages for the entire academic year, but these two months were chosen at random for this study. Categories tabulated were news picture pages; feature picture pages; position of the page; use of captions only, copy only, or both copy and captions; number of pictures; and number of full-page width pictures. A total

Fig. 7.2. Pulitzer prize winner Stanley Forman produced this gripping picture layout of a tragic accident. (By special permission of the Boston, Mass., *Herald-American*.)

Table 7.1.   Frequency of use and location of picture pages

Paper	Total Picture Pages	News Picture Pages	Feature Picture Pages	Inside Pages	Front Pages	Back Pages
Post-Dispatch	57	8	49	3	54	0
Telegraph-Herald	14	6	8	4	8	2
Courier-Journal	23	6	17	9	6	8
Tribune	61	35	26	9	1	51
Journal	53	15	38	45	6	2
News	54	54	0	54	0	0
Totals	262	124	138	125	75	63
		44%	46%	47%	28%	24%

of 262 picture pages were tallied during the 54 days for all papers, with the *Tribune* carrying the most (61) and the *Telegraph-Herald* the least (14).

Figures indicated that feature picture pages were used slightly more than news picture pages, the most frequent position for such pages was inside, almost an equal number of pages used the picture-caption-copy combination as used pictures with captions only, and an average of four to five pictures were used on picture pages (Table 7.1).

HOW TO DEVELOP A PHOTOGRAPHER

A good photographer is less likely to be obtained by a weekly or a small daily than by a large paper, but one can be found, according to Maurice Kaplan, chief photographer for the Huntington, W.Va., *Herald-Dispatch*.

"Photographers can be found through many sources," says Kaplan, "limited only by the extent of the initial operating budget. Usually immediate response can be obtained from advertisements in related trade publications. On the community level, the first place an editor should look for a photographer is at the local high school or, if one exists, a local college. The drugstore operator or photofinisher in the area knows who the local camera bugs are. The area may have a camera club. Any of these sources can turn up amateur photographers. If necessary, an amateur snapshot contest can be run in the paper. This is guaranteed to bring photographers out of the weeds by the dozens."

On any level, however, the photographer must be at the right place at the right time with the right equipment if superior pictures are to result. The cliché, "opportunity plus preparation equals success," applies perhaps even more particularly to the photographer.

BEST CAMERA FOR NEWS

Perhaps the most popular newspaper camera in use today is the 35 mm. The single-lens reflex is used more than any other, according to Professor Clifton Edom. "The 35 mm camera is versatile, easy to handle, and

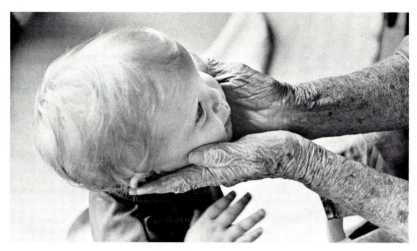

Fig. 7.3. The feature picture can express feelings deeper than words. This was shot by Randy Dieter, chief photographer and picture editor of the Evansville, Ind., *Sunday Courier & Press.*

inexpensive to operate. It has a host of interchangeable lenses which add to its versatility. It even has motor-drive equipment, is adaptable to black and white or color, and lets one take unposed pictures—pictures which look real and honest—not stereotyped snapshots. Among the most popular professional (newspaper or magazine) cameras are the Nikon and Leica."

Professor Edom also makes the following suggestions regarding the positioning of the photographer and the subjects he is to photograph:

A good photographer varies the distance at which he shoots. To shoot from the same distance all the time makes for monotony. With wide-angle, normal and telephoto lenses, one can have close-up shots, overall shots, and normal views. One must, of course, have horizontal pictures and perpendiculars and must know how to select good backgrounds—must keep his pictures simple and uncluttered. His pictures must be interesting (action pictures are more interesting than posed, head-on "mug shots"). So avoid the snapshot; learn how to record the truth as it happens. Obviously, then, the best photographer is the best reporter. He is perceptive and is involved with his subject. He is freezing a moment of life—a capsule of time. He is the eyewitness for the thousands of readers who depend on him to capture the occasion.

POLICIES REGARDING EQUIPMENT

A questionnaire sent to 200 members of the National Press Photographers Association, to which 88 members responded, reveals some interesting facts regarding the equipment they used in taking news pictures:

1. The average number of cameras per photographer was three; the average number of lenses was six.
2. Fifty-one percent of the cameras used were 35 mm; 33 percent were 2¼ x 2¼; 9 percent were press cameras (although none used a press camera extensively); and 7 percent were special purpose, such as view cameras and panoramic cameras.
3. Fifty-eight percent of the photographers had a full complement of lenses, from extremely wide to long telephoto, and 60 percent of the cameras and lenses used by press photographers were owned by them personally.
4. A publication may have essentially four different photoequipment policies: company-owned equipment all of the same brand chosen to conform to the desires of the majority of staff photographers, company-owned equipment chosen by the individual photographer, photographer-owned equipment leased or rented by the publication, or photographer-owned equipment used without reimbursement by the publication.
5. Eighty-seven percent of the photographers who replied used some of their own equipment in their work; 26 percent received an equipment allowance; and 61 percent used their own equipment without reimbursement by the newspaper. Only 32 percent of the publications supplied their photographers with light meters.

LABORATORY NEEDS

Smaller weekly and daily newspapers can manage with far less sophisticated darkroom and processing equipment than the metropolitan publications (some of which employ as many as 30 photographers). "Contrary to the popular myth," says R. F. Garland, marketing specialist for the Eastman Kodak Company, "your 'darkroom on a shoestring' will give you predictable, quality prints for a total equipment layout of just over $200."

As photography demands build up, automatic processors will be a practical consideration. Stainless steel sinks for developing and printing, with fixer and other chemicals piped directly into the solutions, may be added. An air filtration system, to prevent dust, and accurate temperature and humidity controls improve the quality of processing. Ceramic tile walls and floors provide maximum safety and efficiency in cleanup. Any number of enlargers may be needed, depending upon the present capacity and future expansion plans. Color separations may be done with specially built enlargers or with a direct screen process that offers major savings on film.

Before launching into major renovation or planning for new laboratory space and facilities, management should study the successful operations of other newspaper photographic installations as much as possible, since each newspaper's needs will be slightly different. A model black-

The Wichita Eagle and Beacon

LifeStyle

Sun Oct 26 1975 1D

SOCIAL NEWS
  Around Wichita 2D
HEALTH
  Faith Healing 3D
EDUCATION
  Courses by Newspaper 8D

Why, if one were on a hill, surely you could even catch the golden ball for a toy. Staff Photographer John Avery made it all possible one autumn afternoon, with the aid of the setting sun.

FLIRTING
with the sun

His lens watched a girl win the wind-swept race to capture the elusive orb and to, with it in joyous free over the fields then suddenly aware of its greater importance — blow it away with a kiss to set the world to rest

Fig. 7.4. The picture-page layout may express a simple theme in evocative photographs, as in John Avery's sunset series for the Wichita, Kans., *Eagle* and *Beacon*.

and-white photography plant is that of the Boston, Mass., *Globe,* rebuilt to incorporate some of the most modern equipment available.

PICTURES IN COLOR

Color printing continues to grow in favor—another indication of change in newspapermaking. The press manufacturers are turning out equipment that will provide the use of several colors for brightening the news pages and making advertisements more appealing. The publishers, advertising patrons, and readers appreciate this improvement.

The "coloroptics" study made by the Milwaukee, Wis., *Journal* shows that newspaper color can increase advertising readership by 87 percent over black and white. This was substantiated by a later split-run test of the Long Beach, Calif., *Independent* and *Press-Telegram* showing that a newspaper color ad out-pulled a black and white ad by 84 percent in retail sales—that is, the actual translation of increased readership into increased dollar sales.

Color is no longer limited to advertising but appears throughout the newspaper's news and editorial sections. Run-of-paper (ROP) color has increased more than 167 percent during the 1960s and 1970s. Indicative of the increase in use of color is the fact that in 1950 the Milwaukee, Wis., *Journal* was the only newspaper to carry more than a million lines of color advertising. In 1966–67, close to 200 newspapers ran more than a million lines.

"Let's face it," says Richard C. Christian, chairman of the board of the American Association of Advertising Agencies. "We're living in a visual world of color where newspapers appear to be in a learning curve."

Consistent leaders in fine color printing include the St. Petersburg, Fla., *Times,* which led the nation recently with over 5 million lines; the Houston, Tex., *Chronicle,* which has remained in the top ten producers of color linage for the past 20 years; the Syracuse, N.Y., newspapers (the *Herald-Journal,* the *Post-Standard,* the *Herald-American*); the Orlando, Fla., *Sentinel-Star;* the Akron, Ohio, *Beacon-Journal;* and a score of others.

An ink-blending system is saving money and selling color linage for the Dallas, Tex., *Times-Herald.* With this new blending and dispensing ink system, the Dallas paper can create custom colors from bulk supplies instead of buying special colors in kits and drums. With ten base colors, it can get 86 standard colors. It can match colors of dresses, coats, shoes, and purses for its advertisers immediately instead of sending the items out for matching. It can review proof, ordering and then double-checking when the ink finally arrives in the pressroom.

With a three-unit Colorflex-250 press, the Herald Publications of Nutley, N.J., are turning out 750,000 copies of newspapers and other publications per week. The Colorflex is a single-width press with semicylindrical vertical design permitting both straight and collect runs. The

Fig. 7.5. Spot news coverage by the photographer requires quick response. Denis Law of the Seattle, Wash., *Beacon Hill News* heard of a head-on accident on the police radio and arrived on the scene to get this emotional shot.

press has the availability of a color unit with three-color capacity, which has been designed for direct lithographic printing in combination with conventional offset. This arrangement allows three colors to be printed on one side of a web — two by conventional offset and one by direct lithography.

The Omaha, Nebr., *World-Herald,* a heavy user of full color ROP, is able to maintain consistently high quality of reproduction, both editorial and advertising. It runs 365 prints of editorial art per year and one out of every 10 inches of display advertising in color. These figures keep the *World-Herald* consistently in the top 15 newspapers in total ROP advertising.

The Everett, Wash., *Herald* proclaims itself to be the Northwest's most colorful newspaper. The paper has installed a Berkey direct-screen color-separation system that has enabled the paper to produce separations faster and at a savings over the original process with comparable quality.

The *Christian Science Monitor,* Boston, Mass., has installed two five-unit Hoe Color-Convertible presses. Each press is geared to print up to 40 pages at the rate of 45,000 papers per hour and to handle color printing in as many as four colors.

Many daily newspaper presses are equipped with special color cylinders and separate inking arrangements for ROP color printing. The improved tubular (Unitube and Dek-A-Tube) and single-width semicylindrical (Universal) presses have removable fountain pans that lend themselves to convenient color printing with auxiliary attachments, thus simplifying the process.

The all-out commitment to color still has not been made by many of the nation's newspapers. But among those that have gone to lavish use of ROP color, benefits to publishers, to advertisers, and to readers have been manifested.

8

Housing and arranging the plant

A newspaper plant houses operations
that are complex and interdependent. It
must be planned as a unit.

Robert W. Dickerson

Suitable location for the newspaper plant
and its arrangement to provide for efficiency, convenience, and accessibili-
ty to the public are fundamental factors in efficient newspaper publishing.
Improper use of space is just as costly as improper use of machinery or
materials. High-priced equipment cannot produce as it should if it is improperly placed, and many minutes a day can be wasted by employes who
are compelled to take unnecessary steps.

These matters are given careful consideration by the successful newspaper publisher. Competition and heavy operating costs have compelled
the saving of time and labor to make the place of business convenient and
comfortable for employes and attractive to the general public. Consequently, many buildings occupied by newspapers have been enlarged and
improved or replaced with modern structures.

CHOOSING A PLANT SITE

If a new, larger, and more modern building seems necessary, full
study should be given to the location before beginning construction.
Where possible, newspaper buildings are located away from the high-rent
areas of the city or town, although there are notable exceptions to this rule,
especially in the largest cities. Perhaps the most practical location is one on
the fringe of the main shopping area in the city or just off the square or
main street in the smaller town. The newspaper is a manufacturing enterprise, and its industrial operations should not be hampered too much for
the sake of a desirable location in the theater district or on Main Street.
The plant needs to be near a post office, close to a railroad siding, or accessible to trucking facilities, so raw materials may be brought in and the
finished product distributed without delay.

On the other hand, the news and advertising departments cannot
operate at top efficiency unless the plant is located near the nerve center of
the community. Most local news sources are near the city center, and the
newspaper needs to be close to these areas of activity if its reporters are to

be on the spot when news breaks. Retail stores are the newspaper's heaviest advertisers, which means that advertising salespeople can cover more territory and speed up the transmission of copy, revised proofs, and late advertising orders if the plant is near the business section.

Some newspapers have experimented with mechanical plants on the edge of the city, with news and advertising offices downtown. Experience still teaches, however, that the "close-in" location is likely to prove most satisfactory for both metropolitan and community newspapers.

Important points to be considered in choosing a newspaper-plant site are:

1. The lot on which the plant is to be located should be large enough to permit expansion of the building if that becomes necessary.
2. In these times of traffic congestion, parking space by the building is quite important.
3. A desirable location would be a street intersection with an alley at the rear, so that entrances and exits may be provided at three sides of the building.
4. The availability of adequate power, light, and fuel should be carefully considered. Gas pressure varies in sections of a city, and fire hazards are greater in some locations than in others.
5. It is well to remember that the contour of the lot may influence the style of the building. If possible, steps leading to entrances should be avoided.

SPECIALISTS AID PLANNING

Newspaper publishers who have expansion problems can head off costly building errors by employing architect-engineers and by carefully studying well-designed plants of similar size where there are similar problems and possibilities of newspaper growth.

The type of internal plant layout needed to accommodate the newspaper's present operation is vital, but particular attention must be given to possible future development. The minutest details should not be overlooked since mistakes at the beginning are difficult to correct later.

An architect's view

An architect with experience in newspaper-plant planning and construction may be able to see many points for basic consideration that a publisher, limited in knowledge of architectural engineering, might not anticipate. A preconceived and well-studied production plan helps to hold down building costs and, more important, positively reduces operating costs. A well-planned and well-arranged plant can greatly facilitate work flow and save many hours of production labor. All the essentials needed to produce such a plant should be worked into the plan before construction is started. Changes in original plans are always costly.

However, professional architects and planners are not able to provide answers to all the problems that editors and reporters face. For example, when the Milwaukee, Wis., *Journal* installed 64 editing terminals in its newsroom, Managing editor Joseph W. Shoquist found that professional designs lacked the newsroom efficiency he required. "And so," he told colleagues at an editorial conference in Las Vegas, "the assistant managing editor and I, with help from the office designers, moved little squares and rectangles around on a blueprint until we had a floor plan that suited our needs." An individualized arrangement tailored to the news-flow operation resulted, with editing terminals mounted on swivel-type tables adjacent to specially built desks for reporters and editors. Extensive use was made of lateral files at each desk, and concealed cables within structural pillars supported the swivel tables, thus working spaces were achieved that were compact, accessible, and extremely efficient.

STUDY MODEL PLANTS

Before beginning to build a newspaper plant or to alter an existing one, it is advisable that a publisher visit some of the most modern buildings in which newspapers of the same size are published. Valuable ideas for the arrangement and interrelation of departments may be obtained, and ways building costs may be held down will probably be revealed.

Beauty and facility may be as easily provided in a small plant as in a large one. Many handsome one-floor plants have been erected. They provide an easy flow of work in less space and usually with less equipment than other architectural styles.

The Hattiesburg, Miss., *American*

After having been published for many years under crowded conditions from a three-story, wooden-framed hotel building and three adjoining buildings, the Hattiesburg, Miss., *American* now occupies a specially designed plant of one floor under one roof with every convenience needed for producing a modern and growing newspaper (Figs. 8.1A, 8.1B).

The plant, 84 by 204 feet, is in the downtown section, two blocks from the county courthouse, three blocks from the city hall, across the street from a federal building, two blocks from the railway station, four blocks from the bus station, and a ten-minute drive from the airport. Its location near the middle of a large lot makes it possible for traffic to enter and exit on two different streets; it also makes future expansion possible on all four sides. However, enough "extra" space in the building was planned to take care of additional personnel and equipment for years to come. Since there are no inside support walls, it will be easy to rearrange dividing walls to provide more space if that should become necessary.

"Now with the new building," says Robert M. Hederman III, general manager, "the people who write, edit, produce, and distribute the Hattiesburg *American* have a tool to work with, not an obstacle to overcome.

Fig. 8.1A. This attractive plant brings all activities of making a newspaper to one floor for the Hattiesburg, Miss., *American.*

All thoughts and attentions are turned to the contents of the paper rather than to the problems of producing a paper. There are still problems to be worked out and things to learn, but the entire staff is now able to work together as a team to solve the problems. Because departments can now work together, we are putting out a better and stronger newspaper than ever before . . . and faster."

This situation was realized because every detail needed was given careful consideration. The first objective was to plan a building that would provide straight-line work flow.

Ready communication among departments. To get the most benefits from the straight-line procedures, it was necessary to establish strong communications among workers within a department and among departments. This step was accomplished with a central paging system, an intercom system, and wide-open work areas. Private offices, halls, and "off the beaten path work areas" had to be eliminated.

The main office is an example of the wide-open work area idea. The bookkeeping, classified, news, and advertising departments are all located in the same room. These departments are separated by aisles and counters. A receptionist at the front counter greets visitors and customers and directs them to the proper department.

The classified department, in the front right corner of the building, has four employes. Two other desks can be used as needed, and three telephone stations can be used for selling classified ads. All classified ads are sent to the composing room in an air tube, thus saving steps and time.

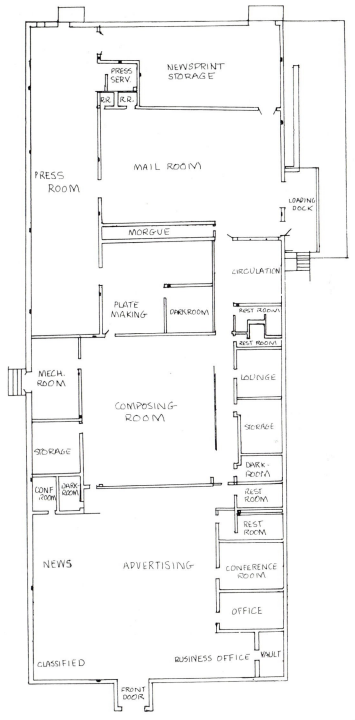

Fig. 8.1B. These floor plans indicate the care used in locating departments and equipment for efficient flow of work in the modern plant of the
Hattiesburg, Miss., *American.*

Speed in handling news. The news department is located in the back right side of the room. The photographers, reporters, and editors use 14 desks. To save steps, there is a conveyor that runs from the front row of reporters' desks all the way back to the editor. When a story is completed, the reporter places the copy on the conveyor and it falls out at the editor's desk. The editor then checks the story, puts it in an air tube, which is located right behind his chair, and sends it to the composing room. Thus stories travel quickly from the reporter to the typesetting machines.

A series of five-drawer file cabinets serves as a picture and story morgue for the reporters. It is an easy and rapid reference system and one that does not take up valuable floor space. The photofax and AP machines are located on each side of the editor and the darkroom is immediately behind. With all copy and picture sources within reach, the editor can keep close control over all material. If it is necessary for the editor to go into the composing room for some reason, it is only a few feet away.

Convenience in ad department. The advertising department is separated from the news department by a counter used to store ad services, layout sheets, and supplies. Under the counter are 80 drawers for filing advertising copy. Thirty-one drawers are used for filing each day's pages for one month. Thirty-six are used to file ads by accounts, and the remainder of the drawers are assigned to the sales staff. By using this combination, a piece of copy is seldom lost. When an ad is finished, the layout is passed directly to the composing room through a chute in the wall.

The bookkeeping department is located next to the front door and across the aisle from the advertising sales staff, who can have the answer to any question about an account in a matter of minutes. Only four people are in the bookkeeping department and two extra desks. Generally speaking, enough desks already are in position in the main office to add 50 percent more people to the staff.

The manager's office is the only private office in the building. Instead of private offices, two conference rooms are available. One is on the news side of the building and will seat four or five people, and the other is on the advertising side of the building and will seat 14 at the table, with ample space for additional chairs when needed.

Spacious composing room. In the composing room, about 1,700 square feet provide more than enough room to double the number of typesetting machines, TTS keyboards, ad pasteup desks, and page makeup tables. Copy comes in from the news department in the air tube or on a conveyor from the wire editor to the markup person, who sorts it out and places it in the carousel. The tape is punched, passed over to the Compugraphic machines, set, proofread, and then sent to page makeup. Ads come in through the chute, borders and illustrations are put on, the ad is marked up, punched, set, and then sent back to pasteup. News and ad corrections follow the same path as the originals. When the copy is correct, it is passed through a chute to the platemaking room.

Another big step taken to help prepare for growth was the installation of electrical conduits on five-foot centers through the main office area and composing room. At each two and one-half feet along the electrical conduit is an outlet. Twelve clean lines were also added in the composing room. This should take care of almost any arrangement of electrical or computerized typesetting equipment. Not knowing exactly what utilities would be needed for future equipment, care was taken to add plenty of hot and cold water lines, extra four-inch drains, compressed air, and many 110- and 220-volt electrical outlets. Plumbing was even stubbed in for a future color darkroom.

When the pages come out of the platemaking department, they are put on a 32-page Goss Urbanite offset press. Only four units have been installed, but space is provided for an additional six.

The circulation department is located next to the mailroom. A large glass window between the two areas gives the circulation manager excellent control over the flow of papers. A view of the dock is also provided to observe the loading of trucks. A 20- by 50-foot canopy over the loading dock makes it possible to load papers in any kind of weather.

Several precautions have been taken to minimize fire hazards. Fire-rated concrete blocks have been used, and 26 fire extinguishers are located throughout the plant. High-pressure sprinklers hang over the areas where papers are handled.

The main office is paneled with antique oak, and the floor is covered with asbestos. Grass, flowers, and shrubs are planted across the front of the building and along the north side. In the back and on the north is parking space for 90 cars and trucks. In the words of the general manager, "The building has been designed for producing a daily newspaper; it was not built or intended to be a showplace."

Making a new start

An experience similar to that of the Hattiesburg, Miss., *American* has come to the Longview, Wash., *Daily News* with its removal to a new one-story plant (Figs. 8.2A, 8.2B).

"Our plant was built to accommodate a complete conversion from hot-metal production to cold type in offset," says J. M. McClelland, Jr., editor and publisher. "Thus we were able to make the move from the old building without taking anything along except the library files and the business files. This gives the newspaper an opportunity to make a new start in a new environment and to make improvements in its contents and ways of doing things."

The *Daily News* adopted a new format, going from nine narrow columns to six 11-pica columns, and narrowed the page width to make it easier for the reader to handle.

Fig. 8.2A. Modernized to provide offset, cold-type, computer-processed tape production of a six-column newspaper, the Longview, Wash., *Daily News* is housed on a three-acre site.

We adopted new headdress, and revised our style book. The editorial page was redesigned and is now five columns rather than the former eight. We give much more space to pictures and emphasize quality of pictures now that offset makes excellent reproduction possible. Our next step is to go into process color, making our own color separations and printing four-color pictures at least once a week.

A unique feature of our building is that all departments were purposely made larger than present needs call for. Thus there is room to grow. Our news room, for example, is only about half occupied. For the first 47 years of our existence, we were always bursting at the seams, and adding on little wings and additions to the old building. When we built the new building we were determined that we would have enough space to last us as far ahead as any of us could foresee.

Daily Record plans ahead

Another newspaper that has moved into a strictly modern plant to accommodate phototypesetting, offset printing, and other electronic equipment is the Roswell, N.Mex., *Daily Record*. Robert H. Beck, the publisher, and Albert M. Geary, production manager, designed most of the plant after visiting other newspapers in the West (Figs. 8.3A, 8.3B). "We believe we are now producing one of the most modern small newspapers in the Southwest," says Beck. "The production facilities are highly efficient—the result of several years of research by staff members."

"I've dreamed for five or six years of having an offset plant—and now it is here," says Geary. "The working conditions are excellent: low noise

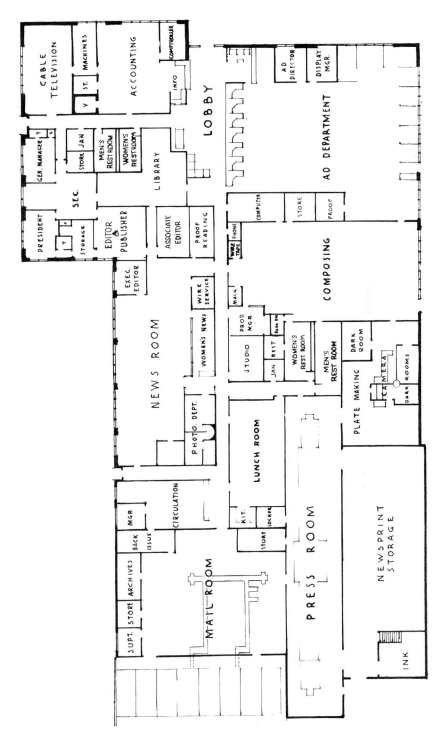

Fig. 8.2B. Floor plan of the Longview, Wash., *Daily News.*

Fig. 8.3A. Offset plant of the Roswell, N.Mex., *Daily Record,* Donald R. Goss and Associates, architects.

level, refrigerated air, uniform lighting conditions, and carpeting throughout except for the pressroom, circulation room, paper storage room, and camera darkroom." Geary was responsible for implementing all the changes made in the new back shop. He visited offset printing facilities on four trips around the country, read books, and talked to people in preparation for the move to the new plant. Says Beck,

> This computerized electronic phototypesetting and this offset printing process have brought us into a new world; no metal is involved. During the first days of publication experts were here representing companies which furnish machines — including the new 32-page Goss Urbanite press — and equipment for the offset operation.
> Previously typesetting involved hot-metal linecasting machines — now the whole procedure is photographic. Tools of the trade include wax, computers which produce "type" on special photographic paper ready for stripping and pasteup, sharp knives, a giant camera which photographs entire pages after they are pasted up, page "negatives" from which thin metal plates are made using light and chemicals and, of course, the new press.

Among worksaving devices installed are carousels, which are centered in the composing room near slots for anything needed to paste up pages. Geary explained, "Carousels are stepsaving, and they keep everything in its proper place. They take the work to be performed to the worker. And they're tied in with the conveyor belt which carries material back and forth between the front and back shops to make work easier and faster."

Additional space

When additional space is needed for new equipment and later expansion, the question always arises as to whether the publisher should add to

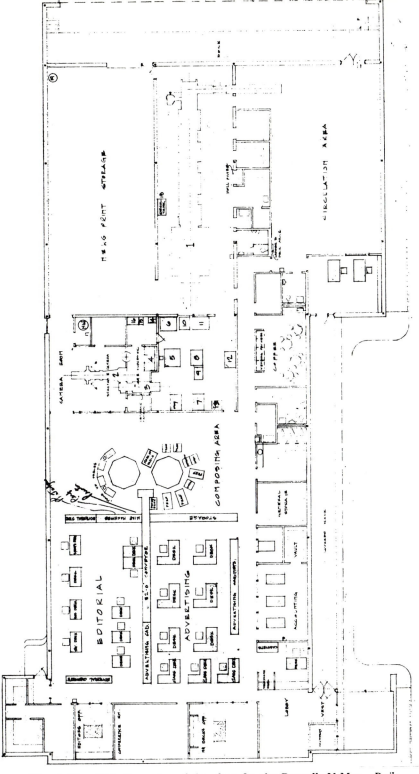

Fig. 8.3B. This floor plan of the plant for the Roswell, N.Mex., *Daily Record* shows how labor costs are reduced by easy work flow from the news and advertising departments through the composing and mailing departments.

the existing building or whether a new site should be chosen for erection of an entirely new plant. It is always a stirring question.

When this question confronted the Johnson City, Tenn., *Press-Chronicle,* careful consideration was given to all phases of the situation and the decision was made to enlarge and remodel the existing plant (Figs. 8.4A, 8.4B, 8.4C, 8.4D, 8.4E).

The existing building provided approximately 27,000 square feet of space. An addition was then planned to provide 17,000 square feet more space, allowing for the expansion of every department of the newspaper operation. The reel room, mailroom, pressroom, and engraving department are now all located in the new addition. The composing room has been remodeled and kept in its same quarters. The newsroom has been expanded by maintaining the portion already in the original building and extending it into the new building. This was true also for the circulation and business offices. By relocating other offices, it was possible to enlarge the advertising department.

"We decided to switch to the Ball Metal System of printing directly from zinc plates," says Tim Jones, administrative assistant.

This enabled us to utilize the advantages of cold-type composition in our composing room and maintain a letterpress operation—to produce a better quality printing job than the standard letterpress printing from stereo plates. We have doubled our press capacity from three units to six units.

Most of our office expansion area has given us badly needed extra room. Our offices were in good condition but simply overcrowded due to the recent growth of our business.

In summary I believe we have a modern up-to-date well-equipped building. We realize that some of our layouts are not ideal from the standpoint of a new building but one must realize that we were simply enlarging our existing building rather than starting from scratch on a new one. In order to maintain a homogeneous relationship between the elements in the old building and the elements in the new building it is sometimes necessary to sacrifice in terms of an ideal floor layout.

Fig. 8.4A. Outside view of the remodeled plant for the Johnson City, Tenn., *Press-Chronicle.*

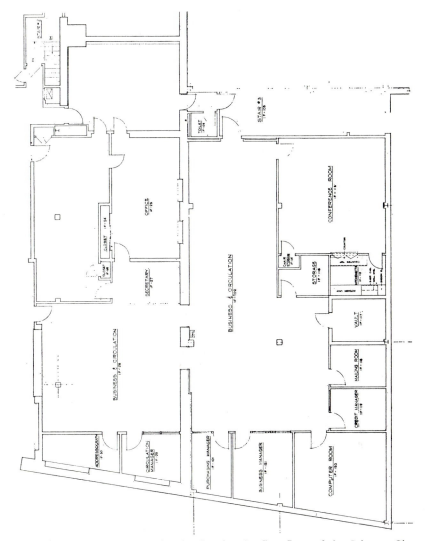

Fig. 8.4B. The architect's plan for the first floor of the Johnson City, Tenn., *Press-Chronicle*'s remodeled plant shows the location of the business and circulation departments.

Arkansas Gazette expands

The *Arkansas Gazette* at Little Rock, Ark., the oldest newspaper west of the Mississippi River, expanded its plant by erecting a unit that houses a new press, the foundry portion of the stereotyping operation, the mailroom, the paper storage, and the distribution-transportation functions.

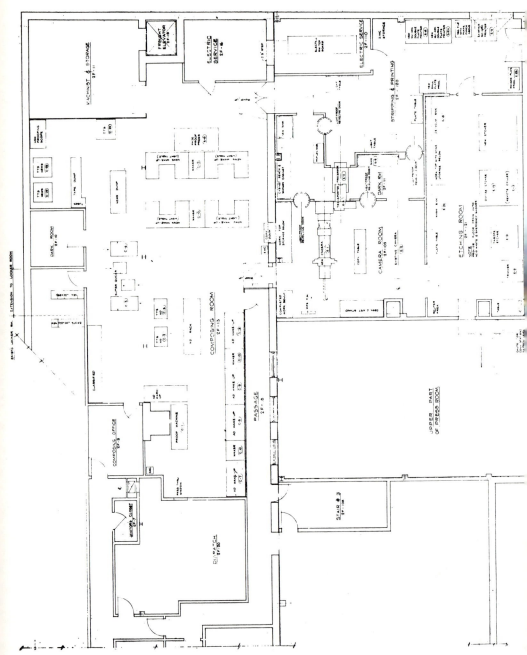

Fig. 8.4C. Composing room layout for the Johnson City, Tenn., *Press-Chronicle*.

106

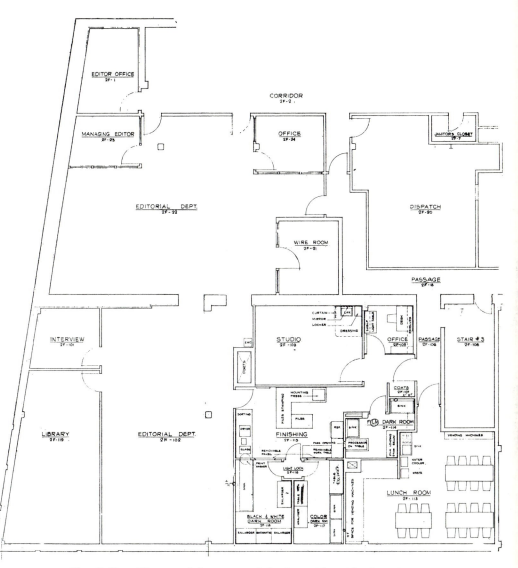

Fig. 8.4D. The second-floor plan of the *Press-Chronicle* plant shows arrangement of the editorial department.

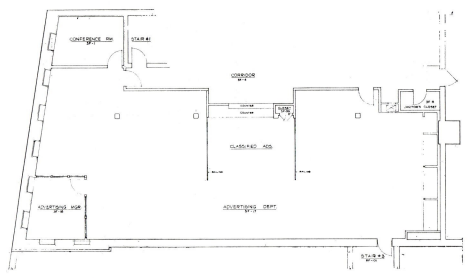

Fig. 8.4E. Advertising department layout on the mezzanine of the *Press-Chronicle* building.

The rest of the newspaper operation will remain in this unit until a companion building is constructed.

The building is a steel frame structure with the exterior of precast and aggregate concrete materials. It is finished with windows containing gold-tinted mirrored glass, framed in bronze-painted steel. It occupies a tract 180 by 170 feet. The newsprint storage area is in proximity to an off-loading facility. The building also contains a covered loading facility for the distribution of printed newspapers (Figs. 8.5A, 8.5B, 8.5C).

The composing room, fully computerized, occupies the entire second deck, a uniquely built feature of the building. A gallery overlooking the pressroom includes access to mechanical and electrical controls for the composing room and for units of the air-conditioning equipment.

Phase two of the expansion program will provide housing for the news and editorial departments, business offices, advertising department, administrative and executive offices, and certain work areas. An enclosed bridge will connect the phase one building with the phase two building, at the second-floor level. The basement of the phase one building contains the ink tank room and the boiler room.

EXPANSION IN SUBURBAN AREAS

Notable changes have been made in newspaper plants located in suburban communities where competition between newspapers is keen. The Monrovia, Calif., *Daily News-Post,* for example, made a thorough survey of its production future from the standpoint of equipment, person-

Fig. 8.5A. This new building is phase one of an expansion program for the Little Rock, Ark., *Arkansas Gazette*.

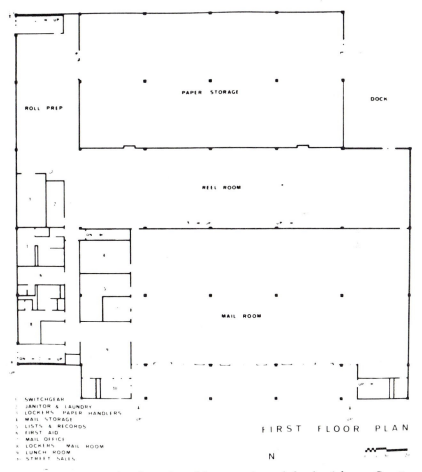

PAPER STORAGE

DOCK

ROLL PREP

REEL ROOM

MAIL ROOM

1 SWITCHGEAR
2 JANITOR & LAUNDRY
3 LOCKERS PAPER HANDLERS
4 MAIL STORAGE
5 LISTS & RECORDS
6 FIRST AID
7 MAIL OFFICE
8 LOCKERS MAIL ROOM
9 LUNCH ROOM
10 STREET SALES

FIRST FLOOR PLAN

N

Fig. 8.5B. First-floor plan of the expansion unit for the *Arkansas Gazette*.

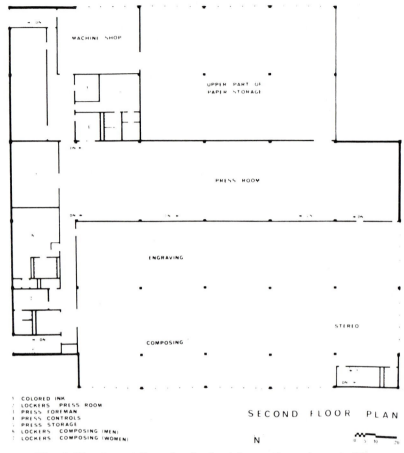

MACHINE SHOP

UPPER PART OF
PAPER STORAGE

PRESS ROOM

ENGRAVING

STEREO

COMPOSING

1 COLORED INK
2 LOCKERS   PRESS ROOM
3 PRESS FOREMAN
4 PRESS CONTROLS
5 PRESS STORAGE
6 LOCKERS   COMPOSING (MEN)
7 LOCKERS   COMPOSING (WOMEN)

SECOND   FLOOR   PLAN

N

0   5   10   20

Fig. 8.5C.   Second-floor plan for the *Arkansas Gazette*'s new building.

nel, plant facilities, and the possibilities of profitable sidelines to supplement the newspaper.

This study indicated a need for high-quality newspaper products with emphasis on process color, for which greater press capacity was needed. An Urbanite web-offset press was ordered, and meetings were held with Goss Company engineers to develop a final press-unit configuration that would meet the needs of the market as defined.

The press and other new equipment would require more space than that provided by the existing plant. Therefore, a careful study was made of plant needs, looking well into the future. A plan was drawn up, showing how the existing building would be used, how additions to the building would be needed at once, and how ground space should be provided for future expansion (Fig. 8.6). The *Daily News-Post* now has constantly before it a definite plan as a guide to its future.

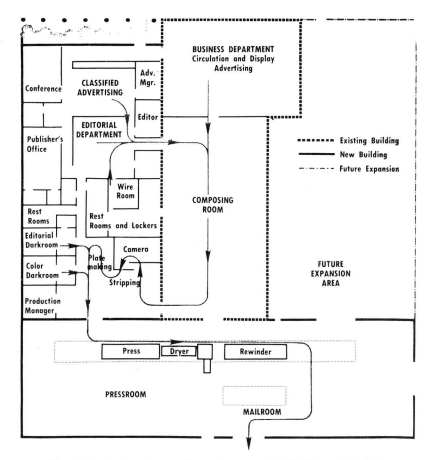

Fig. 8.6. A plant layout shows the expanded facilities of the Monrovia, Calif., *Daily News-Post* as well as future expansion space. Arrows indicate the work flow.

SPECIAL PLANT FEATURES

In designing its modern, tiled-floor pressroom, the Fort Myers, Fla., *News-Press* took pains to include soundproofing for an 8- by 32-foot press control room. Insulation materials and sealants reduced the sound level from 110 decibels to 75 decibels, even when the press units are running at full speed.

The Tampa, Fla., *Tribune-Times* building boasts a service tower concept that provides housing for all inside utilities in the corner areas of the structure. This substantially shortens the length of power lines and communication links for the entire plant.

A unique remodeling plan converted the Guthrie, Okla., *Daily Leader* building into a minimuseum, complete with displays visualizing the era when Guthrie was the state's first capital. The computerized newspaper plant offers an interesting contrast to the 1890s-type facade with which the building has been faced.

Bullet-proof windows, continuous television surveillance, and electronically monitored entrances make the new quarters of the Santa Rosa, Calif., *Press-Democrat* a model of security. These features were incorporated in a $3.5-million expansion program by the *Press-Democrat.*

A real tourist-stopper is the exciting Joliet, Ill., *Herald-News* design. The building, shaped somewhat like a modernistic mosque, appears to be floating in a placid lake. In addition to the island effect, viewers are impressed with the indoor, skylighted lounge complete with trees, pool, and smart furnishings. The work areas are just as up-to-date as the dramatic appearance of the overall structure.

The Houston, Tex., *Chronicle,* in a careful three-year renovation program, has incorporated five older buildings behind a sparkling, unified facade that encloses 100,000 square feet.

PLANNING CONSIDERATIONS

Many points must be considered in planning a newspaper building. A study of the plant designs presented in this chapter shows that the following conditions have been found desirable:

1. It is a distinct advantage to have a one-floor plant with no stairs or elevator. Many publishers are building plants of this kind.
2. The business office and advertising department should adjoin the main lobby and should be near the entrance for convenience of the public.
3. The circulation department should be near the main lobby and at the same time should not be far from the carriers' room and the mailing room, a difficult arrangement but worked out in most plans.
4. Convenient access from the news and advertising departments to the composing room should be provided so there is no delay in getting copy to the machines.
5. The composing room, plateroom, and pressroom should be arranged in that order so that the work flows from one to the other.
6. The mailing room and the carrier room should adjoin the pressroom, with ready access to the outside. Adequate loading space should be provided at the side of the mailing room.
7. Special fire protection for the costly electronic data processing area of the newspaper is mandatory. Modern systems of early detection and "total flooding" with flame-killing gas do no damage to sensitive equipment and protect heavy investments from fire and smoke losses.

Visits to well-designed newspaper plants will provide unlimited examples of how publishers are achieving efficient arrangement of departments and machinery and how money is being invested in better space utilization.

2

Production
and service

9

Factors affecting production

The transition to a new process may result in decreased overall production and increased costs during the changeover period, depending on the magnitude of the change, the local conditions and the amount of training and retraining required.

Walter Hempton

Making the many diverse and independent functions inside the newspaper plant fit together like the intricate parts of a smooth-running watch can be the most challenging and vexing problem facing executives. But there is no substitute for a harmonious blending of these production factors into a unified effort, and nothing else contributes more to the profitable and satisfying rewards to be found in newspaper publishing.

In the same way that a fine automobile spins along on four well-balanced wheels, newspaper production depends on four carefully aligned factors: flow of work, saving of time, capacity standards, and expense regulation.

FLOW OF WORK

Publishing a newspaper requires a steady flow of ingenuity, work, copy, films, and metal. To keep that flow evenly paced and uninterrupted requires clear organization, constant supervision and direction, and the most careful and earnest cooperation.

Editorial-news department

From the start of the publication period until press time, the news department must keep newsworthy information flowing into the office and the composing room. As any good reporter knows, there is nothing so stale as old news. At times a reporter may think the editors or publishers are hard taskmasters, but actually they are compelled by tradition and by the practical reality of competition to stick to inflexible deadlines if they are to keep copy flowing steadily. That's newspapering.

Covering, writing, and editing stories; picture taking; and other news-gathering responsibilities are no different on a weekly than on a daily. They are merely done by fewer persons; and even though the production interval is a full week, a steady flow of copy must be maintained once work on the week's issue is begun.

An alert and efficient editor will do the following:

1. Plan ahead. Once an issue is out, work must begin on the next. In fact, much of the work must be planned days before the date of issue.
2. Keep a date or futures book to reveal what subject matter is to be covered immediately and what news stories are in prospect. This serves a twofold purpose: the paper is not so likely to miss important stories, and assignments can be made according to an organized plan.
3. Use judgment in making assignments. The editor knows which reporters are best equipped by temperament, knowledge, and experience to handle specific types of stories.
4. Plan for early completion of stories to go on inside pages, which are made up first. Interesting copy must be available at all times for quick makeup.
5. See that department editors plan and complete features and stories well in advance. Some publishers measure the worth of department editors as much by how well they plan ahead as by the quality of the copy produced by their staffs.
6. Clear the news wire machines regularly, sort copy in an orderly fashion, and edit it rapidly. For the daily newspaper the wire machines roll out endless sheets of news from all parts of the world. The problem lies in what stories to select and when to send them to the copydesk or into the computer. Only experience will develop the kind of foresighted judgment needed for the job.
7. Keep a backlog of time copy handy — features and other material that may be used to fill in on days when general news is light.
8. Edit copy carefully to avoid revisions in proofs, which may cause delays near press time.
9. Write headlines plainly and transmit them with copy to the composing room. Late headlines cause delay and often are placed incorrectly in makeup.
10. Read proofs promptly. A dilatory and inefficient proofreader may wipe out all the speed put into copy preparation by the news staff.

As important as a steady flow of work is on any day in the newsroom, it is doubly so when extra pages or special editions are produced. "In getting out a special edition the thing to do is to start on it yesterday instead of tomorrow," says Burrell Small, executive vice-president of the Kankakee, Ill., *Journal.* Not long after a 144-page progress edition, the *Journal* published a 176-page centennial edition. This was accomplished by careful organization.

"We made a general outline of the type of material to be used in the edition, the theme of each section and the approximate number of pages," Small explains. "Then we proceeded to assign specific stories to reporters, and the fact that we told them that they should have one in every three or four days seemed to increase their interest. Naturally we had to have close cooperation and a great many staff meetings."

For a fiftieth-anniversary edition, the publisher of a small daily began formulating plans a year ahead and began actual work on the edition six months before it was to be distributed. The publisher first drew up a general plan, deciding that the edition should have ten sections, each dealing with a particular phase of the community's development in which the newspaper had an important part. Next, each section was planned, with a list of the local advertisers who should be represented and the phases of community development to be covered in news and feature stories. Each prospective story was carefully outlined so that the reporter, upon receiving the assignment, had a clear understanding of what facts should be included. A deadline was set for each section. Pictures were taken, copy was prepared, and printing of the section took place within a month after work was begun on the edition.

Work then started on the next section, which was to be written, edited, and printed within two weeks. That two-week schedule continued until the ten sections were completed. Each section was stuffed inside those previously printed, and the constantly developing edition was stored in a protected corner of the pressroom.

The work on the anniversary edition extended over a long period, but by careful planning it was done by the regular staff during some welcomed overtime hours without interfering with work on daily issues.

Business office

Work should proceed steadily and evenly in every section of the business department. Records in the office must be as up to the minute as the news that appears in the day's issue if the newspaper is to meet the standards of a going concern. This can be realized only by:

1. Giving definite instructions to office help.
2. Having proper forms for tabulating required information.
3. Issuing statements and making collections promptly.
4. Avoiding delay in answering correspondence.
5. Acknowledging all advertising and subscription orders immediately.
6. Paying bills promptly and taking advantage of discounts.
7. Maintaining adequate personnel and equipment.

A publisher encourages efficiency, accuracy, and promptness in the business office by requiring up-to-date facts about the business. The secretary of a small daily publisher is required each day to fill in and deliver the form shown in Figure 9.1. Forward-looking business managers are making dramatic use of computers for keeping an almost instantaneous check on minute details of the business operation.

Advertising department

Keeping ahead in preparing and selling advertising and feeding copy to the composing room in a way that will keep the machines busy is the advertising department's job. To accomplish this, most newspapers have deadlines for advertising copy.

The Bloomington, Ill., *Pantagraph* has an advertising deadline of 5 P.M. on the second day before publication, except on advertisements of such perishables as fruit and meat. On those the deadline is 5 P.M. the day before publication. One medium-sized daily has set up requirements as given in Table 9.1.

Table 9.1.   Advertising deadline requirements

Size of Ad	Days Preceding Publication
Double page	5 days
Single page	4 days
Half page	3 days
Quarter page	2 days
Smaller ads	1 day

The composing room refuses copy that does not conform to this deadline schedule. Such a schedule puts the advertising department on its toes and counteracts excuses from the composing room.

When putting out a special edition, the steady flow of advertising copy to the composing room for many weeks prior to publication is as important as a steady flow of editorial copy. The Atlantic City, N.J., *Press* stimulated its advertising force in a unique way for a special edition. To provide competition and thus create a steady copy flow, members of the staff were selected by team captains of the "White Sox" and "Purple Hose." A "nine-inning game" started with the last week in December and continued until mid-February. Each page (2,384 lines) of advertising counted as a run. Each week counted as an inning. The keenness of the competition is reflected in the final score: Purple Hose, 51; White Sox, 50.

Other techniques used to maintain a more even volume of advertising are:

1. A special rate to merchants who carry a minimum amount of daily or weekly advertising.
2. Bonuses and commissions for extra volume produced by salespeople during slack periods.
3. Definite linage goals established with suitable rewards for the staff when the goals are reached.

DAILY REPORT

DATE_____, 195____

NO. OF PAGES:

Today _____ Per Cent Adv. Today _____

Same Day Last Year _____ Special Pages _____

From Jan. 1 _____

Same Last Year _____ No. of Copies Printed:

Today _____

Same Day Last Year _____

ADVERTISING INCHES:

	Today	This Month	Same Day Last Year	This Month Last Year
Local Display				
National				
Classified				
Legal				
Total Adv.				
Promotion				
TOTAL				

CASH ACCOUNT:

Bank Balance This Morning $_____

Today's Deposit .... $_____

      TOTAL .... $_____

Checks Issued Today .... $_____

BALANCE TONIGHT .... $_____

Fig. 9.1.   A daily report form used by some small daily newspapers.

4. Last year's linage figures kept constantly before the staff.
5. Special pages of cooperative advertising produced for otherwise dull periods.

Some newspapers have found it advantageous, as far as stimulating the flow of advertising copy is concerned, to offer discounts to merchants who deliver their copy "camera-ready" to the newspaper. This practice obviously eliminates the work of the advertising representative in obtaining the copy from merchants, and relieves the newspaper of typesetting, composition, proofing, and delivering finished ad proofs for approval by the client.

Circulation department

No department of a newspaper runs more risk of getting off balance in its work flow than the circulation department. Papers must be delivered to homes at regular hours each day or week, and they must be in good order or subscribers are dissatisfied. Circulation totals must rise continually or at least remain stabilized at a profitable level.

A carefully planned adaptation of a semiautomatic bookkeeping machine — the National Cash Register bookkeeping machine, Model 3100, with a 26-inch carriage — has eliminated much paperwork by district personnel in the circulation department of the Santa Rosa, Calif., *Press-Democrat*. Formerly, the district staff posted their "stops" and "starts," then totaled their new draw for each route or dealer and turned in the completed figures to the bookkeeper. Under the new system, the stops and starts for each route or dealer go at once to the bookkeeper who posts them on the daily draw sheets, arriving at the day's draw as well as at the cumulative total for the month. When the total draws at the last day of the month are compiled, figures are immediately available for posting the monthly billings, without the necessity of balancing the month's work.

Rapid circulation growth led the Toronto, Ont., *Star* to modernize its mailing room to speed the movement of papers from the presses to trucks and other carriers. To supplement the equipment it already had in the mailing room, the *Star* publishers had their research-engineering department design a machine to feed bundles directly from a Cutler-Hammer paper conveyor, end on, to the roller-slat conveyor, and then directly through a company-designed automatic self-feeding, wire-tying machine. This specially designed bundle feeder is known as the Starstarter (Fig. 9.2).

To the casual spectator, the mailrooms of modern metropolitan dailies are marvels of mechanical ingenuity, where the pace of activity can become quite feverish as the pressroom hits full production. Conveyor systems are customized to speed freshly printed sections of the newspaper in sometimes bewildering configurations — horizontally, vertically, around curves, and through machines that automatically insert, stack, count, tie in bundles, address, or perform other specialized duties.

The mailroom at the *News-Sentinal* and *Journal-Gazette,* Fort

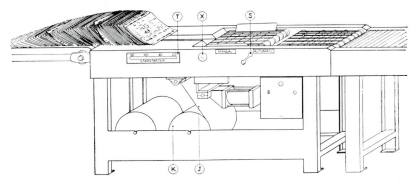

Fig. 9.2. The Toronto, Ont., *Star's* Starstarter. This sketch shows the relation of the Starstarter to the Cutler-Hammer conveyor and the roller-slat stack conveyor on which counting is done and top wrappers are applied.

Wayne, Ind., uses up-to-date equipment in its efficient operation (Figs. 9.3, 9.4). Larry Barr of the production department says,

> We print two daily newspapers in our plant and generally run our press at 48,000 papers per hour. There are two lines in our mailroom, and we try to equalize the workload on each as much as possible. An X switch enables us to go to either of our mailroom lines from either of our presses. We are able to do this while the press is running, "on the fly." A Cutler-Hammer Stack-Pak counts and stacks papers in a configuration determined by the setting of a dial. A pacer squeezes the stack and controls the entry of the papers into the balance of the bundling process. An enveloper puts a 0.5-mil sheet of plastic around the stack and welds it. Our strapping machine, the Signode MLN-2, ties the bundles with plastic straps that are biodegradable. They are easily removed and do not present the disposal problem of wire ties. Our Sheridan 48-P inserting machine is able to insert seven pieces at an average speed of 8,000 per hour. If we seem obsessed with speed, there is a good reason, particularly with the afternoon paper. Studies have shown that if the evening newspaper is not delivered to the customer before the supper hour, it very likely will not be read. This, coupled with ever-increasing traffic problems, makes time more and more important.

The Memphis Publishing Company has added a computer-directed system that determines automatically the distribution of bundles through chutes to waiting trucks four floors below. Some of the specially designed equipment for faster and more efficient mailroom operations can give this part of the newspaper plant an exciting appearance (Fig. 9.5).

A perennial problem facing circulation managers is that of carrier turnover. Frequent changes in carriers interrupt delivery service. Some newspapers deposit to a carrier's credit half the value of a U.S. Savings Bond when he has been on the route three months. To collect the bond, the carrier must stay on his route nine more consecutive months and do good work.

Many circulation problems may be solved by:

Fig. 9.3. Use of equipment such as this Sheridan 48-P inserting machine in the mailroom of the Fort Wayne, Ind., *News-Sentinel* and *Journal-Gazette* is becoming an increasingly important factor due to rapidly escalating postal rates. (Courtesy of the Fort Wayne Newspapers, Inc.)

Fig. 9.4. The complete packaging process at the Fort Wayne, Ind., *News-Sentinel* and *Journal-Gazette* includes the X switch, counter stacker, plastic enveloper, underwrapper, and plastic strapper, all shown here in their relative positions in the bundling process. (Courtesy of the Fort Wayne Newspapers, Inc.)

Fig. 9.5. A typical Goss-Ferag mailroom system for large-circulation newspapers. Tailored equipment includes delivery conveyors and stackers, bundle conveyors, and other devices needed for complete delivery from press to loading dock. (Courtesy of Rockwell International.)

1. Carefully instructing carriers in the best ways to deliver, sell, and collect.
2. Conducting weekly meetings of carriers with the circulation manager or supervisors and keeping carriers mindful of their responsibilities.
3. Providing the carriers a room they may call their own.
4. Providing such incentives as prizes, premiums, trips, and scholarships.
5. Recognizing work well done, through citations and publicity in the press and on radio and television.

Other means of improving carrier service are discussed in Chapter 14.

Mechanical department

   Management once looked upon the composing room more as a necessary evil than as a profitable operating department, but this attitude has been changed by time studies, cost systems, and cost analyses.
   An unusually detailed presentation of desirable trends in newspaper makeup was provided in comments by the judges of the 1976 Typography and Design Contest of the Inland Daily Press Association, as reported in *Editor & Publisher* magazine.[1] The judges were Hayward Blake, Evanston,

---

1. *Editor & Publisher*, Apr. 17, 1976. Used by permission.

Ill., graphic designer; and two educators from the Medill School of Journalism at Northwestern University: Assistant Dean Dave Nelson and Professor Jack Sissors.

Here are some of their observations:

1. The better newspapers use functional rather than formula makeup. Traditional newspapers have a sameness that makes them look designed by formula, whereas the best tend to use makeup that fits the news.
2. Wider columns (four-, five-, or six-column format) appear most functional and attractive.
3. Newspapers do not waste white space but are careful to distribute it throughout any given page.
4. Column rules are disappearing.
5. Newspapers tend to use one type family throughout the paper.
6. Varying the graphic treatment of special sections tends to create interest.

Here were some of their criticisms:

1. Too many nameplates are too large and too ugly.
2. Bad standing heads suggest that many newspaper managements should buy the services of a graphic designer.
3. Too many newspapers use italics too much instead of saving it for use as a contrast face.
4. The use of the same kind of rule borders for boxed stories and advertisements should be avoided.
5. Too few subheads are used to break up body type. Subheads should be boldface and of a typeface that represents a change.

Firm policies on typographical usage and makeup variations will contribute much to the flow of work in the mechanical department.

SAVING OF TIME

Newpapers today buy time as well as talent. The rate of pay to most newspaper employes is as much on the basis of time as ability. The tendency among labor leaders is to have work measured by the time spent rather than by its productive power. Employes work a specified number of hours each week, and for any hours above that figure they are paid at double rate or at time and a half. When manufacturers are buying time of this sort, they want as little of it as possible.

Time clocks used in some newspaper plants not only calculate the hours put in by employees but also make them conscious of their responsibility to make time count and to give full measure. There is some question, however, about the advisability of time clocks since they may have an undesirable psychological effect on employes. This, some publishers have learned, is true for the editorial, news, and clerical department. However, there usually is some form of checking in and checking out where a large number are employed.

Nonproductive work time (which is nevertheless essential) includes such time-consuming operations as repairing machinery, plate removal and storage, cleaning up the composing room, and losses due to machinery breakdown. Daily coffee breaks and vacation periods represent many non-productive hours for which the newspaper willingly pays the same as for productive hours.

In some plants there has been a tendency to abuse the privilege of coffee breaks by staying out longer than the time agreed upon between employer and employes. To avoid this, a number of newspapers serve coffee in the plant.

Vacation policies are established mainly on the length of time a person has been on the company payroll. On some newspapers the employe works for the company for a year before a paid vacation is earned. In addition to the prescribed vacations, six holidays are generally granted during the year: New Year's Day, Memorial Day, Fourth of July, Labor Day, Thanksgiving, and Christmas. Many newspapers make a practice of giving an additional holiday on the employe's birthday. With smaller newspapers, vacations and holidays may be on a less formal schedule.

Editorial-news department

Speed in making assignments, preparing copy, and editing is important in the newsroom. To accelerate work there:

1. Help the reporter off to a quick start by clearly outlining the assignment and explaining its importance.
2. Have sufficient telephones in the newsroom to avoid any bottleneck in phone calls.
3. Organize routine telephone calling, such as that for the society page.
4. Have plenty of copy paper on hand, conveniently placed.
5. Have enough typewriters or editing terminals so that reporters need not wait to write their stories.
6. Keep average sentence length reasonably short.
7. Hold copyreading marks to a minimum.
8. See that reporters as well as copy processors understand copy editing standards and proofreading symbols.
9. Devise simple deadline schedules.
10. Provide chutes, elevators, pneumatic tubes, or other types of carrier systems to convey copy quickly to the composing room.

For covering special events and correcting situations within the editorial-news office, special timesaving arrangements sometimes are necessary.

To achieve quick coverage of the home football games of the University of Miami, the Miami, Fla., *Herald* has a wire machine installed in the press box, and the operator punches out the story on a direct wire to a phototypesetting machine in the composing room. Thus the type is set direct.

Visitors to the editorial-news office to report happenings, to discuss editorial policies, or to complain about how certain items were handled often consume much of the editor's time. To cut down this wasted time, the Winston-Salem, N.C., *Journal* and *Sentinel* carried in its columns a series of "Talks with Readers." One carried an informal photograph of the publisher sitting on his desk, glasses in hand, explaining that newspaper publishers have the tremendously difficult job of managing an operation that is both a business and a public service. Other pictures explained the duties and trials of the editorial director and staff; and copy indicated why certain stories appear in the paper even though the staff, if it could have its way, would prefer not to use them and explained the impossibility of "suppressing" any news story. Discussing one-newspaper towns, the publisher said: "The *Journal* and *Sentinel* are only of moderate size, yet last year it cost something like three million dollars to publish these papers. Publishing costs explain why nine out of ten towns are served by only one publisher."

Business office

In a fast-moving newspaper organization, it is imperative that accounting methods keep pace with other operations. Modern accounting equipment saves many expensive hours of manual labor.

As part of a general modernization program in the accounting department, the Cleveland, Ohio, *Press* installed a Remington Rand accounting machine, which handled the accounts payable record work in less than half the time required under the newspaper's previous system. Under the old system, with six different persons doing portions of the work, the daily time ran to an average of seven and one-half hours. Using the new accounting machine, a single operator handled the same work in an average of slightly less than three hours a day.

Leslie Moeller, former director of the School of Journalism of the University of Iowa, cites other ways to save time and reduce costs in the newspaper business office:

Writing letters costs money and a printed memorandum sheet may take the place of a letter. It is less expensive to print and easier and quicker to type, and you do not have any extended addressing or salutation. The fact that the space is smaller helps to cut down on the long-windedness which often seems to go automatically with the full-size letterhead.

Another step in cost cutting is to shift to a printed postcard. You can carry your letterhead on the reverse side, and if you wish you can make a satisfactory carbon from such a postcard. If you use ten of these cards a day in place of standard letters, your overall saving will be at least $150 a year if you take into account postage, printing, cost of stock, secretarial time and all of the other factors.

Modern dictating equipment will save you much time and money. Many publishers who type their own letters can save real money with this equipment. If your plant is small and you do not use a full-time secretary, you will find it easy to hire a stenographer who would like to work a few hours a day. The equipment is not complicated; you will be able to use it in a few minutes, and any competent typist can learn to transcribe in a little while.

Advertising department

Saving time in the advertising department is a matter of carefully planning copywriting and sales work, giving special consideration to the wants and needs of readers and prospective advertisers and providing proper training for personnel. Some tested timesavers are:

1. Printed layout sheets, for preparing any size ad up to a full page, save many minutes that otherwise would be spent measuring space and ruling borders.
2. Flat-topped filing cabinets permit advertising services to be arranged in order for quick reference and to be opened immediately without going to a table or a desk.
3. A file where advertising ideas for special days each month, anniversaries, special weeks, and the like are compiled.
4. Standard forms for writing classified advertisements and for soliciting want ads by mail enable the ad taker to prepare the ad as it is received and help the mail advertiser to arrange facts systematically and estimate the cost easily.
5. Tilt-top, broad-surfaced copywriting tables raise morale of the advertising department, encourage neat layouts, and speed production.
6. A timetable should be provided for sales personnel to make regular calls on prospects without duplication of effort. Each salesperson should be given a specific list of prospects or a definite territory to over.
7. A sticker on proof to be delivered to the advertiser indicates when proof was delivered and the time proof must be returned to the office to have corrections or changes made.

In many newspaper plants much time is lost in handling general advertising copy in the composing room, due to careless preparation of orders and instructions by the advertising department. To improve this situation in its plant, the Green Bay, Wis., *Press-Gazette* instituted a system whereby ad material was filed by date rather than by product. After that there were few missed insertions, repeat ads were handled almost automatically, and old printing material was eliminated.

Careless handling of layouts is expensive. The copy should be clear, readable, and understandable for the compositor. Much copy prepared by merchants and submitted to newspapers should be redesigned and retyped before it goes to the printers.

Advertising sales personnel for the Chicago, Ill., *Tribune* are trained to sell more than an advertisement — they sell a campaign. The same idea is used by telephone solicitors in the classified department. They are trained to tell a caller "I'll start your ad today for seven days," which often converts a potential one-time ad into a multiple insertion order. It takes no longer to sell a seven-time ad than it does to sell a one-time ad, or to sell a series of 13 display ads than to sell a single ad.

All advertisers are billed at the open rate by the Carroll, Iowa, *Times-Herald* and, if the account is paid by the tenth of the following month, contract advertisers receive discounts ranging from 16 percent to 28 percent depending on the space used. If a customer uses less space than previously and thus reduces the allowed discount, a call is made to suggest ways of qualifying for a larger one. Discounts are listed on the rate card, but the contract states that they are given "for a consistent and adequate advertising program." Since the discount also is based on prompt payment, it serves to keep collections in good order and to eliminate otherwise necessary work by collectors, according to James W. Wilson, publisher.

With the impending conversion to the metric system facing it, the Iowa City, Iowa, *Press-Citizen* was one of the first newspapers in the nation to begin computing all its advertising measurements and contracts in centimeters rather than in column inches. Adjusting early to the new system has already begun to produce savings in time required to educate advertisers and readers to the change. Other pioneers in the transition to metrics include the Bangor, Maine, *Daily News,* the Columbia, Mo., *Missourian,* and the Ypsilanti, Mich., *Press.*

Circulation department

Questions to consider in the circulation department are:

1. How may we lessen time consumed in stuffing when the newspaper is printed in several sections?
2. How may we speed transit of the paper from the press to delivery trucks?
3. Could we reach outlying points of our circulation area by some better delivery methods?
4. Are any of our carriers covering too wide a territory or serving too many customers to do a prompt, efficient job?
5. What can we do to induce carriers to begin and complete deliveries more promptly?

Stuffing papers by hand is a long and troublesome task. Tying bundles and getting them ready for delivery may also be time consuming. The Des Moines, Iowa, *Register* and *Tribune* has made a number of changes in its system of transporting papers from the press to the delivery trucks.

"The overhead conveyor system, once used for moving papers around our mailroom, has been removed," says J. R. Hudson, circulation manager, "and stackers have been installed on the press conveyors. Tying machines now in operation use a plastic tape fastened with a metal clip. The old Pollard Alling machine has been replaced by new Magnacraft equipment and the mail list has been transferred to the computer. We no longer use the Wallastar tying machine. The bottom wrapper on our bundles is now put on automatically with equipment built by our own machine shop people."

In a major redesigning of its mailroom, the Grand Rapids, Mich., *Press* installed high-speed feeder tables and roller conveyors to link inserters, tyers, and loading dock in a timesaving operation (Fig. 9.6).

The importance of getting papers to readers rapidly is never overlooked by an alert circulation manager. At one time, the Salina, Kans., *Journal* served 16 towns in 3 counties with daily delivery by airplane. A licensed pilot flew 180 air miles and delivered 1,000 papers per day, 5 days a week. Another pilot flew 275 air miles to deliver 2,000 papers per day. The papers were wrapped in round bundles and each was dropped from 20 to 50 feet into a field at the edge of the town where papers were to be delivered. The carrier was on hand to pick up the bundle and to begin the route. When weather did not permit use of plane, the papers were delivered by car; but bad weather prevented airplane delivery only a few

Fig. 9.6. The Cutler Hammer Mark II, seen on the far left in this picture, automatically counts and stacks copies of the Grand Rapids, Mich., *Press* and sends them on their way to the tying machines. (Courtesy of Booth Newspapers, Inc.).

days in the year. For four weeks one winter, skis were used on the plane for safe landings at Salina on return trips. Only one forced landing was made in two years, and that was caused by the collapse of an oil strainer. Circulation in the area doubled in the two years of airplane delivery.

Circulation distribution is a continuing problem for all newspapers. They can improve distribution by applying these timesaving methods:

1. By going to press at regular times. Late runs upset the entire delivery system.
2. By providing mailers with good equipment and teaching them how to use it. A mailing machine that operates poorly in stamping addresses on newspapers or wrappers can easily cause late mailings. The same is true regarding a mailer who does not understand the machine operation.
3. By trucking papers to carriers who deliver in outlying districts, thereby enabling them to start promptly.
4. By using motorcycles for delivery in suburban and rural areas, where homes are far apart and routes are long.
5. By rewarding carriers who complete their delivery routes within reasonable time and with no complaints.

Mechanical department

The composing room is one of the most expensive departments of the newspaper organization, and there is consequently a tremendous loss involved in any careless management or waste of time. If materials are scattered, it is hard to concentrate employe operations. Loss also occurs when employes do not have enough material when needed or when they must wait to use a piece of equipment.

To reduce production bottlenecks, the Cleveland, Ohio, *Press* installed a Haploid FotoFlo photocopying camera in its composing room. This equipment produced an advertiser's layout full-page size in seven or eight minutes per photocopy so that everybody concerned could start work simultaneously. In addition, time was saved in the engraving department by furnishing photocopy type proofs in reverse, such as black on white and type with screened backgrounds, for the general run of advertisements.

With an Itek Positive Printmaker, the Lexington, Mass., *Minuteman*, a weekly newspaper with a circulation of 9,500, reports a saving in time of 48 hours per week in production, plus many hours formerly required for editorial layout work. The Itek 1117, made by the Itek Graphic Products Company, requires one minute to make positive prints from original photographs and eliminates tedious "stripping" (placing negatives of each picture into the full-page negative by hand). An additional benefit is that errors are almost totally eliminated (photos were often stripped in upside-down under the old method).

Time reduction in the mailroom was achieved by the San Antonio, Tex., *Express* and *News* when it installed a new Sheridan on-line inserter.

Where inserting used to lag hours behind the completion of the pressrun, the new system keeps up with the press units and the job is finished within four minutes after all newspapers are printed. A twin-delivery arrangement permits a top speed of 36,000 fully inserted copies per hour.

At the New York, N.Y., *Wall Street Journal* satellite plant in Orlando, Fla., fantastic strides have been made in remote-control economy of operation. The six-unit Goss Metro offset press is run by a computer console that provides instant response in the supply of ink, water, or registration adjustments. The management has reported what may be record times for edition start-ups and also believes that losses from newsprint waste have been reduced to the lowest experienced by any newspaper.

The highly-automated Gannett newspapers have found that productivity per person has improved by 9 percent since converting to modern electronic production in the mechanical department. Also the Speidel newspapers have noted that fewer people are turning out greater results with improved equipment so that the average of hours worked has declined 3 percent despite an increase in number of pages and volume of advertising produced.

The Raleigh, N.C., *News and Observer* and *Times* has trimmed its composing room force from 101 to 57 since conversion from letterpress to offset, with electronic data processing equipment added.

Another remarkable achievement in timesaving is that of the Minneapolis, Minn., *Star* and *Tribune*. According to Paul Brainerd, assistant to the operations director, the newspaper is showing up to 30 percent in overall timesaving; 85 percent in markup; 50 percent in pasteup; and lesser reductions in proofreading, keyboarding, making corrections, and the like.

Detailed as some of these time-whittling steps may seem to be, they all add up to increased efficiency and higher profits.

CAPACITY STANDARDS

Another basic factor of production is department-by-department capacity. The desire to increase production always exists, and it is the responsibility of management to be well enough acquainted with each department to anticipate and implement changes wherever practicable and advisable.

Adequate lighting, ventilation, and safety conditions must prevail in all departments before production can reach a satisfactory peak. The reporter becomes drowsy and sluggish if forced to prepare copy under a dim light. Advertising personnel who have difficulty pulling mats from cabinets in shadowy corners lose time that should be spent in copy preparation and selling. Compositors need the benefit of good lighting. Accidents in the pressroom are less likely when there is proper illumination.

Newspaper publishing in many instances is an around-the-clock operation. Consequently, the lighting system must be adequate and independent of natural light. Even during daylight hours natural light is effective only within a few feet of the windows and varies greatly depending on the weather. Illumination must be adequate not only in quantity (foot-candles) but also in quality. The correct combination provides high visibility of detail and overall seeing comfort.

According to William H. Kahler, lighting engineer for the Westinghouse Electric Corporation, Cleveland, Ohio, the composing room should have general illumination of 20 to 30 foot-candles provided by low brightness luminaires such as semiindirect fluorescent equipment, and each machine should be equipped with a supplementary luminaire to furnish at least 50 foot-candles on the copy.

Lighting plays an important role in the pressroom where operators must maintain precise control of modern high-speed machinery. Fluorescent luminaires of the enclosed, vapor-tight type are recommended. Each luminaire contains two 40-watt fluorescent lamps and consists of a steel housing, inner white-enameled reflector, and a hinged dust-tight cover. Illumination along the sides of the press is about 40 foot-candles. The light inside the presses is considerably less, but here again quality is more important than quantity. The direction and diffusion of light from the continuous rows of fluorescent luminaires provides excellent visibility on the press cylinders and permits quick plate changes.

Every newspaper plant presents an individual lighting problem. A combination of careful planning, reliable lighting equipment, and regular maintenance will contribute to high production standards, efficient plant operation, and better morale among the workers.

The physical comfort of employes has a strong bearing on their capacity to produce. Maintaining an even temperature within the newspaper plant the year around eliminates many problems that otherwise would arise. Air-conditioning is expensive, but it contributes greatly to the speed and composure of those responsible for producing a newspaper efficiently and promptly. Temperature has its effect on machinery as well as personnel. An even temperature and humidity should be kept in the pressroom for the proper operation of the presses—static electricity develops easily under adverse conditions of heat and moisture. Some provision must be made for removing surplus heat or fumes that might be produced by a piece of equipment. Efficient ventilation is the obvious answer for all departments where stuffy or odor-laden conditions of air prevail.

Publishers, as well as other manufacturers, are bound by their own responsibility and to a certain extent by law to provide safe working conditions for employes. But machinery around a printing plant presents hazards even under the most extensive protective provisions.

Lack of uniform safety measures for printing plants is the cause of many accidents. A worker transferring from one plant to another usually finds different machinery and different safeguards. A great variety of signaling methods is used in printing plants throughout the country to indicate starting of a machine—bells, horns, whistles, flashing lights.

Another cause of severe and sometimes fatal accidents is the location of the power control button, which is in almost as many different positions as there are machines. This makes it extremely difficult for workers to shut off the power in an emergency if they are not familiar with the machine or if they are on one side and the button is on the other. However, several devices have been created to shut off power automatically when anything happens to prevent smooth operation, and these should be considered in developing plant safety.

Preliminary steps have been taken by the American Standards Association to develop a safety code for signaling devices and controls for graphic arts equipment. In addition, strict regulations codified and enforced by federal and state governments under the general supervision of the Occupational Safety and Health Administration (OSHA) keep the publisher informed of detailed requirements for the elimination of plant hazards.

Fire hazards develop easily in a newspaper plant if the situation is not watched carefully. An analysis made by the National Fire Protection Association of 1,053 fires in the printing industry reveals these general causes: common hazards, 52 percent; special hazards, 27 percent; unknown causes, 21 percent. These special hazards are further broken down into the following types: paper ignited by gas dryer or static neutralizer flame, 35 percent; type-metal melting, 17 percent; ignition of paper shreds by friction sparks from processing units, 21 percent; ignition of gasoline, naphtha, alcohol, and kerosene used in cleaning, 11 percent; ignition of benzol and other ink thinners, 9 percent; overheating of the glue pot, 2.5 percent; ignition of collodion deposits, 2.2 percent; ignition of varnish vapors, 2.5 percent; overheating of wax, 1.8 percent; miscellaneous, 4 percent.

Editorial-news department

In the news department it is difficult to say how much copy a good reporter should produce in a day. That depends to a great extent upon the type of beat to be covered or the kind of copy requested. Some reporters will turn in enough in a day to fill five columns. On some of the large city newspapers the management will be satisfied if its best reporter will turn in one good news story each day or fill one good assignment. The requirement standards on some newspapers are higher than on others, depending on how exacting the editorial-news department is regarding the style and accuracy of copy.

The reporter, as well as the executive, can easily estimate the cost per story or per column of the copy submitted. Employers sometimes remark that a beginner "writes the perfect story, but has yet to learn the tempo of the newspaper. The stories cost too much."

News department production standards may be raised by an alert editor who keeps in close touch with readers and knows how to explain their attitudes to staff members.

The publisher of the Washington, Iowa, *Journal,* in a unique survey questionnaire, asked readers: "If you were the *Journal* editor, how would you change the paper?" The questionnaire was a full newspaper-page size. The questions touched every department, feature, advertising idea, comic, panel, occasional column, regular column, editorial, and so forth that appeared in the *Journal.* Readers were asked to check readership as "always," "occasionally," "seldom," or "never" and to comment on whether the feature or department was liked "very much," "just so-so," or "not at all." The reverse side of the page had space for additional comments and the name and address of the newspaper, with postage prepaid so that the form could be folded and returned. By this means the publisher used reader reaction to point out to staff members the standard of interest created by their work in the news and advertising departments.

The state editor and the public relations director of the South Bend, Ind., *Tribune* made personal visits to public officials of small communities in the circulation area. In each community they called upon the mayor or president of the city council and the superintendent of schools, asking their cooperation in obtaining news of events in their communities. Reception of the idea was excellent. Officials were gratified by this evidence of the *Tribune*'s interest and became good community reporters.

The interest of staff members in better reporting may be stimulated also by:

1. Providing regular and conscientious criticism of stories and methods.
2. Posting samples of excellent reporting and feature writing from other papers.
3. Holding staff meetings to discuss methods that should be used in following important leads and covering outstanding events.
4. Offering rewards to staff members for good story tips.

Business office

Valuable suggestions for improving methods in the business office may be obtained from employes. A suggestion box prominently placed and labeled with an appeal for entries and an announcement of rewards for the best suggestions will stimulate employes to evaluate their own performance and cooperate in improvements.

Bert Stolpe, while director of promotion and public relations for the Des Moines *Register* and *Tribune,* concluded, on the basis of a survey, that American and Canadian newspapers are not getting maximum value from the tens of thousands of minds assembled in their plants. "In the great mass employe mind lies the future of newspaper industry," he contends, "for things don't just happen—somebody makes them happen. In this tight era of mounting costs, revenue-producing and cost-cutting ideas are of paramount importance. Other industries are making hay with suggestion programs. Why not newspapers?"

Other helps toward maintaining a high degree of efficiency in the business office are:

1. Give employes the best equipment the business can afford. A machine that can increase the productive capacity of an employe builds enthusiasm and morale.
2. Recognize accuracy as well as speed. In the accounting department it is better to have statements issued correctly a day late than to have them rushed into the mails without a careful final checking.
3. Pay more for efficiency and less for overtime. In other words, employ efficient help to do a full day's work well rather than low-pay help that will carry you into many hours of overtime.
4. Urge your bookkeepers and clerks to complete the work laid out for the day and carry none over for the next day. Each day then has a fresh beginning.
5. Create a congenial but businesslike atmosphere in the office.

Advertising department

In normal good times the advertising department is expected to produce to the limit. There may be a time, however, when it is necessary to curtail production because of newsprint shortages or mechanical restrictions within the plant. Ordinarily it is more difficult for an advertising manager to curtail production than it is to increase it. No advertising manager likes to draw the disfavor of an advertiser by announcing that only so much space is available and no more. The merchant is bound to feel that the newspaper is favoring another advertiser, probably a competitor.

Many types of accounts are handled in the advertising department. There are users of much space; those who run small but consistent day-by-day ads; and those who use an extremely small amount of copy, probably an inch a week in a business directory, under a special heading, or on the classified page. The salesperson who handles copy for the large-space user naturally produces more revenue than the one who works on very small ads, but at the same time both are important to the newspaper. Small advertisers, if properly handled, may someday be the newspaper's greatest buyers of advertising space.

Incentive plans will raise the capacity standards of any advertising department. To keep its sales force constantly trying to increase the volume of advertising linage over the preceding year, the Mexico, Mo., *Ledger* paid each person, every month, 10 percent of the cash business increase over the same month of the preceding year.

The Wooster, Ohio, *Record* increased its sales of classified display advertising to auctioneers and farmers through suggested copy mailed to the "colonels" of that area. "Public sale season will soon be here; have you contacted an auctioneer?" read one of the suggested ads. "If you are planning a spring sale, book it now for a choice of date." Another provided space for the auctioneer's picture under the heading, "More Dollars, No Worries! Auction Sales Are My Business." This not only brought advertising from the auctioneers but it also recalled the *Record* to farmers when it came time for them to advertise their auction sales.

Production standards in the advertising department may be raised by:

1. Establishing goals to be reached within a limited time.
2. Planning special advertising campaigns for single firms on a communitywide basis.
3. Encouraging repeat selling.
4. Requiring sales personnel to submit reports showing the number of firms served, the number of calls made, and the volume of advertising obtained.
5. Checking other newspapers for ideas.
6. Helping sales personnel to become better acquainted with their community and the possibilities for developing new accounts.
7. Stepping up newspaper promotion.

Circulation department

The circulation department has different classes of clientele to deal with, which require varied approaches in presenting the newspaper's merits. More time per prospect is necessary for selling subscriptions in rural areas than for those in densely populated urban sections. Soliciting is more successful in the fall than in the spring. People do more reading in the winter, when they are indoors, than in the summer, when they are busy with outdoor work and pleasure. The amount of promotion behind a salesperson also helps to determine the number of subscribers added.

The number of new subscriptions that can be obtained on a route does not depend altogether on the personality and sales ability of the carrier. It is also determined by the time available to devote to selling and by the inducements offered by the circulation department. If obtaining a certain number of subscriptions will qualify for a college scholarship, the carrier may give greater thought to that than to the extra revenue the additional subscription will bring.

The accomplishments of the circulation department depend greatly upon the energy, far-sightedness, and ingenuity of the manager. Ed Roberts, former circulation manager of the Denver, Colo., *Post*, decided that circulation could be increased by efficient carrier service and route management as well as by direct solicitation by carriers and special salespeople. To test the theory, he evolved the following simple plan:

1. A monthly point contest within each district based on the success with which a carrier handled the route and produced orders.
2. A suitably engraved award to the carrier in the entire city who was outstanding for each quarter, presented with the pomp and ceremony appropriate to the importance of such recognition.

3. Insignia indicative of outstanding records established over several months or years.
4. Some form of scholarship to reward outstanding carriers on an annual basis.

Result: Within one year the *Post*'s 1,100 city carriers obtained 47,345 daily and 53,213 Sunday subscriptions, almost 8 units per month per carrier at a cost per unit of only 16.8 cents.

Circulation sales personnel will do twice as well in obtaining new subscribers in a given area if they are sent there as part of a well-organized campaign with special incentives and rewards for honest effort and with plenty of promotion behind them.

In developing circulation in a new area, news coverage and special solicitation go hand in hand. If a circulation salesperson has a "nose for news" and gathers items from prospects, they will be convinced of the newspaper's interest in them and in the community and will be more likely to buy subscriptions.

In a summer campaign to increase rural circulation, one newspaper sent a reporter into the country with a member of the sales staff. Before the salesperson began to talk about the merits of the newspaper, the reporter drew news from practically every family visited about the children, poultry, livestock, or crops. On some weekly newspapers, a man and his wife make up the reporter-sales combination.

Mechanical department

The superintendent of the mechanical department knows how much copy a composing machine operator should handle in a day. The way the work is laid out, the encouragement given by the supervisor, and the condition of the plant are important, too. The business manager should have a clear understanding of production possibilities and should confer with the superintendent about conditions in the mechanical department and their effect on production. The abilities of the compositors, press operators, and other employes should be discussed freely with the superintendent; and the poor performers should be worked with to improve their capacities, or they should be weeded out.

The speed with which an advertisement is set depends to a great extent upon its nature and the condition of the copy. If the copy is poorly laid out and instructions are not well outlined, if the layout calls for unusual arrangement of cuts and type, or if it contains much solid matter and few display lines, more time will be required than for a conventional arrangement of type and cuts with much white space. Any simplifications in setting ads will raise capacity standards. Accuracy as well as speed must be sought in composition because careless work means excessive corrections, and that cuts production capacity.

Proper care of presses and paper stock will step up pressroom efficiency. For example:

1. Cleaning the press regularly and oiling it at proper intervals will help to prevent costly stops.
2. Care in adjusting forms on the press increases capacity by permitting top running speed. Even more important, such care prevents accidents.
3. A sufficient supply of newsprint for the run, placed conveniently before starting, will prevent capacity-cutting interruptions.
4. Careful handling of newsprint will prevent web breaks on presses using rolls and will prevent stoppages and waste on presses using flat sheets.
5. Good-quality inks will permit capacity speeds and produce clean impressions.

EXPENSE REGULATION

The necessity for watching expenses and regulating them so that they comply with income has a definite effect on production. When expenses are rising, it is not always possible to keep income within the same range of increase. Management then is compelled to guard expenses with an austere eye and to handle operations with a firm hand.

In the light of these mounting costs, it is important that the newspaper manager analyze the amount and character of all phases of work in the newspaper office and plant. By so doing, standards can be set that will aid in determining hourly pay rates, size of staff needed for operation of a given plant unit, kind of employes wanted, and standard time required for each operation.

Editorial-news department

Expenses mount easily in the editorial-news department, where the best efforts should go into producing copy that will give readers what they want and make the newspaper a credit to its community. Publishers have been interested more in improving personnel than in increasing it. Less help of greater efficiency is better than more help of low caliber.

Reporters and others in the news department should understand the publisher's desire to produce a good newspaper as well as the problem of doing so when expenses are bouncing against the ceiling. Persons in other departments of the newspaper organization and even residents of the community, with the proper approach, may be induced to give assistance that will help to hold down production expenses.

Employes in the advertising and circulation departments should be encouraged to be alert for news tips as they go about their regular duties. Residents of the community who really have a "nose for news" often become helpful part-time reporters and are willing to serve at little expense. The agricultural committee of the National Editorial Association once suggested that newspapers that could not afford to pay the wages offered college-trained reporters could develop good farm reporters in their home communities, and such home-trained reporters could write successfully for farmers who were looking for better ways to increase their farm incomes — incomes that were to be spent at hometown retail stores.

Other ways of curtailing expenses in the news department are:

1. Challenge each member of the reporting staff to produce a feature story a week. Most reporters are busy, yet they will gladly tackle a special assignment. One summer when a member of the staff was absent most of the time, the managing editor of a small newspaper asked each of those remaining on the job to turn in an additional feature story each week. This proved to be a sort of contest to see which could produce the best feature story, with the result that plenty of local material was produced without employing extra help.
2. Have reporters carry cameras. Many newspaper publishers when hiring journalism school graduates as reporters ask for those who know how to use cameras. A combination reporter-photographer is a valuable staff member because the pictures enliven the stories and this saves the publisher the expense of employing a photographer. Almost any reporter, if supplied a camera, can be trained to use it. There is always the possibility, however, that for a time at least interest in picture taking will be so great that more photos will be taken than the newspaper can use. Photographers and photographer-reporters should learn to select their pictorial matter with care because the camera is valuable when used for pictures of unusual interest but expensive when used for routine shots.
3. Engage district reporters on a pay-per-item basis. Select a news-conscious person in each of the four or five main sections of your city and agree to pay so much for each item written that is termed newsworthy by the city editor. This brings in news at minimum cost from sources not usually touched by regular reporters.
4. Invite persons interested in community history to write articles. Facts of extraordinary community interest never before revealed may find their way into the columns of your newspaper by this means.
5. Have some member of the staff devote a certain period each day to other newspapers in search of local interest articles. Newspapers from which such articles are taken are complimented when you consider their copy worthy of your columns and they readily grant permission.

Business office

The care and attention given to cost studies, receipts, and general expenses by those in the business office help greatly to regulate expenses in other departments. A good way to control costs is to set up a budget. Also, use these economy measures for buying materials, supplies, and services:

1. Centralize the buying authority in one person.
2. Wherever practical get prices from two or more suppliers.
3. Be sure you have "minimums" for each item so that repurchases automatically come up well in advance of the "out-of-supply" date. This avoids rush shipments and permits ample time for proper cost-saving buying.

4. Watch your costs for office forms. Many can be produced on a duplicating machine at nominal cost. The copying machine (office variety)
   may cost less than $1,000.
5. Keep purchasing records showing names of suppliers furnishing services
   or supplies, date and cost of the last order, and annual requirements.

The business office must watch expenses and effect economies in other
departments as well as in its own. It knows that contemplated expenditures
must be consistent with the newspaper's financial ability. Administrative
department conferences may result in a change in the newspaper's page
width and column sizes, in elimination of the optical scanner step in computerized composition, or in the sale of company-owned trucks to be
replaced by rented delivery cars.

Advertising department

Not many advertising departments give serious consideration to production costs; their main goal is volume, and often it is *volume at any cost*.
Expense regulation, however, should be applied in this department as in
all others. Consideration might well be given to the cost of producing every
ad, from the two-line local to full-page display.

Some small advertising accounts require so much time and attention
that they cost more than they bring in. Some of that cost is unnecessary.
Salespeople who have been handling accounts on a personal basis may do
just as well by telephone.

The classified advertising department's success at selling by telephone
should represent a challenge to those who sell display advertising. The
manager of a small daily newspaper selected one of the best phone
saleswomen in the classified advertising department to use the telephone a
few weeks before Christmas to see how many small display Christmas
greetings ads she could sell. She made a list of prospects, then clipped from
the ad service all the Christmas greetings material she could find. She laid
out hundreds of small ads, mostly 2 columns by 3 inches, using her own
judgment as to what each prospect might be willing to buy. With the copy
before her she called each prospect, read the copy planned, gave the cost,
and in nine cases out of ten landed the order. She was paid a commission of
10 percent above her regular salary. For two weeks she more than doubled
her income and at the same time sold more display advertising at less cost
than many of the regular sales staff.

Other means of reducing expenses in the advertising department are:

1. Eliminate some of the free service given to general advertisers in promoting advertised products. This is a service feature of the advertising
   department that, in connection with most accounts, may be abridged
   or expanded without seriously affecting results.
2. Insist on customers having their copy ready when the advertising
   representative calls. Many valuable moments, for which the publisher

pays well, are lost when the representative is required to cool his heels while the merchant makes up his mind about copy to be used.

3. Insofar as possible have merchants prepare their own advertising copy. Many newspaper advertising departments have increased department expenses and spoiled advertisers by preparing all copy for them.

4. Urge advertising copywriters to avoid use of fancy composition that requires extra time in setting.

5. Set monthly linage goals for advertising sales staff and pay bonuses to those who exceed. This speeds up selling and increases volume.

Circulation department

Newspaper delivery operations sometimes may be combined to provide more satisfactory service and at the same time reduce delivery costs. The Janesville, Wis., *Gazette* delivers papers to farmer subscribers from trucks that take papers to carriers in country towns. It delivers 2,000 papers to rural residents, while covering 900 miles a day at a cost of 15 cents a mile. Considering the fact that so many farmers receive delivery from a truck used to convey bundles to dealers and distant carriers, a fair portion of the cost is chargeable to delivering to farmers.

At one time the Independence, Mo., *Examiner* had an arrangement with carriers of the Kansas City, Mo., *Star* whereby they delivered the *Examiner* while delivering the *Star*. This was done at far less expense for the *Examiner* than if the paper maintained its own trucks, and it provided additional revenue for *Star* carriers.

The efficiency of a circulation department may be increased and expenses may be reduced also:

1. By inducing rural correspondents to sell subscriptions. Many weekly and small daily papers pay a commission to correspondents for subscription collections in their area. One newspaper puts on an annual subscription contest with its correspondents, offering prizes or bonuses to those obtaining the greatest number of subscriptions. This is in addition to the regular commission paid on subscription collections. Newspapers have found this to be an effective and economical way of building circulation at a reasonable cost.

2. By employing a man and wife as a manager team for the circulation department. With the man as manager and his wife as assistant manager, a unified salary more than takes care of family expenses. Furthermore, the manager is free for house-to-house solicitation, knowing that his wife will take care of details in the office. This arrangement worked out well for the Columbia, Mo., *Missourian,* where Mr. and Mrs. Jack Carr were in charge of the circulation department, and at the Willows, Calif., *Daily Journal,* where Mr. and Mrs. Oscar F. DeSoto directed circulation.

3. By using a simplified form of bookkeeping for the circulation department. The more details to be watched the more opportunities

there are for errors. (See the section on "Circulation Department Accounting" in Chapter 18.)

4. By watching all accounts and seeing that payments are made promptly. Overdue accounts are hard to collect and often are never collected.
5. By closely watching the pressrun each day and the number of papers sold and delivered. Newsprint is costly and much may be wasted by overruns.

Mechanical department

The mechanical department superintendent often has opportunities to reduce expenses by more careful distribution of work and by observing the way employes perform at the machines, at the makeup tables, or in the pressroom. Attention to minor details sometimes results in savings.

The production manager of the Gannett newspapers says that considerable extra cost in a great many pressrooms is due to the fact that papers change in size so rapidly. The trouble begins in the advertising department. Too often the people there do not seem to realize that by adding two pages they increase the number of employes needed in the pressroom by two or three, who a great many times are working at overtime rates. Sometimes it even increases the number in the mailroom.

For many years the Ottawa, Ont., *Citizen* relied on outside help for all its electrical work, care of machinery, and minor repairs; and costs ran high. Finally when a new building was erected and a new press installed, a full-time position was given to the electrician who installed wiring for the new building. Since the electrician also had some knowledge of welding and machine-shop practice, the publishing company set up a modest machine shop with a drill press, arc welding set, grinder, and other small power tools. The savings on minor repair jobs more than covered the expenses of this full-time operation.

Overhead expenses in the mechanical departments of newspapers may be cut down in other ways:

1. By having a superintendent who knows enough about the machinery to make minor repairs.
2. By making negatives or plates for other newspapers and business firms. The rental cost of an offset camera or a platemaker is sometimes divided between several newspapers receiving material from the same machine.
3. By hiring a helper in the composing room to do the office janitor work, thereby combining two jobs in one.
4. By having compositors double as press operators. This is a satisfactory arrangement in the plants of small dailies but could not be worked out in large unionized shops.
5. By arranging working hours in 35-hour or 40-hour shifts to avoid overtime hours.

Many other factors—postage; width of newsprint roll; cost and availability of paper, ink, film, and other materials; general economic conditions; unpredictable personnel problems—will have a bearing on production. Among the constant factors today, it may be said that the degree of modernization of technology will probably have a more direct effect on flow of work, saving of valuable time, capacity potentials, and regulation of expenses than any other single influence over which management may have control.

10

300 ways to cut costs and boost revenue

We seem to have reached the limit of savings through technology.

Helen K. Copley

The problem of eliminating unnecessary newspaper operating costs is by no means a new one, but it is undoubtedly receiving more attention from management now — after two decades of steadily rising inflation — than at any time in publishing history. Most newspaper conventions include one or more special sessions devoted to costs, and some of the best business minds in the country are continuously studying this persistent problem. There is no one answer to the question of how to cut newspaper costs, but literally hundreds. This chapter is devoted to 300 specific suggestions made by newspaper people who live with the problem from day to day.[1]

ACCOUNTING

1. Adopt an annual budget that provides a coordinated plan for anticipated expenses and revenues. A well-prepared budget will indicate whether it is necessary to increase advertising or circulation rates or whether it is necessary to reduce costs.
2. Put each department on a budget, and if the department is operated on less than provided distribute 10 percent of the savings among employes.
3. Social security taxes need not be withheld on amounts paid to independent contractors for their services.
4. Check controllable expenses for possible ways to cut costs. These include stationery and printing, traveling, office supplies, postage, long-distance telephone calls, telegrams, and that catchall "miscellaneous."
5. Carefully scrutinize all entertainment expense to discourage lavishness.
6. Determine the actual cost of producing a column inch and a line of advertising.

---

1. These items are selected from tips collected over a 25-year period.

7. Maintain a comparative study, week to week, of revenue receipts and actual operating disbursements compared with those of the same week one year ago.

8. "We converted an obsolete cash payroll system to a modern machine method of making checks and records in one operation. Many hours of labor were saved. Next, we plan to use the same machine for accounts payable, eliminating book entries and compiling with one operation records that heretofore have taken three. We anticipate saving half the time now consumed in this operation."

9. Take the maximum machinery and equipment depreciation allowed by the Internal Revenue Service.

10. "We reviewed all our printed forms used in connection with the business and were able to establish considerable savings by standardizing various forms, particularly for advertising billing. Some forms were eliminated completely."

11. "We are planning a system for handling purchases and receipts of shipments, bills, and invoices that come into the building. The system itself centers around a new purchase order form that designates in code the department to receive the billing and the stockroom in which shipments or packages are to be placed. This system, we believe, will save time and effort on the part of department heads and department personnel and add to the general efficiency of the entire plant."

12. Wherever possible obtain three bids on all purchases.

13. Keep a close check on inventories to avoid being oversupplied or making rush retail purchases.

14. Use a window envelope in billing procedures.

15. "We require detailed reports on all overtime—slips must be filled out in each case. This has a tendency to discourage overtime."

16. "We made an arrangement with our bank whereby it would accept payment for our transient advertising accounts. In a few instances city circulation accounts also are paid through the bank. The newspaper, not the customer, pays for this service (5 cents per bill, based on a minimum charge for bills under $15 and a maximum charge for bills of $15 and over)."

ADVERTISING—CLASSIFIED

17. Use small type for classified ads.

18. Offer type headlines for want ad display advertisements at high rates. Have a schedule of such type available when the customer places his order.

19. Print the rate schedule with your telephone number in every issue.

20. As a promotion to help sell space, reprint the "Business and Professional Directory" on suitable desk-sized blotter stock along with newspaper want ad promotion. Distribute these where they will help your newspaper.

21. Postcards are used by some newspapers for acknowledging and/or billing classified ads. (The Post Office Department forbids use of cards reflecting on the conduct of the addressee, such as a threat to sue or to collect delinquent accounts.)

22. Have a bookkeeping charge for a transient want ad not paid for in advance. Variation: Lower cash rate if ad is paid for by Saturday noon (weekly) or in seven days (daily); thereafter a higher credit rate.

23. Since reader interest on the want ad page is at least 50 percent higher than on any other, charge extra for classified display as compared to regular retail display advertisement.

24. Offer the lowest classified rate (daily) for three-line daily insertion throughout the year—a volume equal to one half-page of classified ads. Variation: The newspaper offers 10 percent discount to daily want ad users at the end of the contract year.

25. Charge extra for box numbers when run in classified ads.

26. Set classified ads on 10-pica columns or less, running nine or even ten columns to the page.

27. A large city newspaper pays weekly newspapers 15 percent commission on want ad orders received for them. The average order is eight lines, and the average number of insertions is three.

28. Reduce want ad collection losses through a good credit system. Require cash with orders on three classifications: situation wanted, wanted to rent, and household articles for sale. One newspaper uses three card notices and two final collection letters.

29. Install a monitor system in the classified ad telephone room to check on sales technique used by advertising solicitors.

30. Maintain the same word rate for classified ads, but increase the minimum number of words per ad. Additional details in an ad tend to increase results for the advertiser; a higher minimum tends to increase newspaper revenue.

31. Use a postcard to notify the want ad user of the cost and the payment deadline.

32. Carefully edit all classified copy before transmitting it to the composing room.

33. Cut the rule between classified ads from 4 point to 2 point.

34. Sell birth and death notices in classified columns.

ADVERTISING—LEGAL

35. Pay more attention to legal advertising and official notices. Furnish attorneys with necessary blanks.

36. Eliminate losses in legal advertising by requiring advance payment from attorneys through probate court requirement for deposit pending settlement of estates.

37. Issue no proof of publication on any legals until cash is received for full payment of publication.

ADVERTISING—GENERAL

38. Analyze reasons for errors in order to reduce "make goods" of general advertisements.
39. Ask advertising agencies for a five-day leeway on the insertion date so advertising may be run the first part of the week.
40. Urge every retail merchant in your area to ask the salesperson from whom he buys merchandise to encourage placement of more general advertising in your newspaper.
41. Make a reasonable charge for merchandising service in connection with general advertising accounts.

ADVERTISING—RETAIL

42. Sell schedules, not ads.
43. Make one weekly call on frequency contract advertisers — on the same day of the week and at the same time of day. Telephone the advertiser in advance so that he or she is ready for the solicitor, thus providing time for additional sales calls.
44. Have a week-ahead deadline for special editions. "We start picking up advertising copy as much as three weeks ahead and much of it is in the composing room two weeks before the day of publication."
45. After copy is picked up, eliminate going back to the advertiser to show completed layout except when there are questions of size, copy, and so forth.
46. Expand the mat morgue by keeping all reusable mats from monthly service. These can be put in file folders and classified so that they may be found quickly. This gives greater selection and a complete file of all wanted illustrations. Clip extra proofs with the mats to use on future layouts.
47. Allow no changes in copy after a 24-hour deadline (if such is required for copy) and no changes on proofs except strictly marked changes or very unusual circumstances such as sold-out merchandise.
48. Allow a 10 percent discount or bonus to the advertiser who brings copy to the office 48 hours preceding the specified deadline for publication on the date desired. This has been used where mechanical department overtime is a problem.
49. Demand a premium rate for an advertising run in editions given extra coverage. This rate is based on additional distribution and production cost.
50. Conduct a readership study of advertisements and news content to determine actual cost per reader of sales messages and relative popularity of news and feature content. The latter offers a guide to possible elimination of least-read content.
51. Have advertising material correctly prepared when submitted for publication.
52. Reduce or eliminate trick layouts for advertisements.

53. Furnish an absolute minimum number of proofs and charge for every proof over that amount.

54. Set an earlier deadline for large-space advertisements such as half- to full-page ads.

55. Maintain a card file of all retail advertisers, listing dates of their anniversaries and other pertinent information. The anniversary date may be exploited to promote additional linage.

56. Provide proofs only to merchants who ask for them.

57. Use copies returned from newsstands for checking copies to be given advertisers.

58. If you furnish mats of complete ads, make a charge for service comparable to that made by any composition plant.

59. For advance copy, increase your rate twice as much as you think you should, then allow a discount.

60. Set a deadline for display advertising copy at a point where cost of overtime composition may be minimized.

61. Conduct "refresher schools" on principles of retailing and merchandising for advertising sales staff.

62. Take out rain insurance to pay for additional cost of advertising for Dollar Day if more than 0.1 of an inch falls in a three-hour period starting at 7 A.M.

63. "We plan to eliminate all possible tear sheets and checking copies to advertisers, as well as many complimentary copies."

64. Have a roll of white wrapping paper for layouts that do not have to be shown advertisers. This saves expensive layout sheets.

65. "We are setting up a complete layout and copy department in our advertising department to assist the compositors in following a layout more easily and to cut down on corrections. All copy not in a proof-sheet form will pass through the layout department, where a comprehensive layout will be made and all copy will be typed on a standard copy form. Special layout sheets will be used with a faint underprinting ruled off horizontally and vertically in pica widths to enable the compositor to take his measurements right from the layout. The layout artist will indicate typeface and size where a special type is to be used to cut down on composition time, undue corrections due to wrong type size, and illegible copy."

66. A repeat insertion of an advertisement following first publication offers a limited opportunity for savings in production costs.

67. Produce cleaner copy with better layouts. Considerable expense is incurred when the compositor must stop frequently to decipher dirty copy or query the supervisor for instructions on typefaces and type sizes.

68. Adopt the rule that the person who places an ad containing cooperative allowances from distributors and is responsible for the contract is the only one to receive the bill and tear sheets. This eliminates mailing additional tear sheets requested by the dealer.

69. Check on manufacturer cooperative advertising allowances extended to local dealers; make sure available credits are used fully for newspaper advertising.
70. Keep advance copy up to a week ahead in the composing room and see that advance ads are set on light days. Do not keep such completed copy in the advertising department—finish the copy and layout and get it to the composing room.
71. If page-one reader-type ads are permitted, set the rate at double or triple that for similar advertising on inside pages; also charge extra for bold type.
72. Charge full commercial rates, less composition costs, for reprints of ads.
73. Have the advertiser call for tear sheets at the newspaper office—one tear sheet of any cooperative advertisement could be sent along with the bill.
74. Get cash in advance on all noncontract ads unless approved by the credit department.
75. Charge full composition cost where an advertisement is not run after being submitted.
76. Standardize newspaper ad borders and reuse borders each week. With this system, only four pieces are needed for any size ad.
77. Sell extra space by using a cut of the store building at intervals.
78. Develop a list of late-copy advertisers to make sure that advertisers and advertising agencies respect deadlines.
79. Check the number of accounts each advertising solicitor handles.
80. Hold schools for the ad sales staff; get back to fundamentals of advertising sales.
81. Check the use of advertising mat services. Are they being utilized fully? Can any service be dropped without loss of linage?
82. When advertising requires more pages in an issue, increase the percentage of advertising to a greater degree than news.
83. See that mats are properly marked for mortices before they go to the composing room.
84. Mark the advertiser's name and date on all mats for quick and accurate filing after use.
85. Cooperate with other newspapers in your press association to standardize advertising dimension standards; the fewer formats offered, the greater control exercised over advertising profits.
86. Install an advertising department dispatch room where advertising copy, mats, and proofs are handled by service employes rather than by advertising sales staff.
87. Have a schedule of charges for advertising copy revision.

CIRCULATION

88. Do not neglect circulation promotion. The yearly net income from

circulation often is the money the publisher takes out as net profit from the business.

89. Ascertain the milline cost of reaching the newspaper reader in the current years as compared with that of ten and five years before. The director of the Bureau of Advertising, ANPA, says: "Advertisers are studying circulation trends of both newspapers and magazines with more microscopic detail than ever."

90. Analyze inefficient circulation practices that result in heavy returns from some newsstands while others are short of copies.

91. Carrier prizes are more effective in circulation results than premiums to new subscribers.

92. Newspaper puzzle contests should be used only occasionally, if at all.

93. For circulation promotion in a rural town, concentrate heavily on news coverage, conduct five-day samplings of issues delivered to the carrier, and follow by a call from a solicitor who invites prospects to become subscribers. Each sample copy might carry a sticker, with sticker No. 1 introducing the carrier, sticker No. 2 emphasizing news coverage, sticker No. 3 emphasizing the value of advertising, sticker No. 4 emphasizing features, and sticker No. 5 asking "Has the service been satisfactory?"

94. Simplify and standardize circulation department forms.

95. Check the time it takes to count coins brought in by carriers. Mailers Equipment Company, 40 West 15th Street, New York, N.Y., 10011 manufactures an automatic machine, "Coinaudit," which sorts, counts, and wraps or bags coins.

96. Maintain weekly carrier rates and single-copy price at an even coin amount. Odd-penny charges for newspapers are unpopular and result in circulation declines.

97. Introduce a short-term collection plan for mail subscriptions.

98. Review free copies and reduce the amount if possible.

99. A mechanical push-button device, showing in seconds which carrier delivered the newspaper on any street in town, may save time and money.

100. Check constantly on the cause of complaints due to faulty delivery. Reducing complaints cuts expense of phone calls, extra deliveries, and labor.

101. Run a standing box inviting subscribers to notify the newspaper and the postmaster promptly when they change addresses. The cost of "postage due" on returned copies can be high.

102. A "special dispatch" permit may be obtained from the Post Office Department for remailing newspapers at second-class rates from outlying post offices. Copies are weighed at the home post office for charges, then trucked to the outlying post office for delivery.

103. Back issues may be mailed at second-class postage rates.

104. Check returns and files once a week to determine whether the

pressrun can be cut. Continually watch the difference between the net paid and the gross pressrun.

105. "We use taxi service to handle 'kicks' from subscribers, rather than to keep a driver and a car for that purpose. With a special rate from the cab company, this amounts to a slight saving."

106. Better planned work schedules may reduce expense accounts of traveling staff.

107. "We are installing a new system of carrier receipts, using the Uarco interfolding, continuous-sheet type of receipt in a small mechanical dispenser. We are now using a receipt book that costs us about $9.22 per thousand receipts. We use one for city carriers, one for insurance payments, and one for bond payments. We are combining these three receipts on one sheet in the new system at a cost of $9.18 per thousand for three units. The new system also will enable us to make up a book of payments received from carriers, which is arranged numerically by route numbers and will save considerable time in posting for our bookkeeping department."

108. Lay out circulation delivery routes so only right-hand turns are made by drivers—or at least a minimum of left turns. Accident statistics show that left turns are dangerous.

109. Set up cooperative cost sharing of motor route delivery service by competitive newspapers serving the same territory.

110. Check over the delivery route system to hold mileage to a minimum. Can any routes be consolidated?

111. Put twine in a box with wet sponges for three weeks. Dampness toughens twine and permits costsaving use of lighter weight twine. (Rate of usage will preclude the problem of mildew.)

112. "We do not send any mail subscriptions to outlying towns where we have carrier delivery. This permits larger routes and attracts better carriers. We will make more from this plan than we would by mail because we charge $20 a year in first and second zones, whereas we get $28.50 by carrier."

113. File a duplicate set of circulation records in a safety deposit box. Revise them periodically.

114. "We organized the circulation department so that it could be handled by the office staff and eliminated the job of circulation manager. At the same time we reduced the office staff by one."

115. Before you order repair of a circulation vehicle, find out the cost of new or rebuilt parts, which may prove to be more economical.

116. If you are running a circulation contest, be sure to verify each order before awarding prizes.

117. "We have eliminated the old system of having carriers stand in line to pay bills. Now we have a box at the front of the office and the carriers drop their money in the box. Each carrier has a money bag with the route number on it."

118. To interest prospective carriers, conduct a paper-tossing derby.
119. In addition to offering prizes to carriers and to anyone who will send in a few subscription orders, institute a "club subscription plan," offering lodges, youth groups, schools, and churches prizes for submitting groups of subscriptions.
120. If your paper circulates in a wide rural area, investigate the possibilities of economy in airplane delivery.
121. Address a complete set of expiration notices or renewal letters at the same time with address plates. When a renewal comes in, any remaining notices are discarded.
122. Sponsor a limited-time bargain period for renewal of rural mail subscriptions. Prepare a series of three direct-mail letters enclosing a renewal blank and postage-paid return envelope.
123. A $5 subscription offer of so many weeks or months will produce twice as many sales as one for $5.50. Any offer requiring mailing of coins tends to deter action.
124. "A reduced rate or premium of extra issues is best for getting the most subscriptions at the lowest cost."
125. Experience shows that circulation promotion letters mailed under third class postage get new and renewal subscriptions at less cost than those mailed first class.
126. Contrary to the opinion of many, including prospective subscribers, the long subscription letter with detailed persuasive appeal will outpull the short letter. People prefer to receive short letters, but they are less moved to action by a short appeal.
127. Letters outpull circulars in soliciting new subscriptions.
128. Offer a moderate subscription saving for a two-year payment; a larger saving for a three-year payment (weekly newspaper).

CORRESPONDENCE

129. Use note stationery and postcards for short messages, acknowledgments, and similar matter that is not confidential. Routine correspondence on postal cards will save $30 on 1,000 pieces of mail.
130. Check mail to determine whether it should be sent first class or third class.
131. Adopt a central filing department for each floor or for the building.
132. Try a stenographic pool instead of private secretaries; or it might be more economical to use a dictaphone or tape recorders in place of a stenographic pool.
133. To lengthen the life of typewriter and adding machine ribbons, mix a solution of three parts glycerine and one part water and saturate the old ribbon.
134. Use such timesaving equipment as an envelope sealer (hand-operated or electric) and a mail opener.

135. Consider leasing a copying machine to increase filing efficiency and to eliminate cost and time involved in making carbon copies of correspondence.

DIRECT MAIL
136. Meter mail, other than first class, will outpull mail using stamps..
137. If you have a postage meter, you may imprint postage-paid reply envelopes as a substitute for stamped reply envelopes. The meter impression, including name of post office and date when metered, must be printed directly on the reply envelope in the upper right corner. Meter impressions on labels or stickers are not permitted for this purpose.
138. Order forms should be separate from the letter and on colored stock.
139. A beautiful, printed promotion piece may pull no better than a simpler and less expensive one.
140. An inexpensive way to keep a prospect list up-to-date is to imprint a return postage guarantee on unclaimed mail matter.
141. Under U.S. postal regulations you may write or type on third-class matter the name and address of the addressee and the salutation and still send at third-class postage rates; also you may write your signature.

EDITORIAL-NEWS
142. Pay correspondents on a page basis for news published.
143. To save the cost of sending a staff reporter out of town for a news story, maintain an adequate staff of experienced base correspondents.
144. Keep the news staff working on advance copy and have it set to help fill issues on heavy days of the week.
145. Country correspondents are not employes and hence not subject to social security taxes or unemployment compensation, providing they function without news assignments or similar direct controls.
146. Invest in electronic "software" to reduce long-range costs of producing news and editorial copy. Greatest savings have been realized in this area, because 60 to 70 percent of total work hours devoted to prepress operations occurs in the preparation of news and editorial copy.
147. Reduce length of news stories by better editing. This involves better selection of news as well as better editing of copy so that salient facts are made available to readers in less reading time.
148. Run a digest of world and national news of secondary interest that does not merit major news display, as a substitute for complete wire stories, to permit more space for local news.

149. More news items with good front-page headlines will help to give the reader a sense of wider news coverage. Short stories carrying good headlines rather than long stories with fewer headlines enhance reader interest in the news columns.
150. Condense women's club notices and wedding stories.
151. Get wider appeal into women's pages by devoting more space to food, flower shows, and other basic interests and giving less detail of organization meetings.
152. Increase readability of news stories by simplifying words and sentence construction. This gets the story to the reader in less time and at less production cost.
153. Consider elimination of newspaper features that have the least reader interest as measured by readership survey.
154. Eliminate captions over news pictures.
155. Handle births and other vitae usually published in agate-sized type statistically instead of in sentences.
156. Rewrite state news into a readable column.
157. Adopt the rule of having one advance story for coming events.
158. Budget the number of editorial department columns for normal editorial-news usage. Agree on a minimum for community news coverage rather than maintaining a fixed percentage of news and advertising for each issue.
159. Require feature writers to prepare copy well in advance so that it may be sent to the composing room well ahead of the deadline and set prior to the time needed.
160. Make sure that all overset copy is ultimately published and not killed.
161. For the small daily newspaper with nearby large daily competition specialize in local news, local features, and local pictures. Good slogan: "First to the Home People with the Home News."
162. The editorial department should consider very carefully whether to send a staff reporter or photographer to cover an assignment that already is being covered by one of the news services.
163. Minimize the risk of libel-suit damage by making one person on the staff a "specialist" in newspaper libel law. Consult your local libraries for current works on libel.
164. Clean and well-edited copy is essential if pasteups are to be clean.
165. Proofreaders should not edit. They should look only for typographical errors.
166. Replace worn-out typewriter ribbons.
167. News and editorial personnel should be familiar with the style of their paper and adhere to it to save proofroom time in marking irregularities.
168. Prepare and distribute information blanks for obituaries and weddings so information can be mailed to the newspaper.
169. Reduce comics to four-column width.

170. Install a universal copydesk or an equivalent arrangement for closer contact of all persons working there.
171. Establish some agreement as to how important a news story must be to justify delay of the pressrun with possible overtime cost.
172. Review the cost of country correspondents in relation to the number of subscribers served.
173. Instead of using chit-chat items, train country correspondents to emphasize coverage of athletic events, deaths of persons known to readers, meetings of the town board or council, occasional human interest features.
174. Stagger news department staff and reduce overtime.
175. Use bolder headlines for news on pages dominated by advertising.
176. Keep an envelope file on the city desk to contain clippings from each day's issue on every future action or possible development suggested by the stories.

INSURANCE
177. "We had the state fire insurance inspector go over our building as carefully as possible, followed his recommendations, and now have a lower insurance rate. We plan to take this plan one step farther and investigate 'factory type' insurance, which we understand offers an even better rate."
178. If you are carrying coinsurance, be sure that the firm handling your appraisal is recognized by both coinsurers.
179. Make certain your insurance coverage is adequate to match present replacement costs.
180. Every newspaper should have a complete appraisal made by a recognized firm at least once in five years, and it should be revised every two years. Often a business may reduce costs by having the right type of insurance policy written at the right rate. One newspaper obtained comprehensive crime policy coverage — fidelity, forgery, robbery — at material savings.
181. Deposit a complete inventory of plant equipment in your safe. In case of fire, such an inventory would be invaluable.
182. Encourage carriers to protect themselves against death or disability loss through accident insurance available at modest cost.
183. The ANPA-ICMA Safe Driving Campaign seeks a reduction in insurance classification rates and earned credits on current insurance premiums. Newspaper trucks and cars have been classed by the National Bureau of Casualty and Surety Underwriters as one of the most hazardous types of commercial vehicles. Reduction of accident claims should result in reduction of insurance cost.
184. Installing an overhead sprinkler system or smoke detection device will reduce fire insurance rates. Investigate savings.

INTERDEPARTMENTAL COMMUNICATION

185. Professionals in communication industries often must be reminded of simple procedures regarding internal communication that can improve efficiency and cut costs. Do not hesitate to provide guidelines for streamlining the flow of necessary information among offices and departments.

186. Use a standardized memorandum form for all official communications, with adequate routing provisions to concerned editors, supervisors, and business personnel.

187. Reusable envelopes for addressing and identifying memoranda, proofs, or other materials will last many months if simply relabeled for each subsequent distribution.

188. Copy clerks and secretaries should not be diverted from more important responsibilities to substitute for mail runners.

189. Printed directories listing all in-house telephone numbers should be posted conspicuously throughout the plant to reduce unnecessary inquiries, particularly in emergencies.

190. Unmanned telephones are a waste. Some arrangement is needed for automatic "rollovers" to other numbers when certain essential stations are closed down.

MAILROOM

191. Single-wrap machines can help greatly in effecting mailing savings..

192. A Dexter stuffing machine, tested by the ANPA research division, assembles two sections at high speed in time for prompt delivery.

193. Reduce mailroom expense by using bulk distribution in lieu of wrapping and tying separate bundles for dealers and carriers. Have district or route workers count out papers.

194. Install a wire-tying machine. This laborsaving equipment—made by Jampol, Wallastar, and others—reduces the number of people required in the mailroom.

195. Elliott, Speedomat, and Addressograph equipment users may obtain "automatic selector" plates, whereby plates for renewals and new subscribers are selected automatically as needed.

196. When newspapers are sent by bus or truck to local post offices for mailing and charge is made by weight, it is cheaper to bundle the papers than to place them in mailsacks, which weigh four pounds each.

197. Use newsprint for single wraps and old newspapers for carrier bundles. Buy wrapping paper for only a few mail bundles that go out daily.

198. Since jute is high in price and may be hard to get in the future, use gummed tape, wire, or plastic straps to secure the outside wrapper for bundles of loose papers.

199. "Our mailroom has been revamped to increase efficiency

considerably and to cut operating costs and number of employes in the department through the use of two bundlers, a Jampol feeder table, and a completely automatic conveying system."

200. "We installed a Sheridan inserting machine in our mailroom. While this machine cost in excess of $40,000, it will pay for itself within two years in reduced mailroom operating costs."

201. The Cutler-Hammer stack counter saves tedious work and conserves time in speeding counted quantities of the finished newspaper along conveyors to be distributed to waiting trucks.

MAKEUP AND TYPOGRAPHY

202. Reduce or eliminate page-one runovers. How much space do you devote daily to runover heads?

203. Eliminate inside banners.

204. To reduce the cost of composition, condense news and set news content either in larger size type or with the same type on a bigger base. For example: 8 point on a 9-point slug.

205. Where the editorial department is called upon to supply additional news for a special section, anniversary issue, or other expanded issues, set news for such pages in type with a large base.

206. Guard against needless makeovers of editions to catch typographical errors. If you manage to save one or two makeovers a day, it will mean a great saving in the long run.

207. Eliminate mail editions whenever possible.

208. Eliminate the Saturday edition of the newspaper and use saved newsprint for additional advertising on profitable issues. Dropping the Saturday issue also eliminates overtime cost on the sixth workday of the week.

209. "We suspended publication of the Wednesday afternoon issue and went to four issues a week—Monday, Tuesday, Thursday, and Friday."

210. Keep different styles of head types to a minimum. Eliminate all decks.

211. Trim down space size for national news pictures by effective cropping.

212. Eliminate column rules. You reduce expense and give page makeup a modern appearance.

213. Medium-sized dailies may reduce the number of editions, saving mats and replates.

214. Eliminate the women's page layout on Sunday.

MANAGEMENT

215. Prepare an "office guide," detailing operating procedures and policies for employe guidance.

216. Set rigid deadlines and stick to them.
217. Try quantity buying to get full advantage of all price reductions and discounts.
218. Plan buying to cut freight cost per unit purchased to the smallest possible amount.
219. Proper layout of the business office should improve the flow of work and save time.
220. The payroll should be checked constantly to determine the reasons for overtime and to ascertain whether it can be reduced or eliminated by tightening up operations.
221. Centralize purchasing for all departments.
222. Make arrangements for cooperative deliveries.
223. Keep a close check on absenteeism.
224. Supplement income by serving as local dealer for office supplies, wedding announcements, Christmas greetings, rubber stamps, and signs.
225. Invite staff members to suggest ideas for cutting costs, controlling costs, and additional revenue. Reward them for practical suggestions.
226. Waste from newsprint rolls makes good copy paper.
227. If the labor situation becomes difficult, consider cooperation with public schools on the "work experience" feature of the vocational guidance department with a view to possible preapprenticeship training for high school sophomores and juniors.
228. Install air-conditioning to help maintain profitable year-around production.
229. Reduce employe turnover by careful inquiry into an applicant's qualifications and references. Write former employers for a confidential report before you hire.
230. Concentrate on wasteful practices and procedures. Streamline the entire newspaper operation.
231. Investigate duplication of effort among all departments.
232. Reevaluate all jobs and see if shifting responsibilities cannot eliminate one or more.
233. The publisher of a weekly paper with 1,000 circulation says: "I find that two fewer employes, careful accounting, and modern equipment in office and shop make for more profitable operation and less work, worry, and responsibility for the publisher."
234. Install and use pneumatic tubes to distribute copy and messages within the plant, instead of having clerks do it.
235. Install a safety patrol system to eliminate guards.
236. For improved security, have unguarded exterior doors keyed to lock automatically at certain hours; access to the building is thus controlled while push-bars permit egress at any time.
237. Consider the savings of a WATS line (wide area telecommunications

service). For a relatively low fee, the telephone company will provide any number of long-distance calls without individual charges. This is extremely useful in heavy-traffic areas of communication, such as between the state desk and its news bureaus throughout the territory.

238. Make one person in each department responsible for oiling machines.

239. "We are reviewing our entire personnel and intend to replace all employes who have been with us less than five years and have made no progress."

240. "We instituted a plan whereby all maintenance on our company-owned vehicles is done by a local automobile firm at a flat monthly fee for each. Our monthly rate includes a specified number of wash and grease jobs monthly plus all other maintenance, including parts and labor, to keep the vehicles in first-class mechanical condition. The effect was to reduce our expenditures for repair by approximately $2,000 per year and to keep our automobiles and trucks generally in better operating condition. The garage doing this maintenance had the responsibility for all vehicles; therefore, it was in their best interests never to let them get in a condition that would necessitate major repair work."

241. "Our own maintenance crew now does painting formerly handled by contractors."

242. "Reduction in columns of reading matter made savings in newsprint and eliminated the need for two employes."

243. "We will review further to make sure we are not using a top-pay man in a job a beginner could do."

244. "We will have more office conferences to encourage cost-cutting thinking and get ideas."

245. "We are considering a split day shift, with part of the force working from 8 A.M. to 4 P.M., and the others working from 9 A.M. to 5 P.M. and from 9:30 A.M. to 5:30 P.M."

246. "More efficient assignment of personnel and shorter stories have reduced overtime to the vanishing point."

247. "Examine your newspaper's vacation and holiday policy."

248. "We are consolidating the so-called fringe benefits that supplement weekly wages. We are holding fast on what we have, with a firm policy not to add any more holidays. We hope through negotiations to remove part of the prohibitive premium pay allowed for working on holidays, giving straight time only for time worked. We also contemplate underwriting with insurance our severance death-benefit clause and combining this with the existing life insurance policy."

249. "We have surveyed personnel needs and find we still have extras taken on in peak production periods. We are not making replacements in some cases where vacancies occur."

250. "We are tightening personnel practices with more thorough screen-

ing at time of hiring, and we are trying to develop better training programs. In these days of high wages there is room only for producers."

251. "Excess profits tax is too often an excuse for extravagant spending. Its elimination should bring tightening. We favor incentive pay to boost revenue and hold down costs."

252. "We plan to stress quality and increase production per dollar expended in all departments."

253. "We staggered working hours and lunch hours so that we made substantial cuts in overtime and improved our production. We improved the flow of news copy from the editorial room and eliminated 'dead spots' in our machine operations."

254. Independently owned newspapers are published in joint operation in about twenty localities of the United States. This technique has benefited publishers by reducing overhead costs and has benefited readers by preserving editorial identity and integrity of independent newspapers in competitive situations.

255. Newspaper files are better preserved and occupy less space when microfilmed.

PHOTOGRAPHY

256. Save from 3 to 5 percent on purchase price by using camera sheet films in bulk packages.

257. Reprint old photos as "pictorial highlights of the year" in a year-end issue in lieu of type composition.

258. Have a studio in your plant, so the photographer who takes individual and group pictures can sell prints to readers at a price publicized in the newspaper.

259. Have brides pay when their pictures are used in the newspaper.

260. "We are using strobe lights for our photographers, and we believe the saving in bulbs will cover the cost of the lights within a period of six months."

261. If the photo and engraving staff is on the job when not needed, reduce overtime by staggering hours.

262. Train reporters to use cameras, so that photographers are not overloaded when picture orders pile up.

263. See that personnel in the news department get some training in selecting good pictures.

PRESSROOM AND NEWSPRINT

264. The "ton price" on flat paper stock is 5 to 10 percent cheaper than the carton or even the case price. Paper firms will permit you to place an assorted order of bond, book, bristol, and index, for instance, if the total weight is a ton.

265. Be sure to have all cores tied in bundles before returning them to the paper mill and thus save freight.
266. Newspapers can save up to 6 percent on newsprint by using 30-pound paper instead of 32-pound paper.
267. Do not remove the newsprint wrapper until the roll is on the press.
268. Get larger diameter rolls to save core and wrapper waste.
269. To reduce spoiled press copies, try slowing down the press a bit.
270. Pay more attention to temperature and humidity in newsprint storage.
271. Late press starts and finishes add unnecessarily to production costs. Determine who is responsible and correct the situation.
272. Use a device for lowering rolls from truck to sidewalk.
273. Offer a small bonus to pressroom workers for reducing the number of spoiled copies per month.
274. Old newspapers (returns and file leftovers) can be sold to readers at 1 cent per pound instead of to scrap dealers at low market price.
275. Bale your waste paper and sell it at market price.

PRINTING

276. "We are putting more employes on the day side of the composing room to set ads; thus compositors will be paid the lower day rate."
277. Consolidate two editions and thus reduce press running time and extra makeovers.
278. "We have worked with the union to obtain additional journeymen and to reduce excessive overtime."
279. "We require a daily report on composing room production per employe-hour. This enables the supervisor to spot slack days and allot personnel accordingly."
280. Reduce press installation costs by returning to the practice of bidding out the job to contractors rather than to manufacturers.
281. With new ink filtering systems it is possible to recover up to 28,000 gallons of waste ink per year, at a cost of about 16 cents per gallon. The system also removes ink mist from the pressroom area, thus eliminating a possible health hazard.
282. Reduce page margins.
283. Alphabetical files save hours of searching. File live ads and typeset and stereo signatures alphabetically.
284. A four-wheeled dolly with removable shelves can be wheeled about the plant to furnish stock for printing jobs and to provide racks for stacking completed printing matter.
285. Have your power-circuit loads checked. If they are overloaded, correct the situation at once.
286. Buy white rags from subscribers. Use a classified ad.
287. Eliminate cutoffs between all display ads.
288. Install fluorescent lights for saving on electricity costs.

289. Use wastepaper for wrappers, tablets, second sheets, or copy paper.
290. Aluminum paint on the ceiling and posts of the composing room will add to interior illumination.
291. Keep the shop clean. It helps to cut waste in paper stock and encourages printers to work efficiently.
292. Study ways of dovetailing work and otherwise reducing nonproductive labor time.
293. "We carefully reviewed our editorial department's makeover orders for our second edition. We found that by careful planning, we could confine makeover to four pages on an average day; six to eight pages had been the rule. We also discontinued a third edition called the 'Stock Edition,' in which we gave the daily closing prices of a selected list of stocks. We had fewer than ten complaints and lost no subscribers."
294. "Our printed page was lengthened from 279 to 301 lines."
295. "With purchase of photocomp machines, a new composing room layout has given more efficient production."
296. "We installed a 1,000-gallon ink tank and received truck deliveries three or four times a year."
297. "We set up a page-cost committee to make a study and to put into effect measures to reduce composing room page cost."
298. "A Lamson Tube System has been installed to carry want ad copy directly from business office to Teletype department, as well as to carry proofs from copyroom to proofroom and return; and to carry head copy to the head letter machine from the editors."
299. "We have installed a system using colored paper tapes attached to editorial copy, giving the priority system for all phases of production. This helps close pages faster."
300. Total conversion to electronic editing, composing, typesetting, and platemaking does away with most of the former heavy expense for janitorial service. Cleanliness is a dramatic and pleasing form of plant economy.

11

Serving the public through advertising

> Future historians will find in advertising the richest and most faithful daily reflections that any society ever made of its entire range of activities.
>
> *Marshall McLuhan*

Newspaper advertising, popular avenue for consumer approach, is influential in economical living, business growth, and community progress. There is convincing evidence that such advertising can bring about lower prices, greater profits, reduced selling costs, and increased turnover.

Results such as those listed below help to explain why more money is spent for newspaper advertising than for any other form (of more than $23 billion spent annually for advertising, newspapers still get approximately 30 percent of the total in competition with other media, including television, billboards, magazines, direct mail, point of sale, radio, and all others):

1. Enticed by attractive advertising, millions of Americans rush to buy a new summer drink featured in a unique container, and in a single season it becomes the largest selling brand item of its size and class in the nation's food chains and supermarkets.
2. Within 90 days after announcements appear in newspapers, a million cases of chicken pies, offered by a midwestern producer of frozen poultry products, are purchased by an advertisement-reading public.
3. A telephone company, flooded with complaints when demands for service cannot be met instantly on account of the community's rapid growth, launches an advertising campaign in the community newspaper explaining that delays in phone installations were unavoidable due to unprecedented demands. Within a short time complaints fall off 75 percent, and the utility moves forward undisturbed to answer the public's needs.
4. In virtually every town in the country during periodic promotions, housewives meticulously read retail store advertisements in the community newspapers and engage in elbow fights to get the first chance at what is offered at clearance counters.

163

5. In one Christmas season in Detroit when the major newspapers were shut down for ten weeks because of a union strike, the merchants in the downtown area alone reported aggregate losses of $35 million in retail sales — a figure corroborated by the Michigan State University Bureau of Business Research.

The "Eight Reasons" conceived by the Bureau of Advertising, ANPA, are generally endorsed by advertising managers of newspapers, manufacturing concerns, and wholesale and retail businesses:

1. Newspaper reading is a universal daily habit; therefore, newspaper advertising each day reaches most of those who buy.
2. Newspaper advertising is the lifeblood of local trade because it touches all consumer sources in every community. It gives the national advertiser the same opportunity for consumer appeal in any locality.
3. Newspaper advertising cuts selling costs because it entails no waste in the locality of its circulation. Manufacturers use it to cover markets where it is profitable to do business.
4. Newspaper advertising insures quick, thorough, and economical distribution and dealer goodwill because retailers are willing to sell products advertised directly to their own customers.
5. Newspaper advertising enables manufacturers to tell where their products may be bought.
6. Newspaper advertising can be started or stopped overnight and can be prepared between days to meet sudden developments and to obtain immediate results.
7. Newspaper advertising enables manufacturers to check advertising results and costs in every market they enter.
8. Newspaper advertising *costs less than any other kind.*

TYPES OF NEWSPAPER ADVERTISING

New merchandising fields, new typefaces, and better means of illustration have widened the scope and increased the effectiveness of four classes of newspaper advertising: local display, general, legal, and classified.

Local display advertising

A greater part of the advertising carried in a newspaper is that placed by local merchants, manufacturers, and distributors, who depend upon the home newspaper for an economical and effective means of reaching the public they serve. There are four types of local display advertising: retail or price, institutional, cooperative, and promotional.

Most store advertising is of the retail or price type, featuring merchandise with a general description of each item and a price quotation. This kind of advertising appeals directly to the customer's taste and pocketbook and the results are easily checked (Fig. 11.1).

Fig. 11.1. Retail or price advertising.

Institutional advertising deals more with the personality and character of the business or service institution. It may feature the history of the organization, its record of service, the testimonials of customers, an anniversary, or the introduction or opening of a new department or service. Banks, newspapers, and utilities that have services to sell publish more of this kind of advertising than retail stores (Fig. 11.2).

Fig. 11.2.   Local institutional advertising.

Cooperative advertising is used by a group of merchants or individuals to promote an idea, occasion, or movement. It may be a united sales effort on the part of several firms of the same class or it may be an endorsement of a school bond election or some project or campaign within the community (Fig. 11.3). A large advertisement is much more effective than several small ads, so merchants often sponsor a full page and present a strong appeal with their names as endorsers.

Advertising that promotes a community, an institution, or a service department is termed promotional (Fig. 11.4). Advertising of this type often appears as folders or catalogs; but it is also common for cities, utilities, and service institutions to purchase newspaper space for promotional advertising.

You can help us fight cancer
Right here in Columbia

Support

CRƆ

The Cancer Research Center
Business 70 & Garth, Columbia, Mo.
449-3853

CRC's decade of experience in cancer research provides a broad base upon which to build new, advanced and more sophisticated research efforts. Future expansion is restricted only by the current limitations of physical facilities.

INVEST IN COLUMBIA

Help make the Cancer Research Center an economic asset to Columbia as well as a medical and scientific one.

This Promotion is Sponsored by The Columbia Missourian and these Community Minded Businessmen

The Brown Derby	Boone County National Bank
Kruger Plumbing & Heating	Suzanne's
Parker Funeral Service	First National Bank
Miller's Shoe Store	Rollins-Vandiver-Digges Inc.
Nu-Way Lumber Co.	

Fig. 11.3.   Local cooperative advertising.

YOU DO, IF....

you're a retiree who wants to enjoy life to the hilt while on a fixed income.

you're like millions of other people in this world who have ordinary needs, wants, problems, homes and dreams! Classified is the person-to-person advertising medium which lets you communicate with other people . . . quickly, easily and inexpensively. In fact, Classified does more things for more people at lower cost than any other form of advertising! Just dial 869-4411 to place your result-getting Classified Ad.

——BIG WANT AD—— BARGAIN

Order your want ad on the 4 day plan!

10 words
published 4
consecutive
days, only . . .

$3⁴⁰

SPRINGFIELD NEWSPAPERS, INC.

651 Boonville   Ph. 869-4411

Publishers of the:

Morning Daily News   Evening Leader-Press

Sunday News & Leader

Fig. 11.4. Local promotional advertising.

General advertising

General advertising originates outside the newspaper's immediate territory, receives different handling, and is sold by some newspapers at a rate different from that for local display. This advertising is placed through agencies, which prepare the copy, schedule it, and mail it to the newspaper, or it is sent directly to the newspaper from the national advertiser's office (Fig. 11.5).

Although there is a growing tendency to establish similar rates for general and local advertising, many publishers still feel the general rate should be sufficiently higher to cover the commission paid the agency (usually 15 percent plus 2 percent for cash) for placing the order. The argument favoring like rates is that servicing general advertising, including the agency's work, is no more costly and in some cases less so than servicing local advertising. Usually the general rate is on an agate-line basis (14 lines to the inch), and local advertising is priced on the column inch basis. To make them approximately equal, a newspaper with a local rate of $1.10 per column inch would charge general advertisers 8 cents a line, making an inch (14 lines) cost $1.12.

A difference in national and local rates has caused some confusion and controversy in the handling of advertising where the cost is shared by the manufacturer or jobber and the local dealer. This "share" plan is carried out in one of two ways: the advertising agency sends the copy to the newspaper, instructing the publisher to bill the agency for half the space at the general rate and to bill the local dealer for half the space at the rate he pays for advertising, or the copy is sent to the local dealer, with instructions for him to place the advertising in the newspaper, to pay for it, and to send the agency or the manufacturer a statement marked "paid" for the entire amount. The agency in turn sends the dealer a check for half the amount, or the company credits him with that figure toward the purchase of its manufactured goods.

If the general rate is higher than the local rate, the question is which rate to apply in billing advertising. Some newspapers issue two statements to the merchant — one at the local rate, which the merchant pays, and another at the general rate to be marked "paid" and forwarded to the manufacturer. In this way the merchant pays the newspaper at the local rate and collects from the manufacturer for his share at the higher rate. This practice is commonly referred to as "double billing" and is discouraged by both publisher and advertiser on ethical grounds for the very practical reason that it may subject a publisher to action by law. The Advertising Executives Association has resolved "that the practice of double billing be unreservedly condemned as dishonest and that all advertising directors pledge themselves to police their local situations to eradicate any chance of its inadvertent occurrence."

The wisest and fairest policy in billing this "share" advertising is for the publisher to determine at which rate it is to be sold and to issue only one statement, unless the publisher or local dealer is instructed by the manufacturer to handle the matter otherwise.

If your direction is northwestern, go Southern and Eastern.

Southern and Eastern Airlines together make it easy for you to get to Seattle/Tacoma and Portland.

All you do is purchase your Seattle/Tacoma or Portland ticket from Southern and take one of our conveniently scheduled flights to St. Louis. From St. Louis, Eastern will take you the rest of the way to the Northwest area.

And Southern checks your baggage all the way to your final destination.

So, if your plans call for travel to the Northwest, get the most out of your visit. Take time to enjoy the beautiful mountains, rivers and forests.

Southern and Eastern do everything to make it all possible. When you fly with us, convenience and your comfort are our main concerns.

And remember, you'll save with our discount airfares. So if you're taking a business or pleasure trip to the Northwest, Southern and Eastern are the way to go.

For reservations, call your travel agent.

 Southern  EASTERN

Fig. 11.5. General newspaper advertising.

Large city newspapers maintain special general advertising departments, with staff who call on the agencies and manufacturers in the important centers to sell their newspapers as advertising media. This is too expensive an undertaking for smaller newspapers. They usually have special representatives who serve a group of newspapers and work on a commission, which in most cases applies to all general advertising carried by the newspaper.

Weekly Newspaper Representatives, owned by the National Editorial Association, represents a large group of weekly newspapers in the national field. Many state press associations give similar service to newspaper members.

All newspapers are indebted to the Bureau of Advertising, ANPA, for its work in promoting newspapers as effective advertising media. By personal contact with manufacturers, advertising staffs, and advertising agencies and by charts, brochures, illustrated lectures, and campaigns the bureau's representatives sell the idea that the hometown newspaper, read and respected, is the right medium through which to reach the people of a given community. Many of the large advertising campaigns in newspapers may be attributed to groundwork done by the Bureau of Advertising.

Legal advertising

Probably every newspaper publisher has listened to a public office-holder grumble about the expense of publishing a legal notice and has heard the mumbled protests of unthinking readers because a newspaper page contains a few columns of these items. Some persons think the main reason for legal advertising is to provide revenue for the newspaper, but it serves more useful purposes. It safeguards the taxpayer's pocketbook, provides a means of fulfilling in a practical way the constitutional guarantee of security to every citizen, and informs citizens of their duties as voters and of new laws and regulations to be imposed (Fig. 11.6).

Legal advertisements are of three general classes, according to the purposes they serve:

1. Public accounting notices, such as reports and statements from public officials to the public they serve.
2. Information notices regarding new laws, proclamations, election notices, election ballots, announcements of public improvements, bid lettings, and the like.
3. Warning notices (not paid for from public funds) such as financial statements as required of banks, divorce notices, bankruptcy proceedings, probate notices, taxes due, suits to quiet title.

Newspapers must meet specific requirements to become eligible to carry legal notices. Although these vary by states, among the most common requirements are: a second-class publication permit, a specified period of continuous publication, a certain number of paid subscribers,

NOTICE OF PUBLIC HEARING

A public hearing will be held by the Memphis Housing Authority on the plan for the Court Avenue Urban Renewal Area III, Project Tennessee R-49, which is being planned by the Memphis Housing Authority for redevelopment under the Housing Act of 1949 as amended.

The hearing will be held in the offices of the Memphis Housing Authority, 700 Adams Avenue, Memphis, Tennessee at 10:00 A.M. o'clock, CDT, on June 21, 1967. The Project area is bounded as shown below:

The purpose of the hearing is to consider a proposal for this undertaking of an Amendment to the redevelopment plan, under State and Local Law, with Federal financial assistance under Title I of the Housing Act of 1949, as amended, (Public Law 171—81st Congress), to acquire the land in the Project area, to demolish or remove buildings and improvements, to install, construct or reconstruct streets, utilities, park and playgrounds or other site improvements, and to make the land available for development or redevelopment by private enterprise or public agencies as authorized by law. Relocation proposals by the Memphis Housing Authority will be open to discussion by those interested. Any person or organization desiring to be heard will be afford an opportunity to be heard at this hearing.

Plans of the proposed redevelopment plan are on display in the office of the Memphis Housing Authority, 700 Adams Avenue, Memphis, Tennessee.

MEMPHIS HOUSING AUTHORITY

Fig. 11.6. Legal or "public notice" advertising.

and publication in whole or in part in the town where the newspaper office is located.

Because requirements and regulations within a state frequently change, state press association managers and directors spend much time settling questions about charges and keeping member publishers informed on legal-notice laws. Many press associations furnish members with digests of laws and rates governing legal publication. For example, the Missouri Press Association has issued a digest of 470 Missouri statutes that deal with public notices and advertisements. It describes each required legal notice or advertisement, telling the kind and location of the newspaper in which it must be published, the number of times it is to be inserted, the limit of days in which the publication is to begin and end, the legal rate allowed, and the number of the section in the statutes governing publication of the notice.

The rate for legal advertising is prescribed by law. It usually is slightly higher than the newspaper's rate for display advertising because more composition time is required. In some counties and cities, newspapers submit bids on official printing and the low bidder becomes the legal newspaper.

On the smaller newspaper, the publisher or advertising manager usually keeps in close touch with the courts, the city and county governments, and the leading attorneys to receive from them the notices requiring publication. On some of the larger papers a member or a division of the advertising department is delegated to take care of legal advertising.

Classified advertising

Classified advertising is an important service feature of every worthwhile newspaper (Fig. 11.7). It is valuable not only for the revenue it produces but for the reader interest it creates and the goodwill it builds. By reason of this twofold importance, an entire chapter (Chapter 12) is devoted to classified advertising.

DEVELOPING VOLUME AND SERVICE

One of the primary goals of newspaper publishing is to carry a large volume of advertising, the newspaper's chief source of revenue. Another is to keep the advertiser satisfied with results. There are two avenues, therefore, along which the advertising department of a newspaper must work. It must strive to improve the advertising service and to develop advertising volume. This can be done by maintaining a good organization; knowing advertising needs and values; inducing merchants to plan; selling contracts and campaigns; producing dependable and attractive copy; giving point-of-sale aid; obtaining dealer cooperation; handling orders, proofs, and records efficiently; and making a fair charge for advertising.

Maintaining a good organization

At a meeting of the Inland Daily Press Association in Chicago, Clyde Bedell, advertising authority and author of *How to Write Advertising That Sells,* told publishers to:

1. Modernize their selling of advertising.
2. Plan a constructive program of advertising enlightenment for the whole retail community.
3. Use every self-liquidating device or service or facility possible to advance advertising revenues.
4. Determine to start nothing fresh, new, and promising without seeing to it that it is carried through properly, so the fullest possible profit may be achieved.
5. Determine to spend 26 hours (one every second week) becoming thoroughly familiar with what makes advertising interesting and persuasive.

While a publisher needs to have this vision of newspaper advertising

Fig. 11.7. Classified advertising in a ten-column format (for further information and illustrations, see Ch. 12).

possibilities and the willingness to conduct thorough study and research, its full benefits cannot be realized without an adequate and efficient advertising sales organization.

Heading the advertising department should be a person with an appreciation for the opportunities to serve the public and to increase volume, strong organizing ability, and a sales viewpoint. The advertising manager should have selling ability as well as executive ability.

The next requirement is a sales staff large enough to contact and serve every prospective advertiser and qualified to present intelligently and convincingly the newspaper's merits as an advertising medium. This is one department in which the publisher cannot afford to scrimp. With a strong advertising department there is every opportunity to build a strong newspaper. With a weak advertising department the publication can quickly face failure.

Sound organization is just as important to small dailies and weekly newspapers as it is to the large metropolitan dailies. Many newspapers with less than 10,000 circulation have from three to five persons who give full time to selling advertising. A survey of 33 publisher members in the 10,000 circulation class of the Inland Daily Press Association revealed that two employed three salespeople, while ten papers employed two. In cities of 10,000 to 15,000, the number of full-time advertising sales personnel ranged from three to nine for 28 newspapers, with an average of four and one-half.

How the advertising staff is divided and directed largely determines its success in serving its advertising clientele. Regular advertisers must be served, and new advertising patrons must be developed. Advertising staffs often have been enlarged especially to cultivate small advertisers. The salespeople whose principal responsibility is to develop new accounts, however, occasionally should be given some that are easy to handle so they will not become discouraged by too many "cold" calls. Responsibilities within the advertising department should be clearly assigned so that there will be no overlapping and every employe may work at maximum efficiency to cover the advertising market.

Knowing advertising needs and values

Before a newspaper can fully meet the advertising needs of merchants and readers, its publisher must know the possibilities of trade expansion within the circulation area and the distance from which merchants wish to draw business. The newspaper then may widen and intensify its circulation, and the stores may increase patronage by advertising. It is important also for a newspaper publisher to interpret the home market to advertisers. Businessmen appreciate any information that will open new avenues of trade.

But newspapers do not enjoy a monopoly in the advertising business. Other media constantly court the merchants with service claims. It is up to the newspaper to meet this competition with sound arguments and evidence showing why its advertising potential is best. For example, the newspaper can meet television's growing competition with these arguments:

1. The printed word is more reliable than the spoken word, and it cannot be refuted.
2. More accurate information is obtained by reading than by viewing a rapidly changing image on a screen.
3. Newspaper advertisements may be preserved and reread for definite understanding.
4. The ads in a newspaper may be consulted at a time most convenient to the housewife, whereas commercials must be accepted at a definite time regardless of convenience.
5. A better picture of an item of merchandise can be given in a newspaper than over the air.
6. The items in a newspaper advertisement may be compared with items in other newspaper ads much more easily than similar comparisons may be made with television ads.
7. Newspaper space is better suited to retail or price advertising than is broadcast time.
8. For volume advertising, costs favor the newspaper by a huge margin.
9. Many advertisers have wanted to "try" TV, but records indicate as many return to newspaper advertising as leave it.
10. The factor of "excitement" in television does not contribute to the more important psychological aspects of selling — such as recall, retention, and lasting impact — all of which are maximum features of newspaper advertising.
11. The changing role of women means that fewer are watching television during the daytime and more are relying on newspaper ads as a reliable shopping guide for family purchases.
12. The newspaper enters a home assuring the advertiser that every advertisement it contains is available for reading by every member of the family at a time of his or her convenience and choosing.
13. Every issue of every newspaper contains information and features of interest and importance to every member of the family.
14. The newspaper is a medium in which great numbers of people are accustomed to look for advertisements of merchandise and service they wish to buy.
15. People like to read newspaper advertisements: 85 percent want their papers to contain advertising.
16. People read newspapers when they are in an active frame of mind, when they are ready to make decisions and act.
17. Newspaper advertising has versatility and flexibility; it may vary in size and content from day to day or week to week.
18. An advertisement in a newspaper lives for many hours and sometimes for days, weeks, and years.

19. Market coverage by newspapers is high in quantity and quality.
20. Newspaper advertising receives prompt reader attention. An ad inserted today may be in thousands of homes tomorrow.
21. The newspaper makes advertising easy and effective by cooperation in preparing copy and planning campaigns.
22. Most newspapers give the same prominence to small advertisements as to large advertisements by using the pyramid style of makeup.
23. Newspaper advertising occupies a top position in the minds of retailers.

Tailored service

The special services given by newspapers to improve the effectiveness of advertising that appears in their columns are strong factors in building newspaper linage. In an address before the Georgia Daily Newspaper Association, the advertising manager for Swift & Company called newspapers the keystones of local advertising and pointed to seven valuable attributes.

Neighborliness. "Like two housewives talking over the back fence, you've got daily undivided attention in your neighbors' homes. In most cases, you are the only paper there. Four TV channels in Atlanta and 72 radio stations in Georgia blast away all day and Mrs. Housewife can only listen to one at a time."

Economy. "The biggest job facing business today is to find a way of reducing the rapidly and seriously increasing cost of marketing. Newspapers provide an advantage in that, generally speaking, their *line rates are in line.*"

Merchandisability. "Our salesman can't walk into a food store with an outdoor billboard in his hand to demonstrate to Mr. Dealer how our tender-grown Swift's Premium Chicken is being advertised. Many dealers don't have time for radio or television. But what dealer doesn't read his daily paper, if only to watch his competitor."

Flexibility. "We can wire copy to you tonight that will run tomorrow, and we don't have to sign a 13-week contract."

Rhythm. "Your newspapers have no audience rating grief, no star talent grief, and I trust no rebate grief. You've got *rhythm* and it must be sweet music to you."

Personality. "Your paper is as individual as any Georgia citizen. You've got the personality of your editor or publisher and, thank God, in America an editor can say what he thinks without fear."

Retentiveness. "Pa puts his paper in his pocket, until his chores are done, or until after lodge meeting and then sits down to enjoy it. Ma's too busy all day, but gets a chance to read after supper's over and dishes are done, and she can't clip a dress pattern or a recipe or a doctor's column out of a TV show."

The banker, the baker, the florist, the interior decorator, and the insurance man as well as the department store owner and specialty shop operator have found that newspaper advertising builds business. Even lawyers found cooperative advertising helpful in the South Bend, Ind., *Tribune,* sponsoring a campaign to acquaint the public with the many services performed by their profession.

The general tone of bank advertising has changed greatly. Not too long ago, humor in bank advertising had about as much appeal to bankers as counterfeit money. But officials felt that something needed to be done to make the public warm up to them. One of the oldest banks in the country asked a prominent advertising agency to find out just what the people thought about bankers. The results of that survey changed the entire concept of bank advertising and public relations.

Cartoons now appear in some bank advertising. Where cold statistics used to be the rule, attempts are made now to create a warmer, friendlier personality for the institutions that handle people's money. Bankers realize that they need to be close to the family, sharing confidences from birth to maturity and giving advice and assistance in establishing homes and businesses, in planning educations, and in settling estates.

For 18 years a Wisconsin bank frowned on newspaper advertising. Now it carries in the hometown newspaper a series of editorial style ads, two columns by 15 inches, dealing with little-known facts of local history.

Banks are only a case in point. Wide-awake advertising salespeople will turn many firms into regular advertisers by giving them special thought and attention and by developing copy and campaigns for them that bring business.

Inducing merchants to plan

Part of an advertising department's responsibility is to induce merchants to appropriate definite sums for advertising and to plan their advertising copy and schedules carefully.

An adequate budget must be properly determined, its use carefully planned, and its expenditures prodigiously controlled. It is expedient also for the advertising merchant or manufacturer to produce copy that is attractive, honest, and appealing. In selling space to new advertisers, one newspaper always emphasized eight steps to be taken in making sales messages effective:

1. Get an idea of the importance of the month's sales possibilities in relation to annual sales volume; determine whether the month will represent 6, 10, or 15 percent or more of annual sales.
2. Appraise the potentials and set the justifiable dollar-volume goal at which to aim this year; consider all factors that should have a bearing on your objective.
3. Determine the amount of advertising support — in percentage — that is necessary to achieve that volume goal.
4. Determine the space budget for the month; convert the dollars to be spent during the month to column inches of newspaper space.

5. Decide on those departments, items, and types of service that offer the greatest sales potentials for the month.
6. Make a profitable apportionment of space to the items selected.
7. Determine the time of specific ads and the general frequency pattern to use.
8. Advertise what appeals to the customer from the standpoint of season, newness, quality, style, variety, and exclusiveness; show the customer what you can do for him or for her.

For newspapers with computer service available, the information sought in each of the above steps may be readily obtained.

Selling contracts and campaigns

No merchant has a right to expect startling results from a one-time advertisement unless he is offering exceptional values. Most merchants do not jump into big business the first day they open a store in a new community. It requires days, weeks, and months for the community to become acquainted with a new business institution. Successful advertising, too, requires time. The merchant may not get much response to the first ad but as consistent advertising is continued, attention is attracted to the values offered and prospective customers form the habit of watching for subsequent messages.

Advertising departments, therefore, that want to help the advertiser as well as build volume put selling stress on contracts and campaigns. To help stimulate this kind of business, lower advertising rates normally are allowed on monthly and yearly volume and on advertising that appears at regular intervals. A typical schedule of rates, based on the amount of advertising carried per month, is that used by a daily of approximately 7,500 circulation:

All one-time advertisements, regardless of size, per column inch	$1.10
0-25 column inches per month, per inch	.95
25-50 column inches per month, per inch	.90
50-100 column inches per month, per inch	.85
100-200 column inches per month, per inch	.80
200-300 column inches per month, per inch	.75
300-400 column inches per month, per inch	.70
Over 400 column inches per month, per inch	.65

Another medium-sized daily has bulk space rates, allowing discounts from the local open rate when the advertising used during a month reaches specified volumes:

50 inches minimum monthly	19% discount
150 inches minimum monthly	24% discount
250 inches minimum monthly	28% discount
350 inches minimum monthly	34% discount
450 inches minimum monthly	39% discount

A weekly newspaper with a circulation of 2,750 offers advertising at the following schedule of rates on the basis of column inches used during the month:

0–50 inches in same month	$.84 per column inch
51–100 inches in same month	.75 per column inch
101–200 inches in same month	.70 per column inch
201–300 inches in same month	.65 per column inch

Some newspapers base their rates on the volume of inches or lines contracted for during the year. Others offer lower rates to advertisers who agree to use a minimum number of inches or lines every other day, twice a week, or once a week. The lowest rate usually goes to an advertiser who will agree to use a liberal minimum of advertising in every issue of the newspaper for a year.

Another way of building volume is to sell ads in packages, especially to small-space users. It does not take much longer to sell a merchant 13 ads to run for 13 weeks than to sell one ad to run in a single issue. Most advertising mat services include copy suggestions and mats for campaigns of this kind. The plan to be followed is this:

1. Select the store you think is your best prospect at the particular season for a "package of ads."
2. Study the merchant's situation. Set down all the reasons why people should trade at that store. List the products for which there is the greatest natural demand during the next 13 weeks. Prepare a set of the most effective sales arguments in simple language.
3. Put these ideas in concrete form by laying out a series of at least 13 ads. If possible, carry out a theme for the store. Do not hesitate to repeat, for repetition is the essential feature of tested sales psychology. Use illustrations from your cut and copy service and from dealer helps.
4. Take the package to your merchant and present your plan in a straightforward, businesslike manner. Talk about the merchant's business and profits, not yours. Be prepared to meet as many objections as you can anticipate and, above all, stress the advantages to be gained from advertising.
5. Start all over again with the next prospect, using the same procedure.

Campaigns may be sold on a cooperative basis, too. The merchant who seems unwilling to advertise as an individual often will advertise in a cooperative campaign with other businesses. The Rochester, N.Y., *Democrat and Chronicle* sold the florists of Rochester six full-page advertisements to be run immediately preceding St. Valentine's Day, Easter, Mother's Day, Thanksgiving, Christmas, and New Year's Eve.

Producing dependable and attractive copy

Because advertising must build business and goodwill, copy must never mislead. Careless and untruthful claims cause people to lose faith in advertising and in the newspaper. Since merchants never like to be out-done by their competitors, there is a strong temptation to exaggerate. "Highest quality goods at the lowest prices," "lowest prices in town," "lowest prices in the state," and "lowest prices anywhere" are overworked advertising phrases that have become virtually meaningless. One publisher met the situation this way: A merchant who wanted to use the phrase "lowest prices in town" was induced to change it to "our lowest prices"; "the finest quality in town" was changed to "exceptionally fine quality," and "the finest coat you've ever seen" became "the finest coat we've ever sold." If newspaper advertising is to be believed, every statement must be truthful.

Advertising copy must also be attractive. Most large retail stores have their own advertising departments where eye-catching copy is prepared, but smaller stores need help. The newspaper's advertising department can provide the necessary service by having people on its staff who know how to prepare pleasing ad layouts.

How the advertising department of the Sikeston, Mo., *Standard* assisted merchants with their advertising copy was related by Charley Blanton, publisher, at a meeting of the Inland Daily Press Association. Sales personnel prepared and presented to each of their advertisers a case history of the account for the corresponding month of the three preceding years. At the same time they prepared and took new personalized, ap-propriate copy to every advertiser. In most cases the advertiser is sold upon seeing the copy. Mr. Blanton added:

Be prepared to help prepare copy—if you want ad volume, you must be will-ing to draft 75 percent of the copy; the average merchant can't and won't.

Use care in set-up. Many advertisers have been lost because of sloppy work in the back shop. Care in composition . . . will pay dividends.

Offer proofs to advertisers—protect the advertisers and the newspaper and make alterations cheerfully. The customer has the right to have the ad set up as desired.

Give extra service. It will be doubly appreciated.

Encourage window and counter display tie-ins. Furnish display cards and stickers bearing the slogan, "As advertised in the *Standard*." Help make it easy for the advertising to produce sales.

Show an interest in the results—that is what you are selling. Encourage readers to tell your merchants "I saw your ad in the *Sikeston Standard*.

Know what the advertiser has advertised. Nothing is more exasperating to the merchant than to discover you didn't read the ad.

In addition to its work in the general advertising field, the Bureau of Advertising has pointed the way to better preparation of copy for the local advertiser. Its study entitled "More Power in Newspaper Ads" listed these display principles:

1. Photographs excel wash or line drawings as attention getters.
2. A dominant illustration gets more attention for an ad than a small one.

3. Ads with dominant illustrations of premiums, babies, personalities, or animals get more than average notice; those featuring anonymous people or pictures of the package are likely to get below average notice.
4. Large areas of reverse plates (white letters on black background) bring down readership.
5. A dominant timely or newsy note in an ad is usually helpful.
6. In conventional display, as in editorial technique, dominant illustration with a food recipe is better than an unillustrated recipe.

At the fiftieth anniversary celebration of the Advertising Federation of America, John W. Eggers, newspaper representative, compared two Standard Oil Company ads (identical except for color) appearing in the Milwaukee, Wis., *Journal.* The black-and-white ad ran in half the edition, then was replaced for the remainder of the run by the black-and-one-color ad. A readership survey revealed that the color ad scored 55 percent more total readership by men and 31 percent more readership by women. Mr. Eggers concluded that one color and black will increase readership from 50 to several hundred percent over black and white and full color will top one-color-and-black readership by 200 percent for men and 43 percent for women.

Although special position sometimes is requested, in a good newspaper the page on which an ad appears is not so important. Every page contains news of interest to readers. Any page, therefore, is a good advertising page.

The pyramid style of makeup (Fig. 11.8), which places the largest ads at the bottom of the page and the smaller ones in pyramid above them, is the best for advertisers of all kinds and for advertisements of all sizes. Either by position or size it gives almost equal prominence to all ads on the page and reading matter usually touches each advertisement at some point, thereby leading the reader's eye directly from the news to the advertisement. The large ads attract the reader's attention because of their size. The small ads, placed above the large ones, draw attention because of their position.

Giving point-of-sale aid

Most newspapers promote advertising from distant manufacturers and producers by helping to establish outlets and by encouraging dealers to cooperate with the advertising. The point-of-sale aid that newspapers provide should include the following:

1. Information about the market in which the newspaper circulates. Much of this information may be obtained by the advertiser from the federal census report, but the newspaper can give it in more detail. The information includes population of the city where the newspaper is published; population of the trade area; circulation of the newspaper;

Dimensions
by JAMES MILLS

Sculptor 'Freezes' Grid Action

INCONGRUOUS AS it might seem, a Denver sculptor is part of the big Super Bowl scene and even before this weekend, when the Denver Broncos meet the Dallas Cowboys.

A. Thomas Schomberg, whose work is exhibited locally at the Carlson-Alexander Gallery, 240 St. Paul St., is featured in an exhibit of his bronze sculptures of sports figures in the lobby of the St. Louis Hotel in New Orleans.

Schomberg, however, finds no incongruity in this dichotomy of art and Astroturf. Sports, he finds, are a major motivating force of our society, and such activities needn't be represented simply by the brute force of a 280-pound defensive lineman. In his sculptures, Schomberg attempts to make a classic statement about "supreme effort" frozen in time.

"Football is a classic sort of thing," Schomberg said. "It has form. Our society demands that we produce these people. When you look at the classic 'Discus Thrower' and then look at the modern athlete, the pose is still filled with expression and emotion."

In his sculpture, Schomberg strives to freeze the peak moment—in the extremes of both success or failure. He relates well to athletes, as he has been one himself and identifies with the athlete's situation. He now saturates himself in the athletic experience, attending a wide variety of sports matches.

His tennis sculpture, "The Ace," shown recently in Melbourne, Australia, depicts a player at the height of success. His "Overhead Kick" recaptures the phenomenal forms he observed in soccer games in Europe. "The Catch" reflects an ecstatic moment in a football game.

"I think what I'm involved in has super-relevance," said Schomberg. The human body has been reworked by artisan for centuries, so he is using a traditional medium, bronze, to reflect a traditional activity, sports.

"But something new is happening today," said Schomberg. "Denver is fanatical. I've never seen anything like it. And I've been back East, the West Coast, and in Europe. And I think it's my responsibility as an artist to describe it."

One hopes the Denver Broncos provide Schomberg with many peak moments of

EXHIBIT IN NEW ORLEANS
A. Thomas Schomberg's sculptures of sports figures are featured in an exhibit in lobby of St. Louis Hotel.

supreme effort on Sunday, which he may later document in bronze for sports posterity—and, mercifully, without an orange patina.

PAUL MARIONI, West Coast glass artist, will be in Denver for a four-day workshop and a free lecture on Jan. 21, which will sponsored by the Stained Glass School and Supply Inc.

The Saturday lecture will begin at 2 p.m. at Grant Junior High School, 1751 S. Washington St. Marioni will offer a 1½-hour lecture and slide presentation describing his work and techniques.

Marioni has toured the United States and Europe giving lecture-workshops, and is well known for his innovative techniques in glass work.

Although the lecture is free, tickets must be picked up in advance at Stained Glass School and Supply, 1705 S. Pearl St. The school is open from 11 a.m. to 6 p.m. Tuesday through Friday, 10 a.m. to 4 p.m. Saturday and noon to 5 p.m. Sunday. Persons interested in attending the lecture or wanting information on the four-day workshop may call the school at 733-6236.

Evergreen Arts Unit Given $13,140 Grant

The Evergreen Center for the Arts has been awarded a $13,140 matching grant from the National Endowment for the Arts for continuation of the City Spirit Program designed to involve citizens in the planning of a building for the center and its programs.

Allan Coles, center executive director, said the money will be available on a quarterly basis, and that the grant must be matched by local contributions by the end of the grant period on Nov. 30.

"We are very pleased to receive the full amount we requested," Coles said. "The grant backs up statements made by Joseph Golden, City Spirit facilitator, who visited Evergreen in February 1977, and by other NEA staff members, that this is a classic City Spirit community in terms of citizen involvement in meeting community needs through concerted action."

Coles said the City Spirit Program is the key to building community support for the arts center.

Activities to be funded in part by the grant include training for citizens' committees in planning techniques, creation of a volunteer organization, community workshops to advise citizens in planning programs, building designs and finances, joint meetings with diverse bodies of other area organizations, public-information activities, continuing assessment of needs for art programs and involvement of other organizations in specific aspects of planning the center and its programs.

Cosmic Circle Puppets Slated In 'Amazing Dr. Doolittle'

The Storytellers Children's Theater will present the Cosmic Circle Puppets in "The Amazing Adventures of Doctor Doolittle" at 1 and 3 p.m. Jan. 22 at the Children's Museum, 931 Bannock St.

Doctor Doolittle was first created by Hugh Lofting in 1920. Since then the tedious stories of the little English doctor who developed the ability to talk to animals has been very popular.

In the show the Cosmic Circle Puppets will tell the story using the ancient art of Bunraku puppetry. Bunraku is a stylized form of puppetry dating back to 16th-century Japan. Three people dressed in black operate a doll-like puppet more than three feet in height. Both puppeteers and the puppet are in full view of the audience.

'Paris Is Out' Comedy to Open Friday

"Paris Is Out," a comedy by Richard Seff, will open Friday at the Festival Playhouse, 5665 Wadsworth Blvd. The play will be staged at 8 p.m. Fridays and Saturdays through Feb. 4. Faye Jones is directing. For ticket information, call 421-7256 or 424-3429.

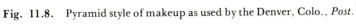
Fig. 11.8. Pyramid style of makeup as used by the Denver, Colo., *Post.*

names of towns in the area and the number of trade outlets in each town; the number of light meters, telephones, and automobiles licensed; volume of retail and wholesale trade; chief manufacturing firms; educational institutions; form of city government; miles of paved streets; value of bank deposits; and other facts that will acquaint the advertiser with the area.

2. A route list of the business places that might stock the advertiser's goods. This enables the salesperson to call upon the outlets in advance of the advertising campaign to acquaint merchants with the advertising and sales effort that is about to take place.

3. A check of stores in the area to see how many stock the item to be advertised. Often the advertiser wants the newspaper to find out the number of packages of the item already in stock. It is vital that stores have enough of the advertised article to meet public demand.

4. A personal call on the merchants by representatives of the newspaper's advertising department or a letter advising them of the nature of the advertising campaign, when it is to start and how long it will continue, and suggesting ways in which the merchants may cooperate through counter and window displays.

5. Delivery of advertising proofs to merchants who handle the item. These proofs usually are posted in display windows or on cards for counter displays.

Agencies are anxious to get all the help they can in merchandising the articles they advertise, and it is to the newspaper's advantage to cooperate within reason and means. The nature and extent of information that agencies would like to receive is indicated by the head of media for the J. Walter Thompson Agency:

How much does it cost people to live in your town and are *you* more of a factor in cheaper rental areas or in more expensive *owned* homes? What about your readers outside your city; in some cases a high proportion of your readers are villagers, suburbanites, or farmers . . . how important is each group? The space buyer is interested in *people* because it is people who buy our goods. Try to turn your *market* into *people* for us!

We are interested in the racial background of your population, both as far as more recently arrived foreign elements are concerned, and in terms of older national heritages of your readers. Such information *humanizes* facts.

If you are so fortunately organized as to be able to do trade checks for us . . . whose results you and we will be really sure of . . . let us hear about it. And set up definite standards as to how you are prepared to go in this direction. Sometimes a detailed trade check is not necessary. If you have contacts with local distributors, a few good interviews at this high level can yield very worthwhile market facts . . . of interest to us, and sometimes tangibly resultful to you.

We would like to know what you are prepared to give us in the way of merchandising help . . . how far you are prepared to go in making sure that the advertiser's printed message will pay off? Can we take it for granted that when an advertising campaign appears in your paper you will follow through a step beyond that, and make sure that the dealer will act upon the campaign, or at least be advised of it?

We would like to feel sure that position request will be watched. . . . The type of advertising and editorial adjacent to our newspaper advertisement is most important to the value of that advertisement in selling the product.

What all space buyers would like to see is a reasonable attitude on the part of newspapers toward publicity. The attitude of the agency is that sending out those free items constitutes a necessary, often important service that has to be performed for the advertiser, and one that will *benefit* the advertiser. We hope you can keep an open mind on it, as we try to do.

The Greensburg, Pa., *Tribune-Review* found that one-third of the small retailers in the average city never advertise. It then designed a specialized 52-week campaign directed toward garden shops, men's hair stylists, florists, travel agencies, jewelers, trade schools, women's boutiques, and similar nonadvertisers. The campaign was pretested and then sold with the added incentive of two feature-story writeups a year on each business signing up for the complete package. The newspaper's total advertising volume was substantially increased by this strategy of point-of-sale concentration.

Obtaining dealer cooperation

Besides servicing general advertisers, the newspaper may do much to obtain cooperation from local merchants that will make their advertising more effective.

Large department stores receive added results when they display tear sheets of their ads on store bulletin boards, on counters, and in windows to attract the attention of prospective buyers and to keep store clerks informed. Newspapers in some cities assist merchants and draw benefits to themselves by providing page-sized display cards with the inscription "As Advertised in the (name of paper)."

Great advantage comes from acquainting employes with the store's advertising. A department store owner instilled the sales force with enthusiasm and gave them a better understanding of their relation to the business at a session where the advertising manager of the home newspaper told them how they could cooperate with the store's advertising. The employes were also told that in reality they were members of the store's advertising department, that without the trained judgment and skill of the store's buyers in sensing bargains there would be no special values to advertise, and that without capable and affable clerks to wait on the trade the store's advertising would be wasted.

Some publishers feel they should protect the local merchants by refusing advertising from merchants in competing towns. The problem of competition, however, is one for the merchant to solve and no amount of sacrifice of revenue on the part of the newspaper will hold business for a merchant who refuses to meet competition. It is practically impossible to protect local merchants when the mail brings in handbills, daily newspapers, and postcard advertising and when local residents listen to advertisements on radio and television. The general economy is based on honest competition.

Lottery advertising, prohibited in newspapers by postal regulations and by some state laws, springs up occasionally to bring about minor strained relations between a newspaper and its advertising merchants. Giving away attractive articles by chance to bring people to town and to stores is a common practice in many communities. Advertising is essential to the success of such a venture and the newspaper is expected to "put it over" in a big way. A publisher is forced to explain that such advertising might cause the newspaper to lose its rights to use of the mails and to run afoul of state laws. Moreover, it can be stressed that such methods of drawing trade are likely to be interpreted as ready admission that the merchants' goods will not sell on their merits alone.

Coupons are one of the most effective ways the advertiser can obtain predictable response to his messages to the public. More than 35 billion coupons are distributed each year to prospective customers, and newspapers provide three-fourths of the total volume of coupon trade.

Another way to involve the dealer, and the reader as well, is the "iron-on" technique. With ROP color, any newspaper can use this process by which material is printed in the advertisement for removal and transfer to T-shirts or other surfaces. The material is simply clipped out of the ad, placed face down, and a hot iron applied. The merchandising possibilities for advertisers are readily obvious.

The attitude of management has to be one that embraces the outlook of both advertisers and readers and utilizes every creative opportunity to stimulate the healthy flow of goods and services and ideas from producers to consumers.

Efficient handling of orders, proofs, and records

Sometimes the goodwill of advertisers is lost and the power of advertising is diminished by careless handling of orders in the advertising department. Agencies naturally complain when ads are run on dates not authorized.

When the advertising manager makes out the daily or weekly ad sheet for the makeup personnel, showing the title, size, and position of all the ads to go in the issue, a recheck should be made to see that all details are correct and understandable. The form generally used calls for the name of the advertiser, the guidelines of the advertisement, the column width of the ad, the depth in inches, the total space, the position, whether or not the ad is to be held for a repeat insertion, and the total charge to be made (Fig. 11.9). Each column of the form should be filled in. If, for example, the guideline is omitted, makeup personnel might have difficulty in identifying the ad or might place a wrong ad in the paper.

Each advertising salesperson helps to keep clients satisfied by seeing that copy is well prepared and the instructions to the composing room con-

DAILY AD SHEET   DATE

Advertiser	Guide Line	Size	Inches	Total Space	Position	Hold	Charge	X ,

Fig. 11.9.   Daily ad sheet.

cerning its setup are plain. The advertising department helps its sales staff to be accurate by furnishing them with large copy envelopes with instructions on the outside or with small instruction forms to be attached to the copy.

To avoid errors in statements to general advertisers and to facilitate handling accounts, charges for such advertising should be entered on a form showing the name of the advertiser, the agency handling the account, the lines inserted on each day of the month, the total number of lines, and the rate and total amount of each account (Fig. 11.10). This gives the advertising department and the accountant a full picture of the month's business in national (general) advertising, and from this monthly record, statements can be made for each of the advertisers.

To determine who is handling certain accounts, who is servicing the most accounts, who is selling the most space, and who may be responsible for any errors in copy or copy instructions, each advertising salesperson in most newspaper offices is required at the end of each day to fill in a solicitor's daily call sheet (Fig. 11.11).

Larger newspapers, like the Miami, Fla., *Herald,* depend entirely on computerized technology for most of the record keeping involved in display advertising. At the *Herald,* the procedure is based primarily on two concepts: posting of linage prior to the day advertising appears in the newspaper (multiple insertion orders are handled as separate transactions) and tight credit controls, which still provide flexibility of operation. Under the present policy, filling is based upon what actually appears in the newspaper, not what is ordered. Nevertheless, a study of statistics in this area indicated a very small percentage of difference between the ordered size of an ad and its actual size.

DAILY NATIONAL CHARGES
THE INDEPENDENCE EXAMINER

MONTH OF _____ 19 ____

ADVERTISER	AGENCY	1	2	3	4	5	6	7	8	9	10	11	12	13	14	15	16	17	18	19	20	21	22	23	24	25	26	27	28	29	30	31	TOTAL INCHES OR LINES	RATE	AMOUNT

Fig. 11.10.   General (national) advertising charge sheet.

Advertising Solicitor's Daily Call Sheet

Salesman ....   Date ....

Account	Ad Size	Insertion Date	Remarks

Fig. 11.11. Solicitor's daily call sheet.

Therefore, information on transactions is entered into the system the day before the paper is issued. This allows more flexibility and time to make credit decisions, ensures prompt billing, and relieves the necessity of maintaining peak personnel requirements for measuring, marking, and posting all the linage after the paper is printed. Measuring and marking merely becomes a verification procedure for what has already been posted and is facilitated through the use of the linage transaction register (prepared during posting), listing each ad in sequence by page number assigned in the paper.

Corrections are marked on the register, punched in cards, and reentered into the system in a minimum amount of time on the same day the ad appears. Statistical reports and others are updated and prepared essentially as a by-product of processing these transactions.

Tight credit control is instituted by the system each day by applying rates and calculating extensions, rather than at the end of appropriate billing cycles. This provides a complete accounts receivable status of an account at any time. Each ad can then be referenced in a minimum time against a credit-risk file that contains delinquent accounts as well as items sent to collection agencies. Applications for credit, new contracts, or renewed contracts can be cross-referenced against all credit risks, including transient customers.

A highly advanced system is used by the Morristown, N.J., *Daily Record,* featuring a specially designed Goss Metrotext unit that interacts with a Harris 2200 ad-layout process. This procedure is described below.[1]

Inserting an ad in a newspaper is a multifaceted task that is not restricted to markup and typesetting, although these are formidable areas of concern. An ad must be entered, made up, scheduled for production, (possibly reviewed by the client and modified prior to production) inserted into the page master, printed in the paper, and billed to the client. It is all of these activities — ad entry through billing — that the Metrotext system is programmed to handle.

At Morristown, all display ads are treated as newspaper items. As an

1. The description of this system is excerpted from an article, Main Features of a Single Data Base System, *Editor & Publisher,* Aug. 23, 1975. Used by permission.

ad comes into the paper (even "slick") it is routed to the dispatch department. Here an insertion order is entered onto a form displayed on a Goss Image V terminal. This entry creates a production schedule and a billing master for each ad. The insertion order permits capture of all data pertinent to the ad. This includes the customer and billing identification, the ad size, proof requirements if any, insertion data, and a display ad classification number. By labeling with a classification similar to that used for classified ads, the system provides breakdowns on ad types such as national, local, split, white goods, automobile, grocery, bank, etc. In the future this facility will allow the sales department to do a quantitative check on all display advertising and linage.

When ads come in a form other than a "slick" they are normally accompanied with a layout text. After dispatch fills in the form on the VDT screen to capture the scheduling and billing information, they type the raw copy into blocks on the text portion of the form. Following a proof against the immediate source document, the ad is then released to the system. A production file by date is established, a billing master is created, and the appropriate market research data is posted onto the system disk file. At the same time, a slug-line report is generated as a makeup control index, and finally a paper tape of the copy labeled with a visual is sent to the 2200 markup machine along with a jacket containing the original dummy layout and source copy.

As the raw copy is called up on the screen, the markup operator, now relieved of the keyboarding task, attends to the direct problem of block layout with the appropriate markup commands. The Harris 2200 then produces a (second) tape output that goes directly to the Metrotext photocomposition area, again accompanied by the job folder. Here the type is set and the layout is made complete with any additional camera work that may be required. Once the ad is completed, it is returned with the job folder to the dispatch area. If a proof is required, the system has automatically, at entry, created a special file to remind the supervisor to send out proofs at a certain time to expedite finishing the ad in time for insertion into the paper.

Finally, at Morristown, if an ad proof comes back with corrections, all the data necessary to reconstruct the ad on the screen is at hand in the job folder. With the tape the job may be called back to the screen and appropriate changes made. Thus in one integrated system, paper size is monitored for current or existing data, a bill is cut, production is scheduled, markup and text errors are minimized and an auxiliary data file is set up to capture market statistics.

Mailing checking copies or proof sheets to advertisers is essential in the processing of accounts through advertising agencies. When these are not provided, there is bound to be a delay in the payment of the account involved. Unless some person in the office is definitely assigned to look after this detail, there is likely to be complaint. Many newspapers engage the services of a checking bureau to provide checking copies for all their advertisers. This seems to be the most satisfactory way.

Making a fair charge for advertising

Years ago, before business fully realized the value of advertising, the rate charged had a strong bearing on the volume carried by the newspaper. Now the rate charged is not as great an influence on volume as the service given by the newspaper and the results obtained from the advertising. The merchant today measures the dollar spent for advertising on the basis of the increased sales it produces rather than upon the amount of money paid for an inch or line of newspaper space.

The accustomed standard for rate setting heretofore has been the newspaper's circulation, but the business public is beginning to realize that something more than paid subscribers determines the value of a newspaper as an advertising medium.

Some businesses give better service to their customers than others. They provide attractive lounges and rest rooms, maintain a special delivery and mailing service, and listen to complaints and make adjustments when merchandise does not come up to the proper standards. Because of these services they tend to receive a higher percentage of profit. Customers do not object to prices because they appreciate the special service. Good newspapers also give special services to their customers. Subscribers and advertisers are provided idea mats, attractive display type and illustrations, special features, and valuable assistance in preparing copy. Special consideration is given to advertisers' ideas and requests, so they may realize more from their advertising.

When a newspaper buys a press or a phototypesetting machine that sets better display lines, it helps to make a stronger newspaper that prints more effective advertisements. When a newspaper employs qualified people who understand how to write effective copy and plan productive campaigns, it benefits the advertiser. When a publisher continually strives to improve the service to the advertiser and is more interested in adding equipment than in producing profits and dividends, a better advertising medium is provided to the merchants. The progressive newspaper publisher fixes advertising rates at a level that will make these improvements possible.

One of the most perplexing situations facing newspapers and advertisers alike is the multitude of sizes and formats resulting from the sudden changes in production methods. The shift from letterpress to offset printing and the conversion from mechanical typesetting to electronic photocomposition, described in earlier chapters, has precipitated a confusion of dimensions. This in turn has had an effect on advertising charging practices.

Otto A. Silha, president of the Minneapolis, Minn., Star and Tribune Company, told a group of publishers, "A recent compilation shows that 976 newspapers with eight-column makeup publish 87 different formats and 40 sizes. One hundred and fifty newspapers with six-column makeup use 47 different formats and 32 sizes. Eighty newspapers with nine-column makeup use 24 different formats and 19 sizes." Silha is leading a national drive toward uniformity and standardization through such organizations as the American Newspaper Publishers Association and the International Newspaper Advertising Executives Association.

By agreeing upon advertising dimension standards (ADS), newspapers representing 95 percent of the daily circulations in the United States and Canada have made great progress toward the solution of the format problem. A special format committee working with the Newspaper Advertising Bureau has promoted ADS codes and symbols to simplify communication among advertisers, agencies, and newspapers. "The problem of formatting," Silha said, "reflects the fast pace of change in our very exciting business. . . . These advertising standards will make our medium easier for our customers to use, adding convenience to [advertising] results."

Commenting on the changes in dimensions, James F. Boynton, manager of J. C. Penney's media planning, observed that "newspapers have been the prime mover of our business for 70 years and still represent the backbone of our advertising effort. . . . The recent changes in column widths, source of continuing discussion in the advertising industry, weigh heavily on a retailer like J. C. Penney." He added that newspapers would "all be better off if they could inject a big dose of standardization into their scheme of things." Apparently, the medicine has already been applied and is bringing about the desired results.

Newspapers are confronted with fair charging for advertising services in many other areas. Discounts for camera-ready advertising copy are regarded with caution by most publishers because the rate structure is based on basic costs, and it is questionable whether camera-ready copy from a few advertisers will affect those costs. Actually, many newspapers prefer that ads be prepared entirely within the plant, so that control can be exercised over conflicting type styles and specifications, and argue that merchants who submit camera-ready copy enjoy options and variations not available to the majority of advertisers. Some even feel that these special privileges deserve an additional charge.

Other factors involved in arriving at reasonable charges include position within the newspaper, proofing service, advertising deadlines, follow-up service, reproduction quality, and billing policy. Management is compelled to weigh all such matters conscientiously and fairly to maintain an advertising rate structure it can live with.

Increasing display advertising volume

The following suggestions for building display advertising volume are gleaned from the experiences of successful advertising salespeople:

1. Find out the date a merchant started in business and annually prepare a suitable anniversary advertisement.

2. The anniversaries of organizations are good for congratulatory ads each year from local citizens, for example, Boy Scouts, Girl Scouts, Camp Fire Girls, and the American Legion.

3. Make use of pictures of local merchants, their employes, and their stores in newspaper advertising.

4. Encourage merchants to time their ads for best results. Start Easter and Christmas advertising early so that the buying season may be prolonged.

5. Be quick to welcome any new business coming to the community. A personal letter followed by a visit from the publisher makes a helpful contact between the newspaper and the merchant.

6. Feature merchants who have been in business 25 or more years with ads and stories in a special section of the newspaper.

7. A department store may effectively honor a long-time employe by having him sponsor a storewide sale.

8. To stimulate Monday retail sales, each week in the Saturday issue run a page of "Shop on Monday" ads for local merchants.

9. Sell insurance firms a full-page cooperative advertisement to be run whenever there is a disastrous fire in the community. This should stress the importance of being fully insured.

10. Sell churches a section in the Saturday issue to advertise their Sunday services.

11. Point out to the city administration the value of publishing the city's annual statement in a full-page space rather than as a legal advertisement in small type.

12. Make the annual report of Chamber of Commerce or Downtown Association activities the basis of a special section, setting forth in news and advertising the business and industrial developments of the preceding year.

13. Prepare a series of full-page ads on the advantages of reliable plumbing and sell it to the plumbing firms, carrying their names, addresses, and telephone numbers at the bottom of the ad.

14. Follow regularly suggestions provided by the Bureau of Advertising.

15. Sell a series of full-page cooperative ads to banks, commemorating Thrift Week, Christmas, Thanksgiving, Commencement, Labor Day, and other special days and weeks.

16. A few weeks before the opening of school, sell ads to local bookstores that carry books that students use.

17. Run a sponsored "Welcome Page" whenever a convention is held in your city.

18. Start a "Home Building Page" in January and run it weekly throughout the spring building season.

19. Encourage farm boys and girls by putting out an annual 4-H Club edition. Let merchants feature in their ads the prize-winning livestock or grain produced by club members and congratulate youth on their achievements.

20. A few items out of "Fifty Years Ago" make an attractive attention-getting feature for a bank's weekly ad.

21. Sell automobile dealers a series of cooperative ads on safety to be run preceding school opening in the fall and on the days preceding holidays.

22. Pay advertising personnel a bonus on all advertising sold above a certain volume during the year. One paper paid a flat bonus of $50 to each person for 10,000 column inches and $50 more for each additional 1,000 column inches.

23. Hold monthly dinner meetings for the newspaper's advertising sales force and salespeople of manufacturing and distributing firms who live in and serve the community.

24. Conduct an advertising clinic for advertising personnel of local business firms.

25. Make use of the various advertising booklets put out by manufacturers. These contain descriptive phrases, headlines, copy, and layout suggestions for advertising.

12

Building classified advertising

Classified pages may look gray, but they
are gold.

Robert Witte

The classified advertising pages are strong
revenue-producing areas of a newspaper and growth is almost limitless.
These little ads, piled up in convenient alphabetical arrangement and
classified according to the needs they answer, contain an abundance of interest for readers and provide astonishing results for advertisers.
"Classifieds" produce one-fourth of the total advertising revenue for the
newspaper. At the same time they are vigorous builders of readership, thus
contributing to circulation income.

Emphasizing the extreme importance of a good classified advertising
section, Stan Finsness of the Providence, R.I., *Journal* says, "Here is revenue worth protecting and enhancing. It isn't peanuts. Every newspaper
should have on its advertising staff people who can improve the productivity and profitability of classified advertising. Some of those ads in the back
of the paper are pretty small, but there are lots of them. And they do add
up."

Close to a billion dollars are spent each year by the American public
for classified advertising. Some daily newspapers carry more than a million
lines of classified per year, almost 25 percent of total advertising linage.

The term "linage" has the same meaning for all advertising—the
number of lines of agate or 5½ point type required to fill the space occupied by the advertising. Not all newspapers set their classified ads in
agate type. Other sizes are 5, 6, 7, and 8 point, normally set solid (on a slug
of the same point size) with little spacing between.

A survey conducted among 100 persons attending an Ohio newspaper
classified clinic from all sections of the state showed that more than 26
million classified ads were placed annually in Ohio newspapers, or nearly
nine per family or business firm as an average. This indicates the
significance of classifieds in the everyday lives of newspaper readers.

READER INTEREST

That the classified pages of a newspaper have reader interest is evident to anyone who sells newspapers on the street or sells subscriptions by

house-to-house calls. Often when a prospect expresses no interest in the local news, the world news, comics, pictures, and sports, he or she may buy a copy or subscribe for a period of time when shown the paper's volume of classified ads. The classified section has *news* to interest readers as well as *values* to interest buyers.

History has been written in classified ads from colonial days to the present. George Washington sold lands he held along the Ohio River with want ads. Benjamin Franklin placed a classified ad when someone took his wife's prayer book from the family church pew. President Thomas Jefferson obtained someone to fill the position of Secretary of the Navy with a classified ad. Dr. Samuel Johnson, the first president of Columbia University, ran a want ad in the New York *Gazette* or *Weekly Post-Boy* to announce he was about to "set up a course of tuition in the new school house adjoining Trinity Church." Sir Ernest Shackleton ran a classified ad in 1900 to seek companions for his hazardous North Pole expedition. These historical facts appeared in editorials in the Tacoma, Wash., *News-Tribune* and in the Jacksonville, Fla., *Florida Times-Union* in recognition of the 250th anniversary of classified advertising in this country.

Of all the material in the newspaper, classified was checked as "most helpful and useful in everyday work and activities" by 172 persons of 652 queried in a readership survey for the Louisville, Ky., *Courier-Journal* and *Times.* The 652 respondents checked their frequency of reading the section as follows: almost always, 31 percent; usually, 20.2 percent; sometimes, 24.7 percent — a total of 75.9 percent that read classified with some frequency. In a similar survey for the Milwaukee, Wis., *Journal,* 28 percent of all men and 29 percent of all women queried said they read the want ads every day.

Classified in weekly papers is as closely read as in dailies. A typical example is the *Plain Dealer* in St. James, Minn. A Readex reader-interest survey showed that the classified page of the *Courier* was read by 74 percent of the men and 79 percent of the women and that no other, including the front page, had as high a readership.

BUYER INTEREST

While many persons read the classified advertisements for the interesting news they contain, many more read them for the opportunities they provide to buy, sell, trade, find, lease, or lend. They are indeed a marketplace where many human needs are met.

A typical classified section offers for sale such widely diverse items as used and new furniture, automobiles and trucks, trailer homes, garden produce, real estate, grain, livestock, household appliances, sporting goods, photographic equipment, musical instruments, farm equipment, building supplies, fuel, feed, and scores of other articles. Owners advertise for lost items and strayed pets, landlords offer houses for rent, employers advertise job opportunities, finance companies offer to lend money. Only on the classified pages is such a wide variety of goods and services handled so efficiently and economically.

Traditional leaders in the classified pages are real estate, merchandise, automotive, and employment advertising. Research conducted by the National Advertising Bureau indicates that people who move from one home to another are major buyers of appliances and furniture—82 percent make such purchases. Whether bought new from dealers or secondhand from other individuals, an enormous volume of this merchandise is moved by means of classified advertising.

CLASSIFIEDS BRING RESULTS

Most newspapers carry a large volume of classified advertising because of the results obtained for advertisers. Newspapers are literally flooded with testimonials from classified users. The San Antonio, Tex., *Express* and *News* carries streamer lines almost daily at the top of classified pages containing enthusiastic testimonials. Typical examples are:

"GREATEST HELP IN MY BUSINESS," REALTOR JIMMY WARD SAYS, "I make more contacts at a minimum cost."
"RESULTS BEFORE NOON—CALLS WOKE US UP BEFORE BREAKFAST" said annoyed but happy advertiser when she cancelled ad.
C. D. SHOCKLEY SAYS: "I SURE DID SELL MY CAR—ON 2ND DAY." Had 7-time order. Cost only $2.10 in *Express* and *News.*
HOW QUICK CAN THE EXPRESS-NEWS SELL LIVESTOCK? A. N. Langston sold cows, calves, pigs first day ad appeared.
15 CALLS ON HOUSE ADVERTISED IN EXPRESS-NEWS. Sold home in 2 days—"Splendid results," says realtor.
2 ADS—2 CARS SOLD—1 DAY—EXPRESS-NEWS WANT AD. "It just shows people really read the *Express-News*"—Mrs. Parrish.

The Houston, Tex., *Chronicle* regularly uses a 6-inch column space in which to feature result stories similar to the one below:

DACHSHUND PUPPIES
Purebred, very fine litter, $150. Males, females, 665-3619.

Mrs. T. B. Peebles, 3612 Carnegie, who raises Dachshund puppies, ran the above ad in the *Chronicle.* She sold five of the six puppies right away.

A farm equipment dealer at Longmont, Colo., regularly runs in the Denver *Post* such ads as that shown below. The dealer wrote the *Post:* "I have estimated that my advertisements in the Denver *Post* the past five years have sold well over one million dollars worth of top quality farm equipment in seven Rocky Mountain Empire states."

```
┌─────────────────────────────────────────────────────────────┐
│                     FOR SALE—ON HAND                          │
│                                                               │
│  J. D. and OLIVER wire—$9.65. Ready-made teeth for your Farm- │
│  hand stacker $2. New Farmhand pumps, $50. New Farmhand control│
│  valves, $25. New Farmhand loaders, complete, $475. New Farmhand│
│  hay sweeps, $75. New Liberty grain blowers, $50. Like new offset│
│  disc, $100.                                                  │
│                     Safe—Cord Twine                           │
│         Baler—$8.50              Binder—$9.50                 │
│                                                               │
│         NORM STAMP OF LONGMONT                                │
│                                                               │
│         You name it—We'll furnish it to you—                 │
│                 At a lot less money.                          │
└─────────────────────────────────────────────────────────────┘
```

A hardware merchant found the classified columns of the Akron, Ohio, *Beacon-Journal* to be an effective means of selling a wide variety of merchandise. He told the classified advertising manager that he sold 48 Lyman boats and an even greater number of motors and lesser pieces of marine equipment as a result of the ad below and another of the same size, both costing $10.08:

```
┌─────────────────────────────────────────────────┐
│                    EVINRUDE                       │
│                 Outboard Motors                   │
│                     LYMAN                         │
│             Inboards and Outboards                │
│                  SCOTTY CRAFT                      │
│             Sport Cruiser, Sleeps Two             │
│                   STERLING                        │
│                  Boat Trailers                    │
│               MARINE SUPPLIES                     │
│                                                   │
│                Hibbard Hardware                   │
│                124 Portage Trail                  │
│      928-1181          Evenings, 864-6432        │
└─────────────────────────────────────────────────┘
```

Classifieds have a peculiar power to sell even outmoded merchandise in competition with, for example, modern air-conditioning. At the Illinois state capital the following 7-line classified ad, costing $4.34, in the Springfield, Ill., *State Journal* and *Register* sold $2,439 worth of window fans the first day the ad appeared, according to a report from the store manager to the classified advertising manager:

```
┌─────────────────────────┐
│    20" WINDOW FANS      │
│   3-Speed Reversible    │
│        No Belts         │
│       No Pulleys        │
│        $81.95           │
│    Montgomery Ward      │
│     508 East Adams      │
└─────────────────────────┘
```

These remarkable results are the rule, not the exception, in every section of the United States. Classifieds are truly the "little wonders" of newspaper advertising. (See Fig. 12.1.)

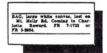

Fig. 12.1. The Charlotte, N.C., *Observer* calls attention to quick service by classified ads.

METHODS OF PRICING

Three methods are commonly used to price classified advertising — count line rate, agate line or space rate, and word rate. Most classified advertising that is set solid is sold by the "count line," meaning the advertiser pays a specified price for each line actually appearing in the newspaper. Ads with large headlines, space between lines, and other display effects usually are sold at an agate line rate or a space rate (number of column inches occupied by the advertisement). Some papers, partly to avoid confusion over count lines and agate lines, sell their classified by the word. Still others have a combination of word count and agate line or space rate, using a word count for the first seven lines and then measuring the rest of the ad to apply space rate.

There are advantages and disadvantages to each pricing system. The main ones are:

ADVANTAGES	DISADVANTAGES

Count Line Rate

ADVANTAGES	DISADVANTAGES
1. Higher average revenue per page is possible.	1. Hard to estimate in advance the number of lines ad will set and the price to be charged.
2. Waste space is reduced.	
3. Handling and billing are more economical.	2. Greater opportunity for advertiser to be confused and to complain when statement is issued.
4. Makes advertiser less price conscious.	3. Greater tendency to abbreviate ad and make it unintelligible.

Agate Line or Space Rate

ADVANTAGES	DISADVANTAGES
1. Advertiser pays for all space used.	1. Encourages display classified which mars the page.
2. Better understood by heavy advertisers, who also buy display advertising.	2. Puts classified in the same category as display advertising in the minds of users.
3. Preferred by advertising agencies in placing orders for national advertisers.	3. Likely to bring a variety of type sizes to classified page.
4. Cost estimated and charge entered more rapidly.	4. Usually permits use of cuts and logotypes, which deprive page of classified uniformity.

Word Rate

ADVANTAGES	DISADVANTAGES
1. Makes it easy for advertiser to compute accurate cost in advance.	1. One, two, and three words in last line represent only partially paid space.
2. No tendency to use vague abbreviations.	2. Reduces number of ads to the column.
3. Inspires public approval through greater convenience, economy, and readability.	3. Encourages the use of long, descriptive words.
4. Protects integrity of newspaper's rate card by eliminating danger of cost discrimination.	4. Much time is required in estimating costs and entering charges.

Three general terms describe the kind of classified advertising sold: transient, contract, and display.

Transient classifieds are inserted at no regular intervals or in no consecutive order. They come from persons who may never again use the classified columns or who may insert a different kind of classified ad a week or a year later. Such ads are here today and gone tomorrow, but they comprise a great proportion of the classified volume.

Contract classifieds are ads placed under contract to insert so many lines each day or at regular intervals during a year or lesser period.

Display classified (or classified display) is advertising set in larger type than that ordinarily used on the classified page, often with considerable spacing between lines and with a border to attract special attention. Some newspapers allow classified display to be placed under its proper classification on the page, but others pyramid it at the right-hand corner or at both corners of the classified page, just as display advertising would be arranged on a news page.

OPERATION OF THE CLASSIFIED DEPARTMENT

The classified staff operates as a division of the advertising department, but it is separate from the crew that handles display advertising. Four main groups make up the classified department personnel: those who receive voluntary ads at the counter or by phone, telephone solicitors, outside salespeople, and clerks who solicit by correspondence.

As one publisher explains, a classified advertising manager must above all be aggressive and enthusiastic. The "CAM" must be ambitious, with ambitions tempered by tolerance and patience. The manager should have a complete knowledge of the classified advertising business and the many details and problems confronting employes and must be able to set standards of operation and production and to transmit a complete understanding of them to the staff. The CAM must be able to analyze and interpret the efforts and production of employes, be sympathetic and understanding, and be loyal to the company.

The need for adequate personnel

On a weekly and the smallest of daily newspapers, classified advertising may be handled by an employe who waits on the counter and keeps the records. Some ads will come in by telephone, but if the ads are sold on a cash-in-advance basis, practically all copy will be received over the counter. Even with no formal classified department, the alert publisher can build volume by encouraging the entire newspaper staff—reporters, ad salespeople, office and back shop employes, and country correspondents—to sell classifieds. It does not matter whether the encouragement takes the form of a commission or something else. The essential thing is for the staff to be classified minded.

Many small daily newspapers will have one employe whose sole responsibility is classified advertising. This person should train all office help to take and write ads either over the counter or by telephone, but most of the time will be spent in actual selling. The classified department of a metropolitan newspaper may employ from 50 to 150 persons, a large number working entirely by telephone. A switchboard operating exclusively for the department brings calls to groups of experienced ad takers, each group having a supervisor. One group handles advertising from real estate firms; another receives apartment and hotel business; another, home furnishings; another sporting goods, and so on.

Some employes do nothing but receive telephone ads that come in voluntarily; others spend their entire time soliciting ads by telephone from prospect lists. There also are ad takers and salespeople at counters to handle copy brought directly to the newspaper. Some newspapers employ individuals on a part-time or commission basis to sell ads by telephone from their homes.

Street salespeople in the classified department are organized on a territory plan similar to the system used for display personnel. They are assigned to a particular class of business or trade or a specified section of the business district.

In the telephone room of the Chicago, Ill., *Tribune* are 84 ad takers and solicitors, divided into three groups: voluntary ad takers, who handle incoming calls from advertisers placing orders for the first time and from those who advertise spasmodically; transient ad takers, who solicit reinsertions of orders, handle incoming calls, and solicit orders from customers who advertise frequently but do not use sufficient linage to warrant a yearly contract; and contract sales personnel, who handle all telephone orders for contract advertisers and cooperate with street salespeople.

Equipment in the *Tribune*'s telephone department is planned for maximum efficiency and comfort. Good lighting, comfortable desks and chairs, and convenient supplies are provided. Adjoining the department is a training room, where beginners are put through a rigorous course in telephone technique and sales language. The training program, all on tape recordings, covers classifications, censorship rules, rates, deadlines, type sizes, full-run circulation, blind ticket procedure, errors, tact in explaining censorship rules, selling voluntary ads, and soliciting transient ads. An instructor reminds each solicitor, old and new, that the job is to advise an advertiser, not just be a salesperson — to show the customer how to achieve best results.

On the Milwaukee, Wis., *Journal,* 22 full-time and 7 part-time ad takers and 16 outside salespeople handle 2 million ads a year. As an incentive to volume selling, the *Journal* has a "Column Club" and a "Page Club." As soon as an ad taker sells the equivalent of a column, he or she becomes a member of the "Column Club"; when a page of classifieds is sold, the employe receives a membership card in the "Page Club." A page is 2,400 agate lines, and selling classified ads to cover that space is a big job.

The San Jose, Calif., *Mercury* and *News,* which handles more than 2 million classified ads a year, has a staff of 72 persons, including some part-time help. The full-time complement includes 7 men and a sales manager on outside sales, 21 territory women and a supervisor, 4 operators on the 32-trunk PBX, 7 women in copy control, 2 on the mail desk, 3 at the front counter, 2 statisticians, and a secretary. There are 38 women on full time and 19 part-timers.

The Kansas City, Mo., *Star* has a staff of 90 in its classified department, 70 of whom are on full time and 20 who are part-time employes. Twenty-three of these are full-time classified ad salesmen. Twenty women sell by telephone.

The Wichita, Kans., *Eagle* and *Beacon* employs 20 women and 9 men as full-time classified advertising salesmen. Fourteen of these sell by telephone and three by mail. Thirty-eight people constitute the full classified staff.

New equipment reduces staff

Since the installation of a Compugraphic VideoSetter and Unified Composer at the Lynn, Mass., *Item,* replacing a century-old hot-metal system, classified ads are stored in the memory bank of the system's computer center. Setting 45 column inches of type per minute, the operator simply types the ad copy with appropriate coding onto a visual display screen. Any ad may be retrieved within seconds for corrections or deletions or other instructions, then returned to storage. By touching a key on the Compugraphic, any expired ad can be killed instantly and removed from the system's memory file.

The Miama, Fla., *Herald* has a unique system of processing classified advertising—called "integrated classified" because the mechanical and accounting functions have been combined. Classified ads are taken in the classified phone room, over the counter, by mail, and from outside sales staff. They are then typed on ad insertion orders by the solicitors, who fill in accounting information, consisting of the customer's telephone number (which becomes his account number), the date the ad is to run, the number of insertions, the classification under which it runs in the paper, and any special instructions. The text of the ad follows.

IBM Selectric typewriters are used in preparing these orders because the type is more legible and the order blank is designed specifically for this typewriter spacing to aid the ad taker in counting the number of lines. After the ad order is completed, it is sent to a copyreader, who ensures that it is complete and accurate and passes text censorship. Ads are then sent via pneumatic tube to the production department where the integration begins.

In the Teletypesetting (TTS) department, orders are manually block sorted into major classifications. Galleys of approximately ten ads are made up and sent via conveyor to TTS operators, who punch both accounting information and ad text into six-level paper tape, using the

Standard Fairchild TTS perforator. Computer instructions consist of dollar-sign codes preprinted on the ad order form. The operator starts at the top of the order, punching first a code, then the accounting information, another code, then the ad text, repeating this procedure throughout the ten ads.

When punching is completed, the tapes representing the ads are processed through the computer, an IBM 1620 equipped with six-level paper-tape readers and punches. The computer performs two valuable functions. First, it "picks off" and punches into cards all the accounting information; and, second, it justifies and hyphenates the text. The text is then punched out from the computer in six-level paper tape ready to be cast in type. While the computer is performing the typesetting function, it also counts actual linage for each ad and includes this count with the accounting information.

During the typesetting function the computer detects any jumbo type size used in the text. Jumbo here is defined as 14, 18, 24, or 36 point type size. The operator has only to punch the jumbo line once with a code to identify the size. The computer then sorts out these lines and sets them in boldface agate type. It also punches a separate tape for these lines in the actual size used. This tape is run on an automatic mixing linecaster where the jumbo type is set. The agate guidelines are then manually replaced by the jumbo type at a collation bank.

The type is galley proofed and orders are sent via conveyor to the proofreading room. Here proofreaders scan the ad text once more. Corrections are made and the type is sent to the classified makeup area where it is placed in page forms. Classified ads are not alphabetized within classification. New ads are simply placed at the bottom of each section.

Cards containing the accounting information are run into the 360 system, where the data is transferred onto a disk file. Since the *Herald* had a rather high classified advertising credit loss in Miami because of the community's transient nature, it became important to perform a credit check on each ad before the paper was printed.

In the computer is a disk file containing over 50,000 records determined as credit risks. These represent any advertisers who owe money and range from recent delinquent customers to bad-debt accounts. Each of these accounts is represented in detail, showing the customer's name, address, telephone number, and the dollar amount and description of each unpaid ad.

After typesetting and credit checking is completed each day, the computer merges accounting information for new ads into a file containing all ads running from the previous day. Thus a file of ads identical to ads running in the newspaper is contained in the computer. From this file a classified-page estimate report is run immediately after the last classified ad for the day is processed through the computer.

This ad estimate report shows the size of each classification in inches and is used by the classified makeup section to aid in laying out page forms. In addition to this service the computer also prints lists of ads to be canceled because of expiration. These are for sales department follow-up. This procedure has eliminated need for a carbon copy of the ad order in the classified department; reports provided directly by the computer are sufficient.

To satisfy the accounting portion of this system, the computer prints a bill for the customer when the ad expires, applies cash when ads are paid, and provides all required accounting reports. The computer also produces a complete array of sales-statistics reports for the classified department.

Newspapers using the Goss Metrotext system have special classified ad terminals operated by the ad takers and supervisors. As a call comes in, the ad taker keys the form onto the screen and fills in the appropriate blanks with customer name, phone number, text of the advertisement, and coded instructions for the printers. While the image remains on the screen, a transmit button relays the information to the main Metrotext processor, where credit files are checked. Within two to six seconds, the ad copy is on its way in digital form to a magnetic disk review library where it can be held until a final OK is signalled for the copy to be released for publication.

Once released, the ads are sorted into the appropriate classification and put into proper sequence (age, alphabet, key word, size, or some combination of these criteria). The text is then processed into a typesetter-ready output file in a background mode. The billing component of the form is separated from the text and the ad is then electronically stored in multiple input, output, billing and production scheduling files. At this time, linage estimates are available on demand by class, edition, or date.

At the close of the ad-entry cycle, the system is interrogated via a keyboard printer terminal in production control to ascertain the size of the day's paper. Statistics are available by class, column size, classification depth, and running depth totals. These statistics are transmitted from the centrally located computer to the production control terminal. The page makeup dummies are arranged and the various classified or display ads are spotted. The individual ad sections are then marked off and the displays are pyramided, and by assigning individual classifications to be set on either or both of two Metrotext phototypesetters, the individual ad sections then become output to the page makeup department in galley form.

Regardless of the degree of sophistication of production or the number of employes engaged in the handling of classified advertising, the basic principles of effective selling and servicing are of paramount importance to the operation. Prospects must be sought from the columns of other newspapers published in the area, from classifieds scheduled to expire, through direct mail and house advertising, or from a permanent file of former advertisers who should be contacted by telephone from time to time.

In other words, one of the cardinal qualities of a successful classified advertising manager is the ability to create an aggressive sales attitude within the department. An employe not instilled with a sense of enthusiasm, resourcefulness, curiosity, and dedication can be expected to produce the barest minimum essential to holding the job.

Where the classified department may not be as highly developed as on the metropolitan dailies, the newspaper would profit by observing the following guidelines as a means to building maximum volume:

1. Maintenance of a separate sales force consisting of at least a sales manager and a staff of three persons.
2. Complete autonomy of the department so that the sales manager is responsible directly to the publisher, unless the newspaper has a director of advertising who is not antagonistic to classified.
3. Higher net cost per line or column inch for classified than the net local display rates for equivalent space and conditions.
4. A strictly competitive relationship between local display and classified.
5. Unlimited credit to transient classified advertisers.
6. A devout belief that transient volume is the key to classified reading habits of the public (which is itself the greatest selling point a classified ad department can have) and, therefore, the key to all the results.

Factors affecting results

There is more to building a strong classified section than merely selling ads. What is done with the ads after they are sold and brought into the office is as vital as what takes place during the selling.

The advertisers who receive satisfactory results will continue to advertise. The kind of results they obtain depends on the attractiveness of the classified section, the explicitness and sincerity of the ads, and the convenience provided readers in finding the articles they wish to buy or the services they wish to engage. In other words, the pulling power of a classified advertising section depends greatly upon its typography, the kind of copy, and the arrangement of the classifications.

Other factors affecting results, but having more to do with volume and revenue perhaps, are the rates charged for classified advertising and credit privileges.

Typography. It must be remembered that the classified section of a newspaper was not meant to be a *display* of offerings but rather a *catalog* of values and services available to the community. It sometimes is difficult for a classified salesperson to make this understood if a merchant is accustomed to displaying items, prices, and names in advertising. Some classified managers and publishers have yielded to this pressure and have granted classified patrons the privilege of using display in their advertising, at least to a limited degree.

Most metropolitan newspapers and some smaller newspapers hold tenaciously to the theory that the classified section should be just what its name says it is: that everything should be done typographically to make classifications stand out; but pictures, headlines in heavy black type, and logotypes should not be used because they subordinate the classification headlines. The Seattle, Wash., *Post-Intelligencer* illustrates this theory (Fig. 12.2).

Some newspapers do not permit display advertising on their classified pages. All ads are confined to single-column width. Headlines in open-face type are permitted but no black type. If classified display advertisements are allowed, they are placed in pyramid makeup style at the lower right-hand corner of the page.

Not all publishers, however, are convinced that the classified section must be devoid of display. The Knoxville, Tenn., *News-Sentinel* has lifted all restrictions as to size of ad, except that is has to be as many inches deep as it is columns wide. All types of cuts and borders are allowed. "We admit that our classified page is not as clean, neat, and uncluttered as before, but it is bigger," says the newspaper's classified advertising manager. "We have not had one complaint and our sales force is very enthusiastic about the change."

Regardless of the different views of publishers, the fact remains that the foundation of a newspaper's classified section is the large volume of small ads set in small type and arranged alphabetically under bold classification headings. Such an arrangement, uninterrupted by display, provides convenience and facility for the reader. It is most likely, however, that a newspaper's classified section will be built to suit the characteristics of the market, particular situations, the relative position of the newspaper in its field, and the established habits of readers and advertisers. The classified pages of American newspapers appear with a variety of type sizes, column rules, and column widths.

The selection of a body type depends upon whether the newspaper wants to compress as much copy as possible into each column without sacrificing readability or creating mechanical complications or whether it prefers to provide maximum readability without too much concern about the space consumed. The newspaper may wish to create an illusion of large volume by using a fairly large type size set on a base that provides spacing between lines. The style and size of type used for classification headings is largely a matter of taste, but on a page full of display types, such headings would need to be heavier than on a page of light typography. There should be sufficient contrast between classification heads and the ad body type to make them easily discernible.

Rules used to separate columns and cutoff rules between ads are usually a hairline face cast on a 1 point to 6 point base. The 4 point and 6 point bases are the commonly accepted standards for column rules. Most newspapers use either a 1 point or a 2 point cutoff rule.

Until a few years ago the standard classified page contained eight columns. Now many newspapers are setting nine and ten columns to the classified page, while continuing to use a different standard throughout the rest of the paper. This achieves economy in newsprint and provides greater revenue from a smaller number of classified pages.

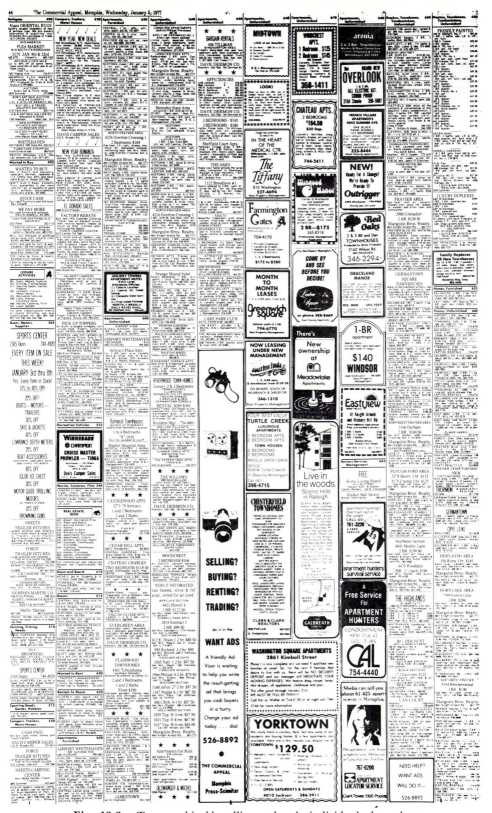

Fig. 12.2. Typographical handling makes the individual ad stand out.

The need for compression into narrower columns has been challenged by the so-called recruitment advertising agencies, which claim that classified deserves to be in larger type because of its high readership value. At any rate, the management is responsible for determining its own specifications for the dimensions of the classified pages.

To break the monotony of uniform setup and to promote the services of the classified section, a banner line may be carried at the top of the page. This generally calls attention to a classification containing items with outstanding appeal, to some service given by the department, or to a linage volume record. Some papers dress up the page with a comic strip or a two-column box containing a result story or a suggestion as to how the classified department may serve readers' wants.

Copy. The classified ad taker probably has one of the most difficult copy-writing jobs on the newspaper. It is relatively simple to write good display copy when words are not limited and illustrations can be used; but putting pull and power into telegram-terse copy, as the classified ad writer is called upon to do, is a different matter.

A classified ad must be concise, complete, and convincing. It must say much in a few very choice words. It should describe clearly the article to be sold. It should convince the prospective buyer of the article's value and that *now* is the time to buy. The following twelve guideposts have been recommended for the writing of a good classified ad:

1. Determine the purpose of the ad.
2. Get the facts.
3. Write without hindrance or restraint.
4. Select words carefully.
5. Use a simple style.
6. State the advantages of what is offered.
7. Appeal to the emotions.
8. Capture the reader's attention and hold it.
9. Make the ad believable.
10. State the price.
11. Create desire.
12. Urge the reader to buy.

An apt choice of words can provide tremendous leverage for obtaining response. The classic example is that of the two blind beggars—one wearing a sign stating "I am blind," the other displaying a sign saying "It is spring, and I am blind." Which do you suppose collected more donations from those who passed by?

The tendency of most transient classified ad customers is to use as few words as possible and thereby cut down the cost of the ad. By doing so, they deprive the advertisement of information, attractiveness, and pulling power. A convincing example is provided by the homeowner who received a position in another town and wanted to sell his property quickly. He inserted this ad in the hometown newspaper, expecting to dispose of the property within a day or so:

> PRIVATE OWNER, 6-room, 3-year-
> old ranch type house, west section, gas
> heat, insulated, large lot.
> Call 445-8473

Four persons called by phone for further details but none came to look at the property. The owner went back to the newspaper and explained that he had received no satisfactory results and wondered why. Together he and an ad taker at the classified counter worked out the following copy to run for three succeeding days:

> WANTED AT ONCE
> A NEW OWNER
> FOR MY ATTRACTIVE
> ALMOST NEW
> RANCH TYPE HOME
> IN CHOICE WEST SECTION
>
> It makes me weep, but it can't be helped; have position elsewhere and must move; 6 rooms, including living room, 12x24, with fireplace; dining room, cozy breakfast nook, three bedrooms; large basement that may be converted into ideal family room; insulated; air conditioned; forced-air gas heat; warm in winter, cool in summer; lot, 100x180, with abundance of shade; $50,000 if taken by July 30. Terms. See it today at 1844 Hamilton Way, or Phone 445-8473.

Before the end of the day the ad appeared the owner had received 15 telephone calls and 4 persons came to see the home. The second person to look at the home bought it.

The striking difference in response is readily understood by the difference in the two pieces of ad copy. The first ad gave an incomplete and not too interesting picture of the property; it in no way reflected the eagerness of the owner to sell or the necessity of the prospective buyer to act quickly. The second ad described the home in simple, understandable, and enthusiastic language—an ad that captured the attention of the reader and held it. The description of the property and the price created a desire for ownership, and the reasons for selling brought immediate action.

The Dayton, Ohio, *Daily News* and *Journal-Herald* believes that the best way to write copy is to keep in mind at all times the term A-I-D-A. The first "A" stands for attention; the "I," interest; the "D," desire; and the last "A," action.

Ad takers and classified sales personnel are doing much to educate the public to use copy that will produce results. Pamphlets containing examples of good copy are mailed with statements to regular advertisers; and promotion ads are run in newspapers, emphasizing the principles of writing effective classified copy.

Some publishers and classified advertising managers require persons entering classified sales work to take aptitude tests and specified courses of training. The Klamath Falls, Oreg., *Herald and News* has evolved an aptitude test that reveals four qualifications about a would-be employe: ability to write a legible hand, to spell, to follow instructions, and to figure simple advertising rates. The *Herald and News* considers this aptitude test a painless method of weeding out incompetent applicants without having to give them a trial on the job.

Classified sales personnel who operate at the counter or at the telephone must be courteous, tactful, and patient and must be thoroughly familiar with the newspaper's history and its rules regarding classified advertising. On most newspapers a new employe is stationed for a few days at the side of an experienced staff worker to observe some of the characteristics and knowledge required. In offices where master telephone sets are used, part of the training will consist of listening in on conversations of ad takers and solicitors with customers.

The Chicago, Ill., *Tribune* is particularly selective in hiring employes for classified sales work because all promotions to the display advertising divisions are made from the classified department after three or four years of training. The steps in the *Tribune*'s training program are:

1. Receive actual office training. During this period they see a motion picture giving the entire operation of a newspaper plant from pulpwood to newsstands. They are also briefed in forms and procedures, type and type measurements, proofreader's marks, rates, and contracts and are given outlines of the work of allied departments by people of authority in those divisions.
2. Go with other salespeople into all types of territories so they may see how successful solicitation is done.
3. Take over a territory of their own or temporarily substitute for workers who are ill or on vacation.
4. Attend weekly meetings on sales psychology and advertising trends. These meetings also provide material about the *Tribune,* its history, and policies.
5. Read books covering specific phases of advertising and selling from the classified department's complete library.
6. Learn how to prepare visual sales presentations.
7. Become acquainted with the work of the research and sales development division.
8. Study bulletins, data, sales material, and charts from the *Tribune*'s advertising divisions.

During their time in the classified department, sales staff are supervised by the assistant classified advertising manager, assistant sales manager, and supervisor of their particular group.

Sometimes an advertiser, for good reasons, may not wish to be identified in an advertisement. An employer advertising for office help would much prefer to have written applications outlining prospective employes' qualifications than to have applicants come in numbers to his office or telephone him during his busiest hours. A person advertising rental property might rather have prospective tenants write to a "blind address."

For the accommodation of such advertisers, most newspapers permit the use of "blind ads," in which a number is used instead of the name, and answers are directed to the classified department. Either they are picked up by the advertiser or they will be mailed upon request. The Kansas City, Mo., *Star* makes a charge of 50 cents for the use of a box number in the ad, and the Wichita, Kans., *Eagle* and *Beacon* makes a charge for bookkeeping and mailing. All blind numbers used in the ads are held confidential unless the advertiser gives the department permission to divulge the identity to an interested prospective patron.

There is the rare possibility, however, that "blind ads" may be used to take unfair advantage or to defraud. In answering ads where the proposition is not clearly stated and the advertiser is not identified, an innocent party might be led into undesirable contacts. The classified department must be cautious to observe the laws regarding civil rights of individuals when accepting such advertisements.

Classifications. The usefulness of classified advertising is due largely to the orderly arrangement under suitable headings of the articles and services advertised. The main classifications in most newspapers that carry a page or more of classifieds are: Announcement, Automotive, Business Service, Employment, Financial, Livestock, Lost and Found, Merchandise, Personals, Real Estate, and Rooms and Board. In small papers with only a column or two of classified ads, quite frequently there is no classification at all; but in metropolitan papers many more classification headings will be provided. Under each of the main classifications are subheadings. For example, under the heading Automotive will be such subheadings as Automobiles for Sale, Automobiles for Trade, Repairing, Service Stations, Trailers for Sale or Rent, or Trucks for Sale. Ads under the subheadings usually are placed in alphabetical order according to the guide word. This enables the reader to find easily the article in which he is interested. Finding specific advertisements is like finding words in a dictionary.

For the convenience of the person who prepares the copy and designates the classification and also for the convenience of the composing room, each heading on the page is given a number, beginning with 1 and following with other numbers in direct sequence to indicate the order in which the headings are to appear. That, of course, is the simplest form of designating the classification. Some newspapers use a system similar to that used in libraries to catalog books to place them in order on the shelves.

For the benefit of readers unfamiliar with classification arrangement, many newspapers publish a directory listing the main headings in the proper order. The directory serves a twofold purpose. Readers may consult the list and find the classification they are seeking without scanning the other columns of advertising. It may also serve as promotional copy, advising potential advertisers of a classification they could use to good advantage and showing readers the great variety of goods and services appearing in the classified section. The main headings in a classified section will depend upon the type of community in which the newspaper is published and the variety of merchandise and services offered. For example, a resort community would have a long listing of rooms and cottages for rent, perhaps with a number of subheads under the main heading, none of which would be found in a newspaper of another city.

Rates. More than 10,000 newspapers in the United States and Canada carry classified advertising. Their classified rate cards are similar in form and function, but the rates charged by newspapers and methods of charging vary greatly. Circulation differences, operation costs, desired profit margins, and competitive considerations account for those variations.

Circulation, however, is less important in fixing the rate for classified advertising than it is for run-of-the-paper display advertising. The worth of a classified ad is judged more by the number of answers it brings than by the number of homes it reaches. As one classified advertising manager explains:

A few lines of copy containing the same advertising message may appear in all newspapers in a given city. Circulation of the papers may be approximately the same. But the advertiser's results from one or two of these papers will be far greater than the others. Why? The message is identical; the circulations are similar; advertising costs are about the same. The essential difference is that the ad-reading public has established a greater value for the advertising in those one or two newspapers than in the others.

Many studies have been made of rate cards on large and small newspapers and in high-income and low-income communities in search of some common yardstick for determining classified rates and values (Fig. 12.3). Apparently, it is not to be found. Ordinarily, the general public will accept an increase in classified rates better than the merchants of a community will accept an increase in display rates. The publisher wants as much revenue as possible in the face of increasing costs but at the same time does not want to have the volume of classified advertising materially reduced, because classifieds are an important factor in establishing the newspaper's prestige with users of display advertising and with the newspaper's readers.

Most newspapers plan to derive more revenue from a page of classifieds than they receive from a page of display advertising, due to the

KENOSHA EVENING NEWS CLASSIFIED ADVERTISING RULES and REGULATIONS

The Kenosha Evening News reserves the right to insert advertisements under such classifications as it deems appropriate, to edit advertising copy by eliminating or substituting words or by making other changes in conformity with its rules and regulations as to content and makeup of advertising matter, and to refrain from publishing any advertisement that it considers objectionable. No representative has the authority to guarantee publication or classification.

CONTRACTS

If lineage contracted for shall not be used the Kenosha News Publishing Company shall have the right to charge and collect for the lineage used the difference between the rate contracted for and the lowest rate earned by the advertiser up to the time of such discontinuance.

Advertising not for the business of the contract advertiser will not receive the benefit of the contract rate. Personal advertising of the advertiser will be allowed the contract rate. BUT will not be considered as fulfilling the terms of the contract lineage requirements.

CLOSING HOURS

Regu
ed for
public
not be
to pub

Will
lined

It is
the co
ment.
repetit
more
same c
liabilit
not ex
part c
occurs
to the

EXTRA SIZE TYPE STYLES AVAILABLE

TRADED NEW TRUCKS
Traded New Automobiles

Caps 17 spaces, lower case 22 spaces. **Permitted only in ads of 12 or more lines.**

Requirements for Displayed Ads

No display permitted in ads of less than 4 lines.

•

Agate caps and white space only display permitted in ads of 4 to 11 lines.

•

nes
or
:ed
ich

ire
sis
ley
re-

nal
er-

Word Rate for Morning and Evening or Sunday

OUTSIDE OF SALT LAKE CITY — MINIMUM AD 10 WORDS

COUNT WORDS	Sunday 10c Word	1 Week Day Both Papers 10c Word	3 Days Includes Sunday	7 Days Includes Sunday	4 Consecutive Sundays	30 Days
10	$1.00	$1.00	$2.00	$4.00	$3.68	$16.00
15	1.50	1.50	3.00	6.00	5.52	24.00
20	2.00	2,00	4.00	8.00	7.36	32.00
25	2.50	2.50	5.00	10.00	9.20	40.00
30	3.00	3.00	6.00	12.00	11.04	48.00
35	3.50	3.50	7.00	14.00	12.88	56.00
40	4.00	4.00	8.00	16.00	14.72	64.00
45	4.50	4.50	9.00	18.00	16.56	72.00
50	5.00	5.00	10.00	20.00	18.40	80.00
55	5.50	5.50	11.00	22.00	20.24	88.00
60	6.00	6.00	12.00	24.00	22.08	96.00
70	7.00	7.00	14.00	28.00	25.76	112.00

PLEASE MAIL CASH OR CHECK WITH YOUR WANT AD.

Word Rate for Either Morning or Evening

OUTSIDE OF SALT LAKE CITY — DAILY ONLY

5 Words To The Line	Daily Rate 46c Per Line Either Morning or Evening Daily	3 Consecutive Days Daily Only	6 Consecutive Days Daily Only
10	$ .92	$1.84	3.68
15	1.38	2.76	5.52
20	1.84	3.68	7.36
25	2.30	4.60	9.20
30	2.76	5.52	11.04
35	3.22	6.44	12.88
40	3.68	7.36	14.72
45	4.14	8.28	16.56
50	4.60	9.20	18.40

RATES APPLY TO EITHER MORNING OR EVENING EDITIONS—DAILY ONLY

Fig. 12.3. Classified rate cards of the Kenosha, Wis., *Evening News* and the Salt Lake City, Utah, *Deseret News* and *Tribune*.

heavy composition and the limited time for makeup, but it does not always turn out that way. Much depends upon whether the advertising volume at the higher transient rate is greater than the volume at the lower contract rates. For example, the Kenosha, Wis., *Evening News* reports an average yield of $390 per page from classified and approximately $330 per page from display advertising.

Special inducements to advertise regularly have proved helpful for many newspapers. Usually a lower rate is granted when the advertiser contracts to use a certain number of lines each day. In this way many business institutions and service organizations become constant users of the classified page. The Wichita, Kans., *Eagle* and *Beacon* makes a reduction in rates to advertisers who use a minimum of lines for a definite number of days.

Credit. Where so many accounts are handled and the items are of small amounts, the question of whether to extend credit arises. Most newspapers keep as close to a cash basis as possible. A common practice is to send out a statement on the day the ad appears, showing a cash price to be paid within seven days and explaining that if it is not paid within that time the item goes to a credit price, which is higher. This generally brings in the cash within a week. Other newspapers wait until the full number of insertions ordered have been run before sending a statement. Where merchants use classified, often it is included in the same monthly billing as that for retail advertising.

The Kansas City, Kans., *Star* offers no discounts and handles all classifieds as cash items. However, it bills on a memo basis and maintains collectors in the city. The Canton, Ohio, *Repository* limits credit on questionable accounts to $10. Transient ads are due on date of expiration, and contract accounts are given a 2 percent discount if paid by the twentieth of the month. The Kenosha, Wis., *Evening News* gives a cash discount to residents of Kenosha who pay for their ads within 6 days and to out-of-town customers who pay within 12. Accounts over 60 days due are refused more credit.

The percentages of loss on credit accounts by these three newspapers were reported as 1, 3, and 1 percent, which is remarkably low considering the large number of ads for which billings of small amounts are made.

FIFTY IDEAS FOR DEVELOPING CLASSIFIED

1. Keep the composing room constantly supplied with a well-rounded assortment of filler ads on classified.
2. Have the supervisor of ad takers visit the classified departments of other newspapers to see how they are handling phone calls.
3. Keep a record of all ads that get results.
4. Offer prizes or bonuses to solicitors who sell the most contracts.
5. Run promotion ads showing linage volume and number of individual ads carried during the month or year.

6. Use classified ads to promote the service of the newspaper's classified department, interspersing them between paid ads.

7. To create reader interest in classified, spot the name of a subscriber somewhere on the page and offer a free want ad to the person who discovers his or her own name.

8. Omit borders from classified display; they draw readership from other ads on the page.

9. Use no mats or cuts because they reduce readership and mar the appearance of the page.

10. Make no new classification until you have sufficient ads to warrant it; eight or nine ads should be minimum in any classification.

11. Keep the classified rate card simple; make it easily understood.

12. Have all members of the newspaper's business department carry a classified advertising rate card. They never know when someone may ask them the cost of an ad or give them copy to be inserted.

13. Carry a blank coupon regularly in the newspaper for the reader to use in writing an ad, estimating its cost, and mailing it to the classified department.

14. Solicit stores in outlying districts and at country crossroads for classified.

15. Clip ads from other papers published in the trade territory and paste them on a form letter to be mailed to advertisers, quoting prices for two, three, and six insertions.

16. Arrange with weekly newspapers to send classified ads of public sales in their communities and pay them on a commission basis.

17. Use a loose-leaf cookbook as a premium for classified ads. Divide the cookbook into 12 sections and give a section for each ad inserted. When an advertiser has inserted 12 ads the recipe book is complete.

18. Solicit bowling alleys to place their scores at classified rates.

19. Sell space on the classified page to undertakers for funeral notices.

20. Have display salespeople query their accounts frequently on the possible need for sales staff, building custodians, or part-time help and suggest they use classified.

21. Grant a low rate to homemakers to encourage them to use classified.

22. Use a seven-day rate even though the paper is published only six days a week.

23. In carrier contests, arrange to give contestants additional points for bringing in classified ads with cash.

24. Carry obituaries on the classified page at the classified rate.

25. Require cash from advertisers with transient addresses.

26. Demand cash with the order on "situation wanted" ads.

27. Have a separate room for telephone solicitation and separate booths for ad takers.

28. Make regular appraisals of the classified department to see if personnel have the proper spirit.

29. See that persons in the classified department are paid on the same basis as in other departments.

30. Have the classified advertising manager address the Motor Car Dealers Association, Real Estate Board, and other groups on the value of classified advertising.
31. Allocate a certain percentage of classified gross to classified promotion and buy space in the paper at the wholesale rate.
32. Make the deadline for classified ads as late as possible.
33. Use homemakers as part-time solicitors for classified.
34. Sell services — not space, words, or lines.
35. Charge for changes in copy, "kills," or insertions made after deadlines.
36. Constantly develop innovative sections such as "Health Care Employment" or "Child Care" or "Private Tutoring."
37. Sell no contracts for less than three months.
38. Use enclosures with circulation expiration notices, calling attention to possible classified advertising results.
39. Equip telephones with shoulder rests to enable solicitors to have both hands free to use the typewriter, or use standard headset.
40. Insert a self-renewal clause in 3-, 6-, and 12-month contracts, automatically extending the contract unless the advertiser cancels it.
41. Solicit appliance dealers for classified ads on "trade-ins."
42. During slump periods feature cut-rate specials to increase linage.
43. Print coupons allowing holders the privilege of placing a classified ad for a specified number of days at a bargain rate and distribute them throughout the city by carrier-salesmen.
44. Observe "National Want Ad Week" with special promotion of classified service or make a special rate to increase volume during the week.
45. Have an ad taker in the classified department call a certain number of persons each day from the telephone directory to explain classified service and solicit ads. Extreme tact is important, as some prospects will be sensitive to any invasion of their privacy.
46. Subscribe to a good classified advertising service and follow applicable suggestions.
47. Issue a rate box, showing the size and style of various ads commonly used on the classified page and the cost of each.
48. Run a special listing on higher paying jobs with its own heading, like the Boston, Mass., *Herald American*'s "Major League Jobs" section, restricted to positions paying $18,000 a year and over.
49. Use a one-order bill system to bring advertising agencies into the classified field, making it easier for them to place ads originating from their clients outside your territory.
50. Check ads of doubtful dependability and accuracy with the Better Business Bureau.

13

Building and maintaining circulation

We in the newspaper industry cannot be
apathetic to the changes and challenges
rushing in around us. . . . It seems now,
more than ever, we in circulation need
flexibility in our thinking.

Joe Forsee

Circulation—the number of newspaper copies sold and paid for—is the foundation of a newspaper's success; it is the basis of all revenue. It is true that newspaper sales account for less revenue than advertising, but circulation is the force that makes advertising pay. Without it, there would be no advertising. Circulation also is a measure of the newspaper's service. The greater the circulation, the stronger the evidence that the newspaper is fulfilling its obligations to the community.

A publisher will place high value on the newspaper's subscribers. In fact, when a newspaper property changes hands, goodwill often is estimated at $25 or $50, or even as high as $150, for each paid-in-advance subscriber. The circulation department is therefore indispensable to the rest of the newspaper organization, and how efficiently it operates largely determines the newspaper's success.

VITAL FACTORS IN CIRCULATION

It is axiomatic that newspapers can be sold only where people live, but size of population does not always determine the volume of circulation. Some communities with small populations have newspapers with large circulations, and some communities with large populations prove to be poor newspaper territory. This can only mean that *internal* population conditions as well as population numbers have a strong bearing on circulation.

While population in the United States is 6 times what it was in 1870, the total circulation of newspapers in the nation has increased to 25 times what it was in that earlier period. Shifts in population, a steady climb in literacy and in education, and a widening of interest in the progress that has been made are factors largely responsible for these changes. Whereas

217

in 1870, 20 percent over the age of ten were unable to read, at present less than 2 percent of this group are in this category. The enrollment of students in institutions of higher learning has increased, bringing the total enrollment to more than 6 million. The opening of new fields of learning, the rapid advances in all phases of science, better methods of teaching, and greater expenditures for education have all contributed to a greater eagerness for information and a wider and more intensive reading of newspapers.

Trend from rural to urban

Another factor that has affected newspaper circulation is the population trend from farm to city. In 1910 the rural population of the United States was nearly 50 million, or 54.3 percent of the total population. Today less than 30 percent live on farms or in rural communities. The profits of agriculture are divided among fewer producers, and the buying power of persons living on farms has increased to such an extent that advertising in the rural press is a significant factor in the nation's economy.

While there continues to be a general country-to-city population trend, there is also a steady flow of city dwellers to suburban areas. To escape congested living conditions, people are moving to the outskirts, but not so far as to be away from the entertainment, cultural, and shopping advantages offered by the city. With this larger proportion of the total population coming within the trade areas of daily newspapers, the tendency is toward an *intensive* circulation rather than an *extensive* one.

Service to a wide territory

It is possible for a newspaper to extend its influence far beyond its immediate trade and circulation area. Former residents of the community now living at distant places are good prospects. During the nation's wars many newspapers are sent to servicemen in all parts of the world; and where permanent forces are stationed, as in NATO or SEATO units, American newspapers are delivered on a regular basis.

For persons on leisure ocean cruises, newspapers are published and distributed on board ships. These maritime journals claim a total circulation of at least a million for each five-day cruise, or an average of 200,000 a day. Wherever there are people, there is an opportunity for newspaper circulation, and the paper that gets there first with the best news presentation gets the subscribers.

The economy as a factor

In times of inflation, unemployment, newsprint shortages, and general market recession, newspaper circulations can be expected to reflect such circumstances by fluctuations from normal figures. For example, during the depressed conditions of the early 1970s, total daily circulations dropped 3.9 percent below their all-time high of 63.1 million to register a ten-year low. However, as adjustments were made later in the decade, newspapers discovered ways to recover lost circulation territory.

As such economic indicators as gross national product, real personal income, and general productivity resume growth in a healthy financial climate, circulations can increase rather dramatically. With the forecast of a 75 percent increase in the number of families earning more than $15,000 in 1985, newspaper readership and sales can be expected to trend steadily upward. The number of adults in the United States—representing the prime market for newspaper circulation—has increased by 27 percent since 1950 to almost 100 million. Population experts see another increase of 38 percent by the year 2000 among this age group. This suggests an enormously expanded purchasing power to support burgeoning newspaper circulations.

Most cities have experienced traumatic changes as the inner-city areas have seen the newsstand outlets all but disappear. Delivery of newspapers has in some cases become most difficult, and collections have become unpredictable because of the shifting tides of urban renewal, population mobility, suburban flight, street crime, and other sociological factors. Whether such conditions are localized or national in scope, newspaper management is obviously challenged to cope in ways that call for resourceful and innovative approaches to the problem at hand.

This presupposes an alertness to and thoughtful anticipation of social and economic changes that might otherwise be blamed for circulation reverses. During the decline mentioned above, many newspapers never registered a decrease in circulation because of shrewd adjustments to changing conditions. Some individual publications actually posted gains during the same period that the national circulation averages showed a slump. It is easy to attribute losses to "business recession," but as William F. Reinhold, a newspaper circulation authority, expressed it, "Circulation sales are like pouring sand into a sieve. You have to keep pouring it in at the top to offset what is being lost. That's the only way to keep up the level." In other words, the real answer to shifting economic pressures is a continuing, bold, creative program of circulation building.

PRELIMINARY TO CIRCULATION BUILDING

Three requirements for successful circulation building are a newspaper that thoroughly and competently covers the news of the local community and the world and carries features the readers will like, a knowledge and understanding of the community in which the newspaper is published, and a well-organized and well-managed circulation department.

As any salesperson knows, good merchandise is essential to any extended selling campaign. Similarly, a good newspaper is needed before subscribers may be obtained and held. It must appeal directly to local people by reporting the news in which they are most interested—home, state, national, world.

They also want other information important to their welfare—markets, highway conditions, weather, and myriad other bits of current data. Business plans its operations and people plan their social affairs by the weather alone.

The modern newspaper, however, offers many circulation-building features that, strictly speaking, are not news: fiction, recipes and menus, sports features, puzzles, comics, pictures, advice.

Local news coverage

Stories about hometown people create reader interest and are more helpful in building circulation than anything else in the newspaper. Some larger newspapers are trying to bring themselves closer to their subscribers by issuing weekly neighborhood sections devoted exclusively to news items of particular interest to those areas.

There is also the question of how the news should be handled to suit readers best. How sensational should it be, or how conservative? Is it well to increase street sales by running sexy pictures, by giving lurid descriptions of murders and suicides? What is the reaction to such news treatment in the homes of the newspaper's circulation area?

The Marquette University School of Journalism gathered comments from a number of Wisconsin editors and presented the findings to the Wisconsin Daily League. This survey was prompted by a discussion of whether newspapers can survive without emphasis on sex and sensation.

The Wisconsin editors' symposium revealed that most newspapers devote priority space and display to news of government on all levels, and that news of Hollywood legs and Broadway bosoms, madams, and mistresses, is given minor position on inside pages. In most newspapers, stories of suicides seldom made page one, and news of divorces was subdued.

The question of how to play individual stories is never settled. But one thing is certain: no newspaper will rise higher than the goals of its owners and publishers. When decisions must be made, each editor and publisher must be guided by sound feelings and judgment in devising a news policy with respect to circulation. After all, in strict merchandising terms, the newspaper is the product the circulation department has for sale. It deserves all the creative talent, attractive layout, exclusive content, and technical excellence in production that can be poured into it. Without an appealing, useful product, selling will be an uphill task and the market will never be developed to its optimum potential.

Roles of the circulation manager

Because there are so many details to be handled in developing circulation, it is possible for the circulation manager to create an unnecessarily expensive and cumbersome operation. But if the department's horizons are narrow, it may not be organized to maximum capability. Then, too, a circulation employe might be handicapped by a publisher or general manager unable to see the possibilities of circulation increase or more anxious to pay the stockholders a dividend than to build up the newspaper.

The head of the circulation department performs in enough ways to easily qualify for ten different positions. To some degree at least the following roles are assumed:

1. A top executive, concerned with overall results of a highly specialized business.

2. A sales manager, capable of directing a large sales crew. The circulation manager of the Des Moines, Iowa, *Register* and *Tribune* has 1,600 carriers who deliver in Des Moines, 6,800 who deliver in other towns, and 1,100 who deliver to farm homes on Sunday. Each of these is as thoroughly drilled in selling as in delivery service. In addition, a force of 10 full-time mail subscription salespeople solicit paid-in-advance subscriptions in the state's outlying sections where motor delivery is provided, and 60 outside agencies and 40 district supervisors are constantly driving for more sales in their respective territories.

3. An auditor with a sound knowledge of bookkeeping and billing. At the Des Moines *Register* and *Tribune,* accounts must be kept for each of the four major divisions of the circulation department: city circulation, agency, independent carrier, and farm service. Statements must be made out each month (some weekly) for every carrier or salesperson in each division, and accurate records must be kept of money that is paid in. Circulation accounts of some sort are kept for one out of every three homes in the state of Iowa.

4. A credit manager who will watch all accounts closely to determine the amounts of credit to be extended and when dealers should be changed and accounts closed. Carriers who do not pay their accounts promptly do not hold their leases long. Newsstand dealers are billed weekly or monthly and are not often allowed to get behind in their accounts. The Montgomery, Ala., *Advertiser* bills news dealers and carriers weekly and requires them to pay for the papers received each week ending on Saturday.

5. A traffic manager who knows the schedules and rates of all trains, buses, airlines, and truck lines. Newspapers employ every means possible to provide prompt delivery to their readers. The Grand Junction, Colo., *Daily Sentinel* delivers 48 percent of its circulation by truck, 11 percent by train, and 14 percent by bus; 27 percent is city pickup. The *Sentinel* owns and operates its own trucks. The bus haul is on contract, based on volume and mileage.

6. A lawyer who particularly understands the laws concerning interstate commerce, child labor, and wage and hour regulations. (For points of law to be watched by circulation managers see Chapter 19.)

7. A public relations person capable of adjusting complaints and handling difficult situations.
8. An all-around advertising and sales promotion expert. (For successful circulation promotion ideas see Chapter 23.)
9. A social service worker who understands youth.
10. A practical newspaper person who knows the problems faced in the mechanical, editorial, news, and advertising departments as well as in circulation.

RESPONSIBILITIES OF CIRCULATION DEPARTMENT

The chief responsibilities of the circulation department are selling the newspaper, delivering it, and collecting for it. Although these functions are distinct and separate, they are closely related. In most newspaper organizations, the carrier performs all three duties; but often there are persons who do nothing but sell, deliver, or collect. Experienced sales personnel and collectors often are used to supplement the carriers' work in these categories.

Selling

Newspaper sales depend upon sound organization as well as upon the paper's quality, contents, and general appearance. Circulation managers select carriers of creditable standing in school, with good personalities and plenty of ambition, because they do much of the home selling. Rewards, contests, and other inducements are used to arouse carriers' interest in selling (Fig. 13.1).

A campaign to obtain subscribers from newcomers to Decatur, Ill., for the *Herald* and *Review* was conducted as a contest between the carriers of these two Lindsay-Schaub newspapers. The purposes were to stimulate carrier interest in selling during a period when circulation activity was quiet, to present the *Herald* and *Review* to newcomers as quickly as possible, and to determine if subscriptions could be sold profitably by this method.

Names and addresses of newcomers were obtained from the Chamber of Commerce and from the reports of the Decatur Credit Bureau. They were then typed on a form and given to the carriers who delivered to those addresses. On the form were these instructions:

The above named person recently moved to Decatur, so we have added an extra paper to your bundle today. Present it to the "newcomer," explain the features of the paper, and try to get this person to subscribe to the paper.

Please call Miss Gregory, circulation department, as soon as you have contacted this "newcomer," and let her know whether you have added a new subscriber. If you already carry to this person, use the extra paper profitably by presenting it to someone on your route not taking the paper and try to sell that person the subscription.

How to SELL New Subscribers

He's "Real George"

He's not afraid to make calls...lots of them. He knows the only way to sell is to tell people about The World-Herald. He knows that prospects won't bite. The worst they can do is say NO.

He'll Make Sales!

He's Fearful Freddie

He's afraid of a door bell. He's afraid to talk to non-subscribers because he thinks they will ask him to leave or slam the door in his face. Fearful Freddie's got the wrong idea. He's afraid to make calls.

He'll Never Sell!

World-Herald Sales Tip No. 1

READ It.. KEEP It.. DO It!

Fig. 13.1. Material such as this impresses upon carriers the right way to sell subscriptions. (Courtesy of the Omaha, Nebr., *World-Herald.*)

As both *Herald* and *Review* carriers are receiving this name, it will be a case of first come, first served, so get your NEW ORDERS FROM NEWCOMERS.

Below is a summary of the results obtained in this campaign:

Names from Chamber of Commerce and Credit Bureau		108	100%
Already taking paper before carrier contacted		35	32.4%
Herald	15	13.9% of total	
Review	20	18.5% of total	
New starts by carrier as result of names sent out		42	38.9%
Herald	17	15.7% of total	
Review	25	23.2% of total	
Do not want either paper*		8	7.4%
Undecided as to what paper to take		10	9.3%
Not moved in yet		5	4.6%
Unable to contact prospective subscriber		8	7.4%

---

*1 is moving; 1 does not want to at present time; 3 single women living in rooms; 1 traveling salesman; 1 does not like city; 1 no reason.

The results were so satisfactory that the plan was continued in succeeding months. From August 1 until December 31 the carriers added 60 "newcomers" to the *Herald*'s subscription list and 109 to the *Review*'s, a total of 169 new residents of Decatur becoming subscribers solely from the carriers' efforts.

Supplying sample copies to prospects before they are approached by carriers or salespeople also has been found effective in subscription selling. Many newspapers pay the carrier 1 cent or more a day per sample. A survey by the Moline, Ill., *Dispatch,* reported to the Central States Circulation Managers Association, revealed that the cost of selling such subscriptions ranged from 50 cents to $1.25 apiece. This included a prize or cash award for the carrier, extra pay for the carrier, promotion material, and newsprint cost of samples.

Selling at counters and on the street. While home delivery service is the backbone of any newspaper's nonmail circulation, many papers are sold at newsstands and on the streets. In the large cities street sales make up a substantial portion of the newspaper's paid circulation. The Atlanta, Ga., *Journal* and *Constitution* has street and newsstand sales equal to one-tenth of the two papers' total circulation. A larger portion of these sales is in the city zone, where street salespeople use coin-box racks to supplement their personal selling. The coin-box money is gathered daily. Ten percent of the circulation of the Little Rock, Ark., *Arkansas Gazette* is handled through coin boxes and 4 percent by newsstands.

A street sales manager with several assistants supervises the racks and street sales of the Atlanta newspapers. The papers are sold directly to the street vendors at a wholesale price and they in turn retail them to the public. Returns are allowed on unsold copies. At the end of the day each vendor pays for the papers received. Allowance is made for "returns" when settlement is made. The newsstands are billed weekly, and collections are made by district managers. In the city no "returns" are allowed from the newsstands and dealers. However, that privilege is extended to some dealers in the retail trading zone.

Success in newsstand and street selling depends greatly on getting the papers to the dealer or vendors quickly, giving them all the papers they are likely to need and being reasonable about "returns," calling their attention to outstanding news or features in the day's issue, and helping them in every way possible to promote sales.

Selling by direct mail. Direct-mail selling cannot be done in a haphazard manner. There are at least four important points to be considered:

1. The material must be made to look interesting, in form as well as in words.
2. It must be written to attract the reader's attention, interest, desire, and action.
3. The writer must forget the *I* and *we* as much as possible and write from the standpoint of *you*.
4. The letter should contain one special offer to stimulate *action* — not more than two. Experience shows that it is a mistake to make more than two offers.

Publishers who do a large volume of direct-mail selling have found that quality paper stock and good printing bring back an average of one more new subscription per 1,000 mailing pieces than cheap paper and printing. This applies to outgoing and return envelopes as well as to the letters.

Another way to attract the reader's attention is to connect the letter's message with some event or condition in which he or she is particularly interested, such as a bumper corn crop in the area, the coming of a large industrial plant, or a national election.

The following letter sent out by the circulation manager of the New Ulm, Minn., *Daily Journal* at the beginning of the fall season, when farmers were beginning to think about winter reading, brought in a 5 percent return:

Here Is a Real Fall Bargain!

Yes! A fall bargain that will give you and every member of your family many things six days a week all winter long. It's a bargain that can't be beat and it will give you—

Entertainment!

Here's entertainment for every member of your family. Yes! A page of comics every day. Entertainment when the sun shines, when it snows, when it rains and any time of day or night. You will find something good, something bad, something humorous, and something glad.

Education!

This bargain will help to educate you and your family. Yes! It will give exercise to the old gray matter. If you digest one-tenth of it, it's a bargain.

World Events!

It's a bargain that will give you the happenings from all over the world: What's doing in the hot war, the cold war, what's our foreign policy, what your elected representatives are doing. Yes! What these United States of America are doing.

Local Events!

What is happening in your county, in your township, in your town and in your school. Yes! This bargain will give you the happenings close to home, about the people you know, about events you will want to know.

Sports!

With this bargain the sporting events of the nation and your home town are yours. Here it is—Football, Basketball, Track, Baseball, Bowling, Golf, Hunting, Fishing, Swimming, and more. You want more? O.K.

Pictures!

All of the above will be enhanced with pictures. Not just pictures of people you read about, but pictures of people you know close to home, about places you know, and happenings you want to know about.

What is it?

This wonderful bargain is the New Ulm Daily Journal, a daily newspaper printed every day except Sunday and a few special holidays. The Journal is one of the best newspapers you can get where you are living.

What will it cost?

You would think that something giving you and your family all of this would cost at least $5 a day. But no, this wonderful bargain is yours for 4 cents a day. Yes! Five months for $6.00. Just think: 150 days for only $6.00. All you need to do is write your name and address on the enclosed slip. Enclose the slip and $6.00 in cash, check or money order in the postage-free envelope and mail. Do it today, and this Fall Bargain is yours.

The Des Moines, Iowa, newspapers also do much direct-mail solicitation to build up their list of subscribers constantly. At frequent intervals they mail attractive form letters to prospects, setting forth their wide coverage of the news and their many features. Enclosed with each letter is a reply card that may be conveniently signed and mailed to the newspaper (Fig. 13.2).

Selling on the installment plan. Installment buying, a sales-promotion accommodation offered by many business firms, is used effectively by a

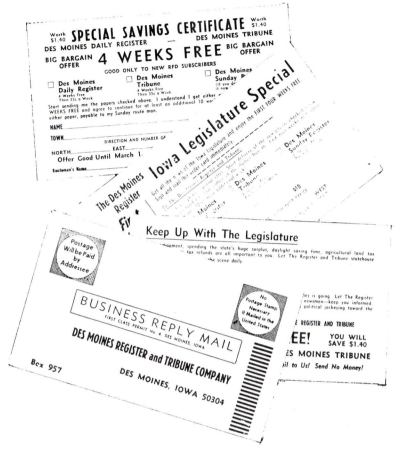

Fig. 13.2. Reply cards used by the Des Moines, Iowa, *Register* and *Tribune* to supplement a letter seeking new subscribers.

number of newspapers, particularly by those with a large percentage of mail circulation. This is usually referred to as "The Economy Reading Plan," "The Pay As You Read Plan," "The Easy Pay Plan," or "The Get Acquainted Reading Plan."

The subscriber pays $2 per month for seven, eight, nine, or ten months according to the annual subscription rate, leaving two, three, four, or five months when no payments will be made. In announcing such a plan to a list of prospective subscribers, the Bloomington, Ind., *Daily Herald-Telephone* sent out the following notice:

PAY AS YOU READ — Pay As You Go!

Most business is conducted on the pay-as-you-go plan. We at the Herald-Telephone are now extending the same service to our readers, old and new.

IT IS SIMPLE—IT IS EASY!

Send two dollars—$2.00—each month for eight (8) months and the last four (4) months are free. Your sixteen dollars pay for the entire year. You may pay more if you like each month. You may pay $2.00 each week for eight weeks and then you are through for the year. As long as the newspaper receives eight payments of $2.00 each, you will receive the Bloomington Herald-Telephone for a year.

Fill in your order card and send $2.00 today. WE PAY ALL POSTAGE.

This offer is open to all present subscribers on completion of your present subscription.

There is no doubt as to the value of this installment-type buying; 400 new subscribers were obtained soon after this plan was announced.

The La Crosse, Wis., *Tribune* found the monthly payment plan particularly good for the region in which it circulates because farmers there depend on bimonthly cream checks for a major portion of their income. Many of them would hesitate about paying for a full year's subscription in advance, whereas they welcome the method of paying monthly.

The *Tribune* explains its easy payment plan to a prospective subscriber in a mailing piece with this information (see Fig. 13.3):

As a special service to our rural patrons, we extend to you the privilege of paying for a one-year subscription on the installment plan.

Save up to $9.00 a year—pay as you read. The regular monthly rate is $2.00, or $24.00 a year, and you save $9.00 by subscribing under the Tribune Payment Plan. You make seven monthly payments of $2.00 each and a final payment of $1.00 for a total of $15.00. If you wish to pay more than $2.00 on any one month, you may do so in units of $2.00.

The only qualification necessary for the Tribune Payment Plan is that you live within 75 miles of La Crosse, where carrier delivery service is not available, and make your payments promptly.

A fourth of the *Tribune*'s mail circulation is sold on this basis.

Developing sales ideas. When daily circulations show signs of losing to economic or sociological pressures of one sort or another, the decreases can be offset by emphasis on Sunday editions. Audit Bureau of Circulations figures reveal a growth pattern for some newspapers whose weekday circulation declined while Sunday sales rose. One six-month audit showed that, for 12 newspaper groups measured, average circulations were down 0.8 percent while Sunday figures for the same groups were up by 1.3 percent. Readers generally have more time to spend with a bigger, more colorful Sunday edition than with daily editions during the week, and many newspapers have taken advantage of that fact by effectively expanding and promoting the Sunday operation.

Other circulation managers have looked into the supermarket outlet, where magazine sales have flourished for many years. Even newsmagazines can be found in supermarkets as well as on newsstands, indicating a ready

SAVE UP TO $9.00 A YEAR

PAY as you READ

You make **seven** monthly payments of $2.00 each and a final payment of $1.00 for a total of $15.00. If you wish to pay more than $2.00 on any one month you may do so in units of $2.00. This same card with another envelope will be sent back to you, at the proper time, as a reminder that payment is due. Payments will be recorded below showing date each is received at our office.

THANK YOU

THE LA CROSSE TRIBUNE   LA CROSSE, WISCONSIN

Subscription is for one year.   See expiration date below name.

Date Paid	Amount	Months		Date Paid	Amount
	$2.00	1	7		$2.00
	$2.00	2	8		$1.00
	$2.00	3	9	FREE	
	$2.00	4	10	FREE	
	$2.00	5	11	FREE	
	$2.00	6	12	FREE	

Do not write on this side of card.

Fig. 13.3.   This card is mailed each month by the La Crosse, Wis., *Tribune* to rural subscribers paying on the Tribune Easy Payment Plan.

market for newspapers. Some authorities have suggested that all printed media — newspapers, magazines, books — join together in a mass effort aimed at increasing readership as opposed to television and movie viewing or radio listening. In this connection, many newspapers like the Louisville, Ky., *Times* issue their own magazines. *Scene,* an attractive leisure-type publication, appears on newsstands wrapped around the Saturday edition of the *Times.* Five years after it was introduced, it had brought circulation up by 20,000.

To combat the difficulties in serving high-rise apartment complexes, the Houston, Tex., *Chronicle* established "news centers" — racks with specially designed key access for subscribers who reside in the building. Each subscriber has a key to the daily newspaper supply within the apartment area and can deposit payments at the "center" on a once-a-week or once-a-month subscription basis. Hundreds of these news centers have proved effective in overcoming the problem of finding people at home, poor communication, protecting the security of apartment-dwellers, and related difficulties encountered by circulation managers in larger multifloored and garden-type residential developments. Other newspapers have depended on delivery contracts with custodians or rental agents.

In a novel campaign to boost circulation, the Columbus, Ga., *Enquirer* and *Ledger* enlisted the aid of all circulation employes and 49 management-level personnel from other departments for a mass door-knocking effort. During the six-week drive a total of 7,847 new subscriptions were added. A spinoff of the campaign was a strong morale-building effect as representatives from all segments of the newspaper recognized together the fundamental importance of readers to the overall operation. John McMullan, vice-president of the Knight-Ridder newspapers, concluded that "there is no substitute for organized, continuing sales efforts on the part of the circulation staff. . . . Sales training has been too much neglected in the newspaper business."

The Lexington, Ky., *Herald-Leader* discovered the same rewards in an all-out monthlong collaboration by 48 employes at all levels—including editors, secretaries, compositors, and the publisher. A total of 3,854 new subscribers resulted, but again the more lasting benefits were counted in friendships and the greatly improved relations the joint effort produced among the members of the staff. The peculiar problems facing the circulation department became better known to employes from other divisions as they all worked together for the general benefit of the newspaper.

Delivering

People used to go to the publishing office for their newspaper or bought it from "hawkers" on the streets. Today most newspapers are delivered to homes, either by carrier or by mail. But the question is not altogether that of getting the newspaper to the subscriber. It is principally one of how *quickly* the newspaper can be delivered and to how wide a territory satisfactory delivery can be made. Newspaper delivery service covers the immediate community and the outlying territory. Each presents a different problem and requires a different method.

In the immediate community. In most localities daily newspapers and nondailies are delivered by carriers 12 years old and over. Sometimes they are hired on a weekly wage basis, but more often they buy the papers at a wholesale rate and sell and deliver them to customers in a specified area at an established retail price. This last mentioned method is known as the "Little Merchant Plan" because the carrier is in business for himself or herself, buying at wholesale, selling at retail, and making a profit on each paper sold, just as a merchant does on each item of merchandise handled. In large cities these carriers comprise a vast delivery army and are divided into districts, with a supervisor over each.

In Ottawa, Ontario, Canada, where homes are widely separated, the carriers for the Ottawa *Citizen* are aided in making rapid delivery by what the circulation manager chooses to call a mobile depot. This is a specially constructed delivery truck that also serves as a conference room and pay station for supervisors and carriers.

The mobile depot travels main streets. Carrier routes are laid out so they start at important street intersections in both directions. Instead of going to the newspaper plant for their papers, the carriers receive them at their starting points from the mobile depot. When they receive their supply, they begin delivering immediately and the load is a diminishing one from the start.

The truck has a rear door for loading and a side door with a curb-high platform for unloading the bundles and receiving carriers who wish to pay their accounts or talk with the district manager, who mans the depot. It is equipped with a pigeonhole for each carrier and a built-up writing platform at the right-hand side of the steering column. Where the left-hand seat would ordinarily be, there is a flat surface for carrying supplies. This also may serve as a seat for the driver's part-time helper. The mobile depot serves about one-fifth of the home-delivered city circulation and one-tenth of the entire circulation.

To outlying districts. Subscribers who live ten or even a hundred miles from the city want to receive the newspaper as promptly as the hometown subscribers do and are not willing to wait until the next day. They want today's news today.

The Little Rock, Ark., *Arkansas Gazette* transports 90 percent of its outside circulation by truck, 4 percent by bus, and 6 percent by train.

The Escanaba, Mich., *Press* has two automobiles on lease for motor route and bundle delivery in surrounding towns. The rental fee includes all expenses except gas, oil, and liability insurance. Each week the cars are taken to the garage for a checkup and servicing, which ensures trouble-free driving. Each year new automobiles are provided.

The Saginaw, Mich., *News* uses a different system. The paper switched from contract trucks to company-owned vehicles, feeling that they could handle the job more efficiently. The newspaper's circulation manager explains it this way: "We purchased a fleet of five one-ton pickup trucks, using night-shift police officers as afternoon part-time drivers. These trucks are for city delivery only, hauling nearly 31,000 copies daily and Sunday. Our savings in operating our own delivery system are not too great. However, we feel that much has been accomplished because we have a greater control over the delivery as well as over those who operate the trucks."

Because the problems and procedures of newspaper delivery have become quite complex and diverse, an entire chapter is devoted to the subject (see Chapter 14).

Collecting

Maintaining a strong circulation depends as much upon a prompt, regular collection system as it does upon a good sales record. Efficient collecting is one of the key factors in building a list of permanent subscribers. If the paper is sold and delivered by independent contractors, there is a dual collecting process. The carrier collects from customers, and the newspaper collects from the carrier. It is just as important to have the carriers keep their bills paid as it is to have the subscribers pay carriers promptly.

Most newspapers require from each carrier or independent contractor a refundable cash bond deposit equal to anywhere from two weeks' to three months' bill. It impresses upon the carrier the importance of keeping up with collections and maintaining a good standing with the newspaper. This collecting system, carried on by the Atlanta, Ga., *Journal* and *Constitution,* is described as follows:

> We usually do not collect the entire amount of the bond at one time, but accept an initial payment and the balance, so much weekly. The carriers are paid 2 percent interest on this cash bond deposit. In addition to this cash bond deposit, we require the distributor or independent contractor to have one surety signature. If the distributor defaults, we are not only protected by cash bond deposit but also by the surety signing an agreement with us. The majority of our distributors collect weekly from their subscribers. We, in turn, bill them weekly for their papers. In this manner, the amount that the distributor owes us is never so great that it is a collection problem.

In city and suburbs. Most newspapers with carriers who are independent contractors require them to collect from the subscribers they serve (Fig. 13.4). Some, however, will permit subscribers to pay at the office. The Norman, Okla., *Transcript* allows city subscribers the choice of paying the carrier weekly, by the month in advance, or to the office for 3, 6, or 12 months in advance. Carriers maintain all records on the weekly and monthly subscribers and receive credit on their weekly bills for the office PIA's (paid in advance).

In rural areas. Two general collecting methods are used for mail subscriptions: mail notices and route collectors. The first method usually is tried initially and, if that is not successful, the second is put into operation.

A first notice is sent out a few weeks before the subscription expires. If the subscriber does not respond by the expiration date, another notice says that it will be necessary to stop the paper if the subscription is not paid by a certain time. A third notice a short time later expresses regret over being forced to take the subscriber from the list. Often the third notice brings results if the others fail.

YOUR HAMMOND TIMES SUBSCRIPTION EXPIRES _____, 19____
RENEW YOUR SUBSCRIPTION NOW.

Name _____

Street _____

City _____, State _____

( )   ( )   ( )   ( )
1 month   3 months   6 months   1 year

Zone _____

Fill out this card; put it with your remittance by check or money order, in an envelope and return it to this office. To avoid interruption in your subscription, you are kindly requested to attend to this matter at once.

THE HAMMOND TIMES
Circulation Department

Fig. 13.4.   The postal card expiration notice used by the Hammond, Ind., *Times*.

Some newspapers use a four-notice mailing. The first one, an illustrated printing in two colors, is sent out 28 days prior to expiration. The second notice, of a different color, is mailed 14 days before expiration. The third notice, printed in red and black, carries the headline, "Don't Wait 'Til The Last Minute; Your Subscription Is Expiring," with the picture of a man who has arrived at a railway station too late to catch a train. This goes out five days preceding expiration. The fourth and final notice, sent out four days after the paper is stopped, is a personal note from the circulation manager, done in his own handwriting, saying, "Exciting days lie ahead! We are sure you will not want to be without your newspaper for long."

The St. Joseph, Mo., *News-Press* and *Gazette* believes in notifying subscripers well in advance of the expiration date. Twenty days before a subscriber's time has expired the following brief letter is received from the circulation manager:

DEAR SUBSCRIBER:

Your subscription is due to expire in a few days. The exact date of expiration appears on the address label of your paper.

We send you this advance notice because the rules of the U.S. Post Office and the Audit Bureau of Circulations require all mail subscriptions of any publication be paid in advance or the subscriber's name promptly removed from the mailing list.

It's easy to renew. Just check the papers of your choice, check the length of the subscription you wish, fill out the handy universal check and mail.

Why not do it right now and avoid the possibility of missing a single issue.

Thanks!

This same letter is used in a second mailing to the subscriber ten days later if in the meantime the subscription has not been renewed. With the letter goes a blank check and a schedule of subscription rates by mail. Then if by five days after expiration date the subscriber has not responded, this more personal note is sent from the circulation manager:

YOU HAVEN'T RENEWED YOUR NEWSPAPER
WE WONDER WHY . . .

Dear Friend:

Judy, who handles our mail records, just showed me where you did not renew your subscription when it recently expired.

Naturally, both of us are wondering why. We're wondering where "we missed the boat."

Would you do us a favor by checking the information at the bottom of this page and returning it? It will help us a lot as we try to improve our newspaper and our service. If you need more room, just write on the back.

At the bottom of the letter are three spaces for the subscriber to fill in, giving the reasons for his delay in renewing:

( ) Delivery was not satisfactory.
( ) Reason for not renewing. . . . .
    . . . .
( ) Have just been putting it off, please renew. Order card and payment
    are enclosed.

Although most newspapers obtain new rural subscriptions and renewals by mail, some papers maintain rural collectors who cover the rural routes at intervals, soliciting prospects and collecting for monthly, quarterly, semiannual, and annual subscriptions previously obtained. They usually work on a commission basis with a car expense allowance. The most common commission is 50 percent for new subscribers and 20 or 25 percent for renewals.

By postponed billing. Frequently, some mail subscribers and persons who phone in subscriptions present a collection problem. Few publishers will demand immediate payment. Instead they usually start the paper and mail a statement later. The Springfield, Mo., *News* and *Leader and Press* collects for such subscriptions by using a combination letter and statement. At the bottom of a regular subscription statement appears this note of appreciation.

Thanks for your order to the Springfield paper. The Springfield *Daily News* or the Springfield *Leader-Press* is $2.70 a month. You may pay for any number of months you wish.

PLEASE NOTE: The postal department requires that mail subscriptions be paid in advance so we are leaving your paper on for 10 days in order to give you time to send in your remittance.

According to the circulation manager, the paper receives almost 100 percent remittances, and the people often order for a longer subscription period than they had originally requested.

CIRCULATION POLICIES

There is no established standard for circulation building. Most papers want all the readers they can get, but there are conditions in some communities where such a circulation would appear to be unprofitable. There seems to be a growing tendency toward concentrated circulation — that is, a more solid coverage of close-in territory.

Eliminating fringe circulation

In one campaign, the Cincinnati, Ohio, *Enquirer* eliminated a total of 11,257 daily and 13,937 Sunday copies of "fringe" circulation and set about to build up a more intensified coverage in its city zone and retail trading zone. Within two years following this drastic trimming of the subscription rolls in outlying territory, the *Enquirer* added an average of 12,936 daily and 13,014 Sunday copies in the close-in area. The *Enquirer* gives three principal reasons for making this adjustment:

1. Records proved conclusively that the *Enquirer*'s circulation trends over the years in those particular areas were more or less static despite consistent hard-hitting promotional efforts; this was because those towns were in the orbit of another city.
2. At the time of the change the newspaper was woefully short of newsprint. Top management gave the circulation department its choice. It could either eliminate "fringe" circulation and continue to promote closer in, or it could cut off all promotion and maintain the status quo.
3. A by-product was a saving in transportation, maintenance, and promotion cost. The manager says, "We've long since absorbed that saving in our expenditures within the close-in territories. This again, seems to make good sense. We now have a compact area to promote. We have better control of our employes and carriers. The *Enquirer* is eminently satisfied with the results. I don't think we will ever try again to establish ourselves in territories that logically do not belong in the circulation area of the Cincinnati *Enquirer* and its local advertisers. We have added a few newsstands in some of the territories cut off, but in each case we are charging more for our paper so we get enough money out of it to pay the distribution and newsprint cost."

The change brought no unfavorable reaction from national advertisers. Some rumblings came from local merchants but nothing that could not be easily overcome with the application of hard, unemotional facts.

This remarkable recovery of circulation volume in a more desirable territory was due to:

1. Short-range and long-range objectives focused so that everyone worked in the same direction.
2. Careful attention to detail in all sales promotion planning.
3. Intelligent merchandising of every campaign and contest.
4. Consistent, enthusiastic follow-up activity in person and in writing through carrier organization, circulation promotion department, field employes, and department heads.
5. Individual quotas and prize awards for every field employe and carrier.
6. Painstaking analysis of individual and group results after each campaign, with corrective measures promptly taken.
7. Constant and cheerful recognition of accomplishment by field employes and carriers.
8. Intelligent understanding and support of top management.
9. Determined elimination of "road blocks to progress" caused by obsession with administrative and routine details in the field.
10. Insistence on sound home delivery service.

Establishing sound policy

Every publisher would prefer to have the subscription list composed entirely of persons who, without outside persuasion, subscribed to the newspaper simply because they needed and wanted it. There are many such subscribers, but a majority who buy newspapers on a yearly or monthly basis are persuaded to do so by strong appeals to their community patriotism, to their family responsibility, to their very personal desires and needs, or to their "pocketbooks." Newspapers require selling just as much as any other article on the market, and every method possible is used in building circulation.

Premiums, prizes, discounts, bonuses, and contests often are used to stimulate a quick response from a large number of people. However, if these methods are used extensively, gains may be lost, at least partially, within a few months or a year. They are not too reliable in building permanent circulation.

The Audit Bureau of Circulations discourages premiums, discounts, and contests by requiring that the money paid for a subscription be at least 50 percent of the established price for the period ordered. When a premium is offered with a subscription, the full price of the premium must be collected in addition to at least 50 percent of the regular price asked for the subscription. Advertising agencies also place less value on circulation obtained by premiums and special offers. For that reason, the Audit

Bureau of Circulations lists in the newspaper's audit report the number of subscriptions sold by that means.

Contests where subscription sales tally votes for someone in a popularity competition or serve as credit toward an automobile have about run their course. Subscription campaign organizations that operate on a high level continue to find favor with some nondailies, but they get little support among daily newspapers. The general feeling is that a good newspaper should have plenty of selling points without resorting to other inducements; its features, news coverage, service to advertisers — the basic factors in circulation building — should be sufficient to do the job well.

Whatever the circulation promotion system, successful selling costs both time and money. In a survey of 159 newspapers of the United States and Canada, L. Richard Guylay, a New York public relations consultant, found that 23.7 percent of all money expended for promotion was used in building circulation.

Loose and tight operations

In its book entitled *Circulation Management,* the Texas Circulation Managers Association says:

> We can accept two fundamental principles of circulation management, the difference and importance of which are frequently overlooked, not only by circulation managers but by publishers as well. . . . At one extreme is a "loose operation," a circulation policy designed primarily to produce a large circulation volume with operating profit or promotion expense of secondary consideration. . . . The other extreme is termed "tight operation," a policy in which operating profit is of first importance, with circulation volume of secondary consideration.

Each has advantages and disadvantages:

ADVANTAGES	DISADVANTAGES
Loose Operation	
1. Produces circulation volume quickly.	1. Usually is excessively expensive.
2. Valuable in highly competitive situations.	2. Does not build permanent circulation.
3. Puts circulation department "on its toes."	3. Not favored by ABC and advertising agencies.
Tight Operation	
1. Is not expensive.	1. Hard to produce increases.
2. Provides greater profits.	2. Deprives circulation department of enthusiasm and enterprise.
3. Builds dependable circulation.	3. Invites competition to enter field.
4. Keeps circulation stable.	4. Makes merchants feel circulation is not adequate.

Every newspaper should have a definite circulation policy, formulated through conferences of all department heads, because the work of all departments has a direct bearing on circulation. When the policy is established, the spirit and the interest must be created to carry it out.

SUBSCRIPTION RATES

As newspaper production costs spiral, publishers naturally look for ways to increase revenue. For example, newsprint price increases have led publishers to reexamine subscription rate policies, and there has been a remarkable change of attitude on this issue.

Not so long ago most publishers felt that newspapers should be sold at the lowest possible price and that advertising should be relied upon to bring in the bulk of the revenue needed to meet publication expenses. Now, however, there is a growing belief that the circulation department must provide its proportionate share. As a result, there has been little hesitancy about raising the subscription price at every advance in newsprint cost.

While publishers are more courageous about raising newspaper delivery prices and street sale prices and give consideration to actual production costs, they still are somewhat reluctant to ask the subscriber to pay all that the labor, material, and time put into the newspaper justify. Their belief that circulation must be kept high to attract advertising is sound. But circulation also must pay its way.

Whatever the newspaper's policy may be regarding circulation rates, a careful accounting of all costs and revenues in the department is one of the principal responsibilities of any circulation manager. Many newspapers keep up with the figures on daily "draw" (actual number of newspapers issued to each carrier or dealer), subscription orders, and collections by standard bookkeeping methods. But more are moving into computerized accounting for circulation, as highly efficient data processing equipment adds this duty to its performances for the other departments of the newspaper.

The 360 data processing system, for example, provides a feasible method for internally storing all basic route-draw records. All statistics, billing, transportation, routing, and press requirements are simply a by-product of recording draw changes, entering them into the system, and producing updated draw records for each route.

Therefore, on a daily basis, once the draw changes enter the system and edition deadlines become due, the system automatically produces the following: press order requirements (by carrying forward new balances on the basis of changes processed), galley route cards and tape labels, mail-subscription labels, transportation routing and loading schedules, and Audit Bureau of Circulation (ABC) statistical figures. Draw summaries are weekly and monthly bills, account summaries for audit control, and circulation revenue reports.

Other functions handled on this mechanized basis include paid-in-advance and mail-subscription procedures; weekly, monthly, quarterly, and annual internal and ABC circulation statistics; and delinquent-account reports.

14

Obtaining and handling carriers

For my ten years as general manager of the International Circulation Managers Association, I have advocated strengthening of the "Little Merchant" youth carrier system. I still know no more efficient and economical way to get newspapers distributed.

Cyrus H. Favor

Experience demonstrates that newspaper carriers are best obtained and held when the circulation manager:

1. Has the sympathetic cooperation of school administrators, youth leaders, and parents.
2. Emphasizes the business training advantages available to carriers.
3. Provides adequate training, proper supervision, sufficient monetary reward, and other inducements to keep carriers interested.

COOPERATION OF HOME AND SCHOOL

Publicity about intangible as well as financial advantages of newspaper carrying has helped sell the position to most school administrators and youth leaders, but a circulation manager still needs to sell these individuals in the community. International Newspaper Carrier Day provides an excellent opportunity to establish a background of favorable public opinion as well as to glamorize the position itself.

A glowing picture of a typical carrier was painted by the governor of Maryland some years ago in this proclamation for International Newspaper Carrier Day, published in Maryland daily newspapers:

Throughout this book, care has been taken to show that no sex discrimination exists as far as employe opportunities on newspapers are concerned. However, because many of the quotes and examples used in this chapter recall the historical precedent associating males with the delivery of newspapers in the United States, the reader will find the concept of "newspaperboy" dominant in this portion of the text. It should be observed that an ever increasing number of female carriers, dealers, and distributors now constitute a substantial percentage of the newspaper delivery work force.

Behind that tune of whistled merriment you hear coming down the street, there is a boy.

He may be wearing his school clothes, or maybe he is happier in his dungarees.

He could be afoot, or he could be riding a bicycle.

He knows every dog in the neighborhood affectionately by name, and tails wag for a word of greeting.

All of the youngsters know him, too, and some of them envy his place of importance in the community.

Adults eagerly await his coming and fret if sometimes he is a little late.

Children, too, look with eagerness for his arrival.

He carries the pulse and the heartbeat, the joys and the sorrow, the serious comment and the daily humor of a varied world in a canvas bag.

He leaves intelligence, matters of great moment, and matters of human interest in doorways and on doorsteps.

He smiles in the sun and laughs at the rain; slides happily on icy sidewalks, despite the burdened sling on his shoulders, and makes the best of the drifting snow.

His is the final service of the day in a task in which many had labored — writers and copyreaders, typesetters and printers, circulation men and mailing room men, advertising men, switchboard operators and others, unknown people and people of note, but none known so well in a given neighborhood as he.

He is the American Newspaperboy.

The purpose of International Newspaper Carrier Day is to honor efficient carriers and outline the advantages to youths who serve in this responsible position. Associations of circulation managers, newspaper publishers, and educators do much to emphasize the valuable training acquired in this field. But publishers and their circulation managers exert the greatest influence in encouraging boys and girls to join the carrier ranks. For example, they might:

1. Obtain permission to place posters on bulletin boards in junior and senior high schools showing the advantages enjoyed by newspaper carriers.
2. Send to each youth group member in the community an attractively printed sheet with a group picture of local carriers and an outline of the benefits they receive.
3. Appear before youth groups to explain the opportunities for valuable business training in newspaper carrying.
4. Have a carrier appear on a television program occasionally to tell about the territory and the number of patrons served and to state an opinion of the newspaper.
5. Run full-page promotion ads containing pictures and testimonials from persons high in public life who were once carriers.
6. Regularly publish the picture of a carrier and a few facts concerning parents, chief interests in school, hobbies, territory served, and standing in the carrier organization.

7. Invite prospective carriers to a meeting at which outstanding carriers are recognized and rewarded.

Depending strongly upon the cooperation of parents in maintaining good carrier service, the circulation manager of the Peoria, Ill., *Journal-Star* has formulated the following six points (applicable to girls as well), which are typical of the newspaper-parent cooperative program followed by many newspapers:

1. *Interview with Boy and Parents*
   Before the boy takes over the route, an appointment is made by the circulation manager with the boy and his parents to go over the entire job of carrying a Journal or Star route. During the interview the manager fills in a report for the office and leaves a copy with the parents. Also all office forms are filled out, such as Identification Cards, Carrier Insurance Application, Office Control Records, and Carrier Merchant Contract. A Birthday Report also is made out and filed so that the new carrier will receive a birthday card on his next birthday. A substantial cash bond also is collected at that time.

2. *Letter to Parents*
   A letter to parents is sent out with a questionnaire to make doubly sure the manager has not misrepresented the route and has explained everything thoroughly to all concerned.

3. *Congratulation Letter*
   A letter of congratulation to the new carrier goes out from the circulation manager together with a Carrier Handbook.

4. *Postcard to School Principal*
   A postcard is sent to the school principal to solicit the cooperation of the school authorities, who help in recommending good carriers.

5. *Ten-Day Notice Cards and Letters to Parents*
   Ten-Day Notice Cards are mailed in by carriers who wish to terminate their contracts. Upon receipt of this card a route list form and letter are sent to the parents. The route lists are used to make up new collection cards for the new carrier taking over the route.

6. *Cash Bond Is Released and Letter to Parents*
   The cash bond is released ten days after the new boy makes his first collection. A check is mailed with a questionnaire to the parents of the boy giving up the route. This questionnaire asks just why their son is giving up route work. If there are any ill feelings or misunderstandings, an effort is made to clear them up.
   It is important that boys leave routes feeling kindly toward the newspaper for they will become advertisers and subscribers in a very few years.
   A close relationship between the newspaper and home is maintained by bulletins and letters from the circulation manager to parents of the carriers, explaining various aspects of service and whenever possible giving commendation for the work that is being done. Parents thereby become as interested as the boys in building up the carrier routes and in keeping customers satisfied.

Circulation managers or supervisors sometimes experience difficulty in persuading parents that their children should become newspaper carriers. Some direct questions and strong arguments have to be met convincingly.

When a youth becomes interested in taking a paper route for the Dayton, Ohio, *Daily News,* the newspaper's circulation manager immediately contacts the parents, realizing that they must be sold on the idea as well. Knowing that some objections probably will be voiced, the manager takes along a list of many of the objections that could be raised and reasonable answers to them, for example:

Objection: Johnny doesn't have time for a newspaper route. He belongs to the Scouts, the YMCA, and takes music lessons. He's just too busy for a newspaper route now.

Answer: I knew Johnny was busy, Mrs. Smith, before I came to see you. We check all boys who are considered for newspaper routes, and the one thing we always look for is the boy who is already busy. We've found that among our 2,500 newspaper carriers, it's the busy boys who always do well. Just look at some of the stories about our carriers, Mrs. Smith. Many of them have the same activities your son has, and I'll bet Johnny could do this job as well as any of these, couldn't he?

Objection: Johnny's dad doesn't want him to have a newspaper route.

Answer: I'm sorry to hear that, Mrs. Smith. However, I'm not here to talk to you about a newspaper route only. I believe after you've seen examples of the fine training I have here, you'll want your son to enjoy this training, too. You and Mr. Smith certainly want him to enjoy the same training benefits and opportunities others enjoy, don't you Mrs. Smith?

Objection: The Jones boy down the street had this route. He had a lot of trouble with it and finally gave it up. I wouldn't want my boy to have the route.

Answer: That's a shame about the Jones boy, Mrs. Smith, and I don't blame you for not wanting your boy to have that same experience. But I wonder, Mrs. Smith, if your son would have the same experience. From what I hear about him, I believe he could do a very good job. With 2,500 carriers, we're bound to have some who occasionally can't make the grade, even as schools and other organizations find those who are not yet ready for the experience. But, as I said, Mrs. Smith, from comments I've heard about your son, I believe he would definitely rank with our carriers. I don't believe we should penalize him by comparing him with another boy, do you, Mrs. Smith?

Objection: I've watched the carriers deliver all during this cold winter weather. I certainly don't want my boy to have to go through that.

Answer: This has been a mighty severe winter for everyone, Mrs. Smith. Just about as bad as they come. However, most boys prefer to be outdoors during winter weather. They spend much more time playing, coasting and ice skating than they would spend on a newspaper route. Actually, I don't believe you would want your boy to spend every cold day by the fireside while others are out enjoying themselves, would you, Mrs. Smith?

Objection: This route is four miles long and too scattered. It would be too much work.

Answer: I don't blame you, Mrs. Smith. It's a long route and it will involve work, but I think you will agree your son's success as an adult will depend primarily upon how he handles each job regardless of difficulties. When Abe Lincoln was a boy he walked miles to school and split rails. That, too, was hard work. Yet I believe the responsibility, development and extra effort helped him quite a bit, don't you, Mrs. Smith?

Objection: You said this route only pays $8.50 a week. That isn't enough money to fool with. I can give my boy an allowance and save him the trouble.

Answer: You're right, Mrs. Smith. You can give your boy $8.50 a week and never miss it. But can you give him the training? After you've given him the allowance for two years, will he be any better prepared for future responsibility? That's the big difference, Mrs. Smith. You know as well as I do the earnings from a newspaper route are secondary. They are unimportant to you as a parent. The main thing you want to accomplish is to train your boy to accept responsibility, meet people, get along in a group, and appreciate the value of a dollar earned. Isn't that right, Mrs. Smith?

Objection: I feel the route will interfere with school work.

Answer: Mrs. Smith, here's what a superintendent of schools says about that (show quotation from local school administrator). A newspaper route can be a supplement to school work. If the boy will follow through and operate his route efficiently it will be an education in itself and the time spent on a route will pay future dividends just as time spent in school.

Question: It seems to me the route will cause added expense such as shoes and wear on his bicycle, so I don't think it will be worthwhile.

Answer: You're right. There will be added expenses just as there are going into any business for yourself. In your boy's case, however, expenses will be low compared with earnings and very low in comparison with the valuable experience he will receive—experience that can't be evaluated in a monetary sense. Here's what the vice-president of a bank says about that, "I'm sure if we can teach him how to budget his money and pay some of his own expenses, he will learn the value of the dollar and grow up with a better sense of responsibility for money. He definitely will have the jump on the boy who has not had the opportunity to earn his own money at an early age."

This usually removes the doubts that parents may have, and they agree for their son or daughter to become a carrier. Then after the boy or girl has served for a few months, the parents are sent a letter with a questionnaire:

This survey is being made in the hope that you will pass along to us observations you've made in your close daily contact with your son on his newspaper route.

As you already know, our greatest responsibility is to provide a sound, well-planned newspaper program . . . that will assure each carrier full training benefits from his newspaper route experience.

This questionnaire will help us considerably in developing these training programs and improving our present methods of counseling carriers.

Your interest and cooperation in completing it will be greatly appreciated.

The answers to the questionnaire were important to the circulation department in helping the new carrier to become fully adjusted to his position.

EMPHASIS ON BUSINESS TRAINING

Economic conditions have some influence. Young people are more interested in working when there is pressure to help supplement the family income — to earn money with which to buy school supplies; tickets to the movies, games, and contests; and some of the clothes they wear. However, under all conditions, in good times or bad, newspaper carrying gives youth the opportunity to learn from experience the fundamentals of self-preservation and business success. Many persons prominent in business, the professions, and in public life give credit to the valuable training they received as carriers.

In a full-page advertisement the Minneapolis, Minn., *Star* and *Tribune* published this description of a typical *Star* and *Tribune* carrier:

He's one of 9,000 carefree teensters who daily whistle their way down city streets and small town avenues, each deftly plunking eighty to ninety newspapers on waiting doorsteps throughout the 225-county area of Minnesota, North and South Dakota, and Western Wisconsin.

What does this typical American junior businessman look like? He's a teenage boy in junior or senior high school. His grades are good; mostly above class average. He owns a bicycle, $50 to $100 in U.S. Savings Bonds, and has a bank account of about $200. He may own life insurance, in addition, paid out of earnings.

He has had his paper route about a year, is probably a Boy Scout, attends Sunday School regularly, and has extra church duties. He also engages in at least one school activity: sports, music, theatricals, or debating.

His father may be a judge, a mechanic, a farmer, or even a corporation president. And like most kids he grins sheepishly when the "Old Man" points with pride to the enviable training his carrier-salesman son is getting in self-reliance, service, salesmanship, poise, and business ability.

Like most Upper Midwesterners, he enjoys his job, his life, and the place where he lives.

ADEQUATE TRAINING, SUPERVISION, AND REWARD

The wise circulation manager selects candidates carefully to insure carriers who will remain on the job. The longer a boy or girl carries a route, the better acquainted he or she becomes with customers and the better he or she understands the possibilities of increasing patronage. A heavy turnover in carriers is costly to a newspaper. Taking on a person who is not fit for the job and has to be relieved in a short time brings about a bad situation. The youth is likely to feel resentment toward the newspaper, an attitude that will persist for many years. But a person who has good relations with the newspaper probably will help find a capable replacement.

The right start

To recruit youths who will develop into first-class carriers, the circulation manager should emphasize the following facts and make sure each person fully understands them:

1. The newspaper represented is worthy. The carrier should be acquainted with the newspaper's history, the features that will interest readers, the editor and manager, other important staff members, and the newspaper departments and how they operate. A tour of the plant should be an early step in carrier enlistment.
2. The position as carrier is important since no one else from the newspaper office will contact many of the persons served on the route. But the office personnel will be judged solely by the attitudes and actions of the carrier, who gives the finishing touches to an important project in which many others have taken part. The work done by others on the paper will be of no account if the paper is not delivered to the readers.
3. The carrier has a threefold responsibility — to sell, deliver, and collect. Each is as important as the others. A carrier cannot excel without also being a good salesperson and an efficient collector. A carrier develops longtime subscribers by giving good delivery service and collecting promptly.

Realizing the importance of giving a carrier the right start, the Gastonia, N.C., *Gazette* sends a form letter to each subscriber on the route, giving the new carrier's name, address, and phone number. In that way the readers at once become acquainted with the carrier and they know how to make contact if they wish to compliment or complain.

It is of utmost importance for the newspaper to show friendly interest and to stress the significance of the positon of carrier for the newspaper. The St. Joseph, Mo., *News-Press* and *Gazette* sends the following letter to a new carrier:

Dear Carrier Salesman:

Welcome to the St. Joseph News-Press and Gazette carrier organization of nearly 500 boys. I am happy you and your parents decided upon a News-Press and Gazette route and want to extend to you my personal wish for every success in this your new business venture.

The service you perform on your newspaper route is a vital one to the people in your community. Many man-hours of work go into publishing the paper each day and unless the paper is then delivered on time after each publication, it is of little value to the subscriber.

That is why the service you perform as a carrier salesman is so important. The people on your route rely on you to give them the best possible delivery service on their paper. You will find good delivery service is the best way to keep customers happy and it will also help you in securing new customers for your route.

I believe you will enjoy your News-Press and Gazette route. You will learn many things from handling a route as your own business. There may be some situations which will arise that may be somewhat unpleasant or difficult to handle. Your ability to meet and deal with these is the thing that is important to you. This you will learn through experience.

Your district manager will personally do everything he can to make your route experience a successful one. Feel free to discuss your route problems with him at all times.

Good Luck!

The right training

The Dayton, Ohio, *Daily News* emphasizes proper training for carriers and indicates the profits to be earned from conscientious effort and efficient work. For example, at a carrier meeting, the circulation manager explained that ten minutes a day devoted to calling on prospective subscribers would bring:

A. INCREASED EARNINGS — 10 minutes a day will increase your earnings, build your profits.
B. VALUABLE EXPERIENCE — 10 minutes a day will provide you valuable experience you can gain in no other way, and it is experience few in your neighborhood can enjoy.
C. PRIDE AND ACCOMPLISHMENT — 10 minutes a day will provide tangible proof to your parents and your friends that you can do an outstanding job as a newspaper carrier.
D. RECOGNITION — 10 minutes a day will help you to be an honor newspaper carrier.
E. FUN AND COMPETITION — 10 minutes a day will permit you to participate in a special newspaper carrier activity which will mean fun, achievement and competition based on your own interest and initiative.

As much care should be given to training the carrier after he or she has taken the job as in selection. Evidence of good character, satisfactory school record, parental backing, and an eager desire to succeed does not necessarily mean the boy or girl is fully prepared for the work ahead. Every good circulation manager impresses upon carriers the importance of these principles:

IN SELLING	IN CARRYING	IN COLLECTING
Neatness in dress	Promptness in	Regularity
Politeness	starting	Correct records
Courtesy	Attending to business	Necessary
Reasonable persistence	Putting paper on	equipment
Businesslike manner	porch	Receipt for amount
Knowledge of product	Giving equal service	collected
Honest presentation	to all patrons	No arguing
Definite number of	Having a substitute	Paying paper bills
calls each day	available	promptly
	Covering route in	Showing apprecia-
	same order daily	tion for money paid
	Protecting papers in	
	wet weather	

Manuals provided by most large newspapers supply carriers with definite information about their work and underscore the dignity of the position they hold.

The Rockford, Ill., *Morning Star* and *Register-Republic* provided a manual entitled, *Tomorrow's Successful Businessman.* The picture of a healthy carrier, smiling, with his hands in his trousers' pockets and chest thrown out, appeared on the cover page. This booklet, in addition to giving explicit instructions about selling, delivery, and collecting, explained each of the forms that a carrier would receive in connection with service to the newspaper and customers: complaint slip, subscriber's statement, collection book slip, carrier's statement, subscriber's receipt card, and "start" and "stop" order forms.

Pictures of its own carriers were used by the Los Angeles, Calif., *Herald-Examiner* in a large manual to illustrate proper carrier service methods. Getting down to brass tacks in selling, the booklet offered these hints on how to overcome the objections most commonly heard:

NOT INTERESTED

Mrs. Greene, I can easily understand why you feel this way, but perhaps you haven't been reading the *Herald-Examiner* lately. You know we have added many new attractive features. (Follow this statement up with points about some feature that would be of interest to a woman; tell her of the interest her husband will have in the *Herald-Examiner*'s sport page.)

CANNOT AFFORD

This objection is easily overcome by showing the housewife many bargains that appear daily in our advertising columns: sale advertisements about articles that are regular items on her shopping list, the purchase of which would save more than the price of the daily and Sunday *Herald-Examiner.* Tell her of the large classified section, where every day there are bargains that would save many, many times the cost of the paper.

NO TIME TO READ

The *Herald-Examiner* is especially designed to meet the requirements of the person who is anxious to keep himself currently informed of the important news of the day yet only has a very few moments to spend reading at the breakfast table each morning. Headlines of all articles are especially arranged by experts to draw your attention to the most important events first, so you may be briefly, yet completely, informed of topics which will no doubt be discussed by your associates throughout the day.

DON'T LIKE DELIVERY SERVICE

That one you know you can overcome. Without doubt this person has some time in the past been a *Herald-Examiner* subscriber, on the route of a careless carrier. You know you can guarantee delivery of the paper in a way that will be completely satisfactory. Just ask them where they expect their paper delivered and in turn assure them it will be THERE.

The training committee of the International Circulation Managers Association prepares excellent publications, like *The Boy with the World on a String,* to be used by member newspapers in their contacts with prospective newspaper carriers and their parents, educators, and civic leaders. Such publications help to promote the in-depth value of newspaper carrier self-development.

Capable supervision and wise counseling

Circulation managers should use great care in selecting personnel to supervise carriers because character as well as ability is involved.

Fred L. Engard, circulation director of the Spokane, Wash., *Spokesman Review* and *Daily Chronicle,* told a workshop group of managers in the Pacific Northwest area that "the fortunes of any circulation department rise or fall on the performance of its district advisors; they hold the key to maintaining a record of good service to our readers and a satisfactory pattern of circulation growth. A newspaper's image and reputation in the community depend to a large extent on the district advisor's responsible leadership in the field. The advisor and carriers form the front line as public relations representatives in every neighborhood and may be the only persons connected with our newspaper that the average subscriber knows."

One newspaper learned from a questionnaire distributed among its district supervisors that only 35 percent felt "dedicated" to their work and 65 percent expressed discontent. A professional attitude among district managers is vital to the health of the newspaper's circulation; and persons who are unable to cope with such problems as carrier recruitment, emergency delivery of routes that may be "down," follow-up of difficult collections, and wise handling of as many as 2,500 carriers in some districts should not be considered eligible candidates for the job.

Proper preliminary training for the supervisor, therefore, is just as important as it is for carriers. Included in training should be the:

1. Relation of the position to overall circulation effort.
2. Importance of getting good carriers and holding them.
3. Need for constant study of the territory.
4. Value of parental cooperation.
5. Handling of service errors.
6. Solution of little everyday problems of carriers.

One of the chief duties of a supervisor is to increase the number of subscribers on each route in the district. Selling efficiency among carriers may be developed in several ways:

1. Make sure each carrier understands the profit earned on each customer.
2. Instruct each carrier in how to sell and in tested ways of convincing prospects.
3. Assist the carrier in working each route systematically so that every potential subscriber is given frequent chances to buy.

4. Encourage the carrier to utilize all promotions to the fullest advantage. Make it easy for each one to get "free sample copies" when approved or other printed promotional material as it is made available.
5. Make the carrier feel important with each and every order obtained.

The supervisors will obviously perform more efficiently within the framework of a planned training program such as the one developed by the El Paso, Tex., *Times* and *Herald-Post*. The 15-week course specializes in motivational techniques for district managers and route supervisors, and uses carefully prepared behavioral science principles. Emphasis is placed on achieving goals through understanding psychological needs of carriers and customers, and then moving to meet those needs in ways that will increase productivity and profit. The El Paso program represents a serious approach, complete with classwork assignments and examinations, to the training of district personnel who represent one of the most critical links in the organization of circulation departments.

Adequate financial reward
How much profit should carriers realize? Perhaps the simplest answer would be: "Enough to keep them satisfied with the job, but not so satisfied that they would not hustle for more subscribers."

From facts provided in a study of 36 newspapers and by using a little arithmetic, the circulation manager of the Charlotte, N.C., *Observer* determined that a fair margin of weekly profit on each subscriber would vary from 8.5 to 22 cents according to the subscription price.

Carriers sometimes work on a straight salary, but more often they lease the route from the newspaper or they serve under a contract. Details of the lease or contract should be fully understood by carriers and parents.

In the lease form commonly used the carrier:

1. Acknowledges receipt of a list of subscribers who purchase the paper and live on a certain route.
2. Agrees to sell and deliver to all subscribers at the established rate.
3. Agrees not to sell or to deliver any other newspaper.
4. Agrees to promote and extend the circulation.
5. Agrees to give notice in advance of intent to give up the route.
6. Agrees not to turn over the subscription list or disclose the name of any subscriber to any person.
7. Testifies that no money has been paid to any person for the list of subscribers and that it will not be sold to anyone.
8. Agrees not to collect in advance from any subscriber.
9. Agrees to pay promptly and regularly at the established wholesale price for all copies allotted for delivery.
10. Agrees to keep a written list of all subscribers with their street addresses and to turn such list over to the newspaper upon cancellation of the lease.

The carrier usually is required to make a cash deposit sufficient to cover two weeks' billing for papers or to provide a surety bond covering any amounts owed at any time during the term of lease or contract. Newspapers often make liability insurance available to the carrier to cover medical or hospital bills in case of on-the-job accidents.

No ethical method to produce results is overlooked by an on-the-firing-line circulation manager, who peppers carriers with a great variety of offers and attractions, never knowing exactly which will bring the greatest results but recognizing in all some merit for the stimulation they give the carrier organization. Chief among these are: trips, scholarships, prizes, contests, honor awards, passes to sports events and entertainment, and participation events.

Trips. Trips are favored as incentives to exceptional service because they are both educational and entertaining. They give carriers an opportunity to learn more about their country and the world, and this perhaps helps to make them more aggressive.

The St. Joseph, Mo., *News-Press* and *Gazette* awarded to two carriers, one from the city and one from the country, an airplane trip to West Germany and Switzerland. Among the cities visited were Berne, Munich, Berlin, Cologne, and Dusseldorf. The carriers won their trips on the basis of sales, service, account payments, scholarship, activities in which they were engaged, and essays that they wrote. Forty-five other carriers in the same contest won free trips to the Mid-Continent Airport and the TWA Overhaul Base.

The Indianapolis, Ind., *Star* and *News* took 85 carriers and 6 district managers to New Orleans for four days one summer. To qualify for the trip, each carrier was required to increase the number of route patrons by 27 or obtain 44 new orders anywhere in the city. Each order was for a 13-week period.

All the employes of the Columbus, Ohio, *Citizen-Journal,* including carriers, were invited to compete for a five-day visit to New Orleans during Mardi Gras. The winner was permitted to take a family member and to receive salary while in New Orleans as if at home on the job. The second highest contestant received an all-expense trip for two people to New York for a weekend at the Waldorf-Astoria Hotel.

Forty-nine carriers for the Buffalo, N.Y., *Courier-Express* were given a weekend trip to New York City at the end of a contest in which each winner sold 25 daily and 16 Sunday 13-week orders. Two carriers of the Waukegan, Ill., *News-Sun* flew to Europe one summer as the newspaper's "cub reporters." Ten others flew to Washington, D.C. The trips were top prizes in a six-week drive for new subscribers. To arouse interest in the contest, letters were sent to parents, employes of the newspaper, heads of civic organizations, school leaders, and Waukegan merchants. Meetings were staged also, and the story appeared in the newspaper and was broadcast over the *News-Sun* radio station.

A red tag identified each of the Champaign-Urbana, Ill., *News-Gazette* carriers working for one of 18 air trips. New subscriptions were rated by points and those who did not get enough to make the trip were paid cash. The carriers wore the red tags when they made their calls.

Scholarships. College scholarships, too, are effective in developing good carrier service. Eight college scholarships with a total value of $12,000 are awarded annually to carriers of the Indianapolis, Ind., *News.* To be eligible, a youth must have carried the *News* for at least two years and have maintained a minimum of a B average in high school.

The Guy Gannett Publishing Company, from whose plant come the Portland, Maine, *Press Herald, Evening Express,* and *Sunday Telegram,* annually awards one scholarship with a maximum payment of $250 and two additional scholarships with a maximum payment of $200 at the end of each school year in June. Carriers in their junior or senior year of high school who have managed their routes for two full years are eligible to compete. Applicants are graded on scholastic ability, citizenship, and ability as carriers.

Four $150 scholarships offered by the Rockford, Ill., *Morning Star* and *Register-Republic* are honored at any college or university in the United States or Canada. The awards are based on: scholastic standing; citizenship, which includes church and youth group activities, extracurricular school work, and the like; salesmanship; service to subscribers; and financial standing, as demonstrated by savings and how earnings are used.

Many smaller dailies have adapted carrier incentive ideas from the larger newspapers, cutting the pattern to fit their operations.

Prizes. Merchandise and other prizes are proven incentives to increase subscription sales and to improve carrier service and collections. Coming to the circulation manager's desk regularly are catalogs with such suggestions as cameras, clothing, pens and pencils, radios, television sets, magician's outfits, games, sporting goods, clocks, watches, pocketknives, telescopes, printing outfits, kites, and bicycles. A random survey made by *Editor & Publisher* revealed that 14 newspapers, varying in size from 22,000 to over 400,000 circulation, spent over $550,000 for such prizes in one year.

One summer the Columbia, Mo., *Missourian* offered a bicycle to the boy or girl who would sell ten yearly subscriptions or the equivalent in shorter term or longer term subscriptions. Those who wanted to enter the sales effort were invited to join the Missourian Bicycle Club and to attend meetings for instructions on selling. A coupon to be filled in for club membership appeared in the newspaper. Pictures of the participants and brief sketches concerning them also were published in the *Missourian.* Twenty youths, about half of whom were carriers, comprised the sales army that besieged homes during the warm summer months, told the *Missourian* story, and obtained subscriptions.

The South Bend, Ind., *Tribune* makes a practice of offering seasonal prizes. At Easter the newspaper awarded a ten-pound ham for six new eight-week starts.

The Des Moines, Iowa, *Register* and *Tribune* developed enthusiasm among carriers and publicity for the newspapers when the promotion department launched a Red Necktie Club. When the number of patrons on a route was increased by two, the carrier was eligible for club membership and was given a red necktie to wear as a badge. The red neckties aroused questioning, carriers were ready with answers, and the conversation usually ended with an effective sales talk.

Contests. Carriers sometimes are pitted against each other in spirited contests to see who can bring in the most orders, show the greatest increase in route patronage, have the fewest service errors, or be the most prompt in making collections. Carriers in one circulation area may challenge their counterparts in another town of similar population, basing the competition on important service points; or the carriers in a town may be divided into groups to compete against each other.

Carriers of the St. Joseph, Mo., *News-Press* and *Gazette* won 204 Thanksgiving turkeys one year in contests within the carrier group. Also awarded were 113 pies, 74 dozen rolls, 40 sacks of dressing mix, and 18 cans of cranberry sauce.

Honor awards. Most newspapers recognize carriers for outstanding service, either with buttons, caps, badges, certificates, and bonuses or by some other means. An interesting plan was designed by the Jackson, Tenn., *Sun*. The basic part of the plan is the base pay of $4.75 per week for beginning carriers, with an additional bonus of $2 per week if they do not exceed one missed copy per week in delivery.

The plan is expanded from this basic wage and bonus. All carriers maintaining a "Perfect Week" receive in addition to the base pay and bonus an "Incentive Reward" of 25 cents. To achieve a perfect week the carrier must meet five principal conditions each day—no missed copies, no complaints on manner of delivery, reporting promptly to receive papers, completing delivery promptly, calling the circulation department each day when delivery is completed.

The incentive rewards are cumulative and increase 50 cents each week of consecutive perfect service up to a maximum of eight weeks. If carriers fail to maintain perfect weeks before a maximum of eight consecutive weeks are reached, they forfeit accumulated incentive rewards and begin again with the base pay and the bonus based on missed copies alone.

The Dayton, Ohio, *Daily News* has a simple, easy-to-operate Honor and Merit Program, which has been used in its circulation area with approval of school officials and other leading personnel (Fig. 14.1). It is based on 25 principles considered essential to a newspaper carrier's success. The principles are in the form of questions divided according to *service,*

Fig. 14.1. This chevron is awarded to each Dayton, Ohio, *Daily News* carrier with one year of service. After the first, a service chevron is awarded for each additional year. (Courtesy of the Dayton *Daily News.*)

collections, behavior, attitude, salesmanship, and *personal appearance.* For example, these five questions are asked about service:

1. Have there been any poor service complaints (late delivery, wet papers, papers not properly placed, papers missed, and the like)?
2. Is a satisfactory substitute available to deliver in an emergency?
3. Is the carrier on time each day for papers and are they delivered promptly?
4. Is every effort made to please subscribers?
5. Are all starts and stops turned in each day, so a complete route list can be maintained to take care of the route in an emergency?

Other questions on the rating form bear just as significantly on the carrier's success. Every question has a maximum value of four points. The year is divided into four periods with a separate award for each period to every carrier who earns a grade of 90 or better. Those earning an average grade of 90 for the four periods receive master honor recognition. Special shows and entertainment programs are planned to build interest in these awards. Each period winner is given an honor pin. Each master honor carrier receives a master honor pin and newspaper sack and is an honor guest at a banquet.

Publishing an Honor Roll in the newspaper, listing the names of carriers who have made outstanding records each month, stirs up pride and effort.

To emphasize the valuable training a youth receives while a carrier, some papers have arranged to issue Business Training Certificates to successful carriers for use when they complete their education and enter business life. Excellent promotional material is available from professional sources (see Fig. 14.2).

To sustain the interest of older carriers in newspaper delivery, the International Circulation Managers Association through its Newspaper Training Committee developed a series of two-color bulletins to be mailed

10 GOOD REASONS
why your boy or girl should have a newspaper route.

1. To earn money.

2. To learn self-reliance.

3. To learn to keep records, and to apply in a practical way math taught in the classroom.

4. To learn to handle money and appreciate its value.

5. To learn to be on time and how to ration time.

6. To learn courtesy and how to get along with people.

7. To learn marketing principles and salesmanship.

8. To experience the principles of the "free enterprise" system.

9. To be operating "a business" of their own.

10. To become sharper, brighter, more mature.

And, we can't think of a single reason why not!

NAME OF NEWSPAPER

For information on newspaper route management for your son or daughter, phone or visit our Circulation Department. They will be pleased to give you full details on available routes. Act now.

Fig. 14.2. A typical promotional advertisement designed to boost the image of the newspaper carrier. (Courtesy of the Hickey-Mitchell Company.)

to carriers in their homes. Twenty-four posters, 8½ by 11 inches, graphically portrayed the carrier in various poses as a young merchant and presented basic selling and service information.

Passes to sports events and entertainment. Passes to major league baseball games, important football games, circuses, basketball tournaments, or weekend outings have great appeal to carriers. The Independence, Mo.,

Examiner each year takes some of its carriers to baseball games in St. Louis and to the Shrine Circus in Kansas City. Eligibility is based on solicitations and a high standard of carrier service.

One winter when the Southern Methodist University football team was playing the University of Missouri at Columbia, Mo., the Dallas, Tex., *News* took a group of its best carriers on a sight-seeing trip through the Ozark Mountains to Columbia to enjoy the football game. Twelve new subscriptions to the South Bend, Ind., *Tribune* entitled a carrier to the Ice Capades in that city one winter.

Other events that may be used to stimulate carrier effort are wrestling matches, state fairs, and track meets.

Participation events. Many carrier organizations throughout the country have their own baseball or softball teams and participate in city tournaments. Suits are provided by the newspaper, and the carriers strive hard to bring honor to the organization they represent.

The Burlington, Vt., *Free Press* has an arrangement with the Burlington Community YMCA whereby the complete facilities are taken each Wednesday evening from 5 to 7:30 P.M. for exclusive use of its carriers. During this period, district circulation managers arrange swimming contests, gym classes, Ping-Pong tournaments, and other activities. Movies and other special events highlight such gatherings on announced evenings.

Shortly after school ends each spring, carriers of the Rockford, Ill., *Morning Star* and *Register-Republic* begin playing in their softball league at Rockford public parks. All playing equipment, such as gloves, bats, and balls, is furnished by the newspaper. Approximately 450 carriers take part in this organized play, which is under the direction of an employed physical education director from one of the public schools. Only *Morning Star* and *Register-Republic* carriers are eligible to compete, and each must have had a route regularly for at least 14 days before qualifying. During the winter months a Carriers' Basketball League is conducted exclusively for *Morning Star* and *Register-Republic* carriers.

MORALE BUILDING

Carriers are individuals, and therefore will not all respond to the same incentive plan. For this reason, a variety of recognition programs must be attempted to stimulate each carrier to maximum performance. The Charleston, S.C., *News and Courier* found that many of its carriers were receptive to the idea of going aboard the aircraft carrier Yorktown for a complete tour. Photographs of "carriers on a carrier" were given wide publicity coverage and proved to be a great goodwill builder.

Another form of recognition occurred during National Newspaper Week when the Nashville, Tenn., *Banner* involved the governor of that state in the celebration. The governor posed for a picture with carriers who were identical twins, which was published along with his proclamation of International Newspaper Carrier Day.

In a novel recognition of its "carrier of the year," the Minneapolis, Minn., *Star* and *Tribune* publicized the contest winner along with his parents at a banquet, then had the carrier chauffeured on his route in a Cadillac limousine. A quarter-page ad in all editions provided full recognition for the carrier.

Experience has revealed that many carriers are motivated more by incentives that satisfy the ego than by outright profits or awards. The knowledgeable circulation manager will be alert to which kind of promotion should be employed for maximum results.

The general morale of the carrier organization is lifted when the circulation manager and his supervisors pay attention to individual needs and abilities:

1. To handle routes properly, carriers must be in good health and not less than 12 years old.
2. Routes must be of such length that they can be covered in reasonable time.
3. The number and weight of the papers that must be carried should not be so great that the load is burdensome.
4. Arrangements should be made to receive papers at a convenient time and place.
5. The time required to carry the route should not be so long that carriers are deprived of time for study and activities they especially enjoy.
6. The bookkeeping required should be made as simple as possible.
7. Consideration should be given to the risks of being injured while carrying the route, often in bad weather, at night, and to homes where there are surly dogs.

To ascertain what is being done by newspapers of varied circulation, the following questions were presented to the Detroit, Mich., *Free Press;* Clinton, Iowa, *Herald;* Terre Haute, Ind., *Tribune* and *Star;* and Levittown, Pa., *Courier-Times.*

1. What is the average number of papers carried by each city carrier?
2. What is the average distance that the carrier goes in covering a route?
3. Does the carrier receive the daily draw of papers at the newspaper office or is it delivered to the home or to a certain spot in the territory?
4. In your opinion what age youth makes the most dependable carrier?
5. Are your carriers covered by liability or accident insurance? If so, is it paid for by newspaper, carrier, or both?

Results of this survey are given in Table 14.1.

The standard of a carrier's service depends to a certain degree upon how well the effect of careful delivery on income is understood. Many newspapers place a service charge against the carrier for every subscriber complaint. The carrier, however, is given the opportunity to erase or

Table 14.1.　Four-city survey of newspaper carrier service

City	Number of Papers	Route Length	Location Papers Received	Age	Insurance
Detroit	65	1 mi.	Branch stations	14	Yes — Carrier
Clinton	79	1 mi.	Home	12½	Yes — Carrier
Terre Haute	80	10 blks.	Home and stations	14	Yes — Both
Levittown	78	1 mi.	Stations	13	Yes — Paper

reduce that charge by going to the subscriber with an explanation and a promise of future good service. The Rockford, Ill., *Morning Star* and *Register-Republic,* which follows this plan, explains in the carrier's handbook its effect upon income (Fig. 14.3). A neatly printed simplified statement detailing the charges against the carrier for weekly or monthly newspaper purchases also is a great help toward carrier morale and efficiency. (See Fig. 14.4.)

The carrier must be dealt with by superiors in a friendly but businesslike manner. Example as well as precept has its effect. The Gastonia, N.C., *Gazette*'s system of keeping records on the number of papers taken by carriers each day, the stops, the starts, service errors, carriers' bonds, and collections is described below.

The carriers are divided into even numbers and odd numbers and there is a record sheet for each. The carriers of even numbers are served at one window and those of odd numbers at another. They receive papers in the order in which their numbers are called. The numbers are arranged in the books according to the distance of the route from the office.

For carriers served by trucks the old "galley system" is used and the draw (the number of papers the carrier is to receive) is revised from day to day. The draw sheet, on which is listed for the truck driver the carriers and the number of papers to be delivered to each, is sent to the mailroom in the morning and the wrappers are labeled to go out in the afternoon. Draw changes are accepted until Friday morning.

Bills are sent out Friday afternoon and most carriers pay on Saturday and Monday. An envelope statement form (with the bill computed on the outside) is used on all accounts. The carrier places the money in the envelope, takes it to the office or turns it over to the district driver, and receives a receipt. The amount is checked in the office and any error is reported to the carrier the next day. Before this plan was begun, carriers had long waits at the counters, piling out pocketsful of change. Now the carrier receives a receipt upon handing in his envelope and leaves. The money is counted during slack time.

When start orders are phoned to the office, they are sent to the carriers served by trucks and their "draws" are increased to insure papers being delivered that day. For carriers who call at the office for their papers, start orders are given when they draw their papers. Stops are handled practically the same way. A regular form is used to notify carriers of complaints.

The circulation manager must understand the importance of making

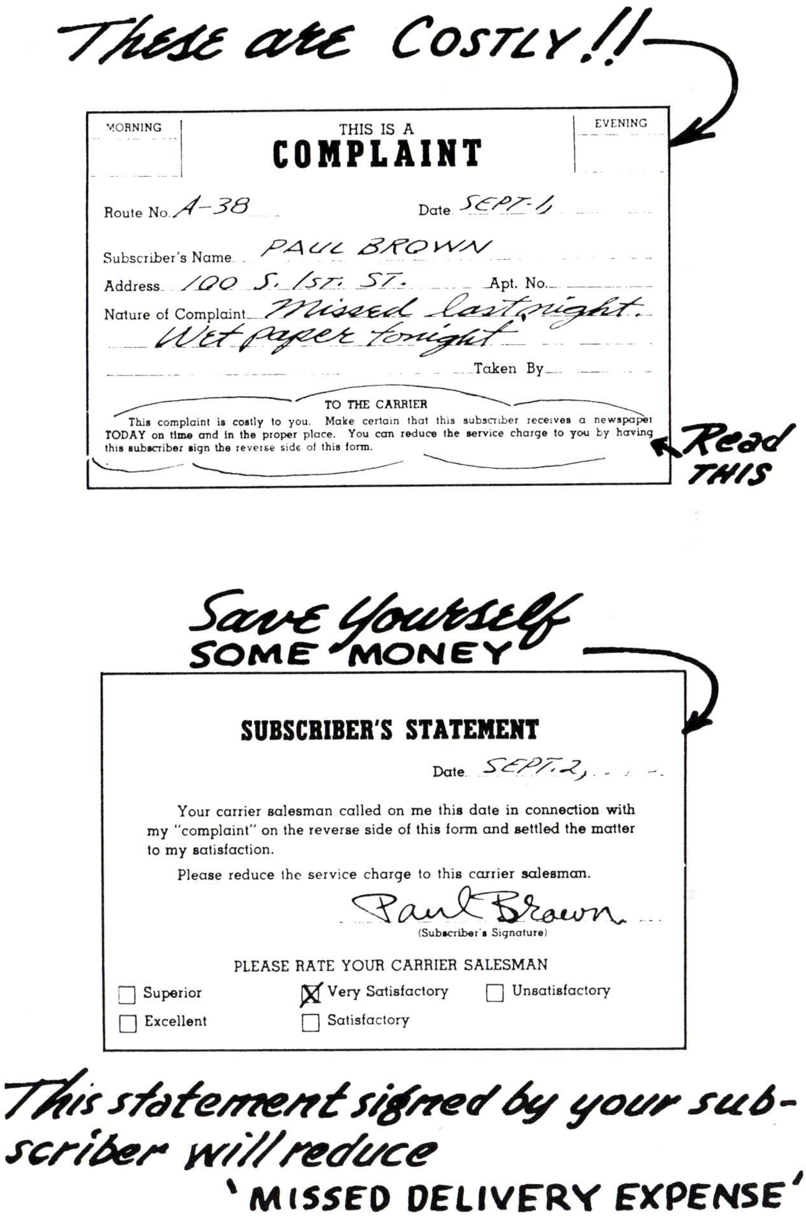

These are COSTLY!!

Read THIS

Save Yourself
SOME MONEY

SUBSCRIBER'S STATEMENT

Date *SEPT. 2,*

Your carrier salesman called on me this date in connection with
my "complaint" on the reverse side of this form and settled the matter
to my satisfaction.

Please reduce the service charge to this carrier salesman.

Paul Brown
(Subscriber's Signature)

PLEASE RATE YOUR CARRIER SALESMAN

☐ Superior   ☒ Very Satisfactory   ☐ Unsatisfactory

☐ Excellent   ☐ Satisfactory

This statement signed by your sub-scriber will reduce
'MISSED DELIVERY EXPENSE'

Fig. 14.3. In this way the Rockford, Ill., *Morning Star* and *Register-Republic* explains to carriers that complaints are costly. (Courtesy of the Rockford *Morning Star* and *Register-Republic*.)

```
                 THE  FREE  PRESS  ASSOCIATION
                         BURLINGTON, VERMONT

                     CARRIER'S  INVOICE


    TO          CM#78    John Allen Jones
                         1223 North Ave.
                         Burlington, Vt.




                 FOR WEEK ENDING    November 15

      CHARGES:
                   300    PAPERS AT  3.6¢                   $   10  80

                   INSURANCE PREMIUMS

                   PAYMENT ON BOND                                  75

                   CARRIER INSURANCE                                15

                   SUPPLIES



                                                               11  70

      LESS CREDITS:

                   PREPAID SUBSCRIPTIONS          $




      TOTAL THIS WEEK                                           11  70
      BALANCE LAST WEEK
      TOTAL AMOUNT DUE                                $

                       RECEIVED  PAYMENT

      DATE                           AMOUNT  $

                      FOR  THE  FREE  PRESS  ASSOCIATION

      BOND BALANCE INCLUDING ANY PAYMENT INDICATED ABOVE $   45.58
                   PRESENT THIS INVOICE WHEN MAKING SETTLEMENT
```

Fig. 14.4. Carrier-merchant weekly invoice. On this sample route of 50 subscribers the carrier would receive $15, pay $10.80 for papers and 15 cents for insurance, save 75 cents on a bond, and retain a balance of $3.30. Such simplified statements prevent arguments and misunderstandings. (Courtesy of the Burlington, Vt., *Free Press.*)

260

Paper Boy.

•Announcer: This is an independent businessman.

(Boy hears horn honking.)

Man: Morning, Joey. How are you?

Boy: Hi, Mr. Martin.
Man: So long, now.

Announcer: He makes his own deliveries,

does his own selling,

keeps the books.

To us, he's just a paper boy.

But 50% of the people on Earth make lower incomes than he does.

That's right. He makes more money than 50% of the people on Earth.

Free enterprise. Sometimes, we forget how well it works.

Free Enterprise.
Sometimes we forget how well it works.

PHILLIPS 66

The Performance Company PHILLIPS 66

Fig. 14.5. This excellent television commercial prepared by the Phillips Petroleum Company gave national prominence to the role of the American newspaper carrier. (Courtesy of the Phillips Petroleum Company and Tracy-Locke Advertising and Public Relations.)

all aspects of the job clear to each carrier. This is particularly true in light of the acceleration of previously unstructured problems confronting circulation departments today. Throw routes (where newspapers are tossed from a vehicle onto driveways or into yards rather than being delivered by hand at the door) have become a necessary routine for larger city newspapers, but some customers have never adjusted to the loss of more personal service. Delivery of magazines along with newspapers has created a new situation for many managers.

A complete overhaul of route delivery and collection methods has occurred in some localities, as in Los Angeles, Calif., where the *Times* implemented a completely computerized Circulation Service Center containing the files of about 750,000 home delivery subscribers. For street sales new distribution centers throughout the metropolitan area were set up for selling direct to retail outlets. This involved a massive realignment of methods, organization, and facilities within the circulation department and necessitated the hiring of 1,200 additional employes. Dozens of video display terminals with on-line access to computer files represent a new concept of circulation record handling.

Price resistance on the part of subscribers has also become a new factor with which circulation departments have had to cope, as rates over a two-year period increased by 25 percent according to the Audit Bureau of Circulations. Discreet and capable management is required under such conditions if total circulation levels are to be kept high.

In addition, new legal restrictions involving contracts with dealers and distributors complicate the work of the circulation department (see Chapter 19). As the president of the International Circulation Managers Association, Donald L. Martz, told his membership, "There is little doubt we are in the same old ball game, but the rules are changing. How much they change depends to a great extent upon the kinds of decisions you make in the days ahead. Everyone is aware that long-established distribution systems are being challenged today like never before." Such a challenge is a stimulus rather than a deterrent to successful circulation management.

It has been said many times that the American newspaper carrier system has evolved as one of the purest products of the free-enterprise system. In an outstanding series of media messages devoted to this subject, the Phillips Petroleum Company prepared a television commercial saluting the newspaper carrier with the observation that "he makes more money than half the people on earth" (see Fig. 14.5). The competent supervision and management of carriers is a contribution not only to the newspaper's success but to the social structure as well.

15

Standardizing circulation facts

> The Audit Bureau of Circulations provides a common language of terms and clear definitions by which advertisers, advertising agents and publishers can converse with mutual understanding.
>
> *C. O. Bennett*

Until the late 1890s true circulation figures were the privileged information of the newspaper publisher. Often even the publisher did not know accurately how many copies of the paper actually were sold. Poor accounting practices, the lack of uniformly accepted standards, and the imaginative claims of advertising agents made "circulation liars" of honest publishers and gamblers out of advertisers.

Today quite the reverse is true. More than 96 percent of all daily newspaper circulation offered to advertisers in North America is verified and reported in accordance with uniform standards and definitions.

CIRCULATION A SALABLE COMMODITY

General recognition of newspaper circulation as a commodity of value to advertisers is fairly recent history. More than any other single factor in affecting this change was a complete turnabout in the role of the advertising agent—from the publisher's space salesman to the advertiser's space buyer.

Volney B. Palmer, the first to call himself an "advertising agent," established an office in Philadelphia in 1841 for the purpose of taking advertising orders for his father's newspaper in Mount Holly, N.J. He rapidly added to the list of newspapers for which he solicited advertising, forwarded copy to the publishers, and collected payments from which he deducted a fee. As more and more agents entered the field, competition and confusion brought on the chaotic conditions that finally forced the issue of verified circulation data.

Publishers established "authorized prices" at which agents were free to solicit advertising. The badgering of agents and the instability of publishers frequently caused these prices to change from day to day and from agent to agent. Seldom did the publisher really know the prices at which agents were offering space in the newspaper, much less the claims being made. The publisher was satisifed with the agent's word and gratefully accepted any payments.

Since the newspaper's circulation was a tightly held business secret, the agent was free to claim any figure that would assist in making a sale. Experienced advertisers shopped around for the best deal, submitting a proposed schedule to several agents and accepting the lowest bid and the most grandiose claims.

In the late 1800s, advertisers called on agencies to add creative services to their functions. The advertising agent now became a part-time employe of the publisher and a part-time employe of the advertiser. Agents who chose not to add the creative services became known as "publishers' advertising representatives." The agency transition continued toward the role we recognize today when advertising agents turned their attention completely to the needs of the advertisers, adding the function of media selection to other services being performed.

Their experience as agents for publishers taught advertising agents much about the problems they were to face in buying space as agents of the advertisers. Their concern, along with that of the advertisers, over suspicious claims of publishers ultimately led to the formation of verification efforts.

ORGANIZATION OF CIRCULATION MANAGERS

With increased attention being given to newspaper circulation as a measure of the advertisers' ability to reach customers, circulation departments began to assume greater importance in the publishing business. Circulation managers began to compare notes and exchange experiences, and in 1898 the National Association of Newspaper Circulation Managers was formed, later to become the International Circulation Managers Association (ICMA).

Sectional associations of newspaper circulation managers were formed to supplement the international organization. The ICMA and these smaller groups served as a clearing house for the best circulation ideas and united the efforts of leaders in that field for the benefit of the entire newspaper profession. Along with other publisher associations, the ICMA contributed much to the effort toward standardizing circulation facts and practices.

ORGANIZATION OF MEDIA BUYERS

While some publishers were at the forefront of the audited circulation movement, most took a dim view of the effort. More concerned with the day-to-day problems of producing a newspaper, they saw in circulation verification the need for additional, costly record keeping.

Anxious to learn just exactly what their advertising moneys bought in the way of a circulation commodity, a group of national advertisers banded together in 1899 to form the Association of American Advertisers (AAA). Financed by member advertisers, the group hired a staff of five "examiners" who began to test the publishers' often repeated assertion that their books were open for inspection at any time. Promises were frequently better than performance. Behind most refusals to permit inspections, despite many reasons given, were a genuine lack of circulation accounting sophistication, an absence of uniform standards and definitions, and a lack of confidence between the three parties in the advertising and publishing industry.

During its 14-year existence the AAA, though it sputtered along underfinanced and with its motives generally not appreciated, did conduct several thousand "inspections." Importantly, it focused attention on circulation values as a key to advertising effectiveness and proved that circulation audits were practical.

AUDIT BUREAU OF CIRCULATIONS

The Association of American Advertisers reached a peak membership in 1913 after which time, far in debt, its examination program came to a virtual halt. Determined in their desire to provide a vehicle for circulation verification, officers of the association developed a plan for reorganization. They proposed to recognize, in membership and direction, the mutual interests of the advertiser, the advertising agent, and the publisher. Advertising buyers would retain majority voice in establishing standards, and publishers would pay the major cost of operating the organization, that of auditing services.

While a splinter group announced a plan to encourage circulation auditing, its plans were later merged with those of the AAA into what in May 1914 became the Audit Bureau of Circulations (ABC). At the time of the organizing meeting, 338 newspapers along with 74 advertisers, 49 advertising agents, 27 magazines, 55 trade papers, and 52 farm publications had agreed to participate.

Objectives of the ABC

In spite of its evolution and preparation, the Audit Bureau of Circulations was introduced to a confused and often cynical industry. Everyone professed to believe in honesty and a "square deal," claimed to be practicing the golden rule, and blamed competitors for practically all that was wrong with the world of business. With no little justification, mistrust was as basic to the industry as were advertisers, advertising agents, and publishers.

Although the ABC was needed primarily to preserve and perpetuate the press as a reliable advertising medium, the organization also reflected to a degree the honor of publishers. Many publishers wanted to give their newspapers' true circulation figures if by doing so they would not be handi-capped by the untruthfulness of others. They wanted a standard measure-ment, and they wanted specific rules for that measurement.

Advertisers also demanded exact information about a publication's ability to produce results from advertising. They wanted to know how many people read the publication, where they lived, and where they bought newspapers. They wanted an honest picture of every circulation. It became increasingly evident that the truth, based on uniform standards, would benefit publisher and advertiser alike.

The objects of the ABC, as outlined in its by-laws, are threefold:

1. To issue standardized statements of circulation data and other data reported by a member.
2. To verify the figures shown in those statements by auditors' examinations of any and all records considered by the bureau to be necessary.
3. To disseminate data for the benefit of advertisers, advertising agencies, and others interested in facts in the advertising and publishing in-dustries.

Basis of measuring circulation

At its inception and for eight years thereafter, the Audit Bureau of Circulations accepted both paid and free publications into its member-ship. Following World War I there was a move to strengthen ABC stand-ards. A major change was the establishment of a paid-circulation eligi-bility requirement, aimed mainly at free-distribution business publications but today considered a competitive deterrent to shoppers and other free-distribution newspapers.

Members justified the paid-circulation requirement with the theory that persons who pay for the publication are persons who read it. In general terms, the ABC defines paid circulation as copies or subscriptions for which at least 50 percent of the basic price has been paid by the purchaser, not for resale.

Under existing standards, a newspaper must have at least 70 percent of its total distribution qualify as paid under the bureau's rules to be eligi-ble for regular ABC membership. A newspaper with at least 50 percent paid, but less than 70 percent, may qualify for provisional membership, agreeing to meet the higher requirement within three years.

The audit bureau has established two market definitions for the areas served by daily newspaper members. The zonal definition provides for a city zone (the central city and contiguous built-up areas) and a retail trading zone (the surrounding area whose residents shop regularly in the central city). The primary market area definition is based on the geographical area within which the publisher concentrates editorial and advertising efforts. Circulation sales are reported by one or the other of these definitions, with sales outside the defined area reported as "all other." (See Fig. 15.1.)

DAILY PROTOTYPE (Evening)

City (County), State or Province

Newspaper Publisher's Statement
Subject to audit by Audit Bureau of Circulations. 123 N. Wacker Drive, Chicago, Ill. 60606

FOR 6 MONTHS ENDING SEPTEMBER 30, (YEAR)

	Evening
1. TOTAL AVERAGE PAID CIRCULATION	85,350

1A. TOTAL AVERAGE PAID CIRCULATION BY ZONES:

CITY ZONE

	Population	Hslds*	
1970 Census:	135,785	44,266	
(Year) ABC Estimate:	144,634	47,324	
Dealers & Carriers not filing lists			33,141
Street Vendors			7,684
Publisher's Counter Sales			116
Mail Subscriptions			450
Total City Zone			**41,281**

RETAIL TRADING ZONE

	Population	Hslds*	
1970 Census:	385,901	116,675	
(Year) ABC Estimate:	425,118	128,430	
Dealers & Carriers not filing lists			31,420
Mail Subscriptions			11,550
Total Retail Trading Zone			**42,970**
Total City & Retail Trading Zones			**84,251**
	Population	Hslds*	
1970 Census:	521,686	160,741	
(Year) ABC Estimate:	569,752	175,754	

ALL OTHER

Dealers & Carriers	76
Mail Subscriptions	1,023
Total All Other	**1,099**
Subscriptions to Armed Forces (Orders for 11 or more only)	
TOTAL PAID Excluding Bulk	**85,350**
(For Bulk Sales, See Par. 5)	

AVERAGES BY QUARTERS:

April 1 to June 30, (Year)	85,561
July 1 to September 30, (Year)	86,011

*Households.

Fig. 15.1. Publisher's semiannual statement to ABC. (Courtesy of the Audit Bureau of Circulations.)

1B. STANDARD METROPOLITAN STATISTICAL AREA:
(Note - figures shown below are optional compilation of circulation data which are included as part of the totals shown in Paragraph 1A.)

Prototype City Standard Metropolitan Statistical Area:

	Households		AVERAGE PAID CIRCULATION
	1970 Census	(Year) ABC Est.	Evening
Central County	56,864	61,385	46,193
Jefferson County	18,212	20,436	10,418
North County	16,801	17,926	8,212
Total SMSA	**93,877**	**99,747**	**64,823**
Population 1970 Census:	300,406		
(Year) ABC Estimate:		318,217	

1C. CITY AND RETAIL TRADING ZONES:

CITY ZONE is the corporate limits of Prototype City, plus in Central County 1970 Census Tracts 59, 63, 68, 73, 80, 84 and 91.

RETAIL TRADING ZONE is, with exception of City Zone, counties of Central, Boone, Jefferson, North South and Wright.

2. AVERAGE PAID CIRCULATION IN PUBLISHER'S PRIMARY MARKET AREA

	HOUSEHOLDS			% of
	1970 Census	(Year) ABC Est.	Evening	Coverage
TOTAL PRIMARY MARKET	**143,620**	**160,334**	**83,431**	**52.04**
STATE				
Central County	56,864	61,385	46,193	75.25
Boone County	31,212	34,860	11,421	32.76
Jefferson County	18,212	20,436	10,418	50.98
North County	16,801	17,926	8,212	45.81
Wright County	18,541	25,727	7,187	27.94
TOTAL PRIMARY MARKET	**143,620**	**160,334**	**83,431**	**52.04**
Circulation Outside Primary Market Area			1,919	
TOTAL PAID (Excluding Bulk)			**85,350**	

3. DISTRIBUTION IN TOWNS RECEIVING 25 OR MORE COPIES IN DETAIL BY COUNTIES. (See Audit Report)

4. NET PRESS RUN AND TIME OF EDITIONS:

Edition	Press Time	Date Printed	Issue Dated	Net Press Run	Sales Release See Note	Approximate Distribution City Zone	Retail Trading Zone	All Other
Evening Issue for Tuesday, September 13, (Year).								
1st	1:45 PM	9/13	9/13	87,045	A-C	48%	50%	2%

NOTE: A—Immediate sales release in City. C—Sales release on arrival at destination in Retail Trading Zone and All Other.

5. AVERAGE BULK SALES IN ALL ZONES: None.

6. AVERAGE UNPAID DISTRIBUTION: Evening

Arrears	
Service, Advertisers, Employes, etc.	92
Agencies, Complimentary, Samples, etc.	184
Total	276

7. (a) RETURNS POLICY:
Nonreturnable to dealers in the City Zone; Retail Trading Zone and All Other, except that two dealers in the City Zone were allowed return privilege.

(b) Were these deducted, so that only paid is shown in Par. 1? Yes.

Fig. 15.1. (*continued*)

268

ANALYSIS OF CARRIER & MAIL SUBSCRIPTION SALES (New & Renewal)

8. PREMIUM, COMBINATION, SPECIAL OFFERS, CLUBS AND INSURANCE:

	1 Mo.	Term Ordered 3 Mos.	6 Mos.	1 Yr.	Misc. Periods
(e) Special reduced prices Par. 11(b)				429	

9. (a) CONTESTS INVOLVING SUBSCRIPTION CONTRACT: None

    (b) CONTESTS NOT INVOLVING SUBSCRIPTION CONTRACT: See Par. 12(a)

10. ARREARS UNDER THREE MONTHS: (See Audit Report)

11. PRICES:

(a) Basic Prices:	By Mail 1 Yr.	6 Mos.	3 Mos.	1 Mo.	By Carrier 1 Yr.	6 Mos.	3 Mos.	1 Mo.	1 Wk.
CITY ZONE:									
E. only	$9.00	$5.00	$2.75		$23.40	$11.70	$5.85	$1.95	45c
RETAIL TRADING ZONE:									
E. only	$9.00	$5.00	$2.75		$15.60	$7.80	$3.90	$1.30	30c
ALL OTHER:									
E. only	$11.00	$7.00		$1.50	Carrier, same as Retail Trading Zone.				

	By Motor Route	Single Copy
CITY ZONE, RETAIL TRADING ZONE & ALL OTHER:		
E. only		10c

(b) Special reduced prices: By carrier in city zone and retail trading zone to employes, 1 year $11.70. By carrier or mail in retail trading zone to postmasters, 50% of basic prices.
By mail to members of Central County Farm Bureau, Tuesday only. 1 year 75c.

(c) For prices lower than basic see Audit Report.

12. EXPLANATORY:

Regular publishing days on which no paper was issued:
May 30, (year); July 4. (year); September 5, (year).

(a) Paragraph 9(b):

A "Gridiron Goldmine" Contest was conducted, beginning with the issue of September 20. 1966 and continuing beyond the period of this statement, in which cash prizes were offered as follows: $5.00 for picking 6 winners; $10.00 for picking 8 winners; $25.00 for picking 10 winners; $100.00 for picking 12 winners; $250.00 for picking 15 winners; $1,000.00 for picking 20 winners.

Answers were submitted on coupons published in the publication Tuesday, Wednesday, Thursday and Friday of each week or answers could be turned in on hand drawn facsimiles. The total amount of cash prizes awarded during the period of the contest as covered by this statement was $1,295.00.

We hereby certify that all statements set forth in this statement are true.

JOHN DOE   JAMES DOE
  Circulation Manager   Publisher
  Date Signed, October 12, (year).

Fig. 15.1. *(continued)*

At the insistence of large chain stores who regularly depend on newspaper advertising, the ABC is considering reporting circulations by ZIP code areas. This would enable retailers to analyze distribution by store locations and by charge account customers — obviously a valuable statistic. ZIP code zone auditing would also assist the newspaper in determining where readership is weak or strong within the retail trading zone. Often those who hold credit cards buy the local newspaper.

Each member newspaper is required to maintain accurate day-to-day circulation and distribution records showing type of sale, location, method of delivery, and price. Subsidiary records to support a general daily recapitulation must also be maintained; and, although many will vary to fit individual publishing conditions, the following are necessary elements of any records system designed to fit ABC requirements:

1. A galley or complete file of addressing devices which has the name, address, and expiration date for each mail subscriber must be maintained as well as a listing of the name, quantity, and delivery instructions for each carrier, dealer, and vendor. Proof lists are prepared quarterly and preserved for the auditor's inspection.
2. A draw sheet is completed each day, including the names of carriers, dealers, and vendors as well as the number of copies sold or distributed to them each day.
3. Accounts receivable and cash receipts records should be maintained. The first should be a permanent record of all items billed: newspapers, insurance, and the like, plus cash receipts, returns, and all other credits, together with balance due. The second is a record of the cash received for mail subscriptions, counter sales, advance payments, and collections from carriers and dealers.
4. A return record should indicate, by zone, the number of unsold copies returned daily by dealers, carriers, and vendors.
5. A pressroom report should include the record of the daily pressrun, number of pages, edition times, spoilage, and any other details required for an accurate accounting of the quantity of newspapers available for distribution.
6. A record of such special subscription offers as reduced prices, contests, premiums, and insurance should be kept, including the number of subscriptions produced through each type of promotion offer. Actual copies of any printed promotion should also be saved.
7. Basic subscription prices should be printed regularly in the newspaper.
8. Post office receipts showing the number of pounds mailed for each issue should be kept on file.

In addition to day-by-day records, the publisher is asked to provide, for incorporation in the annual audit report, a circulation breakdown for a typical day's issue, listing the towns outside the city zone that receive 25 or more copies, with the distribution figures for each. A total figure is given for the city zone, with the listing outside this zone arranged alphabetically by states and counties.

To meet the growing demand for media-to-market data, the ABC includes census-based population and occupied housing unit information in its reports. Additionally, newspaper publishers have the option of providing circulation breakdowns for a self-defined primary market area (abutting census units in which the newspaper has at least 20 percent coverage) and by government-designated standard metropolitan statistical area (census metropolitan areas in Canada).

Population and occupied housing unit data, where reported in ABC reports, is kept current through an annual updating by means of "ABC Estimates."

The growing sophistication of media buying is bringing increased emphasis to audience profiles—the demographic (sex, age, education, occupation, family status) characteristics of a newspaper's readers. The ABC initiated a Newspaper Audience Research data-bank service, a computer storage facility for standardized demographic and readership information, which has been developed and reported within carefully controlled guidelines. Advertisers and other interested members may thus draw specialized reports tailored to the marketing needs of the user.

Benefits to newspaper and advertiser

It would seem that the Audit Bureau of Circulations was set up primarily for the benefit of the media buyer; but if this is so, it is also quite apparent that the publisher wants it that way. Advertisers and advertising agencies are represented by 18 of the 33 members of the board of directors, even though publishers make up almost 70 percent of the bureau's 4,100 members and provide more than 90 percent of the bureau's income.

The advent of the ABC brought stability to media buying by providing the first dependable guide to scientific space selection. It also brought great economies to publishing by requiring auditable circulation accounting and eliminating wasteful and expensive competitive practices.

The ABC gives the advertisers definite facts about media published in the territory they want to reach. It enables them to set up a schedule of advertising with complete knowledge of the circulation behind it. The bureau makes no boastful claims, but presents verified facts that invite conclusions. The newspaper realizes benefits also. Among these are the following:

1. Respect and confidence of advertisers. The newspaper that provides a full picture of its community and circulation earns the goodwill of advertisers and advertising agencies. Even though it may not be able to maintain a circulation figure as great as that sworn to by other

newspapers in towns of similar size, its report will be given respectful consideration when it is backed by an ABC audit.

2. Insight to the newspaper's own practices. The examination of a publication's circulation records by an outside disinterested auditing organization gives the publisher a constantly up-to-date survey of progress. ABC reports visualize the activities in production, distribution, sales, and collections. This information is essential to an efficient operation and also aids the publisher in building and maintaining the volume, type, and distribution of circulation that is inviting to advertisers.

3. Evidence of the newspaper's worth. When a newspaper property is offered for sale, the volume of net paid circulation is an important factor in determining the selling price. Bureau membership makes it possible for the seller to provide unquestioned evidence of the publication's circulation. A study of current and past ABC reports gives the prospective buyer verified history and information essential for making a sound business investment.

Qualifications for membership

When a newspaper applies for membership, a prepayment is made against the anticipated initial audit costs. With its acceptance into membership, the publication pays nominal annual dues. Members are billed quarterly to build up a deposit as prepayment for subsequent audits. Dues are based on the total distribution of the newspaper; audit costs are based on uniform hourly rates for the auditor's time. A schedule of these dues and advance audit deposits is shown in Table 15.1.

The deposit is merely an estimate of the anticipated cost of the initial audit. Types of records and the condition in which they are maintained can affect the number of work hours required. Since charges are based on an actual uniform hourly rate for all publications, the cost of an ABC audit can be materially different from one publication to another of comparable size. If the cost of the audit is greater than the amount deposited, the publisher is charged the difference; if less, the publisher is credited for

Table 15.1. ABC basis of assessing dues and audit deposits, dailies—weekday issues only

Total Distribution	Dues	Amount of Deposit
Under 50,000 to 75,000	$140	$1,100
Under 5,000	$ 40	$ 300
5,000 to 10,000	60	450
10,000 to 25,000	80	575
25,000 to 50,000	110	900
50,000 to 75,000	140	1,100

or remitted the difference. As a rule of thumb, ABC costs are roughly approximate to the cost of a page of advertising in the publications.

While the audit period for all dailies is 12 months, most weekly newspaper members are under an every other year audit plan. Dues for small-town weeklies under such a plan are one-half that of the daily. Dues for urban weeklies, audited annually, are the same as those for the daily.

The 24-month audits recognize that circulation fluctuations are generally very slight on the small-town weekly. Where major fluctuations do occur, they are reported in the semiannual publisher's statement; and reasons for the change are investigated at that time. This plan brings ABC verification within the financial reach of even the smallest newspaper.

For weekly newspapers selling advertising as a unit, the ABC makes a Group Audit Plan available. Participating members of the group select a "group coordinator" who collects and submits per issue data for each of the newspapers. These data are entered in the audit bureau's computer, which generates quarterly recapitulations and semiannual statements for each newspaper as well as a combined Group Publisher's Statement. Participating weekly newspapers must meet all eligibility requirements, including percent paid, initial audit, and auditable records. Obvious advantages are considerably simplified record keeping (the most onerous task handled by the ABC computer), substantially reduced costs to individual publishers, and circulation reports tied directly to either group or individual selling efforts.

For purposes of representation on the board of directors, ABC membership is divided into six groups: advertisers, with 11 directors; advertising agencies, with 7 directors; newspapers, with 8 directors (including a weekly newspaper representative); magazines, with 3 directors; business publications, with 2 directors; and farm publications, with 1 director. An additional director represents Canadian periodicals as an at-large director.

The eight newspaper directors are elected by the members from newspapers published in Canada, in the Eastern Standard Time Zone, in the Central Standard Time Zone, and in the Mountain and Pacific Time Zones; and from newspapers having less than 15,000 paid circulation, having from 15,000 to 100,000 paid circulation, having more than 100,000 paid circulation, and all weeklies. Additionally, newspaper members are involved in ABC activities through liaison committees representing the specialized interests of various newspaper industry organizations.

More dailies than weeklies. More than 1,300 dailies and 550 weekly newspapers in the United States, Canada, Central America, and South America belong to the Audit Bureau of Circulations. A higher percentage of dailies than weeklies hold membership; in fact, weekly newspaper membership has declined. The reasons for limited participation by weekly publishers are many and varied, but here are a few:

Table 15.2.   Daily and weekly newspaper and total ABC membership

Year	Daily	Weekly	Total*
1920	365	25	1,414
1930	1,053	25	2,003
1940	1,028	66	2,049
1950	1,211	763	2,338
1960	1,302	813	3,908
1967	1,307	713	4,063
1972	1,320	559	3,885
1977	1,309	485	4,096

* Totals include magazines and other nonnewspaper publications.

1. The trend toward free or part-free distribution by urban weeklies makes many ineligible for membership under the existing paid-circulation rule.
2. General advertising accounts form only about 5 percent of a weekly's total income as compared with from 20 to 30 percent for a daily. Most general advertising that comes to a weekly is the result of a local dealer's request and not because of verified circulation.
3. Since most weeklies have only shopper competition in their markets, ABC scrutiny and discipline is not of significant concern to local merchants and has a restricting influence on the publisher's practices in meeting this free competition.
4. In most weekly markets, qualified bookkeepers are not in plentiful supply. Sickness and personnel turnover disrupt the continuity of record keeping. Therefore, good business practices recognized by other industries are not normally associated with the weekly field.
5. The freedom and independence of most weekly publishers cause them to guard their parochial practices from outside inspection. What they do and how they do it is largely their own business, they feel, and this extends to their interpretation of the term "paid circulation."

On the other hand, weekly publishers who belong to the ABC are as strong in their support as daily newspapers, and for many of the same reasons. They contend that it gives their newspapers prestige with their advertisers; helps them to run a tighter, more profitable operation; encourages them to keep their subscription lists clean; gives them a better understanding of their newspaper's circulation and financial strengths; and makes them partners with other publishers in a movement for the elevation of circulation standards. The solid membership support shown in Table 15.2 indicates the success of the bureau.

AMERICAN NEWSPAPER PUBLISHERS ASSOCIATION
Not to be overlooked as important factors in the movement toward verified circulation are organizations other than those already mentioned.

The American Newspaper Publishers Association, founded in 1887 to bring about better understanding and closer cooperation between publishers in business matters, quite naturally has given much consideration to circulation and advertising problems. This organization was formed when revenue from circulation was almost on a par with that of advertising. In 1879 the total circulation revenue for daily newspapers amounted to 22 million dollars, while advertising brought in 21 million. By 1909 the circulation revenue of all American newspapers totaled 84 million and advertising revenue 148 million. The great bulk of this revenue went to daily newspapers. It must be remembered also that between 1870 and 1920 the United States doubled its population and tripled the number of urban residents. During the same thirty years the number of daily papers quadrupled and the number of copies sold each day increased almost sixfold. Here was the real beginning of circulation growth and importance. Both in numbers and in total circulation the average daily newspaper rose more rapidly than the city that spawned it.

The cooperation of publishers and advertisers in solving the problem of ascertaining circulation figures was stimulated by the passage in 1912 of the Newspaper Publicity Law, which required semiannual statements of ownership and circulation from publishers using second-class mail service, and the ANPA united wholeheartedly with other organizations and agencies in forming the Audit Bureau of Circulations. The ANPA, through both standing and special committees, has continuously given attention to circulation standards and to laws regulating newspapers in the use of the mails.

OTHER ORGANIZATIONS

Standard Rate & Data, which was launched as a private corporation in 1919, also provides facts helpful to advertisers about each American newspaper — its circulation area, volume, and rates. It goes regularly to more than 4,000 advertising agencies, manufacturers, publishers, public relations organizations, and wholesale and retail firms that advertise extensively.

In 1934 the American Press Association set out to become the country newspapers' representative in the field of national advertising and established offices in New York, Chicago, Detroit, Baltimore, Kansas City, and St. Louis. It issued for advertisers a directory of newspapers — their circulations and advertising rates — and claimed to represent 5,395 weekly, semiweekly, and triweekly newspapers and six daily newspapers.

The American Press Association placed in the advertising media market what it considered to be a select list of weekly newspapers, known as the Greater Weeklies. Afterward, however, this group pulled away from the American Press Association, which later was absorbed by the National Editorial Association, now known as the National

Newspaper Association (NNA). Now the NNA sells national advertising for member newspapers through an organization known as American Newspaper Representatives, Inc.

Regional groups of newspapers, including the Inland Daily Press Association, Southern Newspaper Publishers Association, New England Daily Press Association, and Northwest Daily Press Association, have committees to deal with circulation standards and promotion. Also active in circulation matters are state press associations, many of which issue directories showing circulations and advertising rates of state newspapers. All these agencies are helping to build confidence in circulation facts supplied by the nation's newspapers.

16

Commercial printing— a supplementary service

People have the tendency to lump all periodicals under one head and it is easy to persuade them that a newspaper shop can do a better job of printing for them. And, actually, they can because of their familiarity with news makeup, their equipment and their habit of meeting publication deadlines.

Edmund Arnold

To supplement advertising and circulation income, many publishers operate a commercial printing department or "job shop" along with the newspaper. This is particularly true among weeklies and small dailies. Some weekly newspaper plants realize more than 50 percent of their income from commercial printing. A weekly newspaper in Missouri received 67 percent of its income one year from that source and, contrary to the common view that the smaller the newspaper the heavier the reliance on job printing income, this newspaper was in the highest circulation category.

The average income from commercial printing for weekly newspapers, however, is from 16 to 29 percent of total income, according to surveys made by the National Newspaper Association, the Minnesota Editorial Association, and the University of Iowa Bureau of Newspaper Service. Table 16.1 shows the results of similar surveys made in Minnesota and Iowa.

The income realized from commercial printing by Iowa dailies with circulations of 3,000 to 6,000 was 12.3 percent of the total income, and the job printing income of Minnesota dailies with circulations of 4,427 to

Table 16.1. Percentage income from job printing in various circulation classifications of weeklies in Minnesota and Iowa

Circulation	Minnesota	Iowa
Under 1,000	20	17.8
1,000–2,000	29.4	21
2,000–3,000	18.7	17.4
Over 3,000	25.1	17.3

20,228 was found to be 3.5 percent. One publisher reported a yearly business volume totaling $300,000. Of this sum, the commercial printing department contributed $60,000, an amount that would have been lacking without this important adjunct. In the judgment of the publisher, a daily newspaper "should have a volume of at least $300,000 a year from advertising and circulation combined before dropping the important sideline of commercial printing."

A study in management resources at Syracuse University found that, despite the ready availability of quick photo-offset facilities at neighborhood stationery stores and print shops, commercial printing is still a viable source of income for the community newspaper.[1] Categories of income reported in this study are shown in Table 16.2.

"Though dailies rely on job shops much less than weeklies," Stone and Leibowitz conclude, "the survey found that 30 percent of gross income in America's small-circulation newspapers is still derived from commercial printing. This percentage was so high that the study concluded that community newspapers, even today, would not make a profit without their commercial printing income.

"The study's findings seemed peculiar in light of the advances in printing technology and in light of the increase in central printing, the publishing of shoppers, and the boon insert advertising carried by grassroots newspapers. More questions had to be asked, and a follow-up survey was undertaken in December 1975 to determine if the traditional sources of job printing had drastically changed.

Table 16.2. Income categories (in thousands of dollars) of newspapers responding to management of resources survey

Income	All (n = 172)	Weeklies (n = 114)	Semiweeklies (n = 10)	Dailies (n = 45)
Local advertising	$152	$ 90	$189	$235
National ad net*	15	15	25	10
Classified ads*	25	13	31	39
Legal advertising*	9	7	13	10
Total advertising	$164	$ 99	$216	$290
Circulation gross	39	15	25	88
Total commercial*	81	52	192	71
Miscellaneous*	22	12	47	15
Total gross income	281	155	358	15
Less discounts	− 13	− 10	− 10	− 15
Total Adjusted Gross Income	$269	$154	$348	$436

* Category left blank by at least 20 percent of respondents. Most of the categories are averages based on answers given by less than the entire group of papers in the survey. This explains why the individual items do not sum to the total advertising, total gross income or total adjusted gross income. The data are offered in this manner as the most detailed presentation available for each category.

---

1. Gerald C. Stone and Glen F. Leibowitz, Job Printing Remains Large Revenue Source, *Editor & Publisher*, March 27, 1976, p. 20. Used by permission.

"The follow-up survey netted 75 responses from a single questionnaire mailed to 210 publishers who had participated in the original Management of Resources national random survey. This follow-up study showed that commercial printing is an increasing source of revenue for a community newspaper.

"Some 63 percent of those surveyed said they are experiencing increases in their income patterns from commercial printing (18 percent listed 'large increases' and 45 percent noted 'small increases').

"But even more interesting is that coupled with the 25 percent who said their commercial printing pattern was 'relatively stable,' the figures show that 88 percent of the publishers are not experiencing a decline in commercial printing."

While a commercial printing department is considered an essential secondary operation in the majority of weekly and semiweekly newspaper plants, it seldom is found in daily newspaper plants beyond the 8,000 circulation class. When a daily has grown to that size, the business of newspaper publishing alone usually demands full-time attention and effort.

SEPARATE OPERATION

Sometimes a commercial printing plant is set up as an entirely separate operation. But if that is done, the publisher must be sure there is enough business to absorb the additional expense of maintaining an outside-the-plant department. If job printing is discontinued altogether, the publisher must be satisfied that enough additional income can be developed from the newspaper to make up for whatever commercial printing will be lost.

One example of successfully separating commercial printing from the general newspaper operation is that of the Columbus, Miss., *Commercial Dispatch,* which developed a job printing business volume greater than the newspaper volume. When it became that profitable, it also became unwieldy as a sideline and was divorced entirely from the newspaper to be operated as an independent enterprise.

It is obvious, therefore, that favorable conditions for operating these two types of business in one plant do not always exist. However, ordinarily, there are distinct advantages to be considered:

1. The publisher is able to get double service out of composing machinery and facilities.
2. It provides a way to keep the mechanical staff engaged in productive work between peak loads on the newspaper.
3. It encourages a more even distribution of work hours throughout the week.
4. Through newspaper contacts with advertisers and readers, the pub-

lisher knows the printing needs of the community and has ready access to prospective job printing customers.

5. Advertising columns of the newspaper are always available for promotion of the printing department.
6. Savings in material and labor costs can often be achieved because the same composition used for newspaper advertisements frequently may be used to print circulars or handbills.
7. The newspaper is in a position to quote prices on certain types of job printing that could not be approached by individual print shops.
8. Publishing the community newspaper gives the management a legitimate reason to emphasize "trade at home" appeal in competition with out-of-town printing concerns.
9. Revenue can be increased without more than nominal increase in costs — sometimes with present equipment and personnel.
10. Some genuine production shortcuts are unavailable to the independent printer. For example, employes can be shifted from newspaper work to job work without friction in nonunion shops, and in some instances this is permitted under union shop contracts as well.
11. Because of superior composing facilities and efficient presswork and engraving services, the newspaper plant very often produces large orders such as election ballots or other rush orders that frequently cannot be produced in commercial plants in the same community. On occasion, it is called upon to produce overflow job work for independent print shops in the area.

But there are disadvantages as well:

1. The plant may become so overloaded that the newspaper operation is neglected in order to meet the job department's production requirements. If, for instance, the composing machines are committed to so much job shop composition that some of the news copy or an editorial has to be left out of the newspaper edition, the management must decide whether to hire more help or to eliminate profitable job work. In following either course, management may have to cut into profits; if neither is followed, the quality of the newspaper is threatened.
2. The possibility of additional overtime hours, particularly in composition, is greater than in a single-business operation.
3. Where equal emphasis is encouraged on both operations, the publisher is less likely to become a specialist in either field.
4. The task of accurately assigning expenses to each operation is made more difficult, and standardized cost accounting procedures are rendered less applicable.
5. The effort to maintain two operations in the same plant may lead to crowded conditions and serious production problems.
6. The newspaper publisher is subjected to pressure for lower

prices—particularly by large advertisers who expect concessions from the newspaper they patronize—which they would not expect from independent printers. When yielding to such demands for low printing prices, however, the publisher becomes involved in nonprofitable operation of the commercial printing department or the risk of offending other customers and thus invites losses in advertising revenue as well as in printing. Also, regular newspaper advertisers are likely to be more discriminating than the average purchaser of printing, and it frequently costs more to serve them than customers who have not developed such discrimination.

7. Because labor costs account for approximately 50 percent of the total cost of printing, management may encounter local conditions that render an otherwise successful operation unprofitable.

Comments from publishers in the Syracuse study included the following significant observations:[2]

1. "We run both businesses (newspaper and commercial printing operation) completely separated—both profitable."
2. "In any case, the two operations should show separate profit and loss statements. Each operation must stand or fall on its own, although they can 'help' each other, divest income and expenses to tax advantages, etc."
3. "A couple of years ago our newspapers divorced themselves from the commercial printing business. The company then formed a commercial printing division. This was a very good move."
4. "Our newspaper personnel are just that: newspaper people. And the commercial printing division is just that: commercial printers."

CONSIDERATIONS IN JOB PRINTING

The publisher who hopes to operate a commercial printing department on a successful basis in connection with the newspaper is compelled to evaluate such economic and physical factors as proper apportioning of work time between the two operations; amount and kinds of printing the plant is equipped to produce profitably; methods available for finding costs, figuring prices, and handling stock; requirements of equipment and space; and existing and possible competition.

Apportioning work time

If producing a good community newspaper is to remain the primary and functional objective, the operation of the printing department cannot be allowed to interfere with the plant's basic schedule. During a part of each day or week the machines and the personnel will be producing the

---

2. Stone and Leibowitz, Job Printing.

Table 16.3. Percentage total employe hours spent in job printing in forty-eight Missouri newspaper plants

Circulation	Number Reporting		Mechanical Dept.	Front Office
			(percent)	*(percent)*
Under 1,000	6		29	19
1,000–2,000	25		30	19
2,000–3,000	13		29	8
Over 3,000	4		49	5
Total	48	Av.	34	13

newspaper on an uninterrupted basis regardless of what else goes on in the plant.

In a weekly newspaper plant where job printing is done, Tuesday, Wednesday, and Thursday are devoted almost entirely to newspaper production, leaving Friday, Saturday, and Monday (in that order) as the principal job printing days. Normally, only rush orders are allowed to interfere with this schedule. A survey of 55 Missouri weekly newspapers doing commercial printing revealed that in only 15 plants was job printing a continuous process, and in most plants all employes spent some hours each week in job printing. Table 16.3 summarizes this survey.

Employes of a newspaper with less than 4,000 circulation who spend less than 50 percent of their time on job printing are exempt from wage and hour law provisions.

What kind of printing is profitable?

Listed below are some of the specialties enumerated by the Printing Industry of America as suitable items for profitable production in a commercial printing department:

Advertising circulars and folders
Advertising signs
Anniversary printing
Calendars
Camp and resort advertising
Cardboard novelties
Catalogs
Church printing
Collection reminders
Direct-mail advertising
Display cards
Duplicate books and forms
Envelopes
Financial printing
Fraternal and club publications
Garage forms
Hospital forms
Hotel printing
House organs
Index cards
Insurance forms

Annual reports
Automotive forms
Blotters
Laundry forms
Legal blanks and forms
Letterheads
Looseleaf forms
Mailing cards
Medical and dental forms
Menus
Office forms
Political printing
Postcards
Posters and show cards
Real estate forms
Religious publications
Removal notices
Schedules, football, etc.
School and college forms
Street guides
Theater programs

This is a typical list, but one that can be extended indefinitely. The newspaper job department, however, with limited time to devote to newspaper printing, cannot generally engage in as extensive a program of production as that listed above. The wise publisher limits operations to the kind of printing that can be done well at a satisfactory profit.

Most weekly and small daily newspaper plants are adapted to handle such orders as letterheads and handbills. Other short-production runs and time orders to be printed on similar stock also fit into the job printing schedule of a small newspaper plant. Some examples are:

1. Letterheads for several firms, to be printed on the same stock.
2. Advertising blotters, all on the same stock with different composition for different firms.
3. A series of monthly posters for a mercantile establishment, all on the same stock.
4. Weekly church bulletins with a part of the copy the same from week to week, thereby lessening composition cost.
5. Standing orders from merchants for printing their business forms.

Holidays, anniversaries, special community events, store openings, and similar events present opportunities for printing orders. Most commercial printing departments run a considerable volume of business on Christmas greetings, wedding invitations, and formal social announcements, which may be ordered from large out-of-town printing houses specializing in fancy printing.

A Chicago printer makes this suggestion:

Printers should study every new business, new product, and new service introduced into their community to determine possible applications of printing. . . . The printing industry should study television to determine every possible application of printing. Nationally, the large companies sponsoring television advertising could possibly utilize new printing pieces and ideas in support of their television shows. There are literally hundreds of new activities and new products introduced in the United States each year. The imaginative printer should develop printing relative to these things.

Undoubtedly, many publishers in the job printing business, despite limited time and facilities, increase their volume by creating new ideas and by taking advantage of local events as they occur. However, additional sales expense is seldom justified in operating the department as a sideline. Not only should the publisher be a good printing sales solicitor, but all advertising personnel should be potential printing sales representatives. In small organizations reporters and other staff members often help solicit job orders, and one publisher reports that an employe in the accounting department brings in as much as $1,000 worth of printing a month by intelligent telephone soliciting.

Commercial printing as an adjunct to newspaper publishing is worth

Table 16.4. Percentage of total commercial printing income from each of five categories

Commercial Printing Category	Relative Percent of Income Derived
Stationery, business cards and forms, other job printing	54%
Other paper you do not own (outside contract basis)	25%
Your own shopper	8%
Other papers you own or partially own	8%
Advertising inserts (preprints)	5%

consideration only when it brings an additional profit. Unless it does that, the publisher simply adds to worries that already exist of meeting business expenses. The overall revenue derived from job printing has been broken down into the percentages shown in Table 16.4.[3]

Figuring costs and handling stock

The cash outlay and the overhead charge in producing a given printing order are not the same in any two shops. What may be a profitable price for one printer may be a losing price for another. Several elements enter into determining what is a profitable price on a piece of printing: the adequacy and efficiency of equipment; the wage scale; whether paper stock, ink, and other materials are bought in quantity; the efficiency of the employes; the system of ascertaining production costs; and the care used in pricing the job.

These factors vary in different plants and communities; therefore, prices vary also. A number of studies and investigations reveal, however, that labor and material costs do not vary too widely in the percentage cost of finished work. On the basis of average costs, the Franklin Printing Price Catalog, published by the Porte Publishing Company, Salt Lake City, Utah, provides a detailed schedule of prices for almost every type of printing order. This, however, can be used only as a guide and not as an infallible price estimator for all conditions and localities.

The only safe procedure in pricing a job is to determine as precisely as possible all costs involved and then to add a fair percentage for profit. Every job represents costs for labor, materials, overhead, and taxes; while some of these costs are readily obvious, others are not so apparent. For example, the labor cost of a job includes the time spent in preparing for the printing and in cleaning up after it. Again, the operator requires pay for 100 percent of the working day although the job press may run only 50 or 60 percent of the time, meaning that this idle time must be paid for from printing charges.

The cost of paper is not merely for that used in the completed job, but includes the cost of spoilage and unused remnants of quantities purchased. The cost of ink includes waste that is inevitable in filling, emptying, and cleaning fountains. While good management can hold waste of paper

---

3. Stone and Leibowitz, Job Printing.

stock and ink to a minimum, it is a factor that always constitutes a part of costs.

In addition, printing equipment constantly needs repairs and replacement, and each job should help pay for these "hidden" costs. The printer is not merely delivering printing, but—unless a charge is made for the fraction of equipment used up with every job—actually part of the presses is delivered with every job. The same consideration is applicable, of course, to type and spacing materials.

In quoting prices on a cost-plus-fair-profit basis, the following considerations are also involved:

1. The kind of work ordered. The price is directly affected by such requirements as heavy or light composition, difficult ruling, artwork (requiring engravings), imprinting or overprinting, bronzing, perforating, stitching, and padding.
2. The time allowed for completing the job. If the order is wanted on short notice, the rate is frequently higher because other jobs may have to be sidetracked to handle it promptly.
3. The quantity ordered. The rate ordinarily is quoted in terms of thousands or hundreds and diminishes as the quantity ordered is increased.
4. The kind of paper stock desired. The customer may select from many finishes, grades, colors, and weights of paper. These vary widely in cost.

Before pricing a printing job, the publisher must find satisfactory answers to many questions to be sure the final price will be fair to the customer and to the business:

1. Is my equipment really suited to handling this job? Can I subcontract the part I am not able to handle?
2. How much service will be required, and am I prepared and equipped to give that service?
3. Will this job help to fill a production valley in my plant and thereby stabilize employment?
4. Will this job upset the flow of work in my plant?
5. Will this job overload my work force and help create bottlenecks that may involve newspaper production?
6. Will this job help my business from the standpoint of prestige? (It helps a newspaper to have its imprint on church, charity, municipal, and legal printing, provided such jobs can be done without granting costly price reductions.)
7. Is there a possibility that acceptance of this job might push me into a type of work I would not care to handle regularly?
8. What competition is there for this order?
9. Is this a one-time order or will it bring repeat orders? Could it be developed into a profitable contractual relationship?

10. Would I be safe in looking upon this job as a "loss leader" to help develop an account that will eventually become profitable?

The actual formula for working out the price of a given job is of necessity a general and a flexible one. A public accountant in the field of newspaper costs estimates that the revenue from printing a job should be two and one-half times the labor cost, and that the various costs should be in this proportion: wages, 40 percent; job stock and traceable materials, 30 percent; and manufacturing expenses (including telephone, express charges, and incidental costs), 10 percent. This is calculated to leave a profit of 20 percent.

The late W. Percy Williams of the Paris, Tenn., *Post-Intelligencer* explained his method of figuring job prices as follows:

> I put down the price of the stock first. There are several ways of doing this. The wrong way is to take the invoice price. The right way is to take the catalog price. In pointing out the difference between the two, let us say that your invoice price on sulphite bond paper, which you purchase in ton lots, or perhaps 5,000-pound lots, may be 45 cents a pound. The customer may expect to buy only 20 pounds for his particular job. Therefore, in figuring the cost of the job, I put down the catalog price for 20 pounds, which will be at least 66 cents a pound instead of the actual invoice price of 45 cents. You are entitled to this saving as a reward for having ordered and stored in quantity. This difference may appear to be minor, but it often determines whether a job will be profitable or unprofitable.
>
> I then put down composition. All of this is estimated, and I sometimes get these estimates from the machine operator or job printer.
>
> Next, I add the estimated costs for makeup of the forms and make-ready of the press. Then I add the cost of presswork, which can be figured several ways. The wrong way is to put down only the cost of the printer's wages. I always double his wages as I consider my own time, plus my investment in composition and printing machinery worth at least as much as the printer's wages.
>
> I total all of these items of cost and add anywhere from 20 percent up to 100 percent, depending upon the number printed and several other factors. On a 50,000 pressrun, 20 percent gives me a good profit. On 500 I sometimes lose even when I double what I consider to be cost.

Emerson E. Lynn, publisher of the Iola, Kans., *Register,* is satisfied with a simple formula that, over a period of years, has given him the margin of profit wanted from his commercial printing department. His formula is described this way: "Take the cost of stock and add 25 percent for freight and handling, then calculate the total amount of time required and multiply the hours by a figure that is three times the average hourly wage of all employes in the department. This formula gives about a 25 percent gross profit and about a 10 percent net profit after overhead allocations." He adds that the formula can be broken down by charging more for time put in by highly paid employes on expensive machinery and less for time spent by bindery personnel and other unskilled workers.

It is advisable to allow a liberal percentage for profit because certain unpredictable factors, discussed below, may reduce the normally anticipated profit margin in job printing.

Most manufactured products suffer little loss in value if they prove to be imperfect, but this is not the case in printed matter. Nearly every item is made to order and may be rejected by the customer on the grounds of errors or imperfections. Rejected printing has no salvage value and is therefore a dead loss. A typographical error in one printing order may wipe out the profits from hundreds of dollars worth of satisfactory orders.

Jobs the shop is not equipped to handle efficiently seldom prove profitable. They cut down production rather than stepping it up, and the finished product may not be good advertising for the plant unless costly time and additional pains are taken to make it so. It is often more profitable to farm out such work to specialty shops.

"Prestige" printing is a type of work, generally unprofitable, that some publishers consider necessary to the maintenance of goodwill and the furtherance of better public relations for the newspaper in the community. Some newspaper owners consider it a privilege to print jobs at reduced cost or free of charge for churches, civic groups, or charitable organizations as a contribution to public welfare efforts. Others, however, see the danger of altering price policies in favor of such groups and find that the best business methods apply to "prestige" printing as well as to all other kinds of orders. The following example illustrates the sort of problem that frequently confronts the publisher:

The chairman of a heart fund drive is sponsoring a Sunday football game, with all receipts to go to the fund for heart disease. A committee has solicited the town for advertising in the program and has taken in several hundred dollars from the same patrons who use the daily newspaper. The chairman says to the publisher: "We want you to print the programs free of charge so that all the receipts can go to the cause." The publisher has previously authorized an advertisement in the program for the newspaper, and several members of his staff have bought tickets to the game. In addition, the newspaper has given almost unlimited daily publicity to the drive.

The publisher, therefore, feels justified in telling the fund drive chairman that the printing price will be the same as that asked of any other customer. The chairman's reply is that he will have to take bids from the community's three plants— the daily newspaper job shop, the weekly plant, and an independent print shop. The independent print shop, which gives no publicity to the project, submits the low bid and is awarded the order.

Such situations are bound to arise, and each must be worked out in terms of local circumstances and the publisher's own conscience. "Prestige" printing, in terms of price alone, is seldom profitable, but it is a matter of managerial judgment and experience whether such orders may prove valuable in other ways in the long run.

Methods of job handling. Efficiency in handling the job is one of the major factors determining the margin of profit. In most commercial printing departments an envelope, commonly referred to as the "job ticket" (Fig. 16.1) is provided to hold the copy and instructions. On the envelope face are blank spaces for the order number, order date, for whom and by whom, when proof must be submitted, date for completion, a description of the job, and the estimated price. Other sections contain instructions

---

JOB NUMBER

Date   19   Job Taken By

NAME

Kind of Job

Number Wanted

Kind and Color of Paper Stock

Size of Stock

Color of Ink

Pads   Books   No. to Pad or Book

No. Carbons to Book or Pad

Numbered   Start Number At

Remarks

DATE WANTED

Fig. 16.1. Typical job ticket. This is the basic form used for routing orders in most commercial printing departments. It is printed upon an envelope in which the original copy can be kept while the job passes through the phases of preparation and completion and in which the order can be filed indefinitely. (Courtesy of the Paris, Tenn., *Post-Intelligencer*.)

about stock, composition, and presswork. The order clerk places the copy inside the envelope and gives it to the production manager, who enters the customer's name and job description on the daily order register (Fig. 16.2). The production manager next enters the job with others listed on the presswork sheet (Fig. 16.3) and sends both the sheet and the envelope with the job order to the composing room supervisor.

In smaller plants, the order is less elaborate and goes through fewer hands, but precise instructions are issued for handling the job and a record is made of details in much the same manner. Under all systems, the ticket or order envelope is filed for easy reference upon completion of the job in case of repeat orders.

Apportioning costs among departments. In determining what profit a publisher can reasonably expect from the commercial printing department, the percentage of total expenditures must be determined.

One method of allocating expenditures is to consider only two items— labor and material. According to this method nothing is charged to the department in the way of overhead. Even machine composition is not charged, except in cases where the regular newspaper employes work overtime to produce type for commercial printing. Thus all composition during regular working hours is donated to the department on the grounds that the total payroll expense is not increased because of this additional load. When job printing is conducted strictly as a sideline operation in conjunction with newspaper publishing, it adds very little overhead to total expenses, with the exception of damage and depreciation within the department itself. In most small plants, for all practical purposes, the overhead for the entire operation would be the same with or without commercial printing.

In some newspaper plants—particularly those that extensively engage in job printing—costs of labor and upkeep on the composing machines and presses, of electricity and heat for the department, and other general expenses and depreciation are figured on an hourly basis and charged to each job according to the time required. One weekly newspaper has a chart posted at the side of each press and composing machine to show the hourly operation cost.

The actual percentage of profit derived from commercial printing is frequently difficult to determine because the department is usually operated as part of the overall business rather than as a distinct and separate enterprise. In cases where increased revenue is needed and a demand for printing exists in the community, such a department often develops inside the well-equipped weekly or small daily newspaper plant, with a fraction of the investment that would be required to open an independent shop.

Stock inventories

Printing profits depend to a large degree on intelligent buying and management of materials and paper stock. For example, there should

KELLY PRESS DAILY JOB ORDER REGISTER

SHEET NO. _____

DATE _____

JOB NO	DATE WANTED	CUSTOMER	QUANTITY	DESCRIPTION	INVOICE NO

Fig. 16.2. Job order register sheet. (Courtesy of the Kelly Press, Columbia Mo.)

KELLY PRESS WORK SHEET

DATE

Today	Ready for Press	Paper Cut	CUSTOMER	JOB DESCRIPTION	Press run	Ink

Fig. 16.3. Job printing work sheets. (Courtesy of the Kelly Press, Columbia, Mo.)

always be enough supplies on hand for speedy production of routine printing orders. As long as the printer is certain that all supplies will be used, buying should be done in quantity to benefit from the best rate. Saving from 10 to 14 cents per thousand on envelopes may double later profit on envelope orders. The difference between a broken-case price of paper and the cheaper price on four cases might spell the difference between profit on a job or none.

It is unwise to overstock such unusual items as a peculiarly finished or oddly colored brand of paper that a customer wants for a particular job. It is better to have the customer pay the extra cost of buying from a broken case, explaining that the item is not kept in stock.

Most departments keep on hand a minimum amount of the following stock items to take care of regular trade:

1. Bond paper in several grades.
2. Office forms.
3. Letterhead-size stock in several grades.
4. Envelopes in sizes 6¾ and 10 to match letterheads.
5. Colored poster stock for handbills and other miscellaneous materials.

Stock, which will undoubtedly include more than the minimum listed above, is kept in storage cabinets after it is received from the distributor and inventoried. Each time stock is delivered in lots to the presses, a check is made for regular weekly and monthly inventories; a report is sent to an order clerk when more stock is needed to replenish the supply. In smaller organizations, it is the publisher's or manager's responsibility to keep a close watch on stock reserves.

Storage facilities range from entire rooms set aside for the purpose to shelved cabinets installed in the job department. Regardless of size, the storage space should be free from dampness, dust, and bright light, as all these are harmful to stored paper. It should be located as conveniently as possible in relation to the job presses and the paper cutter.

Necessary equipment and plant arrangement

In the plant that accommodates both a newspaper and job printing, additional space is needed not only for current operation but for possible expansion. Adequate floor space is essential for traffic in the printing department and for convenient flow of work to and from the newspaper plant.

The commercial printing operation in even a small plant requires some specialized equipment. The following items are normally needed for a department, based on the use of a 12- by 18-inch offset press and a minimum of composing and bindery equipment:

One 10″ × 15″ job press with motor and standard parts (automatic feeder)
One 12″ × 18″ small automatic press
Two numbering machines
26½″ lever paper cutter
Heavy-duty stitching machine
Two 80″ × 36″ bindery tables
Paper drilling machine, perforator, punch
Folding machine, with suction pile feeder, 17″ × 22″
Padding compound, glue, etc.

The above list assumes that basic phototypesetting, pasteup, and offset camera equipment, along with platemaker and auxiliary facilities, are already available in the newspaper plant (see Chapter 5).

Perhaps no other single piece of equipment plays a more direct role in determining the operating efficiency and production capacity of the printing department than the kind of press used. There are many excellent models of small offset presses for job work, each designed for a particular type of service (Fig. 16.4).

Fig. 16.4. The Heidelberg K Offset press is ideal for job printing of all kinds. It will deliver 6,000 printed sheets per hour and is suitable for both rush-order and long-run jobs. (Courtesy of the Heidelberg Company.)

With the inevitable fluctuation of equipment prices, it is impossible to estimate accurately the cost of outfitting a new printing department in a newspaper plant. An estimate of $18,500 would be considered a minimum investment for adding a job department; this assumes that the plant already has adequate composition facilities for both the newspaper operation and the job department. If the newspaper plant were not already adequately equipped in these respects, this investment would be insufficient. The cost of stock inventory would also be additional.

Competition as a factor

In some communities the newspaper has almost exclusive control of the job printing market. Often there are no other printing establishments in the town where the newspaper is published, and the newspaper plant is depended upon by businesses and various organizations to supply their printing needs. This is not true, however, in every situation; no publisher knows when such favorable conditions (if they do exist) may change because when printing opportunities increase, competition often moves in.

The dangerous competitor for the publisher-printer is not the mail-order printer or the price cutter, but the independent printer in the community who introduces new and better ideas in printing and thereby attracts customers. A newspaper publisher who has been printing office forms for a manufacturer for years may lose that business instantly to a competitor new to the community who, filled with new ideas, suggests important improvements in the composition or stock used.

OTHER SUPPLEMENTAL NEWSPAPER SERVICES

While commercial printing is by far the most common and highly developed supplemental service offered by a newspaper, some newspapers have expanded their business opportunities and increased total revenue in other ways.

The newspaper office is well suited to cater to the needs of the community as far as writing materials, typewriters, adding machines, bookkeeping records, desks, poster paper, and even some artwork materials are concerned. By the simple addition of shelves and showcases in one area of the office space, some newspapers have developed a business that contributes as much as 20 percent of the total newspaper revenue. In office equipment sales, a 30 percent profit is to be expected; this requires a markup of about 42.8 percent on wholesale costs. One publisher invested $500 to add a stock of office supplies, and by the second month new business was paying enough profit to cover the rent on the whole newspaper plant. It has never failed to do so since that date; and the volume of business on office supplies alone runs about $65,000 and shows the largest profit of any single department.

A publisher may service nearby newspapers with offset camera and platemaking facilities, presswork, photography, or some other specialized

process that may be needed regularly or occasionally. Quoting from the
Syracuse study mentioned earlier in this chapter, "A Pacific Coast
publisher said that with virtually every small shop converted to photocomposing, the high capital investment required to install web-offset presses,
the shortage of skilled offset press operators, and the tremendous comparative speed of web-offset, it makes more sense for the plant with the
press to print for all his neighbors for miles around." He said that the
average small-town newspaper could not survive if each had its own
pressroom today: "The fellow publishers for whom we print could not inventory paper, pay for press investment and maintenance, employ competent operators, or, in short, produce their product for anywhere near the
price they pay for our services. On the other hand, without their volume,
we could not afford the quality and quantity of equipment we have, nor
afford to compete in the labor market for the caliber of people we employ,
buy supplies at volume prices, or produce for the costs we can now."[4]

Rental property may be developed within the newspaper plant. This
method is highly exploited by some metropolitan newspapers that occupy
several floors of a multistoried building in a high-rent area and rent the remaining floors as offices. Many smaller newspapers are designing their new
plants to include rental space for suitable enterprises.

In addition, news and advertising features may be syndicated and sold
to other newspapers, and business profits may be invested for additional
revenue.

Newspaper publishers have found such means helpful in keeping
abreast of rising costs and in maintaining a reasonable profit on their
overall business operations.

---

4. Stone and Leibowitz, Job Printing.

3
Financial and legal questions

17

Evaluation and financing

> While freedom of the press is the staff of life of democracy, economic prosperity is the lifeblood of the press. The future of our cherished editorial freedoms and democracy demands that the press be profitable.
>
> *Jon G. Udell*

Financing anything as complex and variable as a newspaper — whether it be a small weekly or a metropolitan daily — presupposes a sound concept of newspaper values. Long before the actual financing and purchasing, there must be a painstaking evaluation of the newspaper in question as well as a thorough survey of the market community it serves.

EVALUATING THE NEWSPAPER

At least eight basic factors should be considered in evaluating a newspaper: annual volume of business, actual circulation, actual revenue per inch of advertising, goodwill and prestige, equipment and machinery, the newspaper building, personnel, and owner's salary.

Annual volume of business

Perhaps the readiest guide to a newspaper's approximate worth is its annual business volume. The prospective buyer is not so much impressed by what is seen inside the walls of the plant as by what is found on the company's books. A prospect will be interested in determining from actual records exactly what the financial history of the newspaper has been. The buyer will not be satisfied with current figures alone but will examine averages for at least five years preceding — preferably ten years — to ascertain in what direction the business has been moving.

Only by learning how much cash has been taken in and how much has been paid out each year can a buyer know whether the investment will prove to be an enterprise that is making or losing money. Gross revenue is only part of the picture. What must be considered and calculated, if necessary, is the newspaper's net income after taxes. The buyer must be alert to determine the normal net; certain items may be quickly reducible

to increase the net income, such as overpaid executives, excessive depreciation, or high interest on long-term debts that may be eliminated in the
purchase contract.

Circulation

Of primary interest to the buyer is the *real* circulation of the
newspaper — that is, the number of copies that are being paid for. He will
not consult the counter mechanism on the press to determine true circulation; he will not accept the word of the publisher or the figure that may be
given on printed forms or promotional pieces; he will even question the
sworn circulation figure that must be submitted to the postmaster annually
and published on October 1 or shortly thereafter. The buyer must be
suspicious of padded circulation totals because the whole profit-making
structure of a newspaper hinges on the number of paying readers the
publication can claim.

The only safe way is to examine office records that show the amount
of revenue from circulation and give the individual subscription price. By
dividing the price charged for the paper into the income from this source,
the real circulation can be verified. If necessary, an auditor should be
hired to obtain an accurate circulation figure. Until the buyer has this item
defined, all other attempts to evaluate the newspaper will be unreliable.

It is particularly important to know what percentage of the subscriptions are paid in advance because those more than a few months in arrears
are not recognized as bona fide circulation by the Audit Bureau of Circulations, the post office department, and many national advertising agencies.
It may be said that circulation — actual or potential — is the key to
newspaper value. Some formulas actually place a literal value on circulation, like $50 per subscriber, or 35 times earnings — thus creating a tangi-
ble yardstick by which to evaluate this vital ingredient of newspaper worth.

Advertising rate

Since more than half the newspaper's income will probably come from
the sale of advertising, the prospective buyer will be as vitally concerned
about advertising rates and volume as he is about circulation. Once again,
the buyer must find the *actual* revenue per inch or per line collected by the
newspaper for all advertising published in its pages; it would be foolish to
be satisfied with the printed rate card. Many advertisers get special concessions and discounts that might make a difference between the advertising
rate claimed by the newspaper and the rate actually paid by the advertiser.
The buyer is obliged to check the books again, for only by dividing total
advertising income over a given time by the number of inches or lines run
can the rate be determined accurately. In this case also, a five- or ten-year
average will give a truer picture than one-year figures alone.

The buyer may discover that the rates are too high to allow for increased volume or too low to return a reasonable profit. In either event the

decision will be difficult. Will it be safe to lower the rates to sell more advertising and thereby risk a decrease in advertising revenue, or will it be possible to raise the rates without losing existing accounts? The answers will depend not only on the wisdom of management but also on the potentialities of the market the newspaper serves.

The bulk of advertising revenue should come from local display advertising, but the buyer will want to learn the extent to which general advertising has been cultivated and the amount of attention that has been devoted to building up classified and legal advertising. Evaluation of the advertising department, in other words, will involve thorough checking to see if the rates are sufficient to cover the cost of producing advertising and to provide a profit and if the volume of advertising can be expanded. Such projections are not easy, but the time and effort spent in advance investigation may help the buyer avoid a costly experience.

Goodwill and prestige

Usually a newspaper purchase is made by someone who has been familiar with the business and has already formed an opinion of the publication and its standing in the community. Frequently, however, the buyer does not have a background of acquaintance with the newspaper or a knowledge of public attitude toward it. Failing to investigate the goodwill value of the newspaper would be as foolish as neglecting to observe the press in operation.

Most larger newspapers actually value this item out of all proportion to the material worth of machinery and equipment. The Chicago, Ill., *Tribune* in a financial report once listed "goodwill" at approximately three times the value placed on its physical plant. The purchaser may have to pay handsomely for this commodity — and rightly so, because it is one item that cannot be replaced or protected by insurance coverage. Newspaper executives have learned that the goodwill of the public must be built gradually and methodically over many years yet may be destroyed easily in a matter of months.

If goodwill is such a precious asset to the newspaper, how does one define it? The answer must remain indefinite because it involves the changing reactions toward the newspaper of many different kinds of readers and nonreaders. Goodwill is bound up with the tastes, feelings, attitudes, and prejudices of an indeterminate population whose behavior patterns may vary from day to day; and the newspaper publisher can expect the prestige of the newspaper to fluctuate perceptibly. But the newspaper that maintains, over a long period, a high level of public confidence, public support, public interest, and public approval can be said to have the goodwill of that public. The term must be operationally defined if it is to have meaning — that is, it is applicable in situations where *most* of the time the newspaper is enjoyed, used, trusted, and respected by most of the individuals in the public served.

The buyer must gather information that will reveal the true community standing of the newspaper. It must be known whether the newspaper is delivered to the door or is kicked around on porches or yards until the accumulation is thrown out as trash. If it has a history of incompetent publishers, the buyer must decide whether its standing can be raised at all. Its very name might be its greatest handicap. When the buyer has learned all that is possible about the newspaper's place in the community, another sound basis for evaluating the purchase has been determined.

A dramatic example of the value of a name can be seen in the purchase of the defunct Fort Worth, Tex., *Press,* which the former owners declared had "not made a profit in the last 25 years." Nevertheless, the newspaper has been resurrected under new management, which paid a reported $300,000–$500,000 for the property in preference to introducing a new publication with an unstructured image and reputation.

Equipment and machinery

The worth of the physical plant is extremely important, but too often it is considered ahead of everything else by the inexperienced buyer eager to own a newspaper. This is to be expected, perhaps, because it represents the most tangible part of newspaper operation. But machinery and equipment should be regarded only as the means of producing the intangible services and functions that really determine newspaper value.

When purchasing an existing newspaper plant, a buyer, even one with some knowledge of back-shop operations, should certainly have a skilled technician inspect the machinery and equipment. It is not too difficult to "soup up" any piece of machinery to make it appear to operate efficiently for a limited time, especially to the casual observer. Only a technical expert is qualified to estimate the value of printing equipment — even new units are sometimes defective or ill-suited to the type of production for which they are needed. There are many technological leakages through which the new buyer's initial investment can drain unless they are accounted for before the transaction is completed.

It is just as important, on the other hand, that the plant not be over-equipped for the purposes of the new owner; otherwise the buyer may be paying heavily for machinery that will stand idle a good portion of the time.

By all means, the cold-type method of composition should be in use along with modern offset presses. To invest in old-fashioned letterpress equipment, or even in interim facilities such as optical character reading (OCR) of conventional electric typewriter copy and direct printing adaptations on traditional presses (as explained in Chapters 5 and 6), is to invite the prospects of huge financial layouts for later conversion to electronic data processing and offset printing. The buyer who invests in obsolescent machinery in today's rapidly changing technology is inviting losses, not profits.

The newspaper building

The building that houses the newspaper plant is likely to be a better investment if it was originally designed for the purpose. The buyer will want to consider renting or leasing the building, if possible, in preference to purchasing. While complete ownership is desirable, the original purchase price will be considerably smaller if the real estate is not included; and in some instances the renter may assume obligation for maintenance, taxes, and insurance on the building. If the building is to be rented, the length and terms of the lease are important. It costs money to move printing equipment and to have it rewired. By the same token a newspaper rental is one of the most stable in a small town, and most landlords are willing to tie up property for long terms on this basis. Regardless of whether the prospective owner decides to purchase or to rent, the building should be substantial, well located, and adaptable to efficient production and the purchase price or rental terms should be within the newspaper's financial means.

Personnel

If the appraisal of a prospective newspaper purchase is to be complete, the buyer must evaluate the present staff with as much objectivity as possible, trying to ascertain, in a short time prior to the transaction, the identity of the most valuable staff members. Personnel adjustments and replacements almost invariably result from a change of ownership. Many times, a worker who has performed splendidly under the former employer finds it difficult to transfer loyalty to the new owner, particularly if changes in policy are contemplated. The buyer must be diplomatic in winning the confidence of key employes but must also be realistic in evaluating staff in terms of the part each will play in the program, which will involve considerable financial investment and risk.

Not only is it important to determine whether the personnel will remain loyal but attention also must be given to the size of the staff. If there are too few employes to accomplish what the new owner or manager plans, this means future expense for additional employes or overtime pay. If the staff is too large for adequate operations, the publisher is paying too much for labor and a new owner would face the disadvantage of discharging some staff members, thus inviting some ill will at the outset.

Owner's salary

In summing up evaluation of the newspaper, the buyer should consider the actual salary of the present owner. The publisher, after all, is as interested in a regular stipend from the newspaper as anyone else connected with it; and if the present owner is not drawing an adequate salary in one form or another, this should be cause for concern to the prospective purchaser. If the salary is small, it is well to investigate living expenses in the community or to consider other conditions that may constitute compensating factors, such as dispensing with the services and expense of an employe and assuming those responsibilities and salary, or making a place on the staff for the wife, a son, or a daughter, thus increasing the family income.

Where the salary figure itself may not satisfy, the buyer would do well to investigate such marginal benefits as a managerial expense account allowance, access to company vehicles for travel to conventions or for use on business assignments, the publisher's "line of credit" with lending institutions, or other practices that legitimately enhance the owner's income situation.

EVALUATING THE COMMUNITY

While the newspaper itself may appear to be a good buy, its value cannot be determined without a thoroughgoing survey of the field it serves. There are hundreds of questions the purchaser might ask about the community where the newspaper is located, but there are four or five basic answers that must be obtained before it is safe to decide to buy.

General prosperity

Is the community able to support a newspaper? This might well be considered the most fundamental question involved in purchasing an existing newspaper; it is without a doubt the primary consideration in any plans for establishing a new one. A study must be made of local business conditions, both past and present. Many a prosperous town has ridden the crest of a boom for a short period before withering on the vine along with all its enterprises and industries. A city of less than 5,000 could hardly be expected to support a daily newspaper comfortably, although a smaller community might provide fine opportunities for a weekly or nondaily publication.

Some idea of the community's economic status can be obtained by looking up the latest business census report. A more immediate impression, however, can be gained by observing the number and variety of retail outlets that will supply the newspaper with most of its advertising. If there is more than one furniture, clothing, grocery, hardware, department, or novelty store, and particularly if there are several chain stores, a fairly lively amount of retail activity is indicated.

The appearance of the residential section, the dress of the people on the streets, the number of new automobiles, and similar tangible evidence may also furnish clues to whether the population represents a buying market or a static territory as far as sales are concerned. The buyer might check the volume of bank deposits, which is a good index to community wealth, and the amount of sales tax collected locally and then compare these figures with the same measurements in similar market centers. It is expedient to check each industry of the community to determine seasonal fluctuations. If agriculture is the leading industry, reports from the county agent on productivity of the land, rainfall in the area, diversity of crops, totals of livestock and grain shipped out of the county, and other such concrete information can be obtained. It is not too difficult to find out whether a community is progressive or at a standstill.

Most state governments issue periodic "blue books" providing statistics about the economies of cities and communities within the state, and university bureaus of business research have frequently compiled helpful information on market areas within a wide radius of their campuses.

Competition

The prospective owner must be satisfied not only on the question of whether the community can support a newspaper but also on the possibility of its having to support two publications. Competition may already exist or may enter the picture soon after a new buyer has assumed the responsibilities of the newspaper. If a competitive newspaper already is in operation, the new owner must prepare to find community needs that are not being filled and must be sure of a segment of the market under all conditions. Competition should not be feared, provided the community is capable of supporting two newspapers, because that very competition may be the best guarantee against poor writing, sloppy presswork, and indifference to community needs on the part of each newspaper. Competition is actually a healthful influence and an incentive to better service; nevertheless, it is the better part of reason to consider the nature of competition and to realize that the greater the number of established competitors in one market, the smaller the slice each can expect from the profitable business pie.

Of utmost importance to the person who buys a newspaper in an exclusive field is a written commitment from the seller agreeing not to start a newspaper or job shop in that city (or, say, a radius of 20 or 30 miles) for a period of at least ten years. This will protect the buyer from facing the immediate prospect of competition from the person who is ostensibly selling out but who might decide to get back into business later and regain much of the former trade and goodwill. Also, the purchaser should insist on a bill of sale or other assurance that the seller will assume all debts except any specified in writing and should ascertain how far in advance subscriptions are paid. One new owner discovered, after purchasing, that some friends and creditors of the former owner were credited ahead for several years— and that one dentist's subscription was marked "paid in advance" for 20 years!

Community makeup

The nature of the community also has a bearing upon a newspaper's success. Certain types of communities are more conducive to newspaper development and growth than others.

If the community is in a metropolitan area, powerful competition can be expected from city dailies or large weeklies. The new paper's best opportunity for establishing prestige and operating at a profit in heavily populated areas normally lies in developing the community-type newspaper with a particular appeal, for example, the *Village Voice,* which confines its interests to residents of Greenwich Village in the heart of New York City. Language newspapers, labor publications, and suburban journals of limited territorial appeal have all been able to withstand successfully the competition of metropolitan newspapers by being slanted toward interests not emphasized by the larger dailies. Unless conditions are exceptionally suitable, however, the possibilities of establishing or expanding newspaper operations in big-city areas are extremely limited.

In Atlanta, where the heavily financed *Times* lasted only 14 months, a new tabloid newspaper has nevertheless been established to compete with the *Constitution* and the *Journal.* A morning daily known as the *Press,* under the leadership of Timothy D. Jones, is out to fill a particular need of Atlantans. Because the city is installing a rapid-transit system, Jones, pointing to similar trends in northern and eastern cities, feels that commuters will readily prefer his tabloid over the large broadsheet editions issued by his competitors.

The person who does not know and like rural life should not consider the rural weekly field unless other reasons warrant venturing in this direction. The interests of farm people must be understood by such a newspaper and therefore must be represented by it. The rural area that depends upon one crop for its prosperity is not ordinarily as reliable for newspaper investment as one that has developed a diversified agriculture. The prosperity of the newspaper can be expected to fluctuate with the prosperity of the farmers who read it — a further argument in favor of the publisher who has a grasp of rural economics.

Business is brisk and newspaper opportunities are good in manufacturing, mining, or lumbering towns when the industries are in full operation. Large labor groups mean a transient population, which requires retailers to advertise heavily to a changing market. However, a production decline on the national market means a serious slump in local industry and consequently a business slump for all in the industrial community.

Some successful newspapers are located in resort areas, but this type of community is to be avoided unless the owner can depend upon the income from the tourist season to carry the operation through the lean months. Some resort newspapers publish during the vacation season and close down for the rest of the year, but this means either double expense or operating on a shoestring. Moreover, machinery and equipment deteriorate more rapidly and run with less efficiency when allowed to stand idle for months at a time.

Personal reaction

Finally, in sizing up the community that may be the scene of newspaper experience, buyers should consider honestly whether they like what they see, or at least can learn to do so. They will have to live in the community, be interested in it, promote it. They cannot reside in a town with the detachment enjoyed by those in many other types of work but must immediately set about winning the confidence and friendship of readers, advertisers, and the general public.

The townspeople are quick to recognize whether the publisher has the community interests at heart or whether the move is for monetary reasons only. Those who love the big city should stay out of the small town because they are venturing into a situation that will require their whole personality, not just time and money. An owner who wants a newspaper investment in a certain community but does not plan to live there can always hire local management to offset the stigma of absentee ownership; but the overwhelming advantage is in favor of the publisher who lives in the local community, pays taxes and votes along with fellow citizens, and raises a family and establishes friendships there. Liking a community is a tremendous factor to consider in evaluating the newspaper; disliking it can mean the difference between lifelong satisfaction in the profession and an experience that may be both unpleasant and unprofitable.

PROBLEMS OF THE BEGINNING PUBLISHER

For the person just entering upon a newspaper career, the purchase of a newspaper is a much more treacherous proposition than for an experienced publisher. The novice is guided only by the knowledge obtained from others and personal ideals and desires, whereas a person who has been engaged in publishing knows from experience and contact how to judge a newspaper property. The chief capital of the beginner usually is courage rather than collateral.

William A. Bray, former publisher of the Odessa, Mo., *Odessan,* acquired a half-interest in that newspaper immediately upon his graduation from college, and in a short time became the sole owner. He had very little capital and no experience except that acquired during high school student days on the hometown paper; but he had a strong ambition to own a weekly newspaper in a prosperous community. In order of their importance these are the steps taken to realize that ambition, as outlined by Bray:

1. Determined how much money he had or could raise immediately to invest in a newspaper.
2. Listed newspaper properties within his possible price range that were on sale in Missouri or whose publishers might be induced to sell.
3. Went to the towns in which these newspapers were published and sized up the communities. He had to be convinced he would like the town in which he was to locate.
4. Observed the business possibilities of the town, studied the bank deposits, and visited the stores and saw how they were patronized.
5. Studied the newspaper and observed its contents, typography, makeup, advertising, and news volume.

6. Obtained from the owner full facts concerning the volume of business done by the newspaper and compared it with the net profit realized by the owner; observed the percentages of income from advertising, circulation, and job printing; checked the income tax report of the publisher for the previous year.
7. Considered the existing and possible competition in publishing and job printing.
8. Observed the equipment to see if it was in condition to continue service (on the basis evidenced by the newspaper at that time) and estimated its inventory value.
9. Engaged the services of a reliable newspaper broker to investigate the property, check the valuations placed by the seller, and assist in working out details of financing the deal.
10. Worked out an agreement for purchase, made a down payment, and in a short time closed the deal.

A good newspaper broker may benefit both the buyer and the seller in a transaction by protecting the buyer against inaccurate and incomplete information and by making known to the seller experience in previous transactions. In addition to supervising the transaction, the broker may act as appraiser of the property; some provide contract service and legal forms. Reputable brokers, who usually are working, practical newspaper people themselves, generally do not charge more than 5 percent of the selling price. Some may charge a flat fee for papers selling at less than $30,000.

Where it was once standard for the seller to pay the commission, it is now customary for the buyer to pay the broker's fee. When George J. Cooper, a successful newspaper broker for more than 25 years, handled the sale of the New Orleans, La., *Times-Picayune* and *States-Item* to Samuel I. Newhouse, the final price was around $34 million. Brokers involved in such huge transactions are also depended upon for appraisals, consultation, stock analysis, and many corollary advisory services. Many publishers have depended entirely on the advice of newspaper brokers before entering into a purchase contract.

The buyer can learn from past clients if the broker actually knows anything about newspapers and is fully licensed, as well as learning the broker's financial standing and reputation regarding malpractice. An accrediting system for newspaper brokers has been encouraged by Malcolm Donald Coe of the University of South Carolina, who says in *Nieman Reports:*

> In a business as specialized as the newspaper business, the newspaper broker has a legitimate place and function. In the newspaper profession, however, where the professional elements are still not conclusively established, the broker's function could be much improved. The way to this improvement is through an accrediting system voluntarily set up by the profession for brokers meeting approved standards.

METHODS OF FINANCING

After the buyer is satisfied as to the value of the newspaper under consideration, there is the prospect of financing the purchase. Volumes have been written on the brilliant salvaging of the New York *Times* by Adolph Ochs, the failures of Frank A. Munsey in newspaper financing, and other case histories in the realm of publishing economics. Here, however, such experiences will be left for the history books to treat in detail, and the whole subject of newspaper financing will be boiled down to its simplest terms. Chief matters to be considered in financing are possible securities and capital requirements.

Securities

Assuming that an out-and-out cash payment is not available at the time of purchase (which is almost invariably the case), there are five types of securities that may be used in financing the newspaper: straight mortgage, mortgage bond, corporation stock, life insurance, and government guaranty of loans under the Servicemen's Readjustment Acts.

The most common of these is a straight mortgage on the property, with the principal due for payment in a fixed number of years and interest accruing at an annual rate. This is the simplest way to obtain a loan from any source — a bank, the former owner, or some other lender — and it makes possible the purchase of an expensive property with a minimum of cash. To ease repayment of the loan, the total amount frequently is amortized; that is, part of the principal is retired regularly with a sufficient additional payment to bring interest on the entire loan up-to-date, thus avoiding the prospect of a huge interest debt in the future. The recognized hazard of the mortgage is the equity it gives the lender in the owner's property; payment default can lead to forfeiture of the entire investment. Moreover, the credit rating of a mortgaged business is necessarily lower than of one that is clear.

Mortgage bond issues usually are arranged in the sales of large newspapers. These are generally prime rate debentures maturing in ten years. The Chicago, Ill., *Daily News* issued $8 million in such bonds at one time. These bonds are taken by private investors who are interested in putting their money to work.

Issuing corporation stock is another favorite method of financing newspapers. The common stock, which carries voting power in the corporation's affairs, is rarely offered for sale. Instead, preferred stock, which carries no voting power (unless the business consistently fails to show a profit) but shares in all corporation dividends ahead of common stock, is sold to investors. Management usually retains 51 percent of the common stock and thereby keeps control of the business, even though some shares of common stock may be sold. The family-owned newspaper corporation, in which officers and stockholders are the publisher, immediate family, or near relatives, has become a familiar pattern in newspaper financing.

Life insurance is frequently resorted to after the principal financing has been accomplished. Heavy policies are sometimes taken out on the owner, the manager, and other executives; and investors are named as beneficiaries. This furnishes additional security for the newspaper's backers and induces them to purchase more stock in the corporation than they might feel justified in doing otherwise. Such a method has its obvious limitations but is used when raising money for the initial payment is a primary problem. A popular adaptation for the use of insurance as a security is found in the partnership form of management, in which the businesss buys insurance to provide for purchase of stock at the death of either partner. If premium payments on such partnership insurance are made by the business and the business is made the beneficiary, the premiums are tax deductible as an operating expense. This device is especially helpful in cases where the business desires to purchase the stock of a deceased partner to avoid an unworkable arrangement with an heir who may not understand management problems.

Capital requirements

The prospective buyer must make a studied inventory of the capital requirements in the purchase about to be made. For example, from at least $1,000 to $5,000 in cash may be needed to take an option on a piece of property or as earnest money to satisfy the seller of firm intentions to trade. At the time of purchase, the buyer may be required to make a down payment of from one-fifth to one-third of the total sale price. If starting a new enterprise, the buyer must have enough to invest in a plant; if preparing to make some changes in an existing plant, the buyer may have similar expenses. If the business is to be incorporated, there will be some expense on the charter and setting up the organization. There must also be some assets available in the bank for operating capital to take care of immediate expenses like rent, bills for utilities and expendable materials, weekly payroll, interest on the loan, and domestic living expenses.

Capital requirements also include immediate expenditures for adequate insurance protection. Fire represents the newspaper's greatest hazard next to libel suits, and full insurance coverage is of extreme importance. Guaranty and fidelity insurance is needed for bonding employes assigned to handling company funds. A casualty policy to cover possible property damage is as necessary as on any other property. Bodily injury liability insurance can protect the management from disastrous lawsuits. It covers bodily injuries to employes and liability for injuries to others as well. The estate or owner of the newspaper should be fully protected against any settlements that may be made against the business. This protection is given in the form of life insurance.

A form of insurance that has become more widespread in recent years is business interruption coverage. In case of damage to the plant that would prevent its continued operation for a time, the policy provides funds sufficient to have the paper published in another plant or to provide temporary facilities. This kind of insurance is considered worthwhile, particularly by the larger newspapers. In a sense, the worst thing that can happen to a newspaper is to be deprived of its means of going to press and serving its readers. There are also some forms of libel insurance that can be bought by newspapers, but the premiums are high.

ILLUSTRATIONS OF NEWSPAPER FINANCING

In financing a newspaper of $105,000 value, the purchaser borrowed $66,000 from the bank on a straight mortgage (the maximum amount the bank would allow on the property); assumed 13 promissory notes in the amount of $3,000 each, payable annually, which had been made by the predecessor to the original owner of the newspaper; incorporated the business to achieve personal immunity from possible financial liens against the newspaper but retained all stock issued; and set about the task of making a profit at a sufficient rate to retire and amortize the $66,000 loan and to pay off the annual promissory notes plus the accrual of interest on both obligations.

The purchase of a small weekly newspaper for $22,500 was handled in this way. At the time of signing the contract, the buyer paid $1,000 in cash. Upon closing the deal $4,000 more was paid. For the balance of the purchase price ($17,500) 101 promissory notes serially numbered from 1 to 101 inclusive were given. Notes numbered 1 to 100 inclusive were for $125 each, and a note with interest was to be paid off each month. Note 101 was for $5,000, the amount that would still be due on the purchase after the other notes had been paid. All the notes were secured by a chattel mortgage on all the newspaper property.

Another buyer, who purchased a $300,000 newspaper with almost no personal capital, took an option on the property for a small amount, applied for incorporation papers, and set up a stock company capitalized at $600,000 to allow for future expansion. The buyer then issued 1,000 shares of preferred stock, which was sold to local investors at $300 per share, thus raising $300,000 in cash with which to pay off the former owner and assume the ownership. Also issued were 1,000 shares of common stock, some of which were sold at $300 per share to provide working capital for the business; but care was taken to retain more than 51 percent to keep a controlling interest. The buyer secured a three-year grace period in which to make the business show a profit, thus permitting concentrated effort on plowing profits back into the enterprise at the beginning, thereby getting it into shape for prosperous operation over a long-range period.

In another community the business people realized the need for a good newspaper if the community was to progress. Led by the banker, they invited a young man experienced in newspaper and public relations work to buy the local paper, which was not doing well. They raised the difference in the price asked for the paper and the small amount the prospective purchaser was able to provide. The bank served as the escrow agent so that the purchaser did not have to deal with those who put up the money.

As a result the new publisher had strong support from the leading businesses who had their money invested in his success.

In a more sophisticated transaction, the American Financial Corporation, owner of the Cincinnati, Ohio, *Enquirer,* received from a purchaser, Combined Communications Corporation of Phoenix, Ariz., $30 million in cash and $16 million in secured notes, plus stock considerations bringing the total sale price for the *Enquirer* to $55 million.

The threat of a "takeover" of local newspapers by burgeoning groups or chain operations has long been a subject of academic debate; but with limited stock ownership rules and a pattern of family control in most corporations, such a trend has never developed. Some economists have suggested that alien investors not friendly to the United States could easily gain control of American newspapers through realignments of minority investors holding blocks of shares. However, such a threat has yet to be demonstrated.

A number of large newspapers have found it profitable to add small weekly properties as training grounds for the dailies, to discourage competition from new suburban nondailies, or simply to broaden the investment base. When the Newhouse group purchased the Birmingham, Ala., *News* and *Post-Herald,* it rather reluctantly agreed to accept a small subsidiary property, the Huntsville, Ala., *Times.* Since the date of purchase, the Huntsville newspaper has become one of the fastest growing of all the properties held by Newhouse.

A unique way of retaining local ownership is for the publisher to sell the newspaper directly to the employes. C. W. Snedden, owner of the Fairbanks, Alaska, *Daily News-Miner,* chose this route when he found the business too large for family management. Rather than sell to an outside investor, Snedden opted to pass ownership on to those men and women who had made substantial contributions to the newspaper and to the community over the years. "We have made provision," he said, "to allow each employe who so desires to invest either 5 percent or 10 percent of his salary for purchase of stock for his account." This generous plan guarantees local control of the newspaper as well as financial independence for its employes.

FINDING THE OPPORTUNITIES

To the enterprising young person in search of opportunity, a poorly managed and financially suffering newspaper may be the ideal prospect for a profitable venture. If all other factors are favorable, the purchase of an ailing newspaper is often the beginning of a rewarding career. The Damascus, Md., *Courier* was grossing only $25,000 a year when Lonnie Anderson, 25, and Jim Skillington, 24, invested $500 in a corporation charter, financed the purchase, and went to work. Within eighteen months the circulation had grown from 2,500 to 5,500, and the newspaper was grossing $150,000 a year. Modern phototypesetting equipment and other improvements have helped make the *Courier* a paying property, but the human ingredient remains the most valuable asset in successful newspaper management.

Buying into a newspaper property is a major undertaking, both in amount of capital that must be raised and in risk. Beginners may have to be satisfied with very small operations in out-of-the-way locations, but with sound planning, any property can be enhanced in value. The optimum type of newspaper for profit making, according to Robert G. Marbut, president of Harte-Hanks Newspapers, is not the metropolitan giant but the small to medium-sized publication.

Marbut, whose newspapers reach 1.8 million households daily in a number of cities, told a group of San Francisco stockbrokers that he looks for the following criteria in a profitable community newspaper operation:

1. Small to medium population (less than 350,000).
2. General advertising revenue under 5 percent of total ad revenue.
3. Classified advertising revenue under 25 percent of total.
4. Growing and/or isolated primary market area.
5. Little direct competition.
6. Relatively quick response to change.
7. Low newsprint usage (15 to 20 percent of total newspaper cost).
8. Little or no unionization.
9. Relatively simple distribution procedures for circulation.
10. Sound profit margin potential (over 20 percent before taxes).
11. Equipment and facilities of adequate, simple, and low-cost replacement nature; new technology is a must.
12. Relatively low unit labor costs.
13. Small to medium circulation (under 100,000).

Given the required set of economic and demographic conditions, it is up to management to improve the product, provide effective employe training, upgrade the equipment, encourage professional skills, enhance customer service, and maintain a solid base of advertising and circulation income. The inevitable result will be profitability.

18

Accounting and cost control

It isn't how much money the newspapers have to work with, but what they decide to use the money for, that counts. Wise investment leads to good editorial products.

Roscoe Ellard

The accounting department is the heartbeat of the newspaper operation. Modern bookkeeping deals with the task of making proper entries and balances. Accounting explains the results furnished by the bookkeeper and analyzes the health and conduct of the business. Both are necessary for the publisher to know how expenses compare with revenue in all departments, whether the departments are operated without waste, whether investments are being safeguarded, and whether tax liabilities are being accounted for. In the accounting department of a newspaper, four main functions are performed:

1. General accounting—everything necessary to give management and owners a true picture of the financial condition and fiscal operation.
2. Departmental record keeping—the tabulating necessary in each department to reveal to management, the department head, and to department workers the business being carried on there and the progress being made.
3. Cost finding—the process applied in determining the actual cost of a given salable unit of the newspaper, such as a column inch of advertising or a single issue of the newspaper. It is used also in determining the efficiency of a department, an employe, or piece of equipment.
4. Budgeting—outlining in orderly form contemplated monthly or annual receipts from all possible sources and the monthly or annual expenditures considered necessary. This preliminary estimate of the financial possibilities of a newspaper or a department is to be used as a guide and a goal for the period ahead.

GENERAL ACCOUNTING

Most record-keeping functions common to newspaper accounting have their counterpart in less specialized industries, but such phases as

312

daily reports and circulation and advertising billing and analysis apply especially to the publishing industry. Even the small newspaper wants information about the business for each day or for each week including:

1. How much business has been put on the books.
2. The amount of money deposited.
3. The amount of money paid out.
4. The number of pages in each issue and in the same issue the preceding year.
5. The inches or lines of advertising in each classification carried in each issue and in the same issue the preceding year.
6. The paid circulation of the paper for that issue and for the same issue the preceding year.
7. Total papers printed, spoiled copies, and net pressrun.

At the end of the month, additional statements giving more detailed business information are required by most publishers, including:

1. Profit and loss statement for the month and year to date and previous month and year to date.
2. Statement of application of funds.
3. Balance sheet comparing the previous month.
4. Advertising revenue and statistics.
5. Circulation revenue and statistics.
6. Editorial expense.
7. Mechanical department expense.
8. Office and administrative department expense.
9. Advertising department expense.
10. Circulation department expense.
11. Building maintenance and service expense.
12. Newsprint and ink expense.
13. Payrolls.
14. General expense.

The newspaper's financial condition at a given time is revealed by a balance sheet and its financial operations by a profit and loss statement. These usually are issued monthly, showing current and year-to-date figures. Weekly financial statements are not as useful generally, as they do not cover a complete business cycle.

Balance sheet

The balance sheet includes a statement of assets, liabilities, and net worth (Fig. 18.1).

Assets are divided into four classes: current, fixed, intangible, and "other." Current assets must meet two important requirements: be liquid,

BALANCE SHEET

DECEMBER 31, 19—

Assets

Current Assets:

Cash on hand and on deposit		$21,534.56
U.S. Government bonds (Par or maturity value $38,000.00) (Quoted value $36,860.64) — At cost		37,797.00
Accounts receivable — Trade	$ 38,105.06	
Less: Reserve for discounts and losses	2,502.86	35,602.20
Accrued interest receivable		402.82
Inventories — Estimated (At cost or market if lower)		13,723.78
Prepaid values and deferred charges —		
Unexpired insurance	$ 1,330.38	
Stationery and supplies	1,404.22	2,734.60
		$111,794.96

Other Assets:

Cash on deposit for plant expansion fund	$50,000.00
Deposit on equipment purchase	550.00
Advance on architect's fee	600.00
Deposit to guarantee postage	60.00
	51,210.00

Fixed Assets — At Cost Plus $46,000.00 Appreciation Entered on Dec. 31, 1977 (No provision for amortization of such appreciation has ever been made):

	Gross Value	Depreciation of Cost	Net
Land (Including $10,000.00 of appreciation)	$ 24,498.24		$24,498.24
Buildings (Including $6,000.00 of appreciation)	28,174.56	$ 14,711.90	13,462.66
Machinery and equipment (Including $20,000.00 of appreciation)	106,782.48	73,558.24	33,194.24
Furniture, fixtures and bound files (Including $10,000.00 of appreciation)	26,624.66	10,444.98	16,179.68

Automobiles		4,991.50	1,199.92
Inventory of type metal		3,482.56	3,482.56
		3,791.58	
	$194,524.00	$102,506.70	92,017.30

Intangible Asset:

Circulation structure at appreciated value of $20.00 per subscription		130,940.00
Total Assets		$385,962.26

Liabilities and Capital

Current Liabilities:

Accounts payable—Trade			$ 10,511.08
Accrued liabilities—			
Carriers' deposits	$ 1,400.00		
Payroll taxes	1,081.84		
Withholding tax	3,652.16		
Prepaid advertising	835.16	6,969.16	
Provision for income taxes (Subject to final review by taxing authorities)		10,113.50	$ 27,593.74

Reserves:

For subscriptions paid in advance		$ 2,600.00
For plant expansion and improvement		50,000.00
		52,600.00

Capital:

Capital stock—200 shares authorized and outstanding—At par value			$ 40,000.00
Surplus—			
By appreciation of fixed assets and circulation structure	$176,940.00		
Paid-in	20,000.00		
From operations	68,828.52	265,768.52	305,768.52
Total Liabilities and Capital			$385,962.26

Fig. 18.1. Typical balance sheet.

including cash and accounts that by their very nature become cash within a short time, and be used in the normal course of business to pay current liabilities. They may include cash on hand and on deposit; U.S. government bonds; accounts receivable; accrued interest receivable; inventories and prepaid values; and deferred charges such as unexpired insurance, stationery, and supplies. Fixed assets include such items as land, buildings, machinery and equipment, furniture, fixtures, bound files, automobiles, and inventory of type metal. An intangible asset might be the circulation structure at an evaluation of $10, $15, or $20 per subscriber. "Other" assets might be cash on deposit for plant expansion, deposit on equipment purchases, advance on architect's fees, and deposit on postage guarantee.

Liabilities are current and fixed or long term. A rule of thumb for current liabilities is that they are due in a very short time (paid with current assets). Among these are accounts payable, withholding tax, prepaid advertising, and a provision for income taxes. Fixed liabilities are long-term obligations such as a mortgage or bond issue.

The excess of the total assets over the total liabilities is the net worth (what is actually owned). This net worth in corporation structure is made up of capital stock outstanding, capital surplus paid in or created by appreciation of fixed assets or a recorded value of circulation, and earned surplus or the accumulation of undivided or undistributed profits retained in the business.

Profit and loss statement

A profit and loss statement (Fig. 18.2) shows the revenue from advertising and subscriptions less rebates and allowances minus the operating expenses of newspaper printing—editorial, advertising, delivery, general, and administration—to give the operating revenue. Next are shown the income charges and the income credits, including recoveries from bad debts, rentals earned, interest earned, and miscellaneous income. This, subtracted from the operating profit, discloses net income before extraordinary items and income taxes are deducted. Still to be deducted are profits from sale of capital assets and any refunds of prior years' expense to get the true net income before taxes. Deduct income taxes to find the net profit.

Comparative statements are helpful in interpreting figures in balance sheets and profit and loss statements. They indicate whether the publisher is getting ahead or falling back financially. The annual audit report should include a surplus statement, a comparative statement of newspaper printing cost, and a comparative statement of operation expenses for the year.

For many newspapers, accounting goes beyond that already described. According to Robert P. Hunter, secretary-treasurer of the Birmingham, Ala., *News,* the accounting department must "provide and coordinate plans to safeguard the newspaper's assets, check the accuracy and reliability of its accounting data, promote operational efficiency and en-

COMPARATIVE PROFIT AND LOSS STATEMENT

	For Year Ending December 31, 1977		For Year Ending December 31, 1976	
Revenues:				
Advertising—				
Local	$220,758.20		$189,169.64	
National	22,772.14		24,862.40	
Classified	62,875.46		58,667.06	
Legal	3,581.58		3,212.64	
	$309,988.30		$275,911.74	
Less: Rebates and allowances	1,183.88	$308,804.42	931.56	$274,980.18
Subscriptions—				
City	$ 40,950.24		$ 40,977.68	
Mail	5,989.14	46,939.38	6,739.06	47,716.74
		$355,243.80		$322,696.92
Operating Expenses:				
Newspaper printing	$129,329.80		$107,569.70	
Editorial and advertising	92,960.82		82,243.86	
Delivery	2,930.96		3,184.12	
General and administration	82,631.78	307,853.36	81,134.48	274,132.16
Operating Profit		$ 47,890.44		$ 48,564.76
Income Charges:				
Discounts allowed		$ 8,648.48		$ 7,852.36
Income Credits:				
Recoveries on bad debts	$ 44.14		$ 204.46	
Rentals earned	360.00		360.00	
Interest earned	936.00		931.00	
Miscellaneous income	54.84	1,358.98	1,495.46	6,356.90
Net Income Before Extraordinary Items and Income Taxes		$ 40,636.94		$ 42,207.86
Extraordinary Credits to Income:				
Profit on sale of capital assets	$ 120.00		$ 55.00	
Refund or prior years expense— Gas refund	1,612.00	1,732.00		55.00
Net Income Before Income Taxes		$ 42,368.94		$ 42,262.86
Provision for Income Taxes:				
Federal income taxes	$ 9,472.26		$ 9,445.46	
State income tax	641.24	1,113.50	640.36	10,085.82
Net Profit		$ 32,255.44		$ 32,177.04

Fig. 18.2. Typical comparative profit and loss statement.

courage adherence to prescribed managerial policies. Such a system might include budgeting control, standard costs, periodic operating reports, statistical analysis, and the dissemination of such statistics. The system, however, should be simple to the extent that such simplicity is advantageous from an economy viewpoint; it should be flexible so that expansion or changing conditions would not materially disrupt or disarrange the existing arrangements; and it should lend itself to the establishment of clear-cut lines of authority."

John Raymond Harrison, president of the New York Times Affiliated Newspaper Group, each six months implements a "funds-flow" evaluation of the ten newspapers under his supervision. The cash-only revenue and expense figures from the profit and loss statement of each newspaper give him a net cash flow figure. He then subtracts from that total the capital asset expenditures used to support the newspaper operation during the same period of time. This provides him with a picture of the actual gains or declines on a specific funds-flow basis.

General accounting requirements

The least number of accounting books a newspaper can get along with are books of original entry and a general ledger. A single book, known as the cashbook journal, may take care of all original entries; or there may be five books of original entry to show money received, money disbursed, purchases, sales, and accrual and accounting adjustments. From these books of original entry the monthly transactions may be grouped and entered in the general ledger, which on larger papers is supported by subsidiary records known as customers' accounts ledger, plant ledger, and others. The general ledger will show:

ON THE CREDIT SIDE	ON THE DEBIT SIDE
Accounts payable	Capital assets
Notes payable	Investments
Contracts	Cash on hand and in bank
Accrued liabilities	Accounts receivable
Reserves for bad debts, taxes, contingencies	Notes receivable
	Inventories and expense accounts

The larger newspapers have three important finance officers: the *treasurer,* a corporate officer in charge of all money, securities, and books of account; the *controller,* who supervises accounts and accounting procedure and generally operates under the treasurer as an administrative officer; and the internal *auditor,* who is responsible for the accuracy of the company's financial and accounting records. The auditor is entirely independent of the controller and may check the controller's records at any time under the treasurer's jurisdiction.

For small newspapers the duties of these three officers are carried out by a single official, who may be the business manager, treasurer, or cashier—more often the treasurer. This person keeps the accounts, receives the money, and pays out funds. When such a situation exists, a certified public accountant usually is brought in at the end of each quarter or year to make the general audit and to compile the tax returns.

The certified public accountant submits a report to the company's board of directors or to the owner or owners, depending upon whether it is an individual proprietorship or copartnership. The auditing firm makes an independent examination of the balance sheet, the profit and loss statement, and all the supporting records. While the firm may make use of the accounting staff, it is responsible to the stockholders for an accurate job. The income tax returns are prepared in conjunction with the audit report.

Mechanized accounting

Computerization has transformed traditional bookkeeping methods into lightning-fast electronic accounting, with data stored in memory components and retrieved instantly on demand—either on video terminal screens or as permanent and periodic printouts. Equipment includes:

Adding machines	Calculating machines
Addressing machines	Card interpreters
Accounting machines	Card-punching machines
Autographic registers	Collators
Billing machines	Computer control center
Bookkeeping machines	Dictating machines
indexing aids	Document-originating machines
loose-leaf equipment	Duplicating equipment
mailing equipment	Facsimile posting machines
registering machines	Filing equipment
sorting devices	Terminals
tabulating machines	
timekeeping devices	
verifiers	

The advantages of mechanized accountancy are obvious:

1. Improved appearance and legibility of machine-written records—particularly important in documents such as checks, invoices, or accounts receivable statements that are sent to customers and others outside the business.
2. Control over bookkeeping procedures, achieved as a result of machine-imposed routines that must be followed in carrying out assigned record-keeping activities.
3. Reduction of fraud potential involving record manipulation, since those untrained in machine operation are precluded from tampering with the records. Some machines can be locked so that only authorized persons who hold a key can operate them.
4. Improvement of accuracy through automatic proofs that verify the

accuracy of work as it is performed, thus eliminating time-consuming searches for errors disclosed when balancing is attempted at the close of a bookkeeping period.

5. Increased writing speed through machine methods as contrasted with hand methods.
6. Inscription of common information on separate records in a single writing of the information—for example, recording a sale on the customer's statement, his ledger sheet, and the sales journal.
7. Automatic addition or subtraction of figures as they are written. In hand methods, figures are first written on a record, then the entries are added or subtracted to arrive at a total.
8. Simultaneous addition or subtraction of a figure in the calculation of different totals. In the preparation of payroll records, one writing of an employe's withholding tax figure can cause the amount to be subtracted from gross earnings as one step in computing net pay, added to the employe's previous withholding tax balance to compute the withholding tax balance to date, and added to the total of other employe's withholding tax amounts to compute the total of such taxes withheld for the payroll period.

Qualifications for personnel to operate punch-card equipment are not essentially different from those of other accounting and clerical functions. Key punch operators are easily trained, especially if they have had previous typing and clerical experience.

General accounting practices

The chief responsibility of any newspaper accounting department is to keep management informed of the newspaper's current business and financial status and to assist in relaying the same story effectively and clearly to stockholders.

Many newspaper accounting departments now depend on sophisticated equipment that can be tailored to the individual user's needs and can be expanded as requirements change. The NCR data processing system, because of its variety of options, can be found in use in a growing number of plants (Fig. 18.3). The operator can easily shift controls to handle such chores as accounts receivable, accounts payable, payroll, and general ledger. A system compatible with the procedures of each department becomes increasingly valuable as future planning is taken into consideration.

At the Miami, Fla., *Herald,* elaborate data processing equipment has completely mechanized payroll procedures. The IBM 360 system includes given hours worked, rate of pay, and miscellaneous payments and adjustments plus calculation for gross pay, Federal Insurance Compensations Act (FICA), and withholding taxes. Deductions are automatically applied, resulting in net pay. The system then prepares payroll and deduction registers, listing each employe, and prepares department summaries for

Fig. 18.3. An operator can enter data using the standard keyboard on the new NCR 499 data processing system. Optional continuous-forms feeder automatically feeds, holds, and spaces continuous forms such as checks, statements, and journals. The system can accommodate two feeders where a high volume of printing is needed. (Courtesy of the NCR Corporation.)

analysis and input to general ledger, as well as the payroll checks themselves.

Information is updated back to one year while the payroll register is processed. Information retained internally from these procedures is used to develop monthly departmental labor distribution summaries, employer's tax liability, tax reports, annual expenses paid, insurance coverage, and retirement reports.

The procedure for accounts payable on the *Herald*'s mechanized system enables batching work and allows reduction of repetitive functions. Expense distributions (made to various accounts) that eventually become input to general-ledger work are handled at the time a liability is created, thus allowing all input to be documented and balanced at the same time.

The system retains both payables distributions and open accounts payable records created weekly and entered into the system. At the appropriate times of the month, the 360 can produce the cash requirements by due date for open accounts payable items to be paid that period to various vendors, as well as producing checks and remittance advices.

Fig. 18.4. The Miami, Fla., *Herald* depends on this electronic complex for many administrative and production applications. (Courtesy of the IBM Corporation.)

Monthly, the system automatically generates a listing of all payments made to vendors throughout the month, a detailed report of each distribution transaction, and the summary of each expense distribution account. In addition, a trial balance of all open items in the accounts payable file is generated. Furnished on an annual basis is an analysis of purchases made for the year, by vendor, for an analysis of buying.

General ledger operations require only cash vouchers and miscellaneous journal entires as direct input (from punched cards). The majority of payables distribution to accounts payable procedures are used as direct disk file to disk file internal communication input to general ledger. The trial balance, income and expense, and balance sheet are then produced, showing not only current figures but comparative budgetary and previous-year information as well. (For a view of the *Herald*'s mechanized accounting facilities, see Fig. 18.4.).

DEPARTMENTAL ACCOUNTING

In addition to observing the details of general accounting, wise management applies efficient methods for recording specific financial information about each department.

Advertising department

Accuracy in keeping advertising accounts and care in collecting help in maintaining a fluid operating revenue for the newspaper and keep patrons of the department as continuous users of advertising space.

The equipment and personnel needed in advertising accounting depend upon the number of advertisers the newspaper serves. Some newspapers with no more than 100 accounts post their ledgers and make out statements in a single process by using a carbon between two statement forms of different color, one to be mailed to the advertiser at the end of the month and the other to be a permanent ledger record. A journal record of each day's business is made first, and posting is done from that. The ledger sheets are fitted firmly into a strong binder in alphabetical order. It is easy then for the bookkeeper to go through the book at the end of the month, to tear out the top sheet of each account, and to mail it in an open-faced envelope to the advertiser.

Large newspapers. Such a system would not be practical for a large newspaper with many accounts, where great speed is required in bookkeeping, billing, checking, and mailing. For example, ten clerks take care of a multitude of details in the display advertising accounts unit of the accounting department of the Washington, D.C., *Post.*

The clerks get help from the IBM room, where five operators process work for the entire accounting department, using two accounting machines, a reproducing summary punch, a collator, a multiplying punch, an interpreter, an electronic sorter, and three alphabetic duplicating punches.

Small and medium papers. Mechanical equipment also is used to good advantage in the accounting departments of small and medium newspapers. The Ontario, Calif., *Daily Report* uses a ten-total cash register in the advertising department to control all cash and charge advertising sales. The register keeps separate records of the following transactions:

1. Cash sales.
2. Charge sales.
3. Money received on account.
4. Cancellations and allowances.
5. Discounts and commissions.
6. Money paid out and refunded.

Totals of each of four different cash drawers also are available so that the drawers may be balanced separately. Each employe using the cash register has an individual cash drawer, which fixes responsibility for handling money and records.

Orders for advertising are written on a duplicate office form and both copies are "certified" on the printing table of the cash register. The original copy, which when certified is the only authority for setting an advertisement in type, goes to the composing room, where all original copies are filed alphabetically. The duplicate copy is filed under expiration date and later goes from the expiration file to the billing clerk.

On cash sales a receipt is automatically issued by the register and given to the customer. The receipt is the only authority for refund in case of cancellation. When charge advertisements are paid, the accounts receivable copy of the advertising order is certified through the register. If there is a discount, commission, or allowance, the amount involved is also certified through the register. If a charge advertisement is cancelled before expiration date, the actual amount earned is certified, using the received-on-account key; the difference is certified on the same form through the cancellation key.

The net amount affecting accounts receivable is arrived at by deducting from the charge total the sum of the received-on-account total, the cancellation and allowance total, and the discount and commission total. Petty cash paid out and refunds issued to customers are also recorded on the register, using the vouchers shown in the illustration.

By requiring every transaction to be recorded on the register, the publisher is provided with a complete printed history of every day's business. The system furnishes protection against publishing advertisements that have not been properly charged or paid for. If money paid on account is not credited or is credited to the wrong account, the error can be quickly located by tracing the certifications. (The mechanization of transactions for advertising is further discussed in Chapter 11.)

Classified accounting. Classified advertising, with its great number of small-space users, presents the greatest accounting problem. No matter how simple the plan, recording the many items accurately and collecting for them remains a task. Classified advertising managers have given much thought to a uniform system of bookkeeping for classified, but none has been devised that seems acceptable to any large number of newspapers.

To control revenue from want ad sales, the Columbus, Ohio, *Dispatch* uses a six-drawer cash register, equipped with six clerk keys. Separate totals and cash drawers make each clerk individually responsible for transactions handled. It also has separate totals for transient, contract, bill, miscellaneous, and refunds.

After the customer has written his advertisement on the special form provided, it is inserted into the machine. The amount the customer pays is certified both on the portion of the form given as a receipt and on the main portion, which is forwarded to the composing room for processing. At the end of the day the totals on the register are read, and each clerk's total is entered in a statement book. Thus, each clerk is responsible for the amount of money called for in his or her total. Too, by keeping a daily report of each clerk's activity, management has the opportunity to praise or criticize where warranted.

The Athens, Ohio, *Messenger* has a bookkeeping system it uses in connection with a cash register specially built for it. All transient advertising is entered on triplicate order forms, and contract accounts are kept on ledger sheets. One classified manager explains: "On transient ads we do not extend the charges or invoice them until they are cancelled or expire. On contracts, charge extensions are made on the day of insertion and posted on monthly invoices. Duplicates of both transient and contract invoices are retained in the department until paid. No ledger entries are made. Our accounting department has but one account with us — charging us for our accounts receivable." (Computerization of classified advertising accounts and records is also described in Chapter 12.)

Circulation department

Circulation accounting should fulfill three highly important functions: maintain customer accounts, account for every paper in every pressrun, and analyze circulation statistics to determine the results of current operations and to predict future trends.

Since advertising rates and revenue depend largely on maintaining or increasing circulation, the circulation manager must know the market potential, present coverage, and how and where to expand distribution. Furthermore, the Audit Bureau of Circulations requires a semiannual report, subject to audit, of each member newspaper's circulation through all channels of distribution.

The circulation department of the Sharon, Pa., *Herald* maintains its own ledgers and turns over its daily cash collections to the business office. An effective summary has been devised to control 94 percent of its circulation and goes to city dealers, subdealers, country dealers, and motor route carriers.

Each carrier's bond is typed in full before it is presented to the boy or girl and parents for their signatures. The signed bond is turned over to the business office, which maintains records and controls each bond account. The carrier is billed for papers each week and must pay the account in full every Saturday. The actual number of papers required for each route is listed daily in black ink and each day's total is recorded in red (Fig. 18.5). At the end of a week, a statement is issued for each carrier's papers. The statement is prepared in duplicate and a copy is handed to the carriers with their money bags, when they check in each Saturday morning. Carriers receive written credit notices for prepayments made at the office by subscribers. Accuracy is proved by the carriers' accounts record, which must show that the "total charge" tape less the "total credits" tape equals the "amount of bill" tape.

The dealer accounts record operates in the same manner as the one for carriers with one basic difference: dealers are on a monthly basis (Fig. 18.6). Because of the many small payments made during the course of a month by motor route drivers, separate ledger accounts are maintained for them.

For ABC records a daily circulation summary (Fig. 18.7) is prepared, detailing the sale of papers in city zone, retail zone, and other territory by

CARRIERS' ACCOUNTS

Rate - 3½¢

SHARON

Week Ending _____ 19 _____

ROUTE	CHARGES										CREDITS				BALANCE
	Mon.	Tue.	Wed.	Thur.	Fri.	Sat.	Total For Week	Amount Billed	Previous Balance	Total Due	Cash	Pre-Payments	Allowances		
1															
2															

Fig. 18.5. Carrier accounts record form. (Courtesy of the Sharon, Pa., *Herald*.)

DEALERS

Month of _____ 19 _____

Rate	CITY DEALERS	1	2	3	4	28	29	30	31	Total	Amount Billed	Previous Balance	Total Due	CREDITS					UNPAID BALANCE	CREDIT DATE 19
														CASH	Discounts & Allowances	Discounts & Allowances	RETURNS No.	RETURNS Amt.		
3¼	Farrell News Agency																			
	Sharon News Agency																			
	Donald Knox																			
	Robert Tate																			
	Walter's Restaurant																			
3½	Collin's Motel																			
	Ward's - Hermitage																			
3¾	Ellsmore Ser. Sta.																			
	Golden Dawn, Rt. 18																			

Fig. 18.6. Dealer accounts form. (Courtesy of the Sharon, Pa., *Herald*.)

DAILY CIRCULATION SUMMARY
For A B C Circulation Record

.... 19....

	Detail		Total
CITY ZONE			
1—Independent Carriers			
2—Dealers			
3—Counter Sales			
RETAIL TRADING ZONE			
4—Independent Carriers			
5—Dealers			
6—Mail Subscriptions			
ALL OTHERS PAID			
7—Dealers and Carriers			
8—Mail Subscriptions			
TOTAL PAID (Gross)			
SERVICE COPIES			
9—Advertisers			
10—City Employes			
11—			
UNPAID COPIES			
12—Advertising Agencies			
13—Complimentary by Carrier			
14—Complimentary by Mail			
15—			
TOTAL DISTRIBUTION			
16—Office Use			
17—Left Overs and Spoils			
18—Unaccounted For			
NET PRESS RUN FOR THE DAY			

Fig. 18.7. Daily circulation form. (Courtesy of the Sharon, Pa., *Herald.*)

327

carriers, by dealers, at counters, and by mail. The semiannual ABC circulation report, which summarizes the monthly ABC circulation record totals, is prepared from this information.

The pressroom superintendent compiles a report and files it with the circulation department at the end of each day. Figures in this daily report complete the information required by ABC.

The double-page cash receipts record form is a complete daily record of the cash received. The entire left-hand page provides a cash record of carrier accounts. It contains the names of carriers and route numbers, the periods for which they are paying, and the amounts—with a column to show prepaid subscriptions. The other side of the sheet summarizes dealer accounts, counter sales, and cash.

Three figures are given to the business office every morning for its daily report to management: gross pressrun from the pressroom report; total paid (gross) circulation from the daily circulation summary; and daily total of spoils, free papers, and so forth, which is found by subtracting total paid from gross pressrun. The daily circulation summary is transferred to the standard ABC journal, from which the ABC report is prepared.

In the total monthly circulation report, revenue is subdivided into the following categories: carriers, dealers, motor routes, and mail subscriptions. Counter sales are included under dealers. In additon to the foregoing breakdown, the number of pounds of newsprint used and the number of pages published for the month are included.

A permanent change fund of $20 is maintained in the cash drawer for daily use in making change. For balancing, cash and checks in excess of $20 must equal the total daily receipts for the day as recorded in the cash book.

A permanent petty cash fund of $10 is available for sundry expenditures as they occur in the daily course of business. The only requirement is that whenever any of this money is spent, a slip properly dated and signed, explaining the nature of the expense and the amount, must be placed in the petty cash box. Large cash expenditures, such as repayment of the carrier's bond and payment for extra help in the mailroom, are paid by the business office upon presentation of proper vouchers.

Wholesale billing

Keeping accounts with carriers, newsstands, and street salespeople, who in reality are wholesalers, is quite different from keeping accounts with mail subscribers and purchasers at the counter, who buy direct.

The Grand Rapids, Mich., *Press* wanted a more efficient method of handling its wholesale billing and resolved to develop a system that would answer its problems, using only the limited machine capacity already in the office.

William J. Raubinger, circulation manager, says:

We checked and analyzed and cross-checked each little piece of our operation until we were thoroughly familiar with the necessary minimum requirements and the desirable additional luxuries. We compared our carrier accounts with our newsstand and state dealer accounts; our weekly billings with our monthly billings; our accounts subject to discount with those not subject to discount, until we finally evolved a machine system that would work on all our circulation ledgers, regardless of the conditions involved. Consequently our accounting has been set up on what we believe to be a rather unusual basis for circulation records. It is on an open-item basis, sometimes referred to as stub accounting, and is very similar to the accounting used for classified ticket ledger accounts in many newspapers. Under this method we do not punch credit cards or balance forward cards, and therein lies the speed and simplicity of the system.

Handling mail collections

The Allentown, Pa., *Call* and *Chronicle* controls its mail subscriptions by using a single ledger punch card, such as the IBM card 710655, and a set of billing punch cards. The ledger card contains an imprint of the mailing stencil for use in filing and in comparing the mailing list and billing cards. This card is filed in town and county sequence, alphabetically by surname, which eliminates sorting for cost ascertainment and zone analysis. The ledger card contains a written record of all transactions, such as date started, payments made, changes, and expiration date of accounts. The billing cards are filed by date and then alphabetically by subscriber. The expiration date from the ledger card becomes the control for filing. No date is punched on these cards.

When billing is required, the operator merely picks out the date to be billed and lists the charges on statements with the electric accounting machine. When payments are made, the cards are simply moved ahead to the new expiration date, again without punching any date into the billing cards. This eliminates punching new cards and saves time. The *Call* and *Chronicle* operates on a paid-in-advance subscription basis with billing fifteen days before expiration. Any subscription accounts that are not paid by expiration day are listed on the IBM machine and then stopped.

Approximately 9,000 cards in the ledger file are scanned every two months for past-due expiration dates. This manual operation requires about two hours. The billing file, consisting of approximately 36,000 cards, is checked every two months by sorting on a file code to find any ledger cards that may have been misfiled with the billing cards. A set of billing cards consists of individual cards for name, street and number, town and state, and "subscription to," if paid by someone else.

"These files have been in operation approximately ten years," says the assistant office manager, "and have given us very satisfactory control of subscriber billing and payments, as well as ease of handling." (Additional comments regarding computerized record keeping for the circulation department may be found in Chapter 13.)

Purchasing department

Purchasing for smaller newspapers (under 10,000 circulation) is ordinarily under the direct supervision of the business manager, the publisher, or the secretary of the company, if incorporated. On larger newspapers, a purchasing agent or purchasing department is maintained to check buying needs and limitations of all departments and to work closely with the newspaper's accounting department. By using printed requisition forms (usually made out in duplicate or triplicate), which are made available to all departments, the purchasing office can efficiently "ride herd" on the entire operation.

Greater economies can be effected for the newspaper as a whole when all the buying is centered in one person or special group of persons who are close to management. For example, much of everything purchased may be bought under contract at a special rate in wholesale lots, affording a saving over buying in small lots for one department at a time.

Mechanical department

For the mechanical department, records must be kept of the hours worked and those hours must be classified as to regular or overtime, so payment can be made on the right basis. Consideration also must be given to productive and nonproductive hours.

There are no cut-and-dried answers to the many questions that might arise concerning productive and nonproductive hours. If a publisher has a hunch that a machine is costing too much for repairs and unsold hours, how would such facts be ascertained? How can management determine whether a mechanical employe is satisfactorily productive? Should an employe be fired if unproductive work time amounts to more than $66\frac{2}{3}$ percent? These problems contain variable factors that must be observed on the spot before decisions can be reached. But one sure aid in arriving at wise conclusions is a knowledge of what should be expected — that is, some basis for comparison.

This information is supplied by carefully kept records. The costly machine can be studied in light of other pieces of equipment in the same plant or similar newspaper plants and its worth measured against the records; the performance of the costly employe can be compared with that of others who do the identical sort of work for the same, or perhaps different, consideration. By checking the profits against the employe-hour costs of the individual, it frequently becomes quite obvious that the management is either paying too much for employe-hours or selling them for too little. Adjustment then may be made depending upon the facts of the particular situation and upon the judgment of the publisher or manager.

COST FINDING

Cost finding is another important function of newspaper accounting. Publishers need to know as accurately and analytically as possible the expenditures for plant operations, so costs may be controlled and income may be sought to offset them.

What does it cost to produce a column inch of advertising? A column of news material? An eight-page issue of the paper? What is the labor cost per hour in the mechanical department? In the news department? The advertising department? The circulation department? How much is being paid for features? For telephone calls? For telegrams? For transportation?

These and similar questions are often directed to the accounting department, and accurate answers are expected. Such information is needed as a basis for price making and budgeting.

Determining depreciation

The U.S. Treasury Department recognizes three methods for determining depreciation:

1. Straight-line method, whereby the useful life of the equipment is the basis of depreciation; e.g., a machine with a useful life of 20 years yields an annual depreciation charge of 5 percent of the original cost.
2. Declining-balance method, whereby a rate twice the straight-line rate per year is applied to the balance of cost after subtracting all depreciation charged off in previous years. Example—an asset that costs $20,000 and has a life of 20 years would be depreciated at 10 percent of $20,000, or $2,000 the first year; 10 percent of $18,000, or $1,800 the second year; 10 percent of $16,200, or $1,620 the third year; and so on.
3. Sum-of-the-year's-digits method, which is a variation of the declining-balance method, resulting in the complete write-off of the cost of an asset over its useful life. It works this way. The annual depreciation charge is a fraction of the cost, with the fraction declining each year. The numerator of the fraction is the number of years of useful life remaining. The denominator is the figure obtained by adding together all the digits representing each year of the life span. Example—using a 20-year life, the sum of 20 plus 19 plus 18 and so on to 1 is 210. The first year's depreciation is 20/210 of cost, the second year's is 19/210, etc.

(Depreciation is further discussed in Chapter 20.)

Although it may be a useful method, it is perhaps not the best practice to devise a formula for allocating all overhead expenses to various departments, then making these allocations each month as the expenses arise. Such formulas tend to be arbitrary, and the manager gains nothing by assuming that certain costs are actual and final when they may be in reality only the result of the application of theory.

COST-FINDING SYSTEMS

For a cost study of weekly newspapers the Weekly Newspaper Bureau of the National Editorial Association recommended the cost-finding chart shown in Figure 18.8.

Cost analysis for daily newspapers

Realizing the newspaper industry's need for a practical uniform cost accounting system, the Institute of Newspaper Controllers and Finance Officers has issued a manual containing cost analysis procedures that may be applied by any size daily newspaper.[1] The manual, prepared by a committee with G. H. Phillips, secretary-treasurer of the Washington, D.C., *Post* as chairman, is step two in a plan for working out a uniform cost system for newspapers. Step one is the Institute's Standard Chart of Accounts for Newspapers, which has the following main classifications with basic account numbers.

Assets	100-
Liabilities and equities	200-
Newspaper operating revenue	300-
Newspaper operating expenses	400 through 600-
Nonnewspaper operating revenue and income credits	700-
Nonnewspaper operating expense and income charges	800-
Income taxes and surplus charges and credits	900-

For purposes of this cost analysis, the newspaper consists of two general products: news and editorial content and advertising content. A unit for news and editorial content is a paid copy of the paper. For advertising, the product unit is a unit of billed space in whatever measurement is used in billing, such as an agate line or a column inch. The use of a paid- copy or billed-space unit absorbs additional cost resulting from overset and the like and develops a proper cost relationship to the units of revenue.

The manual suggests that cost analyses should cover the operations of each month or each four-week accounting period and of year-to-date periods. If monthly analyses are not feasible, analyses for longer periods either singly or in comparison will have material value. By planning for current accumulation of required data on advertising linage, circulation, and so forth, monthly analyses can be made immediately following completion of the month's expense statement.

Expense items that are in the nature of proprietary distributions are not allocated as a cost of individual products. However, the total profit from all products must be adequate for such expenditures. The excluded items include interest on bonded or other indebtedness, taxes based on income or profits, and dividends on common or preferred shares. Operations of properties not connected with newspaper publishing and investment income are excluded from the analysis of publishing operations. If expense

---

1. Cost Analysis Procedures for Newspaper Publishers, Institute of Newspaper Controllers and Finance Officers, 230 W. 41st St., New York, N.Y. 10036.

INCOME ANALYSIS

Revenue

Advertising Income ....
Circulation Income ....
Job Printing Sales ....
Office Supply Sales ....
Other Income ....
     Total Revenue ....

Statistics

Inches of Advertising ....
Inches Editorial Content ....
Pages Published ....
Av. No. Subscribers ....
Pounds Newsprint Used ....
No. of Regular Employees ....

EXPENSES

Wages and Salaries

Job Printing ....
Newspaper Mechanical ....
Owners or Managers ....
Front Office ....
Others ....
     Total ....

Editorial and News Expense

Correspondents ....
Feature Services ....
Readyprint ....
Cuts and Photos ....
Other Expenses ....
     Total ....

Advertising Expense

Mat Service ....
Discounts and Commissions ....
Other Expenses ....
     Total ....

Material Costs

Newsprint Used ....
Ink Used ....
Job Stock Used ....
Office Supplies ....
Miscellaneous ....
     Total ....

Circulation Expense

Delivery and Carriers ....
Postage and Mail Room ....
     Total ....

Building Expense

Rents ....
Repairs ....

Utilities

Utilities ....
Insurance ....
     Total ....

Machinery Expense

Repairs ....
Upkeep ....
Supplies ....
     Total ....

Business Office Expense

Office Supplies and Expense ....
Travel ....
Dues and Exchanges ....
Bank Charges ....
Bad Debts ....
     Total ....

Taxes

Real Estate and Personal ....
Social Security ....
State Sales ....
Other (not Federal) ....
     Total ....

Capital Expenditures

Building Improvements ....
New Machinery ....
Furniture ....
Other ....
     Total ....

Depreciation

Total ....

TOTAL ALL EXPENSES ....

Fig. 18.8.   Cost-finding chart for weekly newspapers.

accounts include items incurred in operating other enterprises, such as radio or job printing, the portion of such items not applicable to the newspaper should be excluded from the operating statement for cost purposes.

The manual also points out that in allocating expenses, the items in each account under functional grouping should be reviewed to determine whether, due to unusual circumstances or conditions, different allocation should be used for specific items. In some instances allocations must first be made to the general products of news and advertising, and then each part is allocated to the specific products on appropriate bases.

No attempt is made in the analysis to assign to the subscribers any valuation for advertising content nor to assign to the advertiser any value for circulation. These values are determined and given consideration by management. The purpose is to ascertain the actual cost of news and of advertising. Once these facts have been determined, pricing these products to achieve a net profit for the newspaper is definitely in the realm of newspaper management (Fig. 18.9).

The importance of accurate cost finding was dramatized to delegates attending a meeting of the Association for Education in Journalism, where statisticians reported that administrative costs alone for the typical newspaper had increased from 11 percent of all expenses to 27 percent or more over the past quarter-century.

Cost-finding formulas

Individual publishers have worked out formulas for their own use in cost finding. The one most commonly applied in determining the cost of a column inch of advertising follows:

1. Determine the total cost of producing the newspaper for a fixed period.
2. Deduct from this total all income from every source of revenue except advertising—this step is based on the generally accepted theory that the advertising function is of primary importance in newspaper revenue and income from circulation and other sources should be regarded as reductions in the overall cost of maintaining the advertising functions.
3. Divide the remainder (which is cost of advertising for this period) by the total number of inches or lines sold during the period. The answer represents the cost per column inch or line of advertising.

It is important for the circulation manager to know, approximately at least, the cost of producing and delivering the newspaper to one subscriber for one year, in order to have a basis for establishing or revising the subscription price of the newspaper. For computing this, the following formula is sometimes used:

1. Determine the cost of producing and delivering one issue to all subscribers.

AN EXAMPLE OF A MODERATE SIZE SIX-DAY NEWSPAPER

UNIT COST AND UNIT REVENUE

YEAR 19...

	News Content	Retail Display	General Display	Classified
UNITS SOLD				
Net paid circulation (copies sold)	17,374,588			
Column inches of advertising		712,883	126,544	188,379
REVENUE				
Revenue received by publishing company	$ .0362	$1.6323	$1.6790	$1.4466
Adjustment for carriers' and dealers' income	.0138			
TOTAL ADJUSTED REVENUE	.0500	1.6323	1.6790	1.4466
EXPENSES				
Newsprint and ink	.0118	.2907	.2907	.2907
Composing Room	.0095	.3562	.0449	.1644
Platemaking department ....;.....................	.0028	.0306	.0306	.0307
Pressroom	.0011	.0283	.0283	.0284
Editorial and news department	.0187			
Advertising department		.1378	.4373	.2902
Circulation department	.0051			
Mail room and delivery	.0033	.0806	.0806	.0807
Indirect and general expenses:				
Administrative	.0030	.0740	.0740	.0741
Building and plant	.0019	.0449	.0449	.0449
Business office	.0010	.0252	.0252	.0252
Business taxes	.0007	.0183	.0183	.0183
Depreciation	.0007	.0178	.0178	.0178
Doubtful accounts	.0001	.0028	.0028	.0028
TOTAL EXPENSES...............................	.0597	1.1072	1.0954	1.0682
ADJUSTMENT FOR INCOME OF CARRIERS AND DEALERS	.0056	.1384	.1384	.1384
TOTAL ADJUSTED COST	.0653	1.2456	1.2338	1.2066
OPERATING PROFIT OR (LOSS) PER UNIT	$(.0153)	$ .3867	$ .4452	$ .2400

Fig. 18.9. Allocation base for six-day newspapers. (Courtesy of the Institute of Newspaper Controllers and Finance Officers.)

2. Multiply this figure by the number of issues printed in one year. Ordinarily this would be 52 issues for a weekly newspaper but will vary widely for dailies, depending upon whether the newspaper is a 5-day, 6-day, or 7-day publication and whether it publishes morning and/or evening editions.

3. Divide the result by the total circulation.

The estimate is a rough one at best because it fails to consider varying delivery costs of issues distributed by mail, rural free delivery, street carrier, plane or truck, or other methods. Nevertheless, a more accurate idea of the unit subscription cost can be gained in this way than by the "guesstimating" that long characterized efforts of publishers to determine circulation costs.

When daily records are kept on departmental expenses, the data will be helpful in estimating the unit cost of the newspaper's reading content exclusive of advertising. An often used formula follows:

1. Total the costs charged to the news and editorial departments. These should include departmental expenses for materials and labor employed in acquiring and preparing all copy except advertising.
2. Add to that the total of costs charged to the mechanical department for all work on reading content copy. This information is provided on the daily work sheet or time-clock card maintained by most mechanical department superintendents; the total number of hours spent on each operation by each employe is recorded for just such purposes. Even the cost of metal, ink, and newsprint chargeable to editorial content can be calculated and added to the grand total.
3. Into the grand total divide the number of columns of reading matter printed during the given period. Thus, the approximate cost per column will be obtained.

BUDGETING

Like any other substantial business, a newspaper should have a budget, at least a tentative one, on which to operate. At the beginning of the year the revenue should be estimated, and whatever developments are planned for different departments should be given full consideration. These should all be reflected in a budget, which provides a guide chart for the financial program. Some newspapers operate on a departmental budget plan, with an annual consolidated forecast system based on those individual budgets. Since local cost factors may vary radically from community to community, no two budgeting plans will be alike. For example, living costs or living conditions in a given community may make it absolutely necessary to pay higher wages or salaries to get highly qualified people.

A necessary step before undertaking a budget is establishing the desired amount of net income before income taxes. Past records covering total annual expenditures by departments must be consulted. The next step is to analyze carefully and to estimate in round figures the amounts of gross revenues to be yielded by each of the newspaper's revenue-producing departments, being guided by past averages and current business trends. Totaling the aggregate expenses of all departments and deducting this from the anticipated revenue is the logical next step.

To be determined are the minimum operating figure with which the publisher will be satisfied and the sum of money allotted to each of the revenue-producing departments necessary to produce that revenue. With a little educated guesswork, this calculation of potential revenue from the market in the year ahead can be analyzed to a round figure and becomes the business goal of the year ahead.

A serious effort should be made to follow the budget, but it need not be absolutely ironclad. As conditions change from month to month or as emergencies arise, whatever adjustments are necessary can be made by authority of the budget committee or by the executive supervising the budget. The contingency item is designed to take care of unexpected needs, but it may not always be sufficient. Monthly reports to major executives and department heads will keep them informed as to whether they are within the individual budgets.

Formulating the budget

The Santa Fe, N.Mex., *New Mexican* at the close of each year prepares a complete set of departmental budgets, allotting fixed sums to each department for the entire year. The total amount is varied monthly in line with the seasonal curve of business as it has been established by past experience. A set of work sheets is then built up to forecast revenues and expenses month by month for the entire year. These form the basis for information that goes into added columns of monthly profit and loss statements. The management gets a complete picture of actual performance for the current month and the accumulated forecast for the year to date. An additional column on the profit and loss statement carries the "over" or "under" figures accumulated to date against the forecast.

The entire operation of the newspaper, department by department, comes up for careful review at the close of each month. Any radical increase in a budgeted item for any particular department shows up immediately. The system permits absolute control over the hundreds of small items that when accumulated throughout the numerous departments could amount to as much as $2,000 in any given month.

In this way the quotas for circulation revenue and all departments of advertising revenue are fixed by the forecasts made for each of the 12 months. Day-to-day linage records and circulation collection reports are maintained. These check the progress of revenues and tell what is being done toward quotas at the end of any week or other period. Therefore, if a department needs some prodding, it can be done before the month is over.

Conferences among departments

The Glendale, Calif., *News-Press* prepares its budget by means of many conferences among the accounting department, the publisher, and all the department heads. The budget is made up in exactly the same form as the profit and loss statement except that estimated figures are used instead of actual figures.

The local advertising manager, the general advertising manager, and the classified manager submit their estimates, in inches (or lines) and by months, of the amount of advertising they expect to run in their respective categories. These are usually based on the amount run in the same period the previous year plus or minus, on a percentage basis, what they think the year's business will be in the light of current trends. These figures are converted into dollars and cents by the application of current average rates, at the same time taking into consideration any rate increases anticipated or currently going into effect. This gives the estimated advertising revenue for the year.

The circulation manager submits an estimate of average daily net paid circulation by months, which is projected into money by means of an average rate. This gives the circulation revenue, which with the advertising revenue provides the bulk of income. Small miscellaneous income is included at a flat sum per month.

A spokesman for the *News-Press* says:

> The expense estimate is a little more complicated. Over the years we have established a more or less constant pattern for total expenses for each department. I set up on work sheets the total expenses, by departments for November, December, and January, to see at about what point they have leveled off for the current year. Then, by comparison with the same month last year, I establish the anticipated expense for each department for each month of the year, taking into consideration any known factors of increase or decrease, such as special editions, unusual promotional expenses, increases in contract wage scales, and so forth. This takes care of everything but newsprint.
>
> Newsprint being such a considerable expense item, I figure pretty carefully on a formula that begins with the amount of advertising to run as estimated by the department managers, and on a 50 percent advertising basis, so that our total number of pages to be run is just twice the amount of advertising pages.
>
> Having arrived at the total pages for the month, this figure is multiplied by the average daily gross pressrun and by the number of publishing days in the month to get the total number of one-page papers for the month. This amount is multiplied by 14½ pounds per 1,000 pages for the total tonnage for the month, and the tonnage times the cost per ton gives the total newsprint cost.
>
> Then we have the total departmental expenses for each month, which include all fixed charges and management, promotional, and general expenses, as well as production expenses. Adding to this the cost of newsprint, we have total expenses. Applying this to total revenue, we have our estimated profit and loss. To do this takes much more time than to tell about it, but it is time well spent.

Cooperation

An essential of successful budget operation is complete understanding and cooperation between management and the accounting department. This was pointed out by Lyle L. Erb, formerly assistant treasurer of the Federated Publications of Michigan, in an address before a group of newspapermen in Chicago:

Not only the blessing but the active force of management is required. Otherwise, no amount of cajolery or threat by the budget officer with responsibility but no authority will turn the trick. Even top management must use tactful salesmanship if the department heads are going to operate the budget aggressively, rather than accepting it as a necessary evil forced upon them in "another" economy wave by a penny-pinching management.

The techniques involved in determining expense budgets fall into three categories: the regularly recurring or fixed expenses, which are not affected by volume; the variable expenses, or those that vary in proportion to volume or other operating conditions; and expenses that are determined by appropriation and have no direct relation to routine operations or to volume.

One of the greatest hazards to the integrity of the budget lies in the third category. Many of the expenses there include such things as illustrations, promotional activities, travel, and charitable contributions; they are largely dependent on management decisions. It is important, therefore, that the budget officer be kept constantly aware of management's plans.

The budget alone cannot cut costs for a newspaper, but it can help to control them. It also can reveal the way business is going and, if the business is getting out of line, can point the way back to sound operation.

POINTS TO CONSIDER IN NEWSPAPER ACCOUNTING

1. Five elemental and preliminary calculations are required in preparing a master budget. They are the sales budget, the production and purchase budget, the expense budget, the plant addition and plant change budget, and the cash budget. Most of these may be further subdivided by departments.
2. To have a workable budget, management must know what its costs have been before it can determine what they should be.
3. The operation of a good budgeting system calls for constant, regular, periodic review of the operation — not just at the month's end.
4. A budget alone cannot cut costs, but it can control them.
5. A budget should be used only as a guide to good management.
6. Budgets defeat their own purpose unless the human relations problems aroused by their use are solved.
7. It is useless to spend time preparing a good budget if in the course of the year it is not adequately and properly supervised.
8. Without the full cooperation and interest of top management, even to the extent of disclosing some of their secret plans, no budget system will work effectively.
9. An account properly opened is an account half collected.
10. Many accounts turn into collection problems because they are not watched after they have been on the books a few months.

11. Bad debts that have been charged off should be kept under control and followed up.
12. A spasmodic follow-up on collections is much worse than no follow-up at all. It indicates to debtors a slovenly run credit department and makes for poorer payments than before.
13. A check on arithmetical accuracy of total billing should be provided by a statistical analysis.
14. Each day's receipts should be deposited intact and without delay.
15. Important to solving composing room cost problems are a realistic outlook on costs, regular and accurate information, and a working agreement on future productivity.
16. It is helpful to identify three classes of expenses: fixed, semifixed, and variable.
17. Paper consumption must tie in with revenue. For example, if paper consumption increases without any substantial increase of revenue, an error has occurred in the reporting of paper consumption, or editorial content has gone over its percentage in relation to advertising. This means a "loose" paper and should be watched in light of current paper prices.
18. Certain expenses not affected by increased business volume should be placed below an imaginary deadline and should not be permitted to move upward without complete understanding and authorization.
19. One of the fundamentals of composing room cost accounting is to make sense of labor-hour data.
20. Any dependable accounting system for newspapers must comprehend a variable number of pages from issue to issue, variables in the percentage of editorial to advertising space, variable circulation categories, variables in labor costs as related to production, and the relation of fixed salaries and overhead costs to the unit cost of producing and distributing the paper.
21. Comparisons between newspapers sometimes become dangerous because figures have interpretations that are not always consistent.
22. All statements and schedules pertaining to a particular phase of operations should be included in one report. Management can then review all related phases at one time, rather than having to scrutinize each document without benefit of related reports.
23. Reporting systems fail when there are too many uncoordinated reports or when reports are received too late to be effective.
24. Periodic financial statements should be prepared for submission to management, and they should be sufficiently informative to bring to light abnormal fluctuations in expenses and revenues or other discrepancies.
25. Goodwill often is defined as the ability of a corporation to maintain and increase its earning capacity and is a primary element in valuation.

26. All journal entries should be approved by the controller or a comparable official and should be supported by vouchers bearing adequate substantiating data.
27. Ledgers should be balanced at least monthly, and totals should be made to agree with control accounts.
28. Purchases should be made only on the basis of requisitions signed by the respective department heads and routed through the purchasing agent.
29. Invoices should be approved for payment by a responsible executive.
30. All disbursements, with the exception of petty cash, should be made by prenumbered checks.

SUMMARY OF OPERATIONS

"What's past is prologue" applies to newspaper cost control as well as to other situations. Much can be learned by reviewing the cumulative records of revenues and expenses over the years immediately past. Such trends can generally be expected to continue, at least for a portion of the coming fiscal year, and are valuable ingredients to be weighed in determining future budgets.

Newspaper Analysis Service annually prepares such a summary based on a typical metropolitan daily newspaper with a circulation of 262,000. This information, which presents item-by-item and department-by-department data covering the past four years, appears in Tables 18.1–18.7.[2]

---

2. *Editor & Publisher*, April 10, 1976. Used by permission.

Table 18.1. Four-year summary of operations.

		1975	1974	1973	1972
Advertising Income					
Retail	$	15,861,452	13,643,424	12,112,058	11,314,658
National		2,048,267	1,612,038	1,336,427	2,152,991
Classified		6,450,424	6,136,531	5,634,152	5,435,101
Circulars/Inserts		602,997	531,827	553,395	600,373
Total	$	24,963,140	21,923,820	19,636,032	19,503,123
%		79.1	81.1	83.7	84.6
Circulation Income					
City	$	4,527,040	3,401,590	2,480,606	2,283,353
Country		2,034,239	1,566,298	1,245,408	1,163,574
Total	$	6,561,279	4,967,888	3,726,014	3,446,927
%		20.8	18.4	15.9	15.0
Other Income	$	42,547	149,404	82,329	91,517
%		0.1	0.5	0.4	0.4
Total Income	$	31,566,966	27,041,112	23,444,375	23,041,567
Expenses					
Editorial	$	2,465,514	2,339,433	2,155,731	2,040,851
%		7.8	8.7	9.2	8.9
Advertising		1,369,871	1,206,174	1,132,435	1,064,807
%		4.3	4.4	4.8	4.6
Mechanical		4,384,087	4,001,338	3,588,078	3,340,491
%		13.9	14.8	15.3	14.5
Newsprint & Ink		9,306,095	8,029,952	6,683,677	6,495,802
%		29.5	29.7	28.5	28.2
Total Direct	$	17,525,567	15,576,897	13,599,921	12,941,951
%		55.5	57.6	57.8	56.2
Building	$	634,717	511,312	399,205	384,562
%		2.0	1.9	1.7	1.7
Circulation		2,279,890	2,037,088	1,638,559	1,621,570
%		7.2	7.6	7.0	7.0
Administrative		3,348,123	2,300,940	1,978,010	1,763,851
%		10.6	8.5	8.4	7.7
Total Indirect	$	6,262,730	4,849,340	4,015,774	3,769,983
%		19.8	18.0	17.1	16.4
Deductions					
Supplements	$	32,812	49,034	23,893	97,920
Bad Debts		51,246	33,715	35,597	42,600
Depreciation		544,334	543,265	520,177	481,980
Misc/Adjustments		274,195	275,487	250,648	240,000
Total Deductions	$	902,587	901,501	830,315	862,500
%		2.9	3.3	3.6	3.7
Total Expense	$	24,690,884	21,327,738	18,406,010	17,574,434
%		78.2	78.9	78.5	76.3
Profit Before Taxes	$	6,876,082	5,713,374	5,038,365	5,467,133
%		21.8	21.1	21.5	23.7
Average Net Paid Circ.		262,035	260,350	260,766	261,082

Table 18.2. Administrative department expenses

	1975	1974
Business Office		
Salaries	$ 391,616	363,791
Other	138,414	109,086
Total	$ 530,030	472,877
%	1.7	1.8
Average Monthly Salary	$ 815.87	765.88
Executive Office	$ 352,100	328,980
%	1.1	1.2
General Unallocated		
Professional Services	$ 154,079	83,089
Taxes	664,346	662,597
Insurance	251,937	253,200
Other	1,395,631	500,197
Total	$ 2,465,993	1,499,083
%	7.8	5.5
Total Administrative	$ 3,348,123	2,300,940
%	10.6	8.5

Table 18.3. Editorial department expenses

	1975	1974
Editorial		
Salaries	$ 1,667,970	1,575,838
Features	158,048	161,075
Wire Service	217,869	208,192
Tel. & Tel.	58,690	59,545
Travel & Auto	96,568	86,366
Other	92,796	92,031
Total	$ 2,291,941	2,183,047
%	7.3	8.1
Art & Photo		
Salaries	$ 138,823	132,487
Other	34,750	23,899
Total	$ 173,573	156,386
%	0.5	0.6
Total Editorial	$ 2,465,514	2,339,433
%	7.8	8.7
Cols. of Reading Matter	90,093	95,837
Cost per Column	$ 27.37	24.41
*Man Hours	287,721	292,050
Man Hours per Page	25.55	24.38
Premium Hours	601	1,222
Average Monthly Salary		
Editorial	$ 102,961	98,183
Art & Photo	$ 105,169	100,369
*Library Hours Excluded		

Table 18.4. Advertising department expenses		1975	1974
Retail Advertising			
Salaries	$	327,734	310,893
Other		72,784	54,709
Total	$	400,518	365,602
%		1.3	1.3
Columns-Retail		141,213	148,994
Income per Column	$	112.32	91.57
Sales Cost per Column	$	2.84	2.45
Man Hours		53,901	53,567
Man Hours per Page		3.05	2.88
Average Monthly Salary	$	1,040.43	996.45
National Advertising			
Salaries	$	59,650	55,959
Other		73,497	77,591
Total	$	133,147	133,550
%		0.4	0.5
Columns-National		14,187	12,630
Income per Column	$	144.38	127.64
Sales Cost per Column	$	9.39	10.57
Man Hours		10,430	10,407
Man Hours per Page		5.88	6.59
Average Monthly Salary	$	994.17	932.65
Classified Advertising			
Salaries	$	366,356	340,030
Other		61,166	43,157
Total	$	427,522	383,187
%		1.3	1.4
Columns-Classified		69,404	75,721
Income per Column	$	92.94	81.04
Sales Cost per Column	$	6.16	5.06
Man Hours		87,488	86,258
Man Hours per Page		11.35	10.25
Average Monthly Salary	$	725.46	685.54
Dispatch & Make-Up			
Salaries	$	142,861	125,985
Other		26,690	30,945
Total	$	169,551	156,930
%		0.5	0.6
Average Monthly Salary	$	600.26	583.26
Administration & Promotion			
Salaries	$	85,498	79,036
Other		153,635	87,869
Total	$	239,133	166,905
%		0.8	0.6
Total Advertising	$	1,369,871	1,206,174
%		4.3	4.4

Table 18.5. Circulation department expenses

		1975	1974
Mail Room			
Wages	$	383,548	364,541
Wages-Extras		91,666	77,399
Other		69,495	47,048
Total	$	544,709	488,988
%		1.7	1.8
Man Hours		87,692	88,775
Man Hours per 1,000 Circ.		.92	.93
Premium Hours		1,494	1,302
Average Monthly Wage	$	1,028.28	977.32
Circulation			
Salaries	$	498,844	489,947
Promotion		250,882	120,897
Other		102,767	93,408
Total	$	852,493	704,252
%		2.7	2.6
Man Hours		107,278	110,276
Man Hours per 1,000 Circ.		1.12	1.16
Average Monthly Salary	$	807.19	771.57
Delivery			
Transportation	$	783,460	741,773
Second Class Postage		99,228	102,075
Total	$	882,688	843,848
%		2.8	3.2
Delivery Cost per 1,000 Circ.	$	9.23	8.88
Total Circulation	$	2,279,890	2,037,088
%		7.2	7.6

Table 18.6. Newsprint and ink expense

		1975	1974
Newsprint & Ink			
Newsprint.	$	8,982,434	7,736,007
Storage & Handling		105,268	93,935
Ink		218,393	200,010
Total	$	9,306,095	8,029,952
%		29.5	29.7
Tons of Newsprint		36,764	38,867
Cost per Ton	$	244.33	199.04
Pounds of Black Ink		1,193,138	1,314,658
Cost per 100 lbs.	$	12.24	9.97
Pounds of Color Ink		98,174	125,820
Cost per 100 lbs.	$	73.66	54.17
Building Maint. & Security			
Wages	$	254,208	236,800
Other		380,509	274,512
Total	$	634,717	511,312
%		2.0	1.9

345

Table 18.7. Mechanical department expenses

	1975	1974
Composing Room		
Wages	$ 2,152,663	2,035,832
Other	197,793	164,797
Total	$ 2,350,456	2,200,629
%	7.5	8.1
Published Pages	38,686	40,990
Cost per Page	$ 60,76	53.69
Man Hours	306,210	320,503
Man Hours per Page	7.92	7.82
Premium Hours	1,943	2,590
Average Monthly Wage	$ 1,121.18	1,049.94
Photo Engraving Room		
Expense	$ 635,668	542,416
%	2.0	2.0
Square Inches Purchased	5,190,631	4,558,019
Cost per Square Inch	$ .1225	.1190
Stereotype Room		
Wages	$ 397,628	361,779
Other	75,929	76,289
Total	$ 473,557	438,068
%	1.5	1.6
Mats Used	64,043	81,284
Plates Cast	152,697	195,292
Cost per Plate	$ 3.10	2.24
Man Hours	55,654	56,704
Man Hours per Plate	.36	.29
Average Monthly Wage	$ 1,149.21	1,086.42
Press Room		
Wages	$ 741,971	700,179
Other	76,985	42,755
Total	$ 818,956	742,934
%	2.6	2.8
Man Hours	109,781	114,228
Man Hours per 1,000 Circ.	1.15	1.20
Premium Hours	1,984	2,921
Average Monthly Wage	1,110.74	1,052.90
Production Control	$ 105,450	77,291
%	0.3	0.3
Total Mechanical	$ 4,384,087	4,001,338
%	13.9	14.8

19

Legal questions

We should also remember that our
freedom depends in large part on the con-
tinuation of a free press, which is the
strongest guarantee of a free society.

Richard M. Schmidt

Every business enterprise is involved in the
laws of the nation, the state, and the community in which it operates.
Newspaper publishers find themselves more "hemmed in" by legal restrictions than many other businesses do — despite the fact that freedom of the
press is protected by the First Amendment to the Constitution of the
United States and that the U.S. Supreme Court has established this freedom in many areas.

Because publishing is by nature a sociological or public-oriented activity, the newspaper in a sense offers itself and its printed information as a
hostage for public approval or disapproval. With news stories, photographs, editorial opinions, and advertising information about so many
types of persons, products, and organizations day after day, the management of a newspaper must remain alert to the myriad legal dangers
through which a safe but fearless course must be charted.

In addition to the laws that are familiar to every newspaper publisher,
new laws are going into effect or existing ones are being amended. National laws applying to newspapers or to particular phases of their work
have multiplied greatly, and many state laws have been enacted, some of
them strange and unreasonable. However, the laws with which newspapers
are chiefly concerned are: libel laws; laws regarding access to public
records; laws pertaining to right of privacy; laws defining contempt of
court; antitrust laws; wage and hour laws; obscenity laws; child labor laws;
laws regulating advertising; postal laws; and laws regarding lotteries,
fraud, and other questionable activities.

LIBEL LAWS

Reduced to the simplest terms, libel is universally defined as visual
defamation. Defamation means anything that tends to hold the libeled
person up to public hatred, ridicule, or contempt. Slander is a term
sometimes used synonymously with libel, but in more general usage slander
is oral defamation as distinguished from libel or graphic defamation.

Three facts must be established before libel can be proved: that the words, pictures, signs, or other visual means employed actually are defamatory; that the identification of the libeled person or persons is clearly obvious; and that the defamation has been published — that is, revealed to a third party.

If libel is proved and civil or criminal action is brought against the newspaper, the publisher then has recourse to three defenses in most states: truth of the charge; privilege, meaning whether the published matter is allowable under law; and fair comment and criticism, strongest when the subject of comment is a public figure whose performance is open to criticism (as in the case of actors, candidates, and authors).

Management should understand libel statutes in the state where the newspaper operates because the laws vary from state to state. For instance, where truth is an adequate defense in one state, truth plus good motives must be shown in another. In most states, however, the publisher is protected if it can be proved that the libel was published with the consent or permission of the libelee.

In the New York *Times* v. *Sullivan* case in 1964 the Supreme Court of the United States held that public officials were precluded from recovering libel damages from a news publication unless it acted with "actual malice" — that is, with knowledge that the published statements were false or with reckless disregard of whether or not they were false.[1] In this case the Supreme Court reversed a $500,000 Alabama judgment against the New York *Times* in a suit brought by Montgomery officials. However, the interpretation as to what constitutes a public figure has been somewhat more limited in subsequent cases (*Gertz* v. *Welch*, 1974; *Time, Inc.* v. *Firestone*, 1976). Despite the fact that the plaintiff in the Firestone case held a number of press conferences during her trial, the Supreme Court held that she was not a public figure.

Regardless of changing legal attitudes, the principle remains unchanged: the publisher is generally held responsible for all the material printed in the newspaper. A libel may occur in a headline, in the news columns, in photographs or cartoons, in letters to the editor, in editorials, or in paid advertising; and in any of these instances the publisher may be sued separately or named in a joint suit. Thus the possibility of libel constitutes one of the most persistent risks of publishing. Even though it may be obvious to the court that no malice of intent was present in publication of the libel, the law is designed to restore to the complainant any damages suffered from the effect of publication.

Unavoidable errors or honest mistakes made in reporting or in typesetting can be pleaded in mitigation of damages in a libel suit, but they must be proved in court. Other mitigations may result by publishing a re-

---

1. Similar decisions, as in *Associated Press* v. *Walker*, 388 U.S.130, 1967, have served to modify the emphasis on individual state interpretation.

traction or an apology for having committed the libel. Where no malice can be proved, the publisher may be liable for only nominal, compensatory, or actual damages; but heavy punitive damages may be inflicted if malice is established. In any case, the consequence of the plea for mitigation would be up to the jury.

Advertisements sometimes contain libel in the form of charges by one social or political group against another, as when a candidate attacks his opponent. Or the libel could be the result of a simple error made in the advertising department or in the composing room. The publisher is accountable for the statements in advertisements as well as in the news and editorial columns and may be sued jointly with the sponsor of the advertisement. The newspaper is responsible also for libel growing out of an error, no matter whether the error was committed by the advertiser, an advertising employe, or an advertising agency. All parties involved in the libel could be sued jointly or severally.

To protect themselves from the sudden expenses that can result from libel suits, many newspapers carry libel insurance; but premiums are relatively high for the small newspapers. Accuracy and knowledge of the law are the newspaper's chief safeguards against libel.

LAWS REGARDING ACCESS TO PUBLIC RECORDS

Newspaper reporters sometimes experience difficulty in gaining access to public records. What should be done under such circumstances?

The answer depends upon whether the information sought is part of a public record and how far the newspaper wishes to go in establishing its right to see the record and publish it. Not all records of public officials are public records. For instance, in some states the record of assessments for tax purposes is not a public record until the assessments have been completed and transferred to the permanent record book in the office of the county treasurer. On the other hand, the marriage license record in the office of the recorder or county clerk is a public record, even though the clerk, for a fee or at the request of the applicants, attempts to withhold names. A good working definition might be that a public record is any that a public official is required by law to keep and is not specifically closed by statute.

If a public record is being withheld, one way to make it available is to file suit mandating the official to open the record to the public. Usually, this is not necessary. A newspaper ordinarily can get results by informing the balking official that the people will be told in print that he is withholding information they are entitled to have. No official likes this kind of publicity.

The city of Pawtucket, R.I. adopted an ordinance providing that "no city officer, official, agents or employee shall permit any person to examine any tax abatement record or any copy thereof, nor shall any such officer, official, agent or employee disclose the contents of any such record to any person, unless such person has permission of the City Council to examine such record." The Providence, R.I., *Journal* and *Bulletin* had sought during a previous month to inspect tax-abatement records, after a large number of abatements had been put into effect. The ordinance was the city government's hostile answer to these requests for inspection.

The newspaper then brought an action of mandamus in the state courts seeking to compel the city officials to open the tax-abatement records. The city government responded by passing two additional resolutions providing that title searchers might examine the tax-abatement records without special permission and that a local Pawtucket newspaper might do so also, but still excluded everyone else from the information.

After dismissal of the mandamus suit on certain technical grounds, the *Journal* and *Bulletin* applied for relief to the United States District Court, under the federal Constitution and the Civil Rights Act, and succeeded in obtaining an injunction restraining the city officials from withholding tax-abatement records from Providence newspapers. The ordinance and resolutions passed by the City Council were declared unconstitutional. The court said, among other things:

> Where such records as these are public records and where there is no reasonable basis for restricting their examination and publication, the attempt here to prohibit their publication is an abridgment of the freedom of speech and of the press. They (the ordinance and resolutions of the Pawtucket city government) seek to place in the discretion of the City Council the granting or denial of a constitutional right. . . .

The Pawtucket city officials applied to the Supreme Court of the United States, which upheld the decision of the lower court. Thereupon the city officials had to open the records for inspection, under the mandate of the United States District Court. Thus after four years of litigation the Providence *Journal* and *Bulletin* established the right of the newspapers to inspect the tax-abatement lists and to inform the public concerning who had been granted tax concessions.

To have many public records opened, a person must show a special interest. Common-law interpretation seems to accept the newspaper's newsgathering function as a special interest, but this does not apply uniformly. Laws of access to proceedings and records on administrative levels differ widely from state to state. Louisiana throws open "all" records; but in Massachusetts many records, "public" on the face, are opened only when the interested person can prove reason to believe that the administrator of them is guilty of malfeasance in office. Records are more jealously guarded in the New England states. Freer access to records is granted in the western states.

Thus the right of newspapers to report public meetings is interpreted variously by the different states. The Constitution of the United States and those of ten states of the union contain no provision at all regarding the right to attend and report legislative meetings.[2] Only in one state, Texas, does the constitution provide for unlimited publicity for legislative meetings.

The most significant development on the federal level, hailed by some as a landmark in freedom-of-access legislation, came during 1967 in the form of Public Law 89-487, popularly known as the Freedom of Information Act.[3] Briefly, this congressional action imposes upon the executive branch of the government "an affirmative obligation" to adopt new standards and practices for publication and availability of information.

In a memorandum to federal agencies regarding the law, the U.S. Attorney General outlined the practical requirements of the act as follows:

1. That disclosure be the general rule, not the exception.
2. That all individuals have equal rights of access.
3. That the burden be on the government to justify the withholding of a document, not the person who requests it.
4. That individuals improperly denied access to documents have a right to seek injunctive relief in the courts.
5. That there be a change in government policy and attitude toward those seeking information.

It must be reported, however, that implementation of this broad law has been disappointing. Whether public officials have succeeded in finding ways to discourage or to block access to information or whether newsmen have simply failed to utilize effectively the legal provisions made available to them, the free flow of information from government to citizen has not shown substantial improvement.

In June, 1971, the New York *Times* began publishing the famous "Pentagon Papers" — a series of articles based on a top-secret history of the Vietnam War prepared by the Defense Department. The publication of the report was stopped by court order after threee days on grounds that the national security was jeopardized; but after two weeks the Supreme Court ruled that the *Times* could continue publishing the data as belonging in the public domain.

While the dramatic decision was regarded as a victory for press freedom, it was not considered an overwhelming defeat for the critics and opponents of traditional liberty in communication. Newspaper executives generally agreed that the incident should be interpreted as a sign of more trouble ahead.

In a later landmark case the Supreme Court in June 1976 overturned a "gag order" ruling restraining the publication of news in a Nebraska

---

2. Maine, Massachusetts, Rhode Island, New Jersey, Virginia, North Carolina, Georgia, Louisiana, and Kentucky.
3. Effective July 4, 1967.

criminal proceeding. The state ruling, which had been hotly contested by newspapers and journalistic organizations as prior restraint, was termed unconstitutional, and the federal decision was hailed as a significant victory for freedom of the press. But, as the Des Moines, Iowa, *Register* commented editorially, "the victory ended a battle, but not the war." According to the Reporters Committee for Freedom of the Press, 173 similar restrictive court orders were issued against newspapers in a 10-year period.

On county and municipal levels local ordinances are not uniform with respect to "closed" and "open" meetings. Generally, the meeting of councils and boards within the council are specified by the municipal charter as open to the press and the public unless an "executive" or closed session is called. Meetings of subcommittees of the council are frequently closed. Proceedings of the school board or the county court, for example, may be reported without great difficulty; but local policy may exclude reporters from meetings of a county commission created to study the road needs or from sessions of a special committee investigating school discipline.

The aggressiveness of newspapers and the reticence of legislative or administrative bodies on the local level has more than once resulted in litigation concerning the right to access, but each case has been adjudicated as an isolated instance rather than in terms of a fixed principle applicable to the country as a whole.

LAWS PERTAINING TO RIGHT OF PRIVACY

The principle that a person is entitled to his privacy is universally recognized in a democracy, yet not more than a dozen states have attempted to define privacy legally. Statutes designed to protect the individual against invasion of privacy are almost nonexistent. The laws of trespass are concerned with the invasion of property rights only. Invasion of privacy, therefore, is not necessarily trespass; neither is it a form of libel unless defamation of character should result from the invasion.

The right of privacy has not been judicially recognized in Alabama, Arizona, California, Connecticut, Delaware, District of Columbia, Florida, Georgia, Illinois, Indiana, Iowa, Kansas, Kentucky, Louisiana, Maryland, Michigan, Missouri, Mississippi, Montana, New Jersey, Nevada, New Mexico, North Carolina, Ohio, Oklahoma, Oregon, Pennsylvania, South Carolina, Tennessee, and West Virginia; is denied in Nebraska, Rhode Island, Texas, and Wisconsin; and is established by statute in New York, Utah, and Virginia.

In Washington there is a conflict in authority that has not yet been resolved by the highest court in the state. In Alaska, Arkansas, Colorado, Massachusetts, and Minnesota the courts have referred to the right without directly passing on it. Only in Hawaii, Idaho, Maine, New Hampshire, North Dakota, South Dakota, Vermont, and Wyoming has there been complete silence.

The right of privacy has been defined as the right to be let alone, the right of a person to be free from unwarranted publicity, the right to live without unwarranted interference by the public about matters with which the public is not necessarily concerned. Even in the states where the right of privacy is recognized as a common-law right, it is agreed that the right yields to matters of public interest and matters of a private nature in which the public has a legitimate interest. Also, any publication that is privileged under the law of libel—that is, a privileged report of a judicial, legislative, or other official proceeding cannot be made the basis of a recovery on a right of privacy.

Generally, the following rules may be laid down:

1. One may *not* use a person's name or photograph in an advertisement or for purposes of trade without consent.
2. One may *not* use a person's name or photograph without consent in an article of fiction appearing in a newspaper or a fictionalized account of a past event.
3. One *may* use a person's name or picture without consent in a current news item.
4. One *may* use a person's name or picture without consent for illustrative purposes in educational, informative, or entertaining feature stories, such as travel stories, articles of historic events, reproduction of items of past news, and surveys of social conditions.

If a news picture is to be used for promotional purposes, the faces of the persons involved should be blotted out so that they will not be identifiable. Special care must be taken in stories or pictures about emotionally disturbed children, rape victims, or juvenile offenders.

An important suit involving invasion of privacy reached the U.S. Supreme Court in January of 1967.[4] Under a New York law, the plaintiff had been awarded a $30,000 judgment against *Life* magazine for publishing pictures posed by professional actors in the James J. Hill home, where the family had been held captive by three escaped convicts. No member of the family was harmed; but a novel, a play, and a movie based on the experience had portrayed the family as suffering violence.

The *Life* article, entitled "True Crime Inspires Tense Play," contained pictures allegedly showing Hill and members of his family being mistreated. *Life* contended that the article was "basically truthful." In setting aside the decision of the New York court, the Supreme Court held that newsworthy persons may not seek damages for invasion of privacy unless deliberately false publication can be proved. The high court ruled that the jury had not been instructed that the defendant should be liable only for deliberate, reckless falsehoods.

"We create a grave risk of impairment of the indispensable service of a free press in a free society if we saddle the press with the impossible burden

---

4. *Hill* v. *Time, Inc.*

of verifying to a certainty the facts associated in news articles with a person's name, picture or portrait, particularly as related to nondefamatory matter," the majority opinion in this case stated.

A famous test case involved a Siamese twin who, after appearing in sideshows with her sister, married and gave birth to a normal child. A newspaper story referred to the boy some years later as "the only person in the world with two mothers." Suit was brought against the newspaper on the grounds that the boy's privacy had been invaded, but because of the rare news significance attending his birth, the suit was unsuccessful.

In another case, a child prodigy graduating from Harvard University at the age of sixteen was hailed as a genius and received a great amount of newspaper publicity. Immediately after graduation he assumed a normal, commonplace life. After several years, a newspaper article referred to him as a disappointment to a society that had expected some brilliant contribution from one with such intellectual endowment. The newspaper was sued for invasion of privacy and libel. The invasion charge was dismissed by the court because of legitimate public interest in his unusual record.

Newspaper photographers, eager to obtain unusual and interesting pictures, are at times accused of invading private rights, and as a result their newspapers are involved in lawsuits. As in news stories where obvious news values can be shown to exist, the newspaper has no difficulty in building an adequate defense. The unauthorized use of pictures for advertising purposes is indefensible, and few publishers today permit such risky and unethical practices.

As newspapers are forced to deal aggressively with the courts and law enforcement agencies in maintaining their constitutional responsibility to safeguard the public right to information, it is inevitable that some delicate cases involving libel or privacy may bring them into the area of liability for contempt actions.

LAWS DEFINING CONTEMPT OF COURT

Newspaper editors, publishers, and reporters may face contempt citations for any one of a number of actions calculated by the court to interfere with the administration of justice or the rights of an individual to a fair trial. Among these are:

1. Any disobedience of a court order, such as taking pictures in the court without permission or over the judge's objections or publishing what has been stricken from the record of a trial.
2. Publishing criticism or comment on the conduct of a trial while it is still in progress, which might influence the jury.
3. Refusal of a reporter or his superior to testify as to news sources when subpoenaed and brought to the witness stand. To protect the newspaper, which believes that if confidential news sources cannot be protected freedom of the press may be endangered, a number of states

have passed so-called "newspaper shield or confidence laws." These laws admit newspaper people to the class of those whose confidential communications cannot be brought involuntarily into court testimony.
4. Publishing grossly inaccurate reports of court proceedings.

When conflicts develop between the press on the one hand and the bench and the bar on the other, fundamental principles of each — of paramount importance to society — are usually at stake. They are freedom of the press, based on the right of the people to know and the need to give the widest publicity to the activities of the courts so that the judges may act with a sense of public responsibility, and the judges' sworn duty to see that justice is administered with the greatest care. When one considers the goals of the other, conflicts usually can be averted. Troubles develop when either the press or the judiciary, or both, have acted arbitrarily.

In its report on events following the assassination of President John F. Kennedy, the Warren Commission roundly criticized all the news media for crowding the Dallas police station and other public buildings and thus tending to "prejudge" the case of Lee Harvey Oswald. "Trial by newspaper" has been cited as the greatest evil of the American press. Sometimes newspapers may, in their eagerness to carry full details to their readers, go too far in reporting charges and trials, thereby bringing damage to the individuals in question or interfering with the orderly administration of justice in the courts. On the other hand, the threat of contempt has sometimes been used by court officials as a club to force newspapers to suppress news that the public is entitled to receive.

LAWYERS REVIEW POLICY

An advisory committee of the American Bar Association has debated at length the whole topic of fair trial and has recommended the following major revision in its "canon" affecting newspapers:

(1) While retaining, in modified form, the essential provisions of its proposed canon of ethics governing attorneys, the Committee has narrowed and clarified the specific restrictions on public statements after the verdict, so that they apply only pending the imposition of sentence in the trial court and not while the case is pending "in any court." In addition, while recognizing that jurisdictions differ on the point, the Committee has confined its recommended sanctions for violation of the proposed canon to disciplinary proceedings and has eliminated its proposal for use of the contempt power.

(2) With respect to law enforcement agencies, the Committee remains convinced that restrictions on release of certain information during the critical pretrial and trial periods is essential if the right of fair trial is to be preserved and strengthened. In many communities, however, substantial progress has been made in recent months in the effort to achieve effective self-regulation on a voluntary basis. In view of this development, the Committee is now recommending that law enforcement agencies adopt their own regulations governing this matter, and that

only in the event that they fail to do so should steps be taken to implement the recommendations by court rule or by legislative action. In addition, recommending regulations for law enforcement agencies to adopt, the Committee has sought to place greater emphasis on the appropriateness of releasing certain information, including the fact and circumstances of arrest and the nature and substance of the charge, in order to guard against the danger of secret arrests and secret law enforcement.

(3) With respect to its proposals for limited use of the contempt power, the Committee believes, as stated in its original draft, that there are certain instances when the use of that power is appropriate and fully consistent with the Constitution, but it has attempted to clarify those instances still further. As modified, the recommendation is that the power be exercised (a) against a person who knowingly violates a valid order not to disclose information revealed at certain closed hearings or (b) against a person who during the course of an ongoing trial by jury makes a statement relating to the defendant or to the case itself that goes beyond the trial record, that is "wilfully designed" to affect the outcome of the trial, and that seriously threatens to have such an effect.

At its meeting in Chicago in February 1968, the American Bar Association adopted the Reardon Report against the request of newspapers and broadcasting officials that action be delayed until a survey of opinion of judges across the country could be completed.

The major consequences of the bar association's move may be summarized as follows:

1. It is unethical for a prosecutor or a defense lawyer to tell the news media anything about a pending case except basic identifying facts about the defendant and the circumstances surrounding the arrest.
2. Lawyers are forbidden to mention a defendant's record of arrests or convictions, if any; whether there was a confession; the result of any tests made; the identity of witnesses; or any other suggestions about the possible guilt of the accused.
3. Police departments are urged to impose similar restrictions on their officers. Judges are called upon to use their contempt powers to enforce the restrictions on both lawyers and police, if necessary.
4. The courts are called upon to adopt the report's judicial standards, which would make it easier for defendants to get trial delays or transfers to other communities, and to keep prejudiced jurors off jury panels.
5. These standards would also bar reporters and the public from pretrial hearings and any part of a trial held outside the presence of the jury.
6. It clears the way for judges to punish reporters or publishers for contempt if during the course of a trial they publish articles that are deemed to be willfully designed to affect the trial outcome.

Trends during the early 1970s gave reason for alarm, as the number of incidences involving the jailing of newspaper people sharply increased. Many courts adopted a harsh attitude toward reporters who refused to reveal their sources of information to various official investigative bodies. The debate between "gag law" and "shield law" once again became a major issue for all the news media and their readers, listeners, and viewers.

Two prominent examples in 1976 were the jailing of the managing editor and two reporters on the Fresno, Calif., *Bee* for their steadfast refusal to identify the source of information contained in an article to which a state superior court objected; and a United States House Ethics Committee inquiry reprimanding television reporter Daniel Schorr for releasing details of an intelligence report to the *Village Voice,* a New York publication.

In the discussion, which focused on the conflict between national security and a reporter's claim to First Amendment protection, Schorr made this statement: "For a journalist, the most crucial kind of confidence is the identity of a source of information. To betray a confidential source would mean to dry up many future sources for many future reporters. The reporter and the news organization would be the immediate losers. The ultimate losers would be the American people and their free institutions."

Only by a thorough knowledge of press law and a deep sense of dedication to the public's right to know can a publisher operate without fear of costly violations in the disputed area of court contempt. It is not so much the newspaper's privilege as it is its responsibility to publish news of legal proceedings and principles in a manner that is fair both to government officials and to the reading public.

ANTITRUST LAWS

Economic pressures on newspaper management have necessitated a succession of decisions involving outright suspension of publication or merger with other newspapers for survival. Frequently, the latter course has resulted in court action by the antitrust division of the Department of Justice, which bases its charges on the Sherman Act controlling monopolistic practices in business.

One newspaper firm facing such a test was the Times-Mirror Company of Los Angeles, which had purchased the San Bernardino Sun Publishing Company properties, including the morning *Sun,* the evening *Telegram,* and the Sunday *Sun-Telegram.* The government obtained a court order in May 1968, requiring the parent company to divest itself of the Sun newspapers and enjoining the Times-Mirror Company from purchasing any newspaper in Southern California. The publishing firm contended that its Los Angeles *Times* had no intention of monopolizing the newspaper business in Southern California as charged, and that there was in fact no competition between the *Times* and the San Bernardino *Sun* because the latter served "a completely separate market."

The Justice Department also challenged the joint operation of the Tucson, Ariz., *Arizona Star* and the *Citizen.* When the *Citizen* faced financial disaster earlier in its history, the *Star* combined its advertising and business departments with the other newspaper, although both remained editorially separate. When the *Star* decided to sell its properties, the by then prosperous *Citizen* was the purchaser. The government charged that this constituted an economic monopoly and filed suit to nullify all agreements linking the two newspapers. The publisher of the *Citizen*, William A. Small, Jr., testified that his newspaper was on the "brink of death" when rescued by the *Star,* and that Tucson was not a big enough city to support two independent dailies. Nevertheless, divestiture was eventually ordered and the case was closed.

The question of whether a publishing company that puts out two newspapers daily — a morning and an evening issue — and also a Sunday edition can force an advertiser to buy space in combination rather than be permitted to buy space in either of the issues he desires has been debated in a number of suits filed against newspapers. Typical was the experience of the Kansas City, Mo., *Star,* found guilty by a jury of pricing advertising and circulation "in restraint of trade." The newspaper was fined and its publisher was cited on a criminal charge, which was later dismissed.

The case of the government versus the New Orleans, La., *Times-Picayune, States-Item,* and Sunday *Times-Picayune* was appealed from a lower court to the U.S. Supreme Court. Entering the case as "friends of the court" were 98 publishers, who published 167 daily newspapers and most of whom sold advertising space in their morning and evening and Sunday editions under combination rates similar to those of the New Orleans newspapers, which the government attempted to outlaw.

The Supreme Court reversed the decision of the lower court in this case, contending that the government had failed to prove that the *Times-Picayune* enjoyed a "dominant" position in a peculiarly defined market and that the competing newspaper had been injured. However, the broad question of whether forced combination rates, as practiced in varying form by 168 daily newspapers, are legal remained unsettled by the Supreme Court's decision. The Court did establish that "dominance in the advertising market, not in readership, must be decisive in gauging the legality of the company's unit plan."

In another significant case, the Supreme Court imposed restrictions on a publisher's privilege to accept or reject advertising. It decided in the Lorain, Ohio, *Journal* suit that the newspaper violated the Sherman law when it refused to publish advertisements of merchants who patronized a radio station at nearby Elyria, Ohio.[5] The Court ruled that a newspaper may not legally deny advertisers the use of its columns as a means of forcing them to stop purchasing radio time (or space in another medium).

The chief complaint of publishers regarding antimonopoly legislation, as directed against newspapers, is that the charges are provoked not so much by actual monopolistic practices as by the inescapable results of the struggle for economic survival. Consolidations of morning and evening

---

5. *United States* v. *Lorain Journal Co.,* 342 U.S.143.

newspapers, mergers of competing publications, unification of advertising schedules and rates, joint use of printing plant facilities, conflicts with independent dealers who wish to set their own prices on the newspaper copies they distribute, the question of exclusive rights to the publication of syndicated features in a given newspaper territory, and other moves to cope with rising costs of production have forced management decisions that are sometimes interpreted as legal transgressions. Whether these measures create conditions that are in effect "restraint of trade" and "unfair competition" is a question that can provide the courts with much lengthy and involved argument.

Newspaper preservation act

A reaction against the restrictions of the antitrust laws as now applied has developed in the form of legislation, known as the Newspaper Preservation Act of 1970, that would allow limited antitrust exemption to agreements between two newspapers, one of them financially failing, to merge production and business functions while maintaining editorial competition.

Publishers hope the effect of such a law will be to extend competition by preserving in many communities two or more healthy newspapers where there would otherwise be only the one most able to survive.

A monopoly newspaper situation is by no means a monopoly *news* situation. In addition to outside newspapers that come to every community through the mail or on the newsstands, there are many other channels of communication — radio, television, periodicals, motion pictures, and other sources — that make monopoly of news by one newspaper physically impossible. While antitrust suits generally are concerned with monopoly of trade and elimination of competition in a business sense, the charge of "control of information" is not infrequent, particularly where both newspaper and broadcast facilities are under a single management.

Publishers are confronted with a hardening trend in the attitude of the Federal Communications Commission toward joint ownership of electronic properties. Newspapers with such broadcast subsidiaries have felt that the granting and renewing of FCC licenses should be entirely on the basis of performance rather than ownership. The FCC, on the other hand, tends to prefer that newspapers divest themselves of radio, television, and cable facilities partly on grounds that "fairness doctrine" would be better served by independent owners. Actually, each situation fares best, as far as the public interest is concerned, when judged on its own merits.

WAGE AND HOUR LAWS

In 1966 the Congress amended the Fair Labor Standards Act to increase the federal minimum wage and to extend the law's provisions to 8 million more workers. For most of these newly covered workers the amendment insured a minimum of $1 per hour effective February 1, 1967, with

15 cents per hour increases over the next four years to a minimum of $1.60 per hour by 1971. For the 29,500,000 workers already under the law, the minimum wage was raised from $1.25 per hour to $1.40, effective February 1, 1967, with a subsequent increase to $1.60, effective February 1, 1968. Subsequent legislation has brought this minimum to $2.65 per hour, with further guaranteed increases.

The wage and hour law undoubtedly has caused publishers more worries than all the other laws affecting newspapers. It has been difficult to determine the proper application of the law in all cases. When it was discovered that the wage and hour law in its original form had some restrictions that could not be applied well in the plants of smaller newspapers, the law was amended to allow exemption for weekly and daily newspapers of 4,000 circulation or less. That, however, did not remove all the confusion, because the law further specifies exemptions for executive, administrative, and professional employes and outside sales personnel with qualifications for each that are difficult to interpret. Basic requirements for exemption are:

1. An executive employe whose primary duty must be the managing of the enterprise or of a recognized department or subdivision must be paid at least $155 a week.
2. An administrative employe primarily must perform office or non-manual field work directly related to the management or operation of the business and must draw $155 on a salary or fee basis.
3. A professional employe primarily must perform work requiring advanced knowledge in a field of science or learning or primarily perform creative work in an artistic field, and the pay must be at least $170 a week.
4. An outside salesperson customarily and regularly must be engaged in making sales or obtaining orders or contracts away from the employer's place of business.

Ordinarily newspaper publishers class their help in the news, advertising, and circulation departments as professional help; but many publishers, in order to be free from any possibility of violating government regulations, have put their entire force under the wage and hour provisions, paying them on an hourly basis with time and one-half for time over 40 hours.

Due to the difficulty of fitting labor legislation to all situations in a newspaper plant, many questions have been raised with the National Labor Relations Board about applying the law. For example, there are persons who write for a newspaper but do not work on a full-time or hourly wage basis. They sell their copy at a space rate, and in some cases they are under contract to sell only to one newspaper and to submit copy at regular intervals. Do such persons have an employment relationship?

One newspaper editor made a practice of giving copies of books to staff members for reading and preparation of reviews at home on their own time, with the books serving as their remuneration. The wage and hour division decided that in such cases an employment relationship exists—the time spent in reading the book and writing the review should be considered and a regular rate of pay and payment for overtime should be applied accordingly.

Practically all weekly and daily newspapers have persons in rural communities who send in news from their neighborhoods. The correspondents are rewarded in some manner, sometimes with a free subscription to the newspaper. Few publishers had looked upon correspondents as regular employes or had thought they could be so classified until the labor board decided that under certain conditions they were.

The decision arose from the demand of the American Newspaper Guild that 35 correspondents of a certain newspaper be included in a collective bargaining contract. The publisher resisted on the ground that the correspondents were independent contractors, were paid 15 cents an inch for whatever copy was published, and had no contract of employment or job security; neither did they share in any of the benefit plans for regular employes. At the hearing it developed that 8 of the 35 were on somewhat of a full-time employment basis, although some of them had other employment, made daily calls to the newspaper, and their compensation ranged from $2,200 to $2,800 a year. The National Labor Relations Board held that the 8 were employes. On the other hand, it held that the rest of the correspondents, known as "stringers" who sent in news occasionally, were not employes but independent contractors.

OBSCENITY LAWS

The "moral revolution" of the late 1960s and early 1970s drew most of the mass media perilously close to involvement in a new kind of litigation. Pornographic magazines, films, and literature flooded American markets in a reversal of most established standards upheld since the founding of the nation.

Newspapers, while seldom sharing the criticism leveled at paperback books, movies, magazines, and television shows, found themselves pressed primarily in the area of advertising content. Those that attempted to limit or edit the titles and copy of advertising submitted by X-rated movie houses were repeatedly accused of acting as censors and were occasionally faced with lawsuits (as in the case of the Fort Wayne, Ind., *Journal-Gazette* and *News-Sentinel,* which was sued by America's Best Cinema Corporation on the day the newspapers put into effect a new "cleanup code" governing its own editorial and advertising content). Out of 300 letters from readers concerning the ban, reported Ernest Williams, editor of the *News-Sentinel,* all but a half-dozen approved the newspapers' decision to reject display advertisements and publicity stories for the so-called "adult" films.

The long-standing posture of the Supreme Court on what constitutes pornography was that the published material must appeal to prurient interest only; must be totally without "redeeming social value"; and must be "below the national community standard." These rather vague guidelines were somewhat tightened by a ruling of June 21, 1973, which narrowed the third requirement from "national" to "local" standards. The effect of this was to return enforcement of obscenity laws to state and local governments, as illustrated in the Supreme Court's refusal in October 1973 to hear a number of such cases appealed from lower courts.

Newspapers have clearly fought a better fight for the standards of morality than the other mass media, with the possible exception of radio. Legislation in this field will always be muddied, because such qualities as decency and morality are more dependent upon the character and personality of individual publishers and editors than upon court-ordered minimums of conduct.

CHILD LABOR LAWS

In engaging the services of carriers, newspaper publishers are required to observe child labor laws, both state and federal. It is easy for a newspaper to become involved with the law if it is not vigilant in its relations with carriers, especially in matters concerning their age, sex, and length of working hours.

A number of papers reported the use of youths under 12 years of age. One newspaper in the Midwest marred an otherwise excellent presentation of a newspaper carrier story by running on the front page a picture of a child who appeared to be from 6 to 8 years old selling newspapers on a corner.

To set up standards for newspapers in all states, which would not violate child labor laws, the Newspaper Carrier Committee of the American Newspaper Publishers Association has compiled the following simple rules.

The minimum age of carriers should be 11 years; for street sales a minimum of 14 years is required except in cities with populations of 50,000 or less where carriers between ages 12 and 14 would be allowed to sell.

Work should not be performed during school hours. On school days there should not be more than three work hours per day for carriers or four hours for street sellers; work for carriers should begin not earlier than 5 A.M. and end not later than 7 P.M. in winter and 8 P.M. in summer; work for street sellers should begin not earlier than 7 A.M. and end not later than 7 P.M. in winter and 8 P.M. in summer.

The importance of obeying the child labor laws has been so strongly emphasized at meetings of circulation managers that most now guard against violations. Furthermore, they see the advantages of using older and more dependable carriers for the selling and delivering of papers.

LAWS REGULATING ADVERTISING

Honesty in advertising has been a goal of publishers, advertising personnel, and business people for many years. An attempt to improve advertising practices started in 1892, when the *Ladies' Home Journal* announced that it would not print any more medical advertising and launched a fight for its reform. *Collier's Weekly,* other magazines, and many daily newspapers joined in the campaign. Later there were federal laws to prevent the adulteration and misbranding of food products.[6] The Securities and Exchange Commission, established in 1933, was instrumental in demonstrating that existing state laws were inadequate to deal with false stock promotion advertising. Also, dishonesties in retail advertising were brought to light by the Better Business Bureau, which was formed to point out violations to merchants and manufacturers and to create a sentiment for honest merchandising and honest advertising everywhere.

A Federal Trade Commission was set up in 1914 "to prevent persons, partnerships, or corporations, except banks and common carriers subject to the Act To Regulate Commerce, from using unfair methods of competition in commerce." The commission established a board to inspect and examine advertising in newspapers and magazines for examples of misrepresentation. As the system works today, when misrepresentation on the part of any firm is suspected, the board sends a questionnaire to the advertiser asking for facts about both the advertising and the merchandise. If the investigation indicates misrepresentation or fraud, the board may file a complaint through the Federal Trade Commission. The advertiser against whom the complaint is filed is then given opportunity to show cause why the complaint should not be issued. In most cases the advertiser enters into an agreement with the Federal Trade Commission to cease and desist from making the specified objectionable claims in future advertising.

The commission's authority to issue cease and desist orders depends upon three prerequisites: that the methods complained of are unfair, that they are methods of competition in commerce, and that a proceeding by the commission to prevent the use of the methods appears to be in the interest of the public.

Many states also have laws to protect the public from fraudulent and misleading advertising. These statutes prohibit false statements about quantity, value, and price of articles advertised. To encourage compliance with the laws and to place public opinion behind them, the Better Business Bureau has set up a fair trade code for advertising and selling, which has been approved by newspaper organizations, merchants' associations, advertising agencies, and professional groups. The code urges all business agencies to:

1. Serve the public with honest values.
2. Tell the truth about what is offered.
3. Tell the truth in a forthright manner, so its significance may be understood by the trusting as well as the analytical.

---

6. Laying the foundation for still later acts were: The Wiley Food and Drug Act, 1906; the Food, Drug, and Cosmetic Act, 1938; and the Wheeler-Lea Act, 1938 (amending the Federal Trade Commission Act of 1914).

4. Tell customers what they want to know and what they have a right to know and ought to know about what is offered, so that they may buy wisely and obtain the maximum satisfaction from their purchases.
5. Be prepared and willing to make good as promised and without quibble on any guarantee offered.
6. Be sure that normal use of merchandise or services offered will not be hazardous to public life or health.
7. Reveal material facts, the deceptive concealment of which might cause consumers to be misled.
8. Advertise and sell merchandise or service on its merits and refrain from attacking competitors or reflecting unfairly upon their products, services, or methods of doing business.
9. If testimonials are used, use only those of competent witnesses who are sincere and honest in what they say about what you sell.
10. Avoid all tricky devices and schemes such as deceitful trade-in allowances, fictitious list prices, false and exaggerated comparative prices, misleading free offers, fake sales, and similar practices that prey upon human ignorance and gullibility.

The Better Business Bureau helps keep watch on advertising in newspapers, pamphlets, and other printed material; and when it receives a formal complaint that the code or any laws pertaining to advertising are being violated, the person or firm suspected is called upon.

Many newspapers also have set up standards for all advertising in their own columns. The New York, N.Y., *Times* excludes from its columns the following:

1. Fraudulent or doubtful advertisements.
2. Offers of something of value for nothing; advertisements that make false, unwarranted, or exaggerated claims.
3. Advertisements that are ambiguous in wording and may mislead.
4. Attacks of a personal character; advertisements that make uncalled-for reflections on competitors or their goods.
5. Advertisements holding out the prospect of large guaranteed dividends or excessive profits.
6. Bucket shops and offerings of undesirable items.
7. Matrimonial offers.
8. Advertisements that are indecent, vulgar, suggestive, repulsive, or offensive.
9. Objectionable medical advertising of products containing habit-forming or dangerous drugs; offers of free medical treatment; advertising that makes remedial, relief, or curative claims (either directly or by inference) not justified by the facts or common experience.
10. Offers of homework.
11. Mailing lists offered for sale.
12. Advertisements of preparations to "grow new hair."

13. Advertisements of fortunetelling, dream interpretations, individual horoscopes, and nativity writings.
14. Any other advertising that may cause loss or injury in health or morals to the reader or loss of confidence in reputable advertising and honorable business.

These are typical of standards being adopted by an increasing number of newspapers. Publishers are anxious to earn and to hold the confidence of all who read the advertisements in their newspapers and often go beyond the restrictions imposed upon advertisers by law.

To protect the public from being misled by so-called "reader" advertising (similar in appearance to editorial matter), the Post Office Department requires that it be labeled "advertisement." The problem is to determine when paid advertising ceases to qualify as display and becomes reader advertising. There never has been a clear official opinion that can be used as a guide, but publishers would be wise to take the cautious view and insist upon labeling any advertising approaching the "reader" classification. Violation of the regulation is punishable by a fine.

The newspaper has a right to accept or reject advertising copy as it desires, so long as it does not attempt to create a monopoly in advertising. Test suits, in most instances, have held that the newspaper is a private business and as such can accept advertising from whom it chooses and refuse it upon the same basis.

Political advertising must comply with both federal and state regulations. On the federal level, the law requires that all political advertising carry the name of the individual or organization publishing the advertisement. If the sponsor is an organization, the names of its officers are needed. Simply to include the words "political advertisement," is not adequate — as a matter of fact, even though that designation is often used, it is not mandatory at all. State laws are not uniform. Some have no regulations at all; others merely require the "paid advertisement" inscription.

The owner of a dry-cleaning establishment once sought by injunction to compel a newspaper to publish his advertisement. Copy and payment for it had been accepted by the publisher, but later the publisher changed his mind and returned the copy and money to the would-be advertiser. Suit was filed and the matter was appealed to the state's Supreme Court, which delivered the following opinion:

The newspaper business is . . . a business essentially private in nature — as private as that of the baker, grocer, or milkman, all of whom perform a service on which, to a greater or lesser extent, the communities depend, but which bears no such relation to the public as to warrant its inclusion in the category of businesses charged with public use. If a newspaper were required to accept an advertisement, it could be compelled to publish a news item. If some good lady gave a tea, and submitted to the newspaper a proper account of the tea, and the editor of the newspaper, believing that it had no news value, refused to publish it, she, it seems to us, would have as much right to compel the newspaper to publish the account as would a person engaged in a business to compel a newspaper to publish an advertisement of the business that that person is conducting.

Thus, as a newspaper is a strictly private enterprise, the publishers thereof have a right to publish whatever advertisements they desire and refuse whatever advertisements they do not wish to publish.[7]

The question of the newspaper's responsibility in case of an error in an advertisement has appeared in the courts from time to time. Generally, the law has regarded an advertisement as nothing more than an "invitation to bid" and not as a contract between the advertiser and the customer. Consequently, an error in an advertisement does not impose a legal obligation on the advertiser to sell at the prices or under the conditions erroneously stated. In accordance with this legal policy, if the newspaper can prove that it was not responsible for making the error, it has not been considered under obligation to either the advertiser or the customer.

Even though publishers may be absolved of legal obligations for errors in published advertisements, they may nevertheless be ethically or morally responsible. To keep advertiser goodwill and to demonstrate the newspaper's desire to give good advertising service, the publisher could correct the error and rerun the advertisement in the succeeding issue without additional cost to the merchant.

Occasionally advertisers fail to live up to their contracts with the newspaper. If an advertiser buys space for a year, agreeing to use a definite amount each week, and after three months discontinues all advertising, the contract is broken and the publisher is entitled to recover for the loss of profits. Usually an advertising contract of this kind is on the basis of a space rate according to volume used; and when the volume of space specified in the contract is not used, the rate goes to a higher bracket and settlement is made on that basis.

POSTAL LAWS

The importance of newspapers to the immediate communities in which they are published has long been recognized by the government. Consequently, lower postal rates for newspapers have prevailed. A newspaper is permitted to go "free" through the mail to rural route subscribers in the county within which the newspaper is published. For papers delivered outside the county, the rate per pound is determined by zone.

Before a newspaper can gain access to the mails as second-class matter, it must be regularly issued at stated intervals, at least four times a year; bear a date of issue; be numbered consecutively; and be issued from a known office of publication. It must be formed of printed paper sheets, without board, cloth, leather, or substantial binding. It must be originated and published for the dissemination of information of a public character

---

7. *Shuck* v. *Carroll Herald*, Iowa, 1933; 215 Iowa 1276; 247 N.W. 813; 87 A.L.R. 975.

or devoted to literature, the sciences, the arts, or some special industry. In addition, a newspaper must have a list of legitimate subscribers.

The regulations require that all advertisements in periodicals must be permanently attached thereto and sheets containing them must be substantially as large but not larger than the pages of the publication. Advertisements printed on sheets larger than the regular pages are inadmissible even though folded to that size.

To be accepted for entry as second-class matter, a newspaper must publish certain information "conspicuously printed" on one of the first five pages, preferably the first. This applies to each copy. The required information includes title of publication, date of issue, and regular period of issue or frequency; serial number; known office of publication; subscription price; and notice that it has been entered as second-class matter. A publisher who submits false information or evidence to obtain second-class privileges for a publication shall, upon conviction in the federal courts, be fined not more than $500.

Failure to file an annual statement giving information required by the post office subjects the offending publication to denial of the use of the mail. This statement includes the names and post office addresses of the editor, managing editor, publisher, business managers, and owners; if the publication is owned by a corporation, the names and post office addresses of all stockholders owning 1 percent or more of the capital stock; the names of all bondholders, mortgagees, or other security holders owning 1 percent or more of such bonds, mortgages, or other securities; and a statement of the average number of copies of each issue of such publication sold or distributed to paid subscribers during the preceding twelve months.

Offsetting the original advantages of the second-class mail permit for newspapers and magazines have been the recurrent increases in basic postal charges over the last few years. These costs have risen to the point that publishers have had to question whether the Postal Service is carrying out the intent of Congress in creating special periodical rates in the first place. For example, some newspapers that depend heavily on mail distribution for their total circulations find postal charges a constantly increasing aspect of budget considerations where it once represented a fairly fixed estimate. Magazines with giant circulations, like the late *Look* and *Life,* complained that higher postal rates helped put them out of business.

Even under the preferential rates they enjoy, newspapers have seen the cost of mailing rise as much as 142 percent in a matter of a year or so. The American Newspaper Publishers Association is expected to seek relief in Congress from the costliest decade in newspaper history as far as mail "subsidies" are concerned.

LAWS REGARDING LOTTERIES AND FRAUD

To protect the public, the federal government has imposed certain restrictions on both news and advertising copy. For example, no advertising or news that features lotteries or contains fraud is allowed. Several states have lottery laws stricter than the federal regulations, although others have recently legalized lotteries and their advertising.

The provisions regarding lotteries have led newspaper publishers to many controversies with Chambers of Commerce and other organizations that have been interested in promoting and publicizing lotteries on a communitywide basis. Congress helped to bring about a more positive understanding of lotteries when in 1948 it enacted a Code of Crimes and Criminal Procedure, the effect of which was to revise and rectify all criminal statutes under Title 18 of the United States Code. The revised specification relative to lotteries, gift enterprises, and similar schemes as affecting newspapers is as follows:

[The publisher of] any newspaper, circular, pamphlet, or publication of any kind containing an advertisement of any lottery, gift enterprise, or scheme of any kind offering prizes dependent in whole or in part upon lot or chance, or containing any list of the prizes drawn or awarded by means of any such lottery, gift enterprise, or scheme, or whether such list contains any part or all of such prizes, shall be fined not more than $1,000 or imprisoned not more than two years, or both; and for any subsequent offense shall be imprisoned not more than five years.

The enforcement of this law is vested primarily in the U.S. Attorney General and district attorneys. Three elements are included in the legal definition of "lottery"—*chance, compensation,* and *consideration.* That is, prizes are awarded by means of chance or lot to participants who have paid in terms of money, time, or effort. If a person is required to be present at a drawing of door prizes, that requirement may be interpreted as the "consideration" involved, and thus the drawing would be classified as a lottery. The registering of names alone, in order to qualify for prizes, would not be deemed a lottery because the "consideration" is negligible or nonexistent. This is the blanket ruling used by the Post Office Department in determining whether or not a lottery exists.

The effect of this ruling is to say that if the consideration is not present, the matter is mailable and the Post Office Department has no objection, even though the statute expressly prohibits gift enterprises and schemes of any kind offering prizes awarded by lot or chance. However, there is nothing to keep the Attorney General from prosecuting a defendant for conducting a gift enterprise even though the Post Office Department has permitted the use of the mail for the same scheme.

Although lotteries have been legalized in a few states, many have laws making it a criminal offense knowingly to print or to distribute any advertisement of any lottery ticket or scheme. The statute usually takes this form:

Whoever knowingly prints, publishes, distributes, circulates, or knowingly causes to be printed, published, distributed, or circulated any advertisement of any lottery ticket or scheme, or any share in such ticket or scheme, for sale, either himself or by another person, or sets up, or exhibits, or devises, or makes for the purpose of being set up and exhibited, any sign, symbol, or emblematic or other representation of a lottery, or the drawing thereof, in any way indicating where a lottery, or any share thereof, or any such writing, certificate, bill, token, or other device before mentioned, may be purchased or obtained, or in any way invites or entices or attempts to invite or entice any person to purchase or receive the same, shall, for each offense, be fined not exceeding $100.[8]

OTHER LEGAL QUESTIONS

Other interesting legal questions arise from time to time. Newspapers are sometimes guilty of improperly using the American flag in advertising. It is against the law in every state, and a violation of a congressional resolution, Public Law 829, 1942, to use the United States flag for advertising purposes. Significantly, such regulations cover the use, not only of the flag, but of the "standard, color or ensign" and in many cases of "any device, crest, shield, emblem, or insignia, containing or purporting to represent red and white stripes surmounted by white stars on a blue field, and simulating the shield of the United States government, or the crest, shield, emblem or insignia appearing on the flag of the President of the United States, or on the coat-of-arms of the United States."

Newspaper publishers have in some instances become involved in litigation concerning property rights to material that is either reprinted or published for the first time. The provisions of the Copyright Act of 1909 are clearly defined, and should be read thoroughly before the publication of copy whose ownership is likely to be in question. These regulations were updated in Public Law 94-553, effective Jan. 1, 1978. Publishers may find it necessary to consult the detailed provisions affecting use of copyright. It is well to be aware of the fact that unpublished works are protected by common-law copyright, even though formal certification may not have been obtained by the author. Contractual agreements with syndicates usually provide for legal entitlement to the copyright privileges of all feature material supplied to the newspaper.

---

8. Illinois (Smith-Hurd Anno. State Perm. Ed. c. 35, Par. 409).

20

Tax problems

Questions concerning taxation will arise
but, if possible, should all be settled
before the books have been closed for
the year.

A. S. Van Benthuysen

Tax problems of a newspaper are of two
types: taxation as a source of decisive news for its readers and the effect of
tax reporting and taxpaying upon the newspaper organization itself.

TAXES AND READERS

A newspaper has an opportunity for discharging a public service
obligation to its readers by keeping them informed on all federal, state,
and local taxes. So much tax information is provided by various governmental bodies and tax service organizations that a newspaper editor has
only to "select" items of interest to readers. Occasionally, the editor may
decide that readers should be urged to sponsor, amend, or defeat tax
legislation before it is finally acted upon.

In many cases a newspaper may have or develop special knowledge of
good or bad aspects of proposed tax legislation and should keep itself keen-
ly alert in reporting seemingly unfair assessments, wasteful administration,
conflicts of interest on the part of officials, and evidence of self-service
toward favored taxpayers and many others.

IMPACT OF TAXES ON THE NEWSPAPER

Tax payments and tax returns required of all businesses, in addition
to newspaper owners, include property taxes; state franchise taxes for
newspaper corporations; income taxes (federal, state, and city); taxes
based on payroll; sales, use, and service taxes; state or local occupational
taxes or licenses; federal excise taxes; information returns; and
nonoperating taxes. Nomenclature varies among states but an understanding of each type of tax and its impact on the newspaper is essential to
management.

370

Property taxes

Property taxes, sometimes known as "ad valorem" taxes, are assessed annually against real and personal assets, based usually upon a percentage of their value as at a certain date. Valuation procedures, rates applied, and methods of payment vary by state, county, city, or taxation district.

Special assessments for capital improvements affecting real estate are assessed by improvement districts, weighted by proportion of estimated benefits, and are usually paid over a period of years. Interest is added for deferred payments.

If realty taxes are unpaid, the property may be auctioned, and under certain conditions the tax buyer can obtain a "tax" title to the property. If personal property taxes are unpaid, the methods of enforcement vary greatly, including an automatic increase of a substantial percentage for each year of nonpayment.

A special kind of newspaper personal property is the inventory of imported newsprint. A great part of the newsprint used in this country comes from Canada and is delivered in mill-wrapped rolls to a newspaper's storage facility. In a number of decisions, it has been held that stock of unopened imported newsprint beyond "immediate need" is exempt from local property tax under Article I, Section 10, Clause 2 of the Constitution, prohibiting states from imposing taxes on material imported for manufacturing purposes until the material is used. The "immediate need" stock has been variously interpreted as a 1-day, 6-day, or even 19-day supply.

Newspapers endeavor to obtain the contract for the publication of tax delinquencies from which they derive substantial revenues at legal rates. (See the discussion of legal advertising in Chapter 11.)

Franchise taxes

Franchise taxes relate primarily to the privilege extended to a corporation to do business within the state that grants the charter or license. Annual reports are required, covering the stock issued, the proportion of business done within the state, balance sheet statements, report of earnings, and many other features. The state taxation board may be authorized to tax the tangible and intangible values based on formulas prescribed by legislation.

In some states, there is a combination of franchise tax and a state income tax on the same form. Failure to file and pay franchise taxes may forfeit the company's charter and the right to do business in the state.

Newspapers in some states derive revenue from publication of annual reports of nondomestic corporations, allocated by the local secretary of state.

Income taxes—federal, state, and city

Under the laws and regulations of the United States and in some states and municipalities, annual reports of net income from individual proprietors, fiduciaries, partnerships, and corporations are required. Indiana, for instance, uses a combination of gross income or adjusted gross income as a base. Tax payments may be assessable in advance under a system of declaration of anticipated tax, or paid at the time of filing the report, or on a deferred basis.

The basis of reporting income may be on the "cash basis" (as the income is received and the expenses are paid); on the "accrued basis" (as the net income is earned); or on a "hybrid basis" (a combination of the "cash" and "accrual" factors), which clearly reports the taxable income of the taxpayer. The first accepted report of the taxpayer determines his basis and cannot be changed without approval of the taxing authority.

Within a single return the taxpayer may be assessed at one set of rates for normal operations and at another rate for profits on the sale of capital assets. Any of the five following classifications may apply to newspapers, depending upon their organization:

1. Individual proprietors operating one or more businesses, such as a newspaper and a farm, will include separate schedules for each type of operation, the total taxable income becoming subject to the tax brackets scheduled by law. Federal individual returns are due three and one-half months after the end of the taxable year. Individual proprietors are also subject to taxes imposed by the Federal Insurance Contributions Act (FICA), which provides social security benefits to them as "self-employed persons" when they become eligible for retirement or disability payments.
2. Fiduciary income tax reports are required of certain trusts when they become operative according to their terms or during the process of settling the estate of a deceased taxpayer. While the exemptions and deductions differ, the rates of taxation follow the general pattern of an individual taxpayer.
3. Partnership income tax returns follow the terms of the copartnership agreement and act as a source for an individual partner's individual income tax return. Federal partnership returns are due three and one-half months after the end of the fiscal year. Limited partnerships require special treatment.
4. Corporate income tax returns report on business operations authorized under their charters. Federal returns are due two and one-half months following the close of their taxable year. The due dates of state returns vary. Federal corporate tax rates, as fixed in 1964, are 22 percent on taxable income up to $25,000 and 48 percent on taxable income in excess thereof. Where there are two or more related corporations, special rates apply.

Taxes based on payroll

The entire social security system, except for supplemental medical service, is financed through payroll deductions and contributions. These taxes include payments by the employer to the state unemployment compensation funds, the federal unemployment insurance program, and the remittance of payroll taxes due from the employer and the employe under FICA.

Federal and state income taxes also are withheld from an employe's compensation. The newspaper is required to deposit all tax withholdings in an approved institution, and detailed reports are generally required on a quarterly basis.

For all payrolls the employer is charged with complete responsibility for keeping comprehensive and accurate records, and penalties against the employer for failure to comply may be severe. Many businesses, including newspapers, have been padlocked for failure to remit the taxes withheld from employes.

Sales, use, and service taxes

Each state has its own laws and regulations covering sales, use, and service taxes. In most the sale of newspaper copies is exempt from taxation. Purchases made by the newspaper, whether in or out of the state, are subject to these taxes in most areas, though there are notable exceptions. Exemptions for materials purchased for conversion or resale are usually granted.

There is a conflict in court decisions covering interstate commerce versus the sales and use taxes. The attorney general of a state is possibly the most reliable authority for situations not covered by the local regulations on sales and use taxes.

The taxation of "services" is very limited, although there are repeated attempts to tax newspaper advertising. A famous decision in 1936 (*Grosjean* v. *American Press Company*) gave Supreme Court authority to the principle that a license tax on a newspaper's advertising services was an invasion of First Amendment press freedom. A similar case in 1975 (*Bigelow* v. *Virginia*) reaffirmed the position that advertising is entitled to the same constitutional protection.

State or local occupational taxes or licenses

Many state and municipal governments have enacted a business occupation tax or licensing system sometimes known as a retail merchants license, usually requiring a small outlay.

Licensing of automobiles is a recognized source of revenue for the state and the city or county, primarily for building and maintaining roads and streets.

In some cases, newspapers have resisted the application of license or occupational taxes on the ground that they conflict with the first Amendment to the Constitution of the United States, which specifies that "Congress shall make no law respecting an establishment of religion or prohibiting free exercise thereof; or abridging the freedom of speech *or of the press;* or of the rights of the people peacefully to assemble and to petition the Government for a redress of grievances."

Federal excise taxes

Most excise taxes are war-financing measures, but many that were easily collected — such as on telephone calls, utilities, and airplane tickets — have been continued in peacetime.

Newspapers are exempted from excise taxes on telephone calls for the gathering and dissemination of news.

Information returns

Various businesses and individuals are required to submit to the Internal Revenue Service annual information returns on payments to individuals, including salaries, contributions made by employes under FICA, and income taxes withheld from the employe (Form W-2); interest, dividends, and rents paid to individuals (Forms 1099 and 1096). A copy of these reports is to be sent to the payee for his use in preparing his tax return.

Nonoperating taxes

An individual taxpayer, whether he is a proprietor, a partner, or a stockholder, faces federal estate and state inheritance (death) taxes. If the total estate tax is substantial, a taxpayer can make provision for reducing the tax and administrative expense in closing his estate by properly reducing its total value. One method available is to make sure of his "gift" tax exemptions and exclusions.

A method of evaluating the newspaper to determine estate taxes permits the newspaper owner to estimate his potential tax and to plan to minimize the shrinkage in his estate by taxation or administration expenses. (Evaluation methods are outlined in Chapter 17.)

Besides the usual capital gains tax of 25 percent, the seller of a business has been subject since 1962 to an ordinary tax on the total depreciation of depreciable equipment. This device, called "recapture of depreciation," bunches the total recapture into one year and can expose the selling taxpayer to a tax rate bracket much higher than he faced in any year during which the annual depreciation was accumulated.

A seller is also subject to a recomputation of the investment tax credit already claimed on such items purchased as have been on hand for less than the full depreciable life originally set up for the asset.

TAX PHILOSOPHY

The attitude of most good citizens is one of general tolerance toward paying taxes they owe. Some newspapers view paying taxes as a cruel necessity, others as a necessary expense of doing business. Still others seek to take advantage of opportunities for decreasing the tax burden—available through planning their tax program, either on their own or with the assistance of an acceptable tax advisor, a certified public accountant, or a tax attorney.

Form of business organization

In planning a tax program the publisher must first decide what form of business organization best limits total tax expense: an individual proprietorship, a family partnership, or a small corporation entitled to a lesser tax rate or subject to taxation as partners.

For instance, as soon as an individual proprietor begins paying 22 percent on personal income, the corporate form should be considered in order to take the fullest legal advantage of personal and corporate rates. The adoption of a partnership form with a taxable working family member (not the spouse) can reduce taxable liability if such a plan is feasible. The adoption of a "Subchapter S Corporation," wherein the stockholders are taxed as partners, may yield some important tax advantages. Many other acceptable plans can be evolved with the aid of a competent tax advisor.

Under certain conditions a newspaper can be operated on a cash basis, deferring income from accounts receivable until they are collected and paying all expenses promptly. Also, under certain conditions a newspaper can choose to pay income taxes on circulation as earned rather than as received, under the regulations governing prepaid subscriptions. Under other conditions an enterprise can obtain the benefits of the investment tax credit on the purchase of tangible personal property used by the taxpayer in the business.

DEPRECIATION OPTIONS

A newspaper business can continue the depreciation rates established in the past or can adopt the Printing & Publishing Guide guidelines, made available in 1962, which set the average life of its manufacturing equipment as 11 years. Special depreciation methods available on equipment purchases are straight-line method; sum-of-the-year's-digits method; and 150 percent, or the double-declining-balance method.

Other newspaper assets unrelated to manufacturing may use such lives as: office furniture and fixtures, 10 years; automobiles, 3 years; general purpose trucks, 4 years; land improvements, 20 years; and buildings (minimum), 45 years.

Taking care of taxes for a newspaper is not a minor detail. The business office must be organized to keep accurate records and to be financially prepared when taxes are due. Most large newspapers have found it advisable to retain extra legal counsel and accountancy assistance.

4
Public relations

21

Relations with the community

A newspaper and its community are interacting forces; one cannot prosper without the other.

C. A. Oliphant

Newspaper publishing is a profession as well as a business. In that respect it is different from most avenues of service that depend upon public support. The successful newspaper must make a living for the publisher and the great number of persons on its staff, but it has a much higher purpose than that. It exists not simply to get all it can from the community but to give to the community all that it can. And its life depends more on the latter than on the former.

The newspaper should reflect community affairs, events, and attitudes. It must keep the community abreast of the news made by its own people and serve the business institutions by providing a medium through which they can talk to their customers and prospective customers about their merchandise and services. It must serve the leaders of the community by helping them to see the community's needs, by supporting them in their efforts to give good government and to make improvements, and by holding over them the constant threat of exposure should they become negligent of their duty or attempt to defraud the public.

Broad understanding of community needs and a keen sense of journalistic responsibility are reflected in a newspaper's performance. Educational advancement, community cooperation, better agriculture, and transportation development have been strong planks in its program of community improvement.

COMMUNITY SERVICE PROJECTS

In determining a year's program that would benefit the city, the St. Louis, Mo., *Globe-Democrat* discovered that better transportation facilities were badly needed. It lamented the fact that St. Louis, eighth largest city in America, lagged badly in the matter of airline service. It published a series of articles and editorials, which resulted directly in competitive nonstop service from St. Louis to New York and to Washington, and similar service to San Francisco, Miami, and New Orleans, as well as greatly improved service to Chicago, Minneapolis, Cincinnati, and many other points.

The *Globe-Democrat* also sensed the need for a new bus terminal. Photographs and a series of news articles appearing in its columns were given credit by the Greyhound company for its decision to build a new terminal in downtown St. Louis. For more than two years this newspaper campaigned to give people of the surrounding area at least one free bridge across the Mississippi River and supported the construction of the now famous Gateway Arch.

Smaller newspapers as well as large ones in great cities expend themselves with equal effect in promoting community progress. The persistent, aggressive attitude of the Farmington, N. Mex., *Times* was largely instrumental in bringing the Navajo Dam project in northwestern New Mexico to prompt realization. This, along with other important projects authorized by Congress, was threatened to be held up when funds previously set up for construction were cancelled.

Immediately the *Times* put its news and editorial staffs to work. Day-by-day coverage was given to all that took place in Washington, and close touch was maintained with New Mexico senators and congressmen by telephone and telegraph. Resolutions for signatures were submitted to groups throughout the state. In the face of such constructive information and statewide influence, together with mounting unemployment, funds for the Navajo Dam were restored to the budget and construction was resumed.

The Aspen, Colo., *Times* was given a community service award during the University of Colorado's Newspaper Week in recognition of leadership in community development. The honor was based largely on a ten- article symposium on the goals of education, which included an honest appraisal and constructive criticism of the Aspen school situation.

The Dayton, Ohio, *Daily News,* sponsor of many public service features, joined with the University of Dayton one year in promoting a course in family financial management entitled "Better Living for Your Money." Weekly discussion meetings were held at the university with special tie-in features published in the *News.* This constructive help drew warm response.

A newspaper promotion that typifies the constructive approach to the newspaper's community and to its advertisers is "Homearama," sponsored by the Cincinnati, Ohio, *Enquirer.* Homearama is a single-site promotion featuring fully decorated model homes built by a variety of builders. It appeals to a wide segment of the public by stressing new home design, interior design and landscaping, and a wide variety of supplier services that will attract present homeowners as well as those who are establishing a new home or moving up in their living standards.

The *Enquirer* has cooperated with the Home Builders Association and has drawn over 100,000 people to the Homearama site during the two-week show. The quality of the homes, $35,000 up to and beyond the $75,000 price range, reaches the type of readers the *Enquirer* serves (*Enquirer* reader's incomes are above the market median).

WAYS TO HELP

In addition to the service it performs by completely carrying out its fundamental job of reporting the news, any newspaper may be helpful to its community in specific ways.

Pointing out needs and solutions

The newspaper may point out community needs and means to meet them. Its responsibility is to light the way and to drive for action. How similar situations are solved in other communities of like size may be learned from fellow publishers. Commendation by the press for important community accomplishments always is desirable because of the lift it gives to community spirit, but there are times when a community must be shaken out of its indifference and lethargy.

A reader wrote to the Washington, D.C., *Star:*

The way some people talk about our town you might think we all had been forced to come to Washington. You'd think we'd been sentenced to live in Washington. Whereas really and truly the great majority of us live here because we love it.

Love it? Love Washington? Of course, we do. Even with all its troubles, it's the greatest, the most beautiful city on earth. And it's ours. Our town. Our town to love and cherish.

Sure it has things wrong with it. But it has things right with it, too. Good things. Beautiful things. I wish everybody in this town of mine — this town of yours — would sit down and make a list of the good things, the beautiful things. If we had such a list — things that give us pleasure and strength — then we would know what the right things are so we can work to get more of them. Then we would be able to say to ourselves, "See, this is what is good and beautiful about Washington. These are the things we want more of. . . ."

In response to this letter, the *Star* announced a contest to encourage letters "To Washington with Love," pointing out the city's most beautiful attractions. Ten weekly prizes, consisting of a "Wonderful Weekend in Washington" and a grand prize of one full week in the nation's capital for two, stimulated widespread interest and helped to point out the fact that one of a community's basic needs is the love and loyalty of its citizens.

The Dallas, Tex., *Times-Herald* decided that more incentive was needed for junior and senior high school students in the creative aspects of homemaking, art, and industrial and vocational education. In cooperation with the State Fair of Texas and the Central Dad's Club of Texas, the *Times-Herald* sponsors an annual Student Crafts Fair. The Dallas Independent School District supports the program by selecting classroom projects at the individual school level for display in the fair. At the final showing, more than 6,000 projects are exhibited at the State Fair Park. The State Fair provides the display area at no charge, the Dad's Club donates trophies for the outstanding pieces of work, and the *Times-Herald* contributes ribbons and promotional support. Robert H. Kurz, director of newspaper promotion, says, "It is an excellent opportunity to display the work of these youngsters to the people of the community."

Another program aimed at the need for improved dialogue between a community and its youth is the Los Angeles, Calif., *Herald-Examiner* Youth Forum. Each year some 600 teenagers serve as delegates to an all-day convention held at the Ambassador Hotel. Divided into groups of 100 each, they meet in six conference rooms where they discuss, debate, and argue on subjects of importance to themselves and their futures. Present are the governor of California, mayor of Los Angeles, and about 200 civic and industrial leaders, all gathered to hear firsthand how youth thinks, speaks, and reacts.

Following the addresses by the six youth speakers are talks by the governor and the mayor, who comment on what they have heard. In more than a few instances, the governor and the mayor have taken action based on suggestions contained in the youth speakers' remarks. A digest of the addresses presented by the youth speakers is published in the *Herald-Examiner* editorial pages so that its great readership may know the thoughts, ideas, and aspirations of young people. "We are confident," the *Herald-Examiner* Forum Committee states, "that young people who feel that they are part of a community which recognizes their individual needs, views, and goals will more than live up to their role as responsible citizens."

The alert newspaper notifies its community of improvements made in similar towns. Digging up and presenting helpful and stimulating facts about specific projects encourages the community to move ahead. John McClelland, Jr., editor of the Longview, Wash., *Daily News,* says:

> Every paper, no matter how small, needs to show some gumption, some backbone, some courage on local and regional issues. A paper doesn't need to have a BIG crusade under way all the time. But, the readers of a paper should realize that their paper will go to bat for what is right and decent and best when the need arises.

Establishing state and national contacts

The newspaper may help its community by establishing connections with community, state, and national organizations and movements. The publisher, editors, and department heads of a newspaper find it to their advantage to hold membership in organizations that serve the newspaper's circulation area. There also are state and national organizations through which the newspaper may benefit its community by direct affiliation.

Frank R. Ahlgren, as editor of the Memphis, Tenn., *Commercial Appeal* held the following affiliations to link his newspaper in a vital way with the community, the region, and the nation:

Trustee, University of Tennessee.
Former chairman of the board of the Southern Education Reporting Service.
Member of the board of Collins Chapel Hospital.
Trustee, Memphis University School.
Member of Kappa Tau Alpha, national journalism honorary.
Chairman, Memphis and Shelby County chapter of the American Red Cross.
First state chairman of the Crusade for Freedom.
Member of the board of the National Safety Council.
Former chairman of the Citizens of Memphis Utilities Study Committee.
President of the American Council on Education for Journalism.
Chairman of the Journalism Education Council of the American Society of
    Newspaper Editors.
Member of the board of managers of Methodist Hospital.
Director of the Memphis Public Library board.
State chairman of the Society of Professional Journalists, Sigma Delta Chi.
Director of the Memphis-Arkansas Bridge Commission.
Vice-president of the Memphis Committee on Community Relations.
Member of the board of the Tennessee Hospital Education and Research Founda-
    tion.
Member of the Tennessee Tax Study Commission.
Director of the American Press Institute.
Member of the Citizens Committee to Improve the Administration of Justice in
    Tennessee.
Member of the Advisory Committee to the President of the National Cotton Coun-
    cil.
Member of the board of the Mid-South Medical Center.

It is not essential that the executive on the smaller newspaper be as
elaborately involved as this, but representative contacts are just as vital.
Len Kholos, managing editor of the Erie, Pa., *Times,* has served as a
member of the board of the American Cancer Society, the Council on
Volunteers, the annual Gannon Crime Symposium, the Drug and
Alcoholism Council, and the Salvation Army. Such interests bring benefits
to the newspaper in many ways that cannot be measured.

An increasing shortage of doctors in Indiana pointed to the necessity
of establishing a second medical school in the state. South Bend was one of
the cities seeking the new facility. In addition to giving continuing editorial
support, the South Bend, Ind., *Tribune* published a special 16-page section setting forth the need of a medical school in the northern part of the
state and outlining the advantages the school would enjoy if located in
South Bend. Subscribers received this section as part of their regular
newspaper. It was placed on the desks of all members of the Indiana
general assembly in Indianapolis so that they would be familiar with the
advantages offered by South Bend when the legislation for establishing the
medical school came up for action. As many other newspapers throughout
the nation have done, the *Tribune* sensed a community need, "rolled up its
sleeves," and went to work in the community's behalf.

The question of whether a newspaper publisher should be the chairman of a great community movement often has been debated. Publicity is

needed for every worthwhile cause; and when the editor or publisher is connected with it, that name is drawn into the publicity. In the eyes of the public, perhaps, the newspaper figure becomes a self-promoter. But if someone else is the leader, the newspaper can more lustily and heartily throw its influence behind the movement. What is best must be decided by the editor or publisher. As one newspaper publisher said, "The editor who does not attract some dispute is one who is advocating nothing. He is a public relations man, not an editor. He will take any side of a controversy so he can be comfortable. He is a discredit to the profession."

The degree of involvement, then, is always a matter for local judgment. "The very nature of our profession dictates that an editor has no choice except to be involved," says Clement J. Sweet, managing editor of the Harrisburg, Pa., *Evening News.* "Most of use are joiners. Everyone likes to 'belong.' OK — belong, but be careful."

Participation in national activities

The newspaper may help the community to join and to promote national movements. Health campaigns, the drive against gambling and other crime, and the campaign for highway safety are all national in scope. The most influential newspaper is the one that brings the issue home to its community and shows its own people what they can do to help.

Jack Parish, promotion manager of the Miami, Fla., *News,* embarked some time ago on a promotion that has been very rewarding in personal satisfaction as well as earning national recognition. It concerns a safety program involving small children — the Miami *News* Safety Town. Here is Mr. Parish's outline:

We started this promotion at one shopping center and it was so successful that we repeated it again at three shopping centers simultaneously. It involved constructing a miniature town at the shopping centers, which included buildings (we used children's playhouses), real traffic lights, school crossing lights, stop signs, yield signs, and railroad signs. All lights, signs, and the like, were loaned and installed by the Dade County Engineering Department.

Any newspaper that wishes to hold this promotion must obtain the cooperation of a local law enforcement body who must furnish officers to instruct the children. One hundred percent cooperation must be obtained from a shopping center to provide the space for the complex.

We ran our promotion for 11 weeks, three classes per day, five days per week and processed over 3,500 children this year. The shopping center merchants could help liquidate some of the cost of the promotion by purchasing the houses in the town, which they can decorate with their own signs and other advertising material. It is a good idea to obtain the help of the Girl Scouts, Boy Scouts, and other civic groups as volunteer instructors to assist the police officers.

We developed the actual instruction in three phases: (1) the cyclist, (2) the driver, and (3) the pedestrian.

For this, miniature pedal cars and bicycles were supplied. Coupons run in the newspaper took care of the registration for the children for the Safety Town. The main purpose was to allow children between the ages of four and nine to experience traffic situations by walking, riding bicycles, and operating miniature cars. Their experiences will enable them to cope with real traffic hazards they will be exposed to later.

Newspapers are at least partly responsible for the large voter registration turnouts in recent years. In some instances, other means besides publicity are used. For example, the Jackson, Mich., *Citizen-Patriot* fostered a "First-Timers Club." Two women reporters, who qualified for membership, took the initiative in organizing a dozen youths who would cast their first votes in the national election. That nucleus grew to a membership of more than 500 before the registration deadline.

Interpreting state and national news

The newspaper may help to interpret the news from Washington and the state capital to the people of the home community and thereby emphasize their relationship to the national and state governments.

Washington authorities often are unjustly criticized. People are more inclined to criticize those who are far away than those who are near. Congress and the administration, therefore, receive their full share of brickbats. Editors do not always assume the role of severe critics. They sometimes come to the defense of those who are targets. As one Marietta, Ga., editor said:

I feel the State Department knows better how to deal with foreign affairs than I do here.

On the other hand, I can speak with more authority than the diplomats in the shadow of the Capitol dome when it comes to the need for doing something about a four-lane intersection or the urgent necessity for street markers in Marietta.

Carl Wright, editorial promotion manager of the Honolulu, Hawaii, *Star Bulletin,* reports his newspaper has been engaged in an unusual promotion activity. It has adopted a country—Botswana, Hawaii's antipode (the country on the other side of the globe, diametrically opposite).

Hawaii is the only state with an inhabited antipode. As the idea grew it became steadily more serious. As of now, it has the backing of the United States State Department, of Hawaii's governor and both senators. The President appointed Hawaii's governor to represent the United States at Bechuanaland's Independence Day ceremonies when it became officially Botswana.

Support to local groups

The newspaper may give news space and editorial support to existing community organizations and bring them into close working relationship. No Chamber of Commerce, service club, youth organization, or religious organization of any kind can get very far with its program without the support of the newspaper. Some of the most effective community service work the newspaper does is through existing organizations. The honest, unselfish, conscientious publisher cares little if the organizations get all the praise and the newspaper gets none. What the dedicated publisher is interested in is "getting the job done."

In addition to bringing community organizations to a better understanding of their aims and opportunities and to a closer working relationship through the news columns, the newspaper may conduct guided tours into community areas and thereby bring about a fellowship between the newspaper and community leaders.

For example, the Port Huron, Mich., *Times-Herald* took Port Huron merchants on an all-day tour through Michigan's "thumb area," acquainting them with industrial plants, a special farming project, and resort districts there. One hundred and fifty merchants rode with members of the newspaper staff in chartered buses and at noon enjoyed a luncheon program as the newspaper's guests. Opportunity was taken to explain news coverage and circulation, but the important result was a friendly relationship between merchants and newspaper for the community's good.

Community promotion

The newspaper advertises the community to the outside world. A community is judged by its newspaper. Copies that go out each day into other parts of the nation and the world give outsiders an impression of the city in which the paper is published. If the newspaper is progressive, the community is considered progressive. If the newspaper is sloppy, it is likely that the community will be considered indifferent to its general appearance. If the newspaper is attractive in appearance, thorough in the handling of news, and fair and fearless in its editorial columns, the town is judged to be attractive, progressive, and fair.

An annual, international airline ski race—sponsored by the Anchorage, Alaska, *Times*—each March brings in from 150 to 250 skiers who are employes of airlines in Europe, the Orient, and the United States. It provides four days of activities built around the races. Anchorage boasts of being the most air-minded city under the American flag. Statistics are available to support this claim. It has five international airlines operating over the North Pole between Europe and Anchorage and Tokyo. It has one domestic carrier operating between New York, Chicago, and Seattle to Anchorage and Tokyo. In addition, there are many supplemental airlines operating charter and contract flights to and from the Orient. Anchorage always has more than 100 crewmen stopping over between flights, and they enjoy the summer and winter sports along with Alaskans.

Through the annual ski races, Anchorage attracts airline employes who become active boosters for the community when they are mingling with travelers on the other continents. The ski race has been most successful in publicizing the winter sports, the strategic location of the city on the global air routes, and the facilities for entertaining and accommodating visitors; and it has also resulted in hundreds of new friends as far away as Africa, Tahiti, and Yugoslavia.

The newspaper often uses other tools to make its point. A good example of this is illustrated by a handsome color brochure called "Peoria, a City of the Century," which issues an invitation to "take a tour with one of the new families arriving every nine hours." David J. Schlink, sales promotion manager of the Peoria, Ill., *Journal-Star,* says:

> The book is actually the product of a committee of civic-minded businessmen who got together and, with the backing of their parent companies, conceived and agreed to underwrite the costs of printing, etc. The front cover picture and most of the pictures inside were produced by our people at the paper, who worked with our local advertising agency in putting out the complete product.
>
> It was first introduced to the public as an insert in our regular Sunday edition, and that version contained a mail reply order card enabling Peoria families to send copies to relatives, friends, and business acquaintances anywhere in the world. About 300,000 were printed. Our circulation accounted for 115,000 of these books.
>
> The booklet contains striking full-color photographs of the new airport, the downtown area, homes, urban parks, universities, hospitals, industry, recreational facilities, cultural activities, entertainment, and shopping facilities and a nuts-and-bolts two-page spread making the point that this is the future Ruhr Valley of America.

The publisher owes it to the community to put out a good newspaper; and the newspaper owes assistance to every worthwhile local organization, so that they together may make a better community and advertise it to the outside world.

When recognition does come to the newspaper for a job well done, it is welcomed. Each year, for instance, the Associated Press Managing Editors Association publicizes newspapers that have been distinguished for community service. One year, ten finalists chosen from more than 150 outstanding newspapers included the following:

The Detroit, Mich., *Free Press* for a series on escaped mental patients.

The Northampton, Mass., *Daily Hampshire Gazette* for its disclosure of financial irregularities at the University of Massachusetts.

The Charlotte, N.C., *Observer* for revealing political contributions by the Southern Bell Telephone Company.

The Chicago, Ill., *Tribune* for a newspaper campaign to improve the administration of federal housing programs.

The Providence, R.I., *Journal* and *Bulletin* for a series calling community attention to the dangers of drug abuse by doctors issuing prescriptions.

The Fort Myers, Fla., *News-Press* for articles credited with protecting the public from real estate frauds.

The St. Louis, Mo., *Globe-Democrat* for bringing to light threatening irregularities in the construction of a luxury apartment complex in the city.

The Des Moines, Iowa, *Register* for exposing unlawful practices in grain shipments abroad.

The Louisville, Ky., *Courier-Journal* for a broad-based campaign educating the public on the school busing issue.

The Fort Worth, Tex., *Star-Telegram* for alerting the community to police corruption.

FINDING THE OPPORTUNITY

Good public relations has been defined as the art of discovering and furthering a mutuality of interest between one activity and others in a society. Its purpose is to achieve the most harmonious adjustment possible between an institution and its community. This means, therefore, that public relations is a creative endeavor, and successful management understands that it must search out opportunities for improving relationships with all its publics. A newspaper must be mindful not only of the general public it serves but of its direct consumers (advertisers and subscribers); its employes; its stockholders; its suppliers; its colleagues in the communication industry; and a multitude of social, political, and govermental interests to which it must relate on a daily basis in one way or another. The manner in which the newspaper reaches out to cultivate and to maintain all these relationships at the optimum level is a measure of its effectiveness in the community.

Suburban publications have demonstrated an awareness of ways to tap this source of community interest. The Prince Georges, Md., *Journal* is typical of efforts to focus directly on community needs that exist around the greater metropolitan area served by the Washington press. In its opening issue, the *Journal* stated that "unlike the larger newspapers in our area we have the time — and the space — to look at the local scene. We will never appeal as the Washington *Post* did recently for people not to contact us on local stories because we don't have the room."

Even in the largest cities some smaller newspapers are seeking out new fields of profitable operation where no real sense of community would be expected to exist. By concentrating on the cultural, political, and social nature of the neighborhood area, such newspapers as the *East Side Express,* the *Chelsea Clinton News,* and the *Westsider* can function well as part of the Manhattan scene in densely populated New York City. In Cleveland, Ohio, the *Call & Post* draws great support from the black community to which it is addressed, as do the Pittsburgh, Pa., *New Courier,* the Houston, Tex., *Forward Times,* and the Baltimore, Md., *Afro-American.* The Miami, Fla., *Herald* produces a Spanish-language edition for the minority community made up largely of Cubans, thus meeting a specific need that would otherwise be neglected.

The opportunities for community service are virtually inexhaustible. The challenge to the newspaper is to explore them and to meet the needs.

22

Building reader goodwill

Newspapers have unique facilities for
reaching into the homes and hearts of the
people. . . . They come close to people
where they live.

Grove Patterson

The most important members of the com-
munity, as far as the newspaper is concerned, are its subscribers—the people who think well enough of the paper to buy it and to supply it with much
of the news and many of the features that make it interesting. Even in
metropolitan communities, where newspapers carry a vast amount of state,
national, and world news, the local news and features provide the touch
for winning subscribers.

Many suburban newspapers published in the circulation areas of large
newspapers are able to survive and actually to thrive by featuring local
news and giving editorial comment and support to distinctly local problems, as reviewed in Chapter 21. Local news coverage is never overdone,
and when done well it builds reader interest and support as nothing else
can do.

GAINING READER PARTICIPATION

Average readers are always interested in items about themselves and
their families and articles they have written or for which they have given
"tips" to the newspaper. To obtain either of these important types of news,
the editor must have the cooperation of the newspaper's readers.

One small newspaper, soon after it had advanced the subscription
price and the circulation needed a boost, launched an intensive campaign
for personal news items. The circulation manager gave a reporter a complete list of persons receiving the paper before the advanced price went into effect. Each morning at 8:30 the reporter started telephoning a selected
number of those homes, asking for personal items and urging subscribers
to form the habit of phoning in any news about their families and friends.

In one call out of every three, the reporter picked up a news item.
Some that were called did not have news items immediately but responded
with one or more later. This plan underscored the newspaper's personal interest in its subscribers, gave them an opportunity to help make the news,

and was useful in holding subscribers at a time when some might have discontinued their paper because of the higher price.

The amount of good material that may be obtained from community-minded citizens when they are made to feel that their contributions are wanted is surprising indeed. Indian stories written by readers have always been given special play in the *Daily Journal* of New Ulm, Minn., seat of an early Indian uprising. A teenage high school student, encouraged by the editor, became an enterprising historical researcher and feature writer for the Moberly, Mo., *Monitor-Index and Democrat.* High school football team histories, written from facts supplied by students and former students, have proved to be popular features in an Ohio newspaper. An Illinois daily was flooded with historical material from trunks, following a front-page "box" asking readers to explore their attics.

Readers are always ready and willing to contribute material for anniversary and progress editions. For its anniversary edition one newspaper decided not to emphasize the historic past, as is usually done, but instead portrayed the community as it was "today" and as its citizens would like it to become "tomorrow." Pictures, write-ups, and advertisements of persons and organizations then active in community affairs took care of the "today" part of the edition; and a series of articles by community leaders on "The Three Outstanding Needs of Our Community and How They May Be Realized" provided the "tomorrow" angle.

The practice of inviting guest writers from among qualified townspeople is an excellent means of inducing reader participation. One editor, before leaving for an extended vacation, made arrangements with community leaders to continue his daily newspaper column in his absence. The result was highly readable copy and widened interest on the part of the newspaper's readers.

The mayor talked frankly about the difficulties of filling speaking engagements and acting upon the peculiar requests that come to a public official. A monument dealer, who was president of the Chamber of Commerce, discussed the traffic problems of the city. A well-known lawyer, fond of dogs, contributed a heart-moving dissertation on a boy and his dog. A woman leader of a study class argued the need for a better public library. The superintendent of schools analyzed the job-finding problems of young people just graduating from college. A furniture dealer wrote on the issue of trading at home. The chief of police discussed safety, and the county highway engineer pointed out the need for county zoning. A minister fashioned an illuminating article on the recreational needs of the community.

Those volunteer columnists probably would not have been able to write a column day after day, but as one-day "pinch hitters" they were masters. Their output was a diversion that readers enjoyed, and it gave freshness to the editor's material when it reappeared. But perhaps the greatest virtue of the idea was that 22 leading citizens joined the newspaper staff for a day and afterward felt they had at least a small part in helping to make the community a better one. Guest editors or columnists may be called upon at any time.

The Independence, Mo., *Examiner* strengthened its relationship with business and professional people of the community when it invited the Kiwanis Club to put out one issue of the paper. For several nights preceding the issue, the 62 club members met at the newspaper office and, with the assistance and counsel of the managing editor, planned every step of their issue.

Every Kiwanian was given a definite staff role, from that of copyboy to managing editor. Every department found in the largest city daily was included in their issue. A "lonely hearts column" was edited by a dentist. The manager of an air-conditioning plant took care of sports. The president of a large church organization, who often made trips to the nation's capital, was the Washington correspondent and produced an account of capital happenings under a Washington dateline. An insurance man produced a lively movie page with four times the amount of advertising carried in the usual issue. A prominent local physician wrote a column that the hometown readers thought ranked in interest and educational value with syndicated health columns. Two bankers collaborated in a financial column. Every article carried its author's by-line. The regular ad personnel helped the Kiwanis business staff prepare copy, but the selling was by the Kiwanians.

The publisher and the staff were pleased to see a front-page box under the heading "We Mean Every Word" with this note of appreciation signed by the Kiwanis Club president:

> Day in and day out, the *Examiner* passes out the bouquets. It plays down our mistakes and expands our smallest virtues to make good reading in our home circles. Today is our day and we can say what we please. The Kiwanis Club pleases to say that the *Examiner* is the best little paper in fifty states. We love the members of the staff for their friendliness, their honesty and their cleverness. Their advertising department multiplies our sales and the paper's public policy advances all our interests.

Those civic leaders, from then on, were more than mere readers of the paper or mere patrons of the advertising columns. They felt the pride of "partnership" in the paper. And that was the way the newspaper wanted them to feel.

Variations of this idea are carried on in many communities. At South Bend, Ind., the *Tribune* arranges an annual newspaper project consisting of handling street corner and bulk sales for one day by a civic club. Proceeds support community service activities of the club. Although this money represents proceeds of a day's sale, the actual news hawking takes place for only one hour. The club members fan out through the business district during that one hour and put on a forceful selling campaign.

Most newspapers give space to reader comment on matters of community interest. A "public pulse column" can have greater reader-interest than the editorial column. At the very least it indicates the newspaper's respect for the readers right to express their views.

A service labeled "Yesterday and Today in Memphis" rates high on the readership surveys of the Memphis, Tenn., *Commercial Appeal.* The section lists pertinent information that readers must have on a regular basis (Fig. 22.1).

When readers are allowed to have "their say" and when the newspaper invites their counsel and expression on matters of community importance, they feel that the newspaper is something created *by* them as well as *for* them. The general manager or editor of a newspaper who can make the people of the community say, "Look what we did," is doing a great thing for the community as well as for the newspaper.

MAKING FRIENDS

A friendly relationship enjoyed by both parties is a binding relationship. That is what every publisher would like to create between the newspaper and its readers. And there are ways of doing it.

The newspaper can be made a personal friend of its readers by dealing with them in a personal way. People enjoy the human side of other people's nature. They appreciate the natural things others do, and reporting these human interest vignettes helps to build an understanding and a comradeship among readers as well as between readers and the newspaper.

Not enough attention is given to local news of the "about town" order — items strong in emotional appeal that the reporter might overlook in covering bigger events. A column containing grist of that kind is enthusiastically read and thoroughly enjoyed. Stories of dogs, cats, ponies, parakeets, and all other kinds of pets always are interesting. For example, this paragraph in the Bedford, Va., *Bulletin-Democrat* undoubtedly brought chuckles from many readers on farms, where Puss was an important member of the household:

> I don't think the stingiest farmer would deny that every farmhouse has a right to at least two cats — one to catch rats and mice and one to keep the other company. One to sit by the fire and purr at night and let the baby smooth his black coat. The other to go to the barn and sup on the rats in the corn crib. One to follow the mistress of the farmhouse around during the busy day and receive the confidences she would not like to impart to anyone who could speak English and repeat them, such as the amount of coloring she was putting in the butter for curb market, and the little financial deal involving the extra eggs she was selling on the side; the other cat to sit by the early spring garden and pounce on the little rabbits trying to eat the young sprouts in the bean patch. You see what I mean? One cat for utility and one for companionship. This is the absolute.[1]

---

1. This and other human interest illustrations in this chapter were provided by John M. Henry, collector of interesting newspaper columns and coauthor of *How To Write Columns,* Iowa State Univ. Press, Ames, 1952.

Attractions

MEMPHIS BOTANIC GARDENS — Goldsmith Civic Garden Center. Open 9 a.m. to 5 p.m. Monday through Friday, closed Saturday, 2 to 5 p.m. Sunday. All gardens and W. C. Paul Arboretum open daily in daylight hours.

BROOKS ART GALLERY—Overton Park. Open 10 a.m. to 5 p.m. Tuesday through Saturday, Sunday 1 to 5 p.m.

CHUCALISSA INDIAN VILLAGE — 5 miles west of U.S. 61, off Mitchell Road. Open 9 a.m. to 5 p.m. Tuesday through Saturday and 1 to 5 p.m. Sunday.

OVERTON PARK ZOO AND AQUARIUM — Overton Park. Open 9 a.m. to 5 p.m.

MEMPHIS QUEEN — Riverboat sightseeing trip daily on Mississippi River. Call 527-5694 for further information.

FONTAINE HOUSE — 680 Adams. French Victorian mansion, built in 1870. Open daily 1 to 4 p.m.

MALLORY HOUSE — 652 Adams. Preserved Italiante-Victorian landmark with heirloom antiques. Open daily 1 to 4 p.m.

MEMPHIS ACADEMY OF ARTS — Overton Park. Open 9 a.m. to 5 p.m. Monday through Friday. 9 a.m. to noon Saturday and noon to 5 p.m. Sunday.

MAGEVNEY HOUSE — 198 Adams. Pioneer home restored. Open 10 a.m. to 4 p.m. Tuesday through Saturday, Sunday 1 to 4 p.m.

DIXON GALLERY AND GARDENS — 4339 Park. Open 1 to 5 p.m. Tuesday through Sunday.

THEATRE MEMPHIS — "A Midsummer Night's Dream" 8 p.m.

Driver's License

Tests given at Highway Patrol Station at 6348 Summer, 8 a.m. to 6 p.m. Monday through Friday, at 2507 East Shelby Drive and at 3756 Fite Road. 9:30 a.m. to 5:30 p.m. Monday through Friday. All stations closed from noon to 1 p.m.

Animal Shelter

Open Monday through Friday 9 a.m. to 4 p.m., Saturday 10 a.m. to 3 p.m. Located at 3456 Tchulahoma Road. For further information call 362-5310. 24-hour answering service 272-1753.

Auto Licenses

Monday through Friday County Court Clerk's office, 160 North Main and 5705 Shelby Oaks Drive, 8:30 a.m. to 4:45 p.m. To avoid penalty newcomers to the state must obtain title and license upon establishing residence. Residents who change vehicles have 15 days to secure title and license without penalty. For further information, call 528-3244.

Crisis numbers

Chest X-Ray

Gailor Clinic, 42 North Dunlap, Room 140. Open 8 a.m. to 4 p.m. Monday through Friday and 9 a.m. to noon Saturday. Also at 1362 Mississippi Boulevard and 1064 North Breedlove Monday through Friday 8 a.m. to 4 p.m.

Auto Inspection

Open Monday through Friday 7 a.m. to 9 p.m. at 136 High.

Welfare

State Office Building, 170 North Main. Open 8 a.m. to 4:30 p.m. Monday through Friday.

Pregnancy Counseling

Planned Parenthood. 525-0591
Birthright. 327-8109

Voter Registration

Shelby County Election Commission, Room 121, Shelby County Office building. 8 a.m. to 4:30 p.m. Monday through Friday.

Need help? For information on health and social welfare problems call 327-4111 or write to 3485 Poplar. 24-hour answering service.

For specialized help:

Al Anon — 526-2332.

Alcoholics Anonymous — 726-1114.

Birth Control — 528-3800.

Child Abuse, Neglect — 534-6849.

City Information and Complaint Center — 528-2500.

Deaf Interpreting — 528-6491.

Emergency Medical Services — 523-1313.

Family Service — 525-1681.

Med-Help Taped Topics — Symptoms — 458-3361.

Poison Control — 522-3000.

Rape — 726-5531.

Runaway House — 276-1745

Suicide and Crisis Intervention — 726-5531.

Fig. 22.1. Reader interest is served daily by the Memphis, Tenn., *Commercial Appeal* with a detailed personal information guide. (Used by permission of the *Commercial Appeal*.)

The unexpected sayings and acts of the town's youngsters provide other material that can pop up any time to enliven the news columns and bring the newspaper into friendlier contact with its readers. A good illustration is this from the Cedar Falls, Iowa, *Record:*

Children at the Campus Elementary School went home this week telling their parents they wished all the people at school were like Mr. Harland, the custodian. Why? Because on the occasion of his birthday this week he served ice cream to the kindergartners, nursery school and first grade children. Each year Mr. Harland celebrates his birthday in this fashion. He loves it and the children love him.

And undoubtedly the custodian and all the children were pleased with the mention given them in the hometown newspaper.

The town's good-natured men and women and changeable youth also help to keep the newspaper alive and interesting. A columnist for a Los Angeles suburban newspaper, the Van Nuys, Calif., *Valley News,* writes:

I don't know why some people resent growing old. This year I've been older than ever before but I've never been as busy, had as much social life, or as many successes and kicks in the teeth. I know more people than ever, like more people and use more sense and heart in dealing with them. In fact, I like me better now than I liked me when I was young. And though it's nice to get whistled at when walking down the street, it's also nice to have the teenage gang come in and say, "Hi, Maw, got any coffee and cookies?"

When reporters keep their eyes open for the unusual, they will write many interesting paragraphs such as this from the Santa Paula, Calif., *Chronicle:*

Most embarrassed young man in town is one who rushed forward Galahadlike to pick up a handkerchief dropped at the Main Street curb by a smartly gowned miss. He found to his dismay it was one of those paper affairs now so much in vogue. As the young man sulked from the scene he was heard to mutter: "Nuts to chivalry."

Whenever a newsworthy event takes place, such as a fall festival, a Santa Claus visit, or a home talent show, the city editor should alert reporters to be on the prowl for human interest material. There is always the opportunity to pat some good citizen on the back or to comment on some humorous or otherwise interesting character trait.

The Dixon, Ill., *Telegraph* assigned a different reporter each week to fill column one on page one with any human interest material that could be dug up. The editor was somewhat doubtful about the idea at first but, after hearing comments by people around town, concluded the column drew as much attention as any feature in the paper. It provided an opportunity to write about many who were well known to all readers — the sanitation worker, the person who delivered milk, the city employe who spread salt and sand to make the icy streets navigable, and the newspaper carrier. One reporter wrote an entire column about trouble with an alarm clock. A human interest column is a goodwill builder as well as a stimulator of readership.

A newspaper may win reader loyalty by writing about organizations to which subscribers or their children belong. A story about a youth group, reporting the year's achievements and listing the members, arouses interest. An outlying town or community where many of the newspaper's subscribers live is always good for a story featuring the community's history, institutions and organizations, public improvements, and city officials. Pictures of the residents add greatly to the story's impact.

School essays, papers read before clubs, and articles voluntarily contributed by local persons are interesting. Recipes furnished by local homemakers are better than those from newspaper feature syndicates. An article written by a local Parent-Teacher Association member on some phase of child psychology is more closely read than one written by Ann Landers. When home folks talk to home folks through the home newspaper it is good home news.

Readers like the dramatically historic feature, too. Pioneers, trail blazers, Indian fighters, and veterans can supply fact-filled material for many exciting stories. Special days such as Independence Day, Memorial Day, Veteran's Day, Mother's Day, and Father's Day provide the opportunity to make noteworthy local characters of past and present march across the newspaper's pages in such style that their descendants will feel a sense of pride. They enjoy the comradeship such articles provide.

When one of the citizens of Washington, Iowa, died leaving a substantial gift for a new band shell in Central Park, the Washington *Journal,* not content with simply reporting the gift, searched past issues for accounts of previous benefactions and discovered that the community had been given more than $1 million. This generosity was dramatized for Washington citizens by means of a special edition. Soon afterward a local bank officer phoned the publisher to say that four of the bank's customers had been moved by the publicity to make immediate gifts of $10,000 (two), $5,000, and $3,000 toward a home for retired persons of the community.

The publisher also received a letter from the president of the Chamber of Commerce, expressing appreciation and closing with this appropriate paragraph:

Over the years the *Evening Journal* has done much to influence many fine Washington people to provide various benefits for this community. . . . All, no doubt, were encouraged to do these things because of the *Journal*'s willingness to give fitting recognition to those who have been generous. I am sure that such a policy, as in the past, will in the future result in the decision of many other citizens to make available to the community a part of the fruits of their successful lives here so that Washington will be an even finer place in which to live.

This is valuable friendship between a newspaper and the people of its community.

ESTABLISHING CONFIDENCE

Unless a newspaper wins readers' confidence it soon loses them. Goodwill is won and held through thorough coverage of the news, accurate reporting, honest dealing, and courteous attention.

A woman who had been reading the Hemet, Calif., *News* for more than 40 years, wrote the publisher:

> Not long ago when I was reading the *News* it occurred to me that in the files of your paper is the history of my life. Your paper recorded my birth, my childhood parties, my graduation from high school and later from college, my marriage, the arrival of each of my four children and the death of one of them — and now, in more recent years your columns have been recording the arrival, one by one, of my grandchildren. I could go on indefinitely mentioning incidents in my life which have been written up in the Hemet *News*. Is it any wonder that your paper means so much in our home and that we look forward eagerly to receiving it each week?

Such a relationship creates in the reader a strong feeling of confidence in the newspaper. And being honest with readers also goes far in building goodwill.

Another way in which the newspaper publisher may gain a measure of respect and goodwill from readers is by acquainting them with the persons who write for the newspaper and by explaining the problems involved in giving the community a good newspaper.

The cartoonists, feature writers, and columnists who supply much material in newspapers are interesting characters to most readers, who enjoy the features more when they can be made to believe this. Acting on that reasoning the Elgin, Ill., *Courier-News* presented during National Newspaper Week a "Parade of Features," in which it set forth human interest facts concerning its "foreign" contributors, with whom readers became almost as well acquainted as they were with the regular staff members.

In a number of cities the Chambers of Commerce have sponsored Business-Industry-Education Days to acquaint teachers and school administrators with community business and industrial institutions. Schools are closed for an afternoon while the teachers tour manufacturing plants and business places. In the evening the teachers and school administrators are entertained as dinner guests of the businesses.

In most communities where B-I-E Day has been observed, newspaper plants have been among the institutions visited. In one newspaper plant, following an inspection tour of departments, the teachers were assembled in the newspaper's library, where the managing editor outlined a brief history of the newspaper, described its form of ownership, and explained its policies. Teachers were told the number of homes the paper reached and how it was delivered by some of the best students in their classrooms. It was disclosed that approximately 275 merchants of the community spent $115,000 a year for advertising to make shopping easier for the teachers and others in the community. The editor explained how competitive advertising, instead of raising prices, makes lower prices possible and gave specific proof from the experiences of local advertisers.

The editor explained how the newspaper gathered and printed community news, trying always to deal fairly with all interests. Although the paper's two owners belonged to the Methodist and Presbyterian churches, the Methodists and Presbyterians did not dominate the news columns. All denominations were represented. The editor pointed out that the newspaper had at least one staff member in each service club. The teachers were told that the newspaper devoted at least 20,000 column inches of its space each year to the public schools, and that it gave editorial support to school tax levies, school activities, and educational aims.

It was explained also that the newspaper had paid out $118,000 in salaries and wages the preceding year and at Christmas had distributed a bonus of $3,400 to employes. The editor disclosed that in only 22 of the 52 years of the paper's existence had dividends been declared — it was the general policy of the newspaper corporation to turn profits back into plant improvements, additional equipment, and improvement in personnel. By virtually opening all the books and records to the teachers, the editor increased their confidence and interest in the newspaper.

Management that is alert and progressive will heed the spirit of the famous Journalist's Creed written by the late Walter Williams:

> The journalism which succeeds best — and best deserves success — fears God and honors man, is stoutly independent, unmoved by pride of opinion or greed of power, constructive, tolerant but never careless, self-controlled, patient, *always respectful of its readers* but always unafraid . . . is a journalism of humanity, of and for today's world. [Emphasis added.]

Other ways to gain reader respect

1. The Washington, Iowa, *Journal* sponsors a Three-Quarter Century Club, and each year persons 75 years old and older are invited to a dinner at the country club. Usually 150 or more attend.
2. The Madison, Wis., *Wisconsin State Journal* conducts a weekly news quiz. Prizes of $5, $3, and $2 go to readers who send in the most correct answers.
3. To test the community's opinion on important issues of the day, the Rolla, Mo., *Daily News* carried on its front page 18 questions, requiring answers of "Yes" and "No." More than 500 readers clipped the list and turned in their answers.
4. Seniors of the La Porte, Ind., high schools compete annually in an essay writing contest sponsored by the *Herald-Argus*. The winner one

year received a trip to Washington, and runners-up received savings bonds.

5. The Bloomington, Ill., *Pantagraph* sponsored a "Soils Day Show" for farmers and others interested in improved farm methods. More than 10,000 attended.

6. To encourage an interest in art, the Mexico, Mo., *Ledger* sponsored a "Picture of the Week" display at the city library.

7. A series of stories and pictures of rural churches appeared in the La Porte, Ind., *Herald-Argus* and later were compiled in an attractive booklet for county-fair distribution.

8. Each month a farm boy and girl were honored by the Kalamazoo, Mich., *Gazette*. Pictures of the young people and accounts of their activities appeared in the newspaper. Those to be honored were selected by the Farm Bureau staff and FFA advisers.

9. Letters from old-timers were used for an annual special edition published by the Maryville, Mo., *Forum*.

10. Cooking classes for youngsters were sponsored by the Fort Scott, Kans., *Tribune*. Recipe instructions were prepared in nursery rhyme fashion, prizes were awarded for the best notebooks, and certificates were presented to all who completed the course.

11. A baseball clinic for women was launched by the Milwaukee, Wis., *Sentinel,* when the sports editor became flooded with baseball questions from women fans. A panel, composed of the home team manager and players and *Sentinel* sportswriters, answered questions and the women took notes. Each participant was given a booklet, "How to Watch Baseball."

12. The Lincoln, Ill., *Courier* conducts an annual Junior Good Citizen Contest for high school seniors. Each school selects a boy and a girl candidate. The boy and girl who win in the contest's final phase make two appearances at the county fair and receive large trophies. Smaller trophies are presented to other contestants.

13. The Nebraska City, Nebr., *News Press,* published in the heart of the Nebraska orchard country, cooperates with the American Legion and the high schools in sponsoring an annual Apple Bowl football game.

14. When the community failed to subscribe sufficient funds, the Sheboygan, Wis., *Press* sponsored a winter concert series by the civic orchestra.

15. The Danville, Ill., *Commercial News* asked leading men and women to write on the theme, "Your Right to Know — A Constitutional Guarantee."

16. When a long-time subscriber celebrates his 100th birthday, the Jackson, Mich., *Citizen-Patriot* sends a bouquet of roses.

17. The Columbia, Mo., *Missourian,* under the heading "You Should Know," daily ran the picture of a prominent business or professional person and some brief facts about career, business, and hobbies.

18. The Alliance, Ohio, *Review* sponsors an annual Halloween celebration for community children.

19. The Detroit, Mich., *News* sponsors an annual senior citizens art and crafts exhibit at the Detroit Historical Museum. The exhibit features handmade articles, including tablecloths, bedspreads, hand towels, and Lithuanian artwork.
20. The Fort Worth, Tex., *Star-Telegram* conducted a hunting clinic, stressing gun safety. This was held at three Fort Worth area gun clubs in September, under the direction of the outdoors editor.
21. Each day, for 11 days, two pages of the Philadelphia, Pa., *Inquirer* were devoted to examination and explanation of the Delaware Valley's structure, from religion to industry, from education to recreation. Reprints of the full-color illustrated pieces, enclosed in an attractive folder featuring a map of the 14-county area, were distributed by the *Inquirer*'s promotion department.
22. The Richmond, Va., *News-Leader,* in an attractive folder, announced the birth of a new organization, "The Blackeyed Pea Society of America." By-laws of the new organization were included in the folder. Two hundred and ninety-seven devotees of the "noble legume" attended the founding luncheon.
23. "How many home improvements can you suggest?" asked the Washington, D.C., *Star* in a brochure produced by the *Star*'s promotion department. The question, in a mid-Victorian lettering style, appeared under a picture of a turn-of-the-century kitchen. This two-color folder was used to promote a special section, "How to Improve Your Home."
24. At a state constitutional convention the Hartford, Conn., *Courant* gave each delegate an oak seedling to take home and plant as a convention memento. An oak tree served as a hiding place for the charter of the Connecticut colony in 1687.
25. The Scottsdale, Ariz., *Daily Progress* sponsored a "Favorite Father" contest, in which 744,565 votes were cast. The winner and his wife were awarded a weekend visit to Las Vegas.
26. The Columbus, Ohio, *Dispatch* has initiated a program of saluting newly naturalized citizens. An illuminated certificate is given to each new citizen. On the back of the certificate are outlined the responsibilities that go along with the privileges of citizenship.
27. The Cleveland, Ohio, *Press* instituted a reading contest entitled "Easy Street." Readers were asked to identify 60 photos of portions of Cleveland area streets, published daily in the *Press.* To promote the contest, eight gaslights were installed in the plaza in front of the *Press* building, each carrying an "Easy Street" sign.
28. The Scranton, Pa., *Times* spearheaded a drive to raise money with which to buy a new elephant for the city zoo. The drive was started after an elderly elephant, which had been a zoo attraction for many years, had been put to death by officials.
29. The Detroit, Mich., *News* concluded a summerlong community service when it provided free pony rides—by cart and by saddle—to youngsters in deprived areas of the city.

30. The Dallas, Tex., *Times-Herald,* with the blessings of the Texas Women's Golf Association, sponsored a junior girls golf tournament open to all girls 18 or younger who were permanent residents of Texas.
31. The Burlington, Vt., *Free Press,* as a public service, published a list of ZIP codes for all towns in Vermont. Readers were urged to clip the list and use it regularly.
32. The Detroit, Mich., *News* ran a series of ads featuring people involved in various community service programs sponsored by the newspaper.
33. The Aurora, Ill., *Beacon-News* distributed posters in the schools of the city, urging children to "never, never, talk with strangers." The campaign was suggested to the newspaper's promotion manager by his first-grade daughter.
34. The Chicago, Ill., *Sun-Times* series known as "Sunday's Child" resulted in adoptions of at least two-thirds of the homeless youngsters featured. An official of the Illinois Department of Children and Family Services termed it "the best thing that ever happened for Chicago's adoptable children."
35. The Duluth, Minn., *News-Tribune* invites readers to submit humorous captions for unusual photos and pays $5 for the one selected for publication.
36. The Atlantic City, N.J., *Press* awards five pounds of sugar to readers who come up with worthwhile suggestions on how to beat inflationary costs.
37. The Akron, Ohio, *Beacon-Journal* selects various individuals from the community according to their occupations and prints personality-job sketches of each.
38. The Houston, Tex., *Chronicle* invites nostalgia-type questions from readers, looking up answers regarding anything from early automobile models to stars of the silent movie era.
39. The Battle Creek, Mich., *Enquirer* and *News* solicits nominations from its readers of anyone who deserves a "Bouquet Award." Those accepted are displayed on page one of the Sunday edition.

Newspaper involvement with the community is absolutely essential to a healthy operation. The encouragement of reader participation is one of the surest ways to achieve such involvement and to build goodwill for management.

23

Promoting services

Most newspapers are doing investigative work, perhaps more than ever. Many just are not promoting what good their newspapers do.

Earl Truax

If successful public relations can be defined as "doing good and getting credit for it," or "practicing the Golden Rule for profit," then it follows that newspaper management is missing a good thing when it fails to build goodwill by keeping its readers informed on what is new and better as far as the newspaper's services are concerned. All that can legitimately be done to win public approval and broaden influence is summed up under the term "promotion."

From the standpoint of the La Porte, Ind., *Herald-Argus,* promotion consists of "doing something that will help our readers, or at least a part of them, become better citizens as a result of what the newspaper does, or says, or prints. It is an honest effort to make the other fellows feel that we are vitally interested in their welfare and will do all we can to keep them on the right road."

DEPARTMENT RESPONSIBILITIES

The promotion manager of the Des Moines, Iowa, *Register* and *Tribune* says that basically a promotion department is an "idea factory." It supplies suggestions and plans that will help other newspaper departments get their stories over to the buying public. It develops selling aids that produce results.

Convincing evidence of the great variety and volume of work that may be accomplished by promotion departments is apparent in the routine activities of that department at the *Register* and *Tribune.* The promotion manager and 13 assistants had these responsibilities during a single week in early December:

1. Made a sales presentation for the picture magazine of the Sunday *Register* supplement.
2. Prepared a four-page promotion folder, "The Mail-Order *Register,*" for the mail-order section of the picture magazine.

401

3. Arranged for the Christmas party and show, a company-employe activity.
4. Set up Christmas decorations in the building.
5. Put out a four-page scholarship folder for the circulation department.
6. Put out a four-page broadside on a circulation prize offer.
7. Prepared a plaque for the highest corn production in Iowa.
8. Issued four circulation bulletins, 8 by 10 inches.
9. Prepared a full-page circulation comic ad in four colors.
10. Put out a four-page folder for the classified department, promoting spring mail-order advertising.
11. Prepared several small promotion ads for the classified market section.
12. Prepared a full-page ad for the Farm and Home *Register* to appear in an Iowa retail farm equipment magazine.
13. Assembled material for and supervised makeup of two circulation promotion pages, carrying names of Red Necktie Club members.
14. Wrote copy and edited and supervised makeup of *The Spirit,* a four-page tabloid house organ.
15. Wrote copy for 28 radio spots used on six stations.
16. Produced two promotion ads (total 162 lines) for the rotogravure picture magazine.
17. Wrote copy for two black and white ads (½ and ¼ page) for the Sunday newspaper.
18. Prepared a Merry Christmas sign for a television celebrity, to go on a pig crate (received a national TV plug for this).
19. Prepared a page-sized cartoon poster and presented it to the outgoing president of the Des Moines Retail Bureau at an evening dinner.
20. Prepared three promotion boxes for the Sunday *Register.*
21. Did stencil mimeograph work for the *Register* and *Tribune* Christmas parties for employes and children.
22. Prepared two quarter-page ads promoting classified.
23. Prepared Gleem toothpaste presentation for the general advertising department.
24. Prepared copy, layout, and artwork for three advertisements, each two full columns, on the television guide and a new television feature.
25. Prepared copy, artwork, and layout for a rotogravure full-page advertisement on the Washington Bureau. (This ad was torn down and revised three times before it was OK'd.)
26. Prepared copy for two Christmas subscription ads.
27. Took care of the entire production (photography, printing, mounting) of twenty-four 10- and 20-second spot slides for five TV stations.
28. Made layouts for three ads, each one full column.
29. Revised copy on an 11-inch eight-column ad for Sunday.
30. Held a conference and started production on a presentation of 50 color slides for the January circulation meeting.

31. Distributed weekly promotion bulletins to all circulation agency managers, supervisors, and superintendents.
32. Prepared an Iowa map, 18 by 24 inches, for general advertising, showing county coverage.
33. Made a comprehensive full-page layout on an editorial feature.
34. Prepared copy and layout for the local display Christmas ad.
35. Prepared two classified promotion boxes for the *Register.*
36. Prepared three classified promotion ads plugging voluntary business.
37. Prepared a promotion news-story setup and advertisement on the half-millionth want ad.
38. Made the weekly mailing of "World Affairs" to Iowa teachers.
39. Held a meeting and a slide presentation for all advertising sales staff.
40. Deadlined mailing piece to job, then to the McDonald Letter Service for the classified department.
41. Held a meeting on promotion ads for the picture magazine and local display.
42. Met with the classified department and subsequently prepared a letter to go to the Midwest Classified Advertising Managers Association concerning the convention meeting to be handled by the phone-room supervisor.
43. Met with the general advertising department regarding the Bureau of Advertising film and received the assignment to make new slides for general advertising.
44. Made mailing to homes on the "kiddie party."
45. Met with the general advertising department regarding "Markets of America" publicity.
46. Wrote and mailed publicity stories for three trade papers.
47. Conducted 130 persons, in groups of 15, on a tour of the building.

In addition to supervising staff work on these projects, the promotion manager attended the following meetings:

1. Monday—promotion staff, general advertising staff, Iowa Medical Association, executives conference, and Central Iowa Sales Executives Club.
2. Tuesday—Farm & Home advertising force, circulation promotion conference, Chamber of Commerce luncheon, Iowa Duroc Breeders Association, and Manufacturers and Jobbers Bureau.
3. Wednesday—promotion staff, Iowa Savings & Loan Association, and Des Moines Retailers Executive Committee.
4. Thursday—Japan International Christian University, Western Grain and Feed convention, and classified advertising conference.
5. Friday—publicity conference.

For many newspapers the promotion department, in addition to promoting newspaper services and features, organizes and directs campaigns for community betterment, organizes entertainments and recreational programs, and keeps in close contact with all community organizations and movements.

A promotion code

Perhaps the clearest outline of promotion department duties and standards is found in the code devised by Julius Ochs Adler many years ago for the New York, N.Y., *Times* promotion department:

1. A promotion department should be competent to analyze clearly fundamental advertising and circulation problems and to offer sound suggestions for their solution. The promotion department should by no means be an errand boy, merely executing the commands and surmises of other departments. Rather, the promotion staff must create the promotion plan, cooperating fully . . . with other departments — and it must have the force and imagination to carry the program out in its own right.

2. The promotion material should reflect the personality and institutional character of the newspaper rather than the personality and individual cleverness of the promotion staff. Good promotion creates a favorable impression for the institution it serves. Promotion which is conspicuous merely because of its spectacular character does not always serve a newspaper well in the end.

3. A promotion department is expected not only to suggest promotion ideas and themes but to have the patience and ingenuity to stick to them for sufficient time to be effective.

4. It is a responsibility of the promotion department to avoid promotion of a type that is generally designed to please the vanity of your own newspaper or to irritate the competitor.

5. A promotion department is expected to integrate the newspaper's printed and oral selling, and thereby coordinate efforts to obtain business. In other words, the promotion department is a vital coordinating agency which can multiply the effectiveness of the outside sales force.

6. The promotion department has close contact with every department of the newspaper — news, circulation, and the divisions of the advertising department. It should transmit news of what happens in one department to any other parts of the organization where the information would be interesting or useful.

7. The promotion department is expected to make a genuine contribution to the advancement of the general welfare of a newspaper. Its work should reflect credit to the newspaper as a medium and stimulate its intelligent use.

PERSONNEL

Whether a promotion department is successful depends upon the type of person who heads it. Publishers generally agree that the promotion manager should genuinely like to work with people, manage people, meet people, and study people. To plan campaigns, sell features, manage community events, write about the newspaper's services, organize and systematize drives for more advertising and circulation, such a person must realize how fascinating and stimulating a promotion job can be. Moreover, the manager should be well educated, possess an attractive personality, and be a good conversationalist but know how to control and regulate conversational ability. A "promoter" should know how to compliment but never be excessively effusive, and should dress well, but as a business executive, not as a fashion model. A liking and eagerness for work, and a sound background of experience and training are essential.

The promotion manager ranks with other department heads in a newspaper organization and usually is responsible to the publisher or general manager. The number of staff members needed depends upon how the promotion department is organized — whether all promotion work is centered in one department or divided among advertising, circulation, and news.

Any newspaper, large or small, should carry on some systematic promotion. If the newspaper's business is not large enough to justify a separate promotion department with a skilled person in charge, the editor or the publisher may become a promotion manager and sell the newspaper and its services to readers and advertisers.

PLANS AND PROJECTS

In addition to internal policies designed to maintain desirable employer-employe relations, newspaper promotion falls into three classes: promotion of the newspaper's services, including news, advertising, and circulation (see Fig. 23.1); promotion of such features as comics, serial stories, syndicated articles, picture pages, and television and radio programs; and promotion intended to build goodwill through sponsorship of educational, commercial, and entertainment events.

News coverage

News is the predominant feature of a newspaper, and nothing else merits more and better promotion. The expense and labor required to produce news is a story that every newspaper should drive home to its readers. A news story's fascinating journey from source to printed record can be effectively traced in movie films for presentation to service clubs and other community groups.

The New Castle, Ind., *Courier-Times* has produced such a film and has shown it repeatedly to local groups, many of which include publicity chairpersons.

The Hutchinson, Kans., *News* has prepared a handsome booklet containing pictures of *News* staffers at work. A copy is given to every person who visits the newspaper's plant.

The Moline, Ill., *Dispatch* published a full page of pictures and stories, illustrating how *Dispatch* writers strive to serve the public. Editors, reporters, and suburban correspondents were shown on the job; and some of the news sources were explained.

Fig. 23.1. The Northampton, Mass., *Daily Hampshire Gazette* developed a child's suggestion into an outstanding promotional idea. (Courtesy of the *Daily Hampshire Gazette*.)

"Report to the People" was the title given to a tabloid section of the Mason City, Iowa, *Globe-Gazette,* which listed important news sources. A citizen, his wife, and two daughters were pictured viewing the operations of the city through the eyes of a taxpayer.

"The Story of a Good Newspaper," a four-page newspaper-sized promotion piece, issued by the Champaign-Urbana, Ill., *News-Gazette,* emphasized departments, features, and articles of unusual interest appearing daily in that publication.

During a police officers' training program at South Bend, Ind., the trainees were guests of the South Bend *Tribune,* where the managing editor explained the newspaper's policy for handling police and crime news. Afterward the guests toured the plant.

To acquaint teenage boys and girls with the news columns and to stimulate greater readership, the Mason City, Iowa, *Globe-Gazette* for a number of years has run a full page of high school news every Saturday. The Lansing, Mich., *State Journal* observed "Young Editors' Day" during National Newspaper Week by having talented journalism class members from all high schools within 20 miles of Lansing serve as reporters. The Kankakee, Ill., *Journal* runs a weekly two-page "Teenage Section," containing high school news and featuring material about young people. The Canton, Ohio, *Repository* conducted a "Current Events Quiz Contest" for students in Canton high schools. Questions were prepared by *Repository* staff members, and teachers checked the results. A $25 cash prize was given to each freshman, sophomore, junior, and senior winner and a $50 prize to the student who topped them all.

Complimentary copies of the Woonsocket, R.I., *Call* were delivered to English classes at Woonsocket High School, where newspaper reading had been adopted as part of the curriculum.

It is good sense for a newspaper to summarize occasionally the amount of news devoted to schools, churches, the Chamber of Commerce, and to other organizations and movements—space not paid for but valuable promotion nonetheless.

News coverage by the Associated Press, United Press International, or whatever service is engaged and the outstanding columnists and correspondents whose reports appear in the newspaper are all good promotion material. A newspaper may want to feature its independent editorial policy or some special achievement of a department (see Fig. 23.2). Promotion of this kind not only helps to maintain the interest of regular subscribers but also can win new readers for the newspaper.

When the Boston, Mass., *Globe* was honored in the same year for distinguished service in journalism by the Pulitzer prize committee; the Society of Professional Journalists, Sigma Delta Chi; and the University of Missouri, it ran a full page in *Editor & Publisher* (see Fig. 23.3).

The Albany, N.Y., *Knickerbocker News* completely revamped its approach to presenting the news with a "People" section filled with practical information on every imaginable phase of home and family and personal

Have an **important** message
to tell the government?

THE WASHINGTON STAR is THE INFLUENTIAL VOICE in THE NATION's CAPITAL

Fig. 23.2. The Washington, D.C., *Star* proclaims itself an influential voice in the nation's capital.

living. This "extra dimension" to the news, according to one of the editors, makes the publication a "use-paper as well as a newspaper."

Features

If a series of articles on a popular subject is to begin in the newspaper, the public should be told in advance of the first installment. In addition to the newspaper's own columns, circulars, window cards, radio and television time, movie screens, and billboards are good promotional outlets. Unusual fiction, special recipes, patterns, fashions, and other subjects all rate advance publicity. And the sports pages and comic section are constant promotional possibilities.

The New Castle, Ind., *Courier-Times* once featured on its woman's page a series of recipes submitted by local readers. The recipes aroused such interest that the newspaper collected them in a ringbound book and sold more than 1,600 copies at $1 each. The woman's page editor of the Bloomington, Ill., *Pantagraph* gives an attractive wooden recipe box to each person whose recipe is accepted for publication.

The public-spirited newspaper has a vital interest in traffic safety, child welfare, and youth activities that goes much beyond merely printing news about them.

Each week for three weeks the Hammond, Ind., *Times* offered a $25 bond to the person best describing a "crazy driver" incident. Competition for the prize was keen, and the published descriptions emphasized traffic hazards in a unique and telling way.

The Garden City, Kans., *Telegram* gave the receipts from one day's downtown paper sales to a child welfare fund sponsored by the local Kiwanis Club. Club members, pinch-hitting as street salesmen, did so well that many copies sold for 25 cents and more. The Cadillac, Mich., *News* cooperated with service clubs to raise money for the community charities fund by issuing a "Good-Fellow Edition" featuring stories about the service

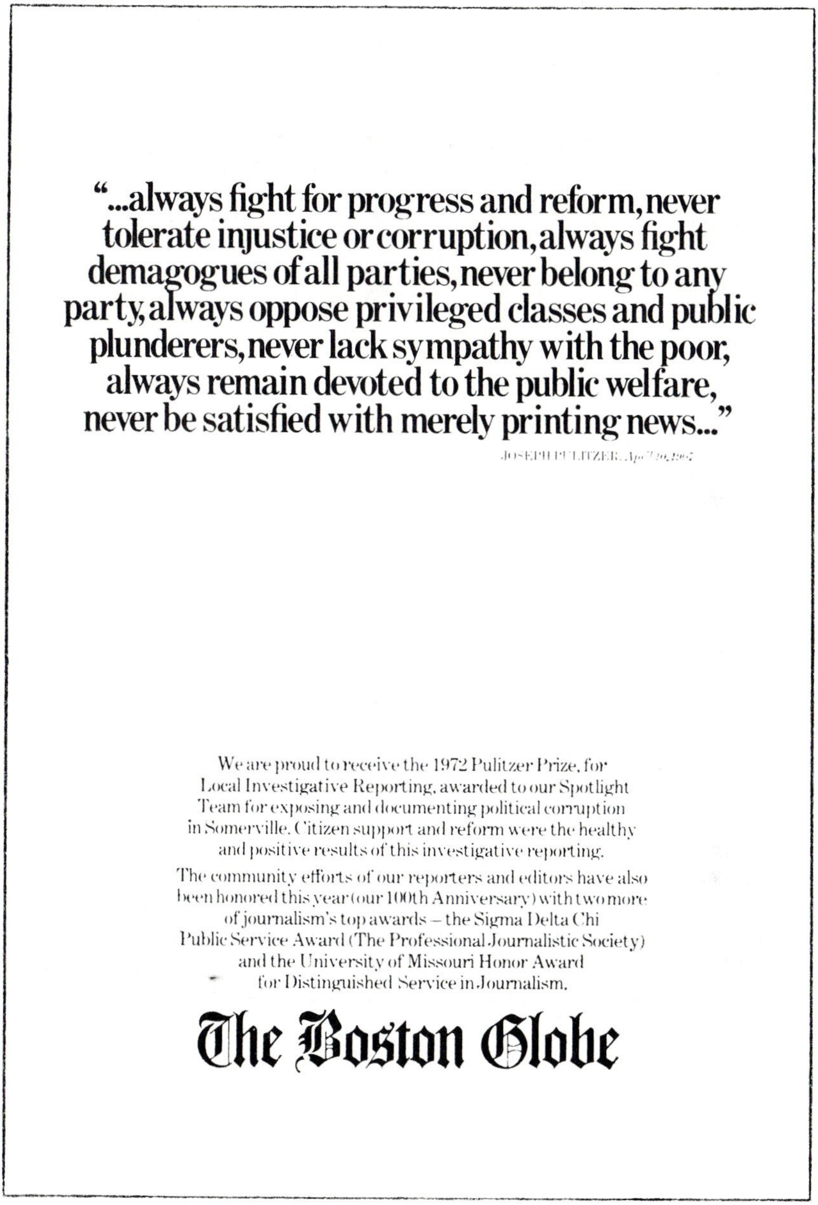

"...always fight for progress and reform, never tolerate injustice or corruption, always fight demagogues of all parties, never belong to any party, always oppose privileged classes and public plunderers, never lack sympathy with the poor, always remain devoted to the public welfare, never be satisfied with merely printing news..."

JOSEPH PULITZER, April 10, 1907

We are proud to receive the 1972 Pulitzer Prize, for Local Investigative Reporting, awarded to our Spotlight Team for exposing and documenting political corruption in Somerville. Citizen support and reform were the healthy and positive results of this investigative reporting.

The community efforts of our reporters and editors have also been honored this year (our 100th Anniversary) with two more of journalism's top awards – the Sigma Delta Chi Public Service Award (The Professional Journalistic Society) and the University of Missouri Honor Award for Distinguished Service in Journalism.

The Boston Globe

Fig. 23.3. The Boston, Mass., *Globe* gains recognition for its investigative reporting.

clubs. The edition was sold on the streets by the service club members and the proceeds provided Christmas baskets for the needy.

The 4-H Club members of a five-county area are honored annually at an all-day event sponsored by the Moline, Ill., *Dispatch.* In Missouri, the Future Farmers of America and 4-H Club members of the county were guests of the Carthage, Mo., *Press* at a winter contest and award day. So popular was the event that one year nearly 1,200 persons traveled over sleet- and ice-covered roads to attend.

Communities and organizations, always newsmakers, often are featured in special ways. The Dubuque, Iowa, *Telegraph-Herald* developed a special section for the Chamber of Commerce, to be distributed by *Telegraph-Herald* carriers at the annual Chamber of Commerce dinner. The section became an important part of a Progress Edition the next day.

Few features have been exploited as successfully as the nationwide "Newspaper in the Classroom" program for effective and constructive promotion. Hundreds of thousands of pupils have been trained in the use of the newspaper as a learning tool. Where the local newspaper has sought and obtained the full cooperation of education officials in the area, the "Newspaper in the Classroom" has made tremendous contributions both to the newspaper's stature in the community and to the teaching experience. This is true because students are motivated to read the newspaper, although they are sometimes poor book readers, and they have felt involved in the world of current events as presented in this "living textbook."

Advertising

Merchants need to be reminded and kept abreast of the service offered them by the advertising department in preparing copy, planning campaigns, and making surveys (see Fig. 23.4). Also worth emphasis are the conveniences provided customers through newspaper advertising and the efficiency and economy of reaching a large numer of homes in the community at nominal cost. Some of the striking results realized from advertising furnish highly persuasive promotion material.

The Denver, Colo., *Post* often features spectacular results of ads. Similar examples are possible almost everywhere. The Memphis, Tenn., *Commercial Appeal* captioned a letter reproduction "More Than 101 Gift Pictures Were Sold from a Single Advertisement in Section 5, the *Sunday Commercial Appeal.*" Here again, the customer's letter appeared in full. The profits of large-space users and the service provided all newspaper readers through the classified advertising department are features to be emphasized constantly. The publisher who neglects this sort of promotion is missing an opportunity to increase revenue and build goodwill for the newspaper.

Advertising promotion is of two classes: that which stresses the general advantages of advertising and that which promotes definite campaigns.

The slogan "You get SO MUCH — for SO LITTLE — with a *Star* and

CALL-CHRONICLE NEWSPAPERS
Allentown, Pa.

SPECTACOLOR • ROP FULL COLOR • PREPRINTS
Represented by Story & Kelly-Smith, Inc.

Fig. 23.4. The Allentown, Pa., *Call* and *Chronicle* makes a major national market of its area.

Tribune want ad!" spearheaded a new classified advertising promotion campaign developed by the Minneapolis, Minn., *Star* and *Tribune* that was instrumental in raising voluntary classified advertising volume to new highs for the last five months of the year. The major "push" behind this successful campaign was more than 90,000 lines of promotion advertising space used in the *Star* and *Tribune*. The result was that voluntary classified linage climbed approximately 20 percent from August to December, and total classified linage reached a new all-time high for November. Because of this gain, the Minneapolis newspaper estimated it had climbed that year, among all newspapers of the country, from fourteenth to sixth place in morning classified linage, from eighteenth to seventh in the evening, and from sixteenth to tenth on Sunday.

A "make things happen" campaign was launched by the Lincoln, Nebr., *Journal* and *Star,* focusing on two themes: the Red Motley slogan, "Nothing happens until someone sells something!" and the color orange. The newspaper and its advertisers stressed both the slogan and spots of color in advertisements for one week and on 4,000 fluorescent orange badges. During the same week, all telephone calls to the newspaper were answered with "Good morning, *Journal-Star.* We make things happen. May we help you?" As a result, increases were reported in retail store sales, bank deposits, real estate transfers, car sales, and advertising linage.

To stimulate classified advertising, the Philadelphia, Pa., *Bulletin* found a "2 + 1" promotion effective. Anyone advertising jobs in the classified section was entitled to a free insertion on Sunday for any two days of paid advertising during the week. A special column on employment and a 16-page booklet of advice were provided to readers as part of the promotion. A remarkable 40 percent increase in help-wanted advertising was only one of the benefits derived from the campaign.

Circulation

The promotion department may help the circulation department in five important ways:

1. Stimulate carrier interest by setting up contests and incentives.
2. Reduce carrier turnover by providing material to acquaint carriers and parents with opportunities for financial reward and business training.
3. Produce material to train carriers in efficiency and dependability.
4. Institute campaigns for circulation development in definite areas.
5. Advertise the newspaper and its services in every way possible to bring in voluntary subscriptions and make soliciting easy.

A small newspaper, as well as a large one, may have a well-rounded program for circulation promotion. For two successive years the Fremont, Ohio, *News-Messenger* won the International Circulation Managers Association award for having the best newspaper carrier program. It was designed to focus public attention on the opportunities for personal advancement and wholesome character development offered to boys and girls through newspaper route management. Carrier activities at the *News-Messenger* one year included basketball, softball, a Ping-Pong tournament, a Christmas party, a free movie once a month, carrier insurance, a savings plan, and an advertising campaign featuring all the carriers. A training plan for new carriers helped the paper to eliminate many of the problems that might have come later.

Five Boy Scouts on the Canton, Ohio, *Respository* carrier force were saluted in a full-page newspaper promotion when they reached Eagle Scout rank. Pictures of the five were shown, and the copy pointed out that

Scouting and carrier training go hand in hand to prepare for the business of living.

A "Forty-Niners Club," complete with gold nuggets for new subscriptions, renewals, and special services, was sponsored by the Bloomington, Ill., *Pantagraph* in connection with a carrier contest. The main reward was a trip to the homes of Abraham Lincoln at New Salem and Springfield. Carriers who did not accumulate enough nuggets for the trip were paid off at the rate of 5 cents a nugget. An "apple for the teacher" in the form of a subscription to the *Pantagraph* was another suggestion used in an early fall campaign to obtain subscriptions from teachers coming to Bloomington. The *Pantagraph* also introduced a "Lay Away Plan" for vacationers who would not be at one address long enough for the paper to reach them but who did not want to miss any of the home news. Issues were held for the subscriber until the family returned home and then were delivered in a bundle.

"Have a Chew" was the invitation extended to potential subscribers to the Owosso, Mich., *Argus-Press* in a circulation letter with a stick of chewing gum pasted at the top. The copy gave the gum manufacturer's slogan, "It is guaranteed to satisfy," and carried out that theme as an invitation to subscribe to the *Argus-Press*.

Whatever the nature of the promotion for circulation, its presentation to the public should be as attractive and as appealing as possible. Such materials are available from well-established promotion firms (Fig. 23.5) or may be made up locally. The emphasis should always be public-oriented rather than in self-serving terms. If the promotion is not in the community interest, it will not be of any lasting benefit to newspaper management.

A striking promotional advertisement by the New York, N.Y., *Times* called the reader's attention to the actual cash value received with a purchase of one copy of the newspaper (Fig. 23.6).

An official high in the newspaper promotion field says:

> About 3 percent is generally what newspapers with well-defined promotional programs spend. This is true both of advertising and circulation promotion, but it varies with the newspaper and its immediate problems. The problem at hand might well cause a newspaper to spend twice that for circulation promotion, or even more, in order to get a new classification of want ads going, or to keep a big classification from slipping; to get or maintain leadership in a classification, a newspaper might spend 25 percent or more of its revenue in that classification for a time. However, there can be no rules in such emergency and temporary situations. Very few newspapers operate on a formal budget system, so far as promotion is concerned.

He adds this concerning promotion department maintenance:

> A minimum promotion department, of course, would consist of a manager, a secretary-assistant, and a general helper. On the other hand, in a small operation, even a part-time hand could function. For instance, a paper that does a sports pro-

Youngsters
who get ahead

manage our newspaper routes.

Is your daughter or son a go-ahead youngster?

Who wants a savings account all his or her own.

Who gets fun out of making a profit.

And likes to meet and serve the public.

And is ready to take on the business of managing a newspaper route. (You will be surprised how well he or she will do, once given responsibility.)

Get in touch with our circulation department today.

New research shows what we have always known . . . boys and girls who do have routes are a step ahead of others . . . both in school and on the playground and in preparing themselves for life ahead and the business world.

Check with us today.

NEWSPAPER NAME
Telephone number

Fig. 23.5. Carrier promotion ads can be fresh and appealing. (Courtesy of the Hickey-Mitchell Company.)

If you were running a newspaper...

9.8 LB

Would you sell 72 cents worth of newsprint for 60 cents?

The December 1, 1974, issue of The Sunday New York Times contained 770 pages, weighed 6 pounds, 2 ounces and the raw newsprint alone cost The Times 72 cents. To figure its total cost you'd have to add ink, printing, distribution and a share of the salaries of some 5,000 Times employes.

Yet you could buy a copy for only 60 cents all over town. It sounds like a short cut to the poorhouse, doesn't it?

Fortunately, The Times is in the *newspaper,* not the bulk paper business. And it takes a big newspaper to cover the rich and varied interests of its more than four million highly educated readers. For instance, on this particular day there were two sections of Main News and a section each on Arts & Leisure, Business-Finance, The Week in Review, Sports, Real Estate and Classified. Plus a 128-page Magazine and a 112-page Book Review.

It also takes a big newspaper to carry the messages all kinds of buyers and sellers want Times readers to see. Whether it's apartments, houses, jobs, cars, boats, bonds or any number of other products or services, The Times is *the* marketplace in print for both the nation and for its Number 1 market. Advertisers spend more dollars to reach high-income, highly placed Times readers than they do to reach readers of any national magazine.

Because of this, that issue of the Sunday Times cost you only 9.8 cents a pound. Can you think of anything else at that price that's nearly as nourishing you can buy for yourself or your family these days?

The New York Times
Makes things happen where affluence and influence meet

Fig. 23.6. This no-nonsense promotional message impresses the reader with the bargain provided by one issue of the New York, N.Y., *Times.* (Courtesy of the New York *Times* promotion department.)

motion could make it a part-time job of a sportswriter. The promotion manager in a small shop might also do layout and have to buy artwork and other needs outside, unless other departments of the paper could supply help, such as the job shop, advertising department, and others. The smaller the department, the bigger the appropriation chunk for salaries. A paper with a $1,000,000 gross, spending $30,000 on promotion, would probably have to spend a third of that on payroll. A paper with a larger gross, spending more on promotion, might still only spend the same as the smaller shop on payroll.

The promotion manager of an eastern newspaper with a circulation near 60,000 reports that the newspaper's annual expenditure for promotion will be from $1\frac{1}{2}$ to $2\frac{1}{4}$ percent of its total annual expenditures. He believes that a newspaper of 100,000 circulation, in order to do an effective promotion job, would be compelled to appropriate a higher percentage of its expendable fund than a newspaper of 500,000. Another publisher says that a budget of $25,000 a year is conservative for a newspaper of 100,000 circulation.

In one of the most elaborate promotions on record, the New York, N.Y., *Press* sponsored two four-day cruises to Bermuda for 2,400 advertising figures representing about 50 leading agencies, advertisers, and market specialists. The promotion was to publicize plans for the appearance of the new afternoon all-color publication. Costs for such an entrée were reported to be near one million dollars, which would be classed as out of the ordinary, to say the least.

Most newspapers do not set up a definite budget but consider the cost of each promotion idea as it is developed. Regardless of the procedure followed, good newspaper promotion pays handsome dividends.

24

Benefits from newspaper research

> Publishers . . . are inclined to appraise themselves and to scrutinize more carefully than ever before the content and form of their output. They are enlisting the aid of research specialists in an effort to substitute research facts for guesswork.
>
> *Ralph O. Nafziger*

Research in its broadest sense is often compared to a mining operation. A great deal of digging is required, most of it in unseen areas. Enormous quantities of unusable material may have to be brought to the surface to be analyzed, separated, and treated in order to glean something of value. In diligent research there will always be an impressive amount of "ore" that must be processed carefully if it is to yield profitable data of any kind.

By far the greatest portion of scientific research into newspapering is being done today in the nation's schools and departments of journalism, where research techniques are refined, academic procedures are established, and expert personnel is available. There are approximately 250 such institutions in the United States, and newspaper publishers generally will find ready access to these and an eagerness on the part of journalism educators to collaborate in research projects. They will find that complete reports on the most significant research undertakings are regularly published in *Journalism Quarterly,* a scholarly journal devoted to research in journalism.

Competition has become too keen and financial risks too great for publishers to depend entirely upon any "sixth sense" in arriving at sound business judgments when at their disposal are valuable techniques and instruments of newspaper research that enable them to minimize the risks of misinformation and guesswork.

Research in journalism is a fairly recent development, and newspapers that benefit regularly from its services are in the undisputed minority. Many publishers still are ignoring one of their best possible sources of business promotion — the community survey — simply because they do not know how to go about conducting one. In spite of the accomplishments of educational institutions, press associations, professional research organizations, and individual publishers in the direction of formalized fact gathering, research in journalism has merely scratched the surface of its potential.

What is research? It is the act of probing for accurate, reliable, useful information and of organizing that information so that sound conclusions can be drawn. Its scope, its complexity, or its cost can vary according to needs and objectives. William Allen White once said that he wrote and edited the Emporia, Kans., *Gazette* for the folks he knew and talked with in his town — but that he made darned sure to know and talk with a mighty lot of them. Research can be just that direct and simple.[1]

But whether simple and inexpensive or elaborate and costly, research that is meaningful to the publisher recognizes the importance of making a genuine contribution to the intelligence of the business — either in producing a better publication for readers or in contributing to more effective use of the medium by advertisers. Research is a means, not an end in itself.

Newspaper research is generally aimed in one of three directions: the market, the newspaper itself, or the products merchandised through newspaper advertising.

MARKET RESEARCH

No newspaper, however small or hard pressed for funds, need deny itself the sales advantages of obtaining complete facts about its own market. Newspapers that do provide factual information on their markets are finding they get extra dividends from the time and effort spent in preparing such data. Some of these are:

1. A sound basis for conducting the overall business operation — a knowledge of the area served by the newspaper.
2. An understanding of the relationship between advertising and sales in the community, insuring better informed ad salesmen.
3. Something tangible to offer prospective local or national advertisers who want to know what they are getting for their money.
4. Ample material for good self-promotional mailing pieces or advertising layouts.
5. Interesting local information for news or feature stories.

The chief problem in undertaking a community survey is identifying and utilizing the sources of reliable market information. Nearly all statistics dealing with business and economic conditions are collected and

---

1. For much of the material in this chapter, the author is indebted to the Advisory Committee on Research of the Newspaper Advertising Executives Association, Inc., and for permission to quote from its publication, *Newspaper Research—How to Conduct It—How to Put It to Work.*

recorded by some governmental or professional agency. Publishers who wish to arm themselves with facts about the market their newspapers serve must know first of all what kinds of facts are of value; then, where they may be found; and, finally, how they may be used to better the business operation.

Kinds of facts

Population factors such as nationality, color, age, sex, education, occupation, incomes, and tastes are of great importance. Housing factors such as number of both owner- and tenant-occupied dwelling units, values of homes, average rentals, types of home heating, cooking fuels used, types of refrigeration, number of television sets, number of telephones, and number of automobiles provide extremely valuable data. Any information that reflects the wants and needs, the preferences, and the ability to pay of the members of the market of a newspaper is of value to some or all of its advertisers.

All advertisers in a newspaper, it must be remembered, do not use the newspaper for the same reasons. A coffee advertiser wants to know how many people of coffee-consuming age are reached by the newspaper. An air-conditioning manufacturer wants to know how many homes with $10,000-or-over incomes are reached. In neither case does total circulation or total population give the answer.

Literally, then, the province of market research extends from teenage fads to industrial trends, from census-tract data to consumer surveys. And only related data tell a real story; the final presentation to an advertiser should always be in terms of the marketing problem of an individual business.

Where to find the facts

The country literally crawls with statistics relating to the United States as a whole. Although such information is of general interest, it is often remote and secondary as far as research on a particular newspaper market is concerned. The interest heightens as the data relates to one's own state, and can become genuine enthusiasm when they get down to the city and county level. "All business is local" is more than a trite slogan, and every alert publisher is interested in understanding and in serving the trading area covered by the newspaper.

To digest briefly the chief sources of economic information, the following checklist of reference material will serve as a guide for individual newspaper market research regardless of local conditions:

1. Bureau of the Census, U.S. Department of Commerce.
   a. Census of Population and Census of Housing (done every ten years in years ending in 0).
   b. Census of Agriculture (done every five years in years ending in 0 and 5).

    c. Census of Business, Census of Manufactures, and Census of Mineral Industries (annually).

    d. Monthly Retail Trade Report (regional summaries).

    e. Statistical Abstract of the United States.

2. Office of Business Economics, U.S. Department of Commerce (*Gross National Product,* quarterly).

3. U.S. Department of Commerce (retail sales of chain stores, survey of current business).

4. Federal Reserve System (business indexes, department store sales).

5. U.S. Bureau of Labor Statistics (building construction, urban areas; cost of living; employment releases; hours and earnings; daily index, 28 basic commodities; monthly report, retail food prices).

6. U.S. Treasury Department, Bureau of Internal Revenue (statement of revenue collection).

7. *Population and Its Distribution,* J. Walter Thompson Company. McGraw-Hill, New York, N.Y.

8. *Editor & Publisher's Market Guide.*

9. *Sales Management's Annual Survey of Buying Power.*

10. Dun and Bradstreet (*Dun's Review* and special reports).

11. *Markets of America* (published by *The Advertiser*).

12. Audit Bureau of Circulations reports.

13. N. W. Ayer & Son's *Directory of Newspapers and Periodicals.*

14. National Retail Dry Goods Association (season sales patterns).

15. George Neustadt Service (redbook of seasonal patterns).

16. *Marketing Research Practice* (Curtis Publishing Company).

17. *How to Conduct a Community Survey* (U.S. Department of Commerce).

18. *Newspaper Research—How to Conduct It—How to Put It to Work* (published by the Research Committee of the Newspaper Advertising Executives Association).

Public institutions in the local community also furnish a wealth of information regarding the newspaper's market area. Indications of business turnover in the locality are to be found in post office receipts, which are available from the postmaster; in sales tax receipts, which are accessible in the state tax department offices; and in bank deposits and debits, obtainable at local or federal reserve banks. Due allowance for price-level shifts must be made, however, in using bank debits as a gauge of business activity levels. Many state universities collect bank debits monthly from communities in all parts of their respective states and publish this information in business reviews or keep it on file for public information.

The county treasurer can supply statistics showing the number of farms in the newspaper's trade area or the number of automobiles in the county. The city auditor keeps records on the number of consumers of electricity or gas or water. Permits and licenses issued by municipal and county offices provide many worthwhile records that shed light on the economic potential of the community. Even the gallonage of gasoline sold in the area can be determined. Monthly employment figures from the state unemployment compensation commission and countless other types of information from sources within the city and county are readily available to the newspaper researcher.

The integration of population, housing, and sales trends sets the pattern of the market's buying power and reveals its present worth as well as its potential and ultimate worth to the advertiser. The newspaper that can give the answer accurately and completely enjoys a marked sales advantage over a competing medium that fails to provide advertisers with adequate market data.

Typical of market research is a ten-page survey of the Rapid City, S.D., area compiled by E. H. Lighter, business manager of the Rapid City *Daily Journal,* and revised annually to include current information. One edition showed that the Rapid City market had one-eighth of the state's population, had property assessed at $79,889,450, was second in the state in school census, had 4,300 persons employed in industries, had bank deposits of more than $48,000,000, and annual retail sales of $63,688,000. Additional facts of importance to anyone wanting to estimate the community's potential were given in tabular form and were well illustrated in a neatly printed report.

How to use the facts

The publisher who has so many other duties that no time can be found to get out any decent market information is perhaps too busy with minor details, because the market survey is one of the most effective tools in dealing with the newspaper's largest revenue-producing customers — the advertisers.

It is not necessary to undertake anything elaborate or expensive. To get a picture of duplication between newspapers in the market, the Phoenix, Ariz., *Republic* and *Gazette* drafted a questionnaire, selected 1,000 families in an accepted sampling technique, and used 21 interviewers. The results were tabulated in the newspaper's promotion department and the whole job was done in three weeks at a cost of $300. A nine-page mimeographed report was prepared and widely publicized.

The beginner in newspaper research should start with something simple. It is possible to use facts already at hand or quickly available. These facts may then be compiled and printed — or multigraphed or mimeographed. For maximum utilization the information should be mailed to a selected list of advertisers and agencies. Mailing lists can be purchased or made up locally and revised constantly.

As soon as the publisher can round up more sources of information and have more facts ready concerning the newspaper's market, that material should be printed and mailed out. It is not enough to keep the facts of research in storage or "available on request." They are useful only when printed in meaningful form, mailed out to prospective advertisers, and followed up with more research material.

Advertisers' budgets are usually limited, and appropriations go to media that can show the highest potential results. Thus a newspaper armed with adequate facts may be in better position to get on a schedule than another with larger circulation but without the facts. Simple statistical devices such as percentages, indexes, averages, bar charts, line charts, and pie graphs add to the effectiveness of presentation.

RESEARCH ON THE NEWSPAPER

Editors get letters from readers expressing approval or disapproval of policies advocated by the newspaper, occasional comments on content or format, or other observations of extreme interest to those who produce the newspaper and are naturally concerned about reader acceptance of their product. But what about the 90 or 95 percent of readers who never write letters to the editor? Can an editor or publisher be sure they feel the way 5 or 10 percent do? Can one be sure the readers do not care one way or the other about the features, the editorials, the method of handling social or church news—or can it be assumed they are completely satisfied?

Since no two newspapers are identical in format, policies, competitive factors, or need for media research, no standardized patterns for research on the newspaper itself can be set. But this type of research does divide itself into several areas:

1. The newspaper as a publication. Here the information deals with its content, policies, reader service, and community service records.
2. Circulation, how many buy the newspaper, who they are, and where they live.
3. Acceptance of the newspaper by the public.
4. Technical data such as advertising rates, mechanical specifications, type of printing available, management standards, operating costs, and any auxiliary services offered by the newspaper.

The newspaper as a publication

This kind of information is most frequently used to show the content of the newspaper and the extent of the service it renders to its readers and to its community. Content may include description of news coverage, wire services, local coverage, feature writers, picture services, columnists, comics, and specialized sections. Physical plant equipment, when it embodies unusual ideas or processes, is always of interest and makes good copy for a research report on the newspaper.

Political policies of the newspaper, the manner of handling news, the type and presentation of "art," rewrite of news stories, editorial policy, and the way local news is played are a vital part of the policy data.

The Columbus, Ga., *Ledger* and *Enquirer* conducts a readership survey so that all will know that the paper is interested in their opinions. John R. Cornett, promotion manager, observes:

> Control of the sample is nearly impossible, but with the help of a local computer operations firm, we allocated returns on the basis of age, sex, and readership in direct relationship to totals from the 1970 census.
>
> A questionnaire is directed to readers involved in news stories that have been printed. This gives us a constant playback, keeps our news staff alert, and gives the readers a good opportunity to sound off. We've spotted many sources of errors through the use of the survey.
>
> It's important that your news staffs know that such a survey is being conducted, their work is being checked, and the project is put in correct perspective. Otherwise they get the feeling that a "black hand" is operating when they find out through the grapevine. We've used it constructively and it's worked out well for us.

Reader service includes special events for the amusement, information, or education of readers, above and beyond the mere publication of an informative and instructive newspaper. A survey of such services provides the publisher with promotional material of striking interest and significance. Also news and editorial campaigns for community betterment, including publicity support for local participation in nationwide drives, can be tabulated and utilized.

As in all research great care must be taken that material is presented without bias and preferably without boasting. The data developed within this area are chiefly of value as a means of picturing the personality of the newspaper, thus pointing out truthfully the type of readers who have been attracted through its behavior patterns.

The newspaper's circulation

By means of surveys, publishers and circulation managers learn from each other what is being done to improve carrier services, how many papers have increased subscription prices and to what extent, how many require carriers to furnish bonds, how many carry accident and life insurance on carriers or make it possible for them to obtain such insurance at nominal rates, how many use country solicitors, how many depend entirely on mail promotions to sell new and renewal subscriptions outside their carrier zones, and many other circulation facts valuable to them in developing their own programs.

The assistant circulation manager of the Oakland, Calif., *Tribune* surveyed 94 metropolitan daily newspapers to determine the policies and techniques employed in handling carriers. He gained helpful facts about general operation, carrier relations, carrier programs, street sales, mailroom procedure, transportation, methods of distribution, and billings. This information was passed back to the dailies that participated in the survey and was made available to other newspapers. The survey is typical of many special studies conducted by individual newspapers in the field of circulation.

Such studies frequently supplement the information provided by the Audit Bureau of Circulations reports, especially where more detailed coverage of local circulation factors is desired. Research in the ABC semi-annual or annual statements is limited to the factual material presented in the reports.

Acceptance of the newspaper

The readership study is the most common research technique for determining the reactions of readers to features, news presentation methods, advertising copy and display, factors of format and typography, and page position. This type of study is ordinarily conducted by means of a questionnaire or checklist on which readers' preferences are recorded or the assisted recall method, which checks not only reading habits but actual readership of news stories, editorial features, classified advertising, and other material that appeared in the newspaper.

The most extensive readership study among newspapers is "The Continuing Study of Newspaper Reading" conducted by the Advertising Research Foundation in cooperation with the Bureau of Advertising of the American Newspaper Publishers Association. Typical of the findings of one of these studies (based upon 62,487 interviews with men and women 18 years or older and including 138 daily newspapers ranging in size from 16 to 96 pages and in circulation from 8,570 to 635,346) are these conclusions:

1. Editorials get higher readership during wartime, while comics and society and sports items undergo varying degrees of readership loss. The pattern changes during postwar years.
2. Men's average readership of classified ads rises 31 percentage points as the size of the city decreases; among women a smaller rise of 20 percentage points occurs as the city size shrinks.
3. In smaller communities, society items attract considerably greater attention than they do in big cities.
4. As the size of a city increases, so does the attention given to television and radio items.
5. Front pages command the highest readership, pictures rank second, sports pages place third among men, and society pages are third among women.
6. Men show greatest interest in pictures related to events, while women prefer photos of people.
7. Picture pages and outstanding news photos attract greatest attention, even outranking top-scoring news stories.

The value of such studies to management and editorial executives of a newspaper is quite obvious. These readership studies also have a dollars-

and-cents value for the advertising department in testing the power of copy, color, or position in advertising. Such surveys make their greatest contribution when the reports are studied for trends and principles rather than for specific details.

In addition to readership studies, reader acceptance can be measured by records of response to published features in the newspaper that require sending (with or without payment) for such things as patterns, health and beauty ideas, and personal advice or merchandising samples. Attendance at cooking schools, sporting events, benefit events for worthy causes, and other newspaper-sponsored activities is another highly acceptable source for readership evidence. Estimates of such attendance should be authenticated by police, park officials, or others, where the crowd fluctuates as in all-day outdoor events or in any case where the newspaper's own estimate may be questioned.

In showing advertiser acceptance of a newspaper, citation of comparative figures from Media Records or other recognized sources of linage reports is common practice. Care must be taken to give full data on all totals reported. For example, if part of the advertising linage appeared in supplementary magazine-type sections of the newspaper such as *Parade* or *This Week*, this should be noted. Sunday and weekday linage cannot be lumped as the basis of an acceptance figure for the newspaper but needs to be classified as such. The advice from national advertisers and agencies on this phase of newspaper research can be summed up in these words:

> Give us the true figures, without benefit of addition and subtraction, to build a better story for yourself, and we'll soon learn to accept your newspaper as a better medium with which to do business. We don't expect you to be first in everything and we often want to use publications which are not first in everything, so don't be afraid to be a good second. Being a good second is the soundest reason we know for proving the urgency of making the schedule as a two-newspaper buy instead of trying to get along with one paper in the market.

Technical data

The purpose of assembling technical data concerning the newspaper itself is manifold: to compute expenditures, to evaluate the newspaper on the basis of costs, to determine mechanical efficiency, to compare business methods, to prepare a list of specifications for advertisements, or any number of similar investigations of the newspaper's services and facilities.

Some newspaper publishers have considered it advisable to have their newspaper operations studied from the broad standpoint of management efficiency. The Cincinnati, Ohio, *Enquirer* had such an appraisal of its operation completed when it passed from trustee to employe ownership. A preliminary audit by an outside organization specializing in management surveys had been followed by frequent checks during a four-year period, providing valuable information about the *Enquirer's* corporate structure, its production and business policies, equipment, personnel, and prospects for improvement in all departments at a time when it was needed most.

The research revealed that the *Enquirer,* an independent newspaper, had great local vitality and national prestige; that it had tripled in circulation in 25 years while competing newspapers had lost circulation; that it had gained in advertising volume continuously until the income from that source came to approximately 68 percent of the newspaper's operating income; that the paper's personnel was of generally high quality; that the average age of the paper's executives was 51 and the average length of service was 20 years; and that despite the *Enquirer's* tendency to be conservative in makeup, it had made several selective changes to streamline the format and improve the readability.

On the other hand, the audit revealed that some changes in operation would be helpful, including sharper coverage of late local news and promptness in meeting deadlines; overhaul of the accounting department, particularly in its relationship to classified advertising; closing the gap between policymaking and execution; and rearranging work schedules. These were improvements that could be more easily carried out under employe-community ownership than under the previous trustee ownership and operation.

An extensive survey of this kind, done by capable analysts and accepted by management, could be of immeasurable value to any newspaper organization. It is not often, however, that newspaper owners feel the need for so general an analysis of their operation. They prefer to analyze their departments separately and to follow each study with definite steps to correct weaknesses. More often still, the study centers on the effectiveness of some service the newspaper offers.

Newspaper publishers and department heads often take it upon themselves to study certain costs to see how nearly they are in line with newspapers of similar circulation. The circulation manager of the Saginaw, Mich., *News* surveyed newspapers belonging to the Central States Circulation Managers Association and discovered that mailers' pay averaged about $3.75 an hour, and that the cost per mile to operate a truck for city deliveries averaged 11 cents. His newspaper had been paying a contractor $6.85 an hour for each truck hired. This survey led him to decide that he could operate his own delivery system at less cost and do a better job.

Before changing from an 8-column to a 9-column format, the Sidney, Ohio, *News* on its own account made a newsprint conservation survey and discovered that by changing to the nine-column format a nonmetropolitan daily of 12,000 circulation might possibly save $5,780 a year. Table 25.1 is a working example, furnished by J. O. Amos, business manager, Cecil Watkins, mechanical superintendent, and Richard McCasland, controller, which adds up to a gain of ten columns a week and a saving of 12 pages of newsprint a week. This indicates that a 12,000-circulation daily newspaper, which printed an average of 118 eight-column pages a week by changing to nine-column pages, would carry 520 more columns of advertising and editorial content and still use 624 fewer pages in a year, with a saving of 91,832 pounds of 32-pound newsprint.

Table 25.1. Comparison of number of pages required for 8-column and 9-column formats

Day	Using 8 Columns to a Page		Using 9 Columns to a Page	
	pages	*columns*	*pages*	*columns*
Monday	16	128	14	126
Tuesday	18	144	16	144
Wednesday	20	160	18	162
Thursday	28	224	26	234
Friday	22	176	20	180
Saturday	14	112	12	108
Total	118	944	106	954

Typical of the cost studies conducted by newspaper associations from time to time for the benefit of their members is the Semiannual Wage and Salary Survey of the Inland Daily Press Association. Similarly, the Annual National Weekly Newspaper Cost Study, a joint project of Newspaper Association Managers and the Weekly Newspaper Bureau of the National Newspaper Association, compiles percentages of income from various sources and percentages of expense borne by such items as salaries, wages, depreciation, services, utilities, building, and equipment.

Research on the newspaper itself varies widely under different sets of circumstances and with respect to local needs and objectives. Examples of surveys of many descriptions are frequently reproduced and often described in detail in the trade publications covering the newspaper field. Reader service departments of trade journals can furnish extensive bibliographies. The National Newspaper Promotion Association sends out to its members a continuing flow of current examples of this kind of research in actual use.

PRODUCT RESEARCH

Product research by newspapers is the newest of the three types of research discussed here. It is also more complicated and frequently more costly than market research or newspaper research. Its value lies in providing the manufacturer with information on the acceptance or sale of a specific brand in a newspaper's specific market. Except in the case of the very large advertisers, this is a kind of information the manufacturer could not develop.

The consumer analysis, originated by the Milwaukee, Wis., *Journal* in 1922, is one form of product research. The data are collected from buyers of the products by means of either questionnaires or personal interviews. The newspaper's consumer panel provides continuous and current information by selecting individuals or families (the Chicago panel consists of 576 families plus about 175 "extras") who agree to keep consumer diaries or inventories in the home over a given period. These records are then tabulated to show such factors as families buying, brands purchased, points of purchase, price lines, and general shopping habits. Store inventories depend for their data, not on the consumer, but on the retail outlet.

The chairperson of the Advisory Committee on Research to the Newspaper Advertising Executives Association gives this advice to newspapers interested in conducting research projects of any kind: "Accuracy is far more important than the extent or number of subjects covered. . . . Put your money into *Intelligence*—not into expensive printing and presentation. Good facts will be studied even if in pencil; poor ones won't be, even if in four colors and gold."

WHAT PUBLISHERS WANT

In an analysis of publishers' views on newspaper research conducted at Syracuse University, the following valuable conclusions were reached:

1. Research can be useful in solving operational problems.
2. The most useful function of research is to solve long-range industrywide problems rather than day-to-day problems or those peculiar to individual newspapers.
3. Needed research should be carried out by cooperative industrywide effort and by universities rather than by individual newspapers.
4. Almost all publishers have a specific study in mind they would like to have performed. For a majority the wanted research is on people rather than on mechanical things or abstract processes; on readers, to improve the editorial product; on nonreaders, to boost circulation; on their own or prospective personnel, to improve the labor situation; on advertising sources and receivers, to improve advertising effectiveness.
5. The most important major information needs for the newspaper industry are on mechanical, production, and technology aspects; personnel; the newspaper image; journalism education; and research itself. From one-half to two-thirds of the publishers say there is great need for information in each of these operational areas.
6. To a lesser extent, there is need for information on editing, circulation, reporting, and advertising, with one-third to one-half the publishers so responding. The least important information needs are in the areas of promotion, management, competitive media, economics, and typography, with one-fourth or fewer specifying each.
7. Information needs vary among newspapers according to such characteristics as circulation size, geographic location, local newspaper competition, production method, and publication time. They are apparently greatest among papers of smaller circulation (under 50,000), in the eastern region of the United States, with no local newspaper competition, produced by offset, and published in the afternoon. In some specific areas need is greatest among newspapers with characteristics opposite to those listed.
8. Opportunities for significant research on newspaper operational problems exist to some extent in almost every area of newspaper operation, in every region of the United States, for all kinds of newspapers.

LARGE-SCALE PROGRAMS

In very large newspaper operations like the E. W. Scripps Company, which publishes the Scripps-Howard group of newspapers in the nation's leading cities, research and development (R&D) are organized on an extensive scale. The following excerpt describes how R&D works there:[2]

The "Operations Research" team of The E. W. Scripps Company, publishers of Scripps-Howard newspapers, since mid-1969 known as the "Research and Development Division," is designed as a broad-based, multidiscipline consulting and basic research job shop for the Scripps-Howard Concern, one of the nation's largest mass communications-mass media complexes.

A unique group of engineering and behavioral scientists, the present team has evolved from a journalism-behavioral science, product-oriented organizational design, conceived in 1958, into a journalism-economics-social science-physical science-systems analysis-engineering Total Systems Operations Research team. Concisely, it may be described as a dynamic management information service, accessing an unlimited data bank.

The objective of Operations Research within The E. W. Scripps Company is to provide all levels of management, according to the priorities of rank and cruciality, with qualitative and quantitative data, analyses, and designs for decision making. The variety of talents and experiences, and flexibility of organization within the team enable a wide selection of research tools and aids. Particular problems may be given parallel, simultaneous analyses by independent disciplines, such as social psychology, systems (hard and software), engineering physics, and marketing analyses all within mass communications-mass media parameters.

EWSCo R&D (the in-house label) provides its management information service on the primary specification that the mode of research, project or problem basis, must adapt to the decision-making needs of management. Blue Sky research required or desired is jobbed out. State of the Art research is continuous but occupies a back burner.

BASIC PHILOSOPHY

The basic philosophy is one of blending the flexible organizational climate with the variety of information systems to produce custom output to the point and within the time frame specified by management. Rigorously, the concept is known as "dissonance resolution," which links the information people have with the way in which they use it. In this environment, one of three things can happen:

1. The organizational climate and the information system both change somewhat to be compatible,
2. The information system is changed, or
3. The organizational climate is changed.

Changing the decision-making climate is not an allowable goal of a good information system. In EWSCo R&D, the change is made in the information system to make it compatible with the management system. In The E. W. Scripps Company, there is both dual management and local autonomy which generate a variety of managements within the same system.

2. Excerpt from "The Application of Management Information Services to the Mass Communications Industry," by special permission of the E. W. Scripps Co.

Principles which govern the relationship between the decision-making authority (Concern General Management) and the information system (EWSCo R&D) at present are:

1. The information must be acceptable. (It must be to the point, valid, implementable, and ready for management's decision.)
2. The information is unbiased. (Management's value system is identified, observed. Exceptions are processed through executive channels.)
3. The information must have value. (Utilities of time, place, and intrinsic value exist.)
4. The amount of information generated is in direct proportion to the number of decision points in management and its receptability. (Generation of data will not be redundant. Effort is made not to duplicate output of other sources, within and without the Concern.)
5. The information system has built-in feedback on the efficacy of initial output, can upgrade, alter, and/or enhance the output. (Projects have been aborted, expanded, reordered in priority. Access to the management decision point is established as the first order.)

These five principles of EWSCo R&D are guidelines for determining the kind, quality, quantity, and viability of information generated for management. Management provides evaluation of R&D's performance in these areas on a proceduralized basis.

ORGANIZATION AND OPERATION

EWSCo R&D's chief executive is its Chairman, who is also a Corporate Vice President and member of the Board of Directors. Policy, planning, and executive oversight are his responsibilities. He is assisted by an R&D Planning Committee, composed of executives from various units with The E. W. Scripps Company plus the executives of the R&D Division, which meets quarterly to determine needs and priorities, review requests, and evaluate progress in terms of the Total Concern.

Supporting the Chief Executive Officer as staff executive is the Division Administrator, who is responsible for the management, operation, and control of the Division itself as a unit of The E. W. Scripps Company. The Administrator performs all staff work required, serves as Secretary of the Planning Committee, coordinates input and output, and oversees the evaluation procedure. He does not participate directly in research activities.

The Operations Research team is headed by a Director of Research, who has been with The E. W. Scripps Company R&D concept since its inception in 1958. His knowledge of the Concern (14 years) and the Industry (31 years) plus a degree in Journalism, a degree in Advertising, and a Ph.D. in Industrial Management and Labor Economics provides both the disciplinary know-how and the industry experience to establish the interfaces required in the information system. He reports directly to the Chairman of the Division, is responsible for all research operations.

The team itself is divided into two classifications: Research Engineers, Behavioral Analysts. Within each classification are three strata, identical in level and salary ranges:

1. Engineers, Analysts;
2. Senior Engineers, Senior Analysts; and
3. Chief Engineer, Chief Analyst, one only of each.

To describe the team itself, it might be best to cite the education and experience brought to bear in its activities:

Education:
- 1 Ph.D., Industrial Management, Labor Economics
- 1 M.S., Engineering Physics
- 1 M.S., Management Engineering
- 1 M.A., Theology, Sociology
- 1 M.S., Advertising
- 3 B.S., Journalism
- 2 B.A., History
- 1 B.S., Economics
- 1 B.S., Mechanical Engineering
- 1 B.S., Industrial Engineering
- 1 B.S., Systems Analysis
- 1 B.S., Education
- 1 B.S., Physics

Experience:	
Mass Media, Mass Communications	52 Years
Industrial Engineering (Multiindustry)	28 Years
Production Engineering (Multiindustry)	11 Years
Engineering Research (Aerospace)	10 Years
Engineering Design (Jet Engines)	4 Years
Systems Engineering (Multiindustry)	4 Years
Economist (Mass Media, AEC)	4 Years
Social Work	4 Years
Mass Media Research (not included above)	8 Years

Typical areas of R&D applications are:

1. Forecasting
2. Production Scheduling
3. Inventory Control
4. Quality Control
5. Transportation
6. Communications
7. Advertising and Sales
8. Maintenance and Repairs
9. Accounting
10. Plant Location and Layout
11. Equipment
12. Packaging
13. Capital Budgeting
14. Market Analysis
15. Demographic Studies

OPERATING MODE

FIGURE 1 shows the levels at which information is generated by R&D. It is a modification of the triangular concept of a management information system. Modification has been made to emphasize the role of middle management in the overall management information system. Note that the R&D function of generating information is greatest at the bottom of the management level.

Progressing up to middle management, the amount of information generated by R&D decreases and, correspondingly, the number of management decisions increases. Note further that in the middle management area, the flow of information generated for decision making is from middle management to top management and from R&D to top management. The path of flow may be from R&D through middle management to top management, or at times the flow from middle management and R&D may be independent of each other. The flow of informa-

FIGURE NO. 1

RELATIVE FLOW OF GENERATED INFORMATION

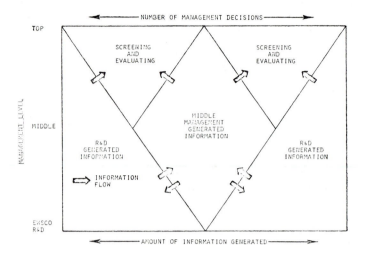

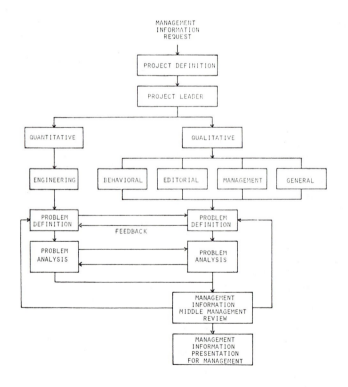

FIGURE NO. 2

MANAGEMENT INFORMATION SYSTEM AND OPERATIONS RESEARCH
PROJECT ORGANIZATION

tion between middle management and R&D is bilateral, that is, there is an exchange of information between R&D and middle management.

On levels above middle management, the flow is unilateral; that is, the flow of generated information is in one direction, toward top management. Screening and evaluation of the information occurs at these levels.

FIGURE 2 shows the management information system and Operations Research project organization as it applies to EWSCo R&D. The functioning of R&D is initiated by a request for information from top management, or possibly middle management. This request is formulated into a definition of the project and its objectives and purpose. Project requirements determine the particular project leader and Operations Research team composition.

The project leader is chosen on the basis of the information sought and the major discipline to which it applies. The team is formed under the project leader and consists of the required member or members from the qualitative and quantitative fields. The quantitative requirements are chosen from the engineering field and the qualitative from the mass media, behavioral sciences, and management fields. In addition, the team consists of at least one manager from the particular Concern Unit involved.

The problem definition, as it applies to the various disciplines concerned, is formulated through feedback between these disciplines. This guarantees that while approaches to the problem may be different for the different disciplines, the overall objectives are the same.

Once the problem definition is ascertained, each member of the team proceeds to problem analysis. The concept of parallel feedback between the various disciplines is encouraged in order that compatibility exists in the final analyses. Conflicts are resolved in transit. Synthesized analyses are presented to middle management, which either forwards to top management or requests addenda or modification.

FIGURE 3 shows the interfacing between the quantitative and qualitative analyses. Feedback, as mentioned before, is considered to be essential so that the engineering analysis is aware of the problems in the mass media, behavioral sciences, and management areas. Interfacing of the quantitative and qualitative analyses is crucial in EWSCo R&D operations, for human engineering is a major factor in the mass media.

Human engineering is defined as the consideration of the intangible human aspects of the problem and must be considered very early in the analyses so that the behavioral-engineering ground rules for individual solutions do not conflict. This process is repeated until the ground rules for analyses are found to be compatible for the various disciplines.

FIGURE 4 shows the EWSCo R&D engineering organization. Engineering is divided into four major areas: Engineering Physics, Systems, Industrial Engineering, and Marketing. Each of these divisions produces information that is basically quantitative in nature.

Engineering Physics includes mechanical and electrical engineering, systems, and mathematical analysis.

Systems includes information generated with computer hardware, computer software, or by engineering systems pertaining to flow charts, plus considerable statistics.

Industrial Engineering includes analysis pertaining to quality control, production methodology, inventory control, and some software applications. Here again, the mathematics is mostly of a statistical nature.

QUANTITATIVE - QUALITATIVE ANALYSIS INTERFACING

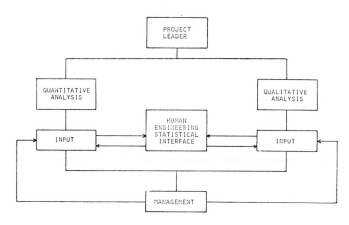

FIGURE NO. 4

ENGINEERING OR QUANTITATIVE ORGANIZATION

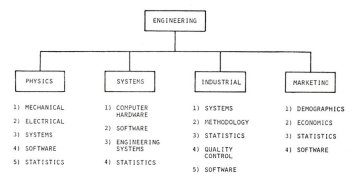

TABLE NO. 1

METHODS OF ANALYSIS COMMONLY EMPLOYED IN R&D PROJECTS

PROJECT	METHOD OF ANALYSIS
RELOCATION STUDIES	STATISTICS, PERT CHARTS, GANT CHARTS, OPTIMIZATION
POPULATION	STATISTICS
PRODUCT AND EQUIPMENT TESTING	STATISTICS
INVENTORY ANALYSIS	INVENTORY CONTROL MODELS
TRANSPORTATION ANALYSIS	TRANSPORTATION MODELS, QUEUING THEORY, STATISTICS
COMMUNICATIONS	QUEUING THEORY, STATISTICS, OPTIMIZA-TION
BEHAVIORAL	STATISTICS

Marketing includes demographic, economic studies, financial analyses and cost evaluations using computer software and statistics.

TABLE 1 shows the methods of analysis employed in R&D projects, mathematical statistics being most commonly used to project data. However, the full range of Operations Research techniques are employed, including PERT charts, GANT charts, Optimization routines, Inventory Control models, Transportation models, Queuing theory, etc. These methods of analysis produce information which fulfills the five basic requirements set forth previously. As the management information system of R&D develops, it is expected that management may demand more sophisticated methods of analysis.

APPLICATIONS OF SYSTEM

FIGURE 5 illustrates the organization and flow of a typical Operations Research project for the R&D Division. This particular project was concerned with evaluating different printing inks considered for printing newspapers. The team, in this instance, was comprised of an Industrial Engineer, an Engineering Physicist from R&D and the Production Manager, the Press Foreman, and the Business Manager of the particular newspaper on test. The Editor of the newspaper has the ultimate decision.

The Industrial Engineer was concerned with quality control; the Engineering Physicist with the power usage, operating environment of the press (such as, the temperature of the rollers), and the optical properties of the ink and paper combination.

The Production Manager evaluated the printability and appearance of the ink (whether the ink smeared, rubbed off, or penetrated the paper, and the blackness).

The Press Foreman evaluated the reaction of the press operators to the ink, considering ink misting, ink distribution control, and wash-up.

The Business Manager evaluated the ink from the standpoint of appearance and comparative costs.

FIGURE 6 shows a typical Operations Research project and its organization for investigating the feasibility of relocating a unit of The E. W. Scripps Company. Included in the technical section was an Industrial Engineer, a Communications Engineer, and an Engineer skilled in the area of economics and marketing.

The Industrial Engineer's analysis included plant layout, methodology of operations and how they would relate to a move, and the operations themselves.

The Communications Engineer was responsible for analyzing the electrical and communications requirements from the standpoint of transmitting news into and out of the facility and problems associated with keeping news flow operational at all times.

The economic and demographic studies determined what problems might exist in the new location, and analysis of population and the degree to which the market for the product would be increased in the new location. Population composition was analyzed for labor supply, etc.

In this instance, no representatives participated in the project as team members.

FIGURE 7 is an example of the proposed milestone chart for such a feasibility relocation study. The chart shows the major milestones to be met in implementing such an operation. This particular relocation study involved four phases. In addition to the major milestones, the total man-hours have been estimated. The mile-

FIGURE NO. 5

TYPICAL OPERATIONS RESEARCH PROJECT
EXAMPLE CASE NO. 1

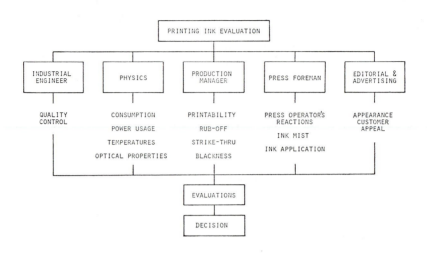

FIGURE NO. 6

TYPICAL OPERATIONS RESEARCH PROJECT
EXAMPLE CASE NO. 2

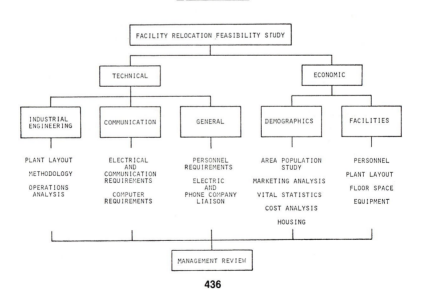

FIGURE NO. 7

PROPOSED MILESTONE CHART OF FEASIBILITY RELOCATION STUDY
EXAMPLE CASE

FUNCTION / MONTH	1 2 3 4 5 6 7 8 9 10 11 12 13 14 15 16 17 18 19 20 21 22 23	MILESTONE
PHASE I		1. Policy Definition Organization of Operation Research Team
Inventory Analysis		
Operations Anal. R&D		2. Complete Inventory Analysis
*Manhours	1250	3. Complete Operations Analysis
PHASE II		4. Go - No Go Decision
Logistics Study		5. Relocation Study Complete
Relocation		6. Scheduling Complete
*Manhours	1300	7. Final Go - No Go Decision
PHASE III		8. Parallel Operation Complete
Relocation Scheduling		
*Manhours	600	
PHASE IV		
Relocation Implementation		
*Manhours	Not Defined	
MAJOR DECISIONS Go - No Go		
MEETINGS Management - O.R. Team, etc.		
EXPENDED MANHOURS (TOTAL)	3150	
MANHOURS	500 1000 1500 2000 3000	

FIGURE NO. 8

TYPICAL PERT CHART DERIVED FROM MILESTONE CHART OF FIGURE NO. 7
EXAMPLE CASE

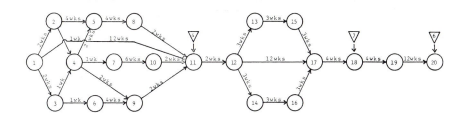

437

TABLE NO. 2

ACTIVITY DESCRIPTIONS
FOR PERT CHART (FIGURE NO. 8)

ACTIVITY	DESCRIPTION
1-2	EQUIPMENT INVENTORY AND EVALUATION (EACH DEPARTMENT)
1-3	PERSONNEL INVENTORY AND EVALUATION (EACH DEPARTMENT)
1-11	REGIONAL ANALYSIS AND PRELIMINARY DEMOGRAPHICS STUDY
2-4	DEPARTMENT LAYOUTS - EQUIPMENT
2-5	PRESENT EQUIPMENT ECONOMIC STUDY
3-4	DEPARTMENT LAYOUTS - PERSONNEL
3-6	PERSONNEL MOVE STUDY
4-5	PARALLEL OPERATIONS REQUIREMENT - EQUIPMENT
4-7	OPERATIONAL PROCEDURES STUDY (EACH DEPARTMENT)
4-9	PARALLEL OPERATIONS REQUIREMENT - PERSONNEL
5-8	NEW OR TEMPORARY EQUIPMENT REQUIREMENTS
6-9	NEW OR TEMPORARY PERSONNEL REQUIREMENTS
7-10	OPERATIONAL PROCEDURES STUDY - INTERDEPARTMENTAL
8-11	GENERALIZED OPTIMIZED LAYOUTS - EQUIPMENT
9-11	GENERALIZED OPTIMIZED LAYOUTS - PERSONNEL
10-11	GENERALIZED OPTIMIZED LAYOUTS - WORK FLOW
11-12	INITIAL EVALUATION AND RECOMMENDATIONS
12-13	POWER REQUIREMENT EVALUATION
12-14	COMMUNICATION REQUIREMENT EVALUATION
12-17	REAL ESTATE EVALUATION - HOUSING, TRANSPORTATION, DEMOGRAPHICS, COST AND PRELIMINARY RELOCATION SCHEDULING
13-15	REAL ESTATE EVALUATION - POWER
14-16	REAL ESTATE EVALUATION - COMMUNICATION
15-17	ADDITIONAL POWER CONSIDERATIONS
16-17	ADDITIONAL COMMUNICATION CONSIDERATIONS
17-18	POTENTIAL PLANT LAYOUTS
18-19	REAL ESTATE EVALUATION AND DECISION
19-20	RELOCATION SCHEDULING

stones for each stage, as well as the major milestones concerning decision points, are shown.

FIGURE 8 gives a typical PERT chart derived from the milestone chart in Figure 7. Here the major milestones have been subdivided into major activities with a time estimate between activities. Orientation is possible between the milestone chart and PERT charts, in that certain of the milestones as indicated on the GANT chart of Figure 7 are also indicated with their corresponding activity number on the PERT chart.

TABLE 2 gives the description of the various activities which appear in the PERT chart of Figure 8.

The two examples cited are typical of the type of projects investigated by EWSCo R&D. These projects have used Operations Research or Management Information System principles and organization to arrive at a solution or solutions to the problem at hand, aiding management in their decision making.

BEHAVIORAL SCIENCE APPLICATIONS

Behavioral sciences in EWSCo R&D, in addition to its interface on projects with engineering, is concerned with the social science disciplines and how research, methodology, analysis, and qualitative evaluation in these disciplines (see CHART 1) can aid in management decision making to provide improved mass media for serving a changing market. Social change is continually observed, analyzed, and evaluated.

CHART NO. 1

BEHAVIORAL DISCIPLINE COVERAGE
E. W. SCRIPPS CO., R&D DIVISION, BEHAVIORAL SECTION

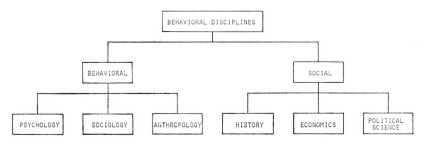

1. RESEARCH

2. METHODOLOGY

3. ANALYSIS AND EVALUATION

CHART NO. 2

AREAS FOR BEHAVIORAL RESEARCH
E. W. SCRIPPS CO., R&D DIVISION, BEHAVIORAL SECTION

MANAGEMENT CONCERNS
(JOURNALISM, EDITORIAL RESEARCH)   SOCIAL SCIENCE CATEGORIES

MEDIA CONSUMER	INDIVIDUAL/FAMILY	ORGANIZATIONS/INSTITUTIONS	SOCIETY/CULTURE
	MOTIVATION	ECONOMIC, BUSINESS	STRATIFICATION
	LEARNING	POLITICAL, CIVIC	ETHNIC RELATIONSHIPS
MEDIA ITSELF	PERCEIVING	CORRECTIONAL	TECHNOLOGY
	THINKING	MILITARY	SOCIAL DISORGANIZATION,
	PERSONAL RELATIONSHIPS	EDUCATIONAL	GEOGRAPHY, CONFLICT,
		RELIGIOUS	DEMOGRAPHY,
MEDIA MARKET	FRUSTRATION, CONFLICT, RESOLUTION	SOCIAL	CHANGE

EWSCo R&D operations in the behavioral area have been primarily concerned with its media applications, or a specific management concern within these disciplines. The structure of project assignment and reporting has been covered in the quantitative engineering discussion. Pure behavioral findings are reported in objective and evaluative statements, organized in a rational manner, and given in "white paper" form, or as statistical compilations.

Behavioral research in mass media-mass communications may be divided into one of three areas:

1. The media consumer,
2. The media itself, and
3. The media market.

This research of necessity is fundamentally the application of social science methodology to what has traditionally been termed "journalism" or "editorial" research. But within the three categories mentioned, specific social science topics do assume their unique identity (see CHART 2). Areas of investigation range from the specific (individual) to the general (cultural). Pure behavioral studies have included "Under Thirty" (attitudes of younger people toward various mass media), "Ecological Problems of Waste Newsprint and Newsprint Recycling," "Economic Support of Mass Media," and "Institutional Reform."

TYPICAL RESEARCH FINDINGS

In a joint research project between Twentieth-Century Fox Film Corporation and the Newspaper Advertising Bureau that tested the effectiveness of movie advertising in Dallas and Atlanta, newspaper advertising was found to be more effective than television commercials. In Dallas, where only newspaper advertising was used, 73 percent reported knowledge of the movie before going to see it; in Atlanta, where television was depended on for 70 percent of the budget, the response was only 54 percent.

When the Advertising Council prepared to conduct a nationwide campaign to provide the public with a better understanding of the American economic system, it hired a private research firm to test the level of information. The attitude survey indicated that only one out of seven Americans understands the system; more remarkable was the fact that only one out of every three business people in the study showed knowledgeability.

The American Newspaper Publishers Association learned in a readability study that roman typefaces are preferred over sans serif (type without end strokes). The testing also indicated that readability is improved with wider column dimensions.

In a project conducted by WomenPoll of Philadelphia, the majority of responses revealed that women are more accurately portrayed in the print media than in the electronic media. Of the total tabulation, the vote was 29 percent for magazines, 21 percent for newspapers, 17 percent for television, and 4 percent for movies; the remaining 26 percent felt that none of the mass media give an accurate portrayal.

A representative sampling of consumer attitudes taken by the American Association of Advertising Agencies favored the newspaper as the "best liked" medium and gave it highest scores on prestige and credibility among the major channels of communication, including magazines, television, radio, billboards, and direct mail.

In a published booklet compiling marketing data, the Portland, Oreg., *Oregonian* and *Oregon Journal* brought to light some remarkable comparisons between the profiles of its marketing area and those of the U.S. population at large. For example:

1. United States: males, 49 percent; females, 51 percent. Portland: males, 48 percent; females, 52 percent.
2. Ages 15-24: United States, 17 percent; Portland, 17 percent. Ages 25-44: United States, 24 percent; Portland, 24 percent. Ages 45-64: United States, 21 percent; Portland, 21 percent.
3. Labor force: U.S. males, 25 percent; Portland males, 26 percent; U.S. females, 15 percent; Portland females, 16 percent.
4. Buying power: per capita, U.S. — $4,176; per capital, Portland — $4,328; per household, U.S. — $12,621; per household, Portland — $12,154.

A Media Records dimensional study of news and advertising content of newspapers showed that, despite a decline in advertising linage over a period of one year, newspapers maintained their volume of news content. While advertising content was down by 2 percent, reading matter in the newspaper was actually up by the same percentage figure, refuting the argument that news space is controlled directly by advertising volume.

The consumer research director of a large media group found in a survey that 21 percent of all suburban males hold college degrees, against 17 percent in the cities; that 33 percent work in managerial positions as compared with 28 percent in the cities; that unemployment runs higher among city residents than among suburban dwellers; and that suburban families earn 20 percent more than their city counterparts.

Like any other precision tool, research must be used with great skill and with appropriate restraint. Properly handled, it can provide the newspaper with invaluable data for decision making, for profit control, and for enhancement of the newspaper product and its promotion.

5

Relations within the plant

25

Cooperation among departments

Efficient management and operation of all departments of a newspaper and an effective cooperation among all of them hold the key to continuing and successful operation.

Charles L. Bennett

Never to be taken for granted, close cooperation among departments is an essential factor in successful newspaper publishing. This is accomplished only when newspaper workers, naturally absorbed in the operation of their individual departments, are able to visualize and fully appreciate the complete newspaper plant performance and their direct relation to it. Routine cooperation can be improved and more precise cooperation can be developed when management supervises and plans to bring it about.

NEWS COVERAGE

Thorough local news coverage can become a reality when all newspaper departments cooperate with the news staff. The Marshall, Tex., *News Messenger* believes:

Advertising personnel run into business stories, plans for expansion, anniversaries, and the like, long before the news crew hear about them. This is because the advertising staff counsel with advertisers and are members of the team developing such newsworthy events.

Carriers are the source of a wealth of small stories. They know of accidents, the unusual slants on fires, and other events where they wiggle right into the crowd. The circulation department knows of an influx of population for one reason or another; the members of that department are the first to sense industrial layoffs; they have their hands on the pulse of the community because they contact so many persons.

The newsroom, unfortunately, does not have too many contacts with the run-of-the-mill reader. Advertising solicitors, circulation people, and the promotion department have a better opportunity to pass on to the news staff what they see and hear. Together, they produce a better product that begets more satisfied readers and advertisers. They ring the cash register more frequently.

445

Other ways in which the news department may be helped by those outside the department are:

1. All staff members can provide story tips about weddings, births, family reunions, birthday parties, and other events in their homes and their neighbors' homes.
2. Camera "bugs" on the staff can keep their eyes open for newsworthy pictures, snap them, and turn them in.
3. All staff members can report activities of organizations to which they belong.
4. Truck drivers for the circulation department who learn of highway and other accidents can report them quickly to the news department.
5. Members of all departments may have hobbies or know of friends and acquaintances with hobbies that would make interesting stories.
6. Carriers can report new home construction to the news department.

BUILDING CIRCULATION

Newspaper publishers in county seat towns know that one of the best ways to build rural circulation is to have a reporter go along with solicitors as they drive through the country selling subscriptions. The good reporter will draw at least one news item from every prospect. Whatever the subject, news items of this sort gathered along with orders for the paper are almost surefire for holding subscribers. And they represent effective cooperation between the news and circulation departments.

The circulation department of the Marquette, Mich., *Mining Journal* gets the full cooperation of other staffers, according to the circulation manager, who says:

When we were building up our circulation on rural routes and in outlying towns, the news department assisted with publicity. The circulation manager was allowed to select the neighborhood correspondents and chose persons who, in addition to writing the news, would sell subscriptions and oversee delivery in their respective areas. Now that the routes are established, there isn't a great deal of cooperation that we need, but we always work with the news, advertising, and mechanical departments. By working smoothly with each other, we seem to hold our own and keep increasing our circulation. The mechanical department helps indirectly by almost always managing to get the paper out on time or even before the deadline, which gives our four trucks, over 100 carriers, and a couple of dozen dealers a break. This keeps customers satisfied and makes our job easier.

The circulation manager of the La Crosse, Wis., *Tribune* received effective cooperation from the news department one summer in getting the paper into new territory. Aerial views of towns in the suburban trade area were published. The pictures were taken before the leaves were on the trees; and all places of interest—famous landmarks, post offices, schools, churches, weekly newspaper offices, factories—were properly identified.

One week before the pictures appeared, doorknob hangers describing the coming feature were distributed to nonreader homes, announcing a "one week free" offer with a six-week order.

In competing with evening television, it is more important than ever to deliver the afternoon newspaper as early as possible. For that reason, the mechanical department is expected to maintain prompt press time; but this can only be done through cooperation between all departments. Active sales promotion also helps meet competition. The advertising department can prepare advertisements and circulars, and the news department can provide front-page publicity when the other departments merit stories.

All staff members can be of real help to the circulation department:

1. Employes can report newcomers in their neighborhoods, so that they may be called upon by carriers or salespeople.
2. The news department can advise the circulation manager whenever a story is to appear that will create a demand for extra copies.
3. The society editor or woman's page editor can let the circulation department know when pictures of weddings and social events are to appear.
4. The news department may cooperate with the circulation department in developing a news section featuring a definite community in which a circulation campaign is to be conducted.
5. The news department can prepare human interest stories about carriers.
6. The advertising department can prepare copy and provide space for promoting street sales and subscriptions.

ADVERTISING DEPARTMENT

All staff members have many opportunities to assist the advertising department. While covering news beats, reporters can pick up advertising copy in stores they visit and at the same time be on the lookout for newsmaking results from classified ads; circulation department employes can deliver checking or advertising copies to merchants while delivering to regular subscribers in the business district; and the compositor can afford the time to give a special touch to an ad to satisfy an important customer.

The news department of the Findlay, Ohio, *Courier* worked with the advertising department in producing a "City and Country" column of ads and local personal items. Carried on the amusement page, it provided a convenient position for last-minute announcements of merchants. Advertisers who brought in display copy too late for the next day's issue were pleased to have the ad in this column, which contained one news item to every three advertisements. The column accommodated about 500 column inches of advertising each month at a higher rate than that for regular display.

Other departments may help the advertising department in these important ways:

1. The circulation and news departments, which often receive the first news about prospective business developments, can tip off the advertising department to opportunities for extensive advertising.
2. The editorial department can run occasional editorials discussing advertising as an economic influence in the community.
3. The news department can inform the advertising department about the historical background of local firms and when anniversaries occur.
4. The news department can cooperate with the advertising department in promoting special sales days and other business promotion events.
5. Staff photographers can take pictures for the advertising department.
6. The news "morgue" can provide suitable illustrations for institutional advertising.

PROMOTION DEPARTMENT

The promotion department works more closely with all departments than any other. The Minneapolis, Minn., *Star* and *Tribune* calls its promotion department a "service unit, devoting the major share of its time to helping the circulation department increase circulation and the advertising department increase its linage."

The promotion department is operated in a manner similar to the advertising department of a manufacturing firm in some other field. The only reason it is not called the advertising department is that the newspapers already have three advertising departments doing business. In practice, the promotion department functions much the same as an advertising agency would. Its "clients" include the advertising, circulation, and editorial departments, plus the performance of occasional chores for personnel, production, and accounting. At some time during the course of a year, it performs some service for almost every department in the building. This ranges from staging a full-scale sales meeting for the circulation department to painting a small sign for the maintenance department.

EXAMPLE OF DEPARTMENT COOPERATION

How departmental cooperation may be developed in a newspaper organization is well illustrated in an attractive booklet published by the Milwaukee, Wis., *Journal.* Entitled *A Week in the Life of a Metropolitan Newspaper,* it contained articles by the publisher, editor, business manager, and chief editorial writer and by the managing editor, who said:

Putting together a metropolitan daily is a complicated manufacturing process. We get out a new product every day, the equivalent of a large, full-length novel. The timing of each phase of this tremendous undertaking must be as nearly perfect as we can make it. Minutes count. The team must click as a unit every hour of the day and every day of the year. This calls for careful planning, direction, and control, so that a constant flow of production is maintained.

"There certainly is no newspaper in the United States whose editorial department enjoys more pleasant relations with the business office," the *Journal's* chief editorial writer says. "We have great admiration for all other departments of our common institution, and I believe they have some respect for us, even if they sometimes think we are off the beam."

The *Journal's* business manager paid tribute to the departments of the newspaper by saying that four things of greatest importance to an ad solicitor are:

1. The operating efficiencies that keep costs and advertising rates low.
2. A product so printed as to be admired, not criticized.
3. A circulation operation that permits selling complete coverage of the newspaper.
4. An editorial product that has earned the advertiser's respect and admiration.

The publisher threw further light on the newspaper's teamwork by explaining the employe ownership plan:

Teamwork has been an important factor in the *Journal's* progress. However, teamwork is not a mere happenstance. It is due primarily to the fact that the men and women who make the *Journal* have been partners in its ownership since 1937. There is motivation beyond mere wages to do the job. There is a unity of effort, which has broken down usual interdepartmental jealousies and barriers.

The policy of a newspaper is compounded from the experience, the knowledge, and the character of the men and women who are its staff — not only its staff today but those whose lives went into the making of the paper over the yesteryears. There is something about a newspaper in the way it handles the news, in the way it comments on events, in the way it solicits and prints its advertising, and in the way it conducts its circulation department that gives it distinctive character.

TEAMWORK AMONG DEPARTMENT HEADS

Newspaper departments are so closely related that teamwork among department heads is vital to successful publishing. The Texas Circulation Managers Association points out the importance of a smooth and pleasant working relationship between the managing editor and the circulation manager:

When such teamwork is lacking, it is possible that the circulation manager has not made much effort to cooperate with the managing editor, or vice versa. When the managing editor is not circulation conscious, a smart circulation manager should create interest by discussing circulation problems, seeking assistance, asking advice, and getting suggestions. Few things are more contagiously interesting than growing circulation figures. Like the circulation manager, the managing editor cannot resist being interested when comprehending the large part that position plays in circulation growth. A truly cooperative editor goes out of his way to do things that help obtain additional subscribers.[1]

When department heads come to a common understanding of a problem that involves all departments, they usually arrive at a solution. The Wausau, Wis., *Herald* wanted in some way to increase linage for Saturday, an otherwise lean advertising day. The news and advertising departments put their heads together and developed "The Camera's Eye," a Saturday tabloid section of pictorial news and advertising. Two or three pages were devoted to well-illustrated local stories. Advertising was sold at a rate higher than that obtainable under contract and the newspaper's sales staff were paid an extra commission on advertising sold for this section. Both advertisers and readers liked the section, which was distributed to all regular subscribers and to an additional 1,136 homes in a suburban area.

The Royal Oak, Mich., *Tribune*—with the news, circulation, and advertising departments cooperating—put on a promotion campaign through its own columns in which the following information was presented throughout the year:

1. How the newspaper gathers the news bit by bit from its territory; assembles it; adds national and world news, features, and local advertising; and presents the entire package to its readers for only a few cents a day.
2. How the busy homemaker can make housekeeping easier, through shopping the advertisements and reading the household hints.
3. Why a newspaper is important to a schoolteacher who must keep abreast of daily news developments while directing the citizens of tomorrow.
4. How the *Tribune* can be enjoyed by all the family by reason of its diversified news, its advertising, and its 51 outstanding columns and features.
5. How the average *Tribune* reader in the course of a year receives enough local news in the paper to fill 83 books and enough national and world news to fill 55 books.
6. Why there is no substitute for newspaper news when it comes to conveying important facts quickly and in detail.

The advertising director of the Richmond, Va., *Times-Dispatch* and *News Leader* explains how department heads cooperate in the Richmond newspaper plant:

---

1. *Newspaper Circulation*, The Steck Co., Austin, Tex., p. 53.

The news department of our papers provides the product the circulation department sells. If it is a good product, and we think ours is, the circulation department's job is simplified and more copies can be sold.

The circulation department sells the papers in areas adjacent to our market where the effectiveness of our newspapers can best be translated into sales for our retail, national, and classified advertisers.

Our promotion department produces speculative layouts and copy for individual advertisements and long-term campaigns, and thus is an important cog in the selling machinery of the advertising department. Another function of the promotion department is the production of our own promotion advertisements for our department as well as for the news and circulation departments.

The mechanical departments make our jobs easy or difficult in direct ratio to the quality of their work in setting and printing both news and advertising.

AVOIDING TROUBLE

"Caring is the drawstring holding a newspaper together," one panelist said at a newspaper workshop session on professionalism. Management, more than at any time in the past, is compelled to develop a conscious concern for the involvement of as many departments and as many individuals as possible in the newspaper's total program. Little "islands" of neglected interests tend to grow into problem areas for any organization, and wise management can take the initiative to prevent any such "identity crisis" buildups inside the plant. If more than 1,000 employes are engaged in the operation, each should feel a kinship to others and all should feel closely identified with the newspaper's reputation, goals, and achievements.

Richard Estrin, an editor of the Long Island, N.Y., *Newsday*, has summed it up this way: "One proposition and one only—that as journalists we are not men; we are not women; we are not white; we are not black. What we wield is at best a very, very imperfect instrument and if we use it in behalf of any cause, any side—for good against evil, for righteousness against wrong, we're making a dreadful mistake. . . . We go out and try to find out what is happening, what is as close to truth as we can get. We come back; we try to tell it so people who want to read it, in descending order of importance, perhaps will understand what we are saying."

If the working personnel in all departments can be infused with a sense of dedication to this overriding privilege and responsibility of keeping the public informed within the framework of a free society, then cooperation among the various internal functions of the newspaper will be assured. To provide the inspiration for that kind of solidarity is one of the primary challenges of management.

Proper security is an increasingly important consideration. Where possibilities for unauthorized visitors, drinking or gambling, solicitation by street vendors or individual fund raisers, loansharking, or threats to personal safety are eliminated, interdepartmental cooperation can be unimpeded. Newspapers located in the downtown areas of large cities generally depend on the services of professional security forces for patrolling, escorting employes to parking areas at night, crowd control during tours of the plant, guarding money transfers, supervising access to the building itself or to restricted areas within the plant, and searching out potential hazards to either visitors or employes.

With management leading the way and eliminating as many chances as possible for problems to develop, each department can be expected to function in harmony with all the others.

26

How to stimulate employe interest

Publishers should avoid parking in the front lot. . . . Walk to your office through the back shop. You can pick up some useful information.

Thomas D. Jones

Few of management's tasks are as exciting and as rewarding as stimulating employes' loyalty to the newspaper and heightening interest in the specific work to which they are assigned. In some respects this interest is not as difficult to develop and maintain in a newspaper as in many other business or professional organizations. Although newspaper work is more or less routine, there is enough creativeness about it to command interest and devotion from those who engage in it. The fascination of printer's ink is legendary.

Management may develop devotion and stability within a newspaper organization by carefully selecting employes, acquainting them with the newspaper's policies, training them in general routines, looking to their special needs, and helping them to help themselves.

SELECTING EMPLOYES WITH CARE

The process of recruiting good employes begins with the first interview. Management realizes there are great differences in employes: some will adapt themselves readily to new conditions and instantly assume responsibilities with enthusiasm; others will approach a new position with prejudice and doubt and consume costly time in arriving at a satisfactory attitude for work. Some persons are never able to become stable employes. Because selecting the right person for the job means greater and better production, less overtime, less personnel turnover, and fewer complaints, many newspapers have established personnel departments.

Hiring people on the basis of how they look, talk, and act is not practical at a time when salaries and wages are high and efficient help is so essential. A better way is to investigate thoroughly before hiring; find out about the person's habits, efficiency in previous positions, ability to get along with people, ambition, and zeal.

The personnel director of the Winston-Salem, N.C., *Journal* and *Sentinel* says these four simple steps give all the needed information about an applicant:

1. Have the applicant fill out a form, which in addition to the name, age, and family background will provide rather complete information on education and performance in other jobs. This step shows whether the applicant is worthy of further consideration.
2. If so, check by telephone with persons who have observed the prospective employe either in school or on previous jobs. Questions should be specific and aimed at getting a true picture of the person's past. Information that could never be obtained by correspondence may be learned by telephone.
3. Personal interview with the applicant. (There is a thorough interview designed by Robert E. McMurray & Company of Chicago. It provides answers to the questions raised by the application blank and the telephone checks and requires about 45 minutes. The executive news editor calls it "the vacuum cleaner.")
4. A complete physical examination by a doctor who knows something about industrial medicine. The examination should include a chest X ray and a blood test where indicated.

There is a fifth step that may be taken in some cases — a series of intelligence, aptitude, and performance tests. These tests have been helpful in selecting typists, compositors, apprentice printers, and press operators; but they have not been used on applicants for other jobs.

Not all publishers will want to select employes with such thoroughness, but how careful they are largely will determine the amount of employment turnover in their offices and plants.

ACQUAINTING STAFF MEMBERS WITH POLICIES

When a person takes a position with any of the large city newspapers, he or she usually is given an information manual (Fig. 26.1). It might contain a historical sketch of the newspaper and an outline of each department's work, the newspaper's policies, and some of its accomplishments. To publish anything so elaborate and expensive may appear impractical to a small newspaper publisher, but some means of acquainting staff members with the policies and history of the newspaper should be provided.

Every new employe of the Portland, Oreg., *Oregon Journal* is given an illustrated handbook entitled *I'm with the Journal* (Fig. 26.2). In it are a brief historical sketch of the *Journal;* some of the highlights of the *Journal's* progress; and the newspaper's labor and special-benefits policies, such as a fair wage, steady position, yearly vacation, old age benefits, medical and surgical care, group insurance, advancement opportunity,

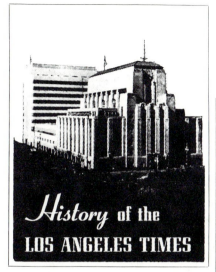

Fig. 26.1. The Los Angeles, Calif., *Times* acquaints employes with the history of the newspaper.

Fig. 26.2. The handbook for employes of the Portland, Oreg., *Oregon Journal* reveals personal interest.

and pleasant personnel relations. The first page of the handbook contains this message from the publisher of the *Journal:*

There is no other business like that of a newspaper. Every day we must manufacture a new product. Today's paper resembles yesterday's only in form and dress; in content it is entirely different. To accomplish this requires close coopera-tion and good teamwork on the part of all departments.

It makes no difference in what department of the *Journal* you may be employed—that department is vital to our operation, and your work is important to that department.

You can take pride in the fact that you work for the *Oregon Journal,* because it is a great newspaper and is known nationally for the many public services it per-forms. Here at home the *Journal* is liked and respected, so much that today it en-joys the largest circulation in its history.

This booklet has been prepared to acquaint you with the advantages, opportunities and responsibilities that go along with your employment here. I know that by reading it you will catch some of the organization spirit that has done so much to build the *Journal* to the position of esteem and leadership it holds today.

In a similar booklet that features a front-page picture of the company's spacious office building, the Oklahoma Publishing Company, which publishes the *Daily Oklahoman* and Oklahoma City, Okla., *Times*, introduces new staff members to the newspaper's history and policies (Fig. 26.3). The president of the company extends a cordial and practical greeting:

The Oklahoma Publishing Company welcomes you to its ranks and wishes you happiness and success in your work. With most of us, our association with the company is a career rather than a job. We have learned that our town progress depends to a very large extent upon that of the organization of which we are a part.

Thus, there are no unimportant jobs in the company. Only by efficient coordination and friendly cooperation can all the complex operations of our organization be joined to achieve the standards of public service that we have made our goal. . . .

Since you are one of us, we know you will take pride in what we have already achieved, and will play a willing part in meeting tomorrow's responsibilities.

Guiding principles, attractively and forcefully portrayed to employes, promote prompt adjustment and efficiency. The creed of the Knight Newspapers is given in the following concise statement by John S. Knight:

The Knight Newspapers strive to meet the highest standards of journalism. We try to keep our news columns factual and unbiased, reserving our personal

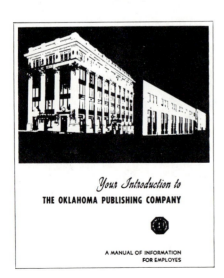

Fig. 26.3. Cover page of the Manual of Information for employes of the Oklahoma Publishing Company.

opinions for the editorial page, where they belong. It is true that we make mistakes. So does every other newspaper that isn't afraid of its own shadow. When our facts are shown to be faulty, we make amends cheerfully and resolve to do better next time. But our newspapers . . . have never been run by the Board of Commerce, the Retail Merchants Association, the manufacturers, the banks or the labor unions. We do not operate them in the interests of any class, group, faction or political party. As my late father said so appropriately many years ago: "We are ourselves free, and our paper shall be free — free as the Constitution we enjoy — free as the truth, good manners and good sense." We shall be for whatever measure is best adapted to defending the rights and liberties of the people and advancing useful knowledge. We shall labor at all times to inspire the people with a just and proper sense of their own condition, to point out to them their true interest and rouse them to pursue it.

Whenever a person joins the staff of the Washington, D.C., *Post,* the newspaper's guiding principles, are presented:

1. The first mission of a newspaper is to tell the truth as nearly as the truth may be ascertained.
2. This newspaper shall tell ALL the truth so far as it can learn it, concerning the important affairs of America and the world.
3. As a disseminator of news, the newspaper shall observe the decencies that are obligatory upon a private gentleman.
4. What it prints shall be fit reading for the young as well as the old.
5. The newspaper's duty is to readers and to the public at large, and not to the private interests of its owners.
6. In the pursuit of truth, the newspaper shall be prepared to sacrifice its material fortunes, if such course be necessary for the public good.
7. The newspaper shall not be the ally of any special interest, but shall be fair and free and wholesome in its outlook on public affairs and public individuals.

While these principles are primarily for editorial guidance, they have a great effect on employe attitudes. A sense of pride and loyalty impels those connected with a newspaper whose policies are so clearly and definitely stated.

TRAINING EMPLOYES

All new employes for a period of time at least, are limited in performance. They first must become familiar with the customs and policies of the paper. Journalism graduates find there is still much to be learned when they take newspaper positions. Training in the classroom and laboratory is helpful, to be sure, but they also have to learn and support the aims and policies of the newspaper.

The Gainesville, Ga., *Times* has instituted a four-part orientation program for new members of its news staff. The editor describes it as consisting of two parts "actual training" and two parts "needling."

The first step is to acquaint the new staff members with the composing room. During their first week, they are permitted to spend the afternoon nosing around the shop, checking on their own work, and finding out what happened after it left the newsdesk. The editor believes that just the sound of the composing room and the confusion of its fast-moving accomplishments impress beginners with the importance of doing their part to prevent difficulties. News staff also learn to appreciate the need for such elementary routine as clean copy, well-read and well-checked copy, and layout placement.

The second step is to stress reporting facility — to show new reporters how to ask questions to obtain complete information and how to dig into background material. Over a period of time the new staffers are required to analyze a score or more topflight stories gleaned from the *Times* and other papers. They divide a sheet of paper into three columns. In the first are listed the bare facts of the story; in the second the beginner enters the questions the reporter must have asked to get the information; in the third, the background knowledge the writer needed to ask particular questions. The purpose is to demonstrate, among other things, the necessity of going on an assignment prepared and loaded with pertinent information.

The third step is to confront the new reporters with their own errors. The proofreader sends the marked galleys to the editorial office, where reporters are called in to face their own mistakes. This not only tends to increase desk accuracy but also puts pressure on reporters to copyread more carefully.

The final step is to require attendance at staff meetings, where policy, style, and general understanding of the paper and its place in the community are discussed. A reading list of the more practical textbooks and professional publications also is given the new reporters and they are urged to do a certain amount of outside reading to become thoroughly acquainted with demands of the profession.

Some publishers have found efficiency is improved by having the superintendents of their mechanical departments tied in closely with top management, where they may discuss human problems as well as production problems. A new superintendent at the plant of the Dayton, Ohio, *Daily News* is carefully acquainted with practices common to the mechanical department. This is done with full respect for the new employe's authority and responsibility. Knowing what the job is and how management wants it done saves times and money and makes the new employe efficient.

The St. Petersburg, Fla., *Times* launched an innovative program to develop latent talent in its employes. This is designated "The *Times* College of Newspaper Knowledge." It is designed to acquaint potential candidates for executive positions with the overall operation of the *Times* and to ground them in the rudiments of modern management. The need for such training became apparent when in a period of ten years eight of the ten top management positions had to be filled from the outside.

A class of trainees is formed on the basis of a candidate selection system outlined by the general manager and a consulting psychologist. During 26 weeks of on-the-job training, candidates spend three days of every two weeks in the newspaper's 18 different departments, seeing and doing what needs to be done. As a supplement to the on-the-job training, each trainee participates in a two-hour seminar each Wednesday night. Topics discussed include the psychological basis of the supervisor's job, basic accounting principles, advertising fundamentals, good executive qualities, mechanics of newspaper production, methods of increasing classified advertising volume, preparation of result-producing ad copy, newspaper history, and terminology.

Free "textbooks" for the course are furnished to each student in the form of subscriptions to *Dun's Review and Modern Industry, Editor & Publisher, Printing Equipment Engineer,* and the Sunday issue of a metropolitan newspaper. An examination is given at "midterm" and another when the course is completed.

The conversion to electronic data processing in nearly all departments of the newspaper (see Chapter 6) has necessitated rather intensive *retraining* programs for a majority of the employes. When the Baltimore, Md., *Sun* installed 76 video display terminals in its newsroom, this meant that almost 300 regular staff members in the news and editorial departments had to be taught how to use the technology. The *Sun* arranged for formal classes of instruction to be set up, using 20 of the terminals for that purpose and rotating personnel from each desk until all had mastered the concepts and procedures involved in the changeover from traditional copy preparation methods.

The *Sun* management found that the training accomplished far more than simply teaching the techniques of equipment usage; it proved essential in overcoming fears and suspicions about the "new system" and in developing an enthusiasm for the tremendous advantages of speed, flexibility, and cleanliness offered by electronic journalism. After the completion of the training sessions, adjustment to actual "on-line production" was a simple matter.

LOOKING TO EMPLOYE NEEDS

Special attention to the physical, moral, and social needs of employes is accomplished through two types of service: that which considers the welfare of the employe during working hours and that which brings him into pleasant contact with his associates.

All those connected with the Des Moines, Iowa, *Register* and *Tribune* spend many enjoyable hours at events planned and arranged by an activities club, composed of departmental representatives elected each year. At the club's annual meeting each member is asked to recommend new events for the following year and to offer suggestions for making regularly scheduled events more enjoyable. After the suggestions have been analyzed and a program is agreed upon by the club's directors, committees are appointed for all events on the year's schedule.

Major annual events are a Christmas party and a summer picnic attended by 1,500 to 2,000 people. Other club functions have included dances, card parties, roller-skating, basketball, camera club, golf tournaments, swimming party, skeet-trap shoot, home talent entertainment, and office forums. A special affair that has been well attended is the "nightside" party for those who work hours that keep them from many other events. The club also maintains a recreation room for Ping-Pong and cards, with tables, a soft drink machine, and easy chairs.

The Minneapolis, Minn., *Star* and *Tribune* has developed a program to make employes feel they are an important part of the organization and have a responsibility toward their associates. The program includes:

1. An employe newspaper with 30 staff correspondents.
2. Dinners for employe committees and luncheons for the union stewards.
3. A "Good Neighbor" campaign with one payroll deduction for all charities.
4. Weekly newsgrams from the company posted on 36 bulletin boards.
5. Fourteen suggestion boxes, conveniently located
6. A special committee to direct the cafeteria.
7. Safety and civil defense committees.
8. Free subscriptions for hospitalized employes.
9. Hospitalization and insurance plans.
10. Twenty-year employes club.
11. A girls' club.
12. A men's athletic club.
13. A social counselor.
14. A medical department.
15. Movies during lunch hour.
16. A "Know Your Newspaper" program.
17. Military leave pay for two weeks.
18. Advice on housing.

Employes of suburban newspapers published in the Pittsburgh, Pa., area by Dardanell Enterprises are treated to a variety of morale-building treats. They were recruited to taste-test the company's own brand of cola used in an advertising promotion campaign; they were presented with gift cigaret lighters of a disposable nature; and women employes are regularly remembered with flowers and candy on Mother's Day and Valentine's Day. A similar publishing firm in Morton, Ill., encloses "thank-you" notes with the employes' federal withholding statements at the close of each year, features Christmas parties, stages bowling play-offs, and maintains a company garden on property behind the plant in which employes are invited to share.

On an increasing number of newspapers where handicapped persons are being employed, special provisions are being made for wheelchair access to parking lots and entrances, and visual communication devices are enhancing the productivity of skilled deaf workers. By meeting the needs of its employes, the newspaper is stimulating loyalty and improving in-plant relations.

HELPING EMPLOYES TO HELP THEMSELVES

So that employes may share in providing benefits for themselves and their associates, management can develop cooperative plans for help in home planning or for providing health insurance, retirement pensions, and profit sharing. The Stauffer Publications, which own and operate several successful midwestern newspapers, share the cost of group hospital insurance with employes. The plan consists of hospital expense insurance, surgical reimbursement, and medical expense benefits for all employes and their dependents. As underwritten by the insurance company, the plan offers each employe an opportunity to participate without medical examination. The Stauffer Publications also share the cost of life and accident insurance with employes.

Other newspapers have similar arrangements with a variety of popular plans such as the Blue Cross Hospital Service and the Blue Shield Surgical Service. In some cases the newspaper pays half the cost. In other cases, the employes pay all, usually on a monthly basis.

Employes of the Memphis, Tenn., *Commercial Appeal* and *Press-Scimitar* have the privilege of participating in a retirement income plan. Under an agreement between the employing company and members of the Newspaper Guild of Memphis, a joint pension committee was established to administer the plan. The employer pays all the costs of the benefits under the plan and all employes are eligible to participate. In the beginning the company paid the sum of $5.25 per week per employe, but this has since been increased considerably. The amount paid to each employe upon retirement at age 65 depends upon the number of years of credited service up to a maximum of 35 years. Disability and death benefits also are provided.

Employes of the five newspapers owned by the Ottawa, Kans., *Herald* and the Hutchinson, Kans., *News* are permitted to become part owners of the newspaper properties by investing a portion of their profit-sharing trust funds in corporation stock.

Some newspapers establish trusts, setting aside a substantial part of each employe's earnings every year, based on a formula approved by the Internal Revenue Service. After providing for a nominal interest on investment, the companies each year pay into the trusts about 25 percent of profits before income tax. Each employe, after reaching 21 and having six months' employment, becomes a participant in the trust. Annual contributions to the trust, plus earnings on funds accumulated in previous years, are divided among the individual accounts of participants. The share that goes to each employe is based half on earnings, half on years of service with the paper.

The employe has the option of withdrawing in cash a portion of the credited profits each year or of having it invested. The remainder accumulates, and can be counted on as supplemental social security. Benefits are available on death, permanent disability, or retirement at 65 (59 for women) in the form of monthly pensions paid over a period of ten years. Each trust is managed by a five-member board of trustees that includes three employes, with at least one from the mechanical department.

The employes are not permitted to invest their shares of the trust in newspaper stock. The trust itself, however, invests under a formula that permits it to have as much as 50 percent of its assets in newspaper stock, up to a maximum representing 25 percent ownership in the paper.

Each participating employe forfeits all money in the individual trust account if he or she leaves the newspaper before five years. At five years, the employe has 50 percent invested interest in this account. It increases 5 percent annually until with 15 years' service it reaches 100 percent.

Howard C. Meadors, senior associate of Edwin Fields Hewitt and Associates, retirement plan consultants, has outlined an 11-step procedure for establishing a corporate pension plan — a procedure that is relatively simple provided management can clarify its reasons for wanting to install the program and can decide definitely what the plan is to accomplish. Here are the steps:

1. Determine the objectives. In many cases, employers have retired a number of older employes without establishing a definite retirement formula. Employers with fewer than 20 employes drawing retirement benefits up to $50 a week should not be surprised to find that they may have incurred retirement liabilities of more than $200,000 as a result of their seemingly modest plan. The primary purpose for developing a formal plan in such a case, therefore, may be to devise a system that will permit an employer to control retirement obligations.

2. Determine the desired type of plan and the desired type of benefit. Retirement plans can be divided roughly into two groups: the fixed benefit (pension) plan and the fixed contribution (profit-sharing or money purchase) retirement plan. If the decision is in favor of a fixed benefit, it is then necessary to decide the type. For example, should it be a flat sum, should it be based on service, should it be based on compensation, or should it be based on a combination of service and compensation?

3. Assemble personnel data. The basic data required for each employe include name or code number, sex, age, service to date, compensation, and classification (active, part-time, layoff, and so forth).

4. Develop the specifications for the plan. This involves determining who will be covered, what they will get, when it will become available to

them, and how the benefit will be provided (will employes contribute or not?). In many cases, employers may wish to fund the plan, which simply means setting aside a reserve to meet future benefit payments. If a funded plan meets Treasury Department requirements, the employer is allowed to take a tax deduction on sums transferred to the reserve.

5. Determine the reaction of key employes. The importance of employe acceptance cannot be overrated. The most liberal retirement plan may fail without employe acceptance.

6. Determine the method of financing. Assuming that a company decides on a funded plan, the question of who will watch the fund is an important one. Adequate consideration should be given to the alternative methods of financing a plan—insurance versus trust.

7. Obtain the approval of stockholders. A plan should be approved by directors or stockholders, or both.

8. Prepare the legal documents. Complicated as the legal instruments may seem, they are simply basic management decisions couched in legal terms.

9. Obtain Treasury Department approval, if required. To obtain Treasury approval of a funded plan, it is necessary to assemble for the local District Director of Internal Revenue copies of the legal documents, a synopsis or summary of the plan, a schedule of compensation, a schedule of coverage, a statement of receipts and disbursements, an actuarial report, a copy of the directors' resolution adopting the plan, a power of attorney (if a third party is to represent the company), and a statement relative to fees.

10. Establish a permanent communications program for explaining the plan to employes. A continuing employe information program may involve individual interviews, group meetings, supervisory manuals, booklets, letters from executives, company publications, posters, and displays.

11. Develop administrative procedures. This step may involve establishing a definite, practical method for determining birth dates of employes, defining length of service, devising a step-by-step procedure for actually retiring employes, and the development of a method for assembling information needed in preparing annual corporate tax schedules.

The loyalty of newspaper employes is heightened when management provides means whereby they may help themselves to pleasant surroundings, better living, and greater security.

27

Management's relation to labor

Easy relationships among its people, respect and affection, understanding, and shared dedication, are the most important qualities of a good newspaper.

Tom Wicker

As has been emphasized in earlier chapters, the change from letterpress to offset printing by so many newspapers; the increased use of color printing in the news columns and in advertising; the introduction of computers and other electronic devices used to develop economy, speed, and accuracy in producing newspapers—all these and other matters affect the relationship between management and labor. Any differences of attitude that may exist must be reconciled if newspaper publishing is to remain a profitable business and a rewarding source of employment.

For example, a contract agreed upon by the Minneapolis, Minn., *Star* and *Tribune* and the Typographical Union's local in that city, assures the publishing company full and complete authority to make decisions regarding the utilization of new technology in any department of the newspaper. Such a clause was recognized as essential to the healthy operation of any publication during a time when processes and equipment are undergoing such rapid changes. Similarly, an agreement between the Tallahassee, Fla., *Democrat* and the union protected the workers' requirement that scanner-ready copy be handled in the composing room with all coding and corrections the responsibility of the news, advertising, or other originating departments. Such jurisdictional understandings are important to all involved.

Newspaper employes generally understand that the success of the institution upon which they depend for family livelihood and future security is in turn dependent upon the degree of their loyalty and cooperation. Neither is it hard to understand the efficiency required of them.

Lee Hills, editor of the Miami, Fla., *Herald,* emphasized the feelings of publishers when he said:

For a newspaper or any other enterprise to be healthy, it is vital to recognize and maintain the responsibility of management to manage the business—to hire, promote, discharge, or discipline for cause, and to maintain the efficiency of employes at agreed-to standards of competence. Management must have the right to change and improve the processes and to determine the schedules and methods of production.

With high labor costs management naturally focuses its attention upon production, realizing that it must convince employes of the importance of conscientious and honest production as a factor in their own welfare as well as in the very existence of newspapers. Year after year, newspaper revenues have increased, but the net profits have dropped because costs have increased disproportionately. A sobering result of this is a substantial reduction in the number of daily newspapers in this country and along with it a reduction in employment possibilities for newspaper workers.

William A. Dyer, Jr., general manger of the Indianapolis, Ind., *Star* and *News,* explained to those attending an annual Great Lakes Mechanical Conference in Indianapolis how improved machinery works to the advantage of those employed in newspaper shops as well as to management.

"More machines are needed in our industry," Dyer said. "They should be welcomed by publishers and unions alike, for it is possible to pay more when machines do more of the work and do it better. The typesetting machine proved that back in the nineteenth century."

Mr. Dyer pointed out that an improved stuffing machine was installed by his papers after a pledge of cooperation was obtained from the mailers' union. "It has paid off in increased production and it has increased the value to us of the journeymen mailers," he declared. "We hope there will be more machines like that available."

An enlightened point of view expressed by the press operators union appeared in an editorial in *American Pressman:*

> Our union must not only keep abreast of new machines, supplies, methods, processes and materials, but it must contribute its full measure to the development and advancement of these things. If we are to retain the respect of management — and the respect of our own members — then we must supply management with skilled workers, willing to accept things which are new; and willing to learn to produce printing by any process, by any method, on any type machine, using any type of material, with any type of supplies, regardless of how new or how far they depart from those things previously used. . . . In this day of astounding research, dynamic development and mass production, there is no such thing as standing still without moving backward. Therefore, let us not anchor ourselves in our thinking or our actions.

WHAT MANAGEMENT WANTS

In this day of rapid and costly production, management feels that it must have:

1. An adequate skilled work force to fill production ranks.
2. Efficient service and loyalty from employes.

3. The acceptance by labor of any modern mechanical equipment that will in any way increase or improve production.
4. An agreement with employes to settle by arbitration any differences that may arise between them and management.
5. A full week of five work shifts before consideration of time-and-a-half pay for employes who work additional hours.

The newspaper publisher wants above all to avoid any dissatisfaction that ultimately might result in an employe walkout. Strikes temporarily upset the newspaper's service program and inflict wounds that do not heal easily. Unfortunately, some strikes have inflicted extreme hardships on both management and labor, as well as on the trade area, where the loss of retail advertising has cost merchants in excess of $50 million dollars through declining sales. Management has at times been forced to provide special training to key executives in the operation of phototypesetting machines, presses, and complex mailroom equipment to continue publication without interruption. Workers and their families inevitably suffer during prolonged walkouts.

In union newspaper shops, employment is covered by contracts running for one or more years, stipulating the hours and conditions of employment and the wage scale. Such a contract may be between the individual newspaper and the individual union, or it may be made jointly by all the publishers and printers in a given city and the different unions involved.

Upon the termination of a contract, it is customary to negotiate for a renewal with such modification of the terms as conditions may warrant. In many cases, the unions present arguments for an increase in wage scales. Some of these increases are granted by publishers, some are approved in part, and some are denied. A denial may be followed by a strike or a walkout.

Controversies between newspaper management and organized labor have been of two main classes: those regarding an application of the Wage and Hour Law and those pertaining to decisions of the National Labor Relations Board. Labor laws are difficult to understand, and there are easy grounds for honest differences of opinion between management and labor. Management, therefore, should know the provisions of all labor laws and the customary procedures and practices of the Labor Relations Board.

Some provisions of the Wage and Hour Law and some decisions of the National Labor Relations Board have been disconcerting and confusing, like a recent ruling that the Madison, Wis., *Capital-Times* should be required to bargain the newspaper's ethical standards in contract negotiations with the American Newspaper Guild union. Labor is determined in its demands. Management, on the other hand, is adamant in protecting the financial structure of its newspaper.

Most of the union difficulties in the printing trades field have been with large city newspapers. However, some small newspapers in metropolitan areas have had trouble because unions tried to bring them under work regulations and wage scales laid down for the larger newspapers published in the same area.

EFFECTIVENESS OF ARBITRATION

Over a long period the American Newspaper Publishers Association has given valuable assistance to newspapers in solving their labor problems. It embarked upon the formulation of a comprehensive labor policy back in 1899. Through it daily newspaper publishers became pioneers in the fields of collective bargaining, conciliation, and arbitration. The position they established contrasted sharply with the belligerent attitude of many contemporary industries.

The American Newspaper Publishers Association created a national labor committee of three members to take up labor questions generally affecting the members of the association and to take necessary measures to protect the interest of members who might be in trouble with labor unions. This committee later came to be known as the Special Standing Committee. Provision also was made for a labor commissioner to work with the committee in settling disputes through arbitration. The committee was not appointed to provoke controversies or to antagonize labor, but, on the contrary, to promote a better understanding between publisher members and employes who represented the union.

The procedure was for disputing parties to resort first to conference and conciliation and then to local arbitration, with possible final appeal to an international arbitration board. Local arbitration boards were to have three members agreed upon by the two parties. The international board was to be composed of the chairman of the Special Standing Committee, the president of the international union involved, and a third disinterested person if deemed necessary. That settlement procedure prevented many strikes and other types of newspaper interruption.

The value of arbitration is evidenced by the number of labor-management disputes brought to successful settlement or ending in contractual agreements. Some of the decisions and agreements arrived at through arbitration have been extremely important to newspaper publishers.

WHAT LABOR WANTS

Labor, realizing that it is one of the foundation stones of the newspaper's success, feels that it deserves living wages, reasonable working hours, pleasant and healthful working conditions, some guarantee of job security, and an assurance of an adequate retirement plan.

Keeping wage level high

The weekly pay schedule is a strong factor in labor relations. Employes are mindful of their paychecks, and management knows well the advantage of a satisfied working force. At the same time the payroll comprises the chief item of newspaper expense and must be kept in line with available operating funds. The newspaper manager, therefore, has a dual problem: obtaining and keeping capable help and holding salary and wage scales under control. This is particularly difficult in years when costs are rising and wage scales are constantly going up.

In an issue of the *American Pressman,* Arthur C. Evans of the Sioux City, Iowa, local of the International Printing Pressmen and Assistants' Union called the attention of the printing industry to the high wages of newspapers in these words:

> Wages followed prices up the economic ladder, and when the leveling-off point was reached it was found that while the pay rates of most workers had doubled over the years the pay rates of skilled workers in a few industries — the printing industry being one of them — had nearly tripled. Thus we can easily see that because those in the printing industry nearly tripled their wages in the same length of time that it took workers in most industries to double theirs, those in the printing industry gained a respectable percentage of buying power more than most workers.

Holding down overtime hours

In few manufacturing plants is it more difficult to establish and maintain definite hours of work from day to day than in a newspaper plant. The news volume and the advertising volume of a newspaper are never the same on successive days. The hours of work required to produce the newspaper, whether daily or weekly, also vary considerably.

The demands of labor for a 35-, 37½-, or 40-hour work week cause overtime hours in most newspaper departments, especially in the mechanical department. Other regulations whereby unions prohibit their members from performing more than one type of work create some problems, particularly for smaller newspapers.

A publisher often has to deal with several unions, unless his employes belong to a company union. Publishers of most papers with circulations of 15,000 and above must negotiate annually with from one to five unions, and the metropolitan publisher may have to deal with as many as 25. As electronic equipment eliminates old jurisdictional lines, however, more and more talk is heard of the possibility of mergers into a single newspaper union.

With these conditions existing in a newspaper plant, management faces a real problem in keeping costly overtime hours to a minimum. Some newspapers have staggered the hours of employes to hold the time put in by each to 40 hours. Others have eliminated the Saturday or Monday issue to put out a newspaper on five eight-hour days instead of six days a week. Weeklies have set up more rigid deadlines and streamlined production schedules.

Maintaining pleasant working conditions

In addition to receiving satisfactory take-home pay and agreeable working hours, the average worker in a newspaper plant wants and deserves congenial surroundings. The strain and speed of newspaper production make the consideration of personal feelings important. Both management and labor have a part to perform in creating a pleasant atmosphere. Where each has confidence in the other, their efforts are related to prompt and efficient production.

A. C. Croft, while president of the National Foremen's Institute, said at a mechanical conference in Chicago that much of the trouble in a newspaper's composing room comes from an irritating supervisor. As an antidote to unpleasant situations, he pointed to seven basic qualities of leadership:

1. A supervisor, first of all, should be loyal—not only to workers, but to management as well. The supervisor should defend both against injustices.
2. A supervisor should be cheerful, and like the job. If not, how can workers be expected to like theirs?
3. A supervisor should practice courtesy. Every worker wants to feel of some consequence and expects to be treated accordingly.
4. A supervisor should be frank and not make the mistake of glossing over situations.
5. A supervisor should be fair and impartial in dealings with workers and should not exhibit favoritism in the assignment of work or in relations with employes.
6. A supervisor should be friendly. Many find it difficult to determine the difference between familiarity and friendliness.
7. A supervisor should have infinite amounts of patience and expend the full capabilities, efforts, hopes, and desires of the working force.

Department heads sometimes wonder whether they should be sparing or lavish in praise. One group says: "Don't pamper the worker." Another says: "Take advantage of every opportunity to say a good word."

Certainly, adequate vacation periods, the usual holidays, and sufficient time off for meals are part of what any employe would expect in an "attractive package." Convenient, safe parking near the plant is no longer a minor item but a major contributor to worker satisfaction. "Fringe benefits" can cost little and be worth a great deal.

Secure employment

Men and women who have devoted a reasonable portion of their career lives—in time, talent, and labor—to a newspaper enterprise, and who therefore have made a real contribution to the success of the business, are generally considered to have earned a legitimate "investment" in that newspaper. With many publications, management calculates a work tenure of ten years to be a fair determinant of eligibility to some form of job security.

While there can be no ironclad guarantee to an employe that he or she will be retained on a job regardless of individual performances and economic reversals, a provision for severance pay in the event of dismissal for cause is considered equitable. Severance may be figured as one week's pay for each six months of accumulated work time. However, formulas may vary widely from one newspaper or group operation to another.

Considering employes' future

It is a common practice of newspapers to provide opportunities for position and salary advancements for employes who are faithful and whose services fit well into the publishing program.

Opportunities for employes to invest in stock of the newspaper, to obtain hospitalization and insurance on an easy-payment basis, and to participate in a retirement plan are offered by most newspapers. Some examples of these are discussed in Chapter 26.

The St. Petersburg, Fla., *Times* and *Independent* offers pension and profit-sharing plans that include carriers and part-time employes. Employes at the average newspaper now feel secure about retirement or disabilities because of a great variety of benefit programs available.

The significance of a harmonious relationship between management and labor in newspaper publishing is well summarized in this statement by George Berry of the Pressmen's Union before a convention of the International Typographical Union:

The newspaper industry of America is not necessarily a growing institution, but there is evidence of disintegration that must challenge the attention of every member of our unions. We must give our best in the stabilization and in the making of a profitable enterprise in the business in which we engage, to the end that there should be more for us — more for the management and more for the investor.

28
Incentives to improvement

The newspaper that is not constantly improving is decaying. What greater incentive could it have than its life, its growth, its health?

L. Dupre Long

Motivation is the raw material of which achievement and success are fashioned. Without this incitement to better performance, the most progressive-minded newspaper manager will fail to reach those ideal goals of staff loyalty, operational efficiency, journalistic excellence, and community support.

No newspaper can afford to be content with what it has done or what it is doing. It must be kept abreast of new ideas and new publishing methods and display management's desire and courage to find means of applying them. That is never easy. It is much easier and much more comfortable to become satisfied with the paper as it is and drift along.

Literacy in the United States is increasing constantly. More than 97 percent of the population can read and write. Each year, college and university enrollments indicate a greater desire for learning and a greater number of educated readers for newspapers. The number receiving master's degrees and doctor's degrees is climbing steadily.

The world moves, and the newspaper that reflects the thoughts and habits of the world must move with it. Unless it is progressive, either its community will pull away from it or it will pull the community down to its level of indifference and stagnation. To reach the heights of service expected of them by an enlightened public and to avoid falling into ruts, successful newspaper publishers set goals for their communities, their newspapers, their personnel, and themselves.

COMMUNITY GOALS

With the power of publicity and promotion and with a knowledge of existing conditions, the newspaper is in a better position than any other organization in the community to acquaint the general public with its needs and possibilities and to show how those needs may be met.

"As newspaper managers, certainly we feel we must carry on a very aggressive and progressive campaign of community and state improvement," says the business and production manager of the Oklahoma City, Okla., *Times* and *Daily Oklahoman.* "We should always support and crusade for everything that will improve the cultural and economic environment of our area. We feel this is a responsibility a newspaper owes to the readers of its community, and certainly we are and will continue to be one of the beneficiaries of such development programs."

For several years the Wichita Falls, Tex., *Record News* constantly reminded readers of community needs under the heading, "A Program for the City," on its editorial masthead. The program as outlined for one year was:

1. Develop Wichita Falls' potential as a wholesaling center through expanded and enlarged warehouse facilities.
2. Support closest cooperation with Sheppard Air Force Base.
3. Strive for a safer city through cooperation with the Citizens Safety Council in its goal of safer streets and highways.
4. Improve agricultural production by increasing interest of farmers in practicing soil conservation; encourage sound methods of poultry production.
5. Remove fire hazards and reduce loss of lives and property resulting from fire.
6. Alleviate heavy downtown traffic burden by acquiring off-street parking and additional highways and traffic arteries.
7. Develop and enlarge public transportation facilities including rail, air, truck, and bus service.
8. Provide for an ample and satisfactory water supply for Wichita Falls on a long-range basis.
9. Encourage public attention and interest in Midwestern University.
10. Sponsor a campaign for remodeling and improving existing substantial and commercial properties. Keep abreast of home-building demands.

One newspaper carried at the top of its editorial column just beneath the masthead a summary of community projects it supported:

THE TEN COMMANDMENTS IN OUR PLATFORM

TOURISM — Provide better markers for route to historic sites.

WATER — Continue fluoride to prevent tooth decay.

SEWERS — Construct an entirely new sewer system.

LIGHTS — Give us a better lighted city, particularly in the neighborhoods.

BUILDINGS — Raze the old city hall. Build a city-county building. Convert courthouse into a museum.

PARKING — Provide off-street parking lots. Tear down the old county jail and use space for parking.

TRAFFIC — Create east-west one-way streets. Pave Madison and Third streets between the tracks, provide more arteries to the south, remove dangerous "island" at 5th and Ash, continue 4th St. over the railroad, widen 9th St.

INDUSTRY — Offer inducements for more industrial plants. Create a citizens-labor committee to bring more factories here.

EFFICIENCY — Employ a central purchasing agent for all city departments as recommended by the Citizens Committee.

TAXATION — Eliminate useless spending, discard boondogglers, overhaul the tax system in the interest of uniformity and equity.

Whether the newspaper has specific objectives like the above or general goals like "Whatever's good for Tallapoosa County, we're for it," the community's welfare and improvement must be a part of the publication's own incentives. (See Chapters 21 and 22.)

NEWSPAPER GOALS

William R. Nelson, founder and editor of the Kansas City, Mo., *Star,* in 1908 wrote a letter to a publisher friend who had purchased a paper in the Midwest and had sent a copy of the newspaper seeking criticism.

"I am not enthusiastic over your paper," wrote Nelson. "It makes the same sort of impression on me that a man would who came into my presence dressed in ill-fitting, gaudy clothing, and talking in loud and vulgar tones. Such a man, I would know at first glance and hearing, was without stability of character. . . . Nothing pays better in the newspaper business than worth and character."

The appearance of a newspaper, what it contains and how responsibly the contents are handled, and the level of service it performs — these are the standards by which a newspaper's success is measured. When the newspaper falls short on any count, it must either change for the better or see its effectiveness and influence diminish.

Improvements in typography

Some publishers have followed a firm policy of making few changes in the typography of their newspapers through the years, believing that readers become accustomed to the makeup and want their paper to retain the familiar appearance it always had. They may have spent millions to modernize their plants, but they keep on turning out newspapers that look about the same as they did a generation or two ago — hard to read and unattractive in appearance. These, however, are the exception rather than the rule.

A noted typographer has said: "To make a favorable first impression, a newspaper must be attractive physically, for the dress of the paper — its physical makeup — is seen and liked or disliked before its contents can be appreciated."

Much attention is given to typography and makeup. Publishers' associations and schools of journalism conduct contests to stimulate interest in typographical excellence and to point out ways of improving a newspaper's general appearance and readability. In competition with 266 papers, the Miami, Fla., *Herald* and the Dubuque, Iowa, *Telegraph-Herald* were named winners of the Edmund C. Arnold Award for newspaper typography (Figs. 28.1 and 28.2).

The most common of the faults of daily newspapers, as revealed by various typographical contests and exhibits, are:

1. Too many front pages are top-heavy.
2. Pages follow too much the same pattern throughout the paper.
3. The print sometimes has a smudgy appearance.
4. Margins are too narrow.
5. Too many lines and letters are broken off or poorly printed.
6. Headline display at the top of inside pages is not strong enough.
7. Too many advertisements have a crowded, jumbled appearance.
8. Small ads lack illustrations.
9. Not enough white space between units on the page.
10. Tendency to treat all ads in a similar manner with little if any change in borders and typefaces.

Many of the faults in typography may be removed by heeding the following suggestions made by contest judges and typography experts:

1. Abandon all-cap heads in favor of caps and lowercase.
2. Eliminate very condensed typefaces.
3. Reduce the number of type styles in headline schedules.
4. Obtain new fonts of type when necessary.
5. Improve presswork by giving more attention to ink control.
6. Consider the entire page as a unit of design.
7. Give more attention to the use of pictures and two- and three-column headlines below the fold to brighten up this area and to give better balance to the page.
8. Use substantial headlines on inside pages to give balance and to attract readers.
9. Omit column rules to give a more open appearance and to make the page easier to read.
10. Provide more white space between stories, between stories and ads, between heads and stories, and between ads to improve the appearance of pages.
11. Give more attention to effective placement of ads on the page so that they will be more inviting and readable.
12. Give more attention to sufficient "breathing space" within ads.
13. Use more pictures in small ads to get reader attention.
14. Strive to fit typography to the personality of the store and the character of merchandise advertised.

The Telegraph-Herald

135th Year, No. 258   2 SECTIONS   DUBUQUE, IOWA, and EAST DUBUQUE, ILLINOIS, TUESDAY, NOVEMBER 16, 1971   22 PAGES   15 cents

Child care tax break voted

WASHINGTON, D.C. (AP) — The Senate has voted 59-24 to liberalize a child-care tax deduction for couples who both work and have children 14 and under.

The Senate vote Monday added to the $19.5 billion tax deduction bill an amendment to the $19.5 billion tax deduction available to couples with joint incomes up to $18,000.

As the bill came to the floor, the limit for such couples was joint incomes up to $12,000.

The amendment would add about $100 million to the previously-estimated $250 million cost of the provision.

Under the amendment, single adults such as widows and divorced persons and couples within the income limits could deduct up to $4,800 per year of child care and domestic help expenses.

Tunney contended the $12,000 limit was not high enough because few couples in this bracket could afford to pay large sums for child care.

Senate leaders are driving for a vote on the bill package by Wednesday.

Senate Democrats have failed in efforts to add a big 1971

How they voted . . .

Voting for the child care amendment were Charles Percy and Adali Stevenson of Illinois; Gaylord Nelson and William Proxmire of Wisconsin.

Voting against was Jack Miller of Iowa. Harold Hughes of Iowa did not vote.

tax cut for individuals to the $23.9-billion tax-reduction bill and to trim benefits for business.

The Senate turns to other issues today in an attempt to finish work Wednesday on the big bill, a key part of President Nixon's new economic policy.

It added $2.2 billion a year to the cost of the measure Monday by voting 56 to 27 to allow parents a tax credit of up to

$325 a year on expenses of a college student. The credit will be subtracted from taxes due.

Democrats tried twice Monday to correct what they said was a major imbalance in the bill in favor of business.

Sen. Adlai E. Stevenson, D-Ill., lost, 44 to 38, in an effort to raise the personal exemption for 1971 to $700, compared with $675 voted by the House and $650 in present law. This would have added $1 billion of tax relief to the bill.

The college-tax-credit rider, sponsored by Sen. Ernest F. Hollings, D-S.C., would be figured on spending for tuition, fees, books and supplies. A credit would be allowed for 75 per cent of the first $200 spent, 25 per cent of the next $300, and 10 per cent of the next $1,000.

Families with incomes up to $25,000 would get the full credit; it would be available in part to those with incomes up to $57,000.

The Senate rejected 58 to 26 another Hollings proposal to provide rebates to poverty-level families for sales taxes paid on food and property taxes paid either as a homeowner or renter. It would have cost $1.7 billion a year.

Kennedy top choice among Democrats

NEW YORK (AP) — Sen. Edward M. Kennedy of Massachusetts is the clear favorite of rank and file Democrats for their party's 1972 presidential nomination, according to the Louis Harris poll.

In a national sampling of 972 Democrats likely to vote in next year's election, Kennedy was the choice of 26 per cent compared to 19 per cent who favored Maine's Sen. Edmund S. Muskie, the poll showed.

But among independent voters Muskie continued to lead with a seven-point margin over Kennedy, according to the mid-October poll results disclosed Monday.

When the preferences of Democrats and Independents are added together, the contest between Kennedy and Muskie is too close to call, the poll reported.

Showers

RUDOLF ABEL
Colonel in KGB

Soviet's master spy Abel dies

MOSCOW (AP) — Rudolf Abel, the master spy who was the top Soviet agent in the United States, died Monday, informed sources reported today.

Abel, probably the most important Soviet spy caught in the United States, escaped detection from 1948 until his arrest in 1957. He was sentenced to 30 years in prison and in 1962 was exchanged for American U2 pilot Francis Gary Powers.

Abel was 68 and had been ill for six months with lung cancer, the sources said.

Abel went to the United States from Canada and set up as a photographer and artist in Brooklyn. His target was American military secrets, and he was exposed after the defection of an assistant, Reino Hayhanen.

Although he was a colonel in the KGB, the secret police, the Soviet government denied Abel was a Soviet citizen. But eight years later, in 1965, the head of the KGB paid official tribute in Pravda to the agent known as Rudolf Abel.

In 1966 the magazine Molodoy Kommunist, or Young Communist, reported that Abel worked in Soviet intelligence for more than 30 years. "His courage, valor and boundless devotion have been highly appreciated," it said.

Field Marshal Rommel disinterred as a myth

By DAVID MINTHORN
Associated Press Writer

FRANKFURT, Germany (AP) — Field Marshal Erwin Rommel was not Hitler's most able war commander — he was a mediocre leader and politically naive according to a West German television documentary.

The program, "The Myth of Rommel," claimed Monday night that the legendary Desert Fox owes his reputation to the Nazi propaganda machine and sentimental postwar biographers.

The documentary's director, Helmuth Rompa, concluded after studying war archives in Koblenz and Washington that Rommel "was at best a good tactician but he couldn't work with large bodies of troops. He panicked when faced with great tasks."

Gen. Ulrich de Mauziere, former inspector general of the West German

Army said Rommel had only slight understanding of large strategic problems and was backward in his political thinking

ERWIN ROMMEL
Legendary Desert Fox

Gen. Wolf von Baudissin, another prominent army commander, suggested that Hitler built Rommel into a folk hero and then used him as a political instrument because "he was no snob and no intellectual.

We would be doing Rommel a favor if we would try to see him today as a person." Von Baudissin told the TV audience

The program showed that Rommel, who was allowed to commit suicide in 1944 after being implicated in the plot to bomb Hitler, retains his almost mystical reputation abroad as well as in Germany.

The commander of the new navy missile ship Rommel reported "I want to emphasize that during the long months of construction of the ship in the United States, the Rommel name always opened doors for us."

The documentary suggests that Rommel's World War I exploits as an infantry lieutenant on the Italian front and his memoirs of the experience were vital to his rise under Hitler.

"Hitler felt that Rommel's book of memoirs confirmed all of his views about war leadership," the film said.

Raised $15,000 for medical expenses

Town rushes to aid of paralyzed player

PETALUMA, Calif. (AP) — The residents of this Northern California community have pitched in to help 15-year-old Robbie Sturla in his time of need.

The youth broke a vertebra in his neck while practicing football for the St. Vincent's High School team Sept. 15 and now lies virtually paralyzed from the shoulders down at Santa Clara Valley Medical Center at San Jose.

Thus far the townsfolk have raised more than $15,000 to offset Robbie's medical and therapy expenses, which run $5,000 to $6,000 a month.

And help has come from as far away as the White House.

"Robbie's a real tough kid," said Mike Gonzalez, athletic director at St. Vincent's. "He's sure he's going to get well and already

is talking about playing baseball next spring."

Robbie's father, Louis, is semi-retired because of health reasons. His mother is a receptionist.

Doctors at the medical center say the boy has regained some feelings in his legs, but they made no predictions about a full recovery.

Robbie himself says, "I feel fine, especially since I got out of traction last Monday. Man, that was a drag. I'm in a wheelchair now."

Robbie's teammates were the first to come to his aid, raising $1,634 by washing windows, raking yards and cleaning chicken houses.

And the football players from Tomales Bay High School, St. Vincent's traditional rival, gave $100.

The St. Vincent's Mothers' Committee

added more than $1,000 to Robbie's medical fund with a seven-hour spaghetti feed.

A three-week auction by radio station KTOB of donated items solicited by the Mothers' Committee raised $11,146.

President Nixon sent a steel engraving of the White House and an autographed card which brought an auction bid of $20.

A Billy Casper golf glove netted $10. A pipe from TV newscaster Walter Cronkite went for $20. A football helmet from Mike McCloy of Notre Dame produced $45. Five neckties donated by Jack Benny brought from $15 to $25 apiece.

"You can't find words for what the people of Petaluma have done for us," the boy's father said. "There is no way to thank them."

Robbie found three words.

"They're kind people."

On a clear day . . .

On any ordinary day, this view of Manhattan Island from Brooklyn is usually hazy with smog, but on one very very clear day photographer Ray Stubblebine took this photo at dusk of the skyline. The star effect on the bridge is produced with a special filter.

Council capsule

Fig. 28.1. Front page of the Dubuque, Iowa, *Telegraph-Herald,* winner of first place in the Smaller Daily Division in the Edmund C. Arnold typography contest.

The Miami Herald

JOHN S. KNIGHT, Editorial Chairman   JAMES L. KNIGHT, Chairman

LEE HILLS, Publisher   ALVAH H. CHAPMAN, Jr., President   DON SHOEMAKER, Editor   JOHN J. JURGENSMEYER, Gen. Mgr.
GEORGE BEEBE, Senior Managing Editor   LARRY JINKS, Managing Editor   JOHN D. PENNEKAMP, Associate Editor

6-A   Monday, July 10, 1972

EDITORIALS

A Forum For A Fair Fight As The Convention Begins

THE Presidential nominating convention opening today in Miami Beach surely is one of the most significant events in the history of the Democratic Party since Andrew Jackson rallied the frontier democracy around him in 1824 and 1828.

Only a few months ago George McGovern ran sixth in the Florida preferential primary on a course that seemed to point to political oblivion.

Today in Florida he is the front-runner, a candidate apparently a whisker away from his party's nomination and thus a target for all the forces intent on maintaining the conventional structure of the Democratic Party.

The party of Jefferson and Jackson grew out of the Roosevelt New Deal into a party of labor, minorities, most of the intellectuals, the durable solid South and a few concentrations of economic power.

Sen. McGovern has put together a coalition of young people, the remnants of prairie Populism, retirees, elements of the Kennedy following and left-of-center political figures.

Organized labor, at least at the top, actively dislikes his candidacy. The Wall Street money left on call for identifiable liberal candidates reputedly has dried up. Some surveys show that some ethnic groups (whose solidarity may be at least a myth) are suspicious.

Yet this is a man who won the primaries, if that is where nominations are supposed to be won, and has inspired a "new" movement of greater proportions than the McGovern forces believe Taft and Eisenhower 20 years ago.

The prize, of course, is control of the party machinery. After that, if possible, it is the Presidency. The Democratic Party under George McGovern would be a new creature just as was the Democratic-Republican Party under Andrew Jackson in 1828.

The issue as the fur begins to fly tonight is the bloc of California delegates which Sen. McGovern won in a winner-take-all primary certified as such under California law. The U.S. Supreme Court, in a ruling overturning a lower court which in turn had reversed a still lower court, found "no case cited to us in which any federal court has undertaken to interject itself into the deliberative processes of a national political convention."

In other words, no precedent. The court left the matter to the "availability of the convention as a forum" in which to decide the delegate issue.

We think this is the proper forum. The courts should never have been involved in an intramural decision, and their actual involvement may well be debated for years as an influence — one way or the other — on the naming of a Presidential candidate.

The silent majority outside the convention hall everywhere in America will watch tonight's decisive action in the traditional wish for fair play, decency and order.

There is too much well-founded cynicism about politics and politicians abroad in the land today. Its countenance and mien, residing in its spread public confidence in the free electoral process which is the be-all and end-all of democracy in America.

Why Miami's The Way It Is

"THE MAGIC CITY" is Greater Miami's nickname, and for good reason. Few other big cities have sprouted from a wilderness in just 76 years—from an Indian trading post at the river's mouth to a population of 1.3 million spread over nearly 1,000 square miles.

In the whole belt around the globe from the Tropic of Cancer to 30 degrees north latitude, only a handful of cities have more people than Greater Miami — Taipei, Chungking, Delhi, Karachi and Cairo. The setting of the Indian and Pakistani capitals is desert-like. So is most of the global band — the Sahara, the Arabian Desert, the Punjab, the parched places of northern Mexico.

At Miami, by a marvelous concatenation of circumstances, rainfall equals a plentiful Moist trade winds flow toward Florida to collide with cooler air from the temperate zone, then drop their water.

The flow of the air currents gives the Magic City two seasons, like much of the tropics. The winter months are dry and mild, with cloudless skies. Summer brings almost daily downpours and mood effects of astonishing variety and majesty, as can be seen by a glance upward.

Currents of water and air also are credited with bringing ashore here the crown palm, now ubiquitous, and such exotic creatures as the rattle egret from Africa and the spotted-breasted oriole from Guatemala, an orange-and-black bird that sways like a woodpecker.

In the doldrums of tropical seas, summer heat and wetness sometimes breed excesses which can come ashore anywhere on the Atlantic or Gulf coast of the United States, including Florida. Danger to life and property has been minimized by strict building codes and the prudence of weatherwise Miamians who get away from low coasts and stay

in safe buildings until a storm has passed.

Hurricanes do some good, too. Their torrential rain augments the flat peninsula's supply of fresh water. Their sudden gusts prune trees and shrubbery which otherwise might engulf men's handiwork in a lush jungle.

So the tiny settlement at the entrance to the Miami River spread ever outward for years. Now it's reaching skyward in high-rises and skyscrapers. Much effort goes into safeguarding the natural scene, including the clear air and sparkling waters which drew thousands of settlers.

Where else is there a great city with a national park on its doorstep, a national monument on islands offshore and vast public preserves for water conservation in its back yard, once the trough of the Everglades, the River of Grass? The outdoors will remain there, untouched, to lift the spirits of dwellers in this subtropical metropolis, surely the Magic City.

Worthy Aim In Broward

THE Broward Area Planning Board has launched an ambitious program to get some input into land development in the fast-growing county.

It will work first to have uniform zoning rules and definitions adopted by all 27 cities and the county. Even more important and more difficult, will be its attempt to get counties-wide support for a long-range plan based either on a rapid mass transit network or a system of expressways combined with clusters of new cities.

The aim is to see that the remaining raw land in Broward is developed in a manner best for the overall environment rather than in a manner that will maximize profits to individual landowners.

History has proved again and again that the latter goal is the one that usually is achieved. But hopefully a dawning public knowledge of the consequences of such short-sighted action will aid the Board in accomplishing its mission.

One-Owner. A Classic

THE JEEP, says our dictionary, is a "demustarr multipurpose motor vehicle" which probably got its name from a pre-WW II combat strip character.

It the jeep has entered the language, still it won't be allowed to park in the family garage. The people who decide what to do with the wondrous piles of U.S. Army surplus say the jeep is too dangerous to be put in the hands of civilians. So the little jobs will be chopped up for scrap rather than be sold to the public.

This is a mistake, we think, for a variety of reasons.

One, obviously, is economic. Another, perhaps, is that the Army's action relieves Ralph Nader of another ulcer. Most of all, it deprives the humble citizen of one of the best back-stretchers, kidney-massagers and arm muscle conditioners in the history of gimmickry. If Uncle will only change his mind we'd be glad, out of nostalgia if nothing else, to buy a used car from That Man.

The Metro Commission is to be commended for taking the first step to remove the South Dixie Expressway from the MUATS map by means of its unanimous resolution July 3. Now, Commissioner Fogg will introduce an ordinance, which is more difficult to reverse than a resolution.

Unfortunately, contrary to jubilant headlines in the press, the South Dade Expressway is far from dead. Dade County planners and the Florida Department of Transportation already are collecting ammunition to keep it alive. A statement from the DOT was admired on July 3, but it will be heard at a forthcoming public hearing commissioners will hold before passing the ordinance.

South Dade citizens who have won this first battle must win again at the final reading of the proposed ordinance (July 25, at the earliest) in order to achieve a second reading. Their next win again at the second reading and public hearing (September)

"At this point, the commissioners still hold the future of South Dade in their hands."

fies S, at the earliest). Proponents of the expressway—the DOT, the local planners and the land developers—also will be heard at that meeting.

If this time schedule is followed, the matter would be settled before the September 12 primary election.

Commissioner Case has cautioned that commissioners may be learned if future population increases cause traffic problems. By the same token, commissioners may be applauded for forcing planners to find new solutions that do not despoil residential areas that now are both economic and environmental assets to the county. These new solutions also can be maybe for federal money.

At this point, the commissioners still hold the future of South Dade in their hands. Are they willing to maintain quash their control to the highway departments, who placed a lone on a map before the affected areas were built up?

The Metro Commission has a rare opportunity to preserve and foresightedness to save South Dade from the irreversible fate of Los Angeles, where more widely scattered highways have generated more widely scattered congestion and more widely scattered pollution.

ROBERTA WRIGHT

Few More Thoughts On The Clock

Your editorial June 26 entitled, "Second Thoughts On The Clock," prompts additional information and education about the mysterious nature of time and our calendar.

According to accepted estimates, an astronomical year contains 365 days, 5 hours, 48 minutes and 46 seconds—or almost 365¼ days. A civil year, however, consists of 365 days — except for a leap year which has 366 days. In four years including a leap year, the calendar will have not only caught up with the astronomical year, it will have actually gained a little bit every four years of a leap year is included, our calendar slides farther and farther ahead of solar time.

To correct this excess, February 29 is omitted on certain centuryending years. (If the last year of a century is not exactly divisible by 400, it is not a leap year.) Three century-ending years are therefore cancelled as leap years every 400 years. Even with this correction, the calendar will still be ahead by one day every 3,323 years. So, an additional change is incorporated into the calendar. The years 4000, 8000, 12000, 16000, etc. are not to be leap years. The calendar thus becomes accurate to within one day every 200 centuries.

ARTHUR J. FRANKEL

Newspapers Are Privileged

We should be thankful that we have the privilege of reading such a paper as The Herald, which "tells it like it is." Without such we would be deprived of knowledge and possibly confused with deliberate falsification.

However, the papers have gotten the best of it. Up to now it has been thought that true reporters were not subject to compellable testimony before grand juries.

Maybe we have to take the honor with the sweet. I recall a situation in Baltimore, when a U.S. held, a reporter was found guilty of contempt of not revealing the source of his information and was sentenced to serve out in jail. The day began at 11:15 p.m. and was terminated at 12:01 a.m. but the power game was going on good he stayed but until the morning hours. Could well be that despite the rule of the Supreme Court, our journalists will retain their common sense and their sense of humor. Let us hope so — or amend the Constitution, which is long overdue for a vacuum cleaning.

HARRY W. ALLERS
Fort Lauderdale

Nixon's Praise Misplaced Here

Jim Bishop's column about Nixon had Nixon faced to mention the auto together Number the President made earlier this month wine or were out of his way to praise the motives of the New York Times who had had no publication of that newspaper because they didn't like the this sum of Jim in one of the advertisements.

It's my impression that the Nixon has long been opposed to a that strikes and to labor's salvation of its contracts.

Even more important is Nixon's approval of this threat to the freedom of the press. What would Republican leaders be saying if the printers had refused to print a pro-Nixon advertisement?

It is more regretable that the President of the United States found it in his nature that important than was we were all snake in this matter.

HARRIET J. CANNERY

Van Didn't Greet New Americans

Prior to the American citizenship ceremonies of May 1, 1972, The Herald published an article informing its readers of the decision of the county manager to send a registration van for the purpose of registering the new citizens after the ceremonies. More than 200 new Americans registered to vote.

It was very sad to note in the last citizenship ceremonies at Barry College, on June 7, that no van was seen to send the registration van on the occasion.

The American Political Association, organized for the purpose of informing, educating, instructing and guiding future citizens of the United States, has asked Mayor Mayor Ben Clark to take the necessary steps to see that the registration van be present at all American citizenship ceremonies. We urge The Herald to help us, too, in this American-ist program.

RAUL ESQUIVEL, Secretary
American Political Association

Criminals Treated With Kid Gloves

I feel I must express my disgust at this unwanted farce so disgust. Why is all the concern given to the rights of the criminals? It seems that nobody is interested in the rights of the majority of law-abiding citizens whose tax dollars pay to provide food, housing, hospital and prison advantages to criminals. To protect them too often results in being put back on the streets to commit another crime, while our ideas and direction are at the low.

I feel that kid-glove treatment of criminals is done to allow them to go scot-free. If a person items, or we was rehabilitating. I we all too "timid, let him live there his time and return to his productive happy life. But the fact that recidivism is over 50 per cent proves to me that it does not work.

When I think of the unspeakable crimes of Charles Manson and Richard Speck and the again that have been suffered before they find California don't think a quick bill of extra truth would be that of unusual that... advance for them. Perhaps the death penalty wouldn't have deterred them from their actions, but it surely would have kept them from doing it again it was that the mental torment of institutionalization.

LYNNE CANNATO

Ban Unnecessary Power Use

Once again South Florida faces a summer power shortage as the past week saw record the reserve power of the Gulf Coast. This means which here have given FPL one reason to say it to have the thermal inversion but this is far less.

Much power may be, as yours, we feel that part of it that matter we can conserve as... thing... it will be our save the reliance on power, but when we turn but a lot of energy and office equipment into a few strange during peak usage days.

BARRY W. SCHUEMAN

Vets' Fees Aren't Too High

Concerning overregulation of jobs, veterinarians have the same accesses all as humans for doctors. The use of an operating room, even when it a new recovery pet when such is its own importance, requires much time and expense, gone.

The fee charged for this longer involves the use of a surgeon, an anesthetist, and post-operative care. Considering what a person would pay for the same fee had the same to care, the veterinarians fees are as clean as a dentist's request.

PHILIP A. RUNALS D.V.M.

Watch What You Call A Slum

In response to Jeanne B... a Miami Newspaper article A R... has the rise for Broadview's reco... I don't think we remarks about t... it. Crawl being a "down all men he ...anted in spare a hard work!"...house so built...

If a and Dictionary definer a slum as a "dirty, crowded area" of a town. Possibly Circus man he is a old all-times congested, but it is not a slum.

I suggest that she turn her attention to the very real slums that exist here in Miami in the so-called rattiest country on earth before writing about slums in other countries.

Needless to say, I am English, and I love Broadview Circus as it is — an old buildings, small shops, traffic, etc. A great many people in bus old Americans such as Paul Gauguin and the late Robert Ruark share my views as seeing to the areas as they know and love.

DEIRDRE M. CLEGG

...(illegible text)... As the conservation opens the elements of another long-waiting area present should George McGovern... fall to emerge to a quick nomination, certainly the intensity between the several appeals above, at the start, little attention to the maneuvering influences of other times.

Let's Go Slow On War Criticism

Often we hand we are hearing an ...tion of protests we see sides the war a hard date, for when that to put a "Stop" or but wasn't. "Slow to extremity the

...(illegible)... a reason to accept it...

I suggest your left want and it address. The sum of insults or premature or signatures will eliminate a letter from consideration for publication. All letters are subject to condensation by the editors.

Sign Your Name

Letters to the Editor must bear the writer's name and address. The use of insults or pen-names or signatures will eliminate a letter from consideration for publication. All letters are subject to condensation by the editors.

IT PROBABLY wouldn't have done much good for the leaders of the Democratic Party to do more harm than a chance of it's defeat both sides of the story. The differences wouldn't have been... and the day was even made the day a recent breath.

SMITH, the next of... ...and he is covering a new stake in the first days...

Undoubtedly the best performance of his career them shot and drew of 78 dividend to finally together was that of Franklin D. Roosevelt, who took the accomplishment to four successful elections.

FOUR YEARS earlier, in 1928, after years of normal party strife he had nominated Alfred E. Smith for the Presidency in a rousing and ringing speech in which he termed the long time New York Governor the "Happy warrior of the political battlefields."

Then, in 1932, he decided to make the race himself, which immediately assured the antipathy of Smith's substantial following, who believed he should be given another chance.

The cause of Herbert C. Hoover,

who had beaten him in four races, but him had been severely charged with and lost the poorer and it's defeat both sides both one way... that is... hard sharp... and.

Roosevelt himself was not an instinctive politician. But he came to office to be a political and dominated dominated the rest and diplomatic party for the end of his career.

Pennekamp

ALSO the contrast of the two men Smith's Brooklyn twang and a supporters' persistent use of the song "the sidewalks of New York," to his 1924 nomination campaign and in 1928 stacked in the Bible Belt state recognized no machine it is not called performance at all.

N. Adam, a member of a distinguished southern family charged and Tennessee had been Woodrow Wilson's secretary of the Treasury, had married Wilson's daughter Eleanor, was wealthy and able as a law-diplomat and railroad executive.

THE BACKED convention finally nominated John W. Davis, who was

born in West Virginia and had won California, the richest electoral honors. A lawyer he had been a member of Congress, would prove of the United States, and many a dominating member of the world bond diplomatic corps at the end of a brief ambassadorship to the Court of St. James.

The nomination fell to him when the of Rustain of Indiana, reached as the most available of the dark cleaves, abruptly removed himself.

Smith also appear after the fall of the which his party had broad could be made a splendid candidate but the convention didn't swallow it.

He was being considered for the nomination when the 34th ballot, the Democrats chose James M. Cox, former governor of Ohio. He was defeated by Warren G. Harding Ohio senator in a vote count of sixty-one against 34.2

As the convention opens the elements of another long-standing area present should George McGovern fail to emerge to a quick nomination, certainly the intensity between the several appeals above, at the start, little attention to the maneuvering influences of other times.

Fig. 28.2. Editorial page of the Miami, Fla., *Herald,* winner of top honors in the Metropolitan Daily Division in the Edmund C. Arnold Typography Contest.

Robert C. Nicholson wrote at one time in the *Linotype News:*

The two greatest enemies of modern makeup and production economies are those two drags on the wheels of progress — habit and tradition. Habit permits actions without thought. Depending on the point of view, it keeps you "in the groove" or "in the rut." Tradition is often the sentimental excuse for habits, and it should have little place in the field of newspapers. Unfortunately, some publishers who wouldn't print a line of yesterday's news today are using dated makeup that was initiated by their grandfathers. . . . The only way to leave the rut of habit and get on the high road of good, economical and attractive makeup is to stand back and analyze each feature of the newspaper in an objective, unbiased manner. There should be a good reason for every head, every box, and every typeface used.

Achievement of a pleasing page appearance has been made much easier with today's photocomposition machines and offset press equipment. With the older processes, it was quite an accomplishment to print a newspaper free of ink smudges or irregular type here and there, but electronic production allows for cleaner, more colorful, and more evenly produced pages. Versatility and innovation in makeup and harmony of typographical elements have also been enhanced by the new technology.

Staff meetings for planning

Department heads, and even persons in the lesser ranks, can help set up goals for newspaper improvement and help to reach them. The editor of the Monroe, Mich., *Evening News* says that one of the most effective aids in the continuing betterment of newspaper service is a weekly staff meeting. All departments heads attend such a meeting, which is regular procedure as soon as the paper goes to press each Monday afternoon. The news department is represented not only by the managing editor but by the city and sports editors. Frequently an additional member of the news staff is called in if the discussion touches upon that sphere of work or interest.

The editor says further:

These staff meetings have been unusually successful, because all matters relating to them are kept in the hands of the staff. The tradition is that the staff members accept the responsibility for organizing and carrying on these weekly meetings independent of management. I sometimes attend but more often do not. The staff group rotates the chair among themselves, each person serving for a month and then passing the responsibility along to the next man in line, who presides and directs the order of discussion. It is the responsibility of staff members to clear among themselves matters of misunderstanding, disagreement, and disharmony. In any matter involving management, they call upon management for decision, correction, or direction as the case may be.

Further, the staff makes it a business to constantly analyze the *Evening News* service and to recommend to management opportunities for improvement. It is the same with consideration of goodwill enterprises to be undertaken by the paper and with editorial objectives that are deemed advisable. In both cases the subjects are discussed at the staff meetings to the end of offering suggestions or making recommendations that will result in effective effort on the part of the paper.

Most of our department heads are people young in years and in spirit. The majority are active citizens in the community. They have varied interests and contacts with people in their personal lives. Out of these symposiums, therefore, we get discussions and suggestions that are exceedingly valuable in the stimulation and guidance of our newspaper service and enterprise.

We have a continuing program of revision and improvement of our services and our editorial objectives. This is somewhat at variance with the practice of some papers of making a formal list of objectives.

DEPARTMENT GOALS

Incentives designed to achieve departmental improvements have been effective in lifting production standards and newspaper quality. More and better style books are being produced and used by newspapers as guides to writing, punctuation, headline writing, and makeup. The style books used in schools of journalism have wide circulation among publishers acquainted with the courses offered in newswriting and copyreading. Newspaper style throughout the country has been improved by a style book issued by the Associated Press and revised periodically to allow for changes in idiom. It is the most definitive and inclusive work ever undertaken by a group of newspapers. Its rules and regulations are becoming the standard in hundreds of composing rooms and on copydesks everywhere.

Training for correspondents

For several years, a former woman publisher conducted a continuous course of instruction for community correspondents of Missouri newspapers. She met with groups of country correspondents in all parts of the state. After each meeting she mailed a resumé of the discussion period to correspondents, so that all had a record of the meeting, whether present or absent. She sent a confidential bulletin to editors and wrote letters of individual criticism for the correspondents. She conducted a monthly contest in which the writers submitted tips or ideas for stories. The winning tips were published in the *Listening Post,* an eight-page monthly magazine mailed to each correspondent. This service was instrumental in improving the copy sent to Missouri newspapers each week by community correspondents.

The Bloomington, Ill., *Pantagraph* gives to each community correspondent and to the publicity chairman of each community organization a four-page guide booklet, explaining what news is acceptable, how to prepare copy, when copy must reach the newsdesk, and other pertinent information. This greatly assists correspondents in submitting timely and well-prepared copy.

To stimulate the interest of rural people in providing news material, one newspaper offered cash prizes for news tips. It also contacts key news sources in smaller towns regularly and obtains many important items from them.

Other means used by newspapers to improve the service of rural correspondents are:

1. Monthly bulletins to correspondents, calling attention to meritorious handlings of news and common mistakes.
2. Monthly or quarterly dinner meetings of all correspondents with the news staff as hosts.
3. Personal calls upon the correspondents by members of the regular news staff to cultivate a closer working relationship and clear up any misunderstandings or inefficiencies.
4. An annual school of instruction for correspondents at the newspaper office.

Training and equipment for ad salesmen

The publisher of the St. Petersburg, Fla., *Independent* and *Times* devised a plan for training advertising salesmen. First, each staff member was presented a copy of a book on how to write effective advertising copy and some of the retail folders released by the Bureau of Advertising. After allowing staff members about two weeks to study the material, an examination was conducted to make sure that they had read and digested the basic principles described in the books. Next, they were required to devote a week to learning how local retailers synchronized their window displays and point-of-sale promotion with their newspaper advertising. Luncheon meetings for staff members were held with a successful local retail store executive present at each meeting as an honor guest. Luncheons were held in a private room where discussion could take place. At least once a week or once a month the publisher bought a dinner for staff members and conducted a copywriting clinic for two hours. At the last meeting of the month the merits of the *Independent* as an advertising medium were discussed.

The Midland, Mich., *News* believes in arming its advertising sales force with plenty of surefire "ammunition." It provides each salesperson with a loose-leaf sales manual containing information on questions likely to be raised in contacting merchants. The manual has eight divisions, each tabbed along the edge so that wanted information is found with little searching. Other divisions may be added as desired. Each page has a transparent covering. The divisions in this handy and practical sales portfolio are:

Promotions — Dates of all sales events of the year sanctioned by the retail merchants and those scheduled by the newspaper. "No longer is it necessary to keep reminding the staff of events to come and find out at the last minute that some event has been forgotten," says the publisher.

Circulation — Map of the complete circulation area, number of families and homes in the area, percentage of coverage by the newspaper, latest ABC report, and comparative circulation data on all competing media.

Market Data — Retail sales figures, effective buying income, payroll, population, homes, number of telephones, automobile registrations, value of building permits, industrial employment and other items showing the outstanding market available to advertisers.

Rate Cards — Both local and national.

Regulations — The newspaper's policy regarding free publicity, use of word FREE in advertising, and the advertising of lotteries.

Type Specimens — Proofs of all type styles and sizes available to advertisers.

Percentages for Advertising Budgets — Listing by Bureau of Advertising to help merchants in making up their advertising budgets.

"Is Your Partner Working with You?" — Presentation prepared by Bureau of Advertising to compare local newspaper coverage with magazine coverage.

Use of aptitude tests

Personality and ability tests are now being given in a number of newspaper personnel offices to would-be employes and are helpful not only in obtaining capable workers but in fitting them to appropriate positions in the newspaper organization.

The executive editor of the Louisville, Ky., *Courier-Journal* and *Times* believes firmly that trained personnel executives must become an integral part of all news operations on the larger newspapers and that smaller newspaper publishers must give attention to this phase of newspaper management. For whatever indifference may exist toward such action, the editor blames "the stubborn newspaper executive who continues to insist that newspapering is 'different'; that it is creative and difficult to define; and that, therefore, employment and training must rest with the individual department" as well as "the personnel executive who insists on using a strange language to define his terms, who has made precious little study of newspaper problems, and who also lends little confidence by office staffing."

Publishers and managers who have established standards and goals for department employes have found them effective in increasing production efficiency and office morale.

PERSONAL GOALS

In addition to setting goals for the newspaper, its departments, and the community, the publisher or manager needs to set for those who work with every phase of the production specific goals that will emphasize responsibilities and help maintain the high ideals of journalism.

Help from journalism schools

Schools of journalism, in addition to providing educated young men and women for the many related fields, are doing much to raise the standard of newspaper work. The entrance requirements of most schools of journalism have been stiffened, some requiring a passing grade in an English proficiency test. Other tests are given to see if the student is entering a field to which he or she is adapted by interest, personality, and ability. When the American Council on Education for Journalism instituted its accrediting program, one point covered the seeking of employer approval of a graduate's work six months after beginning the job.

At most institutions for professional education in journalism, practical experience is provided as a supplement to classroom instruction and guidance. Some schools offer experience on school publications or arrange for students to take assignments on community newspapers.

The practice of providing undergraduate on-the-job experience with newspapers is widespread and expanding. At some schools the internship is optional, at others mandatory. Time on the job ranges from a few hours to a full semester. Some schools give college credit for the work, some insist on payment by the employers at the regular scale, and at some the student receives both pay and credit. There can be no doubt as to the educational advantages of the internship for both student and employer.

Relating theory to practice

A significant step forward in education for journalism and in bringing capable men and women into the newspaper offices of America took place when a system of accrediting schools of journalism was instituted by the American Council on Education for Journalism. The council consisted of five newspaper executives, each representing a newspaper organization, and five educators elected by the American Associaton of Schools and Departments of Journalism. The five cooperating groups were the American Newspaper Publishers Association, the American Society of Newspaper Editors, the National Editorial Association, and two regional groups — the Inland Daily Press Association and the Southern Newspaper Publishers Association. To this group were added the National Association of Radio and Television Broadcasters, the American Business Press, the Magazine Publishers Association, the International Council of Industrial Editors, the Newspaper Advertising Executives Association, the National Conference of Editorial Writers, the National Press Photographers Association, and the Radio-Television News Directors Association. Other groups from the academic world include the American Society of Journalism School Administrators and the Association for Education in Journalism.

With such an all-inclusive representation of the best in education and industry, the accrediting program stimulates the constant improvment of education for journalism through continuing review of programs, objectives, and results and serves as a guide to employers in all mass communication fields.

Executive awareness

Progressive newspaper executives, moved by the demands of readers and advertisers and anxious to improve newspaper service, alert themselves as nearly as possible to all that is going on in the fields of journalism, business, and public opinion. The following practices and habits have become common in the lives of many newspaper publishers and managers.

Study of other newspapers. "In fields similar to my own, what are publishers doing to keep their newspapers up to standard?" Answers to this question are continually sought. By studying other newspapers, the publisher obtains many practical ideas:

1. Opportunities to obtain additional national advertising.
2. Advertising copy that could be used by local merchants.
3. Promotion advertising that may be adapted to the local newspaper.
4. Suggestions for feature articles and for news pictures.
5. Editorials that might be clipped and used with credit lines.

Visiting other plants. Seeing something makes believing easier than just reading about it. There is no better place to learn of the improvements being made elsewhere than by visiting newspapers and observing on-the-scene operations. Many a change has been inspired by discovering firsthand the benefits someone else is realizing from new equipment, improved plant conditions, modified work schedules, innovations in cost control, and myriad other areas common to all executives responsible for producing a newspaper. Unless publishers are competing for the same market, these face-to-face conversations with colleagues in the industry are generally an enjoyable as well as profitable pursuit for all concerned.

Press association membership. Newspapermen receive courage and strength from belonging to a group with like problems and opportunities. The state newspaper association provides information concerning publishing activities, pending legislation that affects newspaters, prospective advertising accounts in the national field, advertising accounts that should be avoided, and many money-saving suggestions. The Michigan Press Association, for example, issued a Cost Checklist for Newspaper Management, which contains more than 200 suggestions for production savings.

Most daily newspaper publishers also belong to a larger area group such as the Inland Daily Press Association or the Southern Newspaper Publishers Association. Publishers of newspapers in cities of 50,000 or more usually are members of the American Newspaper Publishers Association and the Bureau of Advertising of the ANPA. The bulletins of these organizations keep the publishers and department heads up-to-date on newspaper problems, and conventions provide additional information and inspiration.

Circulation managers and advertising managers also have their groups and learn from each other. Those organizations have been instrumental in elevating practice standards in their respective fields. Newspaper controllers and accountants, too, exchange ideas and develop modern accounting practices through the National Institute of Newspaper Controllers and Accounting Officers. Other typical associations that have proved their value to members are the National Newspaper Association for weeklies; Women in Communication; the Society of Professional Journalists, Sigma Delta Chi; the National Newspaper Publishers Association for the black press; the Association of Newspaper Classified Advertising Managers; the Suburban Newspapers of America; and many similar organizations.

Maintenance of a library. Publishers who successfully meet competition keep learning and keep members of their newspaper organization learning. A library of information concerning the best methods to be used in all departments of a newspaper is an important aid to successful publishing. The newest books dealing with circulation and management problems, advertising campaigns, cost accounting, and newspaper promotion should be included in such a library along with ready reference books and the latest on handling news.

A newspaper appreciates selling and costsaving suggestions that can be applied immediately. Robert S. Clary compiled a small book entitled *Seventy-one Ways to Build Up Your Newspaper.* Out of his experience in newspaper promotion he presented practical suggestions for bringing in newspaper revenue and building newspaper prestige. The demand for this little volume was startling, because it gave the "how to" for many angles of newspaper publishing.

Professional journals. Publications valuable to every newspaper publisher are *Editor & Publisher, United States Publisher, Publishers Auxiliary, The Quill, Printers' Ink, Advertising Age,* and *Publications Management.* Giving the news of the profession and the trade, they should be at a reading table for staff members or routed from desk to desk so that all may have an opportunity to learn from their pages. Keeping informed about happenings in the field of operation as they take place is a strong contributing factor to organization and individual success.

Well-informed publishers also read papers, bulletins, and services that keep them up to the minute about business in general, governmental problems, and issues. Among these are *Fortune, Nation's Business, U.S. News and World Report, Newsweek* or *Time,* and the Kiplinger Service or some similar newsletter. Through these, the publisher or manager keeps abreast of world news and happenings that may affect business. The counsel of a newspaper publisher is sought on many subjects. To keep pace with the community, he or she needs to be informed.

Contact with journalism schools. Publishers can give inspiration to journalism students and make a real contribution to their profession by maintaining close contacts with journalism schools. Students stand to benefit from practical lectures by visiting editors and conversations with them.

Furthermore, newspaper executives themselves may learn of new practices and ideas to be applied in their own plans. Conferences, clinics, and bulletins provide valuable information (Fig. 28.3). At most accredited schools and departments of journalism, a professional advisory council made up of practitioners meets regularly on campus to exchange ideas with students. Career days and "job raps" are excellent means of matching upcoming vacancies on the staff with highly desirable young talent. The welding of fresh energies and ideals into the newspaper organization is the surest safeguard against stagnation, and the most promising prospects for the future are being recruited on college campuses where professional instruction in journalism is emphasized.

Compete for awards. Few incentives compare with that of being recognized as a prize-winning newspaper. Prestige and morale are boosted when a reporter, cartoonist, advertising copywriter, feature writer, or any other member of the staff brings to the newspaper state, regional, or national recognition for professional attainment. While only a few may aspire to winning a Pulitzer prize, there are many outstanding competitions that all departments of a newspaper should be encouraged to enter.[1] In addition to state press association recognitions, the following lucrative national awards are worth going after:

The Society of Professional Journalists, Sigma Delta Chi, Award of Excellence
Roy W. Howard Award
Edward J. Meeman Conservation Award
Ernie Pyle Memorial Award
Roy W. Howard Public Service Award
John Hancock Award for Excellence in Business and Financial Journalism
American Newspaper Guild Heywood Broun Award
Worth Bingham Memorial Prize for Investigative Reporting in National Affairs
American Bar Association Gavel Award
World Press Photo Contest
National Association of Science Writers Award
Merriman Smith Memorial Fund Prize
Editor & Publisher Color Printing Award
Jester Comics Award
Elijah Parish Lovejoy Award
William Allen White Foundation Award
National Better Newspaper Contest
National Federation of Press Women Award
Green Eyeshade Award
Raymond Clapper Prize
Penney-Missouri Newspaper Award
Pictures of the Year Award
John Peter Zenger Award

---

1. One of the sound arguments for keeping up with professional organizations and reading their journals is that they are sources of information for most contests and awards in journalism.

Fig. 28.3. Organized class instruction by experienced newspaper people in all phases of journalism is one of the contributions that schools of journalism are making toward elevating the "newspaper business" to the status of a profession.

Best Sports Stories Prize
Golden Quill Award for Editorials
Walker Stone Award for Editorials
Medill Typography Award
Headliner Achievement Award

Many such incentives are offered by special interest groups, foundations, universities, and journalism associations. Management can do much to stimulate interest and pride by seeking out and publicizing to all employes the sources of recognition for achievement and by encouraging participation. After all, somebody is going to win, and it might as well be "our newspaper."

Goals are incentives to achievement. They help to line up a well-connected and workable program. They are an expression of a newspaper's ideals and ambitions and they show what needs to be done to meet progressive standards. Defining, articulating, and implementing them offer newspaper management a challenge and an opportunity.

Bibliography

Aaker, David A., and John Myers. *Advertising Management: An Analytical and Behavioral Approach.* Englewood Cliffs, N. J.: Prentice-Hall, 1975.

Adam, G. Stuart. *Journalism, Communication and the Law.* Scarborough, Ont.: Prentice-Hall of Canada, 1976.

American Newspaper Publishers Association. *Free Press and Fair Trial.* New York: ANPA, 1967.

American Society of Newspaper Editors. *Problems of Journalism.* Proceedings of the annual convention, Washington, D.C., April 16–18, 1975. New York: ASNE, 1975.

Anderson, David. *Investigative Reporting.* Bloomington: Indiana Univ. Press, 1976.

Angione, Howard. *The Associated Press Stylebook and Libel Manual.* New York: Associated Press, 1977.

Arnold, Edmund C. *Modern Newspaper Design.* New York: Harper & Row, 1969.

Ashley, Paul P. *Say It Safely: Legal Limits in Journalism and Broadcasting,* 5th ed. Seattle: Univ. Wash. Press, 1976.

Associated Press Managing Editors Association. *The APME Red Book.* New York: Associated Press, 1977.

Babb, Laura Longley, ed. *Of the Press, By the Press, For the Press, and Others, Too: A Critical Study of the Inside Workings of the News Business.* Boston: Houghton Mifflin, 1976.

Barnett, Michael P. *Computer Typesetting: Experiments and Prospects.* Cambridge: M.I.T. Press, 1966.

Barron, Don, ed. *Creativity.* New York: Art Direction, 1976.

Baskette, Floyd K., and Jack Z. Sissors. *The Art of Editing,* 2nd ed. New York: Macmillan, 1977.

Berry, Thomas Elliott. *Journalism in America: An Introduction to the News Media.* New York: Hastings, 1976.

Blumler, Jay G., and Elihu Katz, eds. *The Uses of Mass Communications: Current Perspectives on Gratifications Research.* Beverly Hills, Calif.: Sage Publications, 1974.

Bogart, Leo. Consumer and Advertising Research, *Handbook of Communication.* Chicago: Rand McNally, 1973.

Burton, Philip Ward, and J. Robert Miller. *Advertising Fundamentals,* 2nd ed. Columbus, Ohio: Grid, 1976.

Bush, Chilton R., ed. *News Research for Better Newspapers.* New York: ANPA Foundation, 1966.

Cavallo, Robert, and Stuart Kahan. *Photography: What's the Law?* New York: Crown, 1976.

Center, Allen H. *Public Relations Practices Case Studies.* Englewood Cliffs, N. J.: Prentice-Hall, 1975.

Chisman, Forrest P. *Attitude Psychology and the Study of Public Opinion.* University Park: Pa. Univ. Press, 1976.

Cirino, Robert. *Power to Persuade: Mass Media and the News.* New York: Bantam, 1974.

Costigan, Daniel M. *Fax: The Principles and Practice of Facsimile Communication.* Philadelphia: Chilton, 1971.

Cowle, Jerome M. *How to Make Big Money as an Advertising Copywriter.* Englewood Cliffs, N.J.: Prentice-Hall, 1966.

Crain, Rance. *How It Was in Advertising: 1776–1976.* Chicago: Advertising Age, 1977.

Craven, George M. *Object and Image: An Introduction to Photography.* Englewood Cliffs, N.J.: Prentice-Hall, 1975.

Croy, Peter. *Graphic Design and Reproduction Techniques.* New York: Hastings, 1972.

DeLozier, M. Wayne. *The Marketing Communications Process.* New York: McGraw-Hill, 1976.

Devol, Kenneth S., ed. *Mass Media and the Supreme Court.* New York: Hastings, 1971.

Doig, Ivan, and Carol Doig. *News: A Consumer's Guide.* Englewood Cliffs, N.J.: Prentice-Hall, 1972.

Dunn, S. W. *Advertising: Its Role in Modern Marketing,* 2nd ed. New York: Holt, Rinehart & Winston, 1969.

Editor & Publisher Staff. *Amendments to the Constitution: 136 Supreme Court Cases Adjudicating Freedom of Speech and Press Issues.* New York: Editor & Publisher, 1976.

Edom, Clifton C. *Photojournalism: Principles and Practices.* Dubuque, Iowa: Wm. C. Brown, 1976.

Emery, Edwin, Phillip H. Ault, and Warren K. Agee. *Introduction to Mass Communications,* 4th ed. New York: Dodd, Mead, 1973.

Emery, Michael C., and Ted Curtis Smythe. *Readings in Mass Communications,* 3rd ed. New York: Dodd, Mead, 1970.

———. *Readings in Mass Communication: Concepts and Issues in the Mass Media,* 2nd ed. Dubuque, Iowa: Wm. C. Brown, 1974.

Enstrin, Herman A., and Arthur M. Sanderson. *Freedom and Censorship of the College Press.* Dubuque, Iowa: Wm. C. Brown, 1966.

Epstein, Edward Jay. *Between Fact and Fiction: The Problem of Journalism.* New York: Random House, 1975.

Evans, Harold. *Handling Newspaper Text.* New York: Holt, Rinehart & Winston, 1974.

Farrar, Ronald T., and John D. Stevens. *Mass Media and the National Experience: Essays in Communications History.* New York: Harper & Row, 1971.

Fedler, Fred. *Reporting for the Print Media.* New York: Harcourt Brace Jovanovich, 1973.

Fowles, Jib. *Mass Advertising as Social Forecast: A Method for Future Research.* Westport, Conn.: Greenwood, 1976.

Francois, William E. *Mass Media Law and Regulation.* Columbus, Ohio: Grid, 1975.

Gerritsen, Frank J. *Theory and Practice of Color.* Cincinnati, Ohio: Van Nostrand Reinhold, 1975.

Gilmore, Gene, and Robert Root. *Modern Newspaper Editing.* Berkeley, Calif.: Glendessary Press, 1971.

Gorden, William I. *Nine Men Plus: Supreme Court Opinions on Free Speech and Free Press.* Dubuque, Iowa: Wm. C. Brown, 1971.

Greene, Richard M., Jr. *The Management Game.* Homewood, Ill.: Dow Jones-Irwin, 1970.

Hafer, W. Keith, and Gordon E. White. *Advertising Writing*. St. Paul: West, 1977.

Hage, George S. et al. *New Strategies for Public Affairs Reporting: Investigation, Interpretation and Research*. Englewood Cliffs, N.J.: Prentice-Hall, 1976.

Hattery, Lowell H., and George P. Bush. *Automation and Electronics in Publishing*. New York: Spartan, 1966.

Herpel, George L., and Richard A. Collins. *Specialty Advertising in Marketing*. Homewood, Ill.: Dow Jones-Irwin, 1972.

Highton, Jake. *Reporter*. New York: McGraw-Hill, 1978.

Hill, Evan, and John J. Breen. *Reporting & Writing the News*. Boston: Little, Brown, 1977.

Hohenberg, John. *Professional Journalist: A Guide to Modern Reporting Practice*, 4th ed. New York: Holt, Rinehart & Winston, 1978.

Holmgren, Rod, and William Norton, eds. *The Mass Media Book*. Englewood Cliffs, N.J.: Prentice-Hall, 1972.

Hosokawa, Bill. *Thunder in the Rockies: The Incredible Denver Post*. New York: Morrow, 1976.

Hulteng, John L. *The Messenger's Motives: Ethical Problems of the News Media*. Englewood Cliffs, N.J.: Prentice-Hall, 1976.

Hulteng, John L., and Roy Paul Nelson. *The Fourth Estate: An Informal Appraisal of the News and Opinion Media*. New York: Harper & Row, 1971.

Hurlburt, Allen. *Publication Design: A Guide to Page Layout, Typography, Format, and Style*. New York: Van Nostrand Reinhold, 1976.

Hutt, A. *Newspaper Design*, 2nd ed. New York: Oxford Univ. Press, 1967.

International Business Machines Corporation. *General Information Manual, Introduction to IBM Data Processing Systems*. Poughkeepsie, N.Y.: IBM Corp., 1967.

Jacobs, Lou, Jr. *Photography Today*. Santa Monica, Calif.: Brooke, 1976.

Johnson, W. Thomas, and L. Lee Moore III. *Automatic Newspaper Composition*. Boston: Nimrod, 1966.

Karo, Jerzy. *Graphic Design Problems, Methods, Solutions*. New York: Van Nostrand Reinhold, 1976.

Kemp, Weston D., and Tom Muir Wilson. *Photography for Visual Communicators*. Englewood Cliffs, N.J.: Prentice-Hall, 1973.

Kennedy, Bruce M. *Community Journalism: A Way of Life*. Ames: Iowa State Univ. Press, 1973.

Kennedy, Fern. *Exploring Photography*. Garden City, N.Y.: American Photographic Book Publishing, 1974.

Kleppner, Otto. *Advertising Procedure*, 6th ed. Englewood Cliffs, N.J.: Prentice-Hall, 1974.

Latimer, Henry C. *Preparing Art and Camera Copy for Printing*. New York: McGraw-Hill, 1977.

Lem, Dean Phillip. *Graphics Master*. New York: Art Direction, 1973.

Lendt, David L. *The Publicity Process*. Ames: Iowa State Univ. Press, 1975.

Lister, Hal. *Suburban Press: A Separate Journalism*. Columbia, Mo.: Lucas, 1975.

McCombs, Maxwell, Donald Lewis Shaw, and David Grey. *Handbook of Reporting Methods*. Boston: Houghton Mifflin, 1976.

MacDougall, Curtis D., ed. *Publication Design*. Dubuque, Iowa: Wm. C. Brown, 1972.

MacDougall, Curtis D. *Principles of Editorial Writing*. Dubuque, Iowa: Wm. C. Brown, 1973.

Massie, Joseph. *Essentials of Management*, 2nd ed. Englewood Cliffs, N.J.: Prentice-Hall, 1971.

Mencher, Melvin. *News Reporting and Writing.* Dubuque, Iowa: Wm. C. Brown, 1977.

Metz, William. *Newswriting: From Lead to 30.* Englewood Cliffs, N.J.: Prentice-Hall, 1977.

Metzler, Ken. *Creative Interviewing.* Englewood Cliffs, N.J.: Prentice-Hall, 1977.

Michman, Ronald D., and Donald W. Jugenheimer. *Strategic Advertising Decisions: Selected Readings.* Columbus, Ohio: Grid, 1976.

Mills, Nicolaus. *The New Journalism: A Historical Anthology.* New York: McGraw-Hill, 1974.

Naylor, Thomas H. *Computer Simulation Techniques,* 2nd ed. New York: Wiley, 1974.

Neal, James M., and Suzanne S. Brown. *Newswriting and Reporting.* Ames: Iowa State Univ. Press, 1976.

Nelson, Harold L., and Dwight L. Teeter, Jr. *Law of Mass Communication: Freedom and Control of Print and Broadcast Media.* Mineola, N.Y.: Foundation, 1973.

Nelson, Roy Paul. *The Design of Advertising,* 3rd ed. Dubuque, Iowa: Wm. C. Brown, 1977.

Newsom, Doug, and Alan Scott. *This Is PR: The Realities of Public Relations.* Belmont, Calif.: Wadsworth, 1976.

New York State Department of Education. *Orientation to Electronic Data Processing: A Basic Systems Program.* New York: Dept. Educ., 1967.

Owen, Bruce M. *Economics and Freedom of Expression: Media Structure and the First Amendment.* Cambridge, Mass.: Ballinger, 1975.

Pember, Don R. *Privacy and the Press: The Law, the Mass Media, and the First Amendment.* Seattle: Univ. Wash. Press, 1973.

Porter, William E. *Assault on the Media.* Ann Arbor: Univ. Mich. Press, 1975.

Read, William H. *America's Mass Media Merchants.* Baltimore: Johns Hopkins Univ. Press, 1976.

Rehe, Rolf F. *Typography: How to Make It Most Legible.* Carmel, Ind.: Design Research, 1974.

Rhode, Robert B., and Floyd H. McCall. *Introduction to Photography,* 3rd ed. New York: Macmillan, 1976.

Rissover, Fredric, and David C. Birch. *Mass Media and the Popular Arts.* New York: McGraw-Hill, 1971.

Rivers, William L., Theodore Peterson, and Jay W. Jensen. *The Mass Media and Modern Society,* 2nd ed. San Francisco: Holt, Reinhart & Winston, 1971.

Roman, Kenneth, and Jane Maas. *How to Advertise: A Professional Guide for the Advertiser. What Works. What Doesn't. And Why.* New York: St. Martin's Press, 1976.

Roman, Murray. *Telephone Marketing: How to Build Business by Telephone.* New York: McGraw-Hill, 1976.

Roshco, Bernard. *Newsmaking.* Chicago: Univ. Chicago Press, 1975.

Rothrock, John B. *How to Research Any Subject for Any Purpose.* Guilford, Conn.: Williams & Barton, 1976.

Ruggles, Joanne, and Philip Ruggles. *Darkroom Graphics: Creative Techniques for Photographers and Artists.* Garden City, N.Y.: Amphoto, 1975.

Sandage, C. H., and Vernon Fryburger. *Advertising Theory and Practice,* 9th ed. Homewood, Ill.: Irwin, 1975.

Sanford, Bruce W. *Synopsis of the Law of Libel and the Right of Privacy.* Cleveland, Ohio: Baker, Hostetler & Patterson, 1977.

Schlemmer, Richard M. *Handbook of Advertising Art Production,* 2nd ed. Englewood Cliffs, N.J.: Prentice-Hall, 1976.

Schmidt, Benno C. Jr. *Freedom of the Press vs. Public Access.* New York: Praeger, 1976.

Schuneman, R. Smith, ed. *Photographic Communication.* New York: Hastings, 1972.

Self, Charles. *How to Take Action Photographs.* Garden City, N.Y.: Dolphin, 1975.

Shaw, David. *Journalism Today: A Changing Press for a Changing America.* New York: Harper's College Press, 1977.

Simon, Raymond. *Public Relations: Concepts and Practice.* Columbus, Ohio: Grid, 1976.

Simons, Howard, and Joseph A. Califano, Jr., eds. *The Media and the Law.* New York: Praeger, 1976.

Stanley, Robert H., and Charles S. Steinberg. *The Media Environment: Mass Communications in American Society.* New York: Hastings, 1976.

Stein, M. L. *Shaping the News: How the Media Functions in Today's World.* New York: Washington Square Press, 1974.

Steinberg, Charles S. *Mass Media and Communication,* 2nd ed. New York: Hastings, 1972.

Stephenson, H. *Handbook of Public Relations: New York: Standard Guide to Public Affairs and Communications,* 2nd ed. New York: McGraw-Hill, 1970.

Stone, Bob. *Successful Direct Marketing Methods.* Chicago: Crain, 1975.

Stridsberg, Albert. *Controversy Advertising: How Advertisers Present Points of View in Public Affairs.* New York: Hastings, 1977.

Survey of Buying Power, Sales Management Magazine. New York, annually.

Tax Systems. Commerce Clearing House, Chicago, annually.

Tebbel, John. *Opportunities in Publishing Careers.* Louisville, Ky.: Vocational Guidance Manuals, 1975.

Thomas, Ella C. *Law of Libel and Slander,* 3rd ed. Dobbs Ferry, N.Y.: Oceana, 1973.

Tillman, Rollie, and C. A. Kirkpatrick. *Promotion: Persuasive Communication in Marketing.* Homewood, Ill.: Dow Jones-Irwin, 1971.

Tubbs, Douglas B. *The Illustrated History of the Camera from 1839 to the Present.* Boston: New York Graphic Society, 1975.

Turnbull, Arthur T. *The Graphics of Communication: Typography, Layout, Design,* 3rd ed. New York: Holt, Rinehart & Winston, 1975.

United States Atomic Energy Commission. *Computers.* Oak Ridge, Tenn.: AEC, 1967.

Van Uchelen, Rod. *Paste-up: Production Techniques and New Applications.* New York: Art Direction, 1976.

Wadsworth, Nelson B. *Through Camera Eyes.* Provo, Utah: Brigham Young Univ. Press, 1975.

Weizenbaum, Joseph. *Computer Power and Human Reason.* San Francisco: Freeman, 1976.

Wells, Alan, ed. *Mass Media and Society: Readings with Text.* Palo Alto, Calif.: National Press, 1972.

Westley, Bruce H. *News Editing,* 2nd ed. Boston: Houghton Mifflin, 1972.

White, Jan V. *Editing by Design: Word and Picture Communication for Editors and Designers.* Ann Arbor, Mich.: R. R. Bowker, 1974.

Wolseley, Roland E. *The Black Press, U.S.A.* Ames: Iowa State Univ. Press, 1971.

Wright, John S., and John E. Mertes. *Advertising's Role in Society.* St. Paul, Minn.: West, 1974.

Wright, John S., and Daniel S. Warner. *Advertising,* 4th ed. New York: McGraw-Hill, 1977.

Zimmerman, John, and Mark Kauffman. *Photographing Sports.* New York: Crowell, 1975.

Index